D1122041

# Great Voyages in Small Boats:
# Solo Circumnavigations

# Great Voyages in Small Boats: Solo Circumnavigations

John de Graff, Inc.
Clinton Corners, New York

GREAT VOYAGES IN SMALL BOATS: SOLO CIRCUMNAVIGATIONS

First printed 1976
ISBN 08286 0079 1
Library of Congress Catalogue Card Number: 76-24261
Manufactured in U.S.A.
John de Graff Inc. Clinton Corners, N.Y. 12514

Reprinted with permission:

TREKKA ROUND THE WORLD by John Guzzwell
First Published 1963
© John Guzzwell, 1963

ALONE THROUGH THE ROARING FORTIES by Vito Dumas
First published in English 1960
© Adlard Coles Ltd.

SAILING ALONE AROUND THE WORLD by Joshua Slocum
First published 1900
© 1899, 1900 by The Century Co.

# CONTENTS

Leaving San Francisco

# TREKKA
# ROUND
# THE WORLD

### JOHN GUZZWELL

# Contents

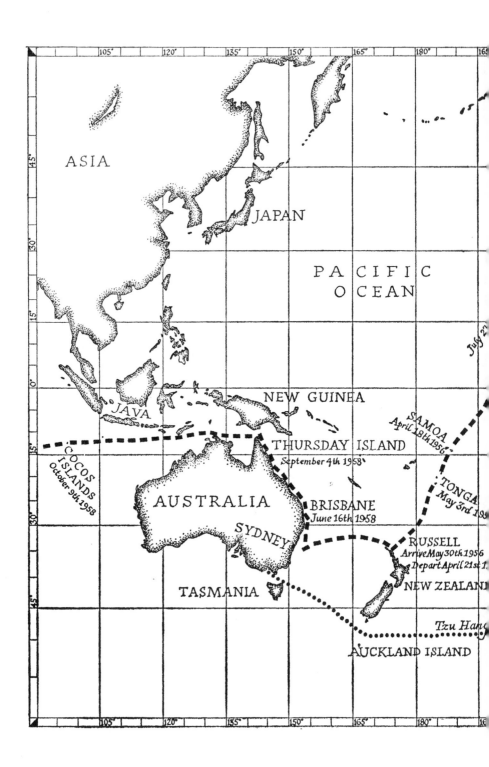

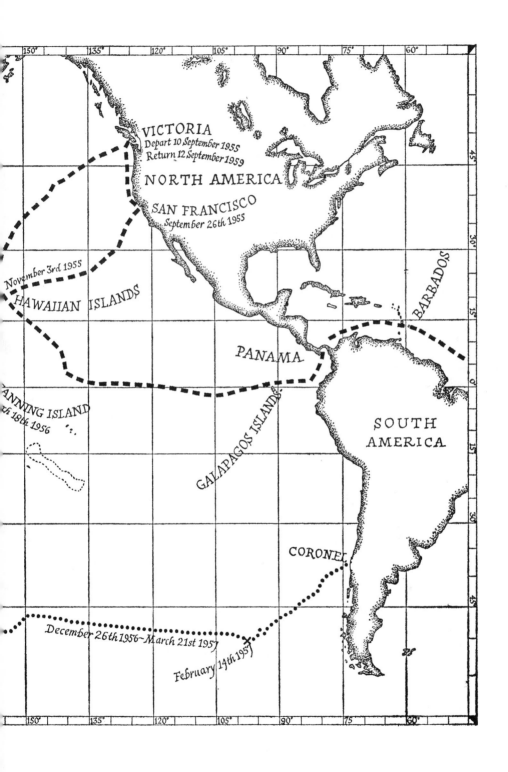

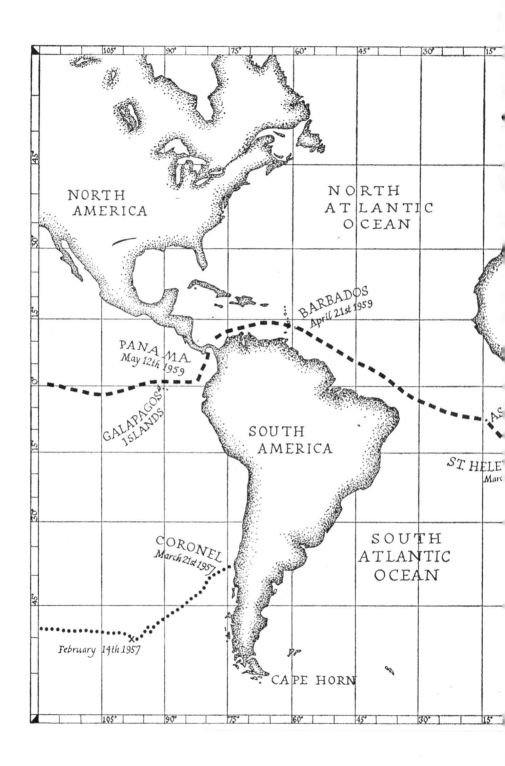

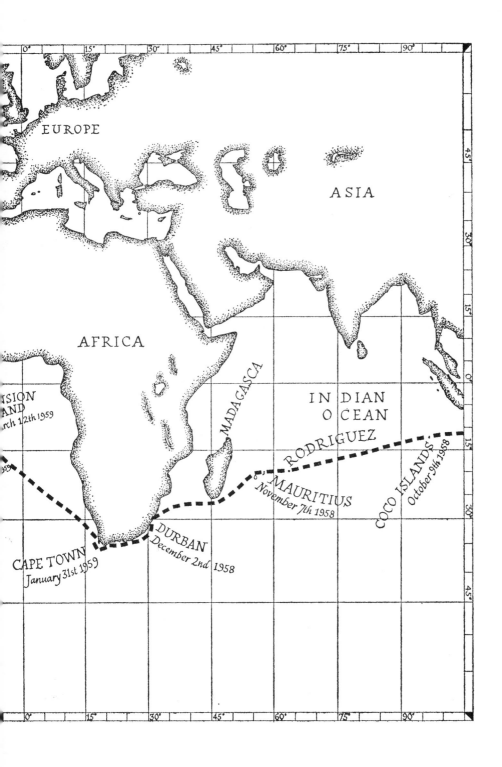

# Illustrations

# CHAPTER ONE

# *Prologue*

Ships and the sea have always been familiar and well-loved friends to me. I inherited this love from my father, also John, who hailed from the English fishing port of Grimsby, which is the home of several hundred deep-sea trawlers. At Grimsby my grandfather's red-sailed smacks were gathering a silvery harvest of codfish from the Dogger Bank long before the era of steam trawlers and mechanised fishing.

When my father was a boy, steam trawling was still in its infancy, but when the time came for him to decide what profession he would follow, he chose to become a marine engineer; the first ship he went to sea in was one of his father's new steam trawlers. After years of wandering about the world, from gold-mining in the frozen wastes of Alaska to pearl-fishing in the South Seas, he eventually met my mother and settled down in Jersey, one of the Channel Islands which lie within sight of the French coast.

Although I was born in England, it was in Jersey that I grew up, and my earliest recollections are of living in a small cottage close to a beach of golden sand with white fishing-boats pulled up near by, and bronzed fishermen in blue jerseys making nets and repairing lobster-pots. I was only three years old when the call of the sea became too much for my father; shore life, though easy, was very unsatisfying to him and it was not long before he decided to have a small yacht built and make a long ocean voyage in her.

The yacht was built by Uphams of Brixham, a well-known West Country firm who had built many trawlers for my great-grandfather. The yacht was constructed on the lines of a Brixham trawler and was also rigged as a gaff-ketch, but she was smaller, being 52 feet over-all and with a maximum beam of 12 feet. *Our Boy* was her name, and with one man helping as crew, my parents and I sailed to Cape Town, where my mother had been born. The voyage out to South Africa took several months, for *Our Boy* called at many West African ports, and Father was in no hurry to end the cruise. We stayed a few months in South Africa, and my father tried snoek fishing at Walfish Bay for a few weeks, but eventually we returned to our home in Jersey, Mother and I by steamer, while Father and two young men sailed the ketch from Table Bay to Penzance in 65 days, making only one stop at Dakar 34 days out.

On her return to England, *Our Boy* was reluctantly sold; she was built for deep-sea sailing and was too large for us to keep around the Channel Islands. My father was not very long without a boat, though, and soon bought an 18-foot cutter named *Try Me* which had long caught his discerning eye.

Living on a small island in close contact with boats and the sea, I naturally grew to know them both, and many of my holidays were spent sailing, sometimes in *Try Me* and at other times with friends on an occasional cruise to French ports in their yachts. I can remember seeing square-rigged sailing ships lying in the port of St Malo, their great yards overhanging the wharves. They were still beautiful to the eyes of a boy, though their rust-streaked hulls told sadly that their sailing days were over.

When war was declared in 1939 it seemed for a while that peaceful Jersey would escape the maelstrom, but soon the German Army was flooding like a tide across Holland, Belgium and France, and we realised that unless something extraordinary happened it was only a matter of time before the Channel Islands were invaded.

Many of our friends queued for hours to get aboard the small coasting vessels that were evacuating the bewildered islanders to the safety of England. In this time of crisis holds were packed with those who had left everything behind them in an effort to escape the advancing German Forces. Rather than risk the danger of being bombed or torpedoed in one of these coasters, my parents decided to try to reach the south coast of England, 80 miles away, in *Try Me*; so we packed what few possessions we could take and hoped the weather would allow us to make a safe crossing of the Channel. Fate decreed that it was not to be, three times we made the attempt to leave, but the weather worsened each time, and we had to return to our home. On the fourth day German Forces invaded the island and put an end to our hopes of escape.

The war years dragged on under German occupation, and food became scarce, but at least we had a comfortable home to live in. Soon, though, even the comfort of that was gone, for the German Commandant of the island gave notice that certain residents on the island would be taken with their families to internment camps in Germany. A few hours after this notice was published in the local newspaper we were *en route* to a prison camp at Wurzach, Württemberg, in the south of Germany. If the time had gone slowly under German rule on the island, it went even slower behind barbed wire. For two and a half years we waited in the camp for the Allied forces

to relieve us. We were never able to discover the reason for our internment, old people of 70 down to babes in arms were with us in the
camp. My schooling suffered as a result of our imprisonment, but my
father taught me navigation, which was to prove so useful years later.

With the war over we returned to Jersey and tried to pick up the
threads of our former life. I decided that I wanted to learn a trade,
and soon after our return to the island I became an apprentice joiner
with a firm of building contractors. Life in the prison camp had
wrecked my father's health, and he died early in 1948. Jersey held
little attraction for my mother after this blow, and so we decided to
return to her homeland, South Africa. We settled in the city of
Pietermaritzburg, the capital of Natal, and I continued my ap-
prenticeship there until I was qualified.

The years had slipped by so quickly and I was becoming increasingly aware of a feeling of restlessness within me. I wanted to travel
and see other countries, and I wanted to make my own way through
life. I knew that as long as I had my box of tools and the skill in my
hands I would never lack a job.

After spending two years in South Africa I decided that the time
had come for me to see what lay over the horizon, so I booked a
passage on a steamer to England.

Leaving home for the first time was a very sad occasion, and my
poor mother was as tearful as I was when the time came for me to
go. About the only thing I can remember was her serious advice that
I should change my underwear and socks regularly.

I spent the summer of 1952 in England cycle-racing, it was a sport
I had enjoyed in South Africa, but somewhere along the road I had
lost the enjoyment of it and I was not sorry when the season finished.

I visited friends in Jersey, but my two years' absence had made
me a stranger amongst them, and I felt I did not belong there. Out
sailing with one of them my old dream of making a long voyage alone
returned to me. I was confident I could do so, providing I had a suitable boat. The best idea was to build my own, and with my skill as
a joiner, I was sure that I could do so. I needed good lumber and
materials and above all I needed new surroundings for this venture.
I remembered the tales my father used to tell me of his life in British
Columbia, of the timber-clad mountains and the logging camps, pan-
ning gold out of the mountain streams and fishing for salmon out of
Pender Harbour. I decided to emigrate to Canada and call Victoria,
B.C., my new home. Looking back on it all, I could not have made a
wiser decision.

# CHAPTER TWO

# The Building of "Trekka"

I arrived in Victoria in March 1953 and soon settled down in my new home. I rented a room on Belleville Street, where I did my own cooking and washing. It proved to be good training for the years ahead. I was soon working at a good job, and with the wages I was earning I realised that it would not be long before I could start building a small yacht. I had a fairly good idea of the type of boat I wanted, she needed to be strong, yet quite light, so that in a storm she would ride to the top of the seas instead of being heavy and sluggish. She would also be quite small, for I was going to sail her alone and, of course, being smaller she would be quicker, easier and cheaper to build.

I used to wander down to Thunderbird Park in the city sometimes and look at *Tilikum*, for she was a proof that my dreams were possible. *Tilikum* was an old Hiada Indian war canoe that Captain J. C. Voss, with various companions, sailed almost, but not quite, round the world at the beginning of this century. Had the Panama Canal been cut then, *Tilikum* would undoubtedly have circumnavigated the globe. As it was she made a really wonderful voyage. I tried to imagine the old canoe in her former glory and wondered if she remembered the gales she had weathered off the lonely capes of the world. She was not the type of vessel I would want to go to sea in.

There is a well-known naval architect in England who specialises in designing small ocean-going yachts; his name is J. Laurent Giles. Many of the boats he has designed have made long voyages, some have sailed round the world, and I knew he was the man I wanted to design my little ocean cruiser.

After work one evening I wrote to him in Lymington and told him of the type of boat I wanted. I said that I would be building her myself and intended sailing her offshore. Would he design her for me? A few days later I had a reply from him, and to my delight he said he would. As the weeks went by, the letters flew back and forth across the Atlantic and the plans gradually took shape. They showed a rather unusual-looking little boat, yawl-rigged and quite streamlined in appearance. There was a surprising amount of room inside the hull, with two bunks forward, and aft of them a chart-table and a small galley where I could cook simple meals on a Primus kerosene stove.

The keel was a ⅜-inch steel plate with two big iron castings bolted to the bottom. It was fastened to the hull in such a manner that by undoing a few short bolts it could easily be removed should I want to store the hull in a garage or similar building during the winter months.

With this keel the shape of the hull was such that even if it turned completely upside down in a storm she would automatically right herself. I was delighted with the plans, for Jack Giles had understood exactly what I wanted. Now I was ready to go to work. But, before I could do so, I had to find a suitable shed or store to work in. The winter time was fast approaching, and I did not want to build the boat out in the open.

It seemed a hopeless search. A couple of times I found the right kind of place, but the rents were too high, so I kept on looking. Then one day I found just what I wanted, it was a store-room measuring 32 feet by 16 with a wooden floor and fluorescent lighting, situated at the rear of Johnny Bell's fish and chip shop on View Street, right in the centre of the city and only ten minutes' walk from my lodgings. The rent was not too expensive, and soon I had moved in with lumber, tools and plans. I felt that I was getting somewhere at last.

I bought a book on boatbuilding and found that the first operation was lofting. This, briefly, is to draw the lines from the plans, full size on the floor so that the measurements are more accurate and the hull is built without bumps or flats in it. I was days doing this, as I made a mistake at the beginning and had to do the whole operation over again, but once done, I was able to start work on the boat itself.

The wooden keel was made of oak and had to be laminated together with waterproof glue. The instructions on the can said that the minimum temperature for the glue to set was 70° F. The thermometer in the store-room read 45° F. I guessed that this was just one of the problems I would have to solve before the day of launching. I went to see Mr Shoemaker, the secretary of the Y.M.C.A., and asked his permission to glue up the keel of my boat in their boiler-room. If he was surprised, he never showed it, and ever since I have wondered what other strange requests he has received during the course of his work at the Y.M.C.A. He asked me to explain again slowly, and to my relief told me to go ahead. A friend helped me to carry the lumber up the street to the Y.M.C.A. building, and later that day with the thermometer reading 80° F. we glued and clamped the keel together. The following day the glue was set and we carried the curved keel back to the workshop on View Street.

There was little I needed help for now, and I was able to get much done, as the winter had arrived and I was working full time on the boat. From the pile of lumber she was slowly taking shape as the bulkheads, ribbons and steamed frames were fastened into position. Soon I had started planking, using $9/16$-inch red cedar strakes, which were edge-glued together and fastened with copper nails through the bent frames.

I feel there is something almost sacred about building a boat. It is a difficult thing to explain, but I have found that other boatbuilders have shared this feeling. It is almost like creating a living being, a boat seems to have a soul and character all of her own. Perhaps it is because of this that boats are usually thought of as being feminine.

It requires more thought to give a boat a good name than it does a child. Yachtsmen the world over have a habit of giving boats nicknames. I met a yacht named *Havfruen*, which was changed to *Half Ruin* by Australian yachtsmen, rather unfairly, I thought, as she was kept in beautiful condition. A Singapore yacht named *Bintang Terang* was immediately dubbed *Orang-utang*. Much thought was put into a name for my little yawl, and I finally decided to call her *Trekka* from the South African word *trek*, to make a journey. I hoped she would have the same dogged spirit of the Voortrekkers who trekked up into the Transvaal and Natal in the 1860s.

When I had planked *Trekka* down to the turn of the bilge, she was ready to be turned over so that I could work on the bottom. After wondering how I was going to do this, I once again made my way to the Y.M.C.A. A friend of mine was a weightlifter there, and I told him and some of his friends about the little boat I was building. They became quite interested, and I invited them to come and have a look at her. Four unsuspecting weightlifters followed me to where the half-planked *Trekka* waited. Another little problem was solved.

When the planking was finished I had to rivet over three thousand fastenings, this was a job I could not do alone and a friend helped me for a few days at this noisy work. We were not very popular with the restaurant next door, and the staff used to hammer on the wall for silence. I got the impression that they did not approve of my boat-building.

My husky friends turned *Trekka* right way up again, and I fitted the laminated deck-beams and then glued and screwed the $3/8$-inch plywood deck down. Spring came, and work slowed, as I was back at a regular job again, and could only work on the little boat at night or at week-ends, but slowly and carefully I finished her. I fibreglassed the deck and made myself even more unpopular with the restaurant next door, as they thought they had a gas leak and would not light the stoves in case of an explosion. The gas man soon discovered that

Building *Trekka*, the framing completed

*Trekka* upside down, the planking finished

It was cold running down the Oregon Coast

The Golden Gate Bridge, San Francisco

the fumes were from my fibreglass. I heard muttered threats and decided that I'd better hurry up before they resulted in sabotage.

Towards the end of August 1954, just over nine months since I started, the blue-painted hull was ready to be launched. On a Saturday morning we skidded her out of the store and took her down to the inner harbour, where there was a crane to lift her. The keel was bolted on, and then she was lowered gently into the water.

There was still quite a lot to do aboard, and as the summer was well advanced I did not try to get Trekka sailing that year. I took things easy, fitted out the interior and made the hollow masts out of silver spruce. I knew that there would be all the sailing I wanted the following year.

In January and February I saw snow on the deck and wondered where we would be when winter returned the following year, somewhere in the tropics, I hoped. The wet, cold days of winter passed slowly, but the sun gradually crept north day by day, and suddenly it was spring. The shoots were bursting out on the tree by my window and there was much activity along the waterfront as the skippers of the salmon-boats prepared for the coming season. I stepped Trekka's masts and spliced up the stainless-steel rigging.

Then came the long-awaited day when I bent on the new suit of sails, let go the mooring lines and felt life in the tiller for the first time. It was a very satisfying moment. I realised that I had a fine little yacht, she was quite fast and stood up to her sail well in fresh conditions. I found that she would steer herself to windward quite easily and just as well as I could do.

During the next few weeks I got to know her better as I sailed about the harbour, sometimes with friends, sometimes alone. I was a very contented young man. There is something very exciting about preparing for a long voyage alone, especially when you have never done it before. It seems that the various jobs and necessary items will never be ticked off the list you have made, instead it just grows longer. My room on Belleville Street now had an enormous amount of gear in it. Every week when I bought my groceries, I got a few extra cans of food, and I now had three hundred stacked away in a cupboard. Scattered about the rest of the room on chairs, on the table, or under the bed was all the rest of the gear I was going to need. Sails, rope, paint and charts, the sextant I had bought at a junk yard, blocks and the patent log. The room looked and smelt like a ship's chandler's. I wondered how I was going to fit it all inside a twenty-footer.

A few close friends knew that I was preparing to leave on a cruise to Hawaii. I asked them to keep it a secret as I did not want the press to send me away in a blaze of publicity. If I came back after a few days and decided that ocean cruising was for the birds, only my friends would know about it instead of the whole city. In August I moved aboard and was getting used to living in the somewhat confined space. All the gear had miraculously been stowed away in the lockers or beneath the bunks, and *Trekka* was sitting much lower in the water. As I had no water-tanks, I bought a dozen two-gallon plastic chemical bottles to keep my fresh water in. I found them ideal; they stowed away easily, and it was useful to be able to see at once just how much water had been used.

I had *Trekka* out of the water for a few hours and painted her bottom with anti-fouling. I hoped the next coat would go on in Honolulu. She was looking very pretty; though she was very small she had the best of gear, and I felt fairly confident.

One morning as I walked into town, I saw a fine-looking ketch moored in the inner harbour. She looked more of a little ship than the usual run of yachts, and I was not surprised to hear that she had been sailed out from England in 1951. She was now about to leave for Australia. Her name was *Tzu Hang*. I did not know it then, but I was to take part in a great adventure aboard her before I came back to Victoria, B.C., four years later.

On Saturday, 10 September 1955, I was all ready to leave. My few close friends had come to see me off from the dock near the Fishermen's Wharf. As they let go the lines and *Trekka* slowly gathered way, their voices carried clearly across the water. "Good luck, *Trekka*! Don't forget to write, John." It was a strangely sad moment, and I wondered when I would see them all again. I remembered the happy sailing we'd had together and how we'd gone over the charts planning the route for *Trekka's* voyage; and now here I was actually starting. As if understanding my feelings, *Trekka* quickly drew away from the little group and headed out towards the breakwater and the open sea beyond.

# CHAPTER THREE

# Victoria to San Francisco

It was already late in the year to be going down the North American coast. July would have been the best time, but I was not ready then. I had one last look at the familiar landmarks, then we shot through Race Rocks Passage with the tide under us, altered course, and headed out along the Strait of Juan de Fuca towards the open ocean.

We passed Sooke, then the wind dropped and left us becalmed on still water. A couple of salmon-trollers motored by towards Victoria, their crews looking forward to Saturday night ashore. I watched them go by with a slight feeling of envy, there was an awful lot of water between *Trekka* and Hawaii—2,800 miles of it.

The sails were just hanging limp, so I lowered them and went below to light the stove for my first meal of the voyage. With the daylight gone, there was quite a nip in the air. The little cabin felt very snug, and the Primus hissed away while the tempting smell of stew floated gently out of the hatchway. I switched on the radio for some music, it was a short-wave portable set, made in the U.S.A., and worked off a dry battery. It proved to be a very good companion at sea. That night I hung a lantern in the rigging before climbing into the warmth of my sleeping-bag and falling asleep.

I had all sail up next morning in an effort to get out of the Strait and into the open sea. The wind was very light, and there were patches of fog about, so I kept close to the Canadian shore and slowly drifted out towards the Swiftsure light vessel.

I had a 4-horsepower outboard motor stowed away in the rear locker. It could only be used in calm weather but as I had only four gallons of petrol aboard, I felt that it was rather early in the voyage to use it. I spent another day drifting along with just a whisper of wind, then it freshened and I streamed the log as we passed Cape Flattery. Before *Trekka* came back to her home port again it had registered more than 30,000 miles.

We were now out in the open sea and bouncing along in grand style. The wind was slowly increasing, but *Trekka* was putting the miles away steadily. As if for a final farewell, a big fishboat appeared from the south and headed over towards us. She came close alongside and a voice with a Norwegian accent hailed across the water, "Vere de hell you tink you are going in dat ploody little pispot?" I sang out, laughing, "Honolulu," and the voice roared back, "Vell, you're ploody crazee, put goot luck." I caught a glimpse of her stern as she rolled away, and read her home port, Victoria, B.C.

With the wind freshening all the while I had to roll a reef in the mainsail, but soon there was too much wind for even the reduced sail area, and I had to take in what sail was set and wait for the weather to moderate. The sea was starting to build up, and I realised that I was about to have my first gale. The barometer was tumbling down and ragged clouds were driving low across the sky from the south-east. I now had to learn how Trekka would lie most comfortably in a gale, so I started to experiment with the sea-anchor out over the bow and the little mizzen-sail set. The idea was to make the boat lie head to the seas, but this she would not do. She lay about 75° off the wind, and had a most violent motion. This was obviously not the answer, for Trekka was complaining bitterly about this treatment. Finally she decided to do something about it and broke away from the sea-anchor. We immediately lay beam on to the seas, and, though it may sound dangerous, she was far more comfortable. I went on deck and lowered the little mizzen-sail; then I pulled the anchor-warp aboard and saw that the shackle-pin at the end had come unscrewed.

With the helm lashed down to leeward and everything on deck secure I went below out of the weather. It was not so much the motion as the sounds that I noticed below. The halyards were beating a tattoo against the mast and the wind accompanied by moaning through the rigging. Somewhere in a locker a tin was rolling backwards and forwards monotonously. I listened to the hiss of a big sea as it approached. There was a bang as it hit the hull and water cascaded over the deck, but Trekka was so light and buoyant that it was only the top of the seas that were hitting her. It is when you are riding out your first gale in a boat you have built yourself that you wonder about some of the doubtful workmanship that went into her. I thought about some of the bent nails I had knocked in, and I remembered one of the splices in the rigging that was not as good as it could have been. But even gales end eventually, and a few hours later the wind had veered to the south-west and dropped enough for us to get moving again southwards. The gale had done me some good, though. I now had confidence in my boat, and a little more in myself, too.

During the next couple of days Trekka slowly beat her way south beneath grey drizzling skies. Even my enthusiasm for sailing was damped, though I had found my sea-legs and was no longer feeling sick. I felt very cold, for my so-called "waterproof suit" was something of a disappointment. Fortunately I had one garment that kept my body warm, this was a hand-knitted Cowichan Indian sweater, it was made from hand-spun raw greasy wool and was virtually waterproof in itself. I became very fond of it and invariably wore it at sea and ashore whenever I felt cold.

I had been edging offshore ever since leaving Cape Flattery, for I wanted to be away from the shipping tracks and have plenty of sea-room in case another gale came along. When we were down to the latitude of the Columbia River, the wind went round to the north. This was my chance to try the twin-staysail self-steering rig I hoped to use once we reached the Trade Winds. Two identical sails were set forward of the main-mast, each boomed out, wing and wing, with the sheets led back through quarter-blocks to the tiller. It was strange to see the tiller correcting the course as the wind filled one sail more than the other. The sky cleared, and I was able to get sights with the sextant and plot our position on the chart. As *Trekka* sailed herself along, I made the most of the sunny weather to dry out my wet clothes and clean up a little.

Later on I decided to take some photographs, and as my camera could be set to take pictures by itself I clamped it to the end of the mizzen-boom, and raced up forward to get in the picture myself.

The pleasant weather lasted for two and a half days, then the wind came in stronger, and I had to lower the twins and set the little storm-jib. I noticed that the two twin-poles had almost wrenched off the sliding ring on the mast. Soon the wind was moaning away in the rigging again, and the sea was running high. I pulled the storm-jib down and lay ahull waiting for the wind to ease. After a few hours it had eased enough to hoist the twins again after I had made temporary repairs to the ring on the mast. *Trekka* fled to the south, going down the seas like a surfboard. It was wildly exciting, but when the wind started to blow hard again I realised that it was time to slow down. I got the twins down and bundled them into the rear locker, then set the storm-jib. This little sail is strongly made and only measures 24 square feet. We continued to roll along to the south at about four knots.

The wind slowly increased until it was blowing a full gale. I joined all the warps I had together and streamed them over the stern to help keep us running dead before the wind, and I sheeted the storm-jib flat amidships. I do not know what force the wind reached. It is so easy to exaggerate, but I think it was touching 70 m.p.h. at times. The sea was an awful sight, *Trekka* plunged to the bottom of a valley one moment and shot to the top of a crest the next. I judged some of the seas to reach a height of thirty feet and watched the top four feet break and roll right down the face of them. It was the worst gale that *Trekka* encountered during her entire voyage around the world.

I dared not leave the tiller, and as the night wore on there was a nightmarish quality about the scene. I would catch myself nodding off to sleep and be suddenly awakened by a sea bursting over the quarter and half filling the cockpit. My weary eyes, stung with spray, would focus on the compass and I'd realise that I was off course.

So it went on, hour after hour, and I wondered dully what had possessed me to leave the friendly earth for this madness. At daybreak the wind faltered a little and I realised thankfully that it was easing. By noon I could stay awake no longer, my eyes felt like two hot coals, and I decided that *Trekka* would have to look after herself for a while. I crawled up to the foredeck and pulled the storm-jib down and then lashed the tiller to leeward. I stood in the hatchway for a few moments watching, she seemed to be quite happy, before I turned to the warm promise of my bunk; I was asleep as soon as my head touched the pillow.

The light was fading when I awoke a few hours later. The wind had eased, but the sea was still running high, so I decided to go back to sleep and wait for the morning to bring us some better weather.

With all the miserable weather I'd had since leaving Cape Flattery, I figured that it would be a good idea to go into San Francisco for a rest. I could fix the mast-ring there, and the rest would be worth a slight delay. I had no detailed chart of that section of the coast, but it would be difficult to miss the Golden Gate if I ran down the coast. In the morning I was able to get a sun-sight which worked out quite close to my dead-reckoning position. We were south of Cape Mendicino and about fifty miles offshore. I decided to make a landfall on Arena Point and altered course to close the shore. On the thirteenth day out from Victoria, I was looking for land and sighted the Point in the early afternoon. I ran along the shore until dusk, and then set the twins and let *Trekka* steer herself for the night. With less than eighty miles to go I was looking forward to a good wash and a steak ashore.

When I awoke, I was conscious of a change. It was a couple of moments before I realised what it was. Fog. It did not appear to be thick, but when I looked towards the horizon I noticed that visibility was down to about two hundred yards. According to the distance run on the log, we should have been quite close to San Francisco, but when I closed the shore I could see nothing but sheer cliffs. Had I passed the Golden Gate, or was it still south of us? It was impossible to get sights and the only thing to do was to wait for the fog to lift. I sailed offshore again for the night, and the fog was as thick as ever. I heard a couple of ships go past, their foghorns blaring mournfully, and I knew that I must be near a shipping track. At daylight I got sail up, and we ghosted along over a very calm sea towards the land. Then the fog lifted a little, and I was able to see the entrance to what appeared to be a small bay. I guessed correctly that it was Tomales Bay, about 20 miles north of San Francisco.

There was very little wind so I decided to motor into the bay and anchor for the night. The outboard was clamped over the stern and roared into life when I pulled the starter cord. As I approached the entrance I saw a couple of black buoys, and, thinking that the channel would be marked with the International system, I left them to starboard. Suddenly we were hard aground, and I saw that the tide was ebbing quickly. I tried to push us off using a spinnaker-pole, but I dropped it and the tide quickly carried it out to sea. I was too late, we were stranded.

*Trekka* lay right over on her side that night, and I was lucky that the sea was so calm. In the morning I jumped overboard and waded out into deeper water with the anchor so that I could kedge *Trekka* off when the tide rose. I got back on board and was waiting for the tide to rise a little more, when a stout-looking ketch appeared from inside the bay and came over towards me. One of her crew jumped into their dinghy and rowed over. "We'll tow you off if you like," he offered, and, as I thanked him, he pulled up my anchor and rowed back to the ketch. In a couple of minutes I was back in deeper water alongside the ketch.

I told them about mistaking the black buoys and said that the chart I had of this section of the coast was too small to show any details. I suspect that when they left me a few minutes later they were convinced that people who put to sea in such tiny boats and approached a strange coast without adequate charts would come to a watery end. I silently agreed with them and resolved never to approach a coast again unless I had a chart of the area.

I watched the ketch motor off towards San Francisco and followed in her wake with the outboard purring contentedly. A gentle breeze came in from the north, and I got sail up and stowed the motor away in the rear locker. We passed the lighthouse on Point Reyes, and I got the spinnaker out and set it without too much difficulty.

Fishboats were making their way towards 'Frisco, and as the light faded, I followed their stern navigation-lights as long as I could see them, but eventually they were lost amongst the thousands of lights on shore and those that marked the approaches to the Golden Gate.

Then the lights on the Golden Gate bridge came into view. Altogether it was one of the most spectacular sights I have ever seen. Though the wind was very light now, it would have been almost sacrilege to have started the motor. I was content to drift in towards the magnificent scene. At five o'clock in the morning, as the fishing fleet was heading out to sea, we ghosted in beneath the great suspension bridge and steered for a yacht basin close by the Coastguard Station. I fastened the motor over the stern, lowered the damp sails and motored in through the entrance to the marina where I moored to a vacant float, sixteen and a half days from Victoria. I climbed into my bunk and fell asleep.

# CHAPTER FOUR

# I Meet Friends

I was awakened by the Customs and Immigration officials, who had some forms for me to fill in and wanted to know how long I was staying. They all seemed satisfied when I said that it would be just for a few days.

A few minutes later I had a very interesting visitor aboard, he was Myron Spalding, the well-known San Francisco yachtsman.

"Come along to the Club," he invited, "you can get a shower there and meet some of the boys."

It was in this manner that I first came across the warm friendship and open-hearted hospitality that is extended to blue-water yachtsmen and which made my voyage so enjoyable. Beautiful scenery and strange places are not enough in themselves to make a visit memorable, it's the wonderful people one meets in different countries that make ocean cruising so worthwhile.

As we walked along to the St Francis Yacht Club, he pointed across the basin and said, "There's another boat that arrived a few days ago from Victoria, B.C. She's got a Chinese name. You could moor *Trekka* just ahead of her." I looked to where he was pointing and saw the masts with the baggywrinkle in the rigging and the sweet white hull of *Tzu Hang*.

Later that morning I moved *Trekka* over to the other side of the basin and a young couple from aboard *Tzu Hang* helped me with the mooring lines. They were Raith and Vivian Sykes from Duncan, B.C.

"Come and have some tea," invited Vivian. "The Smeetons have gone into town, but they'll be back shortly."

Soon we were chatting below in *Tzu Hang*'s cosy saloon, while the Primus roared away in the galley. I learned that they were going as far as Honolulu with the owners, Miles and Beryl Smeeton and their young daughter Clio. The voyage down from Victoria had been a rough one and had taken them fourteen days. A backstay splice had pulled at sea, and the skipper had had to go aloft to fix it.

About half an hour later, when I was about to leave, Vivian said, "Wait a minute, here they come now, I can hear B's voice." We jumped down on to the dock and I was introduced to Miles Smeeton. He was middle-aged, very tall and slim, and carried himself like a military man. I learned later that he had retired with the rank of Brigadier from the Indian Army. Two very friendly eyes twinkled from his craggy features as he gripped my hand. "This is my wife, B.," he said, and I thought I caught a note of pride in his voice.

I turned and looked into two of the merriest blue eyes I have ever seen. They were eyes that had looked at great distances. Her long fair hair was tied in a bun behind her head, and she was dressed in a brown suit with a divided skirt. Her right foot was in plaster, and she tapped it with the walking-stick she was using.

"Don't take any notice of this," she said in a clear English voice, "I trod on the bucket in the cockpit on the way down and broke my big toe. Do come aboard and have some tea, we're dying to hear all about you and your little boat. We've had a simply ghastly trip down. Oh, this is Clio."

Clio was fourteen years old and tall like her father. She seemed to be all arms and legs. "May I go and have a look at Trekka?" she asked, and a few moments later she called out of Trekka's hatchway, "Mummy, you should see his Primus stove—it's polished!"

I knew I was going to like these people.

When we compared notes, I found that on the way from Victoria Tzu Hang had experienced the same sort of weather as I had in Trekka. I was pleased to know that the Smeetons had considered the passage tough going, for although they had only taken up sailing when they bought Tzu Hang in England in 1951, they had gained a great deal of experience when just the three of them had sailed her all the way from England through the Panama Canal to their home on Salt Spring Island near Victoria, B.C.

"If you are going to Hawaii, we should rendezvous there," said Miles. "It's much more fun cruising together than by yourself." So we arranged to meet at Hilo, on the island of Hawaii. The first boat to arrive would wait for the other.

There were a couple of jobs I had to do before I could leave, I needed to make a new spinnaker-pole to replace the one I'd lost at Tomales Bay, and the ring on the mast needed to be fastened on more securely.

I bought the fittings for the spinnaker-pole in the city, and when I got back to Trekka, Myron Spalding was there. "If I was you, I'd get out of here and go over to Sausalito on the other side of the bay," he said. "It's much warmer there and quieter too, you'll be able to work in peace." It was good advice, and later that day I motored across the bay to the lovely little yacht harbour of Sausalito.

I had only just finished mooring Trekka when a tall man approached me and held out his hand. "My name is Bob Frick, I live over here and have a workshop and tools available, if you can use them you're welcome to go right ahead." Through Bob I met more friends, and soon the unpleasant memories of the voyage down the coast were forgotten. Two of these friends had just returned from Hawaii, having taken part in the Trans-Pacific Yacht Race from Los Angeles to Honolulu, and they proceeded to mark on my charts of the islands all the places I should go and see.

*Tzu Hang* arrived a couple of days later and moored just a short distance away. I made the new spinnaker-pole and Bob got the mast ring brazed for me. It was much stronger now and I doubted if it would give me any more trouble.

On Wednesday, 5 October, just eight days after I had arrived, I was all ready to go. The water-bottles were all topped up and I had fresh fruit and vegetables aboard.

I waved good-bye to my friends, and Raith Sykes shouted, "We'll see you in Hilo, John." A launch gave three toots on her hooter in salute, then *Trekka* was away and heading for the open sea in company with an aircraft carrier, which was also bound for the Hawaiian Islands. "She'll be there in about five days' time," I thought. "I guess it will take me at least a month."

I soon found that because of my stay in port I had lost my sea-legs. Whenever I stayed ashore longer than a week I usually felt seasick for the first three days at sea. I did try seasick pills later in the voyage, but I have little faith in them and am quite content to wait until the third day out when I'm usually back on my food again.

With the fine westerly breeze to send us along and lovely sunny skies, it was easy to forget the gales and cold that had been our lot farther north. By noon the next day *Trekka* had run 95 miles to the south-west. Already the weather seemed warmer, and I kept looking at the weather chart and figuring how far we had to go before I could expect to reach the Trade Wind.

Situated almost directly between San Francisco and Hawaii is the North Pacific "High." It is an area of high pressure which has a great influence on the weather in this part of the ocean. Though it is marked on the weather maps in one position, that is only its average position, and it can move very quickly or split into two separate systems. Winds near the centre of the "High" are usually very light, so it is best to try and avoid going anywhere near the centre if your means of power depends on the wind. The fastest course to Hilo for *Trekka* was not the shortest one, but the one that would give the best winds. Looking at the weather chart I saw that I would have to take a curving course to the south before I could steer directly for the islands.

The next few days saw us edging farther south with the weather holding fine. "This is more like it," I thought. "You can keep that other weather farther north."

At noon on 11 October we were nearly 400 miles out. There had been a little rain in the morning, and the wind went round to the east of north. I lost no time in getting the twin-staysails set and *Trekka* rolled along steering herself.

I could make *Trekka* sail herself on most courses, but except for being close-hauled or running free with the twins, it was with a loss of speed that she did so. I usually steered after I had finished breakfast and continued all through the day until sunset when I made her sail herself, perhaps under reduced sail, while I got my main meal of the day ready. Unless there was a change in the weather during the hours of darkness, I did not go on watch again until after breakfast next morning. I would usually wake up a couple of times during the night and have a look out of the hatch to see if all was well; I got quite used to these breaks in my sleep and could return to my bunk a few minutes later and resume sleeping.

It is quite amazing how one can be in "tune" with a boat. I could be lying in my bunk and know almost instinctively when *Trekka* was not happy. Perhaps she had too much sail up or the main-sheet wanted easing a bit more. I think this feeling comes more easily with a smaller boat than it does with a larger one.

The wind was slowly backing to the north-west so I had to change sail and get the mainsail up again. We were really putting the miles away now, and by noon had run 103 miles during the past 24 hours. This was the first time that *Trekka* had run a hundred miles in a day.

Navigation these days was pretty simple. I would go below and switch the radio on, tuned to the American station WWV on 15 megacycles, which broadcasts time signals every five minutes of the 24 hours. With my wrist-watch corrected, I'd take the sextant on deck and get a sight. There was no waiting for a glimpse of the sun these days.

On 15 October we were seven hundred miles from San Francisco and well within the zone of the North-East Trades as shown on the weather chart, but the wind had been north-westerly for the past three days and I was beginning to wonder what had become of the Trade Wind.

That afternoon there was not a breath of air to fill the slatting sails, so I pulled them down to stop them chafing on the rigging. We seemed to have arrived in a different world, the sea flattened out until it looked like glass, and *Trekka* rolled slowly to the remains of the swell. I could see the log spinner hanging fifty feet below, and I hauled it aboard so that it would not get tangled up with the rudder. The sky was beautiful to look at, great columns of cloud towered above each other and reached up into the stratosphere; and yet overhead it was clear and the sun shone down chasing the shadows of the rigging across Trekka's deck.

When I left Canada, a friend had given me a box of paperbacks and said, "Here's some reading material for you. When you've got nothing to do, or you are becalmed, they will pass the time away." I decided to have a look through that box, the last three books had been Western stories. I went below, got the box out and found that the other forty-two books were also Westerns. I returned to the cockpit and was soon sharing the troubles of some rancher who'd had all his cattle rustled, had lost his girl friend to the villain and was being attacked by a party of Indians. I concluded that life at sea was less hectic.

With the sea so calm and no wind about, I though it would be an idea to have a swim and scrub some of the scum from just above Trekka's waterline. The water was quite warm and I soon cleaned off the topsides with some power cleanser.

I swam a few yards from Trekka to see what she looked like and was surprised to see how she was moving and rolling about; on board all seemed quite still. The water was very clear. I looked down into the depths below, a blue world that fell away into infinity, twenty feet below me a jellyfish slowly moved along and I wondered what else was down there. I was suddenly conscious of a horrible feeling that eyes were watching me, and I instantly knew how vulnerable I was out there. With a feeling akin to panic I hurriedly swam back to Trekka and climbed aboard thankfully. No more swimming for me, I decided.

The calm continued. Sometimes a faint breeze would come along and I would quickly get up sail and steer south. We appeared to be right in the middle of the North Pacific "High," and the farther south we went, the better the chance of picking up the Trade Wind. By noon on the 20th we had covered only 120 miles during the past five days, but that afternoon a gentle breeze came out of the northeast and I set the genoa and a staysail wing and wing. Trekka slipped along towards the south-west, the only sound being the liquid tinkling note of the bow-wave.

That night the wind slowly increased, and I set the other twin sail and coupled up the self-steering. The genoa was stowed away in its bag, and I climbed into my bunk happy with the knowledge that we had reached the Trades at last.

By daylight next morning the wind had freshened to moderate, and

*Trekka* was rolling along right on course for Hawaii. It was really grand sailing, small puffy white clouds were all marching in order across a wonderfully blue sky, while down on the sea about us the waves flashed in the sunlight. Every once in a while *Trekka* caught a wave and surfed down the face of it, sometimes she slewed a little off course and I'd watch the tiller automatically correct her and bring back again. So it went on, hour after hour, trekking across the ocean towards the distant islands.

At noon on 23 October, we had reached the half-way point between San Francisco and Hilo. I wondered where *Tzu Hang* was. She was not due to leave Sausalito until a week after *Trekka*, but she'd be eating up the miles by now.

It was time to alter my watch back an hour, I would have to do this once more before I reached Hawaii, for there was a two-hour difference between the longitude of Hawaii and San Francisco.

Every evening I tuned the radio into a Los Angeles station and listened to the soap-box serial I was following. It was on the air for fifteen minutes, and anything I was doing was put aside so that I could give it my whole attention. The radio was certainly a very good companion, and at night-time I listened in to programmes from Australia, New Zealand and the B.B.C. in London. I was surprised one evening to pick up Radio Lourenço Marques in Portuguese East Africa. It is quite a popular commercial station and I had listened to it many times when living in South Africa.

The days seemed to go by quickly, and the little dots which marked our daily positions gradually crept across the chart towards where it was folded. Once we reached that point, I knew that there were only three hundred miles to go.

*Trekka* was still steering herself and doing very well, too. In a week she had covered 741 miles, with a best day's run of 134. She was getting a little help now from the ocean current which was giving us about 10 to 15 miles every day.

On 2 November, my twenty-eighth day out, we were only 120 miles from Hilo. I decided that it was about time I had a shave, and I had just finished that painful operation when the wind shifted from the north-east to the south-east and became quite light. I went on deck and pulled the twins down. They had been up for thirteen days with no attention except that I had altered the sheets on the tiller a couple of times. I set the mainsail and genoa and steered for a few hours; then I put the twins up again at nightfall.

I woke up next morning with the sunbeams dancing across the cabin. I stretched rather lazily and switched the radio on with my big toe. "Let's see," I thought, "one hundred and twenty to go at noon yesterday. From the sound of her she's doing about three now. Yes, if it's clear, I should be able to just see the top of the mountain." I promised myself that if the island was in sight, I'd have a can of peaches for breakfast. Sure enough it was peaches for breakfast, because when I looked out of the hatchway, there, right ahead, but still low down, was the 13,825-foot peak of Mauna Kea. I viewed it with mixed emotions, I was pleased to see it, yet the passage down from 'Frisco had been so enjoyable that I felt a little sorry that it was almost over.

All that day I watched the mountain grow out of the sea; it never seemed to get any closer, but it kept on growing bigger and bigger. By sunset we were still about twenty miles off the coast, and rather than enter Hilo at night-time, I took all sail down and stopped for the night. I was awakened during the night by quite loud squeaking noises, and when I went on deck to see what it could be I was nearly startled out of my wits when a whale surfaced right alongside and spouted with a mighty exhalation. I quickly dived below and shut the hatch tight. "If a whale is going to get amorous with *Trekka*," I thought, "Lord knows what is likely to happen." To my relief he behaved himself and I tried to go back to sleep.

I awoke at daybreak and soon had sail up. The land was only about 12 miles distant, but Hilo was down the coast another five miles, so I decided to close the shore and sail along the coast. It was fun identifying the various points and villages with the aid of the Pilot Book and the binoculars. There seemed to be numerous sugar mills and plantations along the shore, and when we got in closer there was quite a lot of waste from the cane floating on the water. Soon the little township of Hilo itself came into view, and we sailed around the Blonde Reef buoy and tacked up the harbour past a couple of freighters that were loading sugar. I sailed through the rather narrow entrance to the little basin known as Radio Bay where the U.S. Coastguard was located, then I dropped the anchor over the stern and ran up to the wharf with just the staysail set. A Hawaiian took the warp I handed up to him and slipped it over a bollard. "Where have you come from?" he inquired. I let go the staysail halliard and tried to appear casual. "San Francisco," I answered. The expression on his face was so comical that I started to grin. Soon both of us were laughing at each other and he disappeared up the wharf slapping his thighs and chuckling away. "San Francisco," I heard him say again weakly, "San Francisco!"

Soon there was quite a little group on the wharf all firing questions at me, and it seemed only a few minutes later that the doctor, Customs and Immigration officials arrived. The doctor reckoned I looked fit enough after a month at sea, and the other officials said that I could fill in the necessary forms when I arrived in Honolulu. I asked them if *Tzu Hang* had arrived, but apparently she was still at sea, for they had not heard of her.

The officer in charge of the Coastguard Station came along shortly afterwards and offered me the use of their shower ashore, and then he invited me to have lunch with the crew aboard the cutter. I had almost forgotten what a hot shower was like, but shortly afterwards when I had washed all the salt and a good bit of my "suntan" off I I presented myself aboard the Coastguard cutter where the men were soon filling me up with cold ham and salad followed by ice cream. I decided that there were compensations to living ashore after all.

The Smeetons aboard *Tzu Hang* in Hawaii

Iao Needle, Iao Valley, Maui

The view from the trail around the northern cliffs of Kauai

# CHAPTER FIVE

# Hawaiian Interlude

The days passed pleasantly, and I was able to see something of the island. A friend arrived one morning in his car to take me to see the National Park, an area towards the centre of the island noted for its volcanic activity. I was shown the steaming Kilauea crater and the vast lava flows of previous years. We crawled through a lava tube in total darkness for some three hundred feet, and then drove to Keala-kekua Bay where the great navigator, Captain James Cook was killed. It was a lovely bay and I thought it would be a good place to visit in *Trekka*.

My hair had not been cut since I left Canada, and it was getting quite long, so I went into Hilo to get it cut and found to my amusement that all the hairdressers were women. The one that went to work on my thatch told me about the tidal wave disaster in 1950, when many people lost their lives because there was no way to warn them of the approaching danger. Since then a siren warning system similar to that used for air raids during the war has been set up, and this should help to prevent a recurrence of the tragic loss of lives.

A couple of days later I was shopping in Hilo with a friend when I looked out to sea and saw the sails of a ketch approaching. As she got closer I saw that she was *Tzu Hang*. We quickly returned to *Trekka* and put the outboard over the stern then motored down the harbour to welcome her in. We learned that she had been twenty-five days on the crossing and had experienced light weather most of the way. The most exciting event had been when Pwe, the Siamese cat had fallen overboard half-way between San Francisco and Hawaii and Mrs Smeeton had immediately dived in to rescue her. Both of them had been retrieved safely without too much difficulty.

With *Tzu Hang* moored alongside *Trekka*, I got to know her crew better. Mrs Smeeton was always called B. by her friends, and she soon had me fixing some shelves into her galley and repairing the seat in their fibreglass dinghy. One evening we held a discussion in *Tzu Hang's* saloon as to what we should do.

"Look, John, I don't want to appear inquisitive, but where are you heading for in *Trekka?*" inquired Miles.

This was something I had been asking myself the past few days.

The voyage from San Francisco had been so enjoyable that I felt it would be quite easy for me to carry on, there were no ties for me in Canada—or anywhere else, for that matter.

"Oh, I was thinking that I might try to get down as far as New Zealand," I replied. "I think *Trekka* can make it all right."

"Oh, she'll make it all right," said Miles, with a conviction that was heartening to me. "We're on our way to Australia, we've got some friends down there and thought we'd look them up and see the Olympic Games, too, which are being held in Melbourne next year. But there is no sense in going down that way now, not with the Hurricane Season just starting. We don't want to leave the islands here until about the beginning of March. I suggest we cruise together and see as much as we can now. Then we can go on to Honolulu, where we can do any maintenance and get stores for the voyage south." This sounded fine to me and soon we were bent over the chart discussing where we should go first.

"I was over at Kealakekua Bay with a friend the other day," I said. "It's a lovely bay, but it's quite a long way from here."

"We must go there," said B., firmly, "I have been reading the journal of Captain Cook's third voyage, and besides, I'm told that the other side of the island is much nicer."

Thus it was decided that we would sail round the south of the island and up the western side to Kealakekua Bay, where we would meet.

Late one November afternoon the two boats left Hilo harbour together on the 120-mile passage to Kealakekua Bay. Outside the entrance it was blowing the usual brisk Trade Wind, and there was a very lumpy sea running. We sailed together for a few minutes taking photographs of each other in the fading light, and then I put *Trekka* on to the other tack and *Tzu Hang* disappeared into the gathering darkness.

The 30-mile beat to Cape Kumukahi was most uncomfortable after two weeks spent in port. *Trekka* was steering herself and crashing along with the spray flying. I climbed into the windward bunk which helped her to sail more upright, but there was no hope of getting any sleep, the motion was much too violent.

It was still dark when *Trekka* rounded the light and bore away to the south-west with the wind right astern. I waited until daylight then set the twin-staysails and let her roll along, steering herself and surfing continuously. The enormous bulk of Mauna Loa, over 13,000 feet high towered into the sky, and I could see the courses of the lava-flows which ran down the side of the mountain and into the sea. All that day we flew along the coast; it was sailing at its best. *Trekka* would seem to steady herself rather as an athlete does just before he makes his supreme effort, then the bow would dip and we'd quickly gather speed. The hull would level off, then there would be a rumble from up forward and the white water from the bow-wave would shoot up to the lifelines above the chain-plates. The whole boat would tremble as we rode the crest for a few seconds, then as she slipped off it the stern would sit down waiting for the next wave to come along. I looked at the two blue twins etched against the sky, and the white wake stretching aft, and I remembered the winter days at the back of the fish and chip shop when all this was only a dream.

Off Ka Lae, the southernmost point of the island, I got the twins down with a bit of a struggle, as it was blowing quite hard. The staysail was set, and we ran up the west coast, soon coming into the lee of the land where I was able to get the mainsail up. As we went farther up the coast the breeze fell away until we were becalmed. With Mauna Loa effectively blotting out the Trade Wind I realised that I'd have to make very good use of the land and sea breezes if I wanted to get up the coast.

It was very slow going, but gradually I worked *Trekka* up the Kauna coast. That night I dropped all sail so as to get some sleep, and then pushed on again in the morning. By late afternoon we were only four miles from Kealakekua Bay, and when darkness came I could see the light on Cook Point at the northern entrance to the bay, but I waited until the following morning before entering and anchoring close to *Tzu Hang*. She had arrived a full day before *Trekka*.

We spent a glorious week together there, doing very little apart from swimming, having picnic lunches ashore and hiking about the bay trying to locate the sites of the villages that Captain Cook mentioned in his journal. On the southern side of the bay the ruins of the stone marae are still quite impressive, but on the northern side, where there is a monument to Cook, and where once there was quite a large settlement in his day, all has reverted back to the bush and there is not a sign to indicate that once a whole village lived there. We found a bronze tablet set into the rock in knee-deep water which said that the great navigator had been struck down and killed near that spot on 14 February 1779.

I took B. and Clio for a sail in *Trekka* to the little harbour of Keauhou about three miles up the coast. This is the only safe harbour on the west side of the island during south-westerly to westerly gales, but it is only suitable for small craft with a maximum draft of six feet.

There was very little wind, and we drifted back to *Tzu Hang* just after dark.

I sailed on up the coast a couple of days later to the small township of Kailua, which is the main settlement on the western side of Hawaii. The famous Kona Inn is here, and once again I saw tourists clad in Aloha shirts with cameras slung about their necks. Most of them looked very bored and I wondered if they were getting half as much pleasure from their holiday as I was having for a fraction of the cost.

*Tzu Hang* motored in one afternoon, and a little ketch named *Nani* arrived from Honolulu with her owner Jack Randall, his wife, Helen, and a crew of two. Jack was a marine biologist and was on his way to Tahiti where he was going to study a certain type of fish. With the three boats together we had much fun.

The *Nani* boys introduced us to the fascinating sport of skin-diving, and for the first time I knew the thrill of descending into a new world, a world of blue where the living coral grew into the most fantastic shapes and beautiful colours. All about me quite unafraid, swam dozens of multi-coloured fish. Some quite curious, examined the monster that had invaded their kingdom and would only move when I reached out to touch them. Others scurried about the pillars and holes in the coral, very much like people bustling about a city, they even seemed to have the same vacant expressions. With my lungs bursting for air I shot to the surface, but again and again I dived down wishing that I had a breathing apparatus so that I could examine this new kingdom more closely. I promised that I would equip myself with swim-fins and goggles at the earliest opportunity, for I knew that I would be doing more of this in future.

A month had gone by since *Trekka* had arrived in Hawaii, and though I had not seen anywhere near all of it, I decided that it was time to start moving up the islands on towards Honolulu.

I arranged to meet *Tzu Hang* in the little port of Lahaina on the island of Maui a few days later, and then I sailed out of Kailua one afternoon, bound for the island of Maui.

Separating Hawaii and Maui, the two largest islands in the Hawaiian group, is the Alenuihaha Channel, thirty miles wide. This channel has a reputation for boisterous seas, for with the towering mountain of Mauna Kea nearly 14,000 feet high on Hawaii, and the 10,000-foot crater of Haleakala on Maui the Trade Wind frequently funnels through the slot at nearly gale strength.

I had left Kailua in the afternoon on purpose, so that I would be ready to cross the channel early next morning. That night *Trekka* sailed quietly up the coast, and by dawn had almost reached the channel. I could see the wind on the water a couple of hundred yards ahead, so I went forward and roller-reefed about six feet of the mainsail.

As *Trekka* came out of the lee of the land, it was as though some-one had opened a giant door, there was a sudden gust of wind that knocked us down, and I heard pots and pans clanking away merrily from the vicinity of the galley. Then *Trekka* picked herself up and started to go. It was wonderful sailing as we bounced along over the crests with a spray flying, I had just a swimsuit on, and it was just as well, for I was soaked in a matter of minutes.

After five exhilarating hours we came under the lee of Maui and rapidly lost the wind. The occasional puff came along, sometimes from astern, but more often from ahead, and we gradually worked along the shore until off Ahihi Bay, where I anchored for the night. Just back behind the beach I could see four gigantic radio masts, they were the transmitters for station WWVH that broadcasts time signals for navigators. I had listened to their signals nearly every day on the way down from San Francisco, and now I had run the beam down to its source.

Next morning I left for Lahaina, but being in the lee of Haleakala most of the day, did not arrive there until midnight. I anchored in the roads and entered the newly made harbour after breakfast next morning.

I immediately liked Lahaina. It has quite an interesting history and was at one time the capital of the Hawaiian Islands. In the days of sail the whalers used it as their headquarters, and there were some lively times between them and the missionaries. The missionaries became very powerful in the early days and soon had control of large areas of land. That there is still some bitterness felt by the islanders is apparent in what a little Hawaiian told me. "When missionary first come to Hawaii, he see Hawaiian all time happy, fishing, eating and lying on the sand. He say, 'This is no good, you cannot enjoy yourself all time, you must work. We will teach you how to work.' Now you come to Hawaii in your little boat, what do you see? Hawaiians all working, and missionary lying on the sand."

*Tzu Hang* joined *Trekka* in Lahaina and we lay alongside each other. The Smeetons were very keen mountaineers and wanted to walk across the crater of Haleakala, a distance of about twenty-five miles. They wanted me to go along with them, but about three days before we were due to go my left leg was bitten by a small insect and started to swell in a remarkable manner, until it was twice the size of my right one. I went along to the hospital, where they pumped some penicillin into me, but it had little effect. B. reckoned that she could do better than that and got a jar of what she called "anti-phlo" which she boiled in a pan for an hour or so. She told me to put my leg up and then said something about it having to go on hot. She scooped out a large glob from the jar and smeared it on a piece of gauze then slapped it on my leg. Wow!! I gave vent to my feelings and was half-way out of the hatch when she caught me. "Call yourself a single-hander," she admonished scornfully, "making a fuss like that over a little bit of anti-phlo!" Dear B., her methods of first aid are surely kill-or-cure, and if in doubt, just leave it, for Nature knows best.

My leg began to respond to this painful treatment, but I did not want to go hiking on it until it was better, so instead of going off to the crater with them I offered to scrape down *Tzu Hang's* mainmast and varnish it while they were away. The following morning I was working away up the mast when I came across a large patch of rot below the upper spreaders. The mast was a hollow one, and I noticed that the glue seams were also opening. There was little point in me continuing to work on the mast, for it was obvious to me that *Tzu Hang* needed a new one.

When Miles got back from the mountain I told him the bad news and sent him up the mast in the bosun's chair. "I can't understand how we didn't lose it off the Oregon coast when the backstay went," he said, a few minutes later. "We can't go to sea with it like that now, just the mere thought of it is enough to scare me."

"I know what you mean," I said. "It looks as though moisture has been getting behind the spreader fitting and lodging there."

When I returned to *Trekka* from shopping the following day B. called to me to come aboard *Tzu Hang.* "We have found a friend who has solved our problem, come aboard and meet him, his name is Stew Milligan."

I was soon shaking hands with Stew and listening to his pleasant, deep voice, "I'm working in the Public Relations department of a big sugar company on the other side of the island, John, and I know we've got everything over there in the way of equipment and materials."

"Well, that's wonderful," I said, "and have you got someone to make the mast, too?"

"Oh, yes," said B. with an amused smile, "You!"

"Me?" I said, quite startled.

"Yes, you!" she said, and then quickly carried on before I could protest, "You made *Trekka's* masts, didn't you? And you said last night that masts are not very difficult to make, so you can make our new mainmast." I suddenly thought of all sorts of reasons why I couldn't make a 58-foot hollow mast, but when I looked at B. I knew that as far as she was concerned the mast was as good as made.

Stew seemed to sense my hesitation, "It won't be too bad John, there is a young feller called Bobo in the factory, he'll be able to help you."

I looked at Miles a little helplessly, and he said, "We don't want to bulldoze you into it, John. But you can earn yourself some pocket-money and help us out of a difficult spot at the same time."

"O.K." I said, trying to get used to the idea, "but how are we going to work it."

Miles began to explain. "I thought we could go to Lanai Island first and have a look at it while we are here, then afterwards we can sail around to Kahului, which is the main port on the other side of Maui and where the sugar company's workshops are. We can go alongside the wharf and one of their crane trucks can lift the old mast out, so that you can get the sizes for the new one." It sounded all right to me, and the trip over to Lanai would give me more time to think about the project.

"When we get over to Kahului, you'd better eat with us," said B. "It will save you cooking and you'll be able to work longer on the mast." I realised that B. was way ahead of me.

The two boats left Lahaina for near-by Lanai, where we anchored in Manele Bay at the eastern end of the island. Lanai is noted for its pineapple plantations, and is known in the Hawaiian group as the Pineapple Island.

We visited the Hawaiian Pineapple Co., which has 15,000 acres under cultivation in what is the remains of a huge crater. It was most interesting to see the techniques used to get the most out of the soil and to reduce labour as much as possible. The pineapples were spray-irrigated and big combine machines were used to harvest the fruit, the pickers walking along behind a horizontal boom which had a conveyor belt that carried the fruit into big pens in which they were shipped to Honolulu for canning.

From Lanai *Trekka* sailed to Kahului through the Pailolo channel. I left in the late afternoon as the Trade Wind usually eases off at night-time, and beating to windward in the channels is a rough business. *Trekka* arrived off Kahului in the early hours of the morning, and as I was feeling tired I read the chart incorrectly and very nearly ended my voyage there. The leading lights into the harbour were marked on the chart as red and fixed. Somehow, due to being tired or careless, perhaps both, I read the lights to be flashing, and was sailing free on the correct bearing with two lights flashing red when I noticed that I was almost in the breakers. I came up into the wind immediately and beat out of there quickly. On the way out I saw the correct lights about a quarter of a mile to the east, they had been obscured by the rock breakwater. By this time I was fully awake and put the outboard over the stern and motored in.

When daylight came, I saw that the lights I had been coming in on were on a radio mast and were provided for the benefit of aircraft, I was also able to see where I had been heading for and watched the huge rollers breaking on the rocky foreshore.

*Tzu Hang* arrived later that morning and anchored near *Trekka*. Clio came over in the dinghy to collect me and I was relating my narrow escape to Miles and Raith when a man and two children swam out from the shore. When he got close alongside he said, "My name is Guy Hayward. I'm the doctor here, when you're all ready, come ashore and have a drink, my house is right on the beach there." So once again we had made a new friend. Guy and his charming wife, Anita, had five children, they took the invasion of six ocean-travellers as though it were an everyday occurrence and made us feel so welcome that we used their house as a kind of battle headquarters. With their telephone we learned that the crane would arrive at the wharf the following morning and that two gallons of waterproof resorcinal glue had been ordered from the U.S.A. to be dispatched by air-freight.

In the morning we let go *Tzu Hang's* rigging and the crane lifted the mast clear and set it down on the wharf. Until now there had been a faint hope that the damage could be repaired by scarfing in a new piece, but it was now obvious to all that the mast was beyond repair.

The first day I started work on the mast at the factory, a little Hawaiian approached me and said, "Oh, you big man, where you come from?"

I grinned at the stocky figure and replied, "Well, I was born in England, but I've been living in Canada for a while now."

He digested this information and then shot at me, "How high you are?"

"Six feet," I answered.

"Six feet!" he repeated almost reverently; and then he confided, "You know Hawaiian all small people, all dwarf, big sideways, but not high."

He went off muttering, "Hawaiian all dwarf."

The following morning, Raith came along to see how I was getting on and the little Hawaiian rushed up to him, eyes popping with excitement. "How high you are? How high you are?" he said, barely able to contain himself. Raith looked a little startled, but replied good naturedly, "Six feet three."

"Six feet three," echoed the awed Hawaiian, "and where you come from?"

"Oh, well, I was born in England," said Raith, "but my home is in Canada now."

"Hawaiian all dwarf," whispered the other, not able to take his eyes off Raith.

"What's all that about?" inquired Raith, after the Hawaiian had left us.

"Search me," I shrugged. "Maybe he's never seen a tall person before."

I went back to making the mast, which was progressing quite well, the material had been planed, and I was working on the scarfs.

Next day Miles brought the glue along and he had no sooner arrived when the little Hawaiian rushed up and was beside himself with excitement. "How high you are, how high?" he gasped looking up at the towering figure above him.

Miles shot an inquiring look at me, and then, when he saw my grinning face, answered, "Six feet six."

"Big man. Six feet six," gasped the Hawaiian, and I waited for his next question. His eyes never left Miles, and then he said with conviction, "Yes, and I bet you were born in England, too, and now live in Canada!"

Clio arrived later, she was the same height as I was and only fourteen. The Hawaiian was now certain that English Canadians were a race of giants, so we wouldn't let B. come anywhere near the factory as she was only five feet seven.

Bobo, the young Japanese Hawaiian who was helping me, was a good craftsman, and between the two of us we soon had the mast ready for gluing together. Mast-making was something new in the factory, and we seemed to have a never-ending group of spectators. We made over sixty clamps out of scrap lumber and borrowed bolts from the stores. When it came to gluing the mast together we had just about one man to a clamp, and I doubt if any mast was ever clamped together so quickly. Instead of varnishing the new mast it was decided to fibreglass it, and though I was against it at the time, it proved to be very successful and looked almost as good as new varnish and certainly much better than weathered varnish.

We stepped the mast about two weeks after removing the old one, and all agreed that it was a fine-looking spar. Clio's little dog, Poopah, immediately christened it, and we felt it was accepted by him at least. Later a visitor admired the new spar and rubbed his hands on it appreciatively. He smelt them carefully, and then inquired of me what type of oil we used on it to keep the mast in such fine condition. Before I could answer, Poopah appeared on the scene and lifted a hind-leg. I saw understanding dawn in the visitor's eyes and watched him carefully remove a handkerchief from his pocket.

*Trekka* caused me some excitement one night by vanishing. I had noticed that the wind had changed from the normal North East Trade and was blowing quite briskly from the south.

It was quite a dark night, and when at first I couldn't find *Trekka* I was not unduly alarmed, but eventually I realised that she really had gone. I rowed back to *Tzu Hang* and told Miles, who immediately jumped into the dinghy with me, we started rowing downwind, and as we got farther away I began to wonder how close *Trekka* would be to the big rock breakwater. We saw a whitish patch ahead, and I knew it was *Trekka*, but she was drifting downwind quite quickly, and when I climbed aboard a minute later we were only a few yards off the breakwater. I knew what the trouble was, the anchor-warp had wrapped itself around the top fluke of the anchor and pulled the anchor out of the sand. I quickly untangled the fluke and anchored again, and then I put the outboard over the stern and started the motor. Soon I was back alongside *Tzu Hang* again, but that was not the end of the evening's entertainment, for soon we were dragging again. The wind was blowing a solid 35 m.p.h. by now, and I decided I'd had enough of this nonsense, so I went right into the inner harbour and under the lee of a big shed. It blew very hard indeed for the rest of the night and most of the following day, too. I found out later that this was one of the Kona storms which sweep through the group during the winter months, and that on this occasion the wind reached a velocity of over 70 m.p.h.

When the storm had passed I returned to my old place alongside *Tzu Hang*. She had ridden it out to a 65-pound C.Q.R. anchor with a lot of chain out. This anchor had bitten in so well to the bottom, though, that I had to give a hand to break it out when the time came for *Tzu Hang*'s departure.

I went along with the Smeetons on what was to be an attempt at finding the old Hawaiian trail over the ridge of mountains separating Olowalu Valley and the Ioa Valley. We learned that the last party to make the trip had done so twenty-three years before with two Hawaiian guides.

Luckily someone gave us a machete, just before we started, for we had to hack our way through dense tropical undergrowth. The distance was about twelve miles but it took us three days before we came down a stream bed into Iao Valley. Before I started, I bought a pair of blue jeans that were so tight that I couldn't bend my knees, three days later I had lost so much weight that they were almost a sloppy fit.

One evening, when just Miles, B. and I were aboard *Tzu Hang* we got to talking about our future plans, and I asked them both what they were going to do after they arrived in Australia.

"Well, Clio has got to go to school again," said B. "These correspondence courses are all very well, but Miles and I feel she ought to go to a school in England for a while."

"So will you sail her back to England?" I asked.

"No, I think she'll have to go by ship or fly," replied Miles.

"She'll fly," said B. with considerable emphasis. "No daughter of mine will make a long sea voyage alone at her age—not with some of the ghastly types I've seen aboard ships. Believe me, I know."

"If Clio flies to England, that will leave just the two of you on the boat, won't it?" I said. "Vivian and Raith are going back home from Honolulu."

"Well, we sailed *Tzu Hang* out from England to Canada with just the two of us," said Miles. "Clio was only eleven then, and couldn't help us much with the boat."

"Yes, but which way will you sail *Tzu Hang* back to England?" I asked. "If you're going down to Melbourne it will be a devil of a long way to go right up the coast to Torres Straits and twelve hundred miles of tricky sailing inside the Great Barrier Reef, too."

"I suppose we could try to get across the Great Australian Bight," Miles went on. "The winds are not too unfavourable during the summer months."

"Of course, I would like to go by Cape Horn," said B. simply.

"What!" exclaimed Miles and I together, both of us quite startled.

"Well, *Waltzing Matilda* went that way, and so did Conor O Brien's *Saoirse*," said B. "Both boats were about the same size as *Tzu Hang*, but, of course, they had good crews." Then she added a little sadly, "I don't think we could make the trip alone, though, and I can't think of anyone who'd want to come with us."

"I'd come tomorrow," I said, quite surprised at myself.

"Would you really?" asked B. with quickening interest.

"Man, I've always wanted to make that passage," I replied. "I'll never get a chance to do it in a square-rigger, and that's the way I would like to go. But I'd jump at going with you on *Tzu Hang*."

"Now, wait a minute," said Miles cautiously, "We've not even arrived in Australia yet, and you two are already talking about leaving the place."

"What would you do with *Trekka*, John?" asked B., taking little notice of Miles.

"Well, I could leave her in New Zealand and come across with you to Australia," I suggested. "By that time you'd know if you wanted

to take me or not. Single-handers are all supposed to be a bit queer,"
I added mischievously.

"Well, you can say that again," said Miles. "But we don't intend
going to New Zealand, anyway. It's too far off to think about yet,
anything might happen in the meantime."

Just before I rowed back to Trekka for the night B. got me aside and
whispered, "Don't worry, it will be all right. I'll get round Miles
eventually and he'll be just as keen as we are. But you've got to help
me, and for Heaven's sake don't breathe a word to a soul or they'll
talk him out of it."

I rowed back to Trekka thinking, "Miles, you don't stand a hope."

After being in Kahului for nearly a month, it was time to move on
again. We had made so many good friends that it was quite sad
saying goodbye to them all, some of them wanted to come on with us
to the next island, and Tzu Hang had quite a crew when she left one
January afternoon in 1956 for Kaunakakai on the island of Molokai.
Even Trekka had a passenger for the forty-odd mile run. We left early
in the morning hoping to get a good start, but there was very little
wind until about noon when the usual north-easter came in. Trekka
went along very well with the main and spinnaker up and was doing
a steady six knots, but once we came under the lee of Molokai the
wind fell light and we arrived at Kaunakakai just after dark. Our
friends flew back to Maui that night and when we returned to the
two boats we found that a small freighter had arrived to load pineapples. Tzu Hang was in the way so we moved her along the wharf
before retiring for the night. Molokai island is also a great pineapple-
growing centre, and though the plantations did not seem quite as
spectacular as on Lanai, it was apparent that an enormous amount of
fruit was grown there. A friend drove us to the northern side of the
island where we looked down from the pali, a mountainous ridge, on
to the leper settlement at Kalawao, which is one of the three main
stations in the Pacific. There is a very strong updraught near the edge
of the pali, for the Trade Wind blows directly against it and sweeps
up the face and over the top. A trick of the locals is to throw someone's hat over and then watch the wind blow it back again.

We were only a couple of days on Molokai before leaving for
Honolulu some fifty miles away. I left at night so as to arrive in
daylight the other end and made good progress until early in the
morning when the wind fell away to nothing in the middle of Kaiwi
Channel. This is unusual, for the channel is noted for being very
windy.

The U.S. Navy were holding manœuvres, dozens of flying-boats
buzzed about Trekka, and I could not make out if I was in the way

or not. However, we couldn't move as there was no wind, and presently the submarines, destroyers and carriers moved away over the horizon. When the wind came back again, it was from the south. It steadily increased and from the look of the sky I knew that there was bad weather on the way. By the time we reached Diamond Head, it was blowing quite hard, and I had to roll a deep reef into the mainsail. I picked out the leading marks of the Ala Wai Yacht Basin and was running in along the channel when a motor launch came out to escort me in.

Tzu Hang was moored against the gas dock so I ran alongside her and lay there for the night. The wind blew quite hard during the night and this Kona storm did a lot of damage to the neighbouring island of Kauai where 42 inches of rain fell in 48 hours.

Harbourmaster Chick Allen looked after us very well, and soon both boats had moorings in the marina, while we had the use of hot showers and washrooms near by.

We all went out to the airport to see Vivian and Raith off and understood how they felt about returning to Canada in midwinter after spending the past two and a half months cruising in the tropics.

There were some very interesting yachts and people in Honolulu. We met Bill and Phyllis Crowe who had sailed their Block Island schooner Lang Syne round the world, and W. A. Robinson of Svaap fame invited us aboard his lovely schooner Varua. There were many other interesting boats that had made long voyages. I saw Idle Hour, too, which had also made a circumnavigation.

One of the keen yachtsmen we met was Ernie Zimmerer, who had the schooner Kitone. He told us of a lovely walk he had made on the island of Kauai, and showed us photographs taken during the hike into the valley of Kalalau on the northern side of the island.

It sounded so interesting that Miles and B. were determined to go. They asked me to join them, and as it was a good hundred miles to Nawiliwili, the only safe port on Kauai, I decided to leave Trekka in Honolulu and sail aboard Tzu Hang for the trip over. At the last minute Guy and Anita Hayward from Maui turned up and said they would like to come across to Kauai with us, and then fly back to their home on Maui. Unfortunately for them, there was very little wind, and we had to motor the whole way there. I can remember being quite seasick for Tzu Hang's unusual motion was quite different from Trekka's.

We moored off the wharf in Nawiliwili, not far from the Coastguard cutter, and when the four of us were ready to leave on our walk, Miles asked the officer in charge to keep an eye on Tzu Hang while we were away. There was still a lot of damage apparent from the Kona storm, which had blown away roofs and brought prodigious quantities of rain, which in turn had washed away bridges and caused flooding.

A friend drove us out to Hanalei Bay from where we would start our walk. The trail into the valley wound round the coast sometimes high above a cliff, sometimes along a beach. It was very narrow and we had to walk in single file, the views were magnificent, and each new bend in the trail would bring some new vista.

The distance into the valley was supposed to be seventeen miles, and by that night we thought we were only about three miles from our objective. We camped by the side of the trail and pushed on again the following morning reaching the valley about two hours later. Except for the trail around the cliffs, or by landing on the beach in a boat, the valley was quite inaccessible. Great volcanic walls of rock shot up a thousand feet into the air, their jagged skyline looking like the crest of some huge dinosaur. I think the thing that impressed me most was the silence of the place, it was quite deserted, yet with those towering cliffs frowning down upon us I kept feeling that someone or something was watching and waiting for us to go away. There was a strange impressive grandeur about the place that was a little unsettling, and I felt easier that afternoon when we started to retrace our tracks along the cliff trail. The weather looked threatening and all four of us pushed on purposefully.

We camped in a battered old hut, the roof of which had collapsed on one side. None of us could get much sleep and we lay awake listening to rain falling steadily and tried to dodge drips that chased us around the floor.

With first light we were off again, and around midday arrived at Hanalei. Some Hawaiians kindly offered to drive us to Nawiliwili and soon afterwards we were back aboard *Tzu Hang* and changing into dry clothes. The hike had been very interesting, but I for one was pleased to be back aboard the comfort of the ketch.

We left for Honolulu the next morning, a stiff beat of a hundred miles against the North East Trade Wind. The motion was considerable at times but my stomach was much happier now that *Tzu Hang* was sailing instead of indulging in the corkscrew motion I felt when she was motoring. This was the first real sail I had enjoyed aboard her, and I wondered how long it would take me to get used to her if Miles decided to do the Cape Horn passage in her. There was still some doubt that he would, but B. had evidently been working on him to good effect, as he had decided that it might be a good idea to visit New Zealand.

Miles was hesitant about calling there for we had heard some fantastic story that pets arriving from overseas aboard yachts were destroyed by the authorities, who were afraid that New Zealand sheep could become infected with some tropical disease. *Tzu Hang* had a dog and a cat aboard, and this story sounded quite horrible. Of course, it was all nonsense, and when we eventually arrived in New Zealand, officials there were the most friendly and easygoing I encountered during the whole four years I was cruising.

When we got back from our Kauai trip I immediately went to work on *Trekka*. There was quite a bit I wanted to do, and the next two weeks saw me putting in long hours painting and varnishing and doing all the thousand and one jobs that have to be done to get a boat ready for an ocean voyage. When it came to varnishing the masts I moored *Trekka* just below the Ala Wai bridge and lifted the masts out from the top of the bridge. It was easier and better to varnish them out of the boat instead of going up in a bosun's chair.

*Trekka* was on the slipway for five days, and I painted the topsides with two coats of light blue and then the bottom with anti-fouling paint. When someone asked me what shade of blue the paint was, I told them "Trekka Blue." They seemed quite satisfied.

B. was amused at watching me working on *Trekka* because she said that whenever someone started to ask me questions I would go below and start knocking with a hammer or just answer in monosyllabic grunts. This was quite unintentional on my part, but had I stopped to answer every question I got, I would never have got any work done. And the questions: What do you do at night, do you anchor? Don't you get lonely? Why don't you take a parrot with you? What's that white stuff on the wires for? I'm sure all yachtsmen will have been asked similar questions at some time or another.

When *Trekka* slid back into the water she looked almost like a new boat again. Someone asked me what kind of varnish I used as the masts were looking so good. I replied, "Oh, it's some stuff I got in Canada." "Well, you won't get any varnish here like that," confided my visitor. When I arrived in New Zealand I was asked the same question and replied that it was some stuff I got in Honolulu. "Well, you won't get any like that here," I was told. And so it went on at each place I visited. The Australians admired the New Zealand varnish and South Africans the Australian.

I was very pleased to meet "Woody" Brown one day while I was busy varnishing. Woody, Rudy Choy and Al Kumulai designed and built a large sailing catamaran a few years ago which was so successful that it started off a world-wide interest in this type of craft. They named her *Manu Kai*. Catamarans had been built before that were quite successful, but somehow they just hadn't caught the imagination of yachtsmen. It took *Manu Kai* to do that. She was built of marine plywood, scientifically designed and was very light. She sailed like a witch and clocked speeds up to 30 knots. With this first design, Woody had almost attained perfection for none of her off-spring has been able to overshadow her. He had just designed a small 20-foot catamaran which he hoped would become popular in the islands and be raced as a class. The name he had given this class was *Tropic Bird*. I was invited to go for a sail and willingly laid aside my varnish brush. I have sailed in catamarans since but I have never captured the thrill of my first ride with Woody. With a fine Trade Wind to drive us along, she was touching speeds of up to 20 knots at times. After a top speed of 6½ in *Trekka* it was most exciting.

Woody had built close sisters to *Manu Kai*, and was sailing them off the beach at Waikiki taking tourists for trips. If they enjoyed their sail half as much as I did they'd go back for more I'm sure.

*Tzu Hang* had two dinghies, one was a light fibreglass pram which would carry three persons in calm water, and the other was a heavier one that would carry more and was safer in rough water, but it was quite heavy and leaked badly. B. asked me if I would make them a new dinghy out of plywood if they bought all the necessary materials and arranged for a good place for me to work in. I had finished all *Trekka*'s jobs and had some spare time, so I agreed and finally went to work in Ernie Zimmerer's basement.

A week and heaps of shavings later, it was ready for painting, and B. looked after that end of it. It was made so that it would fit over the fibreglass dinghy and still stow between the two side skylights; and, as it was going to stow upside-down, I thought it might be a good idea to make it fit the deck. This had the effect of giving it an almost straight sheer, and though it looked very well stowed it did look at bit odd by itself. There was not time to try it in Honolulu, as the paint was still wet, but I hoped to see it in the water at Fanning Island, which was to be our next port of call. The new dinghy was just over nine feet long and was built of quarter-inch plywood with the keel and chines and removable seats all of spruce so as to reduce the weight as much as possible. For its size it was remarkably light.

I went with B. one day to a little Japanese ship-chandler. We had decided to order plenty of supplies, for once we left Honolulu there would be no good stores available until New Zealand. B. was ordering supplies by the case, and I became infected with her enthusiasm. I also started ordering a case of this and a case of that. At one point she turned round to me and said, "You don't surely think you are going to eat a case of bully beef between here and New Zealand, do you, John?"

"Man, I believe in having plenty aboard, nobody will ever hear of *Trekka* running out of food like some of the voyagers you read about," I answered.

A few days later, when a large truck pulled up alongside the dock and the driver started unloading case after case of canned food, I wondered if I hadn't perhaps overdone it.

"You don't think you are going to stow all that away inside your boat, do you?" asked a passer-by.

"It will go in all right," I answered confidentially, "she's got a hollow mast."

After much sweat and effort I did manage to get it all stowed away, but there was far too much, really. When I finally arrived in New Zealand there was still enough food aboard to take me back to Honolulu had I wanted to go.

Our stay in the Hawaiian group was rapidly drawing to a close. Though we had thought that Honolulu would be just another seaport we had enjoyed it very much. The other islands had been quite different, not commercialised, and the people lived at a slower pace, which suited my temperament better. I had enjoyed it all and hoped that some day I would return.

# CHAPTER SIX

# Off to the South Seas

Miles and I had looked at the charts together and decided to call at Fanning Island, a coral atoll about 12 miles in diameter situated 1,100 miles south of Honolulu. The island is British and has a safe anchorage, it looked quite an attractive place to visit.

On Sunday, 4 March 1956, *Trekka* and *Tzu Hang* left the Ala Wai Yacht Basin for the remote little atoll. After spending the past four months cruising from port to port, it seemed strange to be setting out on an ocean passage again. By that night, *Tzu Hang* had disappeared over the horizon ahead, and I was left alone looking at the diminishing lights astern. My stomach was acting up as usual, and I soon had *Trekka* steering herself while I went below for some sleep. The weather was grand, with the wind just aft of the beam, *Trekka* was going along in her best stride, and the first four days out saw us 390 miles on our way. On the evening of the fourth day, though, the wind fell away and we were left slatting about becalmed. Next morning the sky had clouded over and rain squalls descended on us at times. It was doldrum weather, but as we were only down to Latitude 14° north I couldn't believe that I'd reached the Intertropical Front so soon.

The weather cleared next day, and we started to make better progress, but as we got farther south squalls became increasingly frequent. They would only last for five or ten minutes, but the rain would knock the sea flat. Instead of taking down sail I ran *Trekka* off downwind, which was usually to the west.

I had not been able to get a latitude noon sight for days, but on the 13th we were about 9° north latitude. During the afternoon the wind increased until it was blowing with gale force from the east. I pulled all sail down and lay ahull for a few hours waiting for the weather to moderate.

When the wind eased a little I set the staysail and mizzen and left *Trekka* to work herself south. She sails herself very well under this rig when it is blowing hard.

Twelve days out, Fanning Island was only 95 miles away, but I noticed that we had lost 30 miles off the day's run owing to the Counter Equatorial Current. The following day, too, the current had robbed us of another 30 miles, but we were getting quite close to the island now and I hoped to see it next morning.

The wind left us for a few hours but returned just after midnight, a steady breeze from the east. At daylight, a succession of squalls and driving rain reduced visibility to a quarter of a mile and I wondered how I was going to find the island in these conditions. The highest point of land on Fanning is twelve feet above sea-level and the tops of the coconut palms can only be seen about six to seven miles off from the deck of a small yacht. I was wondering if I had missed the island altogether for navigation these past few days had been difficult with the sun obscured most of the time.

For a fleeting moment I thought I saw a light ahead, but when I looked again there was nothing there. I knew that eyes play tricks when you expect to see something, so I did not take too much notice. Then, a few minutes later, I saw a dark ragged line which extended right across the horizon. I blinked a couple of times, and then I was sure I was looking at the tops of the coconut palms on the northern side of Fanning.

Soon the land itself came into view and I ran along the lee of the island, sailing in strangely calm water. The buildings of the Cable Station peeped out amongst the palms on the western side of the atoll and presently the entrance to English Harbour came into view and I could see the familiar masts of *Tzu Hang* just behind the point.

A glance at the Tide Book showed that the tide was ebbing, and I wondered if the outboard would have enough power to push us into the lagoon. I fastened it over the stern and as usual she started first pull on the cord, but the current was too strong for us, and I was about to give up the attempt, when a small but powerful diesel launch appeared from inside the lagoon and soon arrived alongside. The two men aboard shouted that they had been expecting me the day before.

From their accents I guessed they were Australians, and a few minutes later when we had anchored *Trekka* near to *Tzu Hang* my guess proved correct. The elder of the two introduced himself and his companion. "I'm Phil Palmer, and this is my assistant, Bill Frew," he said in an intriguing drawl. "We're running the copra plantation here," he explained. "When you have time, come ashore and meet my wife and daughters, and I'm sure Bill here will have all sorts of questions to ask you."

Bill was a tall, slim young man with brown eyes, he was very deeply tanned and had a hungry look about him. "What kind of a trip did you have down?" he inquired in a soft, almost lazy voice. "The weather's been a bit crook the past three days here. Miles was fair dinkum when he said *Trekka* was small."

I chatted a few minutes with them, and Phil Palmer suggested that we move both yachts over behind Cartwright Point where we would be out of the tide and in better holding-ground. "We'll take you over at high water this afternoon," he promised.

Soon afterwards I was aboard *Tzu Hang* and comparing notes about the passage. Miles said that they had experienced the same sort of conditions as I had, but had got down in 11 days instead of nearly 14 in Trekka.

"I can't get over how much weight you've lost," said B. laughing.

"Well, what do you expect?" I replied. "Two weeks on my own cooking after two months of your enormous meals!"

"Did you see the new dinghy?" asked Clio.

"Yes," I replied. "I hope it rows better than it looks. It's the ugliest dinghy I've ever seen."

"We're very pleased with it," said Miles. "It rows very easily and will carry a very heavy load, we thought that now you have arrived, we could try your outboard on it when the four of us go across the lagoon."

Later that day Phil Palmer showed us the way through the coral heads to the anchorage behind Cartwright Point. There was a wooden shed with an iron roof just above the beach, and Phil said he would bring us some guttering which we could put up so we could collect fresh water.

I put my outboard on to *Tzu Hang's* new dinghy, and Clio and I went off to the Cable Station to find the doctor, so that I could clear with him and officially be allowed ashore.

He seemed to resent the fact that I had not waited aboard *Trekka* even though he had not been aware of my arrival. He pronounced me fit, rather grudgingly I thought, and said to let him know in good time when I was leaving so he could have the bill ready.

I soon forgot his unpleasantness, the scene outside was too interesting for petty thoughts. As far as the eye could see, the pale green waters of the lagoon stretched out to the horizon. The dark green of the palm-trees contrasted sharply with the blue sky, and in the distance I saw a rain squall darkening the surface of the water. Clio and I threaded our way through the coral heads back to *Trekka* and *Tzu Hang*, the motor trying to drown our speech.

"The skin-diving will be good here," shouted Clio.

"I was told that some of the fish are poisonous," I bellowed. "The Americans dumped a lot of ammunition into the lagoon when the war finished, and it contaminated some of the reef fish."

"I bet they'll be the easiest ones to catch," returned Clio.

We came up close to *Tzu Hang*, I slowed the motor and then cut it as we came alongside.

"Goodness, what a row you two make," said B. from below. "I heard you shouting at one another a mile away. I've got lunch all ready and thought we could go ashore and eat in the Grange. Pwe and Poopah can come ashore too, they would like a run around."

The Grange was the somewhat battered shed on the beach, and it became the centre of our activity during our stay on Fanning. We brought some sails ashore and made a few repairs stitching away in its welcome shade, and Miles decided that such an establishment ought to serve morning and afternoon teas, so a spare Primus was brought ashore, too.

We had several visits from the people at the Cable Station, and we went there a few times, too, but it was a five-mile journey over a very bumpy track, so most of the time it was just the four of us, doing a few odd jobs in the mornings, and then going ashore for lunch, skin-diving in the afternoon, and just taking things easy. It was a complete contrast to the bustle of Honolulu.

The four of us, and Clio's little dog Poopah, motored across the lagoon entrance in the dinghy to Western Point, where Phil Palmer's house was, and I met Mrs Palmer and her two daughters, one the same age as Clio and the other a couple of years older. The girls were soon showing us their pet fish which they kept in rock-pools at the edge of the lagoon. I was most intrigued to see them feed large fish with land-crabs which they held out over the water. The fish swallowed them in one mouthful.

We met Mr Hugh Greig, who was on the island during the First World War when the German raider *Nuremberg* arrived and sent a party ashore to put the Cable Station out of action. He gave us an interesting account of the excitement, and I believe it was he who eventually dived and recovered the cut cable after the Germans had left, so that contact with the outside world was re-established and the Royal Navy warned of the raider's position.

B. decided that we ought to walk round the atoll. According to the chart the distance was about 33 miles, and though there were a couple of other entrances to the lagoon besides the one at English Harbour, they were all shallow ones and could be waded across at low water. We got Bill Frew to collect us in the launch when he was over on our side of English Harbour. B. and I decided that we would travel light and live off the land. I carried a big knife with which I hoped to open coconuts to drink the milk. Miles and Clio thought it would be better to take a few supplies with them and they had two tins of peaches and a few cookies.

We started off from near the Palmers' house and followed the trail which wound around through the groves of coconut palms. The first few miles were quite pleasant, much of the walking being done in the shade, but as we went farther the trail became harder to find and eventually it petered out altogether.

It was necessary to wade across stretches of water which were shallow channels leading into the lagoon from the sea. One of them had the inviting name "Shark Passage." I used to wonder what the scene would look like to a shark, four pairs of legs, one behind the other like some large caterpillar groping its way along a little uncertainly sometimes the front legs stopping as if to test the bottom while the back legs (mine!) fidgeted.

There was an unpleasant stage when we had to cross large expanses of glaring coral sand. It was terribly painful on the eyes, which suffered what I imagine must have been a mild form of snow-blindness. We eventually arrived at a Gilbertese village, the men and their families are brought from the Gilbert Islands to work the plantation. It must have been an unusual sight to them to see four white people walking through the palms and we gratefully accepted the drinking nuts they brought us.

Soon afterwards we pushed on again and had done about a mile and a half when Miles remembered that he had left his camera near the village. The three of us watched him walk back to find it, grateful for the rest, but feeling sorry for the tall figure in the burning sun.

About an hour later he returned, looking tired but undaunted with the camera hanging from his shoulder. My efforts at gathering drinking nuts could hardly be described as successful. Even when I managed to get a nut the vast expenditure of energy required to open it offset the nourishment within. I concluded that there must be a knack to it that I had not discovered. Miles and Clio opened their peaches, and though B. and I protested that we were quite all right we couldn't resist the portions Miles offered us.

We reached the north-west passage and had to wait for low water to get across, by this time the sun had gone down and we were relieved from the energy-sapping heat. With a bright tropical moon to light the way, we crossed the final passage and set about the last few miles. The Cable Station lights came into view, and we went into the office where one of the young men was on night duty. He wanted to get some tea for us, but we realised that if we stopped we'd never get going again, so we just had a drink of water then set off on the last five miles. When we came out of the trees and saw the two boats anchored so peacefully in the moonlight, I promised myself I would sleep a week.

Clio's little dog, Poopah, was the hero of the trek, for with him being aboard the yacht so much he got very little exercise, but except for the wading when we had carried him he had done the rest on his short legs and still had a wag in his tail at the finish.

I had enjoyed Fanning Island very much, but it was now time to move on again. I went to the Cable Station to get a clearance for Apia, Samoa, and found a bill for £4 10s. 0d. waiting for me. This was apparently the "port" dues and the doctor's fee for giving me pratique. Disgusted with an administration that could be so petty and charge that amount for a slip of paper, I paid up. This was the only "port" that *Trekka* visited in her entire voyage round the world where she was charged dues.

*Tzu Hang* was going to Pago-Pago in American Samoa, so we planned to meet again in Auckland, New Zealand, where I would see about laying up *Trekka* so that I could join *Tzu Hang* for the voyage to Australia then back to England.

The two yachts left Fanning Island together late on the afternoon of 7 April, the Palmers, Bill Frew and some of the Cable Station staff came out a little way in the launch, but soon they had turned back and *Trekka* and *Tzu Hang* were left alone sailing quietly away from the sheltered lagoon. At nightfall we separated and I left *Trekka* to steer herself towards the south-west where 1,200 miles over the horizon lay Samoa.

The passage to Apia was a most pleasant one, for the weather kept fine for most of the two weeks it took me to get there. It was obvious that all the squalls and rain I'd had on the way to Fanning had been the doldrums, that area of frustrating weather between the North East and South East Trade Winds.

On 10 April *Trekka* crossed the Equator and slipped along over a very calm sea at three and a half knots. According to the weather charts, I could not expect to pick up the South East Trade until Latitude 7° south, but on Friday the 13th, which has somehow always been a lucky day for me, the wind increased until it was blowing a fine steady breeze. The sky put on its best expression, and I realized that we had indeed reached the South East Trade Wind. *Trekka* went along with the wind abeam, putting the miles away steadily and comfortably; it was sailing at its easiest and best.

Eleven days from Fanning we were only 300 miles away from Apia but then the sky changed and we were enveloped in a terrific electrical storm. Great jagged forks of lightning flashed across the sky, and the thunder cracked deafeningly. Rain fell in solid sheets knocking the sea flat and bouncing a foot off the deck. I never like lightning at sea, I know that there is only one thing sticking up in the air for miles around, and that is the mast. When I built *Trekka*, I fitted extra long chain-plates so that if lightning struck the rigging it could run down the plates into the sea.

The electric storm knocked the Trade Wind for a loop and for a few hours the wind went round to north-west. The sky remained cloudy, and though the south-easter returned I still did not like the look of the sky. That night the electric conditions returned and I downed sail and waited for the lot to move away.

Daylight brought clear weather, but the wind was rather light. *Trekka* kept moving along steadily, and by nightfall we had only 45 miles to go. I left her to look after herself during the night and woke just before dawn to see a light dead ahead. Daylight revealed the cloud-enshrouded slopes of Upolu Island with Apia nestling at the foot of them.

As we approached land, the wind became very light and *Trekka* ghosted along over the calm water. It was a Sunday morning, and all seemed quiet ashore except for a cock crowing, then church bells started to chime, the peaceful sound hanging in the morning stillness. I shackled the anchor and chain to the warp as *Trekka* steered herself into the harbour. When the lead-line showed four fathoms, I brought her up into the wind and dropped the anchor into the clear water. I stowed the sails and put the little yellow quarantine flag up. *Trekka* had completed another ocean hop, 1,200 miles in 14 days.

The doctor and port officials came to clear me a couple of hours later, after they had been out to a freighter which had just arrived from Suva. It seemed a little strange to arrive in port and find no *Tzu Hang* waiting for me, and this raised another problem. How was I going to get ashore?

There was no wharf I could moor against, and *Tzu Hang's* fibreglass dinghy was not available. I was wondering what to do, when a young Samoan paddled past in an outrigger canoe. I called to him and soon we were discussing the problem. We came to terms and I arranged to hire the canoe for the few days I would be in port.

The weather was terribly hot and humid and my shirt stuck to my back like a wet rag. I went into the quaint little town of Apia and brought a few fresh supplies and some bread. Canned food was very expensive, and I was pleased that I had bought so much in Honolulu.

A friend offered me accommodation ashore and rather than try to live aboard *Trekka* in the heat I gladly accepted. Everyone warned me about leaving *Trekka* at night, saying that everything would be stolen, but, although I had no means of locking the hatchway, I never lost a thing all the way round the world.

Just after daybreak one morning, my friend and I walked to the top of the mount overlooking Apia to visit the grave of Robert Louis Stevenson. The trail was quite steep, and though we had started early, it was already hot. A drenching shower when we reached the summit revived us somewhat, and we were able to admire the lovely view. It is a peaceful spot where the great writer was laid to rest.

I went with friends to a beach party a few miles from Apia. We passed through many Samoan villages along the route, and I was intrigued at the way the native houses were built of plaited coconut fronds with stout poles for framing. The houses were set on a level stone platform, and the walls were plaited matting which could be raised or lowered according to the weather. They were ideal homes for the climate.

I would have liked to have seen more of Samoa, and stayed longer too, but winter was fast approaching New Zealand, and I wanted to be there before the bad weather started.

Knowing that it would seem pretty cold as I got farther south, I bought a few items of clothing and an extra blanket.

Five days after I had arrived from Fanning, I was back at sea again running along the northern shore of Upolu Island towards Apolima Strait which separates the island from Savaii, the largest island in the Samoan group. As I approached the strait, a heavy rain squall overtook us, and visibility was down to a few yards for nearly half an hour. When it cleared, we were through the strait and into open water again. I checked the course on the chart and noticed that there was a reef we would be passing that night, so I altered course more to the eastward to make sure that we stayed well away from it. As we were now bound for New Zealand, I had the chart of the North Island out looking at all the interesting places and the natural harbours along the eastern coastline.

In the Bay of Islands, some eighty odd miles south of North Cape I saw a small township marked, named Russell. The name rang a bell in my memory and then I remembered that this was the place my father had spoken of when I was just a boy in the Channel Islands. He had lived in Russell at some stage of his life and was always talking of returning there with my mother and me. The war had put paid to that dream, but I thought I would like to see the place that he had remembered with such longing.

The weather became unsettled and a squall came along which seemed to alter the wind for a few hours. It blew from all points of the compass for a few minutes at a stretch, and finally I became so exasperated at changing sail for the progress of only a few yards that I lowered everything and waited for the wind to settle. The sea gradually flattened out and a faint breeze came in from the south-east. With the masthead genoa drawing well we ghosted along under a clearing sky while I read a book as I was steering. The calm weather continued, sometimes a slight breeze would move us along for a few hours, but there were long periods without any wind at all, and I passed the time away repairing sails or reading.

We were only about 150 miles from Vavau, the northern group of the Tongan Islands, and I decided that as they were so close, I might as well have a look at them. I altered course and started reading the Pilot Book about Vavau. There was a lot of sail changing. For a few hours the wind would be easterly then we'd be becalmed, and it would blow westerly; but slowly and surely *Trekka* kept moving along.

At daybreak on 3 May the north-eastern end of Vavau Island was only eight miles off, and a breeze came in which soon had us sailing along close to the shore towards the entrance to the sound between Vavau and Hunga Island. *Trekka* rounded a point and there before me lay a most beautiful scene, dozens of little palm-clad islands were set in the sheltered water of the lagoon like so many jewels. Small motor launches filled to capacity were ferrying happy, laughing Tongans to their homes on the various islands.

I had to tack up towards Neiafu, the main settlement on Vavau, and though I knew that the settlement was hidden by a point, I thought I must have come the wrong way, but at the last moment buildings came into view and soon *Trekka* had come in close to the wharf where I anchored. A crowd of islanders quickly collected, and presently the port officials arrived. The doctor was a huge man and rather than trust his weight to *Trekka* he asked me to come ashore. This apparently disappointed the crowd who evidently wanted to see how the doctor was going to get down *Trekka's* hatchway.

I was shown a very nice little landing where I could moor *Trekka*, and just step ashore without having to use a dinghy. A Tongan boy who spoke quite good English came and introduced himself, his name was Lino and he had been one of the crew on a large American schooner cruising through the islands. He had been to Honolulu and Tahiti, and said that he had enjoyed his cruising very much and would now try to make me enjoy my stay on Vavau by showing me round.

# CHAPTER SEVEN

# An Underwater Cave

One of the places I wanted to visit was an underwater cave called Mariner's Cave. It is on the island of Naupapu about ten miles from Vavau, and Lino arranged with one of the launchmen who was carrying some freight to the settlement there to take us along. Lino explained that the entrance to the cave was underwater and therefore was difficult to find unless you knew the place on the cliff to look for. The man we wanted as a guide was a fisherman named Benny who lived on Naupapu.

When we arrived Lino found that all the village elders were engaged in some conference, and we were asked to join them. None could speak English, but Lino was able to act as interpreter and the men were most interested in my voyage. One of the old men called to a young girl and spoke to her and presently she brought a large wooden bowl into which she poured some rather muddy-looking water then crushed up some stringy-looking stuff which she put into the water. She mixed the lot up with her hands and then poured a coconut cup of the liquid and handed it to me. Lino whispered that it was *kava* and that I should drink it. I can't honestly say that I enjoyed the national beverage of Tonga; to me the preparations were the most enjoyable part, but soon we were all drinking out of the little coconut cups and chatting away. The proposed visit to the cave was discussed, and someone was dispatched to find Benny. When he appeared I saw that he had only one arm, I learned that he had lost this while fishing—he held on to the dynamite too long.

As the launch had gone on to another island to deliver freight, we decided to walk across the island to the place where the cave was. The trail was very muddy, and as we went farther it petered out until we were just walking through dense bush. There were about fifty islanders accompanying us, and the whole affair had a school holiday spirit about it. Some were singing, others skylarking around, and many of the younger ones eyeing my swim-fins with curious expressions on their faces. Finally we came to the edge of a cliff, which was about forty feet above the sea. Some of the boys were pointing excitedly into the water and when I looked I saw a fair-sized shark swimming lazily away. This seemed to be the signal for everyone to dive or jump into the water. Soon I was the only one left standing on the cliff. I looked down at all the figures in the water beckoning me to jump. I threw the fins and face-mask to them and jumped. A world of blue exploded about me and as I rose to the surface I could see the brown bodies above me swimming and splashing about. I retrieved my fins and face-mask, the fins caused quite a stir amongst the men, as I put them on my feet. It was obvious that they had never seen them used before. Benny beckoned me to follow him, and, when he dived, I followed. There is something a little frightening when you dive for the first time into a cave, like this, not knowing how far you have to swim before you can breathe again, and wondering if you have already passed your point of no return.

Down he went into a large black hole and as I followed he disappeared for a moment into the shadow of the rock, then I, too, was in shadow and conscious of rock above me and the need to go deeper down into the unknown. My ears began to hurt a little with the pressure, then I saw Benny turning towards me and pointing to the surface. With my arms outstretched I shot upwards and broke the surface at the same moment as Benny. We gasped air into our lungs and laughed at each other.

"Is good?" he inquired and I looked about me at the great dome of the cavern.

"Is very good," I replied.

We climbed up on to a rock ledge at the back of the cave, and, as my eyes grew accustomed to the darkness, I was able to see how large it was inside. It was huge; the roof appeared to be a good thirty feet above us, and from the entrance the back of the cavern extended easily sixty feet. The only light was from the tunnel entrance, and, as I watched, it dimmed for a moment, and I saw the brown figure of an islander swimming through the entrance. As he came into the shadow his body seemed to change to dark blue and then he broke the surface and drops of water splashed off his head looking like diamonds and sapphires in the blue light.

Soon everyone was in the cave, and we climbed farther up at the back to make room for the others. One of the young men asked to try my fins, and the others all laughed at him when he put them on, but when they saw how well he swam with them they all wanted to try, and the cave rang with their happy laughter.

I noticed that my sight was distorted every few moments, and it was a little while before I realised why this was so. When the ocean swell hit the cliff outside, the water level in the cave rose a few inches and the air pressure increased, making my sight quite blurred for a few seconds. There was no other air outlet to the cave, and the water always covered the entrance, yet the air was quite pure inside.

One by one the islanders started leaving, and I found that someone had taken my fins with them. However, knowing the distance I had to go now and swimming towards the light it was not too far, and I managed to reach the other side without any help and with a little reserve left.

We climbed up the rock cliff, and I had nearly reached the top when I heard one of the men calling excitedly. Thinking that it was another shark I looked down into the water, but then one of them pointed, and I saw the familiar sails of *Tzu Hang* just entering the sound between Vavau and Hunga Island.

It was a tired and hungry group that made their way back to the village, and when we got there the delightful smell of broiled chicken assailed our nostrils. We only had time to snatch a quick snack as the launch arrived soon afterwards.

The chief shook me by the hand and spoke directly to me. Lino translated, "He says he is happy that he met you, and he wants you to know that he is very pleased that you came such a long way over the sea to see the cave on his island."

The launch drew away from the stone jetty and we waved goodbye. In a few hours I had made a lot of friends and I was sorry that I had to leave so soon.

On the way back to Nieafu, the launch stopped at Swallow's Cave. This cave can be entered in a boat, and we went right inside. Though worth seeing, it did not have the excitement of Mariner's Cave, and I realised that I should have seen this one first.

When we came round the point, I saw *Tzu Hang* alongside the wharf. Soon afterwards we were all exchanging news and comparing notes. I was delighted to find that *Trekka* had made the drift down from Samoa a day quicker than *Tzu Hang*, but, as Miles said, "We weren't trying very hard."

I told them about the cave and of the long way they would have to swim underwater. "Might as well make it sound good," I thought, "then when they make that first dive into the cave, they'll be wondering, as I did, just how much farther to go."

*Tzu Hang* moved from the wharf and moored to a large black buoy that was used for the freighter that called once a month.

"Come on Clio," I called, "let's see how long you can stay underwater. I'll time you with the stopwatch."

"All right," she said, "I'll go and change, you do the same and I'll time you, too."

Clio dived a couple of times. But each time I said, "You'll have to stay down longer than that if you're going to get in the cave."

"Very well, let's see how good you are," she said, just a trifle worried. I dived deep and swam along underwater until I came to the large buoy, I slowly let myself to the surface on the far side so she could not see me, waited a few seconds and dived and swam back the way I had come, surfacing just beneath her and gasping for breath.

"Gosh, that's not bad!" she exclaimed. "Two minutes and forty-three seconds."

"Well, it doesn't take that long to get in," I comforted her. "But you'll have to practise a bit first."

I had intended to sail for New Zealand the day after my visit to the cave, but when I saw *Tzu Hang* again I thought that another couple of days would not hurt.

On the day that the Smeetons went to visit the cave I left Vavau in *Trekka*. As there was no wind I got the launch that they were on to give me a tow as far as the cave. Once there, I couldn't resist another visit and left Lino to look after *Trekka* while I swam once more into the blue cavern.

It took a little persuasion to get Clio in, but after a while she dived deep and went right through the hole to surface inside. We splashed around inside and swam in and out several times. Then I climbed back aboard *Trekka* and said goodbye to everyone.

"See you in Russell!" I shouted. Then the two boats parted company, and I was left alone, sailing along past more islands towards the open sea.

CHAPTER EIGHT

# To New Zealand

By dark *Trekka* had almost put Vavau out of sight over the horizon, and with a fine northerly breeze to drive us along I decided to keep awake while still close to the islands. In the morning we passed the almost perfect cone of Koa Island, which rises to a height of 3,380 feet. Just after noon the active volcano on Tofua Island was abeam, and I watched the smoke from it curling up into the clear sky. At daybreak the next day we passed over the position where Falcon Island used to be. This island was some five hundred feet high in the 1930s and has undergone many changes due to its volcanic nature. It consisted of ash which was easily washed away by the sea after an eruption, so that it frequently disappeared altogether. When we sailed over the spot there was nine fathoms of water over it according to my American chart.

In the afternoon the island of Hunga Hapai was abeam, and we were now in clear water with *Trekka* steering herself under twin-staysails. I had not been feeling too well since the previous day. My throat was quite sore and I was wondering if I should put into Nukualofa just to be safe. This was the only time I ever felt ill at sea during the world voyage. I think, providing you leave port healthy, you are almost certain to arrive well the other end, as there are no germs to be collected at sea, and it's a healthy life away from the smog of cities. I decided to keep going, and the next day I was feeling better.

As we got farther south it started to grow colder. At first I just had to wear a shirt, but soon I was wearing my old Cowichan sweater. The nights, too, were cool, and I wished that I had bought another blanket at Apia.

When about fifty miles north-west of Sunday Island in the Kermadec Islands, the wind increased from the west until it was blowing a gale. It was quite a long time since *Trekka* had ridden out a gale, and I realised that as we got farther south I could expect more of this sort of weather. The wind moaned through the rigging all that day, and the sea built up to quite an impressive height. After darkness I listened to the radio for a while, but there was quite a bit of static and I eventually turned it off. At midnight I swabbed the bilges out with the sponge and was emptying the half-bucket of water over the side when I saw a strange sight. The moon was out and low clouds were racing across the sky, but it was something else that caught my attention. It was a great silver bow across the sky, like a rainbow, but this was night-time, and I felt a shiver go down my spine as I looked at the eerie sight. I concluded that it must be a moonbow, though I had never seen one before.

When the wind had backed to the south-west it rapidly eased off, and I was able to get sights next day and find out where we were. During the gale we had drifted 23 miles back, but soon we were going along again, climbing and dipping over the remains of the gale swell. The weather-cycle hereabouts seemed to be that the wind backed slowly all the time. When the wind was south and even when it was east or north, the weather was fine, but once it went into the west, bad weather usually followed.

*Trekka* crossed the International Date Line, and we went straight from Sunday to Tuesday. It was a little confusing at first, but I managed to convince myself that we were now twelve hours fast of Greenwich instead of twelve hours slow.

One weather cycle after another passed, and when we were about 280 miles from Cape Brett, a fine breeze from the south-east had us going very well. It gradually backed until it was blowing north-east, so the twins were set and I turned in for some sleep. The motion was pretty violent, and when the wind started to increase I decided to slow down and took the twins in. We ran under bare poles for a while, but soon I had set a staysail again, so as not to waste this fair wind. By noon the following day we had run 120 miles on the log in the past 24 hours. We were still going well a couple of hours later, then suddenly the wind just stopped. From a fine, steady breeze one moment it just stopped dead, and the sails came aback as *Trekka* slowly came to a halt. I dropped all sail and we rolled about drunkenly waiting for the wind to return.

A gusty westerly sprang up the next day, and we went along close hauled towards Cape Brett now only eighty miles away, but soon the wind had increased until it was again blowing a gale. I was getting the mainsail down when there was a crash from aloft and the whole boat shook. I was still wondering what had happened when there was a splash alongside and I saw a large albatross shaking his head in a stunned manner, he had evidently flown into the rigging, and I wondered if he had been asleep at the time. He flew away rather crooked, but I don't think he was hurt.

Late that night I saw the loom of the light on Cape Brett. The weather forecast was for westerly winds of 35 m.p.h., and it was quite correct. I remained lying ahull waiting for a break in the weather.

When we got going again the wind was from the north, and soon afterwards I sighted the Poor Knights Islands. I stopped for the night about ten miles off Cape Brett, and with the dawn I got sail up and let *Trekka* sail herself gently towards the Cape while I got breakfast ready.

It was wonderful to see the green slopes and hills of New Zealand and to know that *Trekka* had crossed the mighty Pacific.

All that day we tacked towards the land. There was very little wind, but it was so enjoyable sitting there in the sunshine looking at the coast that I was in no hurry to get in. At dusk we tacked past the lighthouse, and a couple of hours later we were becalmed. I got the outboard motor out of the locker and clamped it over the stern, and soon we were moving along over the calm water.

The moon came up, and I could see the light on Tapeka Point blinking away to guide us in. Around the point we motored, then the red light on the end of the wharf at Russell came into view. Just a few lights were visible and I realised that it was not a very big town. I had expected that it would have grown since my father lived here years ago. I ran in towards the wharf and let the anchor over the stern, then I slipped a bow-line over a bollard on the wharf to complete the twenty-three days' passage from Vavau.

The delightful smell of fresh baked bread came across the water, and I looked sleepily at my watch. It was midnight. I wondered where *Tzu Hang* was and how long she would be getting down, and I thought about the next voyage coming up when I would join her for the crossing to Australia. "Ah, well, I'll think about that tomorrow," I mused, and then I turned to the hatchway and the comfort of my bunk.

I was awakened by the sound of voices from the wharf, school-children were boarding one of the ferry-boats that operate across the bay to Paihia, and several swordfish launches were alongside the wharf, their skippers preparing for the day's fishing. Someone notified the doctor that I had arrived and he came along just after I had finished clearing away the breakfast things. I learned that there were no Customs or Immigration officials at Russell, but was advised to write to Auckland letting them know that I had arrived and would report to them when I arrived in Auckland.

Russell is a charming little place. I think I fell in love with it that first day. Everyone I met seemed so friendly and hospitable, that I felt I was among people I had known all my life. Of all the places I visited in my voyage, Russell has the happiest memories for me. Apart from the good friends I made there, it was easy to like this little township. The scenery around the Bay of Islands is lovely; the green hills, the beautiful islands and natural harbours, a wonderful climate and the peace of the place all combined to make it unforgettable.

Of all the people I met there, I remember Francis and Mille Arlidge best. They took me to their hearts and looked after me as though I was one of their six children. Francis had the game-fishing launch *Alma G.* and took parties fishing for the big striped or black marlin which come to the Bay of Islands from about the beginning of January to the end of May. He had been sport-fishing most of his life and had fished with many famous people, one of the best known being the great writer and big-game fisherman, Zane Grey. The fishing season was almost over and Francis offered me the use of his mooring as he was going to lay *Alma G.* up for the winter. This was very handy for me, as the mooring was just off the beach. He said I could use his dinghy until my friends arrived, so I was able to get ashore easily and quickly.

A friend was going to drive to Whangarei, which is quite a large town almost half-way to Auckland; he offered to take me, and as I had nothing very much to do I went along with him. The drive through the bush along a dirt road was well worth seeing, we stopped at several places to admire the scenery, and I saw some huge kauri-trees, one of the finest boat-building timbers in the world. Whangarei is at the head of a long inlet, about 12 miles from the open sea. It is a very pleasant country town and has a well-sheltered yacht-basin very close to its centre.

When we drove back to Russell that afternoon, *Tzu Hang* had arrived from Tonga and was anchored not far from *Trekka.* Clio saw me and came to fetch me in the dinghy. "Hello," she said, "someone told us that you had gone away for the day."

"Yes, I went down to Whangarei with a friend," I replied. "How many days from Tonga?"

"Fourteen, I think ... and, oh, I've got lots to tell you. We had an island feast after you left Vavau," she said excitedly.

We pulled alongside *Tzu Hang* and climbed aboard.

"Hello, Miles. Hi, B. Did you have a good trip?"

"Yes, not too bad, thanks," said Miles.

"Trust you to arrive in time for dinner," said B. "Well, come on then, you know where the plates are, what have you been doing with yourself?"

We were soon exchanging news over the evening meal and later when I started gathering the dishes for washing-up, we discussed the voyage to Australia and beyond.

"I think there are a few jobs that want to be done before we attempt the southern passage," I said.

"Yes, I know," said Miles. "The point is, can we do them here? If we go down to Auckland there'll be so many visitors we'll never get anything done."

Russell, Bay of Islands, New Zealand, is a charming little place

Francis Arlidge's *Alma G.*

Francis Arlidge and the day's catch

"Well, I can manage my end of it here O.K., once I've got the materials," I answered. "How about both of you?"

"I'm all for staying, too," said B. "And it will be much better for Clio here."

So it was decided we should stay at Russell and go down to Auckland by train to buy the items and materials we would need; and we began four months' intensive work on *Tzu Hang*, getting her ready for a passage round Cape Horn. As I am a joiner, there was much that I could do; and one of the first jobs I got down to was making new skylights, ones that would not leak and did not require a canvas hatch-cover over them in bad weather. The cockpit needed sealing off better, and so we pulled it out and put in a fibreglassed plywood one. It was quite small and little more than a foot-well, as the seating was on deck.

Miles was a little reluctant to adopt the same type of twin-staysail rig I'd had on *Trekka*, but finally agreed to try it. I made two 12-foot poles to boom the twin-staysails out, and these were painted white and stowed along the lifelines amidships.

I asked Miles if I could build a quarter-berth for myself alongside the cockpit, and as some of the tanks had to be renewed and moved he agreed. Meanwhile he was splicing up rigging and adjusting turnbuckles. Then he pulled out the old fuel tanks which were rusty and leaking so that we could replace them with new ones.

Though B.'s jobs were not as spectacular, she was just as busy, making new seat covers with her sewing machine, cleaning up after Miles and me, seeing that Clio kept working at her correspondence course and just feeding us, an all-time job.

It was not all work, though. At week-ends we would sail down to one of the islands where a couple of our friends lived and we also visited other parts of the lovely Bay of Islands.

With the weeks going by quickly, I had to find some place to store *Trekka* while I was away on *Tzu Hang*. Francis Arlidge came to my rescue when he said that I could store *Trekka* in his big shed. And so a few days later I was getting the masts out of her and transferring a pile of canned food to *Tzu Hang*. I put *Trekka* on the hard alongside the Russell Wharf, and removed the bolts that held the fin-keel in position. At high water she floated clear of the fin and I towed her to the beach where I had a cradle ready. By the end of the day *Trekka* was sitting snugly inside the Arlidge's shed along with the masts and sails.

I knew that she was in good hands, and would come to no harm while I was away. Sixteen months were to pass before I saw her again.

# CHAPTER NINE

# A Change of Yacht

The voyage I made in *Tzu Hang* was largely responsible for my completing *Trekka's* circumnavigation of the world, and at the risk of making *Trekka's* story disjointed, I would like to give a brief account of my travels in *Tzu Hang*.

Soon after I had laid up *Trekka* we left for Tauranga in the Bay of Plenty. There was still quite a lot of work to be done aboard, but during the two weeks that we stayed there most of it was finished.

We then sailed for Auckland, and while on the short passage had a bit of a blow for a few hours. We hove to until the worst was over, and then continued. I succeeded in gybing the mainsail and smashing the main boom, and felt somewhat crestfallen about the whole business. To my relief Miles was almost cheerful about it. "Never mind, John, the boom was in pretty bad shape. Now you can make us a new one!" he said.

I made the new main boom in Auckland, and B. got most of her supplies for the Tasman crossing, not too much, as we had heard that Australian Customs had made some skippers pay duty on stores they brought into the country.

We left Auckland on 23 September 1956 bound for Sydney, but decided to visit Great Barrier Island for a couple of days before setting off across the Tasman. The stop there gave us a chance to stow all our gear and try out our two new Terylene sails, a mainsail and a genoa.

We left on the 26th, and, as the wind was north of west, we did not close the shore of the North Island but lay as close to it as we could. I was feeling dreadfully seasick and just couldn't get used to *Tzu Hang's* motion. I'd be quite all right for a few hours. Then I'd be sick again. I told myself I'd be O.K. in a few days' time.

The wind held westerly and we kept going farther north up towards Norfolk Island.

We had just finished our evening meal on the fifth day out when Miles sighted a light. It looked to be too small for a ship, and as we got closer we saw that it was a yacht. To our amazement it was friends of ours, Tony and Bridget Reeves, in *White Hart* from Victoria, B.C., who were on their way to Auckland from Apia in Samoa. They launched their dinghy, leaving one of the crew to look after the boat while we all had a wonderful chat together aboard *Tzu Hang*. A couple of hours later they rowed back and we each went our separate ways. This was one of the most unusual meetings at sea that I know of.

We had a lot of westerly weather on our Tasman crossing, but there was the odd day or two when the winds favoured us. We were about half-way across when we were becalmed for a few hours in the warm sunshine. The sea became quite flat and we just lazed in the sun.

"Let's go for a swim," said B.

"Yes, come on," said Miles and Clio together.

"Not me," I said. "They have sharks off the Australian coast. There could be some out here."

"Nonsense," said B. "I'm going for a swim."

"No, seriously, B.," I pleaded. "Don't go in, it's not worth the risk, you'd never be able to get back aboard in time if you did see a shark."

"But we won't see any out here," she returned. "They stay close to land. Anyway, I'm going in."

"Miles, stop her," I begged.

"Well, I can't stop her," said Miles. "But I'll join her, I don't think there is much risk."

"I'm going, too," said Clio.

Miles could see that I was a bit uneasy about the whole thing. "I'll tell you what," he said, brightening, "you stay on guard with the rifle; I'll go and get it for you."

I watched the three of them swimming about enjoying themselves while I looked about for any signs of a fin in the water. To my relief they all climbed back aboard intact, and I was about to hand the rifle back to Miles when I saw a tin can floating in the water some fifty yards away.

"Oh, Miles, may I shoot at that tin can?" I asked.

"Sure, John," he said. "Wait a minute and I'll load the gun for you!"

When the wind came back we got going again and a couple of days later sighted Lord Howe Island. We closed the shore and thought about stopping for a brief visit, but *Tzu Hang* drew too much water to get inside the reef, and the only other anchorage at Ned's Beach on the north-eastern side of the island looked too exposed. The weather was looking squally, too, and that decided us. We kept going for Sydney.

On our twenty-third day out we entered the heads at Sydney Harbour and anchored in Watson's Bay awaiting Customs. Later in the day we moved to the Cruising Yacht Club in Rushcutter's Bay, where we stayed for just over two weeks. There were a few more jobs to be done, and the mizzen mast needed a new piece scarfed into it near the truck. At Charlie Busch's yard we pulled the mizzen out and I glued the new piece in. The fibreglassed mainmast had been such a success that we decided to do the mizzen, too, while we had it out. I sanded it down well with a machine-sander and Clio helped me to do the fibreglassing.

Miles and Clio were invited to take part in one of Jack Davey's quiz programmes on the radio and came home to the boat that night several hundred pounds richer, having won the jackpot. I regarded this as a very lucky break, for Miles had promised that if they won anything I'd get a new suit out of it, and *Tzu Hang* would be slipped and painted by the yacht yard. He was as good as his word, and I was not the only one to benefit from the quiz show. *Tzu Hang* was equipped with Terylene sheets and a couple of other items which were something of a luxury for a cruising boat.

While *Tzu Hang* was on the slipway being painted we were visited by a certain English yachtsman who had just lost his boat on a reef off the New Guinea coast. He was apparently looking for a suitable vessel in which to continue his voyage, although from his manner I thought he ought to have been in hospital for he had all the symptoms of shock after a trying ordeal. I remarked that I knew of a small boat that was for sale in New Zealand having just been sailed out from England.

"Well, what is she like," he asked me.

"Her name is *Jellicle* and she's a folkboat about twenty-five feet over-all. . . ."

"Twenty-five feet!" he snorted, interrupting me. "What would I do in a boat of that size. I might as well go round the world in a dinghy with an outboard motor. I want to be the first Englishman to sail around the world singlehanded and it's got to be in something not less than thirty-five feet."

I don't think he knew that I had *Trekka* and was also an Englishman. But his contempt for small craft stung me, and I thought, "Just you wait, Mister, and I may show you what a dinghy and outboard motor can do some day."

The first member of *Tzu Hang's* crew left us in Sydney. Poopah, the dog, was sent to England aboard a freighter and would arrive there a little sooner than Clio, who was going to fly from Melbourne and go to school again.

The Olympic Games were due to start in Melbourne towards the end of November, and as B. had some tickets for the opening ceremony we wanted to arrive in Melbourne in good time. The distance to Melbourne is about six hundred miles, and to make sure we'd have plenty of time, we left Sydney with twelve days to get there.

The passage down the coast was a rough one, I was soon feeling seasick again, I just couldn't get used to *Tzu Hang*'s motion. B. persuaded me to try some seasick pills, but I had no faith in them and they did not seem to have any effect. I wondered if I was going to be sick all the way back to England, too. It was rather a grim thought.

We got down as far as Gabo Island off the New South Wales and Victoria border; and there we stayed. The wind came in hard from the southwest, and there was little else we could do except wait for a wind shift and hope that it would moderate. A couple of times we tried some sail up, but there was a big sea running and the motion was awful, we decided to wait.

When we did get going again we went well and passed Wilson's Promontory with still three days to go for the opening of the Games. But then another westerly came along, which blew quite hard for a few hours and we had to lie ahull again. When we eventually arrived at the St Kilda Yacht Club just outside Melbourne the Games had been under way for two days. The St Kilda Club was the headquarters for the Olympic yachting events, and most of their moorings were in use, but we were offered a berth on the Yarra River just below the Spencer Street bridge and opposite the Royal Yacht *Britannia*.

Melbourne was gay with a holiday spirit. Thousands of Olympic visitors thronged the decorated streets and shops, and their enthusiasm infected us. There was little to do aboard *Tzu Hang*. Most of the work had been done, and, except for taking on stores, we were about ready for our long voyage. We decided to have a few days off and see the Games and visit friends.

I was pleased to see some of my South African friends who were members of the Springbok team, and I spent my time seeing as much of the various events as possible. When at last the games were over, and the crowds began to disperse, we watched the Royal Yacht being towed down the river and thought that we would be travelling the same route in a few days' time.

And then the day came when we took Clio out to the airport and watched her climb into the waiting aircraft to be flown to school in England. The three of us felt miserable when we returned to *Tzu Hang*. With Clio gone, there was now a feeling about the ship of wanting to get started on the voyage so that we could all be reunited again.

We loaded six months' supplies aboard and attended to a few last-minute jobs. I'm sure *Tzu Hang* had never looked better. She may have looked newer when she was launched, but she was now a very fine example of a well-equipped ocean-cruising yacht. The months of work had not been spent polishing brass or rubbing down varnish, we had spent the time well, replacing doubtful fittings and gear, stopping any annoying leaks in the deck and making the boat as comfortable as possible at sea. She was a good boat, and because we all loved her, she came first. We were going down the old sailing-ship route to the Horn in a small vessel, but we had confidence in her, and we knew that she could do it.

We left Melbourne on 23 December 1956 bound for Port Stanley, in the Falkland Islands some 6,600 miles away. We sailed down Port Phillip Bay, anchored for the night off Dromana, and left early in the morning, as we wanted to catch the tide at slack water while we went through Port Phillip Heads.

There was quite a slop outside, and we were tossed about a bit as there was very little wind to steady us. Shortly afterwards we noticed that the main gooseneck had broken, it had apparently seized up while we had been in Melbourne. The voyage was still young for this kind of thing to happen, so we decided to go in to Cowes, Western Port, and see if we could have it repaired. It was Christmas Eve but we managed to find a garage in Cowes that was open and someone to braze the fitting.

The wind was starting to blow quite hard from the west and was making *Tzu Hang* surge up against the wharf, so we decided to anchor out in the channel instead.

The following day the wind had moderated and we set off after half an hour's struggling to get the anchor up. Now we were off at last, off on the voyage we had planned in the harbour at Kahului Maui just a year before.

# CHAPTER TEN

# Roaring Forties

I had suffered from seasickness so much on *Tzu Hang* that I did not know what to do about it. A friend in Melbourne told us that seasick pills had to be taken about four days before the intended journey to have any real effect, we had all taken pills for the past four days and I was wondering how long I'd have to wait before the first signs of queasiness. To my delight I found that the remedy worked, and all of us felt quite all right.

*Tzu Hang* seemed to know that we were off on a long passage, for she went along at top speed all that day, and by noon the next had run 168 miles on the log. We went through Bank Straits and then out into the Tasman Sea heading for the south of New Zealand. A strong blustery breeze drove us along over a rough sea and under grey skies. It seemed as though we were following a depression across the Tasman and moving along at the same speed. It was uncomfortable sailing, but we were going well and nine days later we were between the Snares and the Auckland Islands, getting down close to the fiftieth parallel of Latitude.

Then the weather changed and we were becalmed. The sea went down and the skies cleared, it was a welcome change from the grey days, and soon the deck was covered with bedding being aired while we attended to a few jobs that could be done in these pleasant conditions.

I had long decided that the two little doors in the aft end of the doghouse should be changed for washboards and so while the weather was good I made the alterations using some materials that B. had collected. B. never believed in throwing anything away, and, though she collected an enormous amount of junk, some of it became quite useful at times.

While I was in New Zealand, I had bought a 16-mm. movie camera with the intention of making a full-length film of the voyage from Melbourne to England. I had used the camera quite a bit in New Zealand and across the Tasman to Sydney, and had found most of the best angles on the boat for effective filming. I realized that I would have to try to get some shots from the dinghy, as nothing is more boring than endless scenes all shot on board.

Whenever the sea was not too rough and the conditions were good I'd ask Miles if I could launch the dinghy and shoot some film. During the calm off the south of New Zealand we launched the dinghy for the first time. *Tzu Hang* was moving along quietly under twin staysails and as I rowed away with the camera I couldn't help but feel proud of her. There was something rather gallant about the way she carried herself, every line of her was clean and pleasing, she was a lady, and a beautiful one too.

I rowed well ahead, and then shot off a hundred-foot roll of film, some of it from ahead and other shots from the beam and stern views.

"Come and see her from the dinghy, B!" I called, when I came alongside. Miles and I watched as she rowed over the ocean swell, sometimes disappearing out of sight behind a crest. I wondered how many women had rowed a dinghy in those latitudes. None, I decided.

When the wind came back, it was from the north-east, and we held on to the port tack, going south of east. This weather was a little unusual as we had been expecting steady westerlies rather as we'd had across the Tasman Sea.

We drove on until we were down south of Latitude 50° and inside the red line on the weather chart which indicates that ice extends that far north. It was a sobering thought, and rather than go farther south we decided to wait for a shift in the wind.

Slowly we made our way across the vast expanse of ocean, sometimes with fair winds, sometimes beating against head winds, but always moving on with only an albatross or two for company. We were quite content aboard, we had our own little world and were comfortable in it. We were on watch at the same hours every day and got used to our own personal routines. Apart from reading in my off-watch hours, I had other interests, the photography, or making various things from the scrap materials that B. hoarded so zealously. I found myself thinking more and more about taking *Trekka* on round the world, and I passed many pleasant hours sketching on pieces of paper the alterations I planned to make to the little boat.

The days and the weeks slipped by, and we got used to the ever-changing weather systems, the great long swells which always seemed to be with us and the spells of bad weather. On watch at night, I could picture the old windbags loaded full of grain, running the easting down in these latitudes half a century ago, now only the ghosts of them and a 46-foot ketch were going down the old route to the Horn.

We were almost half-way across the Southern Ocean to South America before the winds steadied in the westerly quarter. I had thought that the wind was always westerly down in these latitudes, but it was not. It moved about as each depression came along and sometimes blew from the east leaving us to decide which tack was the best one.

Early on the morning of 14 February I was on watch from 3 a.m. to 6 a.m. *Tzu Hang* was running fast under twin-staysails and steering herself, but the wind was increasing, and I heard the top of the staysails fluttering, which they did when it was blowing quite hard. Miles came up to have a look at the weather, and we decided to take in the twins and run along under bare poles for a while. B, came on deck and took the tiller while Miles and I went forward to pull the twins down. Each sail was set on its own stay and could be lowered one at a time if need be. We let both come down together then unhanked the sails and bundled them down the forehatch and snapped the twin poles to the lifelines.

By the time we had cleared away on deck the wind had quite a bit of weight to it and was sending us along at about four knots under bare poles. There was still an hour to go on my watch, but Miles was well awake by now, and, as he was on watch next, he decided to take over now instead of waiting until six. I went below and pulled my oilskins off and then climbed into my bunk, which was the quarter berth I had built in alongside the cockpit. It was a dry comfortable bunk and I was soon asleep.

I was awakened by Miles tapping on the side of the cockpit, which was the usual way B. called me on watch to take over from her. I was reluctant to leave the warmth of the bunk and wondered if he wanted a hot drink of cocoa or something. I looked out of the hatch and saw that it was light. "What do you want, Miles?" I asked, rather sleepily, hoping that it would be something easy, so that I could get back into my warm bunk.

"You should see some of these seas now, John. They are really quite impressive, and the biggest I have seen so far. How about filming some with your movie camera?"

I thought of getting back into wet oilskins and going out into the cold and part of me rebelled. "The light is not very good," I said, hopefully.

But then Miles was looking aft, and he turned to me and said, "Look at this one coming along now. You've never seen a sea like that before. Get the camera, you may never have a chance to get a shot like that again."

When I looked at the scene I saw what he meant. The sea looked different from the weather we'd had the last fifty days. There was a feeling of suppressed power about it, almost as though it were awakening after a long sleep. I saw another sea a quarter of a mile away roll up astern, higher and higher; then *Tzu Hang* started to climb the long slope until the crest passed beneath her and she sank into the trough behind. Miles was right, I had never seen the sea like this before, and I went below to get my camera. I filmed the sea from astern and got a couple of shots of the wind blowing the crests off the big seas.

"I'll shoot more later on, Miles, when B. is on watch, the light will be better then, and I'd like to have some shots of her steering."

The exposed film I put in a plastic bag, and as the tins I had been using were full, I put the bag in Clio's school-locker. I was pleased later that I had done so.

B. tumbled out of her bunk at seven o'clock and started making breakfast. I ate mine and then went on deck to take the helm while Miles had his breakfast. He was soon back again at the helm and said to me, "Before I called you up to film the sea, two quite large seas broke over the stern and washed me right up to the doghouse. You can see how they burst the canvas dodger."

I thought that he could not have been dead before the sea because during the few minutes I was steering, while Miles had his breakfast, I had been quite impressed at the ease with which the boat steered and rode those enormous seas.

"Goodness, just look at those seas!" exclaimed B. when she came on watch at nine o'clock. "You should be happy now, John, surely. You've been asking for big seas ever since we started for your film. I hope you're satisfied with these."

"Yes, they ought to look good on the screen, even though the sea always looks flat on film," I replied.

I went below to get the camera and noticed that Miles was in his bunk reading. Pwe was sitting on his chest purring. I went on deck again and shot more film and finished the roll with a scene of B. steering.

"I must just go and put another film in the camera B.," I said, and slid the hatch back to go below.

I got a roll of film out of the locker and went aft to my bunk to load the camera. I sat on the seat by my bunk and opened the camera. The exposed film I laid on the bunk, then I started to thread the new film into the spool.

*Tzu Hang* gave a violent lurch to port, and I put my hand out to grab the fuel tank opposite. I had a sudden feeling that something terrible was happening. Then everything was blackness and solid water hit me. I was conscious of a roaring sound and that we were already very deep. "She's been hit by an enormous sea, and is full of water. She is already sinking, I must get out." These were the thoughts that flashed through my mind. I knew that I had to go forward then up out of the doghouse hatch and I started to fight my way against the solid water. Suddenly I was looking at a large blue square. "What on earth is that?" I wondered. Then I heard Miles's anguished voice, "Where's B.? Where's B.? Oh, God, where's B.?" He stumbled past me crying out, "Where's B.?" and I watched him climb into the blue square. I realised that I was lying on my back in the galley and looking at the sky through the opening in the deck where the doghouse had been.

I scrambled out on to the deck and saw B. in the water about thirty yards away. It is a picture I will never forget. She was wearing a bright yellow oilskin, the sea was almost white with spume and overhead the sky was a hard blue. B.'s face was covered with blood and for a crazy moment I thought, "Oh, what a shot for colour film."

B. raised her hand and shouted, "I'm all right, I'm all right." While she started to swim towards us I looked about me and saw that both masts were in the water and all smashed into short lengths as though they had exploded apart. The doghouse had been wiped off at deck level and I noticed that both dinghies had gone. The side skylights were both smashed and the lids had gone too. I looked up and saw another monster of a sea approaching and I thought "What a bloody shame! No one will ever know what happened to us."

"Hang on," I shouted, and *Tzu Hang* lifted sluggishly to meet the crest, she had a slow hopeless feel about her and I watched more water pour down the great hole in the deck.

Miles called to me to give a hand at getting B. aboard. I looked at the ruin everywhere and thought "I might as well jump in alongside her."

B. had something the matter with her arm, for when we hauled her aboard she thought I was kneeling on it.

"Well, this is it, Miles," I said, knowing that we had come to the end of the trail.

He nodded. "Yes, it looks like it, John."

"Hang on!" I cried, as another big sea came along. *Tzu Hang* again made a tremendous effort, but she lifted, and I felt a spark of hope. "We've got a chance," I cried. And just then B. said, "I know where the buckets are."

The two of us climbed down into the waist-deep water that was splashing backwards and forwards in what a few seconds before had been our comfortable little home. My main thought was to prevent more water getting below and that meant we had to cover the doghouse opening with sails or something. I climbed into the forecabin and started pulling the twin staysails aft, they would help.

For bearers to cover the opening I took the rods from Miles's bunk and the door off his hanging locker. My tools were still intact and the box was jammed on top of the galley sink. By some extraordinary luck the galvanised nails were still in the paint-locker though everything else had gone. It was difficult working on deck for there was nothing to hold on to, everything had been wiped bare except part of the aft end of the doghouse, the winches and the mainsheet horse. Miles gave me a hand to cover up the doghouse opening and we spread the Terylene genoa over the bearers I had nailed across, but soon I was able to carry on alone and he went to help B. with the Herculean task of bailing out a few thousand gallons of water from *Tzu Hang's* bilges.

I let go all the rigging-screws except the forestays in the hope that the wreckage of the masts and sails would act as a sea-anchor and hold us head to sea, for a few seconds she came around into the wind but then she broke free and fell back with the wind on her beam.

I transferred the warp trailing aft to the bow, and secured the jib to it in the hope that it would act as a sea-anchor, but there was not enough drag to it and we continued to lie with the seas on our beam. Just inside the forehatch there were two gallons of fish oil together with the canvas bags it was supposed to be used with. I thought I'd never have a better opportunity to try oil on breaking seas, so I punctured both cans and emptied the lot over the side, there was not time to fill the bags. I felt that even a few minutes' respite would help. I also emptied four gallons of engine oil over the side. There was no sign of either on the water and it did not have the slightest effect.

The one thought that gave me hope was that I knew the barometer had started to rise again just before the smash, which indicated that the centre of the depression had passed. If we could keep *Tzu Hang* afloat for a few hours we stood a reasonable chance of getting out of this mess.

Miles and B. were bailing out of one of the side skylights. I covered the other with the red storm-jib, lashing it down as best I could. I could hear B's steady call "Right," as she handed another bucket of water up to Miles who emptied it over the side.

I got a bucket and bailed out of the forecabin skylight, my feet were spread wide on each bunk as I bailed. At first I could easily reach the water bending down with the bucket, but as we slowly made progress I found that I had to climb down to fill the bucket then step up on to the bunks to empty it out on deck.

By dark we had got most of the water out of *Tzu Hang*. But what a pitiful condition she was in! The bilge was full of wreckage, hundreds of cans of food, most of them with no labels, clothing, broken glass jars, books, coal and eggs, parts of the stove and miles of B.'s coloured wool that had somehow tied everything together in a most infuriating way. B. had been wearing a pair of my sea-boots when she went overboard and had kicked them off while in the water. For hours she had stumbled about in the wreckage below with only thick socks on her feet, that night she noticed that one foot was badly sprained.

Miles and I were still vague as to what had happened but B. was able to give us a fairly good idea. She said that she had been steering *Tzu Hang* down wind and had met each of the big following seas stern on, but when she looked over her shoulder again she had a brief glimpse of an enormous wall of water bearing down on *Tzu Hang*. Water appeared to be running down the face of it and she could see no white crests. She could not see how *Tzu Hang* could possibly rise to it but knew that she was dead stern on, there was a feeling of being pressed down into the cockpit then she was in the water and thinking that she had been left behind. She looked around then saw *Tzu Hang* very low in the water and dismasted.

I managed to get one of the Primus stoves working and heated up some soup. Miles had a little, but B. did not want any.

We dozed that night, only to be brought wide awake as big seas hit the boat and water trickled below through the great hole where the doghouse had been. I thought of how I was going to make it pretty watertight if I got the chance. It was an awful night, everything was soaking wet and now that we were not working at bailing or covering the openings, we had time to realise the serious position we were in. A thousand miles from the nearest land, and that was the inhospitable coast of Patagonia and no hope of a passing ship picking us up.

With the masts and booms gone, there was not much to make a jury-rig from either. If we got out of this one all right it would have to be on our own efforts and with a good helping of luck.

In the morning the sea had gone done quite a bit, but it was still running a good thirty feet high, and the wind was about 35 knots. We bailed the rest of the water out of the bilges, then, after we'd had a snack of ship's biscuits and cheese, I set about making a better job of the doghouse opening. I nailed the rods from Miles's bunk round the edge of the hole so that water running along the deck did not go below quite so easily, the hanging locker-door, a piece of cockpit coaming and some plywood that we had stowed away, made quite a strong roof. And when the Terylene genoa was folded several times and laid over, and then nailed down with battens, surprisingly little water came below.

Miles went below to start the awful job of cleaning out all the mess in the bilges and trying to find the parts for the stove.

Pwe the cat was in a bad way and unless she had some warmth she was going to die.

Miles slowly found the missing stove lids amongst all the other mess and soon afterwards the stove was going, though smoking badly, for the stovepipe on deck had gone with all the rest.

We worked away steadily, Miles sorting out the ruin below, B. getting the galley into working order and I doing my best to stop any water from getting below. I sealed *Tzu Hang* up tight and the smoke from the stove below swirled across the cabin making our eyes smart.

Slowly we made progress. There were no worries about going ashore for a few weeks, so we decided to make the boat as comfortable as possible meanwhile.

# CHAPTER ELEVEN

# *Jury-Rig*

Miles came below a couple of days after the smash and announced that the rudder had gone. I went up to have a look, and saw that although the top of the stock was there and still moving, the rudder itself had been torn off and the 2⅜-inch diameter bronze stock had snapped off just where it emerged from the trunk.

Three days after the smash I started making a jury-mast out of two broken booms, one a twin-staysail pole and the other a spare staysail club.

When these two were fished together we had a spar 15 feet 6 inches long. We stepped this spar using jib bridles for shrouds and the old mizzen shrouds for a forestay and backstay. The only sail in the boat that was small enough to use was a raffee that B. had made and which had always been regarded as useless. It now became the best sail we had.

The mast bent badly when we hoisted the tiny sail so we took it down and screwed two splints alongside the mast to strengthen it. When the sail was set again, it did not bend so alarmingly and we noticed to our delight that we were slowly moving along at about two knots. *Tzu Hang* was on the wrong tack, however, and we had to try to get her going north-east instead of south-east. Miles and I struggled with the sheets and paddled frantically with the dinghy oars and finally got her round on to the other tack, we returned below feeling pleased that we were at least pointing in the right direction and moving along slowly.

Miles got some sights that day and to my amazement I found that my radio was still working. We checked the chronometer and noticed that its rate had not altered. Miles's sights put us at 51° 17′ S. Latitude and 98° W. Longitude, just under a thousand miles due west of the entrance of the Straits of Magellan.

During the night *Tzu Hang* went about on the other tack so we dropped the sail and waited for daylight before trying to get her round again.

In the morning we tried just about everything to get her on the other tack, and just got madder and madder. We paddled until our arms ached, we tried towing a drag from the quarter and juggling with the sheets, all to no avail. Miles and I went below, sick at heart, and B. cheered us up by making a cup of tea.

Miles was for trying out some new scheme and I was for making a steering-oar.

"Out of what, though?" asked B.

"Well, there is a lot of material here that I could use," I said. "The bulkheads are all tongue-and-groove boards, and the door-frames are quite solid."

"Well, you make the steering-oar," she decided. After tea I started. Poor *Tzu Hang.* I removed door-frames and any pieces that were not vital to the boat and after a couple of days' work had the most crazy-looking oar imaginable. It was about sixteen feet long and was made up of short lengths all scarfed and screwed together. The blade was a locker door. We took this contraption on deck and screwed it together again. Then I put it over the stern with a grommet to hold it in position. Miles set the raffee and once we were moving I gradually exerted pressure on the oar. *Tzu Hang* slowly responded, and to our delight gybed over on to the other tack. We hauled the oar aboard and altered the sheets of the raffee before returning below, very smug with ourselves. The only compass we had was a small one by Miles's bunk, the main compass had gone overboard with all the other gear. I saw Miles looking puzzled as he looked at the small compass and I went over to have a look. Evidently during the two days I had been making the oar the wind had changed direction and we had just put *Tzu Hang* on to the wrong tack. We went on deck and put her about again. Then we saw that we were now heading north-east.

B. had been below all this time, for her foot was in a bad way. Huge blood blisters were breaking out on her skin, and though I urged her to pop them she was wise to leave them alone. B. had been knocked about worse than we thought. The wound on her head had looked most spectacular, though it proved to be just a deep cut, but her shoulder was very painful, and Miles and I thought she had broken a collar-bone. She sat by the stove most of the time trying to coax the scraps of teak into flame. It smoked horribly, and with every-thing battened down tight, there was no fresh air below and the smoke in the cabin would finally drive Miles and me on deck for a breath of clean air. When we looked aft, we could see smoke emerging from the rudder trunk. Nothing ever seemed to come out of the chimney.

When we returned below the smoke seemed worse than ever, and it was difficult to see from one side of the boat to the other. The figure of B. crouched by the stove, her long hair unkempt and her face soot-streaked, slowly stirring a steaming pot as the cat sat on her lap, gave the impression of a witch's cellar in a Walt Disney movie.

The days passed quickly and *Tzu Hang* slowly crept northwards out of the "Screaming Fifties" and into the "Roaring Forties." One of the nice things about this kind of sailing was that with no rudder no one had to steer, and we all slept in at night.

I would go on deck sometimes and watch *Tzu Hang* limping along. It tore at my heart to see her reduced to such a sorry sight, no more the loftiness of her masts or the delicate upward tilt of her bowsprit, instead just a battered hull and scarred deck. But they were honourable scars, and though she was limping she was still proud. I swore that if she brought us to port safely, I'd help to heal her wounds so that she'd sail the ocean swell again.

The smoky saloon and forecabin were hives of industry these days. I was making a twenty-foot box-section mast out of the stump of the old mainmast and bulkhead material. Miles was splicing up wire rope for the shrouds of this new mast, and B. was unpicking the new Terylene mainsail so that we could make a lugsail out of it.

Meanwhile *Tzu Hang* kept moving along slowly but surely, gradually reducing the distance to Talcahuano, the port we hoped to make in Chile.

Miles was hoping that we might be able to sail to windward if the need arose, with the aid of the sail that B. was altering. When it was ready and I had completed the gaff we took the new mast on deck and screwed it together, and then stepped it next to the small one. The little mast we set up aft as a mizzen.

We decided to try the new rig right away and hoisted the Terylene sail and its gaff. It looked as though we needed something set for a mizzen so we set a tiny jib-topsail as a mizzen with a dinghy-oar as a boom. *Tzu Hang* immediately started to come up into the wind but I was watching the mast when it suddenly broke in half and collapsed.

I went below and Miles passed me the two pieces and I started to repair it. Next day it was stepped again and had two extra pieces fastened half-way up to stiffen it.

We decided to leave the big sail until the wind fell lighter. Meanwhile we had quite a bit of sail up considering what we had before with the little mast. The jib I had used as a sea-anchor had split across the centre. This was now set upside down as a mainsail, with the raffee as a sort of balloon-jib. The tiny mizzen helped to make us point a little higher.

We had done just about half the distance to Talcahuano under the tiny raffee alone, and with the extra sail set we seemed to be moving along very well.

*Tzu Hang* was knocking out some wonderful runs considering the rags she had up and the fact that she was steering herself without a rudder. Our best day's run on the log was 77 miles in 24 hours. There were other days when the total was over seventy, and we really felt we were coming along very well. The ocean current was giving us another 10 miles a day, too.

About two weeks after the smash, B. came on deck for the first time since she had bailed below amidst all the ruin. She had acquired quite a tan from the stove, and though I had seen her looking better, it was encouraging to see her on deck and getting about again.

The cockpit drains had become plugged with pieces of coke and Miles and I tried to unblock them with bits of wire. It took B.'s persistence finally to clear them and let the water drain back into the sea instead of slopping about in the cockpit.

As we crept farther north the weather became warmer and the sea seemed almost calm after two and a half months of the "Roaring Forties." The wind had swung more to the south and we realised that we were coming into the influence of the South Pacific High. All our charts had been lost in the crash except a National Geographic Magazine map of the Pacific which was printed on cloth, and a chart of the South Atlantic which showed just a little bit of the Chilean coast where we were heading for. Miles started to draw a map using the little information from them and consulting the Pilot book. From the look of it, Talcahuano was no good for a landfall, as we would have to beat our way into the bay. The best place to make for was the little port of Coronel some 40 miles south of Talcahuano. It was easy to enter and we could always arrange a tow once we got there.

We had plenty of food aboard, but there were a few items that we missed. Sugar was one of them. The sugar sack had been kept in a bin which formed the seat by my quarter berth. It was quite a large bin and as the sack of sugar took up only half the space, there were a few things stowed with it. B. had a pair of climbing-boots there, and I kept my photographs and magazines there, too.

B. gave Miles and me a surprise one day by producing some fudge she had made while the two of us were on deck.

"Why that's wonderful, B." exclaimed Miles. "May I have another piece?"

"Yes, there's plenty more. Help yourself," said B.

Now when B. starts giving precious stuff like fudge away generously—I get a little suspicious.

"Where did you get the sugar from, B." I asked, quite innocently.

"Oh, I found some," she answered. "Here, have another piece."

Then suddenly I knew what she'd done, I went aft and lifted the lid of the sugar-bin, it was half full of thick brown treacle, and submerged in it was the sugar sack, the remains of my magazines and photographs and B.'s climbing-boots.

"You surely didn't use that?" I said, quite unnecessarily, for I knew she had. "Why, your climbing-boots are floating around in it."

"So what?" she said unperturbed. "They're quite clean, and you said you liked the fudge, didn't you."

There was a wonderful feeling of comradeship between the three of us. We all realised that without the other two we would never have survived, and though we all wanted to get into Coronel, I think we also realised that we would never be this close again.

Thirty-four days after the smash, B. sighted the top of Mocha Island early in the morning. We began to realise that the long journey was almost over.

As we went farther up the coast, we encountered thick fog. This was nerve-racking as we knew that it took us nearly a quarter of a mile to get *Tzu Hang* from one tack on to the other. If land loomed up suddenly out of the fog we might lose the ship.

Three days later the fog was just as thick, but Miles had been able to get sights farther offshore where the fog was patchy, so he was reasonably sure of his position. We went on steadily through the fog, and we took turns up at the bow peering through the whiteness. Then suddenly we emerged into the sunshine and left the blanket of fog behind. Miles had got us right on course and the little town of Coronel was dead ahead. All that day we crept towards it, *Tzu Hang* still steering herself. The sun was low in the sky when we anchored near the wharf, 87 days from Melbourne, having brought our crippled ship into port by our own efforts.

Three days later *Tzu Hang* was towed to the Chilean Naval Base at Talcahuano, where she was lifted out of the water by a gigantic crane and set down on the ground near the sea wall where we hoped to repair her.

Of the months of hard work, the frustration, and the many friends we made, I can do no better than recommend that you read Miles Smeeton's book *Once is Enough*. He has described far better than I ever could the voyage and the repairs in Chile as well as *Tzu Hang's* subsequent voyage.

Technically speaking, there was not very much wrong with *Tzu Hang*. The hull was as sound as the day she was launched in Hong Kong. The new doghouse and skylights presented no difficulty to me to make. But good materials in Chile were very hard to come by. The local wood, lingue, would have been quite good, had it been properly seasoned, but it was discouraging to see it opening up and twisting once it was fastened into position. The masts and spars had to be made out of material that would not have been used as scaffold-boards in Canada, but we put the best we had into her and made it as strong as possible.

I could not leave *Trekka* in New Zealand for too long, I had been away a year already and if I stayed with *Tzu Hang* it would be at least another year before I could return to Russell. Miles and B. said they hoped to leave for England some time in December *via* Panama. I hoped to be fitting *Trekka* out by then as I wanted to cross the Tasman before the southern summer ended.

The last few days I spent in Chile were active ones, although most of the big jobs had been done, there were endless little ones, and I tried to show Miles and B. what had to be done and explain the drawings I had made of the masts and spars and other details.

It was a wonderful experience to know them both, and I think they'll know what I mean when I say that as an achievement, I am more proud of the voyage I made in *Tzu Hang* than my own single-handed voyage round the world in *Trekka*.

# CHAPTER TWELVE

# Return to "Trekka"

From Chile, I flew to South Africa and visited my mother, who was living in Pietermaritzburg, Natal. When I arrived home she told me that she had sold the house and wanted to return to the Channel Islands. I could see that she was not in good health and because of her age it was obvious that I would have to take her there, for she could not travel alone.

I arranged the business of selling the furniture and household effects then saw to the paper side of it, a passport, income-tax clearance and all the nonsense that goes with modern travel. Two weeks later we were on a ship bound for England, and not long after back in Jersey again.

My mother's health had deteriorated while I had been away and she had to have constant attention. This was something I was able to arrange in Jersey, and I felt a little easier that many of her old friends were still living on the island. Towards the end of October I boarded a ship in London bound for Sydney, for it had been impossible to obtain a passage to New Zealand. I watched the daily positions marked on the chart in great five-hundred-mile jumps and remembered the days on *Tzu Hang* when we thought we had done well doing seventy.

I disembarked the ship in Sydney and left the same day for Auckland aboard another one. Three days later I stepped ashore in New Zealand again. It had been a long way back. I spent a few days in Auckland, shopping around for the various materials needed for *Trekka's* refit. Over the past few months I had spent many pleasant hours dreaming of the alterations and modifications I wanted to make to the boat. I knew exactly what was needed, so my shopping was relatively easy.

Loaded with gear I caught a train north and a few hours later boarded a ferry at Paihia for the ten-minute crossing to Russell. A wonderful feeling of peace swept over me when we arrived at Russell and I immediately recognised several friends on the wharf. A little farther on I saw *Trekka's* keel lying in the sand, looking a little rusty, perhaps, but still a comforting sight.

Then, a few minutes later, I met Francis and Mille Arlidge again, and these two really made me feel that I had come home.

"Go on, John," said Mille. "I know you won't be satisfied until you've seen *Trekka* again."

And they both laughed when they realised how true to the mark they were. I walked across the garden to the big shed and opened the door quietly, I am not ashamed to admit that my eyes were wet as I viewed the sweet little hull sitting in her cradle where she had waited patiently for my return. Sixteen months had passed since I last saw her.

Francis and Mille insisted that I should stay with them, and though I was afraid of being in the way, for they had a family of six children, I gladly accepted their kind invitation knowing that there was no one I would rather stay with than these two. The same day that I arrived back in Russell I started work on *Trekka*. Christmas was only three weeks away, and there was much work for me to do before we could leave for Australia. Unfortunately my tools and other gear which I had used on *Tzu Hang* had not arrived in New Zealand. They had been packed in a large crate and dispatched shortly after I left Chile, but had gone astray somewhere. But Francis came to my rescue by lending me his tools, and friends in Russell lent me others.

One of the jobs I wanted to do was to fibreglass *Trekka's* hull. This was something I had regretted not doing when she was being built, but now I had a splendid opportunity to do so as she was very dry from being in the shed for so long. Before glassing the hull, though, I removed the oak garboard-planks and replaced them with mahogany ones which I felt would hold the glass resin better than the old ones. The oak had split badly, too, and was quite unsatisfactory.

With two machine-sanders, one a disc and the other an orbital one, I cut all the paint off the hull and prepared it for the fibreglass cloth. Then, when all was ready, the hull was tipped up to an angle of about forty-five degrees and the glass resin and cloth applied. One side was completed before doing the opposite side, and because there was quite a waiting period for the resin to harden I got busy with some of the other jobs, making new cockpit coamings, painting the interior of the boat and fitting some new laminated knees in the way of the chain-plates to replace the old steam-bent ones.

I then turned my attention to making a small dinghy which could be stowed upside down over the doghouse. I had always thought that *Trekka* was too small to carry a dinghy, but after taking a few measurements with the steel tape I saw that it was possible to have a very small one, providing it was made so that the transom was removable, otherwise I could not possibly get down the hatchway. The voyage down from Canada had shown me how inconvenient it was without a dinghy and I knew it would be used a great deal up the Great Barrier reef if I ever got that far. Trekka's dinghy is about the smallest I have seen, 5 feet 6 inches long and made of fibreglassed ⅛-inch plywood. It was a miniature edition of the normal yacht dinghy, yet it would carry me quite easily. And, providing the passenger was not too heavy or the sea too rough would just carry two if nobody coughed.

With Trekka all fibreglassed she was skidded out of the shed into the summer sunshine where it was easier for me to see what I was doing. The fibreglass was sanded smooth with the orbital sander and any holes filled with resin. Then the hull was painted with the usual undercoating before I finished off with a light blue marine enamel.

Instead of using the original rudder, which had rusted badly, I made a new one out of mahogany. This had more balance to it and was considerably lighter than the old one.

I went down to the wharf one morning with a friend and dug the keel out of the sand where it had been for the last sixteen months. Although it was quite rusty some hard work had it looking more like its former self, and it was generously painted with a rust-preventive paint.

The masts and spars were brought down from the rack in the shed and were rubbed down and varnished several times, then, towards the end of March 1958 Trekka was launched off the beach after the fin-keel had been bolted back on again. When the masts were stepped and the rigging set up I knew that the little boat had never looked better and the past four months' work had been worth it.

While in Chile helping to repair Tzu Hang, I had ordered a new suit of sails for Trekka from England. They were made of Terylene and were now being held at Customs in Auckland together with a short-wave transistor radio from the U.S.A. which was replacing the one I had taken away on Tzu Hang. I decided to collect both these items just before leaving for Australia so that there would be no duty to pay on them.

Most of the work on Trekka had been completed, and what was left could be done more easily from a dock or at least somewhere where it was sheltered. I knew just the place, Whangarei, a small town some sixty miles down the coast and almost half-way to Auckland. Quite a number of overseas yachts stopped there, for it had one of the best-sheltered yacht-basins in the country and was close to the main shopping centre. Most things could be obtained there, but if not, it was only four hours away from Auckland by either rail or bus.

One afternoon towards the end of March I left Russell to sail down to Whangarei but decided to call in at Motu Arohia Island on the way. This island is owned by Colonel Browne and his wife, Myra, who have the island to themselves, except when stray yachtsmen like me drop in on them. I had met Bill and Myra Browne two years before with the Smeetons and had spent many enjoyable week-ends with them, leaving *Trekka* anchored off their crescent-shaped beach in company with *Tzu Hang* and Bill's little sloop *Truelove*, a fine vessel which had been built in England and shipped out to New Zealand.

Bill and Myra must meet more ocean-going yachtsmen than any-one else in the country as, for most yachts visiting New Zealand, the Bay of Islands is the first port of call. I think Motu Arohia is the prettiest of all the islands in the bay. I have always enjoyed going there very much, partly, I must admit, for the wonderful teas that Myra always produced (Bless her!). I'm sure Bill must have found all the visitors distracting, for he was engaged on a most interesting project of making a chart of a section of the coast a few miles north of his island. The existing Admiralty charts of this particular area were not detailed enough to show the passage clearly between the Cavalli Islands and the mainland, and there were a couple of rocks that were marked in an approximate position only. Bill had been able to locate these and fix their position accurately with the aid of his echo-sounder aboard *Truelove*. The chart he was making was a beautiful piece of work, he had been a surveyor in the Army and certainly knew what he was doing. As some people like to collect paintings, Bill collected old maps and charts. I was quite fascinated at some of the ones he had, particularly one compiled by Captain Cook when he surveyed the coast of New Zealand in 1769. It was astonishingly accurate, and I learned from Bill that Cook had an-chored the *Endeavour* right off his beach where *Trekka* and *Tzu Hang* had anchored so often.

When I rounded the point and approached the beach I saw *True-love* on her mooring as she had been two years before, but instead of *Tze Hang* being there, a large blue ketch from England named *Havfruen III* was in her place. When I went ashore, I met her owner "Batch" Carr and his wife, Ann, and I learned that they were on a round-the-world voyage accompanied by a crew of two, a young New Zealander and a West Indian. *Havfruen* was a huge boat compared with *Trekka*, 70 tons against 1½, yet it was interesting to compare the two. I was quite awed at the size of her gear, the enormous blocks and the cordage, yet here were two yachts both doing the same job, carrying their crews safely across the seas, though so different in appearance. She was a very comfortable vessel and beautifully maintained, I was to meet her again many times during the next few months as Trekka followed in her wake for thousands of miles before we finally went our separate ways at Barbados in the West Indies.

The following morning Havfruen left for Sydney, and I got sail up for the run down to Whangarei. There was little wind, and the two yachts were in sight of each other for quite a while before Havfruen passed the Ninepin Rock and disappeared from view. In the middle of the afternoon Trekka rounded Cape Brett passing inside Piercy Island, and I noticed the curious cave through it. There were a few swordfish boats patrolling near by and one of them came close alongside. She was Francis Arlidge's Alma G., one of the most successful boats at Russell and certainly the best kept. With her pink cabin-top she was very distinctive, and it was difficult to realise that she was getting on for forty years old.

The wind fell away, and the next couple of days were spent slowly drifting down the coast in brilliant sunshine and with a nearly full moon at night. It was wonderful to be cruising after the months of repairs, first on Tzu Hang and then Trekka.

I spent a day in the little harbour of Tutukaka, which is one of the loveliest anchorages Trekka ever stopped at, it is a quiet, peaceful place with just a couple of farmhouses backed by the green rolling hills on which sheep graze contentedly. I walked up over a hill to see what the scenery looked like from the top. Trekka looked very pretty anchored in the bay, and I felt that this would be the kind of place I would like to settle down in some day.

There was a good strong breeze when I left the following day for Whangarei and I had a few hectic minutes changing the genoa for the staysail, but finally the sail was bagged and bundled in the aft locker. Working on the foredeck seemed quite dangerous for the life-line stanchions were not fixed yet, this was another job that had to be done before I could leave for Australia.

The weather deteriorated rapidly and by the time we came up to Bream Point it was blowing quite hard and pouring with rain. Willy-waws swept down off the high land with surprising force, blowing sheets of water into the air. Trekka was knocked down with one of these before I hurriedly downed the mainsail and proceeded under staysail only. Once inside the Heads the wind rapidly eased off, and I was able to find a sheltered anchorage for the night.

By next morning the sky was clear and I followed a rather large

ketch that was motoring up the dredged channel to Whangarei.
Later on when I arrived there she was moored close by and I learned
that her name was *Arthur Rodgers*. She was an old Brixham
trawler and her owners, Tom and Diana Hepworth had sailed her out
from England just after the war. She was now engaged in carrying
copra and general freight from island to island, but she had clearly
seen better days.

I was becoming anxious at the way the time was slipping by.
There seemed to be no end to all the work, and I knew that if we did
not get away soon the Tasman Sea crossing was going to be a miserable business. The best month to leave New Zealand was February,
and here it was April. The next few days at Whangarei were very
busy ones for me and I finally completed the remaining jobs, all that
I had to do now was to collect the new sails and radio in Auckland
and put stores aboard for the passage to Australia. On 8 April I left
the yacht-basin at Whangarei and sailed down the coast towards
Auckland, stopping for the night at Kawau one of the favourite
haunts of Auckland "yachties." I promised myself that someday I
would come back and enjoy this part of New Zealand when I was not
in such a hurry. This part of the world is known as a yachtsman's
paradise, and it's easy to see why. There are dozens of islands and
anchorages, calm water and plenty of wind. Yachting is a very popular sport, and yet it is by no means a rich man's pastime, there are all
kinds of boats, both power and sail, but there seem to be far more
sailing boats ranging from dinghies to ocean racing yachts than
powercraft. It seemed to me that every yachtsman I met had built his
own boat; perhaps that was why people from all walks of life were
able to enjoy owning a boat.

One of the unfortunate things about Auckland if you are visiting
in an overseas yacht is that there is no place where you can anchor
or moor close to the city that is well sheltered. Most of the local
boats are kept at Westhaven, Okahu Bay or Devonport, all of which
are some distance from the city centre. A large yacht can lie at
Queen's Wharf near the ferry buildings, but for a little one like
*Trekka* it is too exposed. I went along to Westhaven and moored
*Trekka* to a small jetty, and then caught a bus into the city and
contacted the Harbourmaster who kindly allowed me to moor *Trekka*
in the lighter basin inside the Western Viaduct. Although it was
not very clean there, it was well sheltered and within easy walking
distance of the main shopping area.

Shortly after moving *Trekka* to her new berth I was hustling about
the city collecting stores and the last of the gear I would need for
the Tasman crossing; oilskins and sea-boots, plastic bottles to keep

the fresh water in, and the sails and radio from the Customs. The five days I was in Auckland were one constant rush, and towards the finish I gave up trying to stow the gear away tidily as each time I returned to the boat it was with further armfuls of packages.

On the morning of 16 April *Trekka* went down the harbour on the ebb-tide with clearance papers aboard for Sydney. I thought it would be much easier to go somewhere quiet so that I could stow all the gear properly, but perhaps I was only making an excuse to visit Russell just once more. With a fine blustery breeze from the southwest to send us along *Trekka* reeled off the miles in grand style, and late the following day we were back in the Bay of Islands again.

I spent a day stowing everything away in the lockers and beneath the bunks, topped up the water-bottles and bought some fresh vegetables and bread. It seemed incredible, but I was at last ready, the past five months had been very busy ones, and yet it was difficult to see where the time had gone.

The day had come for me to say goodbye to all the wonderful people I had met in Russell, hardest of all to leave were Francis and Mille Arlidge who had looked after me as one of their own sons, never complaining or asking for anything in return. I have met no finer people than these two, and I knew that I was going to miss them very much indeed. I rowed the dinghy back to *Trekka* feeling very sad at leaving this little place which had so many happy memories for me. The anchor came up from the bottom caked with mud as though it too were reluctant to leave this spot, then *Trekka* gathered way and the figures on the beach waved a final farewell as we rounded the point and Russell disappeared from view.

# CHAPTER THIRTEEN

# The Tasman Crossing

The wind was blowing north-westerly, which meant that it would be blowing right down the coast. There was little point in starting off with a head wind so I went in to Motu Arohia Island to see if Bill and Myra Browne were at home. Their yacht *Truelove* was not at her mooring, and I realised that they must be visiting friends. I anchored near the house and hoped they would return later.

Although I had done a lot of work on *Trekka* during the last five months, one job I had not been able to do. This was painting her bottom with antifouling paint. I was not worried about worms getting into her planking because I knew they could not penetrate the fibreglass, but I was a bit concerned about weed and growth, for I knew that it grows on fibreglass very quickly. The weather always seemed to be wrong when the tides were right and *vice versa*, so I had not been able to put her alongside the wharf at Russell. The bottom seemed fairly clean, though, so I hoped for a fairly quick passage to Sydney where I knew I could get her on the slip at the Cruising Yacht Club.

*Truelove* returned that afternoon, and I went ashore with the Brownes and had one of Myra's delightful teas. It seemed that only the previous week-end Miles, B. and Clio had sat about the same table discussing *Tzu Hang's* passage to Sydney. Now here I was again about to leave in *Trekka*.

In the morning the wind had swung round to south-west, which was fine for going up the coast, so I bade Bill and Myra farewell, leaving them standing in front of the whitewashed walls of their lovely little home, bathed in the warm morning sunshine, an unforgettable picture and two unforgettable people.

*Trekka* slipped along over the calm water and presently the little house was obscured by the point, the Ninepin Rock at the entrance to the Bay of Islands came into view and I altered course for it. I viewed the green hills and the timbered islands and knew that I had come to love this country of New Zealand very much. In some ways it could be considered backward, but I was not sure that this was a bad thing. In fact this was one of the reasons I found the country and people so enjoyable. The pace of life was slower than in any other place I had known and perhaps because of this people enjoyed life more and were not too concerned with making a mint of money. I never met any rich people while I was there, but neither did I meet any poor. I was not conscious of anyone trying to keep up with the Joneses because somehow there didn't appear to be any Joneses. No people could be more hospitable, and sometimes their generosity was almost embarrassing. The climate in the North Island above Auckland is almost tropical in the summer months, and though the winters may be wet, they are not cold.

Towards the end of the afternoon we passed inside the Cavalli Islands, and as darkness fell Stephenson Island was abeam. I went below to start peeling potatoes and prepare something to eat. *Trekka* was steering herself perfectly with the new self-steering gear I had made for her. This was quite a simple arrangement and the idea was really stolen from model yachts. The tiller arrangement on *Trekka* is a little complicated because the rudder-stock is aft of the mizzen-mast and the tiller forward. It is linked to the rudder-stock through two short cables with the mizzen-mast in between. I had made up a fitting for the tiller, which had an arc on the aft side of it, on which it was possible to clamp a slide in a variety of positions. One end of the mainsheet fastened to this slide and it was possible to set it in a position so that the helm was perfectly balanced. This arrangement, sometimes known as the Braine self-steering system, was to prove a most useful addition and saved me many countless hours of sitting at the helm, for though it would not steer on all points of sailing it worked perfectly when the wind was forward of the beam.

I was unable to get any sleep that night as we were so close to the coast but at least I was able to rest in one of the bunks after having a glance out on deck periodically.

By noon the next day we had passed North Cape and were approaching the Three Kings Islands—the lonely sentinels which lie some thirty miles north-west of Cape Maria van Diemen. These uninhabited islands are the scene of many shipwrecks, for they can be quite dangerous to approach owing to the strong tidal currents around them. I steered well to the east of them, but passed through heavy ripplings in the water and was well pleased when we had left them astern.

Sydney was now 1,100 miles due west of us and dead to windward. Had I left New Zealand in February I would have stood a reasonable chance of carrying a fair wind all the way across, but now, at the end of April, I could only hope for westerly winds that were not too strong. It had taken us twenty-three days to get across in *Tzu Hang* and we'd had our share of bad weather then. The Tasman Sea has quite a reputation for these conditions and I knew that I was going to be very pleased when *Trekka* reached the other side.

We carried on close-hauled on the port tack, as there was a better chance of favourable winds farther north, and even if we didn't find them, it would at least be a little warmer.

With *Trekka* going to windward there was no need for me to steer, which meant I could catch up on sleep and stay warm and dry below. I spent much time reading in my bunk, the most comfortable place, for I had not yet found my sea-legs and food was still unattractive. Not for long, however, and a couple of days later I developed a ravenous appetite which threatened to empty the boat of all the stores.

A few days went by with *Trekka* still doggedly working her way to windward, then the weather worsened, and I knew from the way the barometer was tumbling down that a gale was on the way. I went through the procedure of rolling a deep reef in the mainsail and then rolling more down half an hour later, after which it was not too long before just the staysail and mizzen were too much sail area, and we were reduced to riding the swells beam on under bare poles, with only a solitary albatross for company. I stood in the hatchway watching him soar above a crest and then glide down the lonely valleys, the perfection of flight as performed by the king of all birds. I have watched them for hours, endlessly wheeling and banking, sometimes with a wingtip just brushing the surface of the water then doing a half-roll to disappear behind the ridge of the next swell. What do these remarkable birds feed on? I have never seen them eat anything apart from scraps thrown overboard from some passing vessel. They are big birds, with a body as large as a goose and must require plenty of food, yet they never appear to feed off sea life as other ocean birds do. No bird except the Southern Albatross can make flying look so easy, such fun or such a beautiful thing, and if the Good Lord allows me to come back to earth in the guise of some animal I shall ask to return as an albatross and let my spirit roam the reaches of the Southern Ocean.

The wind whined in the rigging, that depressing mournful note that always seems to accompany the low driving clouds that hurry their way across the grey murk as though fleeing for shelter. This is a time when you need patience and confidence in your boat, for there is little that you can do except wait for a return of calmer weather. I reflected that at least it was nothing like a gale in the Roaring Forties, there I really would have something to worry about, for, loyal as I am to *Trekka*, I don't think she could survive a real gale down there.

When the conditions had moderated enough I got sail up again and *Trekka* continued working her way to the westward. Sometimes the wind went round to south-west and we could just about lay the course for Sydney, but the track on the chart showed how we were being forced to the northward.

On the tenth day out, the wind freed for the first time, and I had the masthead genoa up for a few hours before the wind finally backed to east and I joyously set the twin-staysails. *Trekka* surged along quietly, and I stood in the hatchway watching the tiller kick over by itself every so often. With a nearly full moon overhead, I was reluctant to go to sleep now that the weather had at last given us a break. I made a hot cup of chocolate and sat reflecting that this was the kind of sailing many people dream about and knew just how lucky I was to be there.

The weather did in fact remain fine for a couple of days, although the wind became very light and the days' runs suffered badly. All too soon, though, the westerly winds were back again and *Trekka* was bucketing along over a lumpy sea. At least I was not feeling seasick, as I had been over this stretch in *Tzu Hang*. The motion on a small boat at sea can be something wicked. If you were to go through the same motion in a room, you'd be rising to the height of the ceiling every few seconds and jerked back from one wall to the other as well. Yet, after a time you hardly notice it. I have found myself using this motion to advantage sometimes, waiting for the right moment before climbing into a bunk or for the gimballed stove to swing over before I put the kettle on top. At the same time it was easy to be fooled, too. I'd get so used to the movement that I'd forget about it and open a locked door to be showered with the butter, jam and condensed milk. The big bread knife I bought in Auckland attempted to stab me a couple of times before I found a place to stow it where its humour was less likely to cause me bodily harm. This constant motion must also provide good exercise, for I never arrived in port suffering from the somewhat confined space, no matter how long the passage. The addition of the dinghy over the doghouse had provided me with another wonderful source of exercise, for whenever I climbed through the hatch I had to bring one knee up until it touched my chest, other-wise it was quite impossible to get in or out. When I could do this wearing oilskins and sea-boots I felt I was reaching Olympic stan-dards.

The next three days saw very unsettled conditions over this central part of the Tasman. The wind blew hard for an hour or so only to fall away to nothing while the barometer shot up and down in a most confusing manner. I was kept on the move changing sail until

I grew so exasperated that I pulled everything down in sullen rage and went below to wait for the weather to make up its mind what it was going to do.

On 7 May we were only 60 miles from Ball's Pyramid and a gentle breeze from the north sent us along steadily right on course for Sydney. I had been noticing an odd smell below the last couple of days and I decided to investigate. It was not long before I found the cause! Half a dozen eggs had been cracked underneath my bunk.

At nine o'clock in the morning of 9 May I was still in my warm bunk wondering if it was worth getting up to face the day. *Trekka* had been going along all night closehauled, and I had glanced at the spare compass at the side of my bunk at odd hours during the night to make sure she was still on course. Thoughts of breakfast eventually moved me and I stood up in the hatchway to have a stretch... there, just a few yards away, was the towering bow of a freighter. I scrambled out on deck and grabbed the tiller, my knees turning to water and my heart thumping madly. She slid past to leeward and I looked up at her bridge to see several pairs of binoculars examining my somewhat scanty attire. Someone raised a hand in a salute vaguely similar to the V sign Winston Churchill made so famous during the war, though I was doubtful if the gesture was meant to have the same significance. I waved rather shakily and watched fascinated as each of the binoculars waved a hand in reply.

When the stern rumbled past with the blades of her propeller clearly visible, I read her name *Kaitoa* from Wellington, probably bound for Newcastle, as she was well north of the Sydney track.

The wind was slowly backing to the east, and as soon as it was possible to use them I set the twins and retired below to make pancakes which had suddenly caught my fancy. Something went wrong with the recipe, or I must have left some vital ingredient out, for it was quite impossible to flip them, indeed the only possible way to remove them from the pan was with the paint-scraper.

Still smarting from my failure I decided to make a chocolate cake in the pressure-cooker. Now I've made many cakes in the cooker when I've been living ashore and they were very good, satisfying is perhaps a better word, but somehow my efforts at sea have been what I would call disappointing. They always look a bit seasick and usually have a hollow in the centre, this can sometimes be filled up with custard and then the cake becomes chocolate pudding. Some of my other recipes can be altered at short notice like this, and I have found that this can be very useful especially when entertaining visitors.

13 May was the twenty-second day out, and we were only ninety

miles from Sydney and about sixty from the nearest land. I was quite sure that another day would see us moored snugly in Rushcutter's Bay, but then the wind fell away until we were becalmed on a strangely still sea. The following day there was still no wind, but when I worked out our position from sun-sights I realised that we had been set south nearly sixty miles by the strong current which flows down the east coast of Australia.

When the wind came back it was very light from the north-east and we were able to steer the course for Sydney, but although we made sixty miles on the log in the next twenty-four hours, sights showed that we had in fact been set even farther south. I was in a quandary what to do. If we went on like this we might get set a long way south, even as far as Gabo Island, and I knew that the current was likely to be strong all the way in to the coast. One Australian yachtsman took his boat outside Sydney Heads for an afternoon's sailing when the current was running hard, and it took him thirteen days to get back inside again. He was a hungry man by the time he returned, for the boat only had the usual week-end supplies aboard.

All my charts of the Australian coastline were for north of Sydney, and it was this that decided me to sail off to the eastward back the way we had come before going north and having another shot at approaching Sydney from the north-east. It took a couple of days of hard sailing to get north again, but on the 18th we were in just about the same position as we had been on the 12th. Then to cap the lot the wind went around to the south-west, a dead muzzler. It seemed that I was not meant to go to Sydney. I went below to look at the charts. "To hell with it," I decided, "I'll go north to Coff's Harbour." So I went up on deck and altered course. With the wind on the quarter Trekka began putting away the miles and I felt happier to be heading for a definite destination rather than beating about all over the place.

Just after noon on 20 May I sighted land, which turned out to be Smoky Cape about thirty five miles south of Coff's Harbour. But the wind became light and we were still bucking the strong current, so it was not until the following afternoon that we came up to the cape and I put the outboard motor over the stern and motored into Trial Bay where I anchored near a rock breakwater. There were some rather grim-looking stone buildings behind a breakwater, and I later learned that these had been a prison in years gone by.

The next morning after a wonderful night's sleep, I hove the anchor up and set the spinnaker for the run up the coast to Coff's Harbour, but we had no sooner left the bay when the spinnaker collapsed through lack of wind. The morning sun climbed into a cloudless hazy sky, the beach shimmering with heat. There was not a breath of air and the only sound to break the silence was the drone of a fly that was listlessly examining my right knee. It was the start of a typical Australian summer's day. I was surprised at the heat for the time of the year, and had to go below and rummage through one of the lockers to find the sun-awning without which it was quite uncomfortable on deck. There was only a gallon of fuel left for the outboard, which would do for ten miles, so I anchored instead in fifteen fathoms to wait for a breeze.

It was during this calm period that I put a face mask on and looked over the stern and examined *Trekka's* bottom. I had noticed that she had seemed sluggish for the past few days, and now I saw why, for the bottom had become a marine garden. Long streamers of weed and barnacles covered the fibreglass sheathing and steel fin and I knew that this was one job I'd have to see about once we got into port.

It seems ridiculous, but it took me five days to sail and drift the thirty miles to Coff's Harbour, hours went by without a breath of wind. Then a few puffs would goad me into hanging every available stitch of sail up and another couple of hundred yards would be won before the anchor was put to use again to prevent the current from robbing us of our hard-won gains.

On the morning of 26 May, thirty-five days after we had left the Bay of Islands, a breeze came along which finally allowed us to cover the remaining miles and *Trekka* entered the harbour at Coff's where I secured her to a mooring-buoy and then launched the dinghy to go ashore and see the Harbourmaster.

A short time later I was speaking to Captain Merritt, a stocky jovial man who was the Harbourmaster, Customs and Immigration Officer as well as being the Pilot of the port. He went around to various cabinets and cupboards in his office collecting a whole sheaf of forms for me to fill in. "I don't know what the hell you need to be filling all these in for," he remarked goodnaturedly, "but I have to treat you the same as a big ship. I guess it will keep someone in Sydney busy." Between the two of us we completed the forms, and as he stamped them he told me that the stamp had the British Coat of Arms on it and was the oldest one in use by the Australian Customs.

I mentioned the marine growth on *Trekka's* bottom and asked if there was a slipway which could handle her here instead of waiting until I got to Brisbane.

"We can pull her out with one of the cranes on the wharf," he assured me. "We've got wire slings so you need not worry, we won't drop her. All the fishboats here are done the same way whenever their skippers want to paint them. The charge is the same for everyone, to be hauled out and put back in again will cost you eighteen shillings and sixpence. You'd better go and have a word with the crane driver, and tell him when you want to haul out."

I walked back down the wharf and met the crane operator who showed me the wire slings lying beside a fishboat out for an overhaul. I arranged with him to haul out on the Friday afternoon so that *Trekka* could remain in the slings over the week-end without me having to block her up. So that the wire slings would not scar *Trekka's* paintwork, I wrapped some sacks around them which were seized on with marline. On the Friday afternoon when *Trekka* was lifted gently out of the water and set down on the wharf the paint on her topsides was intact.

It was easy to see why progress had been so slow the last couple of weeks, for the whole of the bottom and keel was completely covered with barnacles, long grey watery stalks with a small grey-and-yellow shell at the end. Some of these stalks were over four inches long and they caused much interest amongst the local fishermen, who said they had never seen the likes of them before. However, I was in no mood to exhibit them on *Trekka's* hull, and in an hour had scraped the lot off and washed the bottom down with fresh water.

Over the week-end I painted the bottom, first with zinc chromate and then with anti-fouling paint, so that by Monday morning when the crane driver returned to work he found *Trekka* all ready to go back into the water. This operation was completed without incident, and I went along to the Harbourmaster's office where I paid the eighteen shillings and sixpence charges, sure that it was a very long time since I'd had such good value for my money.

I bought a Sydney paper one morning and read with astonishment that on my arrival at Coff's Harbour I had been "mobbed" by teenage girls. I was described as a "blond Viking" and I could not believe my eyes as I read the rest of it. Australia is such a wonderful country and there are so many really fine people there that I cannot understand how the press, with a few exceptions, can be so incredibly bad. For straight accurate news reporting the New Zealand papers are exceptionally good, but on the weather side of the Tasman are examples of the other extreme.

CHAPTER FOURTEEN

# *Cyclone!*

A couple of days later the English ketch *Havfruen III*, which I had met in the Bay of Islands, arrived at Coff's Harbour and I was very pleased to meet up again with Batch and Ann Carr. That evening I had a meal with them in *Havfruen's* spacious saloon and we passed away a couple of very pleasant hours comparing notes on our progress and planning the future routes.

In the morning they motored off towards Brisbane, leaving me to wait for a breeze so that I too could get started on my way again. I was feeling a little impatient at these calm conditions and regretting that *Trekka* did not have a diesel engine to make use of this long, calm spell. I cursed the weather and the lack of wind but did not know then that in the next few days I would bitterly regret my impatience.

Over a thousand miles away in the centre of the Coral Sea trouble was brewing for me. A mass of air heated by the intense tropical sun was rising and creating a great hole in the atmosphere. Cooler winds moved into this hole, but they too were soon heated up and rose, an intense depression was being formed and with each passing hour it was becoming stronger and stronger. While it waited for its strength to grow, for it was still just an infant, it remained stationary and quite undetected, but then, when its awesome power had reached maturity, it began to move deliberately towards the south-west to wreak its havoc on the eastern coast of Australia. This berserk giant which began to move so slowly was now no longer a mere depression, it was severe enough to attain the title of Cyclone.

Meanwhile quite unaware of what was heading towards me, I was pleasantly surprised to find a steady breeze blowing when I awoke on the morning of 5 June. I quickly got sail up and let go the mooring-buoy. With her bottom clean *Trekka* soon passed between the break-waters and began to knock off the miles. Brisbane was only 260 miles away, and with a breeze like this to send us along, I knew that three or four days' sailing would see us moored snugly in the Brisbane River. I was to be proved quite wrong.

Throughout the day *Trekka* slipped along close to the shore to avoid the unfavourable current, but as darkness fell I edged offshore so that we would not run ashore during the night. By daybreak the following day we had covered some more useful miles, but I edged inshore again as the day progressed and in the late afternoon passed the entrance to the Clarence River. The steady breeze had increased and was blowing at about twenty knots from the south-east, which had *Trekka* really boiling along, but with the sun gone the wind increased instead of easing, and some sixth sense warned me that all was not well. The weather report on the radio gave no indication of bad weather and the barometer was still high, yet something about the sea looked wrong. At first I did not take much notice, but as the hours went by I saw that there was a long swell rolling down from the north-east. There was no shelter along this section of the coast, and with growing apprehension I realised that if this wind was to shift a little we'd be on a lee shore. I sheeted in the main and staysail and furled the mizzen. Then I proceeded to gain as much sea-room as possible by driving hard offshore. What had been exhilarating sailing had now become a desperate bid to gain as many miles as possible before we were forced to heave to. *Trekka* was being driven as she never had been before, sheets of spray stung my eyes and trickled down the collar of my oilskins; drops ran down my back to be temporarily halted by my belt, which acted as a dam before flooding over into the seat of my pants. Then one big sea broke over the beam and completely soaked me; after this there was no point in trying to keep dry.

As the wind increased we were slowly forced to head more north than east and at last I knew that the time had long gone when I ought to have reefed the mainsail. I waited for what seemed to be a lull, then I quickly eased the halyard and cranked the reefing-gear, rolling the wet sail around the boom. Although this was a good reduction in sail area, it did not appear to make a great deal of difference, and half an hour later I stowed the sail, realising that if I left it up any longer it would either blow out or carry away some of the rigging. The sky which had looked so innocent at midday was completely clouded over, and occasional squalls drove the rain horizontally, so that it was impossible to look to weather. *Trekka* staggered on with just the staysail and mizzen up, heading into the long swell that rolled down from the north-east. At times it was like a ride on a roller-coaster as we climbed the face of a swell to plunge down the other side. The queasy feeling in my stomach erupted, and my breakfast and lunch were blown off to leeward to mingle with the elements.

Leaving *Trekka* to look after herself I stiffly climbed down the hatch and removed my sodden garments before easing my weary frame into the lee bunk. Sleep was quite impossible, but at least the bunk was warm and dry and the flickering cabin lamp gave a brave attempt at cheerfulness. Throughout the long night *Trekka* clawed herself offshore until at daybreak on Saturday morning the only sail set was the tiny storm-jib. Our speed through the water was no more than two knots, but it was better than lying ahull and drifting off towards the coast.

My worst fears were realised when late on Saturday the wind backed round to east. I crawled out on to the foredeck and pulled the tiny storm-jib down; then I lashed the helm to leeward and let the little boat ride the seas beam on.

According to my reckoning, we were about 35 miles offshore. I usually figure that in a gale, *Trekka* drifts off downwind at a rate of about one knot, so we had only 35 hours left before the surf on the beach got us. It was a grim prospect.

Through the night at odd intervals I looked anxiously towards the mainland expecting to see the light on Cape Byron, which has a range of 26 miles, but daylight revealed no land in sight, though a haze about the horizon kept visibility down to about three miles. The wind eased a little about midday, and I set the storm-jib for three hours which won us a few miles, before conditions worsened again and the sail had to be taken in.

Another anxious night passed, a night of listening to the shrill note of the wind in the rigging, the halyards rattling against the masts and the sudden hiss of a sea breaking before it burst against the side of the hull. Again I peered off to the west straining my eyes for the loom of a light from the shore. But Monday morning arrived without any sign of land.

I turned the radio on to get the weather report and for the first time learned that this was no ordinary gale but a tropical cyclone. The storm centre was five hundred miles away to the north-east and moving towards us at a rate of 10 knots. The news broadcast told of the damage already inflicted on shore, and of how the beach and sea-wall had been washed away along sections of the coast by huge breakers. My morale was very low now.

Our position was east of Danger Point, not a very cheerful name in itself, but I had no means of knowing how far we were offshore. The correct thing to do was to save as much of that sea-room as possible with the aid of a sea-anchor, but not having one I did the best with what I had. I secured the two manila anchor-warps to cleats, one forward and one aft, then I attached the free ends to an eight-foot length of 2-in. × 2-in. spare lumber, which had the effect of keeping open a fair-sized bight in the water without it sinking. I could quickly tell from *Trekka's* changed motion that the fifty fathoms of warp were checking her drift downwind, although she was not as comfortable as before.

Through Tuesday the wind was as strong as ever, and knowing that there was no more I could do I climbed into my bunk and attempted to get interested in a book. Tuesday night was one of the most nerve-racking I can remember, the insane violence of the conditions outside was bad enough, but the thought of being driven ashore in these seas in complete darkness was worse. I had the feeling that this was a nightmare from which I would soon awake, but it went on hour after hour with no change and little hope.

Wednesday dawned at last, and a searching look to the west relieved my fears, for there was still no land in sight. Greatly cheered by this I had some breakfast, the first real meal I had eaten since the gale started. The weather report on the radio placed the storm centre 500 miles due east of Brisbane and heading more south than it had been. It looked as though the storm was starting to recurve away out to sea. By noon I was fairly sure that this was happening as the sky began to break up and one or two patches of blue large enough to darn a Dutchman's pants appeared. For a few minutes the sun peeped through one of these holes, and I was able to take a sight with the sextant though the sea was still very rough.

The sight placed us on the same latitude as Cape Byron, but I was still unable to determine how far offshore we were. The wind was veering at last from east round to south south-east, and there were periods when the strength of it fell quite noticeably. I set the storm-jib for nearly four hours in the afternoon before another succession of squalls forced me to take it in again.

The radio reported *Trekka* as missing and said that aircraft flying along the coast had been instructed to keep a look-out for me. I was somewhat concerned about this latest piece of news, for the last thing I wanted was a costly air and sea search for me, which might end up in some of the searchers losing their lives. It was my fault in being out in this cyclone, and there was no reason why anyone else should risk their lives to rescue me.

With the wind now in the south-easterly quarter the danger of being driven ashore had greatly diminished, and I dropped off to sleep that night in a much easier frame of mind than I had been for the last five nights.

At daybreak the light revealed the same scene of breaking seas and flying spray, but the appearance of the sky had improved, and when the sun appeared above the horizon it was visible for long periods through the clouds.

After a quick breakfast of porridge, toast and coffee, I went on deck to see if we could proceed on towards Brisbane. The wind was still blowing in excess of thirty knots, and the sea was quite high, but, after being hove-to for so long, I was eager to get moving again. With the wind in the south now I needed to run dead before it, so I decided to tow our makeshift sea-anchor astern and set the little storm-jib. A few moments later when we were moving along at about three knots I saw a large sea approaching, as it came closer it carried the warps forward until there was a lot of slack in them, then the crest reached *Trekka* and she immediately began to surf down the face of it. I held her running true with the tiller, but then she slipped off the back of the crest and sat down in the hollow.

Shortly afterwards a similar sea came along, but this one broke over the stern, soaking me completely and would have taken me overboard but for the lifelines. I was still spitting out salt water when another sea did the same thing. Before it could happen again I got the sail down and lashed the tiller to leeward. It was too dangerous to let *Trekka* run in these conditions, and I decided to wait until the sea had gone down more.

On the radio that evening I learned that the American schooner *Venturer*, sailed by her owners, Jack and Peggy Burke, was also reported missing. She had left Port Stephens going north about the same time I left Coff's Harbour and had probably met much the same kind of weather I had been encountering.

On Friday, 13 June, my usual lucky day, the wind and sea had moderated to such an extent that *Trekka* was able to carry her full mainsail with the staysail boomed out. I hauled in the warps over the stern and we flew along to the north-west looking out for land.

Later in the day I was able to get sun-sights which showed that we were much farther offshore than I had imagined, nearly eighty miles in fact. This was something of a surprise, and the only explanation I could think of was that the East Australian current which flows strongly down the coast had temporarily altered its course during the cyclone when opposed by strong south-east to east winds and flowed offshore at Cape Byron, the most easterly point of the Australian Continent. It had been my usual luck to be in the right place when caught in the storm.

I put *Trekka* on course for Cape Moreton, feeling very relieved to be moving again, and stayed on deck steering long after the sun had gone down.

Saturday was a good day and saw us making good progress with a blustery south-westerly wind, the only sign of the cyclone now was the swell that rolled in from the east, but the storm was moving off into the central Tasman Sea where it eventually blew itself out.

The radio news in the evening reported that the *Venturer* had been wrecked on the reef at Lady Musgrave Island some 300 miles to the north of our position, Jack and Peggy Burke survived being washed across the coral reef and had then swam and drifted nearly three miles across the lagoon to the tiny islet of Lady Musgrave, an incredible escape in those conditions. The news continued that *Trekka* was presumed to have foundered in the storm and that wreckage from her had been washed ashore north of Coff's Harbour. I could well imagine how the Sydney newspapers would lap this lot up—if there is one thing they are quite nutty over, it's yachts getting into difficulties at sea. It never seems to make any difference that usually the vessel turns up safe and sound a few hours later.

At midnight the light on Cape Lookout came into view, and as dawn was breaking we passed the lighthouse and carried on along the shore of Moreton Island.

In the early afternoon we arrived at Cape Moreton, where I anchored in the lee of the high cliffs in company with some fishing launches. One of these was a very able-looking vessel with a flying bridge and a long pulpit on her bow, and the name *Tennessee II* on her transom. She came over to inspect the new arrival. I was hailed and asked if we were the yacht that was reported missing in the cyclone, and on my replying that this was so the skipper on her bridge told me he would report my safe arrival on his radio.

I learned that some of the buoys marking the channel through the sandbanks of Moreton Bay had been washed away in the cyclone, but that if I wanted to go on he would tow me as he knew the channel and also had an echo-sounder aboard. Now that I was anchored and in calm water I was in no hurry to leave again and decided to wait until the following day before going on to Brisbane.

An hour or so later a light plane appeared on the scene, and I could see a photographer taking pictures of us. It looked as though this time we might even make the front page.

Later in the afternoon the *Tennessee II* came alongside, and the skipper invited me to have a meal aboard, which I gladly accepted. I learned that he was Bob Dyer, an American who had a weekly radio show on one of the Australian networks. He and his wife Dolly were very well-known anglers and were looking for a really big shark to break the world record. Two days later they found the one they were looking for, and they got their record with a shark that weighed just over a ton.

Feeling greatly refreshed in the morning after a sound night's sleep

I went on deck to find a warm, sunny day. I tidied up the cockpit and made new staysail sheets as the old ones had chafed badly, this was the only failure of gear that the cyclone had inflicted on us.

Later in the morning the *Tennessee II* came alongside and I secured her nylon tow-line. Shortly afterwards *Trekka* was towing astern like a yacht dinghy.

Brisbane, which lies 11 miles up the river of the same name, is forty miles from Cape Moreton. When one is proceeding to that port from the open sea there are extensive shoals to navigate at the entrance to Moreton Bay. As usual, their positions are constantly changing, but the channels are normally well marked with buoys. In a little over an hour we were clear of the sandbanks and I signalled to the *Tennessee II* that I was casting off the tow-line. She circled around slowly while I got sail up, then, with a final wave from all aboard, she set off back towards Cape Moreton to resume her shark fishing.

*Trekka* could just lay the course for the Pile Light at the entrance to the Brisbane River, a gentle south-easterly breeze sent us along over the calm water at a steady four knots as I sat in the cockpit enjoying the warm morning sunshine. Later in the day a Brisbane yacht named *Alvis* escorted *Trekka* up the river, and that evening, after anchoring for the night, I met Fred Markwell, her skipper.

At the Markwell home the press finally caught up with me and the following day I read colourful accounts in the newspapers, one entitled "The Man who came back from the Dead."

I motored *Trekka* up the river to Bulimba the next day where I berthed alongside a small private jetty owned by Norman and Helen Wright. Many cruising yachtsmen have been fortunate in meeting these two wonderful people. Their house beside the river becomes the home of many yachtsmen visiting Brisbane. Norman and Helen were both keen yachtsmen themselves, and they ran a profitable little business of tending to the mooring-lines of freighters docking along the river waterfront. They owned several high-powered launches, in which they towed the lines to the wharves. Many freighter skippers visiting Brisbane for the first time must have been somewhat surprised to ear Helen's voice call up "Ready for your starboard spring!" Norman, an excellent dinghy helmsman was an expert in the class of dinghy known in Australia as an unrestricted eighteen-footer. You have to be something of an acrobat to sail these dinghies, for with their enormous sail area and as many as six crew sometimes out on trapezes they are not the most stable of craft, to put it mildly. These eighteen-footers are sailed in New Zealand and Fiji as well as Sydney and Brisbane and each year there is a series of races between the best boats of each country. Norman had won the series the previous year in his *Jenny VI.*

Also at the Wright's jetty was a fine little blue-painted cutter from Auckland named *Revel.* I had met her owner, John Smith, briefly in Auckland, but now I got to know him and his wee wife, Marlene, better. Both of them were in their early twenties and were cruising to the Great Barrier Reef in place of the honeymoon they missed when they were married a few months before. I really enjoyed meeting these two, for although I met quite a few couples around the world who were cruising in their own yachts I never met any as young as John and Marlene. John was no stranger to the sea, for like so many New Zealanders he had grown up in boats and had done several long passages in small craft. This was Marlene's first long voyage and she had adapted herself to this strange kind of life quite easily. I was much amused at her remark that the morning after her wedding night, John took her down to the harbour and gave her a brush to scrub the weed off *Revel's* bottom. They were the happiest couple I ever met cruising, and I spent much of my time in their company.

*Trekka* was still very much in the news, and sometimes I would come back to the little boat after shopping uptown to find quite a crowd of people gathered on the jetty. There would usually be someone shooting questions at John, and I would creep up behind to listen.

"Is that the little boat that was out in the cyclone, mate?"

"Yes, that's her," replied John, with a stony look on his face.

"That joker must be crazy sailing about in a little thing like that. When are you leaving, mate?"

John would stifle a sigh and reply, "Oh, in a couple of weeks."

I would work my way through the crowd and suddenly ask, "Eh, mate! Is that the little boat that was out in the cyclone?" John's expression would never alter, and he'd give me the same reply, "Yes, that's her."

Sometimes he got his own back when I was alone on *Trekka* and he returned from the city to find me answering the inevitable questions. One day I received quite a surprise when an elderly lady suddenly shot a question at me: "Which Guzzwell are you? The son of John or James?"

I was quite taken aback, but stammered that I was the son of John.

"Well, young John, I used to work for your grandfather in Grimsby, forty years ago."

Here was an amazing link with the past. I had never known my grandfather, he had been dead long before I was born, so I was most interested to hear about him and her life in the home where she looked after the two sons.

I also met Mrs Palmer and her two daughters whom I had last met on lonely Fanning Island two years before. The girls missed the atoll very much and wondered if their pet fish was still there. I received a telephone call one day from a girl who told me that her Christian name was Trekka and that she would like to see the little boat. My imagination began working overtime, so that I was somewhat disappointed when she eventually arrived to find that she was only twelve years old. The Kiwis on *Revel* pulled my leg for days afterwards.

I was able to visit by road the section of the Queensland coastline known as the Gold Coast, an area famous for its miles of beautiful beaches and the small tourist settlements with many hotels which cater for holidaymakers from Sydney and Melbourne. It is no wonder to me that in many fields of sport Australia leads the rest of the world. With the wonderful climate, people spend more time outdoors than in, and the children are the healthiest I have seen anywhere. Everyone goes to the beaches and all the youngsters threaten to become champion Olympic swimmers. If ever there was a nation of sun-worshippers it's these Australians.

Queensland hospitality can be quite overwhelming, and it was seldom that I ate aboard *Trekka*, so it was not surprising that the days were rapidly going by. I met many friends at the Royal Queensland Yacht Club who kindly presented me with a plaque to commemorate *Trekka*'s visit. The name "Cyclone" was bestowed upon me, and for many months afterwards I received mail addressed to "Cyclone" Guzzwell.

Norman Wright's father, also Norman, slipped *Trekka* free of charge in his small shipyard near by. I gave the bottom two coats of anti-fouling paint, as I had no idea when I would have the opportunity again, perhaps not before we reached South Africa.

*Trekka* and *Revel* were joined by *Havfruen III* for a few days until eventually the big blue ketch departed for parts farther north. It was rather curious that all three yachts were from overseas and all painted blue. But there the similarity ended, for each was as different from the other as could be: *Trekka* with her reverse sheer and light displacement, *Revel* the normal type of small cruising boat, and *Havfruen*, a 70-ton ketch, designed by the great Colin Archer. All three of them were doing the same kind of ocean sailing, which only went to prove that size has little to do with seaworthiness. It's the crew that is the most important factor.

Meanwhile I was preparing to leave and was delighted when John Smith said he would sail *Revel* north in company with me. I went through the usual procedure of putting stores aboard and filling up water-bottles, fuel for the stove and outboard motor and saw to all the little items that needed attention before I could leave.

Friendly yachtsmen warned me of the dangers along the Great Barrier Reef, the tourist resorts where the beautiful sun-tanned Australian girls far outnumbered the men. I was told of other yachts that had been bound farther north, but had not been able to resist the siren calls. I promised to lash myself to the mainmast and let *Trekka* steer herself clear of these islands.

On the morning of 12 July, nearly a month after arriving at Brisbane, *Trekka* and *Revel* went down the river on the ebb-tide bound for the Barrier Reef. The two boats sailed alongside each other across Moreton Bay and had by dusk negotiated the shoals at the entrance without incident. It was now that we parted company, for although *Revel* could stay close inshore and avoid the strong coastal current, I could not expect to stay awake constantly when close to the shore, so I started to edge out to sea. Before the darkness swallowed them up I called to John and Marlene, promising to meet them at Lady Musgrave Island in a few days' time but this was to be the last I saw of them for I learned weeks later that we missed each other by just eight hours.

I set the twin-staysails which just filled to a gentle southerly breeze. The sea was quite calm and I sat in the cockpit feeling very happy to be going north to the tropics at last. The light on Caloundra Head flashed its message every ten seconds against a background of dark blue hills and a few twinkling lights from homes along the shore appeared. Then suddenly it was night and once again I was alone at sea.

# CHAPTER FIFTEEN

# To the Great Barrier Reef

The next three days were spent running before a gentle southerly breeze, and though we made good progress during the day when I came in close to the shore, we sometimes lost quite a few miles in the hours of darkness when I went offshore to avoid running aground. The weather was quite perfect, and though this was the middle of winter, it was more like summer to me after the tough going we had encountered farther south. Owing to the settled weather I was not concerned about staying close to shore except at night-time, and it was certainly far more interesting and profitable to sail well in to the coast.

The wind swung round to the north on the fourth day out, and the combination of wind and current against us resulted in extremely slow progress. On a couple of occasions I anchored off the beach when we seemed to be losing instead of gaining ground.

I spent one night becalmed just south of Sandy Cape and anchored for a few hours while I caught up on sleep. When the wind returned it was still from the north and the following day was spent beating up past Breaksea Spit, a dangerous coral reef which extends northward from Sandy Cape for a distance of nearly twenty miles. This reef is really the southernmost extremity of the Great Barrier Reef, that wonderful coral bastion which protects the Queensland coast for the next twelve hundred miles.

Early in the morning of 18 July I passed the Breaksea Spit light vessel and bore away to the north-west with the wind now abeam and *Trekka* moving really fast. At noon we passed close to Lady Elliot Island which is very tiny and stands only a few feet above the sea. Much shipping passes close to it and there is a prominent lighthouse built on the south-western side of the island and three tin-roofed houses, the homes of the keepers. I passed close enough to get a cheery wave from two figures ashore, then a few moments later the island was astern and appeared to sink beneath the sea.

In the late afternoon the palm-trees on Lady Musgrave Island came into view, but as the wind rapidly eased off it was not until dusk that I came close to the island. There is an extensive lagoon inside the reef and an entrance on the northern side, but as the light was fading

I decided to anchor on a three-fathom patch to the west of the island. I had fastened the outboard motor over the stern in an effort to arrive before dark and was motoring along quite quickly over the still water when suddenly without any warning there was a dreadful Clunk! *Trekka* had hit the bottom hard. My knees all turned to water, I cut the engine and went forward to look the situation over. The bow was about four inches out of the water, but I realised thankfully that she was not seriously aground, and, after a couple of minutes of rocking the boat from side to side, she slid off the coral into deeper water where I gratefully anchored for the night. Thanks to the steel fin-keel there was no damage except to my shattered nerves.

In the morning I motored along the northern edge of the reef to see if *Revel* was behind the island, but unknown to me she had left the previous morning, and when I saw no sign of her I decided to go on to Gladstone and see if she were there.

The sea was like a sheet of glass and just as clear. Beneath the hull I could see a couple of fish swimming along lazily in the shade, occasionally darting out into the sunlight to inspect some morsel, but always returning to their positions by the rudder. The outboard purred away steadily, and every two hours I filled the tank hoping that a breeze would appear and put an end to this motoring. But towards sunset there was still no wind, and so I decided to anchor off the entrance to Port Curtis for the night. The calm continued throughout the night, and in the morning I started the motor again and proceeded on the flood-tide up the South Channel to the small town of Gladstone, where I moored *Trekka* among some small craft in a little creek to the west of the town.

I went ashore and reported in to the Customs, for, although I had cleared at Coff's Harbour it was still necessary to report in to them and have clearance papers from the last port visited. I now handed in my Brisbane papers and arranged to collect a clearance for Townsville in a couple of days' time.

Gladstone itself is quite small and has the rather sleepy air of a frontier town. It lies beside the magnificent natural harbour of Port Curtis, an extensive area of sheltered water which is navigable to large freighters. Because of this it is quite a prosperous little town and much produce from the surrounding districts is shipped out from here. One of the chief items of produce is meat and there is a packing plant in Gladstone which is capable of handling five hundred head of cattle a day. A couple of days later I was given a tour of the meat works which proved to be most interesting, but since that day I have never been able to look a can of bully beef square in the eye. The townsfolk of Gladstone have become very yacht-minded in recent years as a result of the yacht race from Brisbane to Gladstone, which is a very popular event to Australian yachtsmen; Brisbane yachtsmen had given me glowing accounts of the hospitality here, and it was not long before I began to receive similar treatment.

There was a very fine little ketch moored just ahead of *Trekka* which had won the Sydney-Hobart race one year, her name was *Moonbie*, and I was most interested in meeting her American owner, Hal Evans. Hal was about to take her north to the Whitsunday Islands, but what really interested me was that he was going to take the short cut inside Curtis Island, a route called the Narrows instead of taking the outside course which was many miles longer. The mere description of the narrows in the Pilot Book was enough to frighten me off, but I knew that if *Moonbie*, who drew a foot more water, could get through, then *Trekka* could too.

I told Hal that I was also going north to the Whitsunday Islands and asked him if he would mind me tagging along behind through the narrows.

"Sure, you come along," he said. "I've never been through myself, but I was shown the first bit yesterday aboard a fishboat, and I don't think it will be too bad, providing we catch the tide right."

We set off in the morning, motoring across the still water to the entrance to the channel. As we went along we kept careful note of the beacons and markers constantly referring to the Pilot Book. As much of the route wound through mangrove swamps it was often difficult to determine where the true channel lay but usually at the last moment a marker would become visible and our doubts vanish for another mile or so.

The channel became narrower as we went along until we at last reached the Narrows where the description in the Pilot Book became quite frightening. At low water the channel is two feet out of the water at this point. Taking great care now not to let the beacons come out of line, as there are rocks on both sides of the channel, we slowly edged past the worst bit, bucking against the tide, which was flooding from the northern end of the channel. Soon afterwards we were back into deeper water, and in the middle of the afternoon came abreast of the Sea Hill pilot station at the entrance of the Fitzroy River, where I decided to anchor, as there was no wind out in the open water beyond. *Moonbie* motored off into the distance after I had arranged to meet her again at South Mole Island in a few days' time.

Instead of just sitting aboard *Trekka* waiting for a breeze I put the dinghy into the water and rowed ashore to go for a walk. I walked up over the hill near the lighthouse and soon afterwards met the coxwain of the pilot station, Mr Price. He took me along to his house, where I met his wife who in a matter of moments had the table laid with a mouth-watering selection of scones and cakes. There were three families living at the pilot station and I think the women-folk missed a bit of company, for it was not very often that they had visitors. They told me of other yachts that had called there, some of which I knew quite well, and we were pleased to have mutual friends.

When I returned to *Trekka* late that evening after a most enjoy-able visit ashore the dinghy had a pile of magazines aboard and some fresh provisions, eggs and lettuce. This is the kind of hospitality I received so often and remember so well. Perhaps it was easier for me to meet new friends being single than if I had a crew along, for two people can be more difficult to entertain than one.

From now right on up to Torres Straits I would be able to sleep soundly every night, for there were good anchorages all the way, and there was no need to sail at night any more.

Early the following morning I motored out of the Fitzroy River and once outside found a gentle breeze. The motor was stowed away in the aft locker and I got sail up. There was little wind, but just after noon we were close to the Keppel Islands, which looked so attractive that I decided to stop at Great Keppel and go for a swim. I anchored *Trekka* just a few yards off a wonderfully white sandy beach then went ashore in just a pair of swimming trunks for a walk. I saw a couple of homes among the trees but no sign of anyone on the island.

Later in the evening as the sun was low in the sky I made an omelette with the Sea Hill eggs, and afterwards sat in the cockpit listening to the radio news. The air was warm now that we were in the tropics, and it was good to know that I should have this kind of weather all the rest of the way up the Barrier Reef and nearly to South Africa.

The charts were most interesting now, the Great Barrier Reef itself was about fifty miles offshore here at its southern extremity, but close to the Queensland coast were many groups of islands scattered about the calm water, a few of them with people living there, but most of them uninhabited.

Sailing along a strange coastline and passing new islands is always exciting, but to do this with perfect weather, sitting out in the hot sun all day without any need of clothing and with no schedule to worry about, complete in the knowledge that time is of no impor-tance, this to me is perfection.

The next couple of days were spent working north up the coast in bright sunshine but with little wind. The night of 25 July saw us snugly anchored inside Island Head Creek, a very lovely anchorage indeed. The moon came up over the hill, full and so bright that I was able to sit in the cockpit and read a few pages of a book. From the shore the strange call of some tropical bird carried across the still water, and I reflected that this section of the coast was completely unspoiled, this is how Captain Cook saw the Australian coastline, and somehow I think it will be many years before any of this is changed.

I left early the next morning, as I wanted to reach Middle Island in the Percy Group for the night. It was a distance of nearly fifty miles, and though there was little wind to start with, as the sun climbed higher in the sky the breeze freshened and *Trekka* danced along. We did not arrive until after dark, but the moon lit the way into the little crescent-shaped bay where I anchored close to another yacht. Soon after anchoring I was fast asleep in my bunk.

I was awakened in the morning by a voice alongside *Trekka*, I scrambled out of my bunk and stood in the hatchway blinking into the morning sunshine. Sitting in a somewhat battered dinghy was a smallish elderly man with a grizzled beard and bright blue eyes.

"Sorry to wake you up," he apologised in an English accent, as I grasped his hand. "I'm Norman Young from *Diana* over there. We're leaving for Mackay in a couple of hours but would like you to come and have some breakfast with us."

I looked up and saw the yacht I had seen faintly the night before, a stout-looking vessel which I later learned was a Falmouth quay punt and had been sailed by Mr Young from England with a great variety of crews.

A few minutes later I met the four young men aboard who were the present crew. I gathered that they had joined *Diana* in Brisbane, but that three of them were only going as far as the Whitsunday Islands. The fourth member of the crew was a young Queenslander named Gary Turpin, a stocky athletic lad with an infectious grin who later on was to become a very firm friend. He was to sail many thousands of miles aboard *Diana* before he left her in South Africa.

Over an immense breakfast of porridge, bacon and eggs, toast and coffee, I learned more about *Diana* and her owner. Norman Young had retired from the Civil Service after many years with the Treasury and had decided to spend his remaining years cruising in his beloved *Diana*. He was a bachelor and had no ties, so that his yacht was his home as well as being the magic carpet by which he could journey anywhere his fancy chose. He had originally left England for the West Indies with two other elderly men, and I believe that the average ages of the crew on that occasion was more than 65 years. This is quite remarkable when you take into consideration the type of boat *Diana* was, for the gear aboard her was very heavy compared with a modern yacht's. With her big gaff-mainsail I could not see how three elderly men could ever have got it set, but they managed, and the three of them stayed together until Panama was reached. From then on *Diana* collected dozens of different crews, some men staying aboard for months, others getting off at the next port. Norman Young gave many young men their first taste of ocean cruising, and some of them later left to buy or build a boat of their own and follow in *Diana's* tracks.

I was pleased to hear that *Diana* was bound for South Africa now, so that there was a good chance that we would meet many times along the way. Soon after I returned to *Trekka* my newfound friends got sail up, and *Diana* slipped out of the bay bound for Mackay, where I promised to meet them in couple of days' time.

Middle Island is the home of a Canadian family named White who live there all the year round in a homestead up in the centre of the island. They have the reputation of welcoming stray yachts and have a telephone on the beach with a notice above it which says, "PLEASE RING." Later in the morning, when I went ashore, I cranked the phone-handle and when a voice answered the other end of the line told them who I was.

"Good, good," the voice answered, "we heard you were on your way up the coast, please come up and visit us. Just follow the telephone line and you'll find us. It's about a half an hour's walk."

I set off, following the trail, which soon began to climb quite steeply up the timbered slopes. I gathered that this White family must be humorists, as there was a little notice along the side of the trail which read "TIRED YET?" and a little farther a very effective "BEWARE OF THE BULL."

I hurried along the trail and before very long the ground levelled off and I saw the homestead among the trees. A few moments later I met Harold White, a great barrel-chested man with an oddly falsetto voice. He crushed my hand as he greeted me. Then he took me along to meet the rest of the family. There were Claude, who was Harold's younger brother and like him big, and two old friends who lived with them, Dolly and Syd.

I asked Claude why they chose to live up here on top of the island instead of the little bay where *Trekka* was anchored.

"Well, for one thing it's more healthy up here," he replied. "Cooler, too, I reckon. But I guess the main reason is because of the sheep we run. All the best pasture is up here, and we can look after them better where we are almost in the centre of the island than we could down on the beach."

This family was almost self-supporting. They grew their own vegetables and had an almost inexhaustible supply of meat. The few things they needed from the outside world were available from Mackay, but it seemed to me after talking to them for a while that they had about everything they wanted right on the island. The five of us sat down to an enormous lunch and I realised that these were outdoor people after seeing their appetites.

In the afternoon Harold me for a tour of the island in the car, a 1926 Whippet, which appeared to be as sound mechanically as the day it was bought. We bounced and jolted along a few trails on the island from which superb views of the coast and other islands in the Percy Group were visible. I was shown the grove of trees where the two brothers had pit-sawed the lumber to build their boat which they had constructed at the homestead using temporary fastenings before dismantling the whole hull and then transporting everything down to the beach and assembling the lot finally. Harold said that this had saved them no end of time in the long run, for they were able to work on the boat at odd moments at the house, whereas had they been building close to the beach much time would have been lost walking to and from the homestead.

Later in the afternoon I saw the boat and was able to appreciate some of the effort that had gone into her building. She was very similar to Harry Pidgeon's famous *Islander*, having a V-bottom and very strong construction. She was moored alongside a little jetty in a lagoon which was entered through a narrow channel at the northern end of West Bay, where *Trekka* was anchored. The lagoon was quite undetectable from the open sea and was one of the few natural harbours along the Queensland coast that was completely cyclone-proof.

Both Harold and Claude wanted to see *Trekka*, so about four o'clock that afternoon I said goodbye to Dolly and Syd, then walked down the trail with Harold to the little bay. When we got down there we found that Claude was with a party of fishermen and a fine-looking fishboat was anchored near *Trekka*.

The fishermen were also keen to see *Trekka*, and, as all of us were such big people, we had to make it in two trips in the White's run-about. Then we all went aboard the fishboat, *Trade Winds*, where Jack the skipper cooked us a fine fish supper. We talked long into the night before we all said goodbye, Harold and Claude set off to walk back to the house, and I returned to *Trekka*, where I was soon asleep.

Though there was little wind in the morning I decided to leave for Mackay, but we had gone only a few miles when the sun burnt off what wind there was and I had to fasten the outboard over the stern and motor for a few hours. Instead of motoring on through the night I anchored just north of the Beverley Islands in ten fathoms and was surprised when *Trekka* strained at the warp to see that the tide was flooding at nearly two knots.

By noon the next day *Trekka* was anchored close to *Diana* in Mackay harbour, and I went off for some supplies to the town, which is about three miles from the harbour. It is a pleasant little town with a wide main street which has flower gardens planted right down the centre, at the time I was there the street was a riot of colour.

The shops all seem to have awnings extending over the sidewalk so that it is possible to stay in the shade when walking along shopping. I was able to obtain all the supplies and items I needed and was fortunate in getting a ride back to the harbour with my purchases, for there is no bus service in between the town and harbour.

While in Mackay I bought ten gallons of fuel for the outboard as it had been used frequently the past few days, but I was not to know that the fuel would remain untouched for many thousands of miles until I reached South Africa months later. From Mackay north and across the Indian Ocean the South East Trade Wind blew steadily to drive *Trekka* ever onward.

Three days after arriving in Mackay we were off again, this time to the Whitsunday Islands. With a good breeze to send us along, *Trekka* arrived at Lindeman Island just after darkness, and I anchored among some small craft near the tourist settlement.

I went ashore in the morning to the resort where I met the Nicholson family who own and operate it. They kindly invited me to use their facilities and eat with them whenever I wished, and it was not long before I was using their showers and doing some washing.

The resort is set among palm-trees at the head of a white coral sand beach on the southern side of Lindeman Island. Though it is not a large resort the island has a landing-strip and tourists usually arrive by a light plane which operates a regular service with the mainland. When *Diana* arrived and anchored close to *Trekka* the next day, it was not long before her four young crew and myself were entering into the spirit of the resort. We played the various games which we somewhat unashamedly won from the tourists who were paying for their holiday; I seem to remember coming away with a silver spoon for winning the table-tennis competition and between them the boys from *Diana* shared the rest of the prizes.

Early one morning I was awakened by Gary and one of the other lads from *Diana*, who were going to hike to the top of the island to see the sunrise. I pulled a pair of shorts and a shirt on, and a few moments later the three of us rowed ashore leaving the dinghy on the beach. We set off through the palm-trees, stumbling occasionally in the darkness, and shortly afterwards climbed into open grassland. The air had a pleasant chill to it, and as we brushed through the tall grass our legs were wet with dew. It was almost light when we reached the 700-foot summit, and as the shadows faded we were able to appreciate a magnificent view. Off into the distance stretched a string of islands like so many jewels on a necklace, then as we feasted our eyes on the scene the sun slowly lifted above the horizon to tip the island peaks in a pink glow. The three of us were silent as if each wanted to retain the memory of the unforgettable sight, then a few minutes later we reluctantly turned away and began to retrace our tracks in the bright morning sunshine.

We arrived back at *Diana* to find that a massive breakfast was almost ready, and while we ate ravenously we discussed where to visit next.

I was going on to South Molle Island and arranged to meet *Diana* there in a few days' time, so it was agreed between us that the two boats would cruise together going north once we left the Whitsunday group.

After breakfast I rowed back to *Trekka* and a little later sailed out of the bay into the Whitsunday Passage. I steered *Trekka* close to Dent Island, which has a lighthouse on it and was surprised a few minutes later when the keeper rowed out with his assistant in a small dinghy to come and have a chat. I learned the whereabouts of several yachts I knew, for the lighthouses along the coast are in constant radio contact. I was invited ashore, but declined, as the anchorage did not look to be a good one, the tide sweeps through the passage at a rate of three knots. I did not know what the holding ground was like, so I elected to continue on to South Molle. Just before sunset I rounded the northern end of the island and shortly afterwards anchored close to Hal Evans's *Moonbie*.

Of all the places I visited along the Great Barrier Reef, I remember South Molle Island best. Like Lindeman Island, which it resembles in size and height, it is also a National Park and has a small tourist resort situated in a bay on the northern coast of the island.

When I met Hal Evans ashore the following morning he introduced me to the Bowers brothers who were operating the resort and they told me to make myself at home and to use all the facilities.

So much of my time in the last few months had been spent alone or in the company of older people that I had almost forgotten what it was like to relax with someone my own age. The resort on South Molle catered for young people, and now all at once I had plenty of companions both male and female to enjoy myself with. I played tennis in the mornings, usually before breakfast when the air was still cool, and enjoyed the lovely walks along the many trails to various beauty spots. Quite near the resort was a large colony of flying-foxes which hung from the branches of some tall gum-trees. Occasionally they would take fright, and the air was filled with their sharp raucous cries as they circled about in alarm above the tree-tops.

In the afternoons both *Moonbie* and *Trekka* sailed about the island with friends aboard. And one day I took *Trekka* over to Nara Inlet where I was told there was a cave with aboriginal paintings on the walls. The inlet is about two miles long and quite narrow, the shore rises rapidly on each side and is well timbered, so that it is not unlike a Norwegian fjord. I anchored Trekka close to the head of the inlet and then set off through the brush to look for the cave, which I found a few minutes later. It was small, and I was somewhat disappointed with the paintings, for they were quite meaningless. There were two drawings that looked almost like snowshoe-prints but the rest were just daubs of different colours, rather like some examples of modern art.

When we returned to South Molle just after dark, I saw that *Diana* had arrived and was anchored near by. I think Norman Young soon realised the dangers of a place like South Molle to his young crew and knew that too long a stay there could result in him losing them, so I was not surprised when Gary told me that they were departing next day for Cannonvale where the three other young members of the crew were leaving the ship to return to Brisbane. This would leave just the skipper and Gary aboard to take the boat several hundred miles on to Thursday Island unless someone else could be found.

When I awoke the following morning and looked out of the hatchway, *Diana* had gone. A feeling of restlessness swept over me, and I knew that it was time for me to be moving along. I knew now what those friends in Brisbane had been warning me about when they mentioned the dangers along the Barrier Reef. There was a fine yacht moored just a few yards away that had been bound overseas, but her owner had found his green hills here at South Molle, and his voyage had been abandoned.

I spent the day ashore knowing that it would be my last one and walked along the trails taking photographs of the various bays and headlands. From the summit of the island the view is quite spectacular and unforgettable. I watched the wake of a large freighter coming north along the Whitsunday Passage, a white trail on the face of the sea. Then she passed and disappeared beyond North Molle Island. I knew that before another day passed *Trekka* would be following in her wake.

At daybreak the next morning I got the anchor aboard and a gentle breeze smoothed out the wrinkles in *Trekka's* mainsail as we gathered way. Hal Evans stood in *Moonbie's* hatchway watching, and I knew that he too had found his earthly paradise in these Whitsunday Islands. He lifted his hand in salute as *Trekka* glided by, then I eased the sheets and we pulled away from the bay out into the open water bound for Townsville.

# CHAPTER SIXTEEN

# Sailing in Company

As the morning progressed the Trade Wind strengthened and *Trekka* surged along before it with a bone in her teeth. By darkness we had covered over fifty miles, and as the course to Townsville was relatively free of dangers I decided to keep going all night. During the hours of darkness I set the twin-staysails and was able to rest in my bunk for a couple of hours. The light on Cape Bowling Green was abeam just before daylight, and when I had eaten some breakfast I went on deck to set the mainsail which soon had us going near maximum speed.

At noon we were in Townsville, where I found *Diana* already berthed in the river near the centre of the town. Mr Young and Gary helped me to secure *Trekka* alongside *Diana*, and I learned that they had arrived late the previous day. The absence of the rest of the crew did not appear to worry these two very much.

I checked in with the Customs and soon completed the forms which would be handed in at Cairns, the next port up the coast that I would be calling at.

Gary and I went off shopping and returned to the yachts with arms loaded full of packages. Townsville was a good place to shop, and we were able to obtain all the necessary items on our lists.

After a two days' stay in Townsville I decided to continue on up the coast and arranged to meet *Diana* in Cairns some 150 miles farther on. It was now the middle of August, and I was becoming a little concerned at the way time was slipping by, I had traversed less than half the length of the Barrier Reef to Thursday Island so far, and if I wanted to avoid cyclones in the Indian Ocean I had to try to reach South Africa, over 7,000 miles away, before Christmas. From now on *Trekka* had to keep moving.

From Townsville I sailed to Orpheus Island, where I spent the night with tropical raindrops drumming on the deck, but though it was still raining the following morning when I left, the sky cleared later, and I had a most enjoyable day's run to Dunk Island.

Farther south it would have been safe to have kept sailing at night, but the route was becoming more tricky as we went up the coast, and as there were good anchorages in the lee of the many islands along the route there was little point in sailing after the sun had set. This was most interesting and enjoyable cruising inside the Barrier Reef, and I was not going to spoil it through lack of sleep. Providing I left early in the mornings it was possible to sail fifty miles without strain and find an anchorage for the night before it was dark.

I was off again early in the morning, but the wind, which had been steady for the last few days, faltered, and we made poor progress, so that by the middle of the afternoon we had covered only twenty miles. I had intended to keep sailing that night, as the course was clear of dangers and there was little choice of an anchorage farther on, but, on looking at the chart, I decided to go into Mourilyan Harbour instead. This little harbour is really the mouth of the Moresby River and has a narrow entrance between two headlands which are each over five hundred feet in height. Rocks extend out from each shore, so that the channel is only about 170 feet wide, and at springs the tide runs in and out of the harbour at seven knots. The Pilot Book warns strangers not to attempt entering without a pilot, but, on checking with the Tide Book and noting that it was almost slack water, I decided to go in with the outboard motor.

Having safely negotiated the narrowest section of the channel I was congratulating myself on my daredevil pilotage when I was shocked to see a large freighter moored to the wharf inside. I stared at it quite unbelieving that this ship could have entered through such a narrow channel and for a moment was sure that there must be another entrance to the harbour. I learned ashore that there are plans afoot to blast away the rocks in the narrow section of the channel and when this is done it will be a safe harbour and provide excellent shelter during the cyclone season. While ashore I got talking with the navigator of the freighter and he invited me aboard. He was most interested in my voyage and showed me his method of working out the longitude, which was a far quicker way of doing it than the way I had been taught by my father years before.

I returned to *Trekka* later with a full stomach, the result of a fine meal from the cook, and some charts, a present from the navigator.

At slack water in the morning I motored out of the channel and once clear of the entrance stowed the motor and got sail up to a steady south-easterly breeze. The coast was backed by thickly wooded hills, and in the distance the peaks of the Bellenden Ker mountains which rise to an altitude of 5,000 feet were clearly visible. At the end of the day I anchored behind High Island on Tobias Spit, but it was an uncomfortable anchorage and *Trekka* rolled about violently during the night to the swell which came round both ends of the island. I was not sorry when daylight arrived and I could proceed to Cairns,

where we arrived in the afternoon to find that *Diana* had beaten us
in by a few hours having passed *Trekka* during the night, when I
was attempting to get some sleep.

Cairns is a place that has unhappy memories for me. This was the
last big town along the Queensland coast until Thursday Island, and
I had quite a list of shopping which should have been available here,
but apart from foodstuffs I had very little success. Mr Young and
Gary complained of similar failures, and we just had to face the fact
that we would have to do without many items. Disappointed with
our shopping efforts we decided to take a day off and visit the underwater observatory at Green Island, which is one of the true coral reef
islands of the Barrier Reef. Instead of sailing the fifteen miles to the
island we went across on the ferry-boat, the motion of which was so
completely different to *Trekka's* that I felt quite seasick and had the
crossing been much longer would undoubtedly have disgraced myself
in front of my two companions.

The observatory was nothing more than a large tank beneath the
sea which had glass portholes in the sides. It was entered through a
shaft of stairs from the pier but was well worth the visit, for the view
out of the portholes was completely natural, and, as the water was so
clear, it was possible to see quite intimately the living coral and
brightly coloured reef-fish, which frequently swam up to the portholes to examine the strange creatures within.

Later on we walked round the island, which is about a half mile
long and only a few feet above sea-level. The colours of the sea were
a delight to behold, from the palest of greens close to the white coral
sand beach they ranged to every conceivable shade of green and blue.
Shadows moved across the kaleidoscope of colours as Trade Wind
clouds drifted beneath an incredibly blue sky.

We returned to Cairns on the ferry-boat which resumed its
drunken rolling as soon as it left the shelter of the island, and I made
a mental note to apologise sincerely to *Trekka* for thinking that her
antics had been violent at times.

Cairns held little to attract us, so we speedily completed buying
provisions, some of which would have to last until South Africa as
we could not depend on obtaining very much at Thursday Island.

On 23 August the two boats left Cairns together and sailed in
company constantly for the next five hundred miles. Perhaps I remember this stage of the voyage best for the wonderful sailing it
produced, day after day of exhilarating surfing, with *Trekka* going at
her very best to stay up with her larger companion. The miles seemed
to fly past, each one memorable for the very joy of it all. *Diana*,
rather like a sedate old lady, picked up her skirts and really waltzed

along in a welter of foam, *Trekka*, not to be outdone, surfed and skidded down the face of the curling waves in a most unladylike manner, thoroughly enjoying the excitement and sometimes making me shout aloud in admiration of her antics.

We arrived at Snapper Island in the middle of the afternoon, and as there was no anchorage farther on that we could reach that day both boats stopped here for the night. Like the High Island anchorage this was rather an uncomfortable one, for the swell swept round both ends of the island to keep the two boats rolling constantly.

The next day's stage was quite a long one, as we hoped to reach Cooktown, which was a distance of 55 miles, so we all turned in early that night to get some sleep. I was awakened by Gary's hail at four o'clock in the morning, and when I stuck my head out of the hatchway saw that he had got *Diana's* anchor aboard. A few moments later I did the same for *Trekka*, and before I was fully awake had sail up, too.

There was not much wind at this hour of the day, but after the sun showed itself above the horizon the breeze increased until it was blowing a fine steady twenty knots. I set the spinnaker later in the morning, and under this sail *Trekka* had the edge in speed over *Diana*. The hours went by with the sails stretched taut, the mainsail pressed hard against the spreaders and shrouds, while the little blue spinnaker bulged out beyond the forestay, threatening to burst apart at the seams. Everything held together, though, and by four o'clock that afternoon both boats had negotiated the tricky entrance to the Endeavour River to anchor off the little settlement of Cooktown.

On the shore stands a monument to commemorate the landing here of Captain Cook in 1770 where his ship the *Endeavour* was repaired after striking a reef and nearly foundering. Cooktown was at one time a prosperous little town due to gold being discovered near by. But, as with many Australian boom-towns, the alluvial gold was soon worked out, and though gold is still mined inland at the Palmer Goldfields, Cooktown today is little more than a ghost town.

We walked along the main street passing empty derelict buildings that the bush was trying hard to regain. The place held an air of hopelessness and decay that was unsettling. We found a couple of shops where we bought some fresh fruit and bread and a small post office where I posted off some mail, knowing that this would be the only opportunity until we reached Thursday Island.

It was at Cooktown that I first saw the dreaded stonefish. This repulsive-looking creature usually lies on the bottom among the stones, and its naturally brown and greenish body is covered with a dirty coating of slime which makes it very difficult to see. It has thirteen strong dorsal spines which all have a double poison sac, and should some unlucky person step on one and have the poison enter the wound the resulting pain is so immediate and agonising that people have been known to commit suicide rather than bear it. The fish is usually sluggish in its movements, and for this reason is dangerous to bathers who could tread on one. Sometimes stonefish are caught on a line, and you have to take great care in removing them from the hook; moreover they can live for several days out of the water, so they should not be underestimated.

On 26 August after a day and a half in Cooktown, *Diana* and *Trekka* left for Lizard Island, fifty-odd miles up the coast. Another day of fast sailing saw us anchored behind the island well before darkness, but the strong wind which swept off the land prevented me going aboard *Diana* at the end of the day, and I had to be contented with my own cooking for a change.

The wind was just as strong in the morning, and I knew we were in for another fast day's run. The course was almost west today, and it was a change to have the wind coming over the port quarter after so much sailing on the starboard tack.

*Diana's* mainsail was not in use today. It had been made by one of the best-known sailmakers in the world and was made of flax, yet, although it was only two years old, the material had so little life in it that Gary maintained that every time he hoisted it he had to sew half of it back together again. Mr Young blamed the Auckland gasworks for the ruination of his sail and said that *Diana's* berth in that city had been in the lee of the gasometers so that the fumes from them had rotted the cloth. This was an interesting theory, but I thought that fumes from the particular brand of tobacco he smoked were far more powerful and probably more noxious than any the Auckland gasworks could emit. With the wind above 20 knots it was suicide to set the sail, which would only rip into tatters. In any case Gary flatly refused to hoist it, knowing that he would only have to sew it together again, and Mr Young was quite incapable of getting the heavy sail up by himself. I was constantly amused at the battle of wits between these two, and found their company most entertaining.

Of all the sailing along the Great Barrier Reef, I remember the day's run from Lizard to Bewick Island best. The wind was blowing a steady 25 knots once we left the shelter of Lizard Island, and even without her mainsail *Diana* began to pull away from *Trekka*. She was using two big headsails boomed out and her mizzen, while *Trekka* had her usual working staysail and main up. It would have been impossible for me to set the spinnaker in these conditions by myself, but I thought that I might be able to set the masthead genoa and boom the staysail out with one of the twin booms. *Trekka* was doing 6 knots as it was, and I had to be quick on the foredeck to get the genoa hanked on and hoisted before she came up into the wind or gybed, but all went well, and I reached the tiller just as the sail filled. *Trekka* hesitated for a brief moment, then like a racehorse that has the bit between its teeth she bolted towards the fleeing *Diana*. In a series of fantastic surfs on the curling waves, when her speed must have gone beyond 10 knots for seconds at a time, *Trekka* tore through the water at a rate that left me gasping in excitement. I found that by throwing my weight forward at the right moment it was possible to get her surfing on practically every wave, and, using these tactics, it was not long before we caught *Diana* and came up under her stern.

At this moment *Trekka* caught a wave and began to surf down the face of it. I had a momentary vision of Mr Young's startled face and was certain that we were going to disappear down *Diana's* hatchway, then at the last moment we sheered away, just missing her transom as we rushed past. I saw Gary shaking his head in astonishment so then I had to show him my new sport. Waiting for the right moment I ran forward on to the foredeck in the same manner surfers in Hawaii do on their large boards. This had the effect of making *Trekka* stay on a wave even longer, and soon we had left *Diana* quite a long way behind. At three o'clock in the afternoon *Trekka* was anchored behind Bewick Island having covered the 43 miles from Lizard Island at a speed of just under seven knots, this, I think, was the fastest sailing she ever did.

As it was still early in the day Gary and I went spear-fishing from *Diana's* dinghy. Both of us were so leery of sharks that when we had the dinghy anchored the conversation went something like this:

"Water feels quite warm, John."

"Not very clear, though. Don't you think we'd be better farther in?"

"Well, it's not very deep here, John. Let's see you go in and try it."

"Oh, no, I went in first yesterday. It's your turn today, Garry."

"Well, maybe it would be a bit better closer in to the shore."

And so the whole operation was repeated closer in. After much looking under the dinghy we stepped over the side into the knee-deep water, and, as our courage came back, gradually worked farther out. We never did see a shark. But we were not very sorry about that. All about us swam gaily-coloured reef-fish which darted in among the coral whenever they became alarmed. It was not very

The self-steering at work

The resort at South Molle Island, Whitsunday Group

*Diana* keeps me company along the Great Barrier Reef

often that we got one, for we had doubts whether many of these coloured ones were edible, but it was enough for both of us just to look at this beautiful world beneath the sea.

Mr Young invited me to eat aboard *Diana* whenever I wished and I would often do so, for it was far more enjoyable eating with the two of them than preparing a meal for myself on *Trekka*. In the evenings we got the charts out and discussed the route for the following day, deciding where to anchor for the night.

Early the next morning we were off again, and the miles were soon slipping past, though not at the previous day's rate, past Barrow Point and North Bay Point, where the Great Barrier Reef is only four miles away, and then soon afterwards we rounded Cape Melville, where in 1899 a cyclone swept the entire pearling fleet ashore drowning over three hundred men.

In the early afternoon we anchored near a sandspit off the western end of Flinders Island and went ashore to examine a rather dilapidated hut which stood near by. This proved to be quite interesting, for marked on the walls there were names of many yachts and other craft that had called here. We dutifully added ours and then left in *Diana*'s dinghy powered by *Trekka*'s motor to have a look at a wreck which we had noted on Stanley Island about a mile away. The wreck turned out to be a landing craft which had been stripped quite thoroughly, but we were left wondering what had become of its crew, for none of the islands in the group are inhabited.

After eating aboard *Diana* that evening I was about to return to *Trekka* when we noticed that she had dragged her anchor and was fast disappearing downwind and out to the open sea. Gary and I pursued her in the dinghy with the motor and soon afterwards we both scrambled aboard and got sail up for the beat back to the anchorage. This time I made sure that there was enough warp out when I anchored, and the rest of the night passed uneventfully.

From Flinders we went on to Hannah Island where we found four Thursday Island luggers at anchor. They were stout-looking ketches, but were very roughly built. As we got farther north we frequently passed others anchored in the open channels with their mizzens set riding head to wind while their native crews dived for pearl or trochus shell. I was interested to notice that a forestay was rigged to the top of the mizzen-mast when they were lying like this.

A surprising amount of shipping uses this route inside the Barrier Reef, not a day went by without some freighter or tanker passing us, and we usually got a cheery wave from the officers on the bridge, who examined us closely through their binoculars. I'm sure that the sight of the two yachts must have given some of them a twinge of envy, for it would be difficult to find a yacht in more perfect conditions than these.

Another day's run of 45 miles saw us at Night Island, and then we were off again in the morning to Portland Road where there is a jetty and a couple of buildings ashore. We met three white men who lived together in a small house, but they appeared to resent our intrusion into their privacy. One of them offered the information that a crocodile had killed his dog a few days before and advised us to stay away from the creek that emptied into the bay near where the two yachts were anchored, but apart from this they ignored us completely, leaving us puzzled as to who they were and what they were doing there.

The following day we reached Cape Grenville and anchored behind the Home Islands for the night. Gary and I went skin-diving in the afternoon and found the water unusually clear. The coral formations here were excellent, perhaps because of the lack of sediment in the water.

Bushy Island, 50 miles farther on, was the next day's stop; and then we left for Mount Adolphus Island on what was the final day's run inside the Barrier Reef. In the early afternoon we passed close to Quetta Rock named after the British India Company's S.S. *Quetta*, which in 1890 struck this rock and foundered with great loss of life.

The two yachts found a sheltered anchorage in Blackwood Bay, Adolphus Island and soon after arriving we all went ashore to stretch our legs. We were in high spirits at having safely negotiated twelve hundred miles of reef-infested waters, and, though it had all been enjoyable, I was beginning to feel the excitement of setting off across the wide expanse of the Indian Ocean.

In *Diana's* saloon that evening we spread out the charts of Torres Straits, planning the following day's run to Thursday Island. We spent an hour or so attempting to work out the time of high water, as the tides in Torres Straits are reported to be strong, but at the finish we were in such a muddle that we decided to follow our usual practice and leave after breakfast.

Our worries about the tides were quite unnecessary, for we had an easy passage to Thursday Island, arriving off Port Kennedy shortly after noon, and we anchored there among many pearling luggers near a long, pile wharf. It was perhaps appropriate that we should have arrived at Thursday Island on a Thursday.

The island itself is dry and barren with little greenery to be seen anywhere. The town has that frontier look about it, the main street lined with dusty trees backed by a few featureless shops. The air was heavy with the thick red dust that penetrated everywhere. Whenever a vehicle went by fresh clouds of it descended on everything. After a few hours ashore we all looked like Red Indians.

Though the shops did not look very smart they did have nearly all the supplies we had been unable to obtain at Cairns, though prices were considerably higher than in Brisbane or Townsville.

That evening by way of a celebration we dined ashore at the Royal Hotel, which, though perhaps not quite so elegant as the name would suggest, did provide an adequate meal. The proprietress let us use the hotel showers, and though they were perhaps a bit primitive, we much appreciated them.

I had hoped to haul *Trekka* out of the water and anti-foul her bottom on one of the slipways here, but the cheapest price quoted was £A18, which was too much for my pocket. I had a word with the harbourmaster, who thought that *Trekka* might lie alongside the wharf at neighbouring Horn Island, and so, a couple of days later, I motored *Trekka* over to the island, where I found two wooden piles close to the wharf that had four feet six inches of water alongside them at high water.

At the very top of the tide that evening I managed to get *Trekka* alongside the piles and started painting the bottom at five o'clock the following morning when it was still dark. The morning tide was not high enough to float us off, and I had to wait until nearly midnight before we floated off into deeper water. *Trekka's* bottom had been quite clean, but with South Africa still over 6,000 miles away I was pleased to have this opportunity of painting, for it was doubtful if I should have any opportunity of doing so before Mauritius, which was still a long way away.

Though Mr Young and Gary had managed *Diana* by themselves since the Whitsunday Islands, they were not keen to go on across the Indian Ocean without another man aboard. It had been arranged that one of Gary's friends from Brisbane would join *Diana* at Darwin when she reached that port.

A couple of days later I watched *Diana* leaving for Darwin, Gary cranking the anchor-chain aboard, while Mr Young looked after the engine controls from the cockpit. They were an odd pair to be sailing a big, heavy boat like *Diana* together, one a small indomitable man approaching his seventieth year who was quietly sailing around the world in his own vessel as though it was the most natural thing to do, and his companion a young lad of nineteen whose spirit of adventure had led him to *Diana*. I remembered the contrast of their accents and couldn't help but smile wondering which one would eventually win, the precise English of an ex-Civil Servant or the intriguing drawl of the young Queenslander. I was sorry to see them go, for I knew that I was going to miss both of them very much.

On the morning of 10 September, our third anniversary away from Victoria, B.C., *Trekka* left Thursday Island for the Cocos Keeling Islands 2,800 miles away. This was the longest passage I had attempted so far in *Trekka*, but with good favourable winds I hoped to be there within a month.

We rushed out of Normandy Sound on a six-knot tide with a fine easterly breeze pushing us along, too. In the early afternoon Booby Island was abeam, which was to be the last land I saw for the next month. At dusk the twin-staysails were set, and I left *Trekka* to steer herself towards Cocos.

# CHAPTER SEVENTEEN

# The Kindly Indian Ocean

I was standing in the cockpit a couple of nights later when I felt something crawling up my leg. Perhaps it was the surprise that made it feel so horrible, for when I shone a torch on it, I saw it was a creature rather like a shrimp with long feelers, a transparent body and shaped like a grasshopper. I promptly flung it overboard.

We passed many sea-snakes during the next few days. They were quite small, seldom being more than three feet long, with a black back and head, and a yellow underbody. They were excellent swimmers, and wriggled away on the surface of the sea when *Trekka* approached. I tried many times to photograph them but never succeeded.

We had two 24-hour runs of 115 miles, and then the wind rapidly eased off. I saw that we had crossed the Gulf of Carpentaria on the chart and it almost seemed as though we had come into the lee of the Australian coast. For the next week we had very little wind, but the strong, favourable current boosted our mileages and *Trekka* kept going along steadily. What wind there was came from the east so that *Trekka* could steer herself with the twins, but these two sails were meant for blustery Trade Wind sailing and in these light airs they were not large enough to be very much use. Then I thought of setting the small spinnaker from the masthead above the twins, with the spinnaker sheets running through blocks on the end of the twin booms to cleats on the mast. The result was perfect, the twins did the steering while the spinnaker did the pulling. *Trekka* immediately picked up speed and it was largely due to this rig that *Trekka* was able to make such fast passages later on.

It was very hot indeed during the day. The temperature in *Trekka*'s cabin was a steady 98° F., and out in the sunshine it was 20° higher. Though I am a sun-worshipper, there is a limit to what I can stand, and at midday I had to rig the sun-awning over the cockpit. I was also concerned about fresh water, for our total capacity when I left Thursday Island was twenty-four gallons, which would have been quite enough at the normal rate of consumption, but with this heat I was drinking more than half a gallon a day. To stay cool I frequently doused myself with a bucket of sea-water, and as I wore not a stitch of clothing this was a simple and most enjoyable operation.

I was sitting in the cockpit a couple of nights later when I heard a muffled report like a small explosion. I looked round and saw a bright green light falling across the sky until it entered the water. I heard no splash and thought it might have been a Very pistol flare, but as there was no sign of shipping about perhaps I had seen a meteor.

On 25 September we passed about twenty miles south of Roti Island off the southern end of Timor, but the horizon was hazy so I did not see the island. A couple of times the superstructures of tankers showed above the horizon and a plane passed overhead high up, but apart from these signs of civilisation this was a very peaceful part of the ocean.

The calm weather continued, and I wondered what had become of the South East Trade Wind. I had read that the Indian Ocean was a rough place for little boats, yet here we were drifting along, day after day, with just the gentlest of breezes.

At midnight on 1 October we approached what appeared to be a frontal system, a wall of low cloud extending across the sky from horizon to horizon. As we reached this cloud the wind changed direction to the south-east and almost immediately we were enveloped in a tremendous downpour. The rain eased later, but the wind held steady, so that by noon there were 98 miles on the log.

The sky stayed cloudy and frequent rain squalls wet the decks. I caught enough water in the canvas awning during one squall to fill up all the water-bottles, and once I had done this my worries were over. The wind increased until it was blowing a fine, steady breeze reminiscent of the winds along the Barrier Reef, and *Trekka* went along as she had never gone before. On the 3rd she ran 118 miles to noon, and the following day she set a record day's total of 125. Not content with this she made her best run ever the next day with a wonderful 133, to which was added the current which brought the figure up to 146 miles. Considering that she was steering herself for the twelve hours of darkness when I had to reduce the sail area to get her to sail herself, this was extremely good going. The next three days gave us runs of 125, 120, and 127, so that in a week *Trekka* had run 845 miles on the log and made good 910 miles. Towards the end of the week the favourable current left us, but with this kind of sailing we did not really need it.

On the night of 8 October I hove *Trekka* to about 30 miles east of Cocos to wait for daylight before trying to locate the island. Sunsights in the morning showed that we were south-east of the atoll, and, after sailing for three hours on the new course, I saw the tops of coconut palms shortly before noon. After closing the shore and running along the coast of Direction Island we rounded the western point of the island to enter the calm water of the lagoon. I furled the mainsail and beat up to the lee of the island close to where a landing-barge and a crash-boat were moored, and was about to pick up a mooring-buoy when I saw a young man coming out in a small boat to show me where to anchor. He was one of the Cable Station staff, and, after directing me to anchor close off the beach, he took me ashore to meet the members of the Cable Station.

Cocos, I learned, was an important station and was a kind of cross-roads for the ocean cables which connected it with Rodriguez Island, Singapore and Perth. The staff usually spent eighteen months on the island and only the manager and his second in command were married and had their wives on the island.

Dan Griffin, the eldest of the single men remarked, "We're all exiles here, John, and we don't see many new faces, please eat in the mess with us and make yourself at home."

I enjoyed the company of all these single men who were much the same age as myself, but I noticed that the conversation invariably settled down to one topic, sex. One of them said quite ruefully, "Hell, there must be a lot of people think you are living an odd kind of life, sailing single-handed round the world spending days on end alone, but think of us here on this ruddy island, we don't get off for eighteen months at a stretch!"

I gathered that most of them chose to spend their holidays in Singapore and I asked one of them what kind of place it was.

"Never seen it," he chuckled. "I spend my entire holiday in the hotel making up for eighteen months here!"

Cocos, I was sure, would be an interesting port of call for a yacht with an all-girl crew, which would probably be a more effective method of putting the station out of action than the efforts of the German raider *Emden* during the First World War.

The doctor on West Island, where the air-strip is, came over to Direction Island to give me an injection the following day, for there was a mild outbreak of a tropical disease on the island which he thought might prove dangerous for me if I were to become sick at sea with no help at hand.

A couple of days later I visited West Island with one of the young men from the Cable Station. We sailed the six miles across the lagoon in a small boat which the staff used for recreation. It took an hour and a quarter, and was a most enjoyable sail across the sheltered water.

The air-strip on West Island was built during World War Two, but it is now used by Qantas Airlines for their service from Australia to Johannesburg. The next stop from Cocos was Mauritius, and I was told that this route is the longest regular commercial flight over the sea in the world. At the time I was there Qantas were using Constellations on this route, and the stage to and from Mauritius was always done at night so that star-sights could be used for the navigation. I was impressed at the number of men needed for servicing the aircraft and manning the airstrip and wondered at the enormous overhead costs needed to run a modern airline. West Island's men were obviously better off than those at Direction, for fresh provisions, milk and ice-cream were flown in regularly. I had a meal in the spotless canteen that would have done justice to any good restaurant anywhere, and I learned that there were movies and other entertainments to keep the men from feeling too remote.

I collected some mail from the post office on the island and was pleased to receive a chart of the Indian Ocean which Mrs Smeeton had sent from England and which I had been unable to obtain at Thursday Island. Back on Direction Island, I played tennis with the men and went skin-diving in the clear water of the lagoon. Skin-diving at Cocos was one of the most popular pastimes, and many of the young men owned aqualungs and took their diving quite seriously. Some collected shells, and I saw their collections, which were truly beautiful. Many hours had been spent cleaning the shells, and some of them shone like the finest bone china.

Dan was telling me that he knew someone in Canada. "You may know him, as he comes from Victoria," he said.

I wondered how many times before someone had asked me the same thing.

"I'm trying to think of his name," Dan went on, with his eyes screwed up in concentration, "Bill something. Bill . . . Bill . . ."

I thought of the only Bill I could think of, and suggested "Bill Barber?"

"Yes, that's the man. See? I knew you'd know him," said Dan and proceeded with his story as though it were the most natural thing that I should have known his friend.

Cocos had seven yachts call there in the year when *Trekka* visited the island compared with only one the previous year, Irving Johnson's *Yankee*. One of the first to call this year had been Commander Clarke in his *Solace* which he and his West Indian crew had really driven after leaving Cocos, making the 2,000-mile run to Rodriguez in fourteen days, a very fine effort. *Havfruen III* had called two weeks before, but there were two other small yachts ahead of her, *Larrapinta*, a 38-foot ketch from Sydney, and *Vixen*, a 36-foot cutter from Miami.

After spending a pleasant five days at Cocos I was ready to tackle the 2,000-mile stage to Rodriguez. So that I would not run out of reading material my friends ashore presented me with a pile of wormeaten books that the library would otherwise have thrown away. With these stowed away and my water-bottles topped up I was all ready to go.

On the morning of 14 October I set the new Terylene sails as many of the men were going to take photographs from the crash-boat that was going to accompany me as far as the entrance to the lagoon. Dan promised to send me any good pictures he got, and then, a few minutes later, we were off. *Trekka*, as though eager to be on her way, quickly slipped along over the calm water, until, off the lagoon entrance, my friends turned back. I waved for the last time and then ran over towards Horsbrugh Island, where there was a bit of a lee, and proceeded to remove the new sails and replace them with the old cotton suit. When sailing off the wind there was little point in wearing out the new ones when the cotton suit did the job equally well.

A few minutes later we were sailing again, and I streamed the log over the stern. An hour later Cocos was out of sight, and we had the ocean to ourselves again. I went below to get the first wormeaten book, so that I could steer and read at the same time.

The weather was quite perfect, just the right amount of wind, a clear sky and the normal ocean swell. I thought that if these conditions lasted for a few days we'd be able to make some good runs.

Looking back on this passage to Rodriguez I am amazed how easy it was. This was by far the fastest port-to-port passage *Trekka* ever made. The weather was perfect, day after glorious day, and our track across the chart seemed to leap in great jumps with each noon position. By the end of that first week *Trekka* had covered 858 miles with the worst day's run being 115 miles. This was the mileage recorded on the log and run through the water, it proved to be the best she ever did. There was little or no helping current on this passage, so the mileage on the log was what we made good.

I followed my usual practice of steering throughout the day and then letting *Trekka* manage herself when the sun went down. The twin-staysails, mainsail and mizzen were the usual sails set, but sometimes I set the mizzen staysail when I thought the speed was falling off. At night it was easy to furl the mainsail and hook up the twins to the tiller, but I only used one pole for the weather twin, the other one being set as an ordinary staysail. The mizzen was also used as the wind was well on the quarter instead of aft.

On 23 October we were becalmed for a few hours and the day's total sank to 81 miles. This was the only bad day's run we made on the passage.

At night the radio picked up South African stations, faintly at first, but as the days went by with increasing strength. The following evening there was Christmas pudding on the evening menu for we had passed the half-way point to Mauritius. This was a custom I looked forward to partly because it was such an easy meal to prepare. Christmas pudding was served with custard, a whole potful of it, and this comprised the entire meal, there was no filling up on potatoes or stew beforehand, for this was a celebration and I started with the best thing first.

*Trekka* continued to surge along westwards beneath the Trade Wind sky and though we couldn't quite match that first week in mileage we still made remarkable progress.

On 31 October at sunset, just 17 days and 7½ hours from Cocos, I sighted Rodriguez about twenty-five miles off. The wind had fallen light, and so I let *Trekka* drift on towards the island with the twins up during the night. In the morning the island was near at hand, looking wonderfully green and inviting. It is surrounded by extensive coral reefs, but there is an anchorage among them on the northern side of the island in Mathurin Bay. As we approached the bay a motor launch appeared from the shore and guided me into the anchorage, between the reefs. The anchor splashed down into ten fathoms to complete the run from Cocos for an average of 111 miles a day—surely a record for a boat of *Trekka's* size.

The motor launch returned to shore and brought out the Resident Magistrate, M. Toureau, who welcomed me to the island, saying that he had heard I was on the way as the Cable Station had received news from Cocos. I went ashore with him in the launch and soon met his charming wife, who had towels and soap ready—apparently other yachtsmen had called here before. Then the Toureaus drove me in their jeep to the summit of the island 1,300 feet high, from which one can see splendid views of the island and surrounding reef.

It had been some time since the last steamer called at Rodriguez, and because of this I was asked by the Postal Authorities if I would carry the mail to Mauritius. This was an honour I was delighted to accept, indeed I was so keen to do so that I decided to leave the following day for Mauritius, and I was pleased and amused to see a formal notice outside the post office saying that all mail would close the next day at noon, as *Trekka* was carrying it.

I went along to the Cable Station and met some of the young men there. One of them asked me if I would like to send a message to

Cocos, so I wrote out a brief message to Dan Griffin and watched with interest as the young man wrote it down in "cablese," the form of writing which is abbreviated so that the message can be sent quicker and with less expense. A few moments later I was handed Dan's reply in which he said that the photos of Trekka had been successful and that he was sending them on to South Africa for me.

The Manager of the station and his family invited me to lunch and presented me with some fresh vegetables for Trekka's larder. The day after I arrived at Rodriguez, we were off again. I wanted to get to South Africa and spend some time there with many of my old friends and perhaps enjoy Christmas with them.

The green mail-sack was stowed away up forward and some fresh strawberries and vegetables from Madame Toureau put in a safe place, then I got the anchor aboard and hoisted sail.

There was very little wind, and I knew that I should have waited for more settled conditions. A huge black cloud approached from the south and for a few hours we experienced some squally weather. Trekka crashed and banged along with just the staysail and mizzen up, but by the morning the sky had cleared and the wind went back to the south-easterly quadrant.

A couple of evenings later a plane passed overhead going towards Cocos and this showed that we were not far off course.

On 7 November the high mountains of Mauritius were in sight and throughout the day we steadily closed the shore. The island looks very beautiful from the sea with the land rising rapidly in the centre to heights of over 2,000 feet. Port Louis, the main harbour of Mauritius, is on the western side of the island and I elected to sail around the north coast to get there. Extensive sugar plantations were visible from the sea, some of which were being burned off. The smell from them when we came into the lee of the land was as sweet as the cane itself.

At ten o'clock that night we beat up the harbour, passing two lanes of shipping, and then the Customs launch spotted us and came alongside to pass me a tow-line. We were towed into the inner harbour where I anchored and then handed over the mail-sack from Rodriguez. The authorities cleared me in the morning, leaving me free to go ashore and explore what Port Louis had to offer.

Havfruen III, the big English ketch, was in Port Louis, having been in dry-dock for a few days, and I was pleased to see Batch and Ann Carr again and hear how they had been getting on since we last met in Brisbane. I was offered a berth at a private wharf owned by Blythe Brothers which I was very glad to accept, for it was far more convenient than rowing ashore in the dinghy. The offices of this firm

stood close to the wharf and before leaving Mauritius I took a somewhat unusual picture of *Trekka* from the top office balcony.

Doug Reid, the young crew from *Havfruen III*, took me out to the
yacht club at Grande Bay, surely one of the most attractive dinghy-
sailing clubs in the world. I was trying to write mail at one of the
tables on the patio, but soon became aware of delightful young
French girls walking past clad in bikinis. My concentration wavered,
and finally letter-writing was abandoned in favour of admiring the
beautiful scenery.

A young Frenchman took Doug and me to the races, explaining
that this was something we should see. The only horse-races I had
ever seen were the Hollywood variety or perhaps the occasional news-
reel of the Grand National. If you went to the Mauritius Races to see
the horses you'd be wasting your time, I've seen better horses on the
beach at Jersey giving rides at sixpence a time. It was the people
at the races who were worth seeing. There was a grandstand which
was capable of holding almost two hundred, and if you were anyone at all you stood there with the rest of the island's élite. It was
not the grandstand that caught my attention, it was the mass of
Indians in the centre of the course that completely fascinated me, for
whenever one of the four horses in the race went by, there was a
frantic rush by everyone to see it go by on the back stretch. I
expected to see bodies trampled into the ground as each horse passed,
but these racing fans are obviously dedicated ones and are used to
these goings on. The centre of the course was a riot of colour. Indian
women dressed in gaily coloured saris while the menfolk wore
European clothes. Refreshment stands in the Indian style were scattered among the crowd selling various tit-bits which were fried in a
pan over a small fire. At odd intervals people rushed across the track
after a horse had gone by to reach this mass of humanity and I began
to appreciate the obstacles the jockeys faced on the two circuits of the
track, for if the wrong horse was leading, a torrent of abuse, lemonade
bottles and other such missiles were hurled at the riders. The three of
us made our way through the crowd thoroughly enjoying it all, for
it was impossible not to be caught up in all the excitement. I have
never been to a race-track since that day, and any meeting I attended
now would seem a very dull affair after the Mauritius Derby.

Although Mauritius has been British since 1814, most of the popu-
lation are of Indian or French or mixed descent. French is the language more commonly used, but in Port Louis most of the store-
keepers speak English.

I was frequently asked by Indians in Port Louis for work. This was
usually from tailors who were probably eyeing my frame and calcu-

lating how much extra material would be needed. But quite often I got demands for my laundry too. The applicant always had printed references from other satisfied customers. These cards usually stated that the man was a very good tailor or laundryman who took special care in his work, "Signed A. J. Smith (Royal Navy Stoker)."

I would have stayed longer in Mauritius and enjoyed its wonderful beaches, climate and scenery longer but for my desire to spend more time with friends in South Africa. *Trekka's* pantry was stocked with fresh vegetables and fruit, and, being in all respects ready for sea, we left Port Louis on the afternoon of 12 November bound for Durban. There was a gentle north-easterly wind blowing once we were out into the open sea, so I set the twins and then retired below to cook the fresh steak I had bought just before leaving. Another ocean hop was beginning. By the following morning the enormous bulk of the French Island of Réunion was plainly visible, towering up 10,000 feet into a cloudless sky. As the hours passed cloud began to form about the summit and slowly but surely hid the island from view while the rest of the sky remained clear.

The wind was becoming lighter the farther south we went, and it was obvious that we were nearing the limit of the South East Trade Wind. I was sorry to see it go for it had driven *Trekka* so well these past few months. The Indian Ocean must be the best of all oceans for good sailing weather. Perhaps we were fortunate and had exceptional conditions, but I was left with the impression that this ocean has a far worse reputation than it deserves.

There was great excitement one morning when a freighter, the *Crofter* of Liverpool, appeared over the horizon and altered course to come and have a look at us. She came close alongside and an officer hailed me from her bridge asking if I was all right. When I waved back that all was well, he promised to report me in Durban, which I later learned he did. I watched the bulk of her disappear over the horizon and wondered what *Trekka* must look like from the bridge of a big ship.

On 18 November, just 175 miles from Madagascar, we passed a trot line in the water similar to the Japanese ones in the Pacific. A line of glass buoys, each with a stake attached, stretched as far as the eye could see, but there was no sign of a boat or ship about. Perhaps it was indeed a Japanese line for their vessels are reported to be fishing all over the world nowadays.

The wind piped up and *Trekka* started to fly again. By noon the following day we had run 132 miles in the past 24 hours and a favourable current had boosted this to 155 miles, which had surpassed the 146 miles total for a day's run on the way to Cocos. The wind kept increasing, and I had to heave to for a few hours until it moderated enough for us to continue. When it did ease the sea went down very quickly, and by noon the following day we were sailing to a north-westerly breeze 60 miles off the coast of Madagascar. For the rest of the passage to Durban the wind was constantly changing direction, so that my sleep was frequently broken at night by having to go on deck and change sail. Fortunately I was so used to *Trekka's* gear by this time that I could change any sail on the blackest night without getting things into a tangle.

*Trekka's* larder had been particularly well stocked on this passage, the fruit that I had bought green in Port Louis was ripening steadily. There were apples, pawpaw and oranges, as well as litchis, small fruit with white flesh, a brown stone in the centre and a thin brown shell covering the whole. They taste rather like grapes and are delicious. Another interesting buy had been bottles of sterilised milk packed in South Africa. This tasted like fresh milk and I enjoyed it with cornflakes at breakfast time.

The currents in the Mozambique Channel are strong and quite unpredictable. One day would find us set thirty miles north of the course and the next far to the south. It was all very confusing, and I was pleased that there were no islands or reefs in the vicinity for us to hit. I stood well to the northward of the track to Durban knowing that the Agulhas current runs strongly down the African coast and on 1 December sighted land near Cape St Lucia. We were running along the coast with a nice following breeze when I noticed a tiny black cloud on the horizon ahead. It quickly grew in size and I realised that there was a lot of wind behind it. The north-easter held steady until the cloud was almost upon us, then there was a lull which lasted less than a minute during which time I hastily furled the mainsail. There was a sudden blast of air and *Trekka* heeled to the onslaught of the elements. This kind of weather is typical along the Natal coast and is very similar to the southerly Busters experienced along Australia's New South Wales coast. A few hours later the wind was back to north-east again and *Trekka* romped along on the last few miles to Durban.

At dusk we were abreast of Umhlanga Rocks with the lights of the Hotel there clearly visible. Then, a few miles farther on, the illuminations of Durban came into view. It was a wonderful sight after spending twenty days at sea, the lights from the many hotels along the seafront and traffic completely swamped the feeble efforts of the navigational beacons marking the approaches to the harbour. But this was familiar territory to me now, and at 10 p.m. *Trekka* entered the channel between the two long breakwaters and ran into the calm water of the harbour. The signal station on the Bluff fired a salvo of Morse at me with a signal-lamp and kept at it until I did my best with a flashlight to tell them who we were. Amazingly enough they were able to read my fumbling efforts and a pilot boat appeared on the scene and directed me to an anchorage for the night, telling me that the port doctor and officials would clear me in the morning.

# CHAPTER EIGHTEEN

# Penny Whistles and the Cape of Storms

When I had been cleared by the authorities next day the Customs launch escorted Trekka to the yacht-basin where she lay for the rest of her stay in Durban. There I was handed two letters which offered me honorary membership during my stay to the Point Y.C. and the Royal Natal Y.C. This was a gesture which I much appreciated, especially as it resulted in me making a lot of new friends. It was wonderful to be in Durban again, for it is a pleasant city, and one that is easy to enjoy with its permanent holiday atmosphere.

Havfruen III was moored only a few yards away, and it was not long before I met the crews of the other visiting yachts, Peter and Lesley Mounsey from Sydney on the 38-foot ketch Larrapinta and Jim and Jean Stark in Vixen from Miami. Four overseas yachts in port at once was a record for Durban, but a few days later Diana arrived to make it five. Gary and his friend Brian were sporting beards that put Mr Young's to shame, but after I had photographed them Gary and Brian shaved theirs off for they had had a good look at themselves in the Yacht Club wash-rooms.

Durban at Christmas time is unforgettable, the stores all gaily decorated and the very buildings themselves appearing to smile. The thing I remember best about the city at this time of the year is the music, not the dreary old Christmas Carols which are paraded forth every year and which grind on monotonously in the same honeyed tones, but the bubbling happy music of the Zulu Kwela tunes that make even my feet twitch to their wonderful rhythm. After the day's work in the city, Zulu boys get together with their instruments and form small bands which play in the streets to passers-by for the odd coins which are tossed their way. These bands usually number no more than six or seven and the instruments are usually guitars and penny whistles made out of a length of tubing. Sometimes other instruments are used, like a saxophone or clarinet, but some of the best bands get the most magical effects with only the simplest instruments.

*Trekka* at Mauritius after crossing the kindly Indian Ocean

The *Crofter* of Liverpool comes to have a look at *Trekka*

Leaving Cape Town

Whatever restrictions these coloured folk may have in their every-day lives it certainly does not appear in their music, and anyone hearing it for the first time could not help but remark that these are a happy people. Gary and I were listening to one of these bands from the second-floor windows of a friend's flat, the sun had gone and it was the time of the day just before night. A young Zulu girl dressed in black and wearing white shoes was dancing in the street with an open hat in her hands held out for contributions. As the light faded it became impossible to see her at all against the dark background of the street except for a pair of white shoes. We watched quite fascinated as the shoes appeared to dance by themselves among the passers-by to the steady rhythm of the music.

There are few places in the world today where you can hear the true music of a people, and I was very glad to be able to hear these Africans who had far more talent than many so-called stars.

After the Indian Ocean crossing *Trekka* was in need of some atten-tion and I spent several days repainting and varnishing her until she looked more like her former self. The best time of the day to work was early in the morning, when it was still cool. This also meant that there would be no interruptions from interested passers-by for I have been told that I am a poor conversationalist when busy.

In the workshop of the Point Yacht Club I made a small teak table, which fastened to the mast below and could easily be detached and stowed away if in the way. This table was most useful, and once it was installed it was difficult to imagine how I had managed without one before, meals and letter-writing were much easier operations with this new addition.

A few days were spent visiting old friends in Pietermaritzburg where I had once lived, but as so often happens when you return to a place after a long absence it seemed to have changed, and I was glad to return to my little floating home in Durban.

I met a young South African who had recently returned from Canada. He told me about a young man he had met up there a few years before who was building a small boat. I listened carefully and burst out laughing, for it was me he had met! We had forgotten each other, as it had just been a casual meeting. But he was so interested in my voyage that he later joined *Diana* when she left South Africa and crossed the Atlantic Ocean in her.

Durban yachtsman have a somewhat morbid sense of humour when you mention the passage to Cape Town in a yacht, and many of them, knowing that I would soon be off on this stage, told me of the trouble and strife other yachts had encountered while attempting to round the "Cape of Storms." I heard of Tom Steele and young

Ray Cruikshank, who had been rolled over in *Adios* during a storm while attempting this passage, and of Tony Armitt and Brian Loe in the 28-foot ketch *Marco Polo*, which had been damaged by a storm off the coast near Port Elizabeth. These last two New Zealanders went on to circumnavigate the globe in their little ketch which, at the time they completed their voyage, was the smallest vessel ever to have done so.

There were many other tales of woe that set me thinking about the Cape. Was it always bad? Or were most of these other hectic voyages made at the wrong time of the year? On checking, I found that the more hectic passages had nearly always been made at the wrong time of the year or the boat had not been in the best condition. Even so, the crews of the other four visiting yachts that were due to sail for Cape Town eyed each other wondering who would be the first to stick their necks out. We all discussed the 900-mile passage and argued about whether it was better to stay close in to shore or well off. The Agulhas Current was the main bogey. This mass of water flows down the African coast towards the Cape at a rate of about fifty miles a day but it frequently attains double that speed. A gale from the south-west against the current kicks up a vicious short sea, and I think it is this that has caused most trouble to small craft.

My plan on this stage was to keep *Trekka* as light as possible, for although the motion is sometimes quite violent when she is light, she certainly gets hit less by the sea than when well loaded. I put aboard enough stores to last me to Cape Town and filled only three of the water-bottles, which saved quite a lot of weight. As there might be some hard sailing on this leg I bent on the new sails, knowing that the old ones would not stand much rough treatment, they were so baggy now that it was becoming difficult to beat to windward with them. The old cotton mainsail had stretched nearly eighteen inches on the original luff length of 22 feet 9 inches, and it was necessary to roll a reef in the sail if it was sheeted in hard, otherwise the boom rested on top of the dinghy.

On Wednesday, 15 January 1959 the weather had cleared after two days of strong westerly winds. These conditions are usually followed by three days of easterly wind, so I quickly collected a clearance from Customs and within the hour was drifting down the harbour and out to the open sea with a faint easterly breeze smoothing the wrinkles out of the sails. A long swell rolled up from the south-west, and it was not long before my shore-softened stomach paid its toll. *Trekka* began to edge out offshore, for I wanted to take full advantage of the favourable current during this spell of fine weather.

By noon next day we were 100 miles down the coast and 30 miles offshore, but during the night the wind suddenly switched round to the south-west and began to blow hard. The sea became quite steep, but *Trekka* seemed to have the situation under control, and after a few uncomfortable hours we were able to proceed under sail again towards the south-west. Sights the following day showed that during the time we had been hove-to, we had in fact been set over fifty miles to windward by the current—little wonder that the sea had been steep!

The wind switched round to the east again, and *Trekka* surged along down the coast carrying all the sail she could. At noon on the fourth day out we had passed Port Elizabeth, but that evening the breeze fell away and I noticed that the barometer was falling—another depression was on its way. When the wind returned it was from the west, and all too soon it had kicked up the sea to such an extent that we were forced to heave to again. It seems that the winds along this section of the African coastline either blow up or down it, but never off or on to the land, so that there appears to be little danger of being blown ashore.

During the hours of darkness the loom of the light on Cape Recife was clearly visible, and rather than be tossed about while waiting for the wind to change, I decided to run back to Port Elizabeth and shelter.

The passage to Cape Town had now been cut in half and we had done the worst bit, for the section of coastline from Durban to Algoa Bay is barren of shelter apart from the port of East London on the Buffalo River. From Port Elizabeth onward there are several bays that give good shelter during westerly weather, and if I watched the barometer there was a good chance of avoiding gales if I sheltered in time.

I moored *Trekka* close to some other small craft near the Navy landing, The harbour at Port Elizabeth is designed for liners and freighters rather than small craft, but this was a case of "any port in a storm." Soon after arriving I went ashore and bought a large piece of beefsteak as a celebration, which was nicely rounded off with a full eight hours of sleep.

In the morning the westerly wind had gone, to be replaced by a gentle breeze from the south-east, and I lost no time in getting back to sea again. The breeze strengthened, and we sailed down the coast steadily getting closer and closer to the southern tip of Africa. After being so long in the tropics I was feeling that this was something like Cape Horn, but the latitude of Cape Agulhas, the southernmost tip of Africa is only 34° 50′ as compared to the Horn's 56°.

On the afternoon of 24 January I motored into Plettenbergs Bay as the wind had gone and it seemed likely that it would come back from the west. Soon after I had anchored two Navy vessels, a frigate and a Fairmile, entered the bay and anchored about a mile away, close to the settlement ashore. They were still there the following morning when I attempted to leave and as we sailed close by the frigate *Good Hope* an officer on her bridge hailed me with a loudspeaker and asked the name of the yacht and where we were from. He seemed quite surprised when I told him.

The wind was still playing tricks, and I saw that it would be a waste of time to try to sail with so little; so, rather than try my patience, I returned to our anchorage under the cliffs on the south-western side of the bay. Soon afterwards a whaler came towards me from the *Good Hope.* The coxswain said that the officers would like me to have lunch with them, and if it was all right they would come and collect me later. I gladly accepted, and when the officers duly arrived rowing a whaler and clad in shorts I realised that I did not need to feel too much of a hobo in their company. Soon I was enjoying a hot shower and then lunch with these friendly young men.

The sky had a threatening appearance to the west, and soon after lunch I was taken back to *Trekka* with some spoils for her larder, some fresh bread and a pound of butter. I had just got the anchor up and laid on deck when the first quick breaths of the black-looking squall reached us. I wanted to return to the anchorage under the cliffs, which would provide more shelter, and I got the mizzen and staysail set, then a terrific gust of wind hit us, and *Trekka* heeled right over, pots and pans clanking away merrily. It was difficult to estimate what the wind force was in that puff, but I would guess it must have been fifty miles an hour. *Trekka* fled to the shelter of the cliffs, and soon afterwards I had the anchor down and both sails stowed. By the following morning all was peaceful again, a clear sky and a breeze from the east promised good sailing, and I lost little time in getting sail up. The two Navy vessels left shortly before me bound for Port Elizabeth while we departed in the opposite direction towards Cape Town. I had intended looking in at the little harbour at Knysna, and, indeed, the navigator on the *Good Hope* had given me a chart of the entrance of the little port, which looked most attractive, but as we were carrying a fair breeze I decided to carry on and reach Mossel Bay instead.

Throughout the day *Trekka* ticked off the miles on the log, and by nightfall the lights of Mossel Bay settlement were abeam. The distance to Cape Town was now about 250 miles, and as the breeze was holding I passed the bay and set a course for Cape Agulhas. Three hours later a strong westerly wind replaced the helpful easterly one, and, as shelter was close at hand, I put the helm up and headed back to Mossel Bay.

I spent two days sheltering in the little harbour of Mossel Bay feeling very pleased with myself, for it was blowing great guns out at sea. Leaving *Trekka* snugly anchored I set off to see what the settlement ashore had to offer and found it quite a pleasant little place. The main street climbs steadily up the hill and is lined with many cafés and small restaurants, for this is a popular seaside resort. I noticed photographs in a couple of shop-windows of black marlin which had been caught in the waters off the coast and learned that this was a popular spot for keen anglers. Perhaps it was because of the black marlin that the settlement reminded me a little of New Zealand, and even the scenery was reminiscent of parts of the North Island.

On the morning of 29 January 1959 I left Mossel Bay with a fine, steady easterly breeze driving *Trekka* along at almost her maximum speed. By darkness we had covered 60 miles, but unfortunately the sea was getting up and the wind continued to increase. I kept reducing sail until at last the tiny storm-jib was as much as we could carry. By this time the wind was blowing extremely hard, but it was a fair wind, and I didn't want to waste it, so I spent all night at the helm in an effort to help *Trekka* along. The depth of water here on the Agulhas Bank was less than 50 fathoms, but the short seas did not appear to be troubling *Trekka* at all, and steering was not difficult, though, as the hours wore on, I grew very tired.

Daylight revealed a somewhat more cheerful scene, though it was still blowing very hard, and the little storm-jib was ample sail area for these conditions. I climbed stiffly down the hatchway and prepared some breakfast while continuing to steer from inside by simply reaching the tiller with one hand while the other prepared toast and hot coffee. *Trekka* is the kind of boat in which you can do that!

We were well off the coast, and a haze about the horizon hid the land that should have been visible, but, according to the log, we passed Cape Agulhas, the southernmost tip of Africa, at four o'clock that afternoon. The Pilot Book says that after one passes the Cape the weather will often change, and fortunately for me it proved to be for the better. The wind rapidly eased off until just before darkness my wind indicator showed it to be 22 knots. This was still a little strong for the twin-staysails, but as it was easing I set them all the same, and soon afterwards, with *Trekka* surfing along steering herself, I thankfully turned into my bunk and fell asleep almost immediately.

At daybreak I was up greatly refreshed and looking out for the

Cape of Good Hope which, according to my reckoning, was about thirty miles off. I had to wait until noon when the coastal fog lifted enough to show the Cape clearly eighteen miles off. By the late afternoon we were sailing up the lovely Cape Peninsula in the lee of the mountains named the Twelve Apostles. White clouds spilled down off their peaks like waterfalls and ahead I could see that Table Mountain was also wearing its "tablecloth." This is the sign that the south-easter is blowing, but here, in the lee off Seapoint, we were just moving along very quietly. Darkness fell, and we drifted past the Green Point light towards the light on the end of Cape Town's long harbour breakwater.

The view of Cape Town at night from the sea is superb, lights from houses, street lamps and traffic climb high up the slopes of Table Mountain; and this scene seemed all the more unforgettable because I was so elated at having safely rounded the "Cape of Storms." Suddenly, a terrific blast of air hit us and *Trekka* staggered from the blow. I thought it must be just a willywaw from the mountains, but I soon realised that it was continuous. With *Trekka* heeled far over I crawled along the deck and got the mainsail down, then I went on beating with the staysail and mizzen towards the harbour entrance, now less than a mile away.

This furious blast of air was the famous Cape south-easter sweeping around the end of Devil's Peak. During the summer months it blows almost continuously, often with great velocity; one gust at Table Bay Docks Lookout Station was recorded at 102 miles an hour. *Trekka*, well overcanvased, beat her way up the harbour with spray flying. Sizeable waves were slopping against the wharves in Duncan Dock, and, as it was getting late, I anchored close to a Union Castle liner that gave a little protection to the latest arrival from the open sea. With the big 27-pound anchor down I turned into my bunk, knowing that *Trekka* would not wander during the night, even with the gale of wind that was whistling through the rigging.

In the morning the wind was gone and Table Mountain was clear of cloud. A Police launch came over towards us, and shortly afterwards *Trekka* was towed to the small yacht-basin by the clubhouse of the Royal Cape Yacht Club.

On this lovely clear Saturday morning, many yachtsmen were pottering about with their boats, and several of them came over to have a look at *Trekka*. One of them remarked how clean she looked, and compared with some of the other craft in the basin she really looked like a little jewel. The sheets and halyard tails were bleached white with the sun, and the paintwork, fresh in Durban, looked as new.

"She won't look like that very long here," remarked one of the passers-by. This puzzled me at the time, but the following day I saw what he meant when the wind returned. The Yacht Club is unfortunate to have a large area of open lots, railway-sidings and shunting-yards immediately behind it, and, when the south-easter blows, grit and dust from the lots and soot and smoke from the locomotives descend on the unfortunate yachts. It is not surprising that paint and varnish-work do not stand up to this kind of treatment for long.

Offshore sailing in South Africa is a pretty rugged sport, and I was pleased to meet these keen yachtsmen at Cape Town. Some of the old members had met my father when he sailed his 52-foot ketch *Our Boy* out from England years ago, and a couple could even remember the wee three-year-old who had been aboard and remarked that I had grown somewhat since they last saw me.

I was most interested to meet Mr C. Bruynzeel, the owner of *Zeeslang*, an extremely light displacement little sloop designed by E. G. Van de Stadt. Mr Bruynzeel was probably the most experienced ocean-racing yachtsman in South Africa, having owned several large yachts, among them the lovely *Zeearend* and the light displacement *Zeevalk*. We had a long and interesting talk about the relative merits of light boats and heavy ones; and I was very interested to hear that he was planning to build a 72-foot ketch in Cape Town. She has now been built and raced most successfully, her name is *Stormvogel*.

By the time I arrived in Cape Town *Trekka* had very little aboard in the way of supplies, Cairns in Australia had been the last place where I had bought a sizeable amount of canned food, but now with the Cape safely behind me it was time to see about buying stores. Food prices in South Africa were the cheapest I found anywhere during my voyage, and this particularly applied to canned goods, so I tried to put aboard enough stores to see me all the way back to Canada. *Trekka's* designed waterline steadily sank deeper and deeper as every available bit of locker space was filled with cans and boxes.

The Yacht Club gave me six two-gallon polythene bottles which allowed me to carry more fresh water, for there were some very long stages before me in the Atlantic and Pacific when extra water would be needed. Of course, space had to be found for this, too, and though *Trekka* was deeper in the water than she had ever been before, she was not complaining too bitterly.

There wasn't much I needed now before I could sail from Cape Town except charts. I had ordered some from England on my arrival at Durban, but there was still no sign of them, and as the days went by I became increasingly impatient to leave. While waiting for the charts I pulled the mainmast out of *Trekka* and gave it two coats of varnish which had not been done since Thursday Island. The Commodore of the Yacht Club, Basil Lindhorst, heard about my delay because the charts had not turned up, and came along to tell me that there was a pile of outdated charts in the club that had been presented to the Club by one of the shipping companies. I was given the key to a room upstairs and told to pick out what I wanted. From a pile of charts four feet high and boxes of Pilot Books I was able to pick out a wonderful selection of charts—far better than those I had ordered from England.

There had been little work to do on *Trekka* and I had spent much time visiting friends and seeing the wonderful scenery about the Cape Peninsula. What with swimming and walking and sightseeing, the days quickly sped by, but the time had come to put to sea again after being in port for two weeks. The people at the Yacht Club had been most kind to me and I hoped that some day my next boat would revisit this happy port.

On the afternoon of 14 February 1959, two years to the day after *Tzu Hang's* dismasting in the Southern Ocean, *Trekka* edged away from the dock bound once more on another ocean crossing. A cannon at the club fired a salute, and under main and staysail we quickly drew away from the group of friends who had come to see us off.

*Trekka's* motion felt strangely different because of the weight of stores in her—she had certainly never been this low in the water before. We shot down the harbour, and then went out between the pier heads into the open sea with a fine blustery south-easter filling the sails. It was a glorious day to be leaving. The sky was clear, and this good breeze drove us along very quickly. Robben Island was soon left astern as *Trekka* waltzed along to the north-west, where 1,700 miles away the lonely speck of St Helena Island lay. That evening the twin-staysails were set and *Trekka* began what was to be one of the easiest passages she ever made. The wind stayed south-east for days on end, and *Trekka* under her twins steered herself all the time. Whenever the wind eased I set the small spinnaker from the masthead above the twins with the sheets led through blocks on the end of the twin poles. This soon became my favourite rig, for the addition of the spinnaker certainly cut down on the motion which you usually get with just the twins set. *Trekka* coping with her own steering I had much spare time and spent it writing mail on the new table below on my typewriter or reading the many books which friends in Cape Town had given me.

As we got farther north, the weather gradually became warmer. We were making very good time, averaging over a hundred miles a day and not having to steer at all. I liked this kind of passage very much.

One of the things that impressed me was the total lack of bird-life. Previously on other passages there had always been the odd petrel or bosun-bird, but there seemed to be no birds at all over this part of the ocean.

The radio was providing me with a lot of entertainment. My favourite serial, No *Place to Hide* was rapidly reaching the climax, and I hoped that I'd hear the finish of the story before we got too far away to pick up the station. Every night it was a little more difficult to hear, and finally I had to acknowledge defeat. I never did hear the end of the story.

The B.B.C. was now very clear and I noticed how many of the requests in the programme "Listener's Choice" came from St Helena or Ascension Island.

It was wonderful how the little boat kept moving along, the three blue sails without a wrinkle in them hauling us along hour after hour. Every once in a while *Trekka* caught a slide and surfed along on the wave. Sprays of flying-fish fanned out in all directions, some of them gliding over a hundred yards. Others in the panic to get out of the way of the monster that was bearing down upon them shot straight up into the air, and a few landed on the deck, but usually managed to flap back into the sea again.

The decks were dry all the time, and as I was not steering I did a little bit of varnishing. The cleats around the cockpit were not in use these days, as the sheets were made fast to the tiller, so I was able to sand them down and give them a couple of coats of varnish besides touching up a couple of other places that needed doing.

# CHAPTER NINETEEN

# Two Dots in the Ocean

Just before noon on 2 March I sighted the steep cliffs of St Helena dead ahead. We were still about 30 miles off, but slowly the island became more distinct until late that afternoon we were rounding the black cliffs of the "Barn" at the north-eastern end of the Island. St Helena looks a grim and forbidding place from the sea. The steep grey-black cliffs fall sheer into the water like the walls of some medieval fortress; nowhere is there any green apparent, and it looks a very dismal place. I can quite understand how the Emperor Napoleon Bonaparte felt when he first saw those cliffs.

The anchorage at James Bay is on the north-western side of the island, which, during the regular Trade Wind weather, is the lee of the island. It was almost dark when we rounded the north point and tacked down the coast to the bay. A few lights were visible ashore, and in the darkness I could just see the shadowy forms of some lighters moored near by. I anchored close to them in 10 fathoms with my big 27-pound anchor. I didn't want Trekka drifting away here, she might take quite a bit of finding.

In the morning the port officials and the doctor came out to clear me. They thought Trekka had done very well to make the passage from Cape Town in 16 days. The harbourmaster knew all the names of previous yachts that had called here and how long they had been at sea from the Cape. I went ashore with the officials, who told me that there was a boatman who would take me out to Trekka whenever I wanted without my having to use my little dinghy.

Landing in a dinghy would have been quite a hazardous operation in any case, and in mine almost impossible. The landing-place was at the northern side of the bay, near the end of the sea-wall. A strong surge was setting into the bay, and when we got to the landing I could see the water-level rising and falling as much as eight feet. The boatman was an old hand at this, though, and I watched with interest how he approached the landing stern-on and at exactly the correct moment brought the stern up to the steps. When the next swell came along the stern was lifted almost level with the top of the steps and most of us stepped quickly ashore. As the boat fell into the trough the boatman pulled away slightly and the next swell brought the stern in the same position as before. It looked quite easy, but I realised that the St Helenans were excellent boatmen. Later on I saw them launch a whaleboat from the quay by lowering it into the water with the crane. It was a similar exhibition of clever work, for the slightest mistake and the boat would have been smashed to pieces against the quay in the sea that was running. *Trekka* appeared quite safe where she was anchored, though her masts were describing great arcs in the sky as she rolled.

The little settlement of Jamestown is entered through the gate of the fort which stretches across the great gulch from one side of the bay to the other. Situated on the cliffs and commanding the approaches to the bay are all the old fortifications. For in years gone by this was an important call for the big sailing vessels which would get fresh provisions and water here. When steam put an end to sail the island fell on hard times, for there was no need for the smoke-pots to call. The islanders have been poor ever since, as there is little industry on the island except growing flax for making rope, and the odd bit of fishing. A few years ago a small canning plant commenced operations, but as fish catches were not regular the venture closed down. Perhaps with good equipment it could be made to pay, but the bugbear of no harbour is a difficult one to get over, for the weather can become bad at certain times of the year and westerly storms sweep into the bay, so that all craft have to be lifted out of the water with the crane.

Jamestown itself is rather like a small English village. I have seen similar places in the West Country, but if one looks up at the great volcanic slopes the illusion is lost immediately.

I met two keen anglers who had come from South Africa to try the sport fishing. They had to make do with the simplest of boats and were without the usual fighting chairs, but one of them had managed to land a small black marlin weighing just under 200 pounds.

There was no air service to the island, but a passenger boat called once a month, and I gathered that this was a most looked-forward-to event. Many of the womenfolk do embroidery after the fashion of the the Madeira work. I don't think the work is as fancy as the Madeira embroidery, but the materials are probably better, as they use only the best Irish linen.

On my first day ashore I climbed the great flight of steps known as Jacob's Ladder. Six hundred and ninety-nine steps lead up the side of the gulch to a fort at the top, which is now serving a more useful purpose as the school for the island's numerous children. Every day these youngsters climb the steps, and though it may look easy to anyone who has never been up them, I can assure you it is a stiff climb and took me a good ten minutes to reach the top. The children have devised a good means of descending, by spreading their arms wide and gripping one of the handrails and resting their feet on the other, they then slide sideways down the rails, which have become very well polished over the years.

Of course, no visit to St Helena is complete without seeing Longwood, the house where Napoleon was exiled. Much of it has been attacked by borers over the years and the house has been repaired so much that I doubt if much of the original is still standing. Some new teak floors had just been put down and my eyes were taken by the beautiful timber. I could have found better use for it than just to be used for floors. About the only thing that did interest me at the house was a globe of the world which was made in 1808; it was most interesting to compare the coastlines of parts of the world as known then to present-day ones. I noticed that a rock was marked about 40 miles due south of the southernmost tip of Africa, Cape Agulhas. Somewhere close to that spot an 8-fathom patch was discovered a few years ago, and I wondered if there was any connection between the two.

In Mrs Benjamin's store in Jamestown I found all kinds of wonderful buys. One-pound tins of New Zealand butter and some very fine English margarine in tins, which kept better in the tropics than the butter did. Both these items had been unobtainable in South Africa. I was on the hunt for some good ship's biscuits. My large tin that I had bought in Auckland was almost finished, but the only type of biscuit available seemed to be cream crackers. While I was in Mauritius I had bought some "hardtack" from a ship's chandler there. They were enormous biscuits, an inch thick and seven to eight inches across. I tried all kinds of ways to eat them but I never found the knack. When they were broken into small pieces it was like chewing stones. I soaked one in fresh water for three days and then had a go at it, but only the outside had softened a little. The inside was still as hard as rock. I considered putting them in the pressure-cooker, for by this time I was wondering just what kind of supermen ate these things, but I still had other biscuits left and I eventually threw all the Mauritius ones away except a couple which I kept for friends. One I gave to Gary aboard Diana; he went to the dentist the next day, but he confessed that he hadn't even been able to mark the biscuit.

I met two elderly English ladies who had settled on the island and learned from them that there were quite a number of people who had come to the island to stay. Cost of living was very cheap for retired people, and I believe that the one hotel in Jamestown charged only £5 a week all found.

On 5 March, after a very pleasant three days' stay, I left St Helena. Next stop was to be Ascension Island, another lonely dot in the ocean some 700 miles away. I left my two fishermen friends waving in the boatman's tender. I think they would have preferred to sail with me than on the liner that was calling the following week.

Once clear of the island, I set the twins and spinnaker and let *Trekka* take care of herself. I had swapped my store of books with one of the English ladies and was soon settling down to one of her books. There was no doubt about it, sailing was terribly rugged these days!

The wind was light for the first two days, but it freshened until it was back to the normal Trade strength, and we went along as we had on the passage to St Helena. It was much warmer now, and I began to notice a few birds about, mainly bosun-birds with long tails. There was plenty of fish life, the flying-fish shot out of the water in clouds, and I never got tired of watching the dorados chasing them.

One day we had a school of big black porpoises swimming with us. They were of the type known as blackfish, and I watched them for a few minutes before going below for my camera. Suddenly *Trekka* jerked and pulled up sharp, and I realised that we had hit one of the porpoises. We got going again and a few seconds later did the same thing. These creatures are usually so nimble that I was very surprised at colliding with one, this was the only occasion *Trekka* ever did so.

The twin-staysails had done quite a lot of work recently, and the stitching on one of them was starting to let go. I have found that the old saying "a stitch in time saves nine" is very true especially with sails. I had the port twin down for about an hour one day so that I could sew up some of the seams. I think it will be a great day for the ocean voyager when the seams of sails are welded together. Perhaps for synthetic cloth that day is not too far off.

At nine o'clock on the morning of 12 March Ascension Island was in sight just over thirty miles away. The peak was clear, and the island looked very small from a distance, but as we approached it grew out of the sea until I was able to distinguish various points about the island, and the tall rock of Boatswain-Bird Island, which I approached quite closely.

Ascension Island is a strange-looking place. It is volcanic, and numerous craters and lava flows are scattered about the island. Only the top of Green Mountain has any vegetation on it at all, the rest is barren and resembles a lunar landscape.

I arrived off the anchorage at Georgetown at four o'clock that afternoon and anchored near a landing-barge and a couple of other similar craft. A few minutes later I saw a boat being lowered into the water by a crane at the end of the quay, and when it arrived along-side soon afterwards I met Mr Harrison, who was the Resident Magistrate as well as being the manager of the Cable Station. He told me that he was expecting me to arrive that day as he had been notified by the Cable Station in St Helena of my departure, and he guessed that the passage would take about a week. Yachts that had called before had usually taken seven days.

We landed at the foot of some stone steps and it was a similar operation to landing at St Helena. There was also a large swell rolling in, but the men handling the boat were St Helenans and good boat-men, so we scrambled ashore without any trouble.

Mrs Harrison was most kind and insisted that I have a fresh-water bath, though I knew water was rationed on the island. After a long sea voyage that first fresh-water bath is really wonderful, although you invariably find that all your suntan goes down the plug-hole when you have finished washing.

The Harrisons had been stationed at Bermuda and Barbados, and I thought that after being there, Ascension must seem somewhat lonely, yet both of them said they liked it very much. Certainly the climate is wonderful, the island is only eight degrees south of the equator and right in the heart of the South East Trade Winds, so that there is always a breeze to keep the temperature down. With an ideal climate like this there are no apparent pests, flies and mos-quitoes, and the island is very healthy, but there is no denying that it is a pretty remote spot in the ocean. Not everyone would care to live there.

Apart from the Cable Station there are no other people on the island except the Americans who have a base there. During World War II the Americans built an air-strip on the island. If you have seen the desolation and contours of the island you will appreciate what a job this must have been. The only available site was the nesting-ground of millions of wideawake-birds with a hill right in the middle of it. Apparently the hill was easier to remove with bull-dozers than the birds were and millions of nests were destroyed before the birds eventually found quarters elsewhere on the island. With the advent of guided missiles the Americans took over the base again, and Ascension Island became the end station of the rocket range from Cape Canaveral in Florida.

It was rather amusing to come from St Helena where everyone seemed to talk of Napoleon and the old days, and then to hear the talk on Ascension of "Snark" guided missiles and rocket motors. I was invited out to the American Base by the Base Commander, Cap-tain Duch of the U.S.A.F. Though I was not allowed to see anything secret it was an interesting experience to see how the base was run. just about everything was flown in from the States, and I had fresh steak that night that had arrived by the Globemaster transport that day.

There were quite a number of men at the station but no women. To compensate for this wages were very high, but as one man said to me, "That don't help not at all."

The mascot of the base was a donkey called "Hardaway." He had been taught to drink beer out of a can and spent his day bumming drinks off the men. He was drunk from morning until late at night and had such a solemn look on his face that everyone kept offering him drinks. His diet seemed to agree with him, for he looked in very good shape, though one of the men was convinced that beer was no good for him, and swore that he was developing a "gut" from drinking so much.

The Harrisons took me to the farm at the top of the mountain one day, in their jeep. The road winds up the mountainside and is very steep and narrow. The hairpin bends are very tight, and I thought it would make a splendid course for a keen hill-climb motorist. We stopped on one of the bends where greenery was starting to grow and looked at the desolation below. Everywhere were the fantastic colours and hues of the craters and ash. Higher up the mountain it became pleasantly cool, grass and a few trees grew by the side of the road, and when we arrived at the farm it was difficult to believe that this was the same island. A fine drizzle drifted down on us for a few minutes and I realised that it was the moisture from the Trade Wind clouds, no wonder everything was so green up there.

I met Peter Critchley and his wife who were running the farm. As there was only the Cable Station staff to cater for, Peter grew bits of everything, potatoes, onions, carrots, lettuce and cabbage, as well as many other vegetables. There were poultry and pigs, in fact it could easily have been a little farm in the Channel Islands or some parts of Britain.

Staying at the farm were two ornithologists, Dr Bernard Stone-house and his wife Sally. They were part of the party that were studying the wideawake-bird for the International Geophysical Year. They asked me if I had seen any birds on the way up to St Helena, but I told them that aside from a few bosun-birds and storm-petrels I had not seen very many. They told me that the wideawake-bird returned to the island every nine months to nest, but disappeared after staying on the island for three months. No one seemed to know where they went to, but Dr Stonehouse thought that they might stay out at sea somewhere, only returning to the island to nest.

I said that I wanted to walk to the summit of the island as I had heard that there was a dew-pond at the top. Sally Stonehouse offered to come with me, and we set off along a trail which wound round the mountainside circling the summit and giving wonderful views of the rest of the island. The trail to the summit was very muddy, but when we were nearly there we entered a thick grove of bamboos. A few steps more and we came to the very top of the mountain. There, among the bamboos, was a lily-pond about twenty feet across, with a few goldfish swimming lazily about. It seemed most unexpected to find a pond on the summit of a mountain. The moisture from the clouds condenses on the bamboos and provides water for the pond. Close by was a piece of old chain, and Sally said that she had been told that if you held the chain and made a wish your dream would come true. I know it works because my wish came true one day in September six months later.

When we returned to the farmhouse breathless and hungry Mrs Critchley had a wonderful spread for afternoon tea. She seemed genuinely pleased when she saw the massacre of her cakes and pastries.

Before I left Peter put some potatoes, onions, a large stalk of bananas and some lettuce in the jeep for me. These were most appreciated, and I think Peter will be pleased to know that his potatoes are the finest I've ever tasted. I still had some left when I reached Hawaii four and a half months later. They had kept perfectly.

Mr Harrison was a keen yachtsman, and I took him for a short sail in Trekka while I was there. I guessed he didn't get much chance to sail while living on Ascension, and I knew that this was one of the things he missed very much.

*Trekka* anchored off St Helena

Lunar landscape on Ascension Island

"Scarface" on the run to Barbados

Porpoises enjoy *Trekka's* company

# CHAPTER TWENTY

# Fish Friends on the Way to Barbados

On the afternoon of 15 March I left for Barbados in the West Indies. The Harrisons came to see me off, and I sailed close to the quay so that they could get a picture of *Trekka* under sail. With a fine, steady Trade Wind blowing, we were soon putting the island below the horizon as we set off on the longest stage so far, 3,000 miles. The twins and spinnaker pulled away like a team of horses, and the log clocked the miles away steadily.

*Trekka* had been growing some weed about the water-line, but I noticed that while she was anchored at Ascension some small black fish had been eating the weed and it was almost gone. They were curious little fish and would eat just about anything I threw into the water. I tore up some paper and threw that over the side; they loved it.

We continued running before the wind for the next four days, by which time we had covered 430 miles. The wind was starting to get very light now, though, and towards the north I could see heavy black clouds. That night I could see flashes of lightning in that direction, too, and I realised that we were approaching the Inter-tropical Front. Instead of continuing to the north-west, I altered course to the west and ran parallel to the cloud, hoping that we would be able to find a narrower belt of doldrums towards the South American coast. For the next few days I edged farther towards the west, staying close to the same latitude. The wind was light and fluky, but there was a nice current under us that was giving us about 15 miles every day.

I had a look over the stern at *Trekka's* bottom one day and noticed that it was starting to foul up with goose-barnacles. I remembered how they had grown while crossing the Tasman Sea and I hoped they would not slow us down too much. This passage was going to be long enough as it was. I have noticed that if *Trekka's* bottom has barnacles or weed on we soon collect a family of fish friends which will follow us for hundreds of miles. Two yellow-finned tuna had joined the company; they were large fish and would have weighed nearly a hundred pounds apiece.

The sea was very calm and just the lightest of breezes pushed us along, but it was most enjoyable to be out in the sunshine all day. It was quite hot at midday, for we were getting close to the Equator now.

One evening I noticed something odd about the moon. There was a big piece bitten out of it, and I wondered what had happened. I checked in the nautical almanac and saw that there was a partial eclipse of the moon on that night. A few minutes later it was back to its usual shape, and I felt somewhat easier.

When we were about 450 miles from Cape São Rocque, the eastern-most point of South America, the wind steadied in the south-east, so I ran before it for the next couple of days, determined to cross the doldrums at about 33° west longitude.

The sky clouded up, and soon afterwards the rain was teeming down in solid sheets. I had to replace the twins with the working rig and make use of the occasional squalls that blew hard for a few minutes before leaving us slatting around in a jumble of a sea. The wind was trying to go round to the north-east, but it was still very uncertain, and I had to play around with the sheets to make the most of each breath that came along.

I was amazed at the bird-life about the boat. We passed thousands of wideawake-birds, and I thought that Dr Stonehouse would prob-ably be interested to know about all these. Perhaps he is right that they remain at sea for nine months.

On 30 March we crossed the Equator and left all the squall clouds behind. The sky cleared, and we were left becalmed on a still and silent ocean. The water was like glass, and I got my face-mask and inspected the bottom of Trekka again. She was fouling up quite quickly and I wondered if I should try to scrape them off before I got to Barbados. Almost as if to answer that question I saw a shark slowly circling the boat. It was brown in colour and its fins and tail were white-tipped. I decided that the bottom would be quite all right for another couple of weeks.

All about the boat were hundreds of fish, mostly dorado with their young. They circled around slowly as though asking why we had stopped. I noticed one big one with a scar on his side that kept close to the shadow of the hull. He was an easy fellow to recognise, and I immediately christened him "Scarface." The two big tuna were still with us, and a large ugly-looking barracuda nearly five feet long stayed practically motionless well below the surface. The shark tried to catch some of the smaller fish which rushed to the protection of Trekka's hull. The rudder jerked over and I felt the shark beneath the boat trying to get at the little fellows. I felt quick anger that he should try to eat one of my little friends, and quickly got one of the twin poles with which I managed to poke him on the head. He looked quite offended and slunk away leaving us all in peace.

When the wind came back it was from the north-east. Gently at first a faint air stole across the surface of the water, then ripples began to spread, so I quickly got sail up and soon we were ghosting along over the calm swells. I set the genoa in place of the staysail, and away we went towards Barbados, still 1,700 miles away.

All the little fish had gathered astern just behind the transom. It appeared that the wake of *Trekka* pulled them along, so that they did not have to swim to keep up with us. Sometimes a Portuguese man-of-war drifted by, and a dozen or so of the little fellows would dart off to investigate it. Then there would be a mad rush to get back to *Trekka*. Very often they couldn't make it, and the number of tiny fish slowly dwindled until there were less than a dozen.

The big dorado and old Scarface stayed with us, day after day, swimming along at their own stations, some out ahead, others on each side and astern. Every once in a while a cloud of flying-fish erupted from the water, and I saw dorado chasing them at a terrific speed, swimming on their sides and keeping an eye on the airborne fish until it could glide no farther. Then there was a quick splash, and the dorado returned to *Trekka*, flicking their tails with satisfied looks. The dorado were sudden death to the flying-fish and sometimes got so excited that they leaped out of the water in great jumps of twenty feet or more in their efforts to catch up with the speedy flying-fish.

The wind increased until it was blowing quite freshly, the sea was right on the beam and every once in a while a wave lopped aboard and wet the pages of the book I was reading. I had to roll a reef in the mainsail a couple of times and the staysail was quite big enough for a headsail these days.

At night-time I usually stowed the mainsail and let *Trekka* go along steering herself with just the staysail and mizzen set. There was plenty of wind to keep us going, and the runs each day were quite good considering the state of *Trekka*'s bottom.

I had been so amused at all the radio requests from St Helena and Ascension Island on the B.B.C. "Listener's Choice" programme that just before I left Ascension I wrote to the B.B.C. and asked them to play a tune for me. I had the radio tuned in one evening and was busy getting my main meal of the day ready when to my delight I heard the pleasant voice of the lady announcer, with my record. "Calling John Guzzwell of the yacht *Trekka*, who has asked us to play a request for his friends aboard two other yachts at sea in the South Atlantic, *Diana* and *Havfruen III*. The record is 'The Breeze and I,' sung by Catarina Valenta." Neither of the crews on the two yachts heard the programme, but I know that many of my friends at St Helena and Ascension did.

Trekka had been chasing the sun north for days, and our latitude was almost the same as the sun's declination. The day came when I couldn't decide if the sun was north or south of us. The sextant read 89° 45', and by the time I had turned to look at the southern horizon I noticed that the sun was lower in the west. I have had this happen a couple of times. Noon-sights are not easy to get when the sun is directly overhead, and if you are not careful it's very easy to miss a latitude sight. Trying to work a position-line after noon is not much better, either, for with the sun immediately overhead the line runs north and south, giving a longitude but not a latitude. The following day we were north of the sun, and as the days went by gained on it so that the sextant angle decreased, and the noon-sight became easier.

I saw the Pole Star for the first time in Trekka since I crossed the Pacific on the run down to Fanning Island, our latitude was 8° 16' and I wondered how close to the Equator it was possible to be and still see the star. So often cloud on the horizon hides it from view.

As we got farther to the west the wind slowly became more easterly, which brought it farther aft. I was able to set the twin-staysails with only one boomed out, so that Trekka could steer herself at night-time with the wind on the quarter. The wind was also lighter as we got farther north, and sailing was not such a wet business as it had been a few days before.

Each night the West Indies radio stations and Radio Demerara in British Guiana came in a little stronger on the transistor portable, and I realised that we were getting close now. Only another week and I would be snug at Barbados.

The dorado were still swimming along beside Trekka, they had followed us for over 1,200 miles now, and Scarface was still there among them. It occurred to me that I might try to catch one for a meal. I had some line and lures that a keen fisherman had given me when I was at Lindeman Island on the Great Barrier Reef. I had never caught anything on them, but with so many fish about it should not be too difficult, I reasoned.

I secured a good-looking lure to some stout nylon, and then attached everything to some line. The lure had just hit the water when a big dorado had taken it. He swam up towards me and fixed me with a questioning look as if to say, "What's the game, buster?" Then he gave a brief flick of his head and swam away with the lure still in his mouth. I pulled the line aboard and saw that the nylon had parted. But my fishing instincts were aroused now. I thought that there could be no finer thing than fresh dorado, and I was determined to hook another. I unlaid some rigging wire to use as a leader, but though I hooked many more fish afterwards, I was never able to land any. I tried towing them to try to drown them, and I even got them alongside and speared them with the spear-gun, but I never landed one. They were far too big for me to handle with no gaff. Their colours were lovely and changed from green through to silver and almost white and then to the most wonderful electric blue. Some appeared to have brown stripes down to their sides, but they changed colours so often that it was difficult to say exactly what colour they were.

Gradually my stock of lures was used up, and I saw fish swimming alongside with the silver lures hanging from their mouths. I imagine the hooks would quickly rust through and free them of the encumbrance.

On the night of 20 April I sighted the light on Ragged Point, the easternmost point of Barbados. As we closed the land I could see the breakers on the reef, clear in the bright moonlight. I stayed up and ran along the coastline round the south end of the island. Then early the following morning we rounded Needham Point and came into Carlisle Bay, where I anchored not far from a big freighter. There was still a little darkness left, so I went below to snatch a couple of hours' sleep. Trekka had taken just under 37 days for the 3,000 miles.

I was awakened by the port officials, who wanted to know why I didn't have my yellow flag up. They were not a scrap interested in papers or passport, but seemed rather annoyed that I was not flying a quarantine flag. I told them that I had only arrived a couple of hours before and was very sleepy and had forgotten all about it. They accepted this story without too much disbelief, and I promised that if I ever came again I would fly my little yellow flag. The doctor looked at me a bit doubtfully, then said I was fit enough to go ashore. The other port officials told me to go over to the Yacht Club and pointed towards the southern end of Carlisle Bay where I could just see some small craft moored off the beach.

I tacked up the bay and anchored close to the Aquatic Club. A Dutch yacht was anchored close by. She was of the barge type with bluff bows and lee-boards, and I thought her crew must have been pretty plucky to have sailed her from Europe.

It was a delightful anchorage just off the beach. I went ashore in the dinghy and was offered honorary membership of the Aquatic Club for the remainder of my stay. This was very handy as there were showers to be had there, and it was also possible to get meals, too. The following day I met Ian Gale and his wife, Margaret. Both of them were young people around my age and very keen on sailing. Ian was the Commodore of the Dinghy Sailing Club which was right next to the Aquatic Club. He had a little 26-foot schooner named *Simbie*, which was built for him at Bequia. She looked a trim little vessel and was kept beautifully. We decided that we'd take both boats for a sail and try to get some good photographs of them before I left.

Bridgetown, the main town on Barbados, is a fascinating place. I used to love to walk along the waterfront and see the big trading schooners unloading their cargoes from other islands. Many of these schooners had been fishing on the Grand Banks for cod before they were sold and retired to a warmer climate. They make a fine sight under sail, beating up to the island from Martinique or running down the coast, perhaps from Georgetown.

The narrow shady streets of Barbados with the crowds of gaily dressed West Indians are a riot of colour. Fruit vendors sell oranges and limes on the street corners, and all the while I was conscious of laughter and gaiety in the air. I found good produce in the market near the bus depôt, and was interested to see many of the island crafts on sale here, too, from plaited shopping-bags to steel drums all tuned and ready to play.

Early one morning I saw *Havfruen III* motoring towards us. She had just arrived from Ascension Island, too. Later that evening I joined Batch and Anne Carr with their crew to celebrate the completion of their voyage round the world, for *Havfruen* had crossed her outward track at Barbados to complete the circumnavigation. She was bound for England a few days later *via* Bermuda, so this was to be the last time the two boats were to share each other's company.

There was something very satisfying about returning to the beach late at night after visiting friends ashore, pulling the dinghy into the water, and then rowing back home to *Trekka*. She was ridiculously small to be sailing round the world, but she was home to me, and, once aboard, I felt completely independent. I could have a wonderful time ashore and meet lots of friends, but I was never sorry when it was time to return to *Trekka*, where I had everything at my fingertips, no worries, a very good deck over my head and plenty of food.

I cleaned off *Trekka's* bottom while she was anchored. The water was delightfully warm, and swimming about with fins on my feet and mask on my face was a pleasure rather than work as I scraped the barnacles off with a broad knife paint-scraper. The bottom needed painting again, but I thought it would last until I got to Panama, where I wanted to anti-foul it before taking off on the final leg of the journey.

One lovely sunny afternoon Ian Gale and his wife, Margaret, brought an attractive young lady along with them to crew for me so that we could get some photos of each other's boats during the afternoon's sailing. It was a pleasant change to see someone else enjoying the feel of *Trekka*'s tiller, and I was able to change sail up on the foredeck without scrambling aft every few moments to bring the boat back on course.

Day sailing like this is quite different from ocean sailing, and I enjoyed the afternoon very much. Getting pictures of your own boat can be a difficult business, so often if you give a friend your camera to use the pictures either turn out blank because the lens hood has not been taken off the camera or the film was not wound on. Ian got a very nice picture of *Trekka* with the working rig up, and I snapped some good shots of *Simbie* with her new Terylene sails set.

# CHAPTER TWENTY-ONE

# Panama and the Pacific Again

After a week's stay at Barbados I was ready to leave for Panama. I had collected all my mail and had bought fresh fruit and a couple of other items. I still had cases of canned goods aboard, enough to see me to Hawaii, anyway.

On the morning of 29 April I left Bridgetown and sailed past *Havfruen III* for a final farewell. Both boats had put a few thousand miles behind them since they first met in the Bay of Islands in New Zealand, and I was sorry that this was the parting of their ways.

Cristobal, the port at the Atlantic end of the Panama Canal, was 1,200 miles away. The passage started off with light winds and wonderful sunny weather, but a few days later the sky clouded up and there was much rain.

I was startled one afternoon by what sounded like breakers on a reef. It was thousands of porpoises, breaching and leaping out of the water, as they made their way rapidly across the horizon. It was a remarkable sight, and I wondered where they were off too in such a hurry.

Another day we were running with the twins and spinnaker set, when I heard a roaring sound, I looked around the boat then saw a disturbance on the water less than fifty yards away. The water was being whipped about over a small area, and, as I watched, fascinated, a waterspout began to form. The spray was rising from the water so that it was a hollow tube about eight feet in diameter. It was spinning about like a dust-devil and moving across the sea at about eight to ten knots. Though we were so close to it the wind held true, but I got the spinnaker down in record time in case it came closer. The spout overtook us, and when it was a couple of hundred yards ahead it seemed to disappear suddenly. This is the first and only time I have seen a waterspout, and I would rather like to see more for this one interested me very much. I doubt if it would have done any damage to the boat apart from making the sails flog for a few minutes.

I was starting to see plenty of shipping about, and, though I thought it would be very unlikely for a ship to hit *Trekka* at sea, I decided to light the lantern and hang it in the rigging at night, just in case. We were close to a shipping track all right, as the sea was full of rubbish. I saw paint tins and boxes floating about, and quite a few large planks which I thought of when we were sailing fast at night-time. Trekka's 9/16-inch planking wouldn't need a very hard knock to have a hole smashed through it.

As we approached Panama, I saw more and more ships, and I hoped that the lantern was visible, though I had my doubts. We were running with twins and spinnaker set early one morning when I saw a ship coming up astern on the same course as Trekka. She had strangely familiar lines and I thought she looked a bit like one of the meat boats that operate between New Zealand and Britain. When she got closer she altered course a little so as not to approach us too closely and I was able to see her name, Taranaki.

As this is the name of a beautiful part of New Zealand's North Island I was sure my guess was correct. The officers on her bridge waved cheerfully, and I wondered what they thought of seeing a small yacht steering herself and running right on course while her skipper sat on top of the dinghy waving back.

A couple of days later, when I arrived in Cristobal, I met these same officers and had lunch aboard the Taranaki while repairs were being made to her engines. The men said that Trekka looked very lovely but rather small. I would have loved to have seen her myself, for that is the only unfortunate thing when you own a boat, it's so very seldom that you see her sailing.

I arrived at Cristobal just after daylight on 12 May after a 14-day passage from Barbados. There was only a breath of air when I arrived and we drifted in past the breakwaters with barely steerage-way. A Pilot Boat came over to check up on the new arrival and offered me a tow. I said I had a motor and got it out of the locker to bolt it over the stern. I could see that it was looking a bit rusty, but after all I had not used it since Plettenbergs Bay in South Africa. The Pilot looked out of the wheelhouse window, and I could see from the expression on his face that he didn't think I had a hope of starting it. It was a British motor and had marked on the tank somewhere beneath all the rust, "The best Outboard Motor in the World." I felt a stir of national pride as I looked at the battered old thing. The pilot asked good-naturedly, "What's that, an egg beater?" I refrained from answering, but was determined that the motor would uphold the boast of its makers. I flooded the carburettor and mumbled a few prayers over it before pulling on the cord. It fired immediately and roared into life. The expression of amazement on the Pilot's face was worth seeing, and I wondered how many of the American chromium-plated monsters would have survived the passage from the Cape in the rear locker and still started first pull.

I had been anchored only a short while when the doctor and measurer arrived. The doctor said I was fit enough and could go ashore to report in to Customs later. Then I helped the measurer to get Trekka's dimensions so that he could work out the tonnage by the Panama Canal rule, as dues to transit the Canal were computed on a vessel's tonnage.

Later that day I moved Trekka to the Yacht Club in Cristobal. It was a handy place to moor and had water and power laid on at the dock. I was soon joined by a ketch named Sundowner with a crew of five young high-school students from Newport Beach, California. We were soon all good friends and as the boys could speak Spanish much better than my feeble efforts I waited until one of them was going up to Colon before going to do any shopping.

About the only job I wanted to do here was paint Trekka's bottom, and the morning after I arrived Trekka was sitting up on the slipway at the Yacht Club and I was giving the bottom two good coats of anti-fouling paint. The next stage was going to be a very long one, and I didn't want the bottom covered in barnacles again as it had been on the run from Ascension.

The Panama Canal Zone, that narrow strip of territory on each side of the Canal, is kept free of flies and mosquitoes by constant spraying of insecticides and I saw trucks with tanks and spray guns moving along the roads spraying trees and bushes. Once across into Panamanian territory the contrast was amusing. Papers and filth were allowed to remain in the streets, which looked as though they were never swept, and I wondered what the American Health Department in the zone thought about it.

With Trekka back in the water I wanted to get through the Canal and back into the Pacific again as soon as possible. I learned that if I could find someone with a launch-operator's licence I need not take a Pilot, but I was told that I must have two other men with me on board to go through the locks.

I had read various accounts of other ocean-voyagers who had taken their yachts through the Canal, and some of them sounded a bit scary to me. I was determined not to go through Gatun Locks against the side of the lock walls, but to go alongside a banana-boat, one of the motor cruisers that use the Canal all the time.

Jim Gloss, a young man who I met at the Yacht Club had a licence and he offered to come with me through to Balboa, and one of the young men off Sundowner also said he'd come, so I saw Jim, who said that there was a tug locking through the following morning, and we could go alongside her.

I went along to the Harbourmaster and told him that I wanted to

go through the following morning and I was taken upstairs and introduced to a Mr Peterson as Captain Guzzwell of the *Trekka*. Mr Peterson was talking to the Captain of a freighter, and I heard enough of
the conversation to know that the dues for that particular vessel ran
into a few thousand dollars. A few moments later I was being taken
care of.

"Well, Captain Guzzwell, so you want to make the transit tomorrow, do you? I'm sure that will be all right. Has your vessel been
measured?"

"Yes, she was measured when we arrived here, but I do not know
what the tonnage is," I replied.

"Oh, if she's been measured I can soon find that out. Will your
agents here be paying the dues or will you?" he asked.

"No, I would like to pay myself, now," I said. "I have no agents
here."

"Very well, just a moment, I'll phone and get the figure of the
measured tonnage, so that I can work out the dues."

I watched him pick up the phone and heard the following one-
sided conversation.

"Hello? Oh, I've got Captain Guzzwell of the *Trekka* in the office
here. The *Trekka* is making the transit of the canal tomorrow, and
I want the measured tonnage figure so that I can work out the dues
... Yes, *Trekka* ... What's that? ... Three? ... Three what? ...
Three thousand or three hundred? ... Just three!" He turned to me
with a puzzled expression on his face and said, "They say three tons
—is that right?"

I nodded, "Yes, that's about right."

"But three tons at seventy-two cents a ton ... Why, that's only
two dollars and sixteen cents!" he said unbelievingly.

I did not argue about it, but paid up quickly. It was good value
instead of going round Cape Horn.

The following morning Jim arrived with his outboard. He said
mine was not the best-looking one he'd seen and asked where I had
found it. I told him that before the day was through he'd alter his
opinion about my poor old motor.

With the young man from *Sundowner* we set off and reached
Gatun Locks an hour later, after I had set the main and staysail, too.

We were almost an hour early and found a banana-boat that was
about to go through. Jim asked the skipper if we could go alongside
him, and he said it would be all right.

I had borrowed four car-tyres to use as fenders, and these were
ready to hang over the side. A few minutes later we motored into
the great canyon of the lock and moored alongside the banana-boat

and astern of a German freighter, the *Perseus*. The huge lock-gates closed behind us, and a moment later I saw the calm surface of the lock began to boil as water gushed into the lock through the eight-feet-square manholes in the floor.

*Trekka* was tossed about against the banana-boat, but the tyres saved our paint. A few minutes later the gates ahead had opened and we followed the *Perseus* through into the next lock to repeat the operation. Once more we did the same. Then we left the locks behind and motored out into Gatun Lake some 85 feet higher than the waters of Limon Bay we had left behind.

This was supposed to be the rainy season, but the weather was perfect. There was a nice little north-easterly breeze, and it was quite hot. Jim suggested that we stop at the Gatun Yacht Club for some ice before setting off across the lake to Pedro Miguel Lock.

With a bucket full of ice we set off with the outboard running like a watch, she never missed a beat, but the speed was still too slow for Jim, so I put every possible sail up too. The masthead genoa, staysail boomed out, main, mizzen staysail and mizzen. Jim knew the "Banana-boat Passage," a narrow channel that is a short cut and saves a couple of miles. It was rather frightening to me to see all the tree stumps sticking out of the water on each side with the channel so badly marked. I went below so that I wouldn't have to look. Once we came out into the main channel again it was very easy to follow the marks. There was other shipping passing us at times, either going north or south. We passed the Continental Divide and the Gaillard Cut and arrived at Pedro Miguel at four o'clock that afternoon. There was some delay here, but we eventually locked through alongside the wall, which is quite simple when going down instead of locking up.

When the gates opened, we raced across to the Miraflores Locks which would see us out into the Pacific. It was getting dark when the last gate opened and *Trekka* motored out on to the waters of the Pacific. I felt that I was almost home again. Astern the *Perseus* slid out of the canyon to overtake us. She had not made the transit any quicker than we had.

With the motor still purring contentedly we moored alongside the gas dock near the Balboa Yacht Club, where the three of us were soon eating steak celebrating *Trekka's* return to the Pacific. Jim shook his head over my outboard and admitted that for such a horrible sight it certainly ran very well.

At Balboa I met Wally Pearson and his wife Anbritt. They were keen yachtsmen, and Wally had built his own boat, a very fine ketch named *Tondelayo*. They had returned from a cruise to the Galapagos Islands a couple of months before and wanted me to go there and visit the islands, but much as I would have liked to, there was no time if I was going to get back to Victoria before the winter gales set in.

*Sundowner* arrived the following day and moored close to *Trekka*. The boys had stopped here before and knew Panama City quite well. I went with them shopping there and bought some fresh vegetables and some potatoes, for my Ascension Island ones were getting low.

Through Mrs Pearson I got some canned pumpernickel bread and a couple of canned cakes from the Commissary, which could only be used by employees of the Canal Company.

# CHAPTER TWENTY-TWO

# 54,00 Miles across the Pacific

The sailing-route from the Canal to Victoria, B.C., is a difficult one. It is well-nigh impossible to go up the coast, for the winds are very light and head ones at that; the currents are against you on that route, too, and it seemed to me that the easiest way, though by no means the shortest, would be best. This was to go right out to the Hawaiian Islands and then on up to British Columbia. It meant one very long stage, about 5,400 miles, and then another of 2,600 after that, but the long one would be in good weather and had Hawaii at the end of it. I knew that I could have a few more pleasant landfalls to look forward to.

*Sundowner* was off back to California and because she had a good engine she was motoring up the coast and refuelling at Acapulco. We planned to leave together.

On the afternoon of 21 May the two yachts left Balboa together. *Trekka* accepted a tow from the other yacht as there was very little wind and I wanted to be well offshore before nightfall without using up my precious gallons of petrol.

This stage had quite a thrill attached to it, for if *Trekka* reached Hawaii safely, she would complete her circumnavigation of the world and become the smallest vessel ever to do so.

As the light was fading, the boys on *Sundowner* slowed their engine and cast off the tow-line. We shouted goodbyes to each other, and I wished that we could have continued our companionship. I watched them motor off into the gathering darkness, and then I started getting sail up.

The first stage of the voyage would take us out close to the Galapagos Islands, where I hoped to pick up the South East Trade Wind, but before I got there I had to sail nearly 900 miles over a piece of ocean that has a bad name for sailing craft. Between Panama and the Galapagos Islands the winds are very fluky and the currents strong and unpredictable. Some yachts have been weeks trying to reach the islands, but although I knew that there would still be over 4,000 miles of ocean to cover once we reached them, I was not too worried about this stage, for I felt that this was one passage that would suit *Trekka* very well. She was a light boat and needed very little wind to get her moving, and with the new sails I had on I knew that she could outpoint most cruising boats. All I needed was just a little wind.

That first night out, thunder crashed and lightning lit the sky about us. Rain fell as only tropical rain can, in solid lumps, but a faint breeze from the south-east allowed Trekka to sail herself towards the south and Cape Mala.

The sky had cleared the following day, and we slipped along over a very calm sea. I decided that whenever the wind dropped I'd use the motor and so get the maximum use out of it. Though the sky had squall clouds all about the horizon, none seemed to come near us, and we stayed in the sunshine all the time. I was a little worried about fresh water on this stage, because I had only 35 gallons aboard and little idea of how long the passage was going to take. Knowing that this was an area famous for its rain-squalls, I made a little canvas tray which fitted underneath the main boom so that I could catch rainwater from the mainsail. Later that day, a brief squall came along and I saw the tray working perfectly. It looked as though I'd be able to catch plenty of water once some of my containers were empty.

My plan for this stage was to concentrate on getting as far south as possible before going out west towards the Galapagos Islands. On the second day out we passed Cape Mala, and I noticed that we had a nice strong favourable current giving us a boost when I worked out the distance run on the log and the miles covered.

Quite often we passed through strong ripplings in the sea, as though we were on some enormous river. Eddies and small whirlpools tugged at the keel, but Trekka kept on working her way south in beautiful weather and over a very calm sea. I wished that I had more petrol aboard, for with the sea so calm I could have used the motor for long periods instead of only when there was no wind.

On the fifth day out the wind went into the south-west and freshened, Trekka was soon going fast to the south, and at noon that day we passed to the east of Malpeo Island, just a lonely lump of rock, the home of sea-birds only. The sea about the island was very confused and lumpy, almost as though we were in shallow water. The following day, although we had made a good run on the log, I noticed that we had lost thirty miles to a strong northerly setting current. It would seem the rough sea near the island was due to the two currents in opposition to each other.

On the seventh day out of Balboa we were down to Latitude 2° 57′ north and were finding the current very strong. I decided to bear away to the west and put Trekka on the port tack, letting her steer herself close-hauled over an uncomfortable sea.

As the days went by so the wind slowly edged around to south, and, though I could not lay the course for the Galapagos Islands, we were still sailing a little south of west. *Trekka's* daily runs were very good, and five days in a row she clocked runs of over a hundred miles a day. On the fourteenth day out, the log clocked 121 miles, and I found that they were all made good, too. The current was now helping, and I expected to make better progress. That afternoon the two small islands of Wenman and Culpepper, the northernmost of the Galapagos Islands, were in sight. We sailed between the two and close to Wenman, but it was very barren, just being volcanic in nature, and I doubted if it would be possible to land. The chart was very sketchy and the Pilot Book vague, so I decided to keep going.

It was as well that the current was helping us now, for the wind was very light, the sea was calm and the weather really beautiful. The nights were quite cool, though we were close to the Equator. This was due to the water temperature which had dropped from 82° F. in the Bay of Panama to the present 74° F.

It was lovely peaceful sailing. The days were wonderful with blue skies and a gently heaving ocean. I sat in the cockpit reading most of the time without a stitch of clothing on as my shorts had the seat worn out of them from constant rubbing on the fibreglass deck. I preferred to sit on a sail bag instead.

*Trekka* was starting to grow a fine crop of barnacles on her bottom. This was most disappointing as I had anti-fouled the bottom in Cristobal less than a month before with two coats of paint to make sure she'd stay clean on this passage. I knew that it wouldn't be long before I'd have to do something about it.

On 11 June we crossed the Equator, and I noticed that the current had given us a boost of nearly 40 miles during the 24 hours. According to the chart, I was just about in the middle of the South Equatorial Current, which is the continuation of the Humboldt Current that flows up the coast of South America. A few days later I found to my dismay that the current had vanished. Worse was to follow when it turned against us and started to set towards the south-east. I started edging farther north in the hope that I would find the favourable current that had been such a help a few days before.

When just 25 miles south of the Equator the sea became very calm and I decided that the time had come for me to make an attempt to try to remove some of the barnacles off *Trekka's* bottom. The idea of going over the side with swimfins and face-mask was not an attractive one, for if there's one thing I am scared of it's sharks. It is very seldom that you see any at sea, but that does not mean that they are not there, and it doesn't stop my imagination from working, either.

*Trekka* leaving Becher Bay on the last few miles

After four years and two days, 33,000 miles, *Trekka* comes home

Maureen and I on *Trekka*, Honolulu, 1961

I have a mental picture of what the scene looks like to a shark some fifty feet below the surface, Trekka's round red bottom with the keel and rudder slung below it, and a figure in the water alongside with just a body and legs visible. So it was with considerable reluctance that I lowered myself over the stern of Trekka armed with a very rusty old knife and the paint-scraper.

A quick glance about below the surface indicated that I was safe enough for the moment, so I scraped away around the rudder, watching the grey stalks and shells of the barnacles gradually drift down to the depths below. Trekka, with no sail up, was rolling slowly to the ever-present ocean swell and as I hung on to her toe-rail my shoulders would sometimes be pulled out of the water as I tried to scrape down right beneath the bilge.

I kept glancing over my shoulder to make sure that I was still alone while the scraper sliced off great clusters of barnacles and after about fifteen minutes I had cleared off quite a large area on each side of the hull. It was not a very good job, but the bottom was much cleaner than before. I climbed back aboard thankfully and hoped that I wouldn't have to do that again. When I got sail up I noticed how much faster we were moving through the water, now that so much of the drag had been removed.

The wind returned the following day, and it was more like the South East Trade Wind of the Indian Ocean. Trekka was soon going well to the westward, staying just about on the Equator, but slowly edging farther north, where I hoped to find more current.

The wire spinnaker-halyard was chafing badly at the masthead, and I had to put in a new splice as we rolled along under twin-staysails. It was difficult work up on the foredeck with the splice end six feet up in the air, and my arms were very tired by the time I had finished.

A few days later I celebrated my twenty-ninth birthday with an evening meal of canned steak fried with onions, following by one of my cans of Australian Christmas pudding with custard.

Coffee was served in the cockpit as the sky faded to a golden glow which softly stole away from the gathering darkness. The stars began to wink one by one, and I sat leaning against the dinghy, very contented. When I am away from the sea and caught up in the rush of everyday life, I shall try to remember these moments, for they are among the most beautiful I have known.

The little radio was alive with stations after darkness, and I started to pick up New Zealand and Australian programmes again. Trekka had covered a few thousand miles since I last heard these stations nine months previously. I listened in to the heavyweight title fight between champion Floyd Patterson and the Swedish challenger Ingemar Johannsen from a Los Angeles station and was most surprised another night to hear the South African weather forecast from the S.A.B.C.

On 27 June we were 47 miles north of the Equator and I decided to have a go at knocking off more barnacles, our progress was slowing down again, and the past few days had shown that the unfavourable current was still with us.

I was in the water for nearly half an hour, and by the end of that time had made quite a good job of the bottom. It was quite clean now although there were still a few barnacles left along between the bolts of the fin-keel.

The Equatorial Current had been playing hide and seek with us the past few days, but now it started to give us a mighty shove to the west. At noon on the 29th *Trekka* had made good 147 miles in 24 hours, and, as the wind was holding steady, I thought that here was the chance I had long waited for. Every skipper wonders how far he can drive his ship in 24 hours and I had long speculated on what *Trekka* could do, given the best conditions and a good current to help her. The greatest distance she had covered in a day was 155 miles off the east coast of Madagascar, but it looked as though I might be able to beat that now. *Trekka* kept boiling along, hour after hour, and, though the wind was quite strong, I decided to hang on to the spinnaker that night and see if we could set a record run.

Sleep was quite impossible, though I lay in the bunk trying to rest, and finally I got up and stood in the hatchway looking at the gear and hoping that everything was going to hold together. The twins were getting old for this kind of treatment, and the ¼-inch nylon sheets were stretching like rubber shock-cord in some of the stronger puffs. We were really moving fast, and I watched the phosphorescent wake shooting aft like the fiery tail of some big rocket blasted off into space. The governor-wheel on the log would suddenly spin into life, and then slow for a few moments before going mad again.

Hour after hour she kept going at top speed, surfing and sliding along, rolling and bouncing, so that the gear in the lockers below rattled away and the mast squeaked where it came through the deck.

After breakfast I took over steering in an effort to keep her running truer, as sometimes she would sheer off a wave and collapse the spinnaker, which shook the whole boat when it suddenly filled again. By noon the log read 132 miles, but sights showed that we had covered 175 miles with the current added. That night I took the spinnaker in, so that I could get some sleep, but *Trekka* kept on sailing herself under the twins and trekking to the west towards Christmas Island.

I altered my watch an hour every 15 degrees of longitude so that the sun passes the meridian between 12 noon and 1 p.m. On 3 July I put the clock back another hour (there was five hours' difference between Panama time and Hawaiian time) and we had a 25-hour day. I worked out the sun-sights I had taken, and found the latitude close to what I had estimated, but the longitude was nearly sixty miles out from my D.R. position. I took fresh sights and checked the watch with time-pips on the radio but always got a position farther ahead. I finally concluded that the sights must be right, though it was difficult to believe, for *Trekka* had covered the remarkable distance of 192 miles in 25 hours!

The track chart was now a pretty sight, with the past few days' runs contrasting sharply with those on the way out to the Galapagos.

On the chart at Longitude 140° west I had marked in a position which I had named Point X. This was where I had decided would be the best place to turn north and cross the doldrums before heading directly for Hawaii. I had been tempted to turn north days before, but Point X showed the narrowest belt of doldrums in this area, so I held on until we were only 30 miles short of the position, when I thought we were close enough, as the current was still flowing very strongly to the west.

On the afternoon of 4 July I gybed *Trekka* over on to the starboard tack and we went along to the north to try to find the North East Trade Wind. *Trekka's* daily runs continued above the 150-mile mark, and in one week she covered the extraordinary distance of 1,101 miles —surely a record for a boat of her size, and one that would have been quite impossible but for the current.

We kept going north, but when we reached Latitude 7° 30' north, the weather changed, and I realised that this was the end of the South East Trade Wind. It was like losing an old friend. She had driven us along for thousands of miles, sometimes boisterously, sometimes gently, under skies dotted with white cumulus cloud or beneath overcast ones with the occasional rain-squall to darken the faded blue sails and wet the decks. I wondered if *Trekka* would ever know her caress again.

The next two days were typical doldrums weather. Rain fell in solid sheets from the lowering sky, beating the sea flat, only for the next squall to kick it up again. We were now in the middle of the Counter Equatorial Current which is about 180 miles wide hereabouts and sets to the east at a rate of about 30 miles a day.

I motored for a few hours, using up the last of the petrol, and then stowed the motor away in the locker with the tank quite empty. A faint breeze came out of the north-east and gradually strengthened. *Trekka* could just lay the course for Hawaii, 1,300 miles away.

On 12 July at Latitude 13° north and Longitude 145° 7′ west, the wind had increased to such an extent that I decided to drop all sail and wait for the weather to moderate. This was the first time since rounding the Cape of Good Hope that *Trekka* had been hove to because of bad weather. The wind increased until it was blowing with gale force, and I watched the barometer tumble down as the depression approached. I noticed that the wind was backing all the while, and when it was north-west the wind seemed to be at its hardest, but it continued backing until it was south-west, when the fury went out of it. After being stopped for nearly 20 hours, I was able to get sail up again and resume the course for Hawaii over a very lumpy sea.

After the beat out to the Galapagos Islands I had replaced the good suit of Terylene sails with the old cotton ones. These were the sails that I had started from Canada with nearly four years before, and it was not surprising that they were becoming very ripe. After the rough treatment just before the gale, the mainsail gave up the ghost by tearing badly where it rested against the upper spreaders. Instead of trying to mend it I replaced it with the new Terylene sail. Soon afterwards the staysail tore badly, too, and I had to set the new one, and I had just finished doing so, when I noticed that the mizzen had a small hole in it, so I replaced that too.

I was starting to look like a hobo. My hair had not been cut since I left Barbados, and I had not shaved since I left Panama. There was some excuse for this as I was trying to save as much water as possible. I thought I'd have a try at cutting my own hair, so I hunted through the lockers to try to find a pair of scissors I knew I had somewhere. They were found at last and I noticed that they still had bits of fibreglass stuck to them, which reminded me of fibreglassing *Trekka* in New Zealand over a year ago.

I sharpened the scissors with a file and then got my two mirrors and a comb and went on deck. One mirror I jammed beneath the dinghy-lashings and the other I held in my left hand behind my head. While *Trekka* rolled along bouncing over the waves, I started in on my considerable thatch. I made quite a good job of it, though trying to cut hair behind my head while looking in a mirror with a boat constantly moving calls for careful concentration. People often ask me if I didn't find the boredom at sea too much for me!

On 20 July I had been at sea for 60 days and was looking out for the top of Mauna Kea, the 13,825-foot mountain on the island of

Hawaii. We were still 60 miles off, but had the horizon been clear I would have been able to see it, as I sighted it 85 miles away on the run down from San Francisco nearly four years before.

A plane passed overhead going towards America, and a couple of hours later I saw a small tanker also bound for the States. She passed about a mile away.

That night was a very special occasion and I had my last can of Australian Christmas pudding to celebrate it, for *Trekka* had just crossed her outward track, and had completed her voyage round the world, the smallest vessel ever to do so. I felt very proud that she was mine.

The next morning when I tumbled out of the hatch, there were Hawaii and Maui peeping out of the morning haze. *Trekka* closed the shore, and we romped along the northern coast of Maui while I feasted my eyes on the lovely green slopes that swept down to meet the edge of the sea. Past Kahului, we went, where I had made *Tzu Hang's* mainmast, and where her southern voyage had been planned, then on towards Molokai, lit by the last of a lovely sunset.

I stayed at the helm that night, running along the coast of Molokai with a bright tropical moon to light the way. It was wonderful to be back in familiar waters again.

With the first light of dawn, we were entering Molokai channel with about 50 miles left to Honolulu. The spinnaker was pulling steadily, and a couple of hours later the mountains on Oahu became clearer. The lighthouse on Makapuu Point came into view, and early that afternoon we passed it and sailed into more sheltered water.

Towards late afternoon we rounded Diamond Head and came up to the entrance to the Ala Wai Yacht Basin. I tacked up the channel with just enough wind to fill the sails, and then moored against the gas dock, where I waited for the authorities to clear me. It had been a very long passage. 5,400 miles in 62 days.

The next few days were busy ones for me, apart from meeting many old friends and writing mail to others in various parts of the world, there was much to do on *Trekka*. The last time she had been painted and varnished was in Durban, and the bottom needed anti-fouling again, so I set about trying to make her look a bit more shipshape.

I got *Trekka* out of the water on to a cradle and went to work, rubbing down the topsides and painting them, and then cleaning off the bottom and anti-fouling it again.

It was not long before I had the little boat looking near her best again, and once she was back in the water I had many interested visitors to come aboard and sit beneath the sun-awning and swap yarns with me.

I met Jack and Peggy Burke who had lost their schooner *Venturer* on the reef at Lady Musgrave Island. They had a new yacht now, named *Shiralee*, which they had bought and sailed up from Sydney. There were many other friends, some of them I had met in my travels, like Buz and June Champion in their *Little Bear*. They had been in Sydney when I was there in *Tzu Hang*, and Lee and Anne Gregg, who had been in Whangarei aboard their little ketch *Novia*. We had much to talk about, for it had been a long time since we had seen each other.

I wanted to try to arrive back in Victoria, B.C., on 10 September, which would make it exactly four years to the day that I had left. To do this, I estimated that I would have to leave Honolulu not later than 5 August, as the passage was 2,600 miles, and I thought it would take us about 35 days under normal conditions.

By the evening of the 4th I was ready, fresh fruit and vegetables were aboard and, as some of my canned goods were getting low, I bought a few more items to make sure I'd arrive the other end with plenty left. The water bottles were all full, and I had got the sail-maker to repair my oilskins. I figured that I was going to need them on this passage.

Although I was ready to leave on the morrow, I did not, because a hurricane was approaching the Hawaiian group from the south-east. As it got closer the weather slowly worsened, and the weather bureau reported that the wind force near the centre was up to 135 miles an hour. The hurricane was given the name "Dot," and I asked some-one why hurricanes were always given women's names. The reply I got was that hurricanes, like women, were very unpredictable and sometimes did things quite contrary to what everyone thought they were going to do!

As the storm-centre came closer to the islands, reports of strong winds, high seas, and the usual tales of storm damage were broad-cast over the radio and warnings were issued that people should be prepared for the storm centre to come close to Honolulu.

I doubled up on *Trekka's* mooring lines and wondered what kind of a mess there would be in the Yacht Basin if the eye of the storm passed over Honolulu. Some of the craft were moored with lines no stronger than bits of string.

The wind became very gusty as the eye moved closer and I saw the full hurricane warning flying from the Harbourmaster's office—two red flags with a black square in the centre. The storm was moving in a westerly direction at 10 knots, and when it was due south of Honolulu and moving on to the southwest many people thought that it was all over. A couple of yachts left to return to California, but then, just as I had feared, the storm recurved and started back towards us. There was little I could do aboard *Trekka* to pass the time away. I wrote some mail, and then walked up to the Waikiki Post Office clad in my yellow oilskins, sea-boots and wearing a sou'wester. A man who was soaking wet, wearing a short-sleeved Aloha shirt and shorts said to me, "I can see you're one of the locals, I'm just a crummy tourist. They didn't tell me the weather could be like this here, or I would have brought a raincoat or stayed at home."

That night the storm passed between Oahu and Kauaii, and the latter island received quite a battering. The centre had passed about 80 miles west of Honolulu, and as the hours went by so the wind force slowly decreased. I was thankful I was not at sea, for although *Trekka* could probably have handled it without too much bother, it would have been anything but comfortable, and I prefer to miss storms if possible.

Because of "Dot" I was not able to leave Honolulu until 8 August. I could have left the previous day but that would have meant leaving on a Friday and that is something I never do. I am not superstitious, but the only time I ever left port on a Friday was aboard *Tzu Hang* when we left Melbourne for Cape Horn. I had no desire to repeat *Tzu Hang's* pitchpoling in *Trekka*.

# CHAPTER TWENTY-THREE

# Home Again

In many ways it was sad leaving Honolulu. This was now the last passage I would be making in *Trekka* for a long time, perhaps for ever, and though I wanted to get back to Canada I was sad that the voyage was nearly done. Over the horizon some 2,600 miles away were the timber-clad mountains of British Columbia. *Trekka* seemed to know that she was headed home now to the land where she was born, home to the land where the pine-trees scent the air and the white-capped mountains reach to the sky, home to the waters where the Cohoe and the Sockeye run, where busy little tugs tow the log-booms and the early morning fog hangs about the inlets. I, too, was looking forward to getting back, for no matter how beautiful another country may be and the times you spend there, it is not the same as returning home again after a long absence.

Oahu faded into the night, and soon only the light on Makapuu Point blinked a farewell to us. Our course was to the north, and *Trekka*, closehauled on the starboard tack kept working her way along a little east of north, steering herself while the North East Trade Wind sang in the rigging. At times the wind eased, and it was lovely sailing with the big genoa. At other times I had to stow the mainsail and go along with just the staysail and mizzen up while crests slopped aboard into the cockpit and *Trekka* bounced along over a lumpy sea.

As we got farther north the weather began to get cooler. At first it was just a slight chill to the air, but all too soon I had to get my old Cowichan sweater out of the locker to keep warm. Up into the thirties *Trekka* climbed, and each day saw the sun a little lower in the sky and the Pole Star higher at night.

At Latitude 37° north, we were not too far from the centre of the North Pacific High, the area of high pressure that has such a bearing on the weather in the north-west of the American Continent.

There were some lovely cool days with clear skies and a very calm sea, *Trekka* ghosted along with the masthead genoa set, going farther and farther north. The wind still remained north-easterly and I was still unable to lay the course for Juan de Fuca Strait.

It was not until we were up to Latitude 42° north that the wind started to back to the north. I held on to the starboard tack for one more day, and then went about on to the port tack for the first time in eighteen days.

This was a wet, cold and depressing part of the ocean we were in now. For days we never saw the sun except for a brief glimpse through thick cloud, I had to wait for hours sometimes to get sights, and with the big swell that was running from the west it was difficult to bring the hazy-looking sun down on to a reluctant horizon.

I was awakened one morning just after daylight by *Trekka* hitting something. It felt just as though she had run aground, and I scrambled out of the sleeping-bag and rushed to the hatch. She had collided with a huge waterlogged log that was encrusted with barnacles. Fortunately we were only moving along slowly, doing not much more than 3½ knots under twins and spinnaker, there was no damage, and the log drifted astern without fouling the rudder.

On 3 September I knew again the lonely feeling of a gale at sea. All sail was down and *Trekka* was riding the white-crested swells as buoyantly as the big gooney birds, the northern albatross, which had replaced the tropical sea-birds. As the wind moaned through the rigging and the halyards beat a tattoo against the masts, *Trekka* climbed the desolate ridges only to plunge down the other side into the waste of a sea valley. Sometimes I braced myself in my bunk as I heard the hiss of a big sea approaching and waited for it to hit the hull. *Trekka* would lean far over like a prizefighter riding a punch as water swept across the deck.

We had been through all this before at various times, but I don't think I could ever get used to a gale at sea in a small boat, for each one is different from the last, and I always know a great feeling of relief when the smoking seas have spent their fury. I have never been able to forget the awful majesty of the seas in the Southern Ocean just before *Tzu Hang* was dismasted when she was running down the easting towards the Horn, and at the back of my mind is the fear that the sea could build up to the impossible height it reached on that occasion.

I was sitting below on the curved bulkhead seat looking out of the doghouse windows at the endless spectacle of the sea. I watched the crests approaching and the way my little vessel rode them so surely and bravely. I decided to make some tea and had just lit the stove when I glanced out of the window. My heart stopped beating and I saw as if in a nightmare a great monster of a sea advancing towards me. I watched hypnotised as it reared higher and higher and I knew that this was the biggest sea I had ever seen in *Trekka*. For a moment I was sure that it was going to be *Tzu Hang* all over again, then the brave little boat started for the summit with the courage of a Hillary. Up, up, up, she went, then with a final little flick of her stern she was over and plunging down the other side. I heard a muffled boom as the sea broke, leaving a great white swath to leeward. I had lost my appetite for tea and instead climbed back into the warmth of my bunk.

We were riding out that gale for 42 hours before I was able to get sail up again and continue on towards Victoria. The wind was still fresh from the west, and the sea high, but it was a fair wind, and Trekka surfed along under twin staysails steering herself. The barometer was still very low, and after reading up the Pilot Book I reckoned that there was a secondary depression coming along. My diagnosis proved correct, for all too soon the wind was blowing with gale force again, and I had to pull all sail down and wait for conditions to moderate.

A few hours later the wind was easing and the barometer climbing steadily. With the twins up again we rolled along towards Cape Flattery, now only 165 miles away. On 9 September I could see what looked like land away to port and on checking the chart found that it was the top of the mountains on Vancouver Island. Canada was in sight at last!

That night thick fog closed down around us, and I dreaded the thought of another gale when so close to land and with visibility down to a few yards. Early the following morning I was in the cockpit well bundled up with my sweater and oilies on and wearing seaboots too. I wanted to steer as accurate a course as possible, so that I would not miss the entrance to the Strait of Juan de Fuca, which is only 12 miles wide. Even the great navigator, Captain James Cook, had missed the entrance of the Strait when searching for a possible route for the North West Passage. I could easily miss it, too, if the fog did not lift.

Towards noon the fog thinned a little, and soon afterwards it lifted completely, I went below to get the sextant, but I had used it for the last time, for when I looked ahead again, I could see the long-awaited sight of Cape Flattery, some twenty miles away.

The wind fell right away as we closed the coast, and I decided to use the motor and try to reach the sheltered anchorage of Neah Bay on the American shore. We passed many fishing boats, all trolling for salmon, and towards late afternoon slipped past Tatoosh Island in company with some of the trollers that were also heading for Neah Bay.

The sun sank into the sea, leaving the sky a fading gold, the pinetrees on the hills looked aflame, and then the colours faded to purple, to violet and then to darkness. The anchor splashed in the stillness and frightened a cormorant into the air.

Because of Hurricane "Dot" in Hawaii, we were a little late in geting to Victoria. It was 10 September now, and there was still fifty miles to go. In the morning I went ashore and filled up my can with petrol at a garage. Soon afterwards we were running down the coast to Victoria.

Towards darkness we were close to Becher Bay on the Canadian shore and I decided to go in for the night and anchor so that I could get some sleep and get *Trekka* shipshape for the morrow. I moored to a jetty at the head of a small bay and was soon chatting to a man who was pottering about in a small boat close by. He took me up to his house where I was able to phone a friend in Victoria and tell him that *Trekka* had come home again.

That night the press caught up with me and got the story. They told me to be at Ogden Point breakwater the following day at 1 p.m., where the doctor would give me pratique.

*Trekka* left Becher Bay the next morning under power with only 13 miles to go. Once outside the bay, the fog shut down all about us like a curtain, but I was able to creep along the shore with the dia-phone on Race Rocks to guide me through the passage.

William Head loomed up out of the fog, and then Albert Head. There was less than two miles to go now, when the fog started to lift a little and I saw a fishboat heading towards us, the repeated blasts on its hooter carrying clearly across the calm water. I saw figures standing in the bow, their hands waving excitedly, and as they came a little closer I saw that they were the same friends that had waved me goodbye from the dock four years before. A great lump rose up in my throat, and I felt a flood of affection for them all. I gripped *Trekka*'s tiller hard and it seemed to quiver in my palm. We had known many adventures together in those years. They had been most wonderful years, and it was due to her that it had all been possible.

The fishboat slowed as she approached and the voices of my friends floated clearly to my ears across the stillness. Faintly at first then louder, "Welcome home, *Trekka*! Welcome home!"

# Epilogue

When I thought of attempting to write this book and set down on paper the account of *Trekka's* voyage there was one place where I knew all the happy memories would come flooding back, Russell, in New Zealand.

During the northern winter of 1959–60, while *Trekka* was laid up with snow on her decks waiting for her skipper to return, I sat in the sun at Russell before the typewriter remembering all the good times and some of the bad ones we had shared together. In the middle of March 1960 with a somewhat ragged manuscript stowed in my sea-bag I returned to Canada aboard an Orient Line vessel bound for Vancouver. It was during this innocent-appearing voyage that an event occurred which was to make my life even richer, I met Maureen, who was to become mine as well as *Trekka's* mate.

We were married shortly afterwards in Vancouver and for our first few months of marriage set up home in Victoria. Yachts and boats had never entered into Maureen's life until she met me, but gradually I became aware that she too was in love with the little blue-painted yawl. She understood the restlessness that came over me at times and instead of fighting it, she encouraged it—bless her— with the result that early in 1961 she proposed that we take *Trekka* to the tropics again.

The voyage to Honolulu and back to Los Angeles proved two things to me, firstly I had been incredibly fortunate in my choice of mate and, that far from being over, my sailing days were just beginning.

Our beloved *Trekka* was capable of carrying both of us safely, for she made the 2,500-mile passages as easily as she ever did, giving my new crew a love of the sea which she had not known before, but as much as we loved *Trekka* we knew that the time had come for us to build a larger boat. We parted with her to a young man in Los Angeles who had long admired her and who would look after her in the warm climate she had come to know so well. Maureen and I walked away along the dock sharing the deep sorrow at parting with our *Trekka*, the smallest and most gallant little vessel ever to circumnavigate the world.

# "Trekka"

The reader will not be surprised that I consider Trekka hardly the ideal type of yacht for a world voyage, but before crossing her off the list of successful designs it is worth while considering her advantages together with her faults.

Firstly cost: there can be no doubt that Trekka represents about the smallest investment for a world voyaging yacht. Unlike many of her predecessors she was brand spanking new when she left Victoria in September 1955 and returned four years later in virtually the same condition. Most voyagers like to keep their vessels looking smart, and perhaps in this respect I tend to be even more particular, yet friends on other yachts I met always envied the ridiculously small amount of work needed to keep Trekka shipshape compared with their larger boats.

In certain ports charges are levied against yachts for lying alongside a wharf or, as in the case of Panama, making the transit of the canal. These charges are usually based on length or tonnage and the $2.16 charges for the Panama Canal transit illustrate where Trekka scored over her larger rivals.

Many promising voyages fold up because the crew cannot afford to maintain their vessel. Sails cost money, and naturally the larger they are the more they cost. The cotton suit of sails which took Trekka nearly the whole way round the world cost only £29 10s. for the mainsail, staysail and mizzen. How many other craft could get a suit of sails for that price?

On the maintenance angle it took just a pint of paint for her topsides and a quart of anti-fouling for her bottom. It is obvious that maintenance did not take me anything like the time it took other yachtsmen. Therefore when I was in port I could spend more time ashore sightseeing and visiting friends, for this surely is the reason most of us go cruising, we want to see something of the place when we get there. Yet how often I have known other crews to spend their entire time in port fixing all the damaged gear from their last passage.

For a single-handed voyage, therefore, perhaps Trekka was not such a bad choice as some people may think. At sea she proved to be an excellent little sea-boat, making extremely good passages on many occasions, while not demanding excessive attention from her crew.

Naturally enough *Trekka's* chief disadvantage was lack of space. This was most apparent in port and never noticed at sea. In port the lack of space became a nuisance largely because of shoreside customs. Getting dressed into a jacket and trousers required one to become something of a contortionist, and the toilet arrangements were hardly as easy as when at sea!

One of the things I missed was returning some of the hospitality to friends who had been so kind to me on shore. Had I been able to invite some of these people into a more spacious saloon I would have done so, but two persons below in *Trekka* was about the limit. However, on many occasions I was able to take friends sailing for an afternoon which would entail much work aboard a larger yacht, whereas on *Trekka* bending on sails and letting go mooring lines were only a few minutes' work.

If I were to do it again singlehanded?

This is an interesting thought, and one that has passed away many pleasant hours at sea. As a result of spending nearly three years living aboard *Trekka* I tend to think of any boat larger than twenty-five feet as quite spacious. Because of this my boat would be small, so that nothing would get out of hand, and so that I could keep control of the gear. I would want standing headroom even if it was only beneath a small doghouse, and also a reliable inboard diesel engine instead of an outboard as used on *Trekka*. My main consideration would be that the boat be simple, she would have no electricity of any kind aboard, all lights being kerosene-operated, which gives good, safe lighting from a fuel that is available throughout the world. I would again use polythene bottles for fresh water instead of tanks, for the bottles can always be taken ashore and filled, whereas tanks frequently collect sediment and can be difficult to fill when there is no hose near by. A lot of the places I would want to visit have no such things as hoses.

As for the size of this little vessel, she would need to be no longer than 30 feet overall, but I would definitely have a light-displacement hull rather than heavy; draught would not need to be less than five feet, so that if needs be she could stand up to her sail and beat out of a tough spot.

*Trekka's* yawl rig proved to be quite excellent, the chief advantage being the ease with which it was possible to balance it and get the boat to sail herself, but since completing *Trekka's* voyage there has been a marked breakthrough in the design of vane steering systems operating a small tab on the trailing edge of the rudder. Having used one of these since on *Trekka* I would rather go to a cutter rig than that of a yawl, for it is more efficient for its given area and requires only the one mast.

The most important requirement of all would be that this little vessel be constructed with my own hands, for I would want to know every nail and bolt in her and have handled every one of her timbers, perhaps then I would also know the confidence that *Trekka* gave me during her trek round the world.

*Trekka* sail plan
Mainsail      100 sq. ft.
Mizzen         26 sq. ft.
No. 1 Staysail 58 sq. ft.
No. 2 Staysail 29 sq. ft.
Genoa         148 sq. ft.
Mizzen Staysail
                    64 sq. ft.

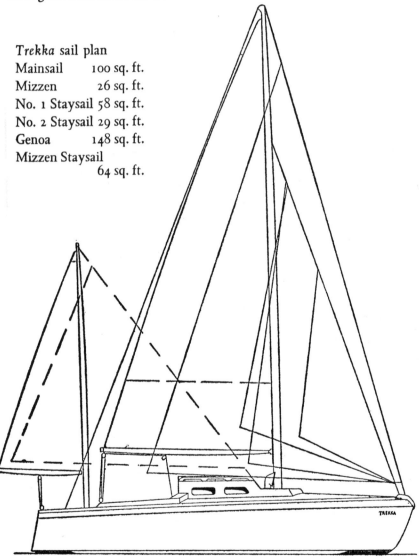

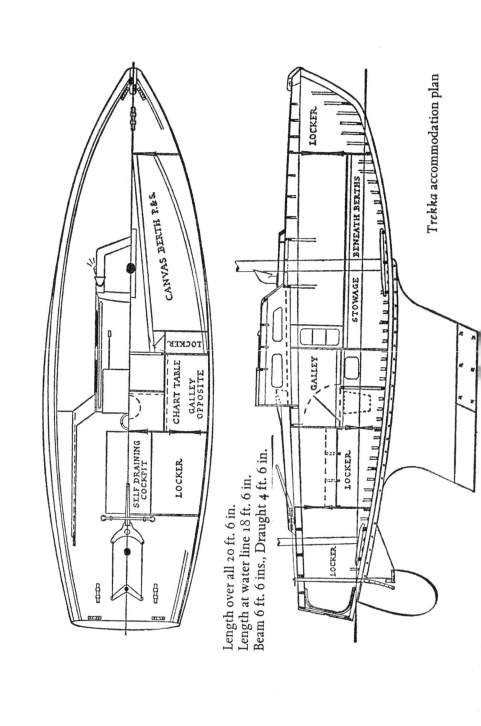

Length over all 20 ft. 6 in.
Length at water line 18 ft. 6 in.
Beam 6 ft. 6 ins., Draught 4 ft. 6 in.

SELF DRAINING COCKPIT

LOCKER

CHART TABLE
GALLEY OPPOSITE

LOCKER

CANVAS BERTH P.&S.

LOCKER

STOWAGE

BENEATH BERTHS

GALLEY

LOCKER

LOCKER

*Trekka accommodation plan*

# What Happened to "Tzu Hang"

One of the questions I have been asked so many times during the second half of Trekka's voyage and since is: What really happened to Tzu Hang down there in the Southern Ocean?

Miles Smeeton in his book Once is Enough has told how on two occasions Tzu Hang was turned completely over during storms in those high latitudes. Many people in their ignorance of what conditions can be like down there have criticized the boat, saying that there must have been something wrong with the design of the hull. Some of these armchair experts have done little coastwise sailing let alone ocean crossing in a small craft.

I do not say that it would be impossible to find a better boat, but anyone who knew her would agree that it would be hard to find a more seaworthy vessel than Tzu Hang. In no way was she an extreme design, her displacement was quite moderate for her size and her seven tons of outside lead ballast with a draught of seven feet gave her excellent stability.

I have never once doubted Tzu Hang's ability, and her behaviour during the 7,000 miles I sailed in her before that fateful day when she pitchpoled over left me with nothing but praise for her sea-kindliness, design and excellent construction.

In my mind the boat cannot in any way be blamed for what happened to her, the sea that was running at the time was in fact too much for her, as it would have been for any other yacht of similar size and displacement.

There was a time when I believed that a small, well-designed yacht in the open ocean would, if correctly handled, take anything the sea had to offer, but since seeing with my own eyes the almost unbelievable state it can on rare occasions reach, my views have changed. I do not see how any yacht less than 50 feet overall could avoid being capsized in the extreme conditions it is possible to experience in the wastes of the Southern Ocean. If you have seen a child's toy bowled over in breakers at the seaside you might be able to imagine what happened to Tzu Hang.

My thoughts on the matter have not been in finding fault with the boat, but rather what could have caused the sea to reach such a staggering height on this one occasion, for, remember, we had been at sea 50 days in Roaring Forties weather before the accident, and another month afterwards without seeing the sea approach the state it did on 14 February 1957.

While in Honolulu towards the end of 1959, I had a most interesting discussion with William Albert Robinson, who, it will be remembered, completed his excellent circumnavigation of the world in *Svaap* towards the end of 1931.

We talked about the more recent voyage he made down into the Roaring Forties in his lovely 70-foot brigantine-schooner *Varua* and on a chart compared her track with that of *Tzu Hang's*. During that voyage he encountered a storm of such severity that he called it "The Ultimate Storm." The scene of this storm and *Tzu Hang's* misadventure were a long way apart both in time and distance, though on similar latitudes. Robinson is quite emphatic that during that storm *Varua* passed over a shoal, though there is no evidence to show on charts of the area that a shoal exists.

The state of the sea when *Tzu Hang* pitchpoled was very similar to what would be encountered with a long swell passing over a shoal area, very steep seas, some of which toppled over and broke like surf on a beach.

Quite recently I wrote to the Hydrographic Department in London seeking information on the depth of water in this part of the ocean, the reply I received is of sufficient interest to repeat an extract here.

"Admiralty Chart No. 789 shows only one line of soundings crossing the meridian of 98° W. longitude in about 50' 42' south latitude. This line of soundings was taken by the United States ship *Enterprise* in 1883–86. The soundings nearest to your position are 2,383 fathoms and 2,291 fathoms. The only other soundings in this vicinity shown on the chart are 2,565 fathoms about 290 miles to the N.E. and 2,555 fathoms about 310 miles to the south."

The closest soundings of 2,291 fathoms are in fact about 40 miles from the scene of *Tzu Hang's* somersault.

In recent years, ships equipped with echo-sounders have discovered many "seamounts" in the North Pacific, shoals like mountain peaks which rise rapidly from the bed of the ocean to within a few hundred feet of the surface of the sea. These discoveries have been made largely by accident by shipping which crosses the North Pacific on the great circle course from the West Coast of the United States to the Far East Ports.

I see no reason to doubt that there are similar undiscovered seamounts in the South Pacific which have remained undetected solely because so little shipping uses the old sailing-ship route from Australia to Cape Horn.

If soundings which were taken in 1883 are to be taken seriously what of other soundings that were also taken during the last century?

Take the case of the Maria Augustina Bank, the position of which *Trekka* passed 120 miles northward of during the run from Thursday Island to Cocos. The Admiralty Pilot Book tells the history of this in these words.

"In 1856 the Captain of the Spanish frigate *Maria Augustina*, when cruising about 540 miles east-by-south of the Cocos Islands, perceived a change in the colour of the water, and soundings taken immediately showed depths of 11, 9, 7, 5, and 13 fathoms, sand and mud; at the same time a black object on which the sea broke was observed about half a mile northward of the vessel. After sailing a further 7½ miles on a course of 211° soundings of 6, 8, and 10 fathoms were obtained.

"From good observations taken at the time, and later verified at Java Head, the southern entrance point of the western end of Sunda Strait the position of the rock was established at Lat 14° 05′ S. and Long. 105° 56′ E. Discoloured water had been previously reported at approximately the same position, by the master of the *Helen Stuart* in 1845 who stated that he ran over a milk-white patch for about 50 miles in an east and west direction, no soundings, however, were taken.

"The existence of the above bank is considered doubtful."

What do you make of that one? The closest sounding to the bank other than those mentioned above is 2,825 fathoms, 120 miles to the northward.

Here is another one in the South Indian Ocean about 600 miles south-east of Durban.

"Slot Van Capelle. The existence of this bank, as well as its position is considered doubtful, but it is shown on the chart in lat. 36° 34′ S. long. 41° 20′ E. It is named after the Dutch vessel by which it was reported in 1748, which vessel stated it to be of considerable dimensions and obtained soundings in 63 fathoms southwestward of it. The bank was again seen by the *Automatia* in 1801 and by Captain Viana of the *Jacques-Elizabeth* in 1856."

Perhaps someday when the oceans of the world have been accurately sounded we may be able to piece together some of the riddles of the sea, of the ships like *Tzu Hang* who survived a catastrophe and of the many who didn't and left their bones rotting on the bed of the ocean, or perhaps some uncharted shoal.

Vito Dumas in oilskins. Taken aboard *Lehg II* at Cape Town.

# Alone Through the Roaring Forties

The voyage of *Lehg II* round the world

*by* *Vito Dumas*

*Translated by*
*Captain Raymond Johnes*

# CONTENTS

# LIST OF ILLUSTRATIONS

# LIST OF DIAGRAMS

*The sketches have been drawn by Mr. C. Kingston from originals supplied
by the Author*

*Reception in Honour of Vito Dumas*

Thursday, the 12th of August at 13.00 hours in the English Club, Calle 25 de Mayo 586, Buenos Aires.

Speech by the Naval Attaché of the British Embassy, Captain H. A. Forster, R.N.

'I have the honour to communicate the following message of congratulation from the Royal Cruising Club of London on the occasion of your magnificent feat.

It reads:

"To Vito Dumas, Yacht Club, Buenos Aires. Commodore, officers and members of the Royal Cruising Club, London, have learnt with great interest that you have arrived at Buenos Aires after lone circumnavigation of world via Cape of Good Hope, Australia and Cape Horn and send warmest congratulations on your magnificent feat of skill and endurance."'

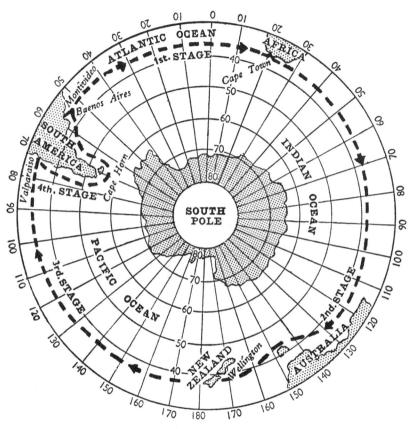

Map of route taken by Vito Dumas in his single-handed
voyage round the world.

# TRANSLATOR'S FOREWORD

The most astonishing thing about this book—as distinct from the feat which it records—is that it should have escaped translation into English long enough for the honour to fall upon me.

Vito Dumas was born in Buenos Aires on September 26th 1900. A keen swimmer from early youth, he won the championship of the River Plate when he was 23 by crossing 42 km. of this estuary, noted for its strong currents, from Colonia (Uruguay) to the Argentine coast, remaining 25½ hours in the water. At the same time he conceived an affection for such sailing in small boats as is always within reach of a tough, willing and handy youngster. These trips afforded him an escape from the worries of a rather straitened family life and it is not difficult to understand how the sea came to be identified in his mind with freedom and the great peace of solitude.

Apart from his voyages and some short periods in Spain and France, Vito Dumas has always lived in the Argentine, ranching and farming until, time after time, the insistent call to the loneliness, beauty and danger of the sea became irresistible.

All his boats with the exception of *Lehg I*, built in France, have been designed and built in the Argentine. His ocean voyages began in 1931 with the crossing from Arcachon to Buenos Aires in *Lehg I*—a distance of 6,270 nautical miles in 74 days' sailing. His boat, an old international 8-metre, had some twenty years in her timbers. Dumas was the first to make an ocean crossing in this type of boat; Alain Gerbault's comment was that he never would have attempted it. Nevertheless it was the *Dorade*, an American built yawl, that won the transatlantic race the same year and her lines were of racing yacht rather than of the conventional types regarded at the time as the most seaworthy.

It was in 1942 that Dumas embarked on the unprecedented cruise of which he tells in this book. The moment chosen for this splendid gesture may not have been quite fortuitous; in those dark days the Swastika was within striking distance of Cairo and Moscow, and the Rising Sun, of Queensland. Perfectly aware of the dangers and hardships confronting him, he flung his gauntlet in the teeth of Fate and, with an Apostolic trust in God and a well-found ship, he set out without wireless, without funds or a spare oilskin.

Dumas's voyage may be summarized briefly as follows:

He left Buenos Aires on the 27th of June 1942 and reached Cape Town on the 25th of August—55 days to cover 4,200 miles. A ghastly misadventure at the beginning of the run very nearly terminated his career. He remained only three weeks in Cape Town before starting on the next leg of his journey, which proved to be the worst; 7,400

204

miles to Wellington in 104 days. After a month's very necessary rest, he was off again on the 30th January 1943. The passage to Valparaiso, which he reached on the 12th of April, was uneventful compared to the other stages of the journey. Dumas lingered there deliberately until the 30th of May, waiting for the crucial moment to tackle his last and most formidible adversary, Cape Horn.

This satanic region has been too well described to require any comment here. Having rounded the Cape with a degree of luck which his judgment and determination had most fully deserved, he reached Mar del Plate on the 7th of July 1943, 37 days and 3,200 miles from Valparaiso. He had made some remarkable daily runs, averaging 120 miles at times, and had even attained 175 miles in twenty-four hours. To achieve this single-handed in a 31 foot-overall yacht is a performance which has been equalled by few fully manned racers of similar size.

His landfalls in the River Plate on the outward and return journey may be discounted; he had circumnavigated the globe with three landfalls in twelve and a half months, of which 272 days were spent at sea; he had sailed 20,420 miles, staying close to the ill-omened 40° parallel. In so doing he broke four records: he was the first lone navigator to round the Horn and survive, Al Hansen having been wrecked shortly after his success; the first lone navigator to round the Horn from West to East; the first—and we may expect the last—to take the 'impossible' route he chose; and the only one to have sailed round the globe with only three landfalls. Anyone ambitious to emulate let alone surpass him can lay claim to a head as well as a heart of oak.

The impossible has been proved possible *once*—by one very tough, gallant and experienced sailor, who on top of these qualities enjoyed a generous hand-out of luck. That should suffice. As Dumas himself says: 'Never, never again.'

But he was by no means finished with ocean voyaging. In 1945 *Lehg II* and her skipper sailed on the 1st of September to Buenos Aires, and after calls in South America set out for Havana, arriving there on the 9th of March 1946 after a run of 5,400 miles from Rio de Janeiro. After leaving Havana on the 2nd of June, *Lehg II* appears to have taken the bit between her teeth, for they passed New York, the Azores, Madeira, the Canaries and the Cape Verde Islands without stopping, to call at Ceará, Brazil, on the 16th of September, having spent 106 days at sea and covered 7,000 miles without a landfall. From first to last this 17,045 mile cruise took 234 sailing days.

No doubt he was at a loss to find some new problem, for it was not until 1955 that he set out for New York from Buenos Aires in a boat of 2½ tons displacement, the *Sirio*. With one landfall, at Bermuda, he sailed 7,100 miles in 117 days.

So it is not surprising that in June 1957 Dumas received the following letter:

'I am very pleased to inform you that the Slocum Prize has been conferred on you by a vote of the members of the Slocum Society. It is normally to be given for the most remarkable trans-oceanic crossing achieved during the previous year, but on this occasion we have made an exception to the rule to honour the extraordinary voyages made by the greatest solitary navigator in the world.

'Will you accept my congratulations on being the first to receive the Slocum Prize? With this prize, which we now send you, we do homage to yourself and to the great captain from whom it takes its name. In spite of its small intrinsic value, I hope that you will have much pleasure in receiving it as we ourselves have in conferring it on you.'

(Signed) RICHARD GORDON MACCLOSKEY,
*Secretary.*

Many yachtsmen have attended many distributions of prizes, cups, medals and trophies; they know how soon the memory of minor prowesses fades like fire in stubble once the freshness of the event and the euphoria of commemoration are past. This is something different. Deeds of quite exceptional skill and courage, involving weeks and months of solitary hardship, have, on due deliberation, been found superior to anything previously known and rewarded on that basis. The Slocum Prize is an Order of Merit which Dumas undoubtedly deserved. For though many since Slocum's time have sailed great distances in small craft, most of them have followed prudently in the well-buoyed channels of previous experience. Dumas had the vision of a Michelangelo to foresee the unforeseeable and accomplish the impossible.

And, like the cosmic artists of the Renaissance, his activities spread over many fields. He is not only a musician but a painter, whose pictures have that transparency, depth of feeling and rhythm which the ocean demands and which those who know it can best appreciate.

All this—and farming too!

Like all original and versatile artists, he has very definite ideas and some of his idiosyncrasies may be criticized. He himself knows best why he dispenses with a sea anchor or a bilge pump. One may well ask why he never caught fish or why *Lehg II* carried only one screwdriver. Never mind: he is justified by faith and works; and the 'dear little cherub that sits up aloft' watched over him.

And if he is determined to die with his sea boots on, I venture to suggest that he should call his boat *La Santita.*

I am indebted to Viscount Traprain, Mr. William Mason and Mr. D. H. Shackles, C.B.E. for their very kind assistance on certain technical points.

RAYMOND JOHNES.

---

*Barometer readings in this book are expressed in millimetres.*
*100 millimetres = 3.94 inches.*

The Author on horse-back on his country estate near Buenos Aires.

*Lehg II* being painted and re-fitted at the Argentine Yacht Club before departure.

# INTRODUCTION

For a long time I dreamt of finding a seaman among my ancestors—a pirate, a 'black ivory' merchant; at the very least someone from a romantic seaport in lovely Brittany. No luck: nothing but landsmen. At the time of the Revolution our great-grandfather was a prelate who escaped the massacres, took refuge in a little village in Italy, became a teacher and got married. No doubt he avoided the subject of his past; this, and the fact that many records were destroyed at that time, has made it impossible for us to trace farther back. All that I can add is that the portrait of General Dumas which was shown in the Arts pavilion of the Colonial Exhibition struck me by its remarkable resemblance to my father and my uncles.

But there was nothing of the sailor in this general's life, nor yet in his descendants: one was a Cavalière of the Order of the Crown of Italy; another, the only sporting one, set up a world motor-cycle speed record in 1910.

Where did I get my love of the sea?

Conspicuous among the memories of my youth are the expeditions we used to make with my father. He took us into the country or to Buenos Aires, especially into the La Boca quarter among the Genoese who could not bear to part from their ships, and so cast anchor there. On those calm Sundays I was impressed by the great masts of the sailing ships, the apparently inextricable tangle of rigging; but I cannot say that this sight gave me any very definite ideas on my own future: it was too far away. And though I loved to read tales of pirates and musketeers, I did not feel a serious call to either of these professions.

But I shall never forget the shock experienced in the little library that provided me with intellectual nourishment, when I was told:

'But you've read them *all!*'

When vacation time came round we used to go to the seaside, and we went by sea. Unfortunately the trip took place by night and thus the longed-for contact with the ocean meant no more than a visit to the ice-cream merchant on board, after which my father sent me off to bed. No, those trips can hardly be counted as sea voyages.

Yet one night I noticed that the passengers were not walking normally; they moved about hesitantly and unsteadily. This was something I failed to understand, so I asked for an explanation.

My mother, fearing that I might be feeling sick, replied with her usual gentleness:

'Don't worry about that, dear; it's because they don't feel well.'

'But why do they travel if they're not feeling well?'

That was my youthful reaction. At no time in my seafaring life have I ever experienced that very common type of suffering.

It must be a great disappointment to those who would like to see in me a reincarnation of some sailor longing to return to his element. No. And I never dreamt of exploring fabulous countries either.

The fine care-free years of my life were spent in the fields, and I know them well. Then came hard times of work, struggle and worry—hardship that became a physical experience. I was only 14 years old when I came to understand what my parents felt as their resources dwindled to the point of hunger. Meals were reserved for my brother and me. So I decided to leave my books and go to work. I pretended to my parents that I had had enough of school; they understood that I was aware of the situation and made no comment.

So my new life in long trousers began; one more man took up the struggle for existence. Neither a pirate nor a musketeer, I embarked on the most commonplace task—washing floors, running errands, polishing brass for a wholesale business. A long way from my distinguished ancestor at the Italian Court!

My former schoolmates seldom missed the opportunity of calling out: 'Look at him; he's working!' with a hearty laugh that was meant to be offensive. It didn't hurt. It was a shock, of course, but I never felt bitter. My feelings were very mixed—a kind of savage satisfaction that I was not the only sufferer from poverty, and a secret exaltation that made light of misunderstandings. This last may be called optimism; it has always protected me from the hard knocks of life. And although I was not quite indifferent to the attitude of former classmates who came to jeer at me as I polished the brasses, the sorrows of my first month at work were amply repaid by the joy of my parents when I brought back the little handful of pesos I had earned.

Then I got organized. In the daytime I worked; in the evenings I went to the Academy of Art to study drawing and sculpture. Still nothing in the least nautical. . . .

I shall tell elsewhere of the train of circumstances which brought me back from France, alone on board the *Lehg I*, setting my course on the Southern Cross. How far away it seems, that evening in 1931 when the sun was gilding the dunes of Arcachon as I set out! Misty, too, my successes—triumphal entries into Vigo, the Canaries, Rio Grande do Sul, Montevideo and, finally, Buenos Aires. Today *Lehg I* rests in the Lujan Museum. And how times have changed!

War . . .

A breath of panic ran round the world. It seemed that all was lost.

All I had to do was to stay quiet. It's so easy and comfortable, and routine presses on the shoulders of whosoever would rise from his seat and go.

Nevertheless, what did I do at home on rainy days? Bending over my charts, in spirit I was on the seas. I was studying the Roaring Forties: the 'impossible route'.

What set me off, to throw off all my normal life and tempt fate? Was it to show that I was not lost after all, that dreamers propelled by their inward vision still lived, that romance somehow managed to survive? The young need examples; maybe, without being too self-conscious, I could provide one. I was torn between two alternatives: to stay, to lunch at a given hour, to wait for someone, receive guests, read newspapers, and tattle with friends outside working hours: the clock would go on telling the hours and I should be one of those creatures chained to the treadmill of today and tomorrow. Or else—more generous and perhaps even more altruistic—to respond to that appeal which John Masefield expresses so well in 'Sea Fever'.

My decision was made, the first step taken. Nothing would stop me now; I had only to say 'goodbye,' perhaps forever. Before me lay the unknown of the 'impossible' seas. My charts, the apparatus of navigation, the chronometer, the old compass, the tables—all those loved objects I had kept would go to sea again with me. And so my life as a sailor began once more.

# 1

# *The Search for a Mate*

On this enterprise a mate was obviously necessary—that is, the boat.

It had to be *Lehg II*, which I had built in 1934 with the idea of sailing around the world. But difficulties had mounted up and, apart from a few trial runs and pleasure cruises, I always returned to the land; pushing a plough seemed to put my dreams to sleep. The seafaring vagabond was getting stuck in the furrows. I sold my boat to buy a tractor, thus putting one ideal in the place of another—less romantic, admittedly, but still an ideal. And in spite of the digs that a sailor's conscience gave me, I had given up the idea of seeing *Lehg II* again. I made real efforts to forget the sea and cling to the land; the earth to which I even dedicated long, secret poems. The sea was so far away that I could hear its voice only in my imagination; yet sometimes, standing on a hill, I sniffed the wind that had passed over the vast estuary of the River Plate; it smelt different from the breeze of the pampas, it had a different quality. But the earth had got such a hold on me that one day, when a woman remarked how wonderful it must feel to be alone on the sea, I replied:

'Man was born into society and he must return.'

Yet that evening, I thought of my 'mate'. I felt I had to find her and see her again.

On the morning on which I left the *campo*, courage failed me after the cordial farewells of the peons. I could not turn back to look at the horses, the plough, the little tree that grew on the stark plain, thanks to my parental care—not even to say goodbye to my dog Aramis. I got into my car and drove to the ring-fence; looking back I saw that the dust of my passing had obscured the tangible certainties behind me; in front lay incalculable hazard.

The whitewash I had put on the fence some time back had stood the weather well. This little detail gave me some pleasure and I almost stopped thinking; but the dust was settling and soon the familiar landscape would be visible. I felt the danger of finding myself back on that dusty road; and with something akin to fear I averted my eyes and slammed the gate.

My kitbag was sitting beside me in the car. In it were the old oilskin that I bought in France for my first voyage, sailmaker's needles and

211

thread, even signal flares. Some of them had been used as fireworks on *fiesta* evenings in the country. The others were returning to the sea in that kitbag that forms part of the sailor; they might be used sometime, with nothing to celebrate. My dear old seaman's knife was there too; in the *campo* I had used it for cutting up meat. Now it was going back proudly to its proper use. The seaman was being reborn in the bag.

Many thoughts were passing through my head to the purr of the engine. A saying came back to be: 'Never let a friend's hand get warm in yours'. One must always say 'goodbye' and pass on. So I must start again saying goodbye to all things—ports, towns, human contacts. The hands of my friends should not get warm in mine, I would not give them time; I would carry the warmth of friendship with me into endless solitude.

The bag did not feel at home in the car. It wanted to go back where it belonged—in the cabin of *Lehg II*. But where, oh where, was the boat?

Dr. Raphal Gamba, to whom I had sold her, still owned her. I took my brother Remo and sought him out.

It was all quite clear: I needed just that boat and no other. It would take too long, perhaps a year, to have a new one built. I could not delay my departure for the favourable season was near, and besides that, now that my decision had been made, something had started up inside me. We discussed a jumble of figures and dreams. The boat was put on the slip and the Argentine Yacht Club offered to stand the expense of making her seaworthy. Manuel M. Campos, the naval architect who supervised the repairs, designed masts and sails to stand up to the terrible seas where I was bound. My old friends the Russo brothers of La Boca, artists in their own way, made the sails without asking how and when they were going to be paid for time and materials. They had no illusions; for them to contribute their bit to the enterprise was enough.

'We're not in the habit of keeping ships waiting,' they said. And everybody worked without unnecessary words.

I was going to leave a lot of debts behind me without a clue as to who was going to pay them. Fortunately my old Fencing and Gymnastic Club in Buenos Aires wanted to help me; they paid for the sails. So that was all right and so were the repairs. Only one tiny problem remained: I had not enough money to pay for the boat. I had hoped to raise the money by selling a batch of cattle; but the unfortunate beasts, having been driven from the ranch to one remote fair and then another, were so weak and thin that they could hardly walk. The irony of it! I had sold *Lehg II* to buy a tractor and I could not sell enough cows to buy her back.

'I'm told that cattle don't sell,' I said to Arnold Buzzi; 'they're going to die on their feet.'

'I was always against your scheme,' he replied, 'but since you've made up your mind, leave the cows in peace to fatten up. Here's the money you need for the boat.'

Furthermore, I had the invaluable collaboration of the members of the Buchardo Club, nicknamed 'slavers'. They worked incessantly on *Lehg II* for the fun of it. They brought their own maté and biscuits; they drove in a nail and had a sip of maté; a screw and another maté. Laughing, always laughing at their work, for which time was of no account. I cannot express the value of their work to me and can never forget it.

The water tanks aboard were inadequate; but time passed and I could not linger over every detail. Here another friend materialized, Innocencio of Lower Belgrano. He was a small shopkeeper, and he left shop-keeping to his wife while he trotted round the town pricing tanks. I also needed tins for sea biscuits. Innocencio dumped out his goods in bulk, took the tins and soldered them up himself. It was high time for my preparations to finish; Innocencio was on the point of losing his business—and his wife, who had had enough of running it single-handed.

One day he said confidentially:

'You're going to some very cold parts—you'll need hard liquor.'

'Can't do much about that,' I replied, 'look what it costs.'

Innocencio found the answer. He persuaded a number of his clients to present me with a few bottles each, and so I got an excellent adver-tisement combined with a fine cellar; they were very useful.

Thanks to the kindness of my friends, I acquired everything I needed as the time for departure got nearer. For example, a photographer from *El Grafico* called on me one day with a request from his director for a picture of me in a fur hat and gloves.

'I'm quite willing,' I replied, 'but I haven't any.'

'Never mind,' said he, 'I'll bring them tomorrow.'

The fur cap might have been made for me and the gloves were mag-nificent. The photograph was taken. I wrote a note to the proprietor of the magazine, saying: 'Dear Gaston: This is just the job: very many thanks'; and I kept the cap and gloves.

And what a piece of luck to meet my friend Bardin. I went to see him to have a talk . . . and next day I had a complete ship's medicine chest. My doctor friends gave me ampoules of antibiotics, adrenalin, caffeine injections, etc. Everyone brought me little boxes labelled 'Medical Samples. Not to be sold.' The law could rest easy: they sold me nothing.

On one evening I spent with the 'Banda di Estribor', Professor Niceto Loizaga expatiated on the dangers of scurvy for navigators. Of course I knew of this sort of organic decomposition which can attack anyone deprived of fresh foods for sixty days. Would I be a victim of the scourge of old-time seamen? With vitamins I should be safe enough: but how to buy them? A few days later quantities of vitamins A, B$_1$, C, D and K arrived on board, together with a mound of glucose to keep my calories up to standard.

My friend Corteletti was working on another line. One day I received 400 bottles of sterilized milk and a quantity of chocolate milk that would keep for a year; all this from the stocks of the Argentine Yacht Club. Another surprise was six tins of cocoa, 20 kilos of lentil flour, split peas, chick peas, 10 kilos of maté, cans of oil and 10 kilos of corned beef. Then came quantities of chocolate of every kind, fifteen tins of condensed milk, 70 kilos of potatoes, ten jars of jam, cigarettes, pipe tobacco, and what have you. I began to wonder whether I was going to sea or starting a business.

On my last day my friend Scotto gave me a log to measure the distance travelled—and I don't know how many boxes of matches. Finally, all I had to buy in this land of corn was—biscuits!

'What do you propose to wear when it rains?' asked Señor Llavallol in the course of a friendly visit.

'A raincoat.'

He burst out laughing and gave me a note for a store; I went there and came out fully equipped.

I shall never forget when my friend Weber came to see me. Rather awkwardly he drew me aside and showed me a fine woolen dressing-gown. He didn't want to hurt my feelings—and I had not so much as an overcoat. Weber could not imagine the pleasure he was giving me. Another very useful gift, from Dr. Torres, was a pair of thick socks knitted by his wife. I wore them so much that I had to darn them with sail thread. For it must not be forgotten that all my ports of call were subjected to wartime rationing and that I could not replace clothing.

Enrique Tiraboschi gave me a leather jerkin. He was an optimist. Praising the garment, he told me to take great care of it, not to get it crumpled or scratched, because I would not feel the cold when I wore it. In fact, I needed this magnificent jerkin—with five or six woolies underneath, two sets of oilskins on top and a thick layer of newspaper next my skin to keep out the polar winds.

Everything aboard had to be stowed so that I could keep an eye on it and that it should not come adrift in the rolling and pitching of the boat. In this respect my worst fears were more than justified. Several times I was on my beam ends in a way I should never have believed possible.

The date of my departure was set for the 26th of June.

# 2

# *My Faith in 'Lehg II'*

The boat was of the build known in France as a 'Norwegian with pointed stern', in Spanish a 'double prow'. Length 31 ft. 6 in., beam 10 ft. 10 in., draught fully laden 5 ft. 8 in., a cast-iron keel weighing 7,700 lb. Apart from provisions I carried 90 gallons of water in two tanks and 21 gallons of kerosene for cooking and lighting. I could stay at sea for a year without revictualling.

*Lehg II* was ketch rigged, that is to say with a mainmast and a mizzen. The mainmast was one made in France for *Lehg I* in 1913. It was therefore thirty years old at the start of my voyage. The suit of sails comprised jib, storm jib, mainsail and mizzen. I carried a complete set of spares, plus a storm trysail and an enormous balloon jib for very light weather. The cabin top was permanently covered with canvas to prevent the waves from beating continuously on it, starting the seams and causing leaks. Furthermore it kept the cabin in twilight, so that I could sleep in the daytime.

I had not forgotten a spare tiller. My provisions were complete: nothing was left to chance. If I did not succeed it would not be from lack of foresight; on this sort of enterprise there is no room for improvisations. Everything must be calculated and measured.

I knew how well my boat could behave in heavy weather on the high seas. In 1937, on a trip to Rio de Janeiro, I was surprised by a *pampero* squall blowing at between 60 and 70 knots—the one which wrecked the *Bonny Joan*[1] and *Shaheen* on the rocks of the Punta del Este. As for myself, I was in the area where the *Cachalot* vanished without trace.

It was in the evening. I was making myself some chocolate and hoping to spend as pleasant a night as possible. The wind outside was so violent that a sail had been blown to ribbons, and the raging seas were something to shudder at. I was hove to, close to the wind.

Suddenly there was a terrific crash. I followed the motion of the boat and found myself sitting on the ceiling of the cabin. This was it. For several seconds of eternity the masts were pointing to the depths and the keel skywards. The chocolate was flowing over the ceiling. I was sealed in, in the total darkness and assumed that I was sinking.

[1]*Bonny Joan*, Norwegian 59 ft. and 41 tons. *Shaheen*, schooner 98 ft., 130 tons.

I was partly stunned and there was nothing that I could do. The end of everything. I felt hot blood running on my hands. There was no way out of the darkness and confusion, and *Lehg II*, keel in air, would soon fill and sink.

It was a coffin more than a prison. Then came resignation and I relaxed. I cannot say whether my mood was one of acceptance, thankfulness even, or a kind of reverence for death, so often defied. I left everything to fate. To struggle was quite useless; I seemed to be returning to infancy.

Then *Lehg II* slowly rolled over; and keeping pace with the movement of the boat, hope came back. As soon as it was possible I scrambled back on deck; resignation was transformed into furious energy. Everything came to life at once, muscles, brains and nerves—a torrent of vitality sweeping over me. I looked at the sea and smiled. The sea and I; face to face.

I was no longer in a coffin but on my own deck. Some distance away the dinghy drifted off, awash; but nothing mattered now that I could fight back with eager eyes, a heart full of hope and in possession of all my faculties. From the bottom of my soul I thanked the boat, I talked to her with endearments that fled down the howling wind.

My faith in *Lehg II* dates from then.

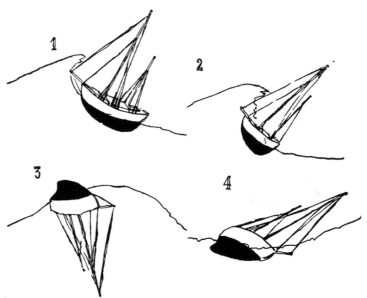

*Lehg II* turns over. (1) The crest of the wave advances. (2) The yacht is overwhelmed. (3) For several seconds the mast points to the depths. (4) She rights herself. The drawing records the Author's impressions and is not to scale.

# 3

# *Good Luck*

On Friday the 26th of June I paid my final visit to Admira Guisasola. His aide-de-camp led me down a corridor and ushered me into a dimly lit office. Through the window behind the Admiral came a single shaft of light. Feeling a little confused by the excitement of the last few days, I tried to express myself properly and say a great many things. And all that would come out was: 'Admiral, I've come to say goodbye.' The words sounded hollow and I felt that it was not I who spoke. Out of the darkness came a reply:

'Good luck, Vito.' And after a long silence the Admiral added: 'That is what I wish you.'

We embraced; and this accolade meant a great deal to me. We did not speak. Then I turned and made for the door in haste. But as I went down the corridor, rather like a clock-work dummy, a hail of good wishes followed me.

As I looked across the square from the entrance I could not pull myself together. I felt stunned, as if I had just realized what was about to happen to me. Up to then, work had kept my mind occupied; now I had to think of the voyage. The two sentries, pacing their beats, took no notice. As I walked on a policeman shook hands with me and made a 'good luck' sign with his free hand.

What did I do till midnight? I don't remember. I only know that I went on like an automaton with a little spark glowing inside that told me I had finished with my friends, with fighting difficulties and correcting mistakes. I longed to feel at peace with this world that I was about to leave and that I might never find again.

For some obscure reason one scene sticks out in my memory; I see myself at midnight going aboard *Lehg II* with some friends, carrying blankets and taking a last look round.

Then I went ashore to sleep.

# 4

# *The 27th of June*

The morning was cold and sunny. I came out and took the Metro, and looked round at the headlines of newspapers the other passengers were reading. They said: 'Dumas's duel with the sea starts today'; 'Vito Dumas's return match with the sea'. I was not at all awestruck; on the contrary, the fuss the press was making filled me with a kind of childish delight. People were staring at me in surprise; whispering and thinking, no doubt, that I was not dressed for the part of the lonely mariner; carrying no luggage, wearing an ordinary and quite inappropriate lounge suit, I looked like any clerk going to an office.

Getting out with the crowd at Carlos Pellegrini station, I went to the hairdresser of my Gymnastic and Fencing Club. There were still patches of white frost on the ground.

Once installed in the barber's chair, I took whatever was coming: a hot towel after the shave? Sure! Manicure? Call the girl! Shoes? I looked at them and thought a polish would do them all the good in the world. I felt like a Pasha enjoying all the pleasures of life; I surrendered to luxury. But presently the hairdresser remarked:

'So today's the day?'

I woke up. I looked at my nails that the manicurist was polishing, at my shining shoes, and asked myself what the use of it all might be. The mirror reflected my image as if to reveal me to myself. No, really, I was not 'in the skin of the part', as actors say. I was not convincing my audience. Should I be serious or laugh? Should I be grave or dramatic? Not an easy part, the lonely mariner. I replied:

'Oh yes, I think so.'

'But all the papers say so!' exclaimed the unfortunate man.

'If they say so it must be true.'

I went on looking at myself in the mirror, making faces and trying to find one that fitted the lonely mariner, while they went on fussing over my fingernails and my shoes. It seemed to me that someone else was being titivated while the solitary navigator was looking for his face.

I lunched at the Argentine Yacht Club and had to leave the table twice to satisfy the press photographers. At 1 p.m. I started off for the boat.

Our Commodore, Señor Antonio Aguirre, was hanging round my neck, when my friend Arnoldo Buzzi drew me to one side.

'How much money have you got?'

Caramba! I hadn't thought of that one. I drew out my wallet: what Buzzi and I saw was a single 10-peso note.

'So you expect to get round the world with that?'

'Where do you expect me to spend money at sea?'

'Oh no, my dear fellow, that won't do!'

And Arnoldo, who is rather more practical than I am, gave me ten British one-pound notes.

A sailor came up to me.

'Must wish you luck, sir. I admire you. I know those seas.'

'Oh, do you?'

'Yes. It was at the Cape of Good Hope that we got dismasted in a storm. Well, all I can say is that I admire you.'

Nothing like encouragement, I thought. But the crowd was getting thicker. Only fifteen steps down to the dinghy that would take me to *Lehg II*.

My mother stood before me, pale and sad as I had not seen her for many years. I don't care for family farewells; no, I never liked them. What on earth was I to say to her?

'Mother dear, smile!' I begged. 'I don't want people to see you looking sad. It'll only be a year.'

I kissed her and turned to go down the fifteen steps. But my brother could not restrain himself any longer; he burst into tears. He hugged me with all the vigour of despair; as I broke loose I cried:

'*Hombre!* you're suffocating me!' A childish effort to hide my feelings, to deceive him—and myself.

The crowd got thicker. I jumped into the dinghy. The last photographs, final good wishes, and handshakes, and away! I was soon on board.

Whilst I was changing, the Russo brothers and the Yacht Club hands were hoisting the sails.

Now I was alone on board. *Lehg II* was making way under the northerly breeze that had been blowing since morning. It was 13.05 hours. Behind me was the country where I was leaving my mother; she had already become, not a being of flesh and blood, but a symbol.

Two hundred yards. For the last time I looked back, scanning the prospect that stretched from the mole where the crowd had gathered to see me off, to the high wall of the Yacht Club; and throwing off the emotion I had suppressed for so many hours in order to conceal my weakness, I cried out:

'*Adios*, my country!'

I sailed slowly down the channel. To leeward, several yachts with friends were escorting me, *Angelita* leading; the Ministry of Works boats sounded their sirens as I passed.

I began to feel the sea getting choppy under the north wind. I reckoned that the run to Montevideo would not take long.

One by one my escorts dropped off. When it came to *Angelita's* turn, whom should I see aboard but my son, Vito Diego.

I had to say something but all that came into my head was:

'Keep well! Do some good work!'

Quite simple—but something he could repeat to himself every day.

Once I was through the entrance channel of the South Basin a sloop, the last of my escort, came alongside with Arnold Buzzi, who had done a few cruises with me in the past and who was to accompany me to Montevideo. He was to see me through the congested traffic of the River Plate whilst I stowed everything that had been put aboard at the last moment.

I got down to it. Off Quilmès, Arnold sang out:

'Ship to windward!'

It was that excellent yachtsman Martinez Vasquez, the director of *El Grafico*, in his *Sea Bird*, to give me a final send-off.

I set the balloon jib to put on more speed. Darkness fell slowly; in the sunset lay Buenos Aires, which I might never see again.

Then it was quite dark; white and red, the light buoys of the channel were winking.

Ashore, the city of La Plata was a blaze of light; here and there a green light marked a wreck; ships went to and fro. On board, only the binnacle and cabin lights were shining. The wind freshened and veered to the N.E. Dinner-time went by as we chatted of this and that. Astern, the lights of La Plata were growing dimmer. I said:

'Steer E. a quarter N. while I get a little sleep. I'll take the watch at midnight.'

'Right.'

I lay down hoping to sleep, but without success. From time to time I would ask Arnold:

'How goes it?'

'Very well.'

'Are we on course?'

'On course.'

These rather futile questions were chiefly put to reassure myself that Arnold had not gone to sleep. By 1 o'clock it was no longer enough for me to ask, I had to make sure that we were on our course. Oh dear! we were heading for Mar del Plata. Arnoldo had lost his bearings. The oddest thing about it is that, once we had arrived, he thought that I made the mistake.

I decided to stay with him. We talked from time to time. The moon peered through heavy clouds. Conversation fell; silences became longer and longer.

'Do you want to sleep, Arnold?'

'Er, not much . . .'

'Right! she's keeping nicely on course, all by herself. Let's both go to sleep.'

We went to bed and *Lehg II* sailed on with no one at the tiller.

As the dawn began to peer through the deadlights, I felt I must see where we were. The lie of the boat told me that the wind had freshened. Leaving Arnold asleep, I went on deck and took the tiller. Forward lay the channel buoys of Montevideo. I passed them at 8 a.m. just as Arnold was beginning to show signs of life. And at ten we anchored in the port of Buceo after some twenty hours' sailing.

This short trial trip had been useful. I had spotted several details that called for immediate attention; for example, the shrouds had got slack and the mast, no longer properly held, had taken on an alarming bend. Two sailors, friends of ours, undertook to brace them up, to change the dead-eyes for others of a more suitable size, etc.; this work being scrupulously paid for ... with a bottle of Muscatel.

Numbers of friends came to see me, bringing welcome gifts: a seaman's knife, a picture of *Lehg I* to decorate my cabin. Another brought bottles of mineral water. Fat Mathos Puig took me in his car to a ships' chandler where I got brushes, paint, an electric torch. Puig kept on at me till I was loaded up with a lot of lumber I didn't know where to stow. What is certain is that the proprietor of the shop, carried away by his eloquence, did not allow me to pay for a thing. Everyone wanted to give me something and ask me to dinner.

For a few days a violent *pampero* caused the authorities to close the port. I did not sleep aboard but at the Uruguayan Yacht Club, where a red flag for danger was hoisted: the wind continued blowing at 30 knots. Nevertheless I decided to sail on July 1st. The wind and the sea were not reassuring, but I had important reasons for haste. The season of fine weather was passing and I wanted to get to South Africa before spring.

# 5

# *The Great Day*

The morning of the 1st of July was very like the preceding days;
the seas were more impressive than ever.

I had arranged to start early in the afternoon; having some time
to waste, I went into the centre of the town. The Avenida del 18
Julio was forbidding and full of hostile wind. I felt like a very frustrated orphan and tried to get rid of my mood by going into a
bazaar and purchasing some kitchen utensils, then some newspapers
which I turned over without reading them. Finally, I got into a bus to
return to the club. Everyone was muffled up on this mean, cold,
surly morning. We arrived at the Plaza de la Libertad, which has
changed little in the course of centuries; it made me think of those
quarters of Paris that remain so strikingly themselves while change
goes on all round.

The Plaza de la Libertad took me back into the past; I saw myself
in my far-off childhood, running or driving in a tiny carriage drawn
by two lambs. O Past, why did you have to haunt me just at this
moment? It often used to happen to me in the years when I was growing into manhood: suddenly I would awaken from my daydreaming
and see what had been hidden. Here was the moment of truth; I had
to tear myself from this spot that I had loved as a child—but beyond
the years I clung to one image that had to be stored away in my innermost consciousness: my intense joy at seeing the Marqués de las
Cabriolas in the Montevideo carnival and the sound of tambourines;
the procession passing under my penetrating six-year-old eyes as I
sat in the little chair my parents had placed at the edge of the pave-
ment. Now the tambourines were ringing in a sad heart that yearned
back from the present to this warm, human little past.

The motor-bus went on and I woke up in front of the club.

As I ate my last lunch there, all my Uruguayan friends wanted
to sit at my table in turn. They were not cheerful.

'Well, Dumas, remember that the bad weather is local; once you're
away from the Uruguayan coast you will be in a calmer zone.'

That was the best encouragement the Harbour Master had to offer.
There was a certain amount of discussion, but many words remained unspoken.

Time was up.

The harbour was still officially closed. But I got my clearance at the Maritime Prefecture. My farewells were almost silent; I went aboard and was towed out to a mooring where it would be easier to set sail.

I set all sail. The boat was dancing; what would it be like outside? Several friends were circling round me. I slipped the mooring and *Lehg II* was quickly under way. The sou'wester was blowing at over 30 knots and the seas were heavy outside. We were soon through the harbour entrance, steering S. to avoid shoals along the coast.

The crossing to the African coast had begun; more than 4,000 sea miles. . . . I would make the acquaintance of those 'roaring winds' of the forties. It was the first time that a man had ventured into them alone. What would those tomorrows bring?

For the moment I knew that my safety, my universe, depended on the security of a few planks. The only yacht that had decided to see me off in such weather was shipping heavy seas with some frequency; she went about and made for the harbour; arms were waving a last farewell.

And as this handful of friends, from a country so dear to me, drew away, I shed tears.

I needed this relief. I had choked them back too long under an outward stoicism; now I reverted to childhood.

At 16.00 hours Flores Island was abeam. I steered due East with a following wind. The sea was still rising and I could not relax my attention for a single moment. I had decided not to rest at all until I was well clear of the coast, on account of danger from congested shipping.

At 21.00 hours Iman Point, Periapolis, was abeam. The boat was bustling along as though she were under power. At 23.00 hours the pencil of light from Punta del Este was flashing at regular intervals on my sails. To the South I could see as I rose on a wave the dark mass of Seal Island.

It was a really dirty *pampero*. From time to time heavy clouds would burst in a cascade which combined with the seas breaking on deck and made it essential to batten down everything. And this went on for an entire day.

Early in the morning of the 3rd of July, dead-beat with sleepiness and fatigue in this hellish weather, I decided to take in the mainsail. I had to cling to the hand-rope and every other hold in sight. At times I had to stop work to avoid being washed overboard.

The night was still black; no sign of life anywhere. I had been on deck for forty hours without a chance to eat or drink.

The flogging of the mainsail as I lowered it made the boat quiver as if everything would break up. Finally I managed to get it lashed down and made fast.

*Lehg II* had lost speed and was easing up to the waves more gently.

I let her lie with her head to the land. I was trembling with cold and fatigue.

Up till then I had been sailing without lights. In order to display one I entered the cabin for the first time since I set sail. What was that sound of water?

I struck a match. But my hands were numbed and stiff. I went through the whole box. It was wet: I threw it overboard. I did not know what was the matter with me: nerves or clumsiness after so many years ashore. At all events it was not till the third box that I began to be methodical. At last I got a light. And sure enough there was water in the bilge. Tired as I was, this was the last straw....

The seaman must not think of himself until he has seen to the needs of his craft. So I set about baling. I must record here that never since I have been sailing have I used a bilge pump. One after another, I threw seven buckets of water over the coaming. *Lehg II* had taken all that in since Montevideo: I was surprised, as she had never made a drop of water before.

To tell the truth, I had only a vague idea of my position; I should have to pass through a good many more trials before I found my sea legs.

I had been thinking of so many things in the last few days and was so tired that I had no appetite; I only wanted to rest. I wedged myself in and went fast asleep, to awake, half-conscious, at midday. I ate a little biscuit and drank a small bottle of chocolate milk.

The weather did not mend; I decided to carry on under the staysail and mizzen. The barometer stood at 769, the thermometer at 13°C., the hygrometer at 90 per cent. No land in sight and no prospect of the wind abating. In the evening I lashed the helm and left the boat to sail herself, taking refuge in the cabin. Enormous waves came and went; *Lehg II* was groaning. From time to time a wave would crash down on the deck; the wind was now blowing at over 50 knots: I was well into the 'roaring winds'. I emptied twenty buckets of water; and this added greatly to the exhaustion caused by the weather.

At midnight I saw with consternation that the floor boards of the cabin were awash. At every roll the water threatened to spoil everything on board. Feverishly I tackled it and threw bucket after bucket of water overboard. I was soon exhausted. Often the bucket would empty itself over me when I had nearly got it out. I was drenched; my hands were scored and very painful. I wondered what could be happening; she had never made a drop of water before—why should she fill so quickly? Unless I could staunch the leak she would sink. I worked desperately to get all the water out so as to trace the damage, but there was a difficulty: the greater part of the space under the floor boards was filled with some five hundred bottles of assorted drinks.

In spite of the movement of the boat in the stormy seas, I had to shift all this cargo, bottle by bottle. And when I had finished I found that the leak was not where I expected.

I inspected the whole hull, from the stern to where the tins of biscuits were stowed forward and where the pitching was most violent. Passing the tins into the cabin, I hurt my hands and knocked myself about considerably. But there was the leak, at last!

There was a shake in one of the planks, which had split. This was not the time to ask how or why. Quickly I mustered a piece of canvas, red lead, putty, a piece of planking, nails and a hammer, and set about stopping the leak. I was so eager to have done and the lamp swung so violently that I kept hitting my fingers with the hammer.

At last the job was done; only a very little water was coming in; and I re-stowed all the tins.

It was four o'clock in the afternoon of the 4th of July. I had worked desperately to save the boat. But I felt the satisfaction of having overcome the first difficulty; I could now indulge in a few moments' rest.

The sea was still bad, but not quite so bad as it had been in the first days. The trouble was that everything was saturated with sea water. I went back to the helm.

The 'roaring winds' were making their weight felt. The English have given them this name because, apart from their violence, they have a peculiar sound not unlike that of a saw cutting through wood. They rule the waves in 40° South, accompanied by low cloud, rain and squalls.

Dusk was falling by the time I had finished with the leak. I did a few odd jobs and looked out at the darkling sea, in the majesty of rolling waves that every now and then cut off the horizon. Stars were showing. The wind, which had touched 50 knots, had now dropped a little. Seagulls were following me and snapping up the bits of biscuit I threw to them.

When I awoke at 01.00 on the 5th of July, I saw that the light on deck had gone out; I decided not to light it again.

I proposed to organize my life as follows: in bad weather, to navigate under the staysail and mizzen and during the night to let *Lehg II* sail herself as best she might while I slept, until 7 or 8 in the morning. Such were my intentions; but an unexpected event came to modify my plans.

That morning at 8 I felt ill. My right arm was infected and there were several open wounds in my hand. I felt depressed and had not the courage to take the helm. I resolved to stay in bed.

On the 6th of July my arm was worse. The sea had gone a little, the wind remained very fresh. At 10 o'clock I set down the storm trysail, a sail for foul weather, smaller than the mainsail under which I had set out. This task, hard enough at any time on a moving deck, was doubly awkward with my right arm useless; I was beginning to get worried about the septic condition.

I remained at the helm on the look-out for a ship, but only albatrosses were to be seen. That night several porpoises, hardly breaking the surface, came to play around *Lehg II*; I was surprised to see them so far from land.

The sea became gradually calmer; for the first time the tranquil majesty of the Atlantic began to impress me. A few clouds in the sky, piling up to N.N.E. and N.N.W.

At midday on the 7th of July I took sights and got 35°47′ S. and 47°W. I was therefore 480 miles E. of Montevideo. The wind frequency chart showed that I was in the zone of twenty-four days of gales out of thirty, on an average.

And I was in a flat calm! The light breeze I hoped for was coy. The boat turned round and round, pointing most frequently to the N.E. Finally, at dusk the wind rose in the N.E. and for the first time the boat really held her course alone. My mind, too, was looking for a course and turned to J. L. Grundel, an old sea dog of the Swedish navy who had become a merchant skipper. I could see his kindly face. I fancied I heard him talking as he did shortly before I left Buenos Aires, in his precise limpid way, the words coming out like the murmur of a spring as he mourned over his seafaring past. He had remained young and strong; only on account of his 'cabin boy', his son, had he renounced the sea. I remembered a great truth he had uttered in the course of one of his soliloquies: 'It's out there at sea that you are really yourself.' I now understood what he meant and smiled at the memory of my despair on the night when I used three boxes of matches to get a light. It is true that the beginning was the toughest, for during those first days the wind blew at times at over 50 knots, tearing out the eyelets of the canvas cover in spite of its considerable strength.

# 6

# *The Arm and the Sea*

I had both hands bandaged and every bit of work necessary to handle the ship caused me acute pain. There was a long road ahead and I had not forgotten to ask God for guidance; but I understand also that a seaman has to suffer and that the picture one sees from ashore, when fit and well, does not include the bitter realities of life afloat. I could accept these—whilst doing my utmost not to lose altogether the illusions of happier days.

I was heading for a zone in which one storm follows another and which had never been sailed by a lone hand. I did not try to deceive myself. I knew before I started that it would not be a joy-ride; but imagination always falls short of the truth. I remembered the experiences of other navigators, but all the accounts I had read dealt with less inhospitable regions. I tried to adapt myself. I would take what was coming: I would face whatever the unknown future had in store. That evening I decided to have a feast to boost my *morale*, my first real meal since I set out. The menu: soup and fried potatoes. Not much, but for me, a banquet. So one goes on expecting less and less; and any trifle may become a source of satisfaction. Perhaps that is truly living.

The wind, which had been shifting continually, had unfortunately settled at E.S.E. on the morning of the 8th of July; I was obliged to take a tack to the S. The sky was completely overcast. I had some sleep and at 8.30 tried again to hold the tiller. As I was making no headway and getting very wet, I decided to return to the cabin, where I spent most of the time lying down. The barometer was steady at 774 and the temperature at 14°C.; wind 30 knots.

As the day went on, the weather grew worse. It began to rain and *Lehg II* sailed on alone under the storm trysail, on a south-easterly course.

During the night we had quite a shaking up. In the morning I decided to steer. At midday, when I went below to rest, I was appalled to find that there was a great deal of water in the hull. My summary efforts to master the leak had not been good enough. But the seas were too heavy for me to work on it in that part of the port bow. I should have to wait for better weather in order to make a proper job of it. But, weather permitting, would I still be able to do so? My hand, swollen and misshapen, was a nasty sight.

This hand and the whole right arm continued to swell, making movement impossible. The pain was getting worse and my temperature was rising.

In the evening I decided to give myself an injection to bring down the temperature; I spent an uneasy and feverish night in my bunk.

The next morning (10th of July) the weather was just as bad; on top of that, on this infernal course, the leak was making a great deal of water; and now I discovered that a 5 kg. jar of honey had come adrift and smashed. A disaster: the stuff had run into the bilges and made everything sticky.

Another injection. I sterilized the needle and succeeded in getting 1 c.c. of the liquid into the syringe; it was not easy to carry out this delicate operation left-handed. The jolting and banging of the boat were so continuous and so violent that I had to be very careful not to inoculate the mattress! On land, with steady hands, there is no difficulty about giving an injection, but here, nothing stayed in its place. An awkward movement, and everything was on the deck. And then—fish the needle out of the bilge, get the apparatus together and sterilize all over again. It took me a whole hour's fidgeting—in great pain, shaking with fever and sick with apprehension.

My will power had sunk to the point when, cowering in the cabin, I no longer cared whether the boat went on her course or sank. I could not sleep—for every jolt of my arm caused intolerable pain— nor think; there was only one thing in the world: my arm hurt.

The next day I gave myself another injection. The arm was monstrously swollen and my temperature never went below 40°C. I began to wonder what would happen unless I could do something more effective. I could not go on much longer like this, weak with fever, sleepless with pain.

A decision had to be made. That night must be the last with my arm in this condition. Land? I could not reach land in time. If by tomorrow things had not improved, I would have to amputate this useless arm, slung round my neck and already smelling of decay. It was dying and dragging me along with it. It was septicaemia. I could not give in without playing my last card.

There were several suppurating open wounds in the hands, but I could not localize the septic focus in this formless mass. With an axe, or my seaman's knife, at the elbow, at the shoulder, I knew not where or how, somehow I would have to amputate. I thought of the rudimentary material available for my purpose. The boat, her course, the voyage, no longer interested me. Feeble, feverish and unspeakably depressed as I was, my torments were increased by the endless rolling and pitching.

Slowly they went by, the hours of this long, long night; I yearned to sleep, to sleep for ever.

I was conscious of the inadequacy of my medical knowledge in this terrible dilemma. Amputation was the last hope, but ... would that be a solution? Was there not a risk of complications, of a more serious and virulent reinfection?

Out of the innermost secret recesses of my soul on that unforgettable night was born a fervent prayer—my only hope. I commended myself to little St. Teresa of Lisieux; I asked her help; and I lost consciousness.

I did not know how long it was; but at about 2 o'clock in the night of the 12th of July I awoke. The bunk was damp. Could a wave breaking on deck have got in through the portholes? But I knew that they were shut tight. As I moved, my arm felt lighter. Thank God! There was a gaping hole about three inches wide in my forearm; pus was flowing from it.

With the marlinspike of my seaman's knife I tried to get out the core of the abscess. It was a sinister scene under the dying light of the swinging lamp. I was too weak to stand the revolting sight of my arm; what I did was to apply a dressing of cotton-wool with cicatrizing oil. Then I gave myself a fourth injection.

That day, as if to celebrate my recovery, the sun rose and the wind veered to S. I began mechanically to put things shipshape; mopping up the honey, disinfecting the bunk, all with my left hand. The future seemed more promising. On the 13th I went back to the tiller, which I had hardly touched for several days.

# 7

# Prevailing Storms

Fresh squalls blew up and continued for a long time; they were characteristic of this zone of the South Atlantic.

The current was favourable. *Lehg II* was forging ahead under storm trysail, staysail and mizzen. Up to then, if the truth be told, I could not make up my mind what sail I ought to carry; I groped and experimented. In any case I could not stay on deck for long, my right arm being protected only by two dressings and a strip of material, which soon got sodden with pus. And I had to avoid getting it too wet.

The wind, which was now aft, required my constant attention and obliged me to attend to many other things apart from holding my course.

I remained at the helm until the first minutes of the 14th of July; then, as the wind did not serve to let the boat sail on her own under the amount of sail I was carrying, I lowered the storm trysail and went below for a well-earned rest. Thus *Lehg II* was heading a little into the current which, however, carried her towards the middle of the Atlantic so that, on the whole, she was on the right course.

In the morning I set the mainsail in order to make up for the delay caused by my illness. The wind was still W., blowing 30-35 knots. After drinking a bottle of chocolate and milk, I spent the day running through squalls. In the evening I was very tired and after dressing my arm—a matter which brooked no neglect—I decided to leave all sail set; every two hours I got up and went on deck to check the course.

The next day I took the helm early and stayed till midday. My arm was well enough for me to shoot the sun, which gave me 36° S. 41°50′ W. So I was 720 miles E. of Montevideo. As expected, I was still in the region of gales prevailing twenty-four days a month!

In the afternoon I baled and from time to time sat down on my bunk to rest and contemplate my surroundings; they seemed quite new to me. For the first time since my departure I was happy; I felt like a guest aboard of *Lehg II*.

The barometer stood at 780 and the temperature in the cabin at 15°C. Outside the sky was strangely overcast, but I was getting used to this outlook.

Next day I was surprised to see that the glass had dropped 5 mm., while the wind had changed to N.E. overnight. The temperature rose to 17°C. Later I was to realize that when the glass falls, the wind invariably shifts to the E., which was what I needed.

One day was not like another. I decided to use the storm trysail which, although it made me lose speed when the wind was light, allowed me to proceed normally when it got fresher. It saved me some worry as well as the labour of lowering the mainsail every evening. I had made a meagre run during the last twenty-four hours, only 55 miles. The wind shifted to the N.E. which obliged me to set a course to the N.; I went on deck to carry out this manoeuvre and was glad to find everything in perfect order.

No sign of life around me except, riding the waves, a great albatross (the species whose wing spread exceeds 10 feet). Up to the present, the Pilot Chart had given me an accurate forecast of the winds; it now indicated that I was leaving the zone of unfavourable weather. I cherished the hope that kinder winds would give me better average runs. The ground swell was very heavy; huge masses of water were moving towards the N.E. My arm was much better, so I took to setting the mainsail when possible and remaining prepared to lower it immediately in case of necessity.

The hours passed in the tranquillity that comes of contemplating always the same view. The mind drifts on erratically; it jumps without pause of reason from a sentiment to a question. Why did the *Copenhagen* sink? An iceberg encountered at night, with no time to steer clear? An idea came to me—what if I met an iceberg in the night? I remembered that at this time of the year there was no thaw. Or did the *Copenhagen* meet a 'white squall'—a wind that gives little notice of its arrival—which laid her on her beam ends. If she had her portholes open she could have filled and sunk to the bottom—some 2,000 fathoms hereabouts.

My thoughts wandered, hopping off hither and thither and returning without a pause for rest. It was hard for me to arrest even the memory of my mother for more than a few seconds. Everything was so strange. Yet my life on board had become quite well ordered; at night I shortened sail and went to sleep; in the morning I went back to my course and my work.

My position was 35°26′ S. by 34°45′ W., my speed very indifferent; some 55-65 miles a day, barely 2½ knots on an average.

The weather, which had been reasonably good for some time, got worse again. The swell was heavier and waves began to break. A wave breaking over the boat threw her on her beam ends and got into the cabin through a scuttle which I had forgotten to shut; the cockpit filled. It was really hellish weather. It was holding me back; I feared that the crossing would be a long one. I still had 900 miles to go before I got to the latitude of Tristan da Cunha. The shaking of the mizzen halyards sounded like a hammer striking an anvil. Waves were constantly breaking on board. I was sailing under the staysail and mizzen.

On the 24th the storm reached its climax; the W. wind was gusting over 70 knots. For thirty hours I kept looking astern, hoping that each blast would be the last; but the squalls followed each other continuously.

For the whole of this thirty-hour stretch I kept on humming the same song, a short catch that kept time with the endless repetition of the waves. I issued a challenge: let's see which will tire first, the weather or I. Wave after wave broke over my wretched waterlogged carcass. I chewed on a scrap of canvas impatiently. As each wave broke over me it would run down to my hand, mingle with a drop of blood and make a little pink puddle in a fold of my oilskin. But my lips still burbled on their monotonous little song; in spite of my irritation the notes came out in perfect cadence to fly down the wind.

The waves appeared over 50 feet high. They came on regularly and shot me down from their crest into the abyss. It was an infernal night; at times the black squall would close round me; and in that blackness one had to feel the wave coming, present the stern to it with a quick thrust of the tiller, then yaw back again. This game continued to the point of exhaustion.

At midnight I took advantage of a momentary lull to bring *Lehg II* up into the wind, and, leaving her to ride it out alone, I went below. The song had stopped; the weather had defeated it. I laid down on the floor of the cabin, sore and soaking wet. My hands, hardened to the cold, were no longer bleeding; they were as numbed as I was. So I spent an uneasy night, waking now and then with a start.

On the 26th of July a lull in the storm allowed me to make sail again and to mend a rent in the mizzen.

I found that in the last twenty-four hours I had made 170 miles with only the staysail and mizzen. At times I felt that the mast was coming down. But anyhow, that was over and done with, the prospects for the morrow were better and 170 miles was so much gained. I was now 1,320 miles from Montevideo; the calculation filled me with such joy that I forgave the wretched storm.

As I had taken nothing hot for several days and cherished succulent memories of my last 'feast', I managed with great efforts to heat up some soup. It was marvellous.

There remained two inconveniences, which had to be borne without any enthusiasm whatever: to bale the hull twice a day and endure the accursed squalls. And then the fatigue. It was quite enough to hold the tiller and to dress my wounds at regular intervals; as a rule I did not find it necessary to add cooking to my other troubles. Instead, I flung myself into the nearest corner to sleep; the need for repose was paramount and everything seemed comfortable so long as I was not working—even the hard planking. Thus, bit by bit, all the refinements of life ashore drop away from us!

Early on the 30th the sea went down; to the E. the sky cleared and the sun shone out.

I regretted that I had no means of announcing my position to those who were awaiting my arrival in South Africa. I had not shipped a wireless transmitter because, in time of war, it might have got me into trouble.

Since my departure I had not encountered a single ship. My solitude in the Atlantic was complete except for the albatrosses and some smaller birds with pretty check patterns under their wings. These were pintado petrels or Cape pigeons. I often saw them during my long hours at the helm.

While I was throwing overboard all the stores that had been spoilt by salt water, it occurred to me that I had not heard a human voice for thirty-one days—nothing but the wind and the slap and swish of water along the hull. It was a kind of living death. My eye would seek a focal point on the enormous leaden mass of the ocean, as it always does in town or country. Here there was nothing; and in the distance the sea itself merged with the sky.

For two days I had been running with all sail set under a southeasterly breeze and *Lehg II* kept on her course practically without attention. Night had fallen, yet at Buenos Aires it was still light; I was getting near the meridian of Greenwich. On the 3rd of August my position was 35° S. by 17° 23′ W.

At last I could undertake to remove the summary repair which was letting water in, and make a better job of it. I found that the nails had rusted, causing further small leaks. I changed the tingle, put on some fresh putty and replaced the nails with screws.

I was making 105 to 115 miles every twenty-four hours. The boat was not very well balanced under sail and had a tendency to luff, which made it necessary to use quite a lot of helm to keep her on course; I felt that I should set a storm jib and this made it necessary for me to work on the end of the bowsprit.

It is common practice when embarking on this operation to make a note in the log: 'Shall I get back?' Many have been carried away when indulging in this very dangerous exercise, as pitching plunges the bowsprit and the man on it into the waves.

After a long and wearisome hour of work, getting completely drenched, I returned to shelter having done the job; the storm jib was set; casting a last look at it before entering the cabin, I savoured triumph. To tell the truth, once it was over, the task that had looked practically impossible now seemed easy.

*Lehg II* now sailed better and had lost the tendency to luff; she was easier on the helm.

On the 5th of August a bank of cloud to the South indicated the presence of Tristan da Cunha about 200 miles away. This island is inhabited by a small colony and is only visited once a year, and that for a few hours, by a ship of the Royal Navy; but for me it represented humanity.

Why did I not call there after these thirty-eight days of isolation? For two reasons: currents and winds had carried me far to the north; and, as the island has no port, I could not have rested there. The revictualling ship has to anchor off shore and send in boats. Furthermore, I was in a hurry to get to Africa to have the boat repaired and let my arm heal properly. And I wanted to give some news of myself as soon as possible.

During the days of light breezes I spent most of my time in the cabin; when I came on deck I had the amusement of seeing some little grey petrels doing aerobatics round my rigging.

The current had carried me off course to the North, and if my meridian of the 6th of August was correct, I was 200 miles too high. That should teach me not to rely too much on my dead reckoning in future. The magnetic variation was very considerable: already 28° and increasing.

I was frequently becalmed and carried along by the current. It seemed to me, contrary to what I had been told, that these calms set in after the full moon; the storms we had to endure—we, for both the boat and I suffered in the struggle—appeared to grow with the crescent moon to a simultaneous climax.

On the 10th of August, thanks to heavy squalls from the South, I was able to make 110 miles with a double gain to the South and West. Latitude 34° gave me more wind; and on the 11th I was only 3°45′ W. of Greenwich. Slowly but surely I was nibbling away the first leg of my voyage.

Up to the present I had not seen the slightest sign of human life; so the sight of a bit of floating cork was an event; another one was the discovery of a tropical cockroach, an insect I have always detested and which I was surprised to find on board. Unfortunately I did not succeed in catching it.

Next day at 07.30 I encountered a monster, a grampus over 30 ft. long; and for the first time I saw a numerous flock of birds, a sign that land was nearer, though still over 1,000 miles away. But what did absolute distance matter, compared with this manifestation of life? I was getting forward, that was all that mattered. A few days more and I would meet people; I would talk and laugh and, most important of all to me, would have accomplished the first part of my task. As if to confirm the prospect, a baulk of timber floated by.

On the 13th of August at 02.00 I crossed the meridian of Greenwich and started to reckon from the East, a thing that had never happened to me before; I felt like a foreigner here! What a lot of things would have happened before I got back into W. longitude: I had still to cross a part of the Atlantic, the immense and desolate Indian Ocean, a part of the Tasman Sea and a large slice of the Pacific. Of course, I was not there yet, but all was going well. This new reckoning of longitude, the signs of human life, a good lunch well washed down (with lemonade)—what more could I ask of life? I noted in my log. I had never experienced so great and simple a joy since I had been at sea; so trivial, to tell the truth, since it caused me to write so naïve a sentence and to see the best of life in such details! There was not much in the way of deeper feelings left in me: to have found my way back to sea, to have saved the boat, so far: and to have experienced the miraculous healing of my arm after a fervent prayer to little St. Teresa of Lisieux.

Yes, all was well; *Lehg II* was sailing much better, took the waves more smoothly. I had become more accustomed to this way of life; in the height of the waves I no longer found awe but amusement: the waves were my friends and I was playing switchback on them.

Today, the 14th of August, I had beaten my own record of lone sailing. In 1932 I had taken forty-five days from the Canaries to the coast of Brazil; this trip so far was one day longer and it gave me a certain satisfaction, although I did not forget that it was the shortest leg of my 'impossible route'.

I had been able to take a series of sights which confirmed the fact that I was nearing the route of ships bound for South Africa. According to my calculation I should arrive on the 22nd; but well before that date I would sight ships. I looked forward to this moment both with joy and anxiety; joy at seeing human beings, anxiety to verify the accuracy of my navigation. I had only one chronometer of which I took the greatest care, winding it each day at the same time, 13.00 hours. Any irregularity would increase my error in longitude. As for latitude, I observed it by sextant with meticulous care. I was quite sure I was making no mistake and certain not to miss that appendage of Africa, the Cape of Good Hope; so sure that I allowed a margin of safety of only 20 miles S. of Cape Town. I could not permit myself an error which, if it proved fatal, would with justice be accounted serious negligence, unpardonable in this region.

Since the last storm the weather had remained reasonable but changeable, demanding perpetual vigilance. I could not rest and allow the boat to sail alone, except when the wind set in the South; so I looked forward with impatience to such moments.

# 8

# *Human Voices at Last*

I do not know how many hours I had been asleep. It seemed to be about dawn. I turned over again. But ... what was that? No, no, impossible! And it was *not* a a dream ... I heard a siren.

The second blast was longer.

I leapt from my bunk like a jack-in-the-box, banging my head on the panel.

Hurrah! about a hundred metres astern the enormous dark olive hull of a ship making towards me. The deck was crowded with officers and sailors shouting and gesticulating. I motioned them to try to come alongside. Slowly and carefully the ship came abreast of me. Only then did I think of speaking to the crew in English, the language of the sea:

'Captain, my position, please?'

I got a reply, but it was not what I wanted to know. I was so disappointed at not getting the information that I imagined that they had not understood. I collected a speaking-trumpet and put my question again. They only replied with words which did not make sense to me and at all events were not what I wanted: I needed figures, not words.

Interminable, useless seconds passed. I thought of asking them whether they spoke Italian and got a loud 'No' in reply. Then I saw the name '*Pyratiny*'. . . . I tried in Portuguese and they replied in the same language:

'Why didn't you come out when we blew the siren?'

'Tell me, Captain, do you never sleep?'

'Ah, you were asleep!'

I asked for confirmation of my position but was told that I could not have it. It was wartime ... they were not allowed to give information.

In the meantime, a member of the crew had recognized me and soon everyone on board knew who I was. It was a Brazilian ship. I asked them to send the following message to the Argentine Minister of Marine when they next touched port: '*Lehg* sailing nothing to report'.

Before we parted, I insisted:

'I'm at 34° S. by 6° 15' E., am I not? About 700 miles from the Cape of Good Hope?'

'No,' replied the captain, but without conviction, 'but carry on as you are. You're on the right course.'

'Yes,' someone corrected, rather irritably, 'provided the wind stays as it is.'

More salutes; we parted and she went her way.

From time to time I popped out of the cabin to convince myself that I had not been dreaming. No, there were the masts and funnel, gradually getting smaller. Soon there was only a smudge ahead on the horizon.

I was left with the happy feeling of having spoken and the satisfaction of knowing from several indications that my navigation had been correct.

The night was calm. The moon appeared on the horizon. I looked into the depths, trying to distinguish something. Everything was phosphorescent. Fish were dashing about: some of the bolder ones passed under the keel. A kaleidoscopic world of strange light.

The whole night would not have been enough to appease my curiosity. But the calm would not last, could not last, in these regions. In fact, it was rather abnormal. The barometer, which always knows best, started to fall. And now a violent East wind started blowing in my teeth—a rare phenomenon in this region and exactly what I did not want.

But I was so accustomed to inconveniences that I accepted this curb on my impatience in the same way that I accepted the routine of baling—which I have passed over in silence but which unfortunately was still necessary—and that of the dressings which continued as well. Sometimes an awkward movement would give the damaged limb a knock. But all that was nothing compared to the satisfaction of seeing the boat rising through the masses of spray that tried to smother her.

For the storm prophesied by the barometer was well and truly there. Everything was creaking. I spent long hours at the helm, with all sail set, except that the mainsail was replaced by the storm trysail. The waves were battering *Lehg II*.

In that series of squalls the only hours had for sleep were from 02.00 till daybreak. During that time I lowered the trysail. I lost 30 miles by doing so, but I had to have more rest; every time I had tried to stay more than thirty hours at the helm the result had been bad.

On the 20th I noticed that the mizzen was coming unsewn in some places. The wind, now blowing from the West with furious squalls, did not permit me to mend it, and I had to wait for the early morning lull to do so. Having done the job, I went below; but at three a terrible crash made me feel that *Lehg II* was sinking. I was in my bunk surrounded by bottles, broken glass and tins of food which had been hurled at me. Fortunately none of these projectiles had hit me fair and square; it might have killed me.

The hull was horizontal and a torrent of water was pouring through the hatch; slowly she straightened up. It was easy to guess what had happened: carrying so little canvas the boat had got blanketed under a breaking wave, which laid her on her beam ends.

Everything below was in a horrible mess. Tins of butter were mixed up with needles and thread. Partitions had been torn out; water, swilling to and fro, was wrecking the cabin. I set to work.

By dawn order was more or less restored. On deck the only sign of the accident was that the metal weather-vane from the masthead had been carried away.

I was 210 miles from my first landfall. During the day I saw one ship, but very far away.

During the night of the 22nd of August the weather improved and invited a contemplative mood. At peaceful moments I find that daydreaming is a spiritual need. I watched the flight of clouds, the relics of the gale, as they drifted slowly eastward; I should have liked to go with them to see what awaited me farther on. I wished for the power to amend or avoid so many errors, to be able to direct lost humanity on to the right path, to achieve something beyond normal human capacity. . . . I felt an urge for unity and harmony with the majesty of the starlit night around me; and words were pitifully inadequate, almost an insult to the grandeur there unfolded. I sang an Ave Maria.

Reality brought me tumbling back to earth. I saw to the S.E. two ships without lights and tried to attract their attention with my electric torch. I imagine that they must have taken me for a camouflaged submarine, for their smoke showed that they were crowding on steam in their haste to avoid me. And soon I was alone again on the sea, looking at the stars beyond my masthead with its missing pennant, the only sign of an incident that might have meant the end of the journey. Perhaps something of me went overboard with that little sheet of metal?

I went below, and before getting into my bunk I knelt down as I did every evening: time for prayers.

When I made the first entries in my log for the 31st of August I certainly had no idea what this day would bring, nor that it would be a milestone, for ever memorable in my life as a sailor.

It was a stormy daybreak; the sun shone fitfully and the sea was getting up under the sou'wester. Between two waves a cachalot whale appeared and vanished rapidly. But astern . . . ? Could I be mistaken? I thought I had a glimpse of a ship. I was more often in the hollow of the waves than on their crest and it was hard to be certain.

But I was not left long in doubt. It was certainly a ship, but she was light, empty. She must have been making over 25 knots in such a sea. What could she be? At times it seemed to me that she was a yacht. She was pitching heavily, appearing and vanishing, but getting rapidly closer. I hoisted Argentine colours and got out my speaking-trumpet. And now she tackled me in Morse with a Scott lamp. I could not reply; I waved my arms to try to make them understand.

The warship, for such she was, came closer. The officers on the bridge asked me my name in English. Now, I had learnt that language, rather badly, at school, and had not spoken it for over twenty years. We had some difficulty in making ourselves understood.

'Where are you bound?'

'The Cape.'

'Why?' I was asked rather testily.

'To rest.'

'Why in that port?'

'There is no other ahead of me.'

'Why choose that one?'

I explained that after doing some 4,000 miles I felt I deserved a rest.

I thought I saw a smile.

At this precise moment I was rather shattered to see something emerging from the waves quite close to me. It was a submarine.

The questions went on. I then asked whether it would not be possible to speak French. One officer volunteered to interpret but soon gave it up, explaining that he had not spoken that language for years. Then a voice, not from the the bridge but from aft, remarked:

'How goes it, old man?' in perfect Spanish.

The first words in my language for fifty-five days! All eyes turned to the stern of the ship, even those of the submarine crew huddled on the conning tower. With these words, which only I had understood—and with what joy!—everyone burst out laughing and gesticulating. The humble sailor, our interpreter, suddenly became important.

No machine gun ever spoke so fast as I. My interlocutor was riddled, harassed, overwhelmed with words. I told him where I came from, who I was, what I was doing or not doing, what I wanted and what I didn't want . . . but suddenly a wave made me lose my balance and deposited me in the cockpit. A gale of laughter arose— I joined in.

The commander asked whether I needed anything. No thanks. When did I expect to make land? That same night.

'Impossible,' he replied. 'You're still over 50 miles away.'

'I shall be in port this very night,' I insisted.

They told me the way—I was on the right course, and after friendly greeting drew away. The submarine, surfaced, passed *Lehg II* hull to hull; we were evidently going the same way.

The weather, the heavy seas, the wind, everything looked rosy. I felt happy, full of love and life. I thought of the pride all my Latin American brethren would feel when they heard that the South Atlantic had been conquered.

It was 16.00 hours; flocks of birds were wheeling round me, birds of species that never go far from land; below me the immense swell of that Cape which was once called the Cape of Storms.

On the leaden horizon to the N.E. I seemed to distinguish a patch that was darker than the rest. I looked, I stared, and thought that I could at last identify Table Mountain.

Land. For fifty-five days I had seen none. The miracle had happened. It was true! Before my hungry eyes the mountain was growing, taking shape; thickening clouds came and veiled the summit but not the foot. I took cross-bearings. Already my mind was at rest; I had made landfall and it didn't matter what time I arrived; I was there.

It was a wise precaution to take bearings, for the land was soon obscured and I was not to see it before nightfall.

*Lehg II* ws spanking along.

Something was floating ahead; as I came closer I saw two seals resting on a baulk of wood. At the sight of me they dived.

Dusk was falling; I passed a mine-sweeper manoeuvring and we dipped flags to each other. But the swell was so heavy that we lost sight of each other at times, less than a hundred yards apart. It got dark; there were many bright lights abeam; it looked like Rio de Janeiro bay. Bit by bit I advanced, hearing sounds of traffic while wind and waves grew less.

As I rounded Greenpoint, two searchlights, one from the top of Table Mountain, the other from Robben Island, were focused on me. No doubt to identify me.

A cutter approached in the darkness; someone hailed me:

'Your name?'

I replied; the vessel saluted and went about. Farther in a little tug offered to pilot me. I declined with thanks.

'You can't come in without a pilot,' he yelled.

I pointed out that I knew my way and that I was a yacht, not a merchantman. I had not forgotten my little store of £10: a pilot would cost £5, and my capital would be halved.

The pilot went off swearing at me; he could not have sailed very many seas.

In the meantime I was nearing the port; its red light had been visible for the last two hours. The lights of the harbour launch appeared ahead; I could hear the pilot telling how his services had been refused.

'Well, it's a yacht.'

'These *verdomde* sailing ships always make us lose money,' he grumbled into the darkness.

The crew of the harbour launch welcomed me and came with me into the port, where I made fast alongside an enormous vessel undergoing repairs. The crew leapt aboard and helped me to lower the mainsail: the staysail had been set for fifty-five days.

I did not feel tired at all. It was 22.00 hours. In a few moments I was boarded by a whole series of official craft; the Harbour Master, the Customs, the police and the camaraderie that unites all sailors in the world took over at once.

Half an hour later I felt that I was dreaming. On board of a motionless *Lehg II* more than ten persons were celebrating her success in rum that had crossed the Atlantic. The bottles passed from mouth to mouth; we drank and drank again. With the stub of the last cigarette of three packets smoked without stopping, I lit a South African cigarette that was passed to me.

At three in the morning these new friends departed; I remained alone and disposed myself to enjoy my rest.

It was far from perfect.

Many nights were to pass before I stopped rushing up on deck with my heart in my mouth, to make sure that I really was in port.

# 9

# *Start Again*

The next morning saw the procession of journalists and photographers. They were all full of congratulations.

With several friends from the British Navy I went ashore. My legs felt very odd—was it an earthquake? No; *Lehg II* who, I could hardly realize it, had crossed this incredible stretch of sea, my darling *Lehg II* was swaying peacefully at her moorings in the calm water of the harbour.

We called at the Harbour Master's office and an officer began to explain how to bring my documents up to date. But his chief interrupted, pushing a pass in front of him.

'This is for Mr. Dumas. He can come and go as he pleases.'

I was taken to the officers' mess and went to have a wash: one handed me a towel, another a comb, a third lit my cigarette. They waited on me hand and foot. The Garrison Commander and the S.N.O. were there; a special cocktail was mixed in my honour. The S.N.O had read the book of my first voyage.[1]

Lunch followed. I was being overwhelmed with kindness without being able to express my gratitude properly.

I was called to the telephone. The telephone? For me? Who in this country can be ringing me up? I was afraid of being unable to cope with a telephone conversation in English, but it was the Argentine Consul, who soon joined us.

At the end of the meal I noticed for the first time that people were staring at me with curiosity. My God! I had driven in a car, been about in the town, met all the V.I.P.s, had lunch in a first-class restaurant . . . dressed in tattered old trousers, a pullover with the elbows out, a handkerchief round my neck and no haircut. The next day's papers described me as being 'picturesquely dressed, with the air of a filibuster'.

I had made a hard-and-fast plan: to stay twenty days at the Cape and not do anything about the boat until the last week. I wanted to put work on one side completely for a while. I was able to moor *Lehg II* in a quiet spot near the quay and spent the first few days looking round.

[1]'Solo Rumbo a la Cruz del Sur.'

242

Cape Town lies in practically the same latitude as Buenos Aires and Montevideo, and the climate is excellent except when the East wind stirs up coal dust in the port area. It is a modern city with a very important port and a network of magnificent roads leading to practically all parts of the Union of South Africa and running through varied landscapes of surprising beauty.

My South American eyes were caught particularly by the trolley-buses in the central part of the town; practically all double-deckers with women as conductors. Another characteristic detail was the helmets worn by the police, as in London.

The segregation between white and coloured is very marked, to the point where teashops display a notice 'Reserved for Europeans'. The buses and cinemas for the whites may not be used by coloured people, who have their own.

A bar, run by an Englishman who talked only with one side of his mouth and smiled only with half his face (probably so that the other half should not know), displayed the same sign. But . . . the most curious circumstance is that adjoining this bar was another, identical in form and decoration, communicating with the first by a door situated behind the barman. One place was for whites, the other for blacks. Two halves of bar, two halves of expression . . .

I was never able to determine which side caught the barman's smile and which his straight face.

# 10

## ... And Carry On

From the world I had left behind me came news: telegrams from Buenos Aires and Montevideo. They were joined by letters of congratulation from South Africa.

I was particularly struck by one of these; it was obviously written by a cultured woman.

She belonged to a seafaring family from Holland and showed her enthusiasm for everything connected with the sea. She lived with her family in a villa nestling close to the sea in a quiet little spot, and asked me to call.

On a sunny afternoon I decided to go and make her acquaintance. The spot—Camps Bay—and the villa made a perfect picture, a little world of its own. Quite close by, the tired Atlantic swell rolled in to die, gently, on the beach. A spot one would like to come back to.

I was received by a fair-haired young woman, some 30 years of age, who was fond enough of nature to go swimming even in winter. She had taken this house in exchange for a finer one on the hillside which she had previously owned, to be nearer the sound of the sea which had an irresistible ancestral appeal to her. She had dreams of living in the Seychelles, near the Equator in the Indian Ocean; she knew them well and spoke with enthusiasm of their beauty and their pleasant climate.

The company of a person with such a taste for beauty and so much understanding of the things that meant much to me was most agreeable; and this house was a refuge for me in days of uncertainty.

My new friend spoke several languages and possessed a very comprehensive background of travel and culture. One day she said:

'Why go on with your voyage?'

Would I not like to settle there?

What she could not understand was that my placidity was that of a calm at sea; it would not last. And whilst reason and inclination urged me to stay, I looked for a way of breaking the spell.

I could neither promise to stay nor say that I was going.

I remembered the proverb: 'Never let your friend's hand get hot in yours'. This calm sea, this lovely spot, this mildness, was balm to me; it mingled with the picture of that island in the Indian Ocean, a dream rather than anything earthly. Why go on with the voyage? Because ...

because nothing else would do; because there remained in my hand a little of the warmth of other hands, that warmth that strikes deeper and deeper till it reaches the heart. I confessed to myself that one day I should say '*à demain*' and that tomorrow would never come.

One evening I was trying to describe our pampa and reading passages of 'Martin Fierro', haltingly translated to illustrate my meaning: I was sitting under the light of a single lamp, which left the rest of the room in semi-darkness. I lifted my eyes to rest for a moment.

Outside, the moonlight on the sea made a track to the West, as if to show me where my home lay. A path of light. . . . A sign, but I hardly knew what it meant at that moment. There was the West, that was where I had to go. And if I did not get there I would get nowhere. Neither the harmony of the South African night on the white beach, nor the generous hospitality, like calm waters where my spirit could rest—nothing could hold me. I had sailed from Buenos Aires into the rising sun; now the moon seemed to be showing me this point of departure and demanding my return. The moment had come. I said '*à demain*'; it was 'goodbye'.

I have kept two letters, the prologue and the epilogue of this moment of my life. The first is the invitation; the second says:

'Lord Byron affirmed that in the course of his life he had only known three hours of happiness. I have had many more: I am happier than he was. I savoured them consciously and lost nothing of them. I understood that the hours you were giving me would destroy in a few moments all those—and they were not many—that I had known before. But I felt that it was better so; and for you I ask only the greatest happiness of all, which is the pursuit of your ideal.'

# 11

# *Buenas Tardes, Señor!*

On one of the last afternoons of my stay at the Cape, I visited my friends of the Argentine ship *Menendez* which was about to sail. I was overwhelmed with congratulations and good wishes and they promised to testify to my good morale when they arrived at Buenos Aires; furthermore the captain gave me some canvas to repair my sails and various bits of ironmongery that might come in useful.

As I was going back to *Lehg II's* berth, not far away, with my parcel under my arm, I heard a voice which said in good Castilian:

'Buenas tardes, Señor!'

I stared at the speaker, for I thought I already knew everyone in the town who spoke Spanish; he must be a South African.

'May I come with you?' he continued.

'With pleasure! Just let me put this parcel aboard, and we'll go somewhere.'

And so it was. We started back through the security areas of the port, barred to the general public but for which he, being a ship's chandler, held a permit. I then learnt that he had spent thirty years in Patagonia. He spoke with deep feeling and enthusiasm of the time he had spent in the Argentine and asked me to have a cognac.

We entered one of the numerous bars; friends arrived and the cognac soon multiplied itself by eight, and all the languages of the world were exploding round us like a basket of fireworks.

One wore a fez, another a white turban, this one a wide sombrero, the next a cap. The atmosphere was very rich and colourful; it was like a congress of survivors from assorted shipwrecks.

Alcohol spontaneously generates good fellowship, especially in the presence of memories in common. And my companion insisted on taking me home with him to Bella Vista in the suburbs. The train we had to take ran through the cemetery, where there are no fewer than three stops. It is said to be the largest graveyard in the world.

We came to a pleasant house.

'Before we start,' said he, 'I want to show you something that will shake you no little.'

From a drawer of his desk he produced twelve Argentine passports.

'My sons,' he said proudly.

Presently the owners of these documents arrived, twelve magnificent young men born in Patagonia. Thanks to one of them, I heard something that I had missed for a very long time, tangoes played on the victrola. A strange sensation—a ghost from the past which one wants to smother and cherish at the same time, which gives pain rather than pleasure. In far-off ports I generally try to get outside myself—outside my memories and my feelings; and that is why I try to interest myself in other people's problems. I therefore listened with great attention when the lady of the house told me of her thirty years in Argentina. She went there young, to seek fortune; she came back home with twelve sons, her only achievement and the only rewards of a long and arduous life.

# 12

# *Washing Up*

It was midday. Tomorrow I was to go back the sea.

The sun shone out of a leaden sky. I was washing crockery in the cabin.

*Lehg II* was moored to a little wooden pier belonging to the Lowus company; its proprietor had given me some waterproof paint, which I needed very badly, in exchange for a bottle of whisky.

The damage forward had been so perfectly repaired that no trouble was to be anticipated. Two fishermen had served my shrouds with sheepskin so that the sails should not get stained with rust.

All this cost me £7 and the necessary charts were another £10 and I had £2 left.

The prospects of the 'impossible route' across the Indian Ocean were not at all encouraging. The distance was 7,400 miles; and from what I had been able to gather, there was little hope of overcoming so many difficulties. The numerous records of voyages with a tragic end in this zone gave me no rosy outlook for the future.

The Pilot Chart, that precious and indispensable compendium for the navigator, which I carried on every voyage, gives for September-December a probable mean of twenty-seven days per month of winds Force 8 (37-44 knots). And it was precisely in those months that I was to attempt the crossing of the whole breadth of the Indian Ocean.

But this was not all. To these twenty-seven days of gales per month must be added the risk of cyclones in the region between 100° and 175° E., which includes the Tasman Sea by New Zealand. In these cyclones the wind force rarely falls below 60 knots (Force 11); and through that zone I must pass. This picture should convey what one means by 'living to keep watch and keep the sails in repair'.

In consequence of the relatively shallow water above the submarine plateau, these winds whip up the sea and create breaking waves which may exceed 40 feet or even 50 feet in height. In the immensity and solitude of this ocean, the second leg of my voyage, I would not encounter any place to put in nor any shelter. On my route lay only two islets, St. Paul and Amsterdam Islands. In case of dire necessity I could indeed take refuge there: on the N. side of the crater of St. Paul there is a store of food and clothing for the shipwrecked; and similar facilities at Amsterdam. But these islands are inhabited only by sea birds, have no beaches on which to land, and above all, one would have to be very lucky to get there.

In this zone the magnetic variation is considerable and magnetic storms severe, the variation reaching 54° W., which necessitates steering a course of 144° by the compass in order to sail due E. This variation changes very rapidly, so that I should have to calculate my route carefully every two or three days, at the same time making a correction for drift to leeward, under penalty of prolonging still further this interminable and wearisome stage.

It was an almost impossible enterprise, but in spite of everything I kept smiling.

What a difference between this trip and a crossing in the region of trade winds, where the boat is quietly, gently wafted across a warm sea; where life flows by in tropical somnolence with marine fauna for company and entertainment during the long hours of watch-keeping, and the journey soon ends in some happy island covered with coconut palms and bordered with beaches of coral sand. And then—to live for the day, far from conventions and civilization so-called, from ready-made ideas, taxation, and especially from the clash of personalities so painful to the sensitive. Lucky are those strong enough to break loose from habit and escape the dreariness of dying on their feet or existing as 'zombies'. But how many reach the end of their life without ever having lived! Not only to embark on the endless tracks of the sea, but to follow the road of everyday life in simplicity.

Thus I meditated sombrely on the eve of my departure, face to face with the monstrous reality written on the next page of my dance programme—the *valse triste* of this 7,400 mile stage eastward, a sequence of bitter unsmiling tomorrows—unable to define clearly why it was my choice. Tomorrow I should set out on the inhospitable road that no lone navigator had ever followed. When I went to buy charts the old skipper in charge of them said:

'I knew that you were bound to roll up here. Alain Gerbault came to see me. Like everyone else who has sailed a bit, he had a project, a reason for going to sea again some day. He said to me: "Do you know that there is an almost unkown little island in the Indian Ocean, covered with seals. Work it out; at £5 a pelt we'll be rich. . . ." We'll go there after the war; will that suit you?'

So I went on washing crocks on board *Lehg II*. I looked through the porthole. On the quay several weary-looking negroes, waiting to be hired, were chatting. One of them was humming a weird tune.

I heard the sound of engines and turned round to see a launch enter the port and manoeuvre to lay alongside the quay. I noticed that her ensign was at half-mast; there must be dead aboard. Some marines were standing on deck with flowers in their hands.

When she had made fast, a lorry arrived and stretchers were brought ashore; bodies were swaying under the blankets. *C'est la guerre.*

*Monday 14 September.*
*Lehg II* was waiting. With my fellow countryman Glessmann, I went to the grocer's. There was such a lot to take. But there were serious obstacles: rationing and my £2. All that I could buy barely filled a carrier bag. Of course I had basic rations aboard; but I saw many things in the shop that would be very welcome on a run of over 7,000 miles! I had to content myself with some preserves and cheese; and when my friend offered to pay I did not refuse. . . .

Once more the hour of parting was about to strike; the minutes were running out. Quickly I set all sail, pausing to greet the Portuguese and Spanish Consuls as well as the representative of the Royal Cape Yacht Club, most of whose members were serving. Other friends were looking on and drinking in every detail. The Argentine Consul coiled down a rope, no doubt in memory of his sailings on the River Plate. Embraces, handshakes, goodbyes that stuck in the throat, and at 13.00 *Lehg II* started off slowly from the berth where she had remained for twenty days.

Workmen stopped work for a moment to wave to me, some climbing to the bridge, others lined up on deck. I was going so slowly as to get a panoramic view of this section of the port. Between the sheds I could see the masts of that famous sailing vessel the *Pamir*. As I neared the pier in the afternoon sun, a group of friends rushed to the pierhead, and Bill Amman, an enthusiastic yachtsman, could not restrain a cry of admiration.

'How fine she looks with all sail set!'

It was quite true, she was lovely. I looked at her with a certain pride myself.

I was about to pass the pier when a British warship came in. As she passed I saluted her ensign; on his bridge the commander stood to attention and saluted me with a fatherly smile.

From land came cries of 'Cheerio, cheerio, cheerio!', the farewells and good wishes of my friends, the stevedores, sailors and what have you.

To get out from under the lee of the land, to catch the wind and get searoom before starting on the high seas, I tacked. This brought me close to a fine American six-master, with a name that thrilled me: it was *Tango*. Some of the crew who had been lying on deck got up as I approached.

'Where are you bound?' they asked.

'For New Zealand.'

'Good luck!'

They could imagine what was in store for me. They added:

'The weather's just right for you.'

(They say that because they long to put to sea themselves; they had been anchored there for several months.)

Penguins and seals were playing round my boat. At 17.00 hours the fine houses of Green Point were abeam. A patrol vessel dashed up, saluted and went off again. The breeze was light and veering to the S.W. As night drew on it got lighter until I was practically becalmed.

Outward bound ships passed me at speed and I took pleasure in contemplating the lights ashore.

As the moon set I raised a little breeze that helped me on. Near me I heard a seal breathing. I tried to go up into the wind to be clear of all obstacles, but I had to struggle against a strong current.

The next day I got to the level of Duyker Point, but was becalmed in the Atlantic current that switches to the North along the African coast and could make no headway; in twenty-four hours I had only progressed some 10 miles.

In the afternoon deceptive breeze gave me a slender hope that I might round the Cape of Good Hope, only some 20 miles away, by midnight. But after passing Hout Bay I was becalmed in front of Slang Kop lighthouse; this obliged me to spend the night on deck because of the traffic. Enormous masses of steel hurtled by without lights, only the sound of the engines announcing their coming.

From the coast I could hear the singing of birds mingling with the other noises of the immense African continent. Shore lights were twinkling under a blaze of stars. This was a generous compensation for my solitude. The dream-like spectacle left me in a kind of trance. *Lehg II* was barely leaving a phosphorescent wake.

On the 16th of September the sunrise was very pale. After fifty hours' calm the wind set in the north. *Lehg II* began to get headway, and I tried to make up for lost time. Hout, Chapman's Peak and Slang Kop were left behind. On my port bow a high promontory jutted into the sea; the Cape of Good Hope, discovered by Vasco da Gama in 1497 on his way to India. This 'cape of storms' was for a long time an unavoidable passage for all the ships of the world.

On this sunless morning its silhouette stuck out harsh and jagged against the sky, cold lines on a cold morning.

Excitement grew as I approached it. The swell was getting up; as it came from astern it helped the wind to carry me on. The cape was now abeam, but I had to continue steering South for half a mile in order to clear two rocks that mount guard seaward. I took a bearing and when I was sure of being clear of danger I tacked due East.

Soon a line of wind-torn breakers showed that I had passed the rocks. The historic moment had come: it was 10.00 hours on the 16th and I had rounded the Cape of Good Hope. Thus the Atlantic crossing was truly finished and I set forth on the impossible journey across the Indian Ocean. Up to the present no one had ventured alone into the regions I was about to cross.

# 13

## *The Worst of All*

I had experienced hardship in the Atlantic, and perhaps that gave me confidence for the future; but the reality, the frightening reality of what lay before me, was to surpass anything that I had experienced before in my life as a sailor. It was more painful and more terrifying than the short passage through the Bay of Biscay on my 1932 cruise.

With all sail set and a fair wind the boat was running at full speed. The swell was irregular and got heavier as I passed Rocky Bank. Two patrol vessels, put out from False Bay, sailed towards me, but they soon gave up the attempt on account of the gigantic swell and returned to the shelter of the land.

In front lay Hangklip Point; farther on Danau, the detached end of a mountain range, jutted out into the sea.

In accordance with my programme I tried by every measure to hug the coast as close as possible, so that when I came to Needle Point the current off the reef, which reaches 4 knots (100 miles in twenty-four hours), should not carry me too far South. The swell was much stronger there; it was already very noticeable here, in a depth of 30 fathoms.

Night fell and I could not leave the tiller for a moment. I was driving with all sail set, without lights, through the inky night and the storm. The glass was falling; the gale had not yet reached its climax. If there was to be any change it would certainly not be for the better. Every sign indicated that I had the worst to fear; I had no confidence whatever.

Out of the trough of the waves dead ahead emerged the dim outline of a ship on the opposite course. She was, of course, without lights and pitching badly. She was making heavy weather, for she was head on to the seas.

Gradually she disappeared astern.

On the horizon to windward, flashes of light from the Needles lighthouse cut through the darkness. As I drew near I got the feeling of blows struck into the empty air, beams that tried in vain to pierce the darkness. This is an occulting light with three eclipses; at times the rays of light seemed like sentient beings, struggling desperately to survive this black night.

I was getting on well to the East. At midnight the wind suddenly dropped, and before I could note what was going on a squall from the South struck me. With it came low cloud; and soon the flashes from the lighthouse disappeared in the murk. Visibility was very bad and I feared that, with this change of conditions, the wind might pick me up and cast me ashore in Struys Bay.

I set about shortening sail in order to get into the wind and so away from the coast.

I had not slept for many hours, to all intents and purposes since I left port.

On the 17th at 03.00 hours I could no longer keep awake; I decided to sleep in spite of the weather and lowered the mainsail. And so I let her sail on alone, waking every now and then to see what was happening.

At daybreak I was able to return to the helm and to check my course properly. I saw an enormous whale. I had sailed 143 miles in twenty-four hours.

In the afternoon I heard the drone of an aircraft and saw a bomber flitting through the clouds. No doubt a patrol; he flew over me and went his way.

Land had disappeared; I was not to see it again for several months.

# 14

## *Legends of the Sea*

On the night of the 19th of September I was sailing in the region where the ghost of the phantom ship has been seen.

She was known as the *Flying Dutchman*. The captain is said to have been seen on stormy nights driving his crew to pile on sail in order to round the Cape of Good Hope.

All sailors tell these stories; and things are actually experienced at sea that seem fantastic to landsmen.

Take for example the case of the brig *Mary-Céleste*, found on the high sea with all sail set and no trace of a human being aboard. The table was properly set and a meal was ready in the galley; everything was in order. This mystery has never been satisfactorily solved.

Another story which I can now tell (for at the time I should have been taken for a lunatic) happened to me ten years ago.

I was two days from Arcachon when one night, off Bilbao, the silence of the sea was broken by a conversation which I heard distinctly; it was almost monosyllabic.

Two people appeared to be speaking.

I was astounded. I asked myself how they could have come aboard, for I had not left the boat for twenty-four hours previous to sailing.

They could only be hidden forward in a locker that I never used, with a small door which separated it completely from the rest of *Lehg I*.

'Listen,' said a voice with a strong Spanish accent, 'I'm going to look for something to eat.'

'Shut up; he'll hear you.'

'No, he won't.'

It was nearly 30 feet from the tiller to that point, which was also hidden by the mast; the fore hatch might well have been open.

At the moment I did not dare to speak, but I sought for a logical explanation of the presence of these individuals.

One of them frequently asked for cigarettes. I also heard a number of unusual sounds which satisfied me that there were strangers aboard.

Twenty-four hours went by; the storm which had blown up did not permit me to leave the helm. My own struggle for life, if it did not make me forget what was going on, at least inspired me with pity for my stowaways; as it was practically impossible to hang on aft, I could imagine what it was like for them forward. I resolved to hail them as soon as the storm had blown over and put them ashore at some port or other.

The wind lasted three days and three nights. Three feet of water was playing hell below.

On the night I was nearing Ferrol, having rounded Cape Ortegal, I called out to them to come forth from their hiding-place. No one answered. I went on, explaining that I understood; I went below and, armed with a gaff, searched every cranny where they might have hidden. I struck matches; I found nothing.

Returning to the helm, very puzzled, I could see no other solution to the mystery than that they had tried to swim ashore.

After this happened to me, nothing could surprise me any longer. What can arise out of the depths of the sea? Who knows what lies beyond this life? Who can sound the unknown? Our poor senses are feeble instruments.

There is St. Elmo's fire, seen by many sailors, which announces a storm. And I have myself heard many voices at sea accompanied by the sound of bells. There is a state of mind, peculiar to the sailor, which is simple and human because it does not deal in subtleties. Alone at sea and near to God, who can know whether the environment is not in tune with strange forces?

On the stormy night when I recalled these memories I was sailing in the area where legend—unless it be reality—places the appearances of the phantom ship. They are actually recorded on one of my charts.

The new day dawned reluctantly. My boat was running with all sail set in a stormy sea; my position was 36°10′ S. by 24°45′ E. The patrolling aircraft went by, as it did every morning. That day I managed to salute the crew by waving my arm.

I had not been entirely successful in overcoming the current that was carrying me towards the South.

I escaped from the helm for a few moments to see whether *Lehg II* had made much water in the last twenty-four hours. Alas! I was distressed to find that the bilge was full; I could not understand it till I discovered that it was fresh water. The hammering we had undergone had started the rivets of the forward tank, which held 40 gallons. A rapid calculation showed that all I had left was a 20 gallon tank, a 2 gallon demijohn and a 10 gallon breaker. I should have to make do with that.

I went back to keep watch and saw that the wind had dropped. The clouds were very low and I was frightened to see three waterspouts approaching from the North. The clouds were whirling as if boiling in a gigantic kettle. I reckoned the diameter of each spout at 300 yards; they were spinning furiously and sucking up water. It is not known with certainty whether these spouts go right up to the cloud mass. The spectacle, terrifying as it is, has a certain grandiose beauty.

They were bearing down on me rapidly. I tacked in order to avoid them, but there was so little wind that this manoeuvre went slowly. Seconds and minutes passed in trepidation; but fortunately the spouts went by at a distance of some 500 yards. My breathing returned to normal; the skirts of death had brushed me.

It is said that an American warship went deliberately through the centre of a waterspout so that her captain could assess the possible damage; it seems that, apart from two smashed lifeboats, the super-structure suffered only minor damage. But is must not be forgotten that the ship was protected by her length. *Lehg II* was only 9 metres 55 long, and if the spout had caught her she would have whirled like the sea-water. I prefer not to think of the result.

I tried to organize for the best in the circumstances, but perfection was unattainable because the situation kept changing. I stayed at the helm as long as possible in order to reach New Zealand before the cyclone season. My daily runs were 120 to 150 miles (an average of 5 to 6 knots), which was excellent. In order to achieve this I had to crowd on all canvas—on this infernal ocean—whilst I was at the helm. The waves were breaking on the whole surface of the sea. I could not avoid those that broke on the deck, drenching me completely and wrecking my outer clothing.

In the cabin the temperature remained about 15°C., but on the deck the cold struck through the Balaclava cap on my head.

I was wearing several pullovers under my oilskin, but the latter was in such a state that it was no longer any protection.

The wind stayed in the West. Weather permitting, usually at dawn, I made myself a large cup of chocolate, accompanied by dates and sea biscuit well buttered. This rather odd diet, supplemented with bar chocolate, kept me in excellent physical condition. I was strong and in perfect health and did not appear to be losing weight. I corrected the diet by adding vitamins A and C to take the place of fresh food and keep scurvy at bay. Before leaving Buenos Aires I had been examined by five doctors, who affirmed that I had nothing to worry about: man and boat were both seaworthy.

For several days I had not seen an aircraft nor indeed any sign of human life.

One day I remembered that it was my forty-second birthday and decided to celebrate. I prepared a feast; to begin with, the inevitable chocolate for breakfast. Then in the evening, a delicious soup of vegetable meal, jam, sweets and other delicacies, washed down with champagne.

I was running against a strong current which worked up the sea. I hoped that as I gained longitude it would be less strong and the sea less choppy.

The spells of bad weather in the part of the Atlantic I had left in my wake and in this part of the Indian Ocean had nothing in common with those of the Bay of Biscay. The mean depth of those oceans is over 2,000 fathoms and no continent is near enough to break the full force of the wind; the latter raises waves with a trough up to 50 to 60 ft. deep and 900 to 1,200 ft. from crest to crest, and in the South Atlantic there is always a ground swell.

The Pilot Chart had been my Bible, but reality surpassed everything I had been told. And if, by careful steering, I had managed up to the present to defend myself against the massive avalanches of water which this chaos unleashes, it was due in some degree to the shortness of my boat, her rig, and the shape of her hull. I do not think I exaggerate when I say that *no* ship, whether under sail or mechanically propelled, can navigate without risk in these latitudes.

Not so far to the North lay Madagascar; farther on, Réunion and Mauritius; still farther away, Rodriguez Island; all ports of call that I must eschew in order to follow my route as planned. There was indeed nothing to prevent me from varying my route to stop there, have a rest and learn some history, but I was riding the seas to demonstrate a possibility, and I stuck to it.

For the first time on this run *Lehg II* was sailing alone under full sail. Squalls came in regular succession, all laden with rain. It was interesting to note that with every one the barometer fell 3 mm.

Fortunately I adapted myself to circumstances and got into the habit of taking this sea and these conditions for granted. Up to the present, life rolled by without any remarkable incident: nevertheless, in the depth of my consciousness was a latent, unsurmountable feeling of apprehension that kept me on the alert. I was very conscientious with my navigation; I watched the barometer, thermometer and hygrometer and took sights whenever possible. This work, which the state of the sea rendered rather tricky, gave me great joy, as I could mark the tiny gain on my chart; each day a little step forward a little dot beyond the last.

On the 28th of September I was 1,100 miles out from Cape Town: in fourteen days, allowing for the initial calms, I had made satisfactory progress.

I had no time to be bored. I have often been asked how I filled in the day in the course of my long cruises; people cannot conceive the idea of life without cinemas, theatres and especially human society.

It is said that solitude is best shared with another. These seas offer joys to anyone who is capable of loving and understanding nature. Are there not people who can spend hours watching the rain as it falls? I once read somewhere that three things could never be boring: passing clouds, dancing flames and running water. They are not the only ones. I should add in the first place, work. The self-sufficient man acquires a peculiar state of mind which may be reflected in these pages.

At nightfall on the 28th big black clouds invaded the sky; as I had been struggling ceaselessly against violent winds and a sea that allowed me no rest, I now decided to set a course that would take the boat, sailing on her own, gradually to the North, where better weather might be expected. The length of my runs therefore began to diminish. On the 29th I made ony 93 miles and 114 on the following day.

The wind set in the North, which allowed *Lehg II* to sail unattended. As I drew away from high latitudes (in relation to the hemisphere) the sun showed itself more frequently and the temperature rose to 20°C.

Although the mean depth of the Indian Ocean is 2,500 fathoms, its colour is a lighter blue than that of the Atlantic. I was sailing along the northern limit of drift ice. I was not specially concerned with ice, although it may have been the cause of many unexplained shipwrecks. The counter-current which traverses the Indian Ocean from West to East helped me along.

The hours of my first day in this part of the ocean passed more slowly. Sky and water. A few Cape pigeons and the inevitable albatross kept me company.

On the 1st of October I made 113 miles, the following day 100. Numerous porpoises played round me. Their presence was probably due to the proximity of the Crozet Islands, discovered by Mallon du Fresne in 1772; they were only 610 miles away. One of them, Hog Island, contains a store of provisions for castaways.

On the 3rd, thanks to the wind, which after backing from N. to W. had set in the S.W., I made 113 miles and sailed even deeper into the region of low cloud with which I was to become well acquainted.

On my first day in those parts wind and sea dropped; I took advantage of this to cook some mashed potatoes and pillao rice—a consolation for the rough days when it was impossible to cook at all. Cooking is not an unpleasant task, it is even a relaxation from an interminable day at the helm.

And so began a series of identical days in light breezes; my daily runs dwindled to 67 miles, then to 40 miles, and this thanks to the current alone. I was in fact well into what the English call 'horse latitudes', where the winds rise above the clouds leaving them motionless. Then the current itself grew slack and I saw no more albatrosses; these birds need a wind. Only porpoises appeared from time to time. That very impressive ocean had become as calm as a lake.

I solaced monotony by imaginary journeys to places like Colombo, Ceylon, Bombay, ancient India, Calcutta, Rangoon—lands of legend, some of them discovered by Vasco da Gama in 1498, others described by Marco Polo, which I hope some day to visit. They were many miles away, but the Réunion group was only 780 miles from my position on the 5th of October.

On the 7th I was amused by an albatross riding on the sea. He was very interested in the activities of a big dorado (*coryphæna*) which was hunting small fish. All this was going on very near him, but outside the reach of his beak, with which he pecked the water at intervals as if to claim a stake in the game. The dorado was making great leaps out of the water in his pursuit. But *Lehg II* drifted slowly away on the current and I never knew who won.

Tiny fish were swimming round the boat. In the night a massive dark bulk passed me, going northwards; a whale, no doubt; the heavy rhythm of his breathing broke the silence of the night. Later on an enormous fish leapt near the bows.

In the afternoon of the 11th I took advantage of a light breeze from the West which soon veered to the N.W., to set a southerly course and get out of this calm.

The zone of the 'horse latitudes' is easily recognized: on their southern edge one can see the high clouds driven by the roaring forties, those terrible winds which I certainly had to cultivate if I were to make any progress.

The roving eye looks out for something new; everything is interesting. Among the clouds of all shapes and colours I picked out two that seemed to give the figure 99. What did it mean? Perhaps the duration of my second leg, to New Zealand. It turned out to be very near the truth (104 days).

Then my attention was drawn to a committee of albatrosses. Ten of them in a circle, their beaks directed to a central point which they were examining with interest. As I got nearer, I saw that the object under discussion was a small jar. They sounded rather like ducks, but with a deeper pitch, and seemed to be holding a conference on the origin of this inedible object.

I was getting on; I had reached 35° S. by 64°45′ E.; course E. a quarter S.E. The seas were getting heavier and I had to put on my oilskins. The wind was changeable, never staying more than twenty-four hours in the same quarter. The temperature in the cabin fell to 15°C. I was nearing the islands of Amsterdam and St. Paul, which were over 500 miles to the east, but which seemed nearer on my wind chart. The wind freshened in the East; the barometer, already at 773, was still rising.

As I had finished my first tin of biscuits, I set about opening the second with a hammer and chisel—unaccustomed labour and so a welcome change. When I had unsoldered the lid a piece of wrapping paper appeared. On it was written: 'I wish you a pleasant journey; your friend Innocencio, 22 June 1942'. Buenos Aires was so far; and in the course of past months I had had so few occasions to refresh my memories of the town I had left, that I felt deeply moved.

Everything round me was so familiar! The things under my eyes were silent witnesses of past struggles, the intimate universe of the seaman; my sail-mending kit was thirty years old, the tobacco box in which I kept my matches, and the pricker for the Primus, had crossed the Bay of Biscay and the Atlantic with me; the ashtray, an empty sardine tin, was an old friend. Indeed wherever I looked I saw some tried and trusted companion. And now a stranger pops up unexpectedly out of the box: a few lines. . . .

To keep matters under control I seized a swab and set about the floorboards; I did not want any witnesses, silent though they were, to my weakness.

The boat was taking a hammering; a big wave broke over the deck from starboard; we shipped a good deal of sea, the cockpit was awash and the water slopped over the zinc coaming into the bottom. More unwelcome work. I did it and returned to the helm; it was very heavy weather and raining hard. The rain was pouring down the mizzen and splashing on my oilskin; sometimes the squalls caught it and dashed it in my face, though I tried to protect myself with a piece of canvas worn as a sou'wester.

Visibility was diminishing; at times I could not see the waves ahead of *Lehg II* as she worked her way to the Southeast. I had run out of this region to find calmer weather, but peace and quiet had palled. Here there was life and movement and, although not a pleasant spot, it was the best for making progress.

The drops falling on my knees formed a pond; to keep the water from running through to my already wet clothes I brushed it off with the canvas of the binnacle housing in a mechanical gesture.

The hull surged and fell again into the trough of the waves. I looked ahead. Nothing in sight but the dark plain of the sea, ridged with white-caps. The lowering sky was like a prison wall. Nothingness—but I was used to it; I threw a cigarette stub overboard and hummed a tune.

Early on the 24th of October I passed Amsterdam Island with its volcanic peaks rising to over 1,000 metres. St. Paul lies quite near it to the North. I had no intention of stopping and in fact I did not see the islands, only a bank of clouds that marks these insignificant and desert spots in the Indian Ocean. All I could possibly find there would be some shipwrecked mariner waiting for death.

The storm did not slacken and the shallower soundings made the sea choppy. Several times when going aft I could not avoid being drenched by a wave. As the days went by I struck deeper into the roaring latitudes and noticed that albatrosses were becoming more numerous.

There is no doubt that these birds are the kings of sail. Their gliding is superb, their weight and power giving them a masterly control over flight.

A smaller bird, the stormy petrel, has a most curious flight, designed perhaps to attract the fish on which it feeds: it flies very rapidly in circles or in zig-zags falling from one wing to the other; then, as if dizzy, it skims the water and with the help of its little feet it dashes up a wave as one going upstairs in a hurry. It carries on with this exercise indefatigably, all day long; and I never saw one settle. It is quite small. I do not know how it can come so far from land unless, being so small, it sometimes settled in this immensity without my noticing it.

*Lehg II* was sailing in a roaring, majestic inferno. The waves exceeded 40 to 50 feet, stood up like walls and rushed along at a great speed. When I was in the trough I could hardly believe that the boat would rise again instead of going to the bottom in 1,500 fathoms. I saw some seaweed floating. The magnetic variation was almost 35° W. I was still more than 1,800 miles from Australia, forty days out from Cape Town.

The cold was intense.

My linen was in a sorry state. Try as I might, I could not allow *Lehg II* to sail alone except for a few hours at night; sailing as she was with a following wind, she occasionally luffed, but this had little effect on the daily run; so I could get some rest and bale the water that was still seeping through some crack in the deck.

I ate what I had; I mixed cockles or peas with rice. As I was constantly drenched, caloric deficiency was making itself felt, and in the evening I found it necessary to drink rum or brandy; I took it down like water.

# 15

# *My Friend the Pigeon*

A new kind of porpoise had appeared. They had white bellies and tails and light brown backs. I saw numerous petrels, little birds with an easy flight which are supposed to announce storms. My daily runs varied from 93 to 103 miles; the temperature in the cabin had fallen to 12°C.

I often amused myself by throwing scraps of biscuit to the birds, who flung themselves upon it. One Cape pigeon stayed by me for nearly the whole of my crossing of the Indian Ocean. He used to arrive and fly round the boat every day and then disappear. Quite one of the family; he would fly ahead of the boat and alight, as though expecting scraps of biscuit as I passed. When the albatrosses came, they would drive him off and I would not see him until the next day, when he came regularly to be fed. He was a great friend; I awaited him anxiously and he must have felt as I did. The albatrosses frightened him, but they too used to quarrel among themselves until only the biggest and strongest remained in the field.

On the 1st of November I decided to mend the mainsail and reinforce it by sewing in large patches. As I worked on it I thought of the friends who designed and made it and who would have been amused to see me at work. To spread the sail out in the cabin, I had to anchor it at every possible point; and each time I had sewn a foot, these points had to be shifted. In the course of the first thirty stitches the needle slipped off the palm and stuck into my hand; this technique was soon abandoned, for however painfully, I got the hang of it. The work was finished in four hours.

I then made a surprising discovery: there was a fly aboard. Where could it have come from? Was it hatched on board? As a good host I offered it some sugar; it buzzed around and then perched on my hand.

Later on, weather permitting, it used to make short flights outside; sometimes it would light on the sunny side of the sail and then, having taken its constitutional, return to the cabin. It was a well-brought-up fly, not one of those impertinent creatures who, out of all the available resting places, chooses your nose; so I took care of it. It was my traveling companion, a good friend who kept me entertained and thus repaid my trouble. Alas! circumstances were too strong for it: it vanished in the course of a storm.

The barometer kept steady at 775, but on the 1st of November I was becalmed and this lasted until the 3rd.

I had done 3,800 miles; what I still had to do was worrying me, for, as the season grew on, cyclones would be more violent; to pass south of Tasmania I should have to go below 44° S.

The glass fell but brought nothing worse than heavy squalls from the N. and N.E. The heavy clouds scattered in the morning and gathered again in the East, which might have led me to believe that I was nearing the Australian continent; but I was sure enough of my navigation to know that these clouds which appeared to be 200 miles away were in reality much farther. My position was in fact 780 miles E. quarter S. of Cape Leeuwin.

One night I was startled to see a whale dead ahead. Fortunately it swerved slightly to port and swam round astern, probably out of pure curiosity. But as it was a dangerous neighbour I persuaded it to go away by flashing an electric torch.

On the 6th of November I felt poorly and was a little feverish; but this passed off. During the night a wave broke over the foredeck with such a crash that I thought *Lehg II* had struck a reef!

The wind, which up to then had been variable, now set in the North, which allowed me to dash along under full sail for several days.

On the 9th I took advantage of a calm to transfer the 50 litres of water from the breaker to the empty tank. It was almost dark brown; and it was all I had left!

After fifty-six days at sea, I shaved for the first time; not that there was any need to do so—I was rather warmer with the beard and would not have minded keeping it. But shaving was something to do for a change.

I thought that the weather was about to improve; but it was wishful thinking and I was disappointed.

The Pilot Chart does not mention fog in this region; nevertheless I became fog-bound for three days. There was, of course, little or no wind; the situation was drastically changed.

'This is the life!' said I to myself. For something to pass the time, I took to reading the accounts of other lone sailors.

I was astonished at the amount of trouble they had with sails and top-hamper; it was doubtless due to the slowness of their crossings. Perhaps they used machine-sewn sails, made of unsuitable material or badly set. I was always careful to leave plenty of grease; the canvas is thus much less susceptible to changes in the weather. On the other hand, my boat was well balanced, and answered very sweetly to the helm; more than ever, I am convinced that two masts is the ideal rig for ocean sailing. This is confirmed by the fact that I had been using the same set of sails since leaving Buenos Aires and that it was to bring me home again. The only changes were to take in the storm trysail or to replace it by the big Bermuda mainsail when weather permitted.

I had forgotten the taste of sterilized milk long ago; on the 10th of November I discovered a bottle whilst inspecting the hold. What a treat!

The barometer fell sharply and I spent an uneasy night; and as daylight crept through the portholes I rose slowly and drearily to get some underwear on my poor old carcass—how it still managed to carry on, I don't know, after all it had undergone in the way of wounds, knocks, strain, cold and near-starvation. Underwear? A sack lined with bits of newspaper and that was that. The contact with my body of something cold, which was not the tepid sea-water of the wash-basin, made me jump. But outside the rising storm was calling. What matter what my body felt? The practised fingers could not be more sensitive; they curved like the talons of a bird of prey, they were claws. See them unfastening a knot here, to make another elsewhere! A mast, a scrap of canvas, what protection are they against the malice of the storm? At least I would not have the wind full in my face.

The ground swell looked harmless enough. The sky was overcast and grey as lead. In the West, low black clouds seemed to be massing for the attack. A gust ruffled the back of the sea. For the moment the minutes were passing rather quickly; later on, when the hurricane was unleashed, they would go more slowly. Up yonder, a scrap of dirty cotton-wool pelted into the East, followed by smaller scraps—like a hyena with its young. Already the sea was breaking into sharp, jagged blades that dissolved to white spray. The new waves clashed against those of a past storm and this battle of giants left great patches of spume; finally, nothing remained but a smooth patch of emerald green water. The wind howled in the rigging.

The glass was at 740 and still dropping. it had never been so low; I knew that one hell of a cyclone was coming, that *Lehg II* would be in the middle of it and that I was about to face a decisive battle. Looking into the cabin and thinking of what was brewing, I put up a prayer to little St. Teresa and sat down. A long look at everything around me, at my bits and pieces, silent friends and companions, at my universe. Returning to the cockpit, I tapped the barometer; it fell to 732. On deck, the view was truly impressive; clouds that looked like black smoke formed a backcloth for a tragedy. An enormous wave shook the boat and by the crash I could guess at the damage below. I peered into the cabin. The bookcase, which was well secured, had been flung across the cabin. The bunks were littered with broken bottles and scraps of cordage in unholy disorder. A horrid sight. One thinks of one's skin and then, noting that the heart still beats, one weeps over secondary matters, one bewails broken bottles and objects which a few moments back hardly counted at all.

I had experienced a miracle.

The weather was and continued to be execrable, but the impact had passed. The crucial instant, the moment of life or death, had produced no more serious consequences. I could not complain; I was able to struggle on. At midnight I lowered the storm trysail and went below to enjoy a well-earned rest. One more battle was won.

After this memorable day the barometer rose. My runs, after one of 113 miles, gradually lessened. On the 13th of November I was only 130 miles from the South-west of Australia, little more than the entrance of the English Channel. But only extreme necessity and real urgency would have made me change my course for a landfall. I had resolved since I left the Cape to make New Zealand in one stage.

Now there were more days of calm, with breezes that died away as soon as they arose.

I had practically crossed the Indian Ocean.

# 16

# *Slow Death*

I had taken to noting each day the distance made and how much was still to be covered; it was something to do.

That day, for example, I had only done 40 miles. It was the first of many similar days; evidently I had entered a zone of calms and I did not know how long I would have to stay there.

On the 15th of November, my position was 37°74' S. by 113° E. When making my calculations I noticed that it was Sunday. When would that word come to mean anything to me again? There was a long way to go: 2,800 miles to the end of this hard, hard stage.

Next day I passed the meridian of Cape Leeuwin. The look of the cloud bank to the North confirmed my calculations. Any mistake in latitude might land me in some very unpleasant surprises and I could run no risks. Having no motor and relying entirely on sail, I should be in danger close to the land if becalmed, as I now was.

That night a cachalot nearly 50 feet long made a couple of passes at *Lehg II.*

I set the mainsail, which I had not used since I patched it twenty-seven days back, and looked upon my work with pride. It was childish but profoundly human. Steering and nautical astronomy are not enough; a sailor must be many men—cook, nurse or doctor; he sews a sail or mends his sock when an insolent great toe has pushed through. I had patched my trousers with a scrap of code flag.

I was beginning to worry over the fresh water question; what I had left was getting dark and muddy and it was dwindling. My gums were painful; and that is the first symptom of scurvy. I knew well how this disease, which in former times would plough terrible gaps in a crew, begins with ulceration of the gums and skin, loosening of the teeth and softening of scar tissue. Common contributory factors are prolonged cold, damp, bad or insufficient food, but especially the lack of fresh vegetables. It usually appears after sixty days at sea; I had done 65. Had I not been careful to dose myself with vitamin C throughout the voyage I might never have made any port at all. And in spite of my precautions the first symptoms had appeared.

On the 18th I was 130 miles South of Albany, a town and port of South Australia. For sixty-five days I had seen neither land nor ships and had spoken to no one; and yet, against every natural inclination, nothing would have induced me to put in there.

I was still a long way from rounding Tasmania, indeed some 1,440 miles. But I remembered the sound Chinese proverb: 'The road of a thousand *li* begins with a step.'

One day followed another in restful monotony. I took advantage of it to sunbathe. Although it was only 14° C. in the cabin, the sun on deck was warm and I was grateful to it for two blessings: these baths and dry clothes. But the latter were so impregnated with salt that as soon as they were in the shade—that is, when I put them on—they became damp again.

No birds around me, no sign of life. I do not agree with those who interpret this as a sign of bad weather. I believe simply that the lack of wind makes it harder for birds to fly.

I took in the log which had registered only 64 miles in the last eight hours because without any way, it simply dangled and acted as a kind of sea anchor. The breeze was soft, gentle, peaceful; but it meant exasperating delay. Bougainville, sailing slowly and painfully towards the New Hebrides, wrote: 'Rations are the same for officers and the lower deck: but the meat is so bad that we prefer such rats as we can catch.' Yet he added: 'The men did not ask for double pay, and ill-nourished though they were, they danced every night.'

Heroic times. A day like today would have brought the word of command: 'Hoist the topgallants!'

In those days they used to say: 'Wind in the tail, not far to sail', or: 'Sea calm, wind in tail, Sancho Panza goes for a sail.' Where are the days of look-outs in the crow's-nest of a galley? 'A capful of wind is better than a galley's sweeps', shows how powerful is the force of wind on sails, compared to the muscles of the strongest crew.

Another saying proclaims that 'each spar carries its own sail'; everyone can carry his own sail without crowding it on others.

Influenced perhaps by these reminiscences of old navies, I set my balloon jib, or spinnaker if you like, for the first time: 645 square feet of light canvas which should catch the least puff of wind. But there was not enough breeze to keep my balloon from deflating gracefully on the foredeck.

# 17

# *'Upon a Painted Ocean'*

'I have practically arrived at the antemeridian of my country; that
is to say, I still have to sail half-way round the world.' I could not
affirm that these lines would or would not be read by anyone else.
Soon, at any moment, my brave boat and I might go together to
our last rest. But I could not find the right words to convey the
atmosphere of that time. Peace, eternal peace, of an inconceivable
profundity. Today, as yesterday and for several days, banks of
glaucous clouds like marble hung motionless in the sky.

Ten days now, of total immobility, of absolute calm, in the
course of which I had not heard the faintest sound. I felt unreal.
I remembered Bruges la Morte, the city of the painted dead. Strolling
there one afternoon I was startled to hear the steps of a *concierge*. A
human being! Here, I required an effort of the imagination to conceive that the world of men existed. I was like a musical instrument
that had vibrated with melodies of every kind—Beethoven's sym-
phonies, Saint-Saens' *Danse Macabre* and Wagner's convolutions—and
was now being lulled by the serenity of an *Ave Maria*. The familiar
objects round me seemed dead; *Lehg II* must be dead. Was I losing
my mind?

At last a manifestation of life—my Cape pigeon, whom I had not
seen for a long time. He flew twice round the boat and disappeared.
I had time to appreciate the magnificent white pattern on his dark
wings.

Then there were whales. The sun struck down on the metallic
mirror of the sea and a faint vapour was rising. The milky clouds
mingled with the water so that no horizon was discernible. The
stertorous breathing of the whales sounded like a far-off naval
bombardment, punctuated by the splash of projectiles.

I lived. I ate, always the same thing. I could only open tins of
corned beef; they were much too large and, once opened, they
went bad in a couple of days. This meat made me feel thirsty and
water was scarce.

The thermometer rose to 22°C. My potatoes had not only
sprouted but were producing new ones. With my constant sun-
baths, I was getting as black as a Papuan. Numerous small fish
played round me; jellyfish a yard wide floated by, trailing long

yellow filaments. Whales came quite close and it was interesting to watch their games.

On the 22nd of November at nightfall I crossed the meridian 120° E., the antipodes of my country. From now on I should be getting closer to it.

The star Actenar rose practically dead ahead. Between the shrouds was Aldebaran and abeam, a little above the horizon, Aries. A moonlit night brilliant with stars, calm, calm and still calm. I took in the balloon jib and replaced it by the storm jib, for the sky was getting overcast.

My hope . . . my hope was a storm. It was all very well to be in the zone of 'roaring winds', they refused to play. At last, at first light on the 23rd, the storm blew up but, to my surprise from the East.

I was no longer accustomed to waves and their size was like a new experience. What was really strange was that the entire sky turned brown. It was the 'williewaws'.

The English chart says: 'Rather rarely one of these small cyclones visits our Australian coasts, accompanied by heavy rain and thick low clouds, with lightning. This spectacular phenomenon usually heralds a gale. It is announced by a sharp fall of the barometer; if the fall stops at the end of the day, danger is to be expected; navigators should exercise great care.'

Well, that was what was happening. I thought of the Rio de la Plata when the *pampero* was blowing up.

There was no doubt; I must receive the williewaws with full honours. In the meantime it was best to get some sleep, for the visitor would certainly not arrive before daybreak.

# 18

## *The Visitor Arrives*

On the 24th at four in the morning I was awakened by a heavy list. I leapt on deck, for the boat was broadside on the waves.

The wind was violent. I got some leeway on, and saw that the jib sheet had parted at the first gust.

Accustomed as I was to heavy weather in the Indian Ocean, I kept under full sail, for I had decided to take a risk in spite of a wind gusting at a speed of over 50 knots. I felt that I had to settle the 'southern Tasmania question' and to make up for lost time at any price.

The gale was very like my familiar *pampero*.

When night fell I did not hesitate to let the boat sail herself under full sail in the South wind; and although some squalls exceeded 50 knots, and the speed was correspondingly high, I went at daybreak to work out on the bowsprit to replace a line that had carried away. Wrapped in my oilskin—two seaman's knives fastened to my arms so that they would come to my hand with a jerk, this operation was not funny. But it had to be done.

The wind was so violent that the flogging of the storm jib shattered the thimble, and another gust broke a new 20 mm. rope off short. I had to keep my eye on two enemies; the flogging jib which could have damaged me severely, and the sea into which I plunged from time to time.

While taking a breather I saw a little whale to port playing under his mother's watchful eye. At last I managed to finish my work and  pull myself together in the cabin, where I stuffed some more newspapers under my wet underwear. My body was covered with red patches and my hands were bleeding, but the job was done.

The wind flew from South to West, the sky being still overcast, and dropped after daybreak. The glass rose very high—to 775—and stayed there. The temperature was 14°C.

On the following night large luminous patches appeared on the water, increasing as I progressed eastward. They were very remarkable. I seemed to be sailing over braziers. Some were over 300 yards in diameter. This phosphorescence is produced by enormous numbers of microscopic creatures called globigerina. Some patches looked like cylinders about 2 feet long. Sometimes they switched off and on like lighthouses and might almost have given the impression of being near an inhabited coast. I thought of the Bay of Naples.

On the 28th of November I was only 400 miles from Kangaroo Island, the southern limit of the great bay of Adelaide. I had been seventy-five days at sea and was aiming for the southern coast of Tasmania. My pigeon friend continued his visits.

Great flights of birds southward bound indicated the direction of the land whence they came and of the quarter from which the wind would come.

My progress slowed up once more. Up to the present the region of calms had not quite tallied with the data of the Pilot Chart. The zone where I was now sailing was shown as being subject to eleven to fourteen gales a month and only four days of calm; whereas I had already experienced ten. I should say relative calm, for my runs were from 50 to 80 miles. On the 30th of November I was 600 miles West of Melbourne.

I began to use salt water for cooking in order to economize my fresh water, such as it was.

The South wind was very welcome; it made it possible to run at 7 knots and to leave the helm and rest. But is was not entirely reliable.

My clothes were in rags, my oilskin covered with patches. But I had to make do with it. As regards food, the position was not too bad.

I was longing to see the coast of Tasmania. At midday I tried to take a sight, for that is the only moment when one can really rely on one's observation. In the middle of this procedure I lost the pencil with which I was noting a series of altitudes; a wave put a full stop to the proceedings by obliging me to take refuge below and search wildly for something to dry sextant, chronometer, and even the log-book.

Days of mist and fresh winds followed. The waves were very different from those which had rocked me up to the present, for the depth was much less, rising gradually from 2,500 to 900 fathoms. It was evident that I was nearing Tasmania, which I could not see for mist, although on the 8th I was less than 50 miles from the coast where Mts. Picton, Adamson, South Cape and others rise up to 3,500 feet.

Low visibility made it imperative to keep a sharp look-out for this coast, which I very much wanted to see in order to confirm the accuracy of my navigation after eighty-five days out of sight of land, and to check my chronometer.

During the night of the 9th the atmosphere at last cleared, and I was able for the first time to observe the Aurora Australis. The rays piercing the night mists flickered fanwise, like searchlights seeking enemy aircraft; had I not been quite certain that only eternal snows and uninhabited lands lay in that direction, I might have believed it to be the reflected lights of a city.

The sun rose in a clear sky. At 06.00, to the N.W., the monotony of so many days was broken by the appearance first of smoke then of a ship steaming at top speed on the same course. I was no longer alone now. Two hours later, a ship steaming south emerged from the morning mists which had not quite cleared. Ahead to the East the conning-tower of a submarine emerged, only to vanish immediately.

A strong current had carried me off my course to the North. I was now only 22 miles W. of South-west Cape; unfortunately, the wind dropped and a heavy mist returned during the morning and hung about for the rest of the day.

I spent a very uneasy night; I was so close to the coast that I might easily have run on the rocks, and I waited anxiously for daylight.

Joy!

On the eastern horizon, between patches of mist, I saw Tasmania!

The South-west wind freshened and allowed me to take bearings, which reassured me that my chronometer was only 1½ minutes fast. Newstone Islands appeared, one after the other, and I left South-west Cape astern.

Land was so near that numerous birds came to inspect me; it looked deserted. Maatsuyken Island seemed to be joined to the mainland by Witt Island. To the West, relatively shallow water (but still 100 fathoms) was causing the sea to break. Ahead lay White Stone, covered with foam (hence the name) and Eddystone, standing some 20 miles off the mainland. Eddystone Rock is remarkable: a cylindrical mass of rock jutting out of the sea.

I did not wish to go far from the coast, for after rounding Tasmania I would run into a current flowing southward along the East coast of Australia, which would carry me well out of my course. I therefore set my course for those rocks; even with mist I would see them soon enough to steer clear, which would not have been so easy on another course. From time to time I tried to spot them with a telescope.

It was barely two in the afternoon when something which at first I took for a sail showed me that they were near. As I drew closer the waves became more dangerous. The green of the sea was a welcome change for eyes accustomed to the blue of great depths. At 16.00 hrs. the rocks were abeam to the North, while the mist gradually devoured the coastline.

The elation I felt at having made a successful landfall was momentary and it was followed by intense depression—a nervous reaction from the long, hard fight. I had not the courage to face the 60 miles that separated me from Hobart, the capital of Tasmania; a town was in front me and I did not react. It was too tempting: another little effort, 1,200 miles, and I would finish my run and be free from the danger of cyclones.

On the morning of the 11th of December the outline of Tasman

Point showed through the mist: it divides Entrecasteaux Channel from Storm Bay. At midday, Cape Pillar, an outpost of the island, appeared far to the North. The wind was still in the South and the cold was cruel.

I dozed off in the cockpit; when I awoke, two cachalots, each over 30 feet long, were swimming alongside. As soon as I made a movement they disappeared.

That night, when shortening sail, I tore a muscle in my left leg.

The weather was now bad; the gale did not let up for a minute. It was quite a job to prepare any food. I took advantage of spare moments to rest. The tack of the storm jib carried away, and once again I had to mend it, playing figureheads against a sinister background. The colours of the clouds were strange and squall after squall came over, laden with rain and hail.

On the morning of the 13th there was a slight lull. The barometer had fallen to 763; the porpoises were rushing round in circles at high speed and for some reason this game worried me. The sea, the air and I were shut up in an atmosphere that varied from mauve to black. A cyclone was coming. I had neither will power nor perhaps strength to lower the mainsail, and I left *Lehg II* under full sail.

The glass fell to 760 and the first blast of the hurricane shook the boat so that I expected to see the mast go by the board. I kept anxious watch for any damage to my sail.

Hope slowly sank as the hours passed; this storm would never let me out of its teeth. An enormous wave over 60 feet high, not uncommon in this zone during a cyclone, broke on board, submerged me and flooded the cockpit. I emerged slowly in a mattress of foam; water was running out through all the scuppers. In spite of my weakness and the troublesome injury to my leg, it was absolutely essential to bale.

Early in the night I tried to keep awake but it was impossible. Gradually, as in a vision, fantastic shapes of ruined buildings flickered ahead. At moments I felt myself falling from a scaffolding. The whistling wind went through the heavy cap I was wearing. The load of innumerable days weighed me down and smothered my reactions; sleep was irresistible.

The boat was no longer on her course; the binnacle light seemed to be mocking me as I yawed from one course to another in spite of myself.

At times I tried to pull myself together, with very temporary success; I soon felt as though I were holding up an iron bridge. I resolved to lower the mainsail. Aching and bleeding, I managed it with great difficulty. The rolling and pitching tossed me from one side to the other like a rag doll, and every blow meant a new wound or bruise.

I cannot express the difficulty I had in mastering that canvas, to stow it away on deck; only I can know what I endured and the relief I felt when at last I could go below and let myself sink down, anywhere.

The boat sailed on without lights. Only the sepulchral glow from the binnacle showed any trace of life on that poor bundle of planks, tossed ceaselessly to and fro by the waves.

# 19

# *No Can Chew*

The nights were short—only five or six hours of darkness.

My mouth was very painful. The first symptoms of scurvy, mitigated by the vitamins I took, were succeeded by an inflammation of the gums which gave me great pain every time I endeavoured to eat hard biscuit.

On the 16th of December my position was 46°39′ S. by 160° E.; less than 160 miles from Cape Providence, the southern point of New Zealand; but my goal was Wellington, on the strait which separates North and South Islands, so I had still 800 miles to sail. The seams of my oilskin had been resewn so often that it was no longer of much use.

A cyclone from the Antarctic reached me; its epicentre, a compact mass of clouds, melted into the surface of the sea. Immense rays like the spokes of some gigantic wheel appeared in a half-circle to the N.N.E. As I was trying to calculate their trajectory in order to avoid them, something delightful materialized out of this inferno; something that I had missed for several days: my Cape pigeon! The faithful bird had not abandoned me.

He settled on the water and I went quickly to get some biscuit. Having fulfilled my side of the contract, I turned my attention to the cyclone, which gave no time to talk to my friend but increased in violence. The waves pursued, caught and pounded *Lehg II*. Next day they were even more gigantic.

But it was a tremendous satisfaction to note that my daily runs exceeded 150 miles and reached a maximum of 175.

Yet I was weak and aching and the hull creaked; I needed all the experience acquired in years of navigation to save *Lehg II*. I would luff or present the stern to the most threatening of the roaring waves that flung me at terrific speed into the troughs. This game went on to the point of exhaustion till, early on the 18th of December, the weather changed. The cyclone? I had already forgotten it: 175 miles in twenty-four hours was rich compensation.

I stripped off my now useless clothes and put on an old raincoat; the short rest and a fine day were enough to put me on my feet again. The wind was a mild south-westerly breeze which carried me slowly towards the coast of New Zealand. Already I could see albatrosses playing; I listened to the rustle of the water along the outside of the hull. I hung my 'linen' in the sun to dry and took advantage of the fine weather to make and mend.

I was careful not to sail too near the coast, for it would have been difficult to claw off it if another storm arose; indeed, the weather was uncertain and the sky was occasionally overcast.

A seal came to keep me company; he was hunting a fish. The pursuit was fascinating to watch, as hunter and hunted dashed around the boat and under the keel. They were unconcerned by the presence of a spectator and sometimes splashed me as they leapt. Now and then the seal would stop for breath, inhale deeply and start afresh. I watched the game for a quarter of an hour but I cannot say whether the seal won; I only know that he followed in the wake of *Lehg II*, no doubt in the hope of another chance.

My bird had not reappeared and I was not to see him again.

On the 23rd, reckoning my position to be 42° S. by 170°45′ E., I decided to set on a course for land and have a look for the coast. Visibility was very bad; the clouds did not allow me to take good sights—only a meridian. Even so, the sun looked misshapen. The wind, which had been from South to South-west for some days, now climbed over West to North-west and dropped to a light breeze. In the afternoon, I estimated that Cape Foulwind lay some 40 miles to the N.E.

As time went on the situation was becoming critical, for if I made the smallest error in navigation I was lost for certain: and that would have been too deplorable after having achieved the 'impossible'.

And that very night the wind went back into the West and blew a gale. No lighthouse in sight; inky darkness and a chorus of groans and creaks.

Imperturbably the boat rode the waves with magnificent courage and toughness; it was really wonderful to see her under way on these stormy nights.

On the 24th of December, Christmas Eve, at 16.00 hrs., through what seamen call the land mist, a precipitous coast appeared about a quarter of a mile away. It was Cape Farewell, the northernmost point of South Island, staring me in the face. After 101 days land ahead. The stupefying fact was that I was only a quarter of a mile out in my reckoning. I could congratulate myself!

I tried to run as far as possible into Cook Strait; as I progressed the coastline that ends at Farewell Spit unfolded itself before me. A tremendous swell helped me on. Around me bits of timber and branches were floating, but the coast was deserted, showing no sign of life. As night was about to fall, I decided to lower the mainsail and let her heave-to to the North, so as to get some sleep before carrying on in daylight; a necessary precaution on an unfamiliar coast.

It was cold on Christmas morning and I suffered from the 11°C.

*Lehg II* is given a good send-off at Capetown.

*Lehg II* starting from Cape Town Harbour at the beginning of her passage through the Indian Ocean.

and especially from my caloric deficiency. Cook Strait is about 65 miles wide. Being at the foot of Mount Egmont, which is 8,260 feet high, I was surprised not to see it. But no matter; I was sure of my navigation.

The day passed by. At four in the afternoon I was absorbed by the battle of Titans going on round Mount Egmont, which had shown itself for a few seconds. The low clouds, striking the foot of the mountain and jostled on by those following, were whirling at such a fantastic speed that, as an airman, I could think of no air-craft to compete with it—the fastest machine would, in comparison, appear to be stalling. The clouds rushed, rolling, boiling and twist-ing, to the summit of the mountain. I could imagine what a roaring inferno it was up there, and by analogy I caught an inkling of the incandescent stages of the earth's formation. Everything here spoke of primeval times, the more so as no sign of animal life appeared. Drifting along the current was the wreckage of forests, roots and broken branches that tossed and beckoned to the sky as they rolled. The latter was overcast with an indescribable palette of tattered clouds, black, blue and red, casting strange shadows on the sea. Wherever I looked I was aware of the harsh exuberance of cold, hostile nature; of cold that pierced into the marrow of my bones—the dark vindictive cold of inaccessible spaces, without pity or mercy for any creatures. And I, with my unfortunate *Lehg II*, was sailing into this hell. I would not give up. Hope and some tiny inward glow sustained and heartened me. I was firmly convinced that whatever lay before me, sinister though it might be, must be mild in comparison with my sufferings on the ocean I had just crossed.

I leapt below to snatch a piece of chocolate, green with mould. I rubbed it on the sleeve of my oilskin and ate it with great pleasure. I followed my course along the centre of the strait, which closes in to the East, as accurately as though I could see the coast. Accord-ing to my calculations, I should have to alter course S.E. at 21.00 hours to follow the curve of the land. At 23.00 the flashes from the lighthouse on Stephens Island pierced the darkness, the first artificial light testifying to the existence of other human beings. I had made no mistake in navigation. The wind was in the West and very fresh; I could not relax my vigilance for a single moment and I longed for daylight.

At dawn I spied Kapiti Island through the morning mist. As the sun rose it showed me Gore Point, Queen Charlotte Point and, farther South, the Two Brothers. The high peaks of this island showed in their full beauty. One of them, its summit white with snow, stood out against a sky of purest blue; below the peak God had adorned it with a mantle of lilac velvet that faded into pale green as it neared the sea. A magnificent present to the lonely pilgrim.

Time flew even faster than my keel; and if yesterday I was uncon-cerned with delay, I was now conscious of an imperious, aching need to have done. I was exhausted, rigid with cold and dreaming of the rest I might perhaps find that very night.

I was quite near Port Nicholson and expected to arrive shortly; but the wind which had been so favourable dropped as I rounded North Point. As if to try me again, *Lehg II* dragged along. At 16.00 hours I was quite near the entrance to the sound; the high walls of that immense corridor were only 10 miles away! With a fair wind, an hour or two would have brought me to the rest I longed for. But what I got was an uncompromising head wind, a fresh breeze from the North. I sailed as close as I could in order to strike the entrance; but, alas! the current was so strong that I lost ground on every tack.

I saw ships coming out and others patrolling quite near me, but would not understand; they did not even recognize my ensign. I attracted their attention, they came near—and off they went again! No doubt they took me for a member of the local Yacht Club out for a spin.

For the sixth time I crossed the entrance channel and for the sixth time I was farther away than before. Finally I got sick of the game. I lowered the mainsail, went below and collapsed.

But not for long. After a few hours I picked myself up. My first instinct was to get something hot inside me; and seeing the uselessness of my efforts to make port today against a head wind, I decided to wait. Perhaps the old saying: 'North wind lost, look for it in the South' would fulfil its promise.

During the night I took bearings on the lighthouse to get my position. I could see the reflection of the city lights in the sky.

Early in the morning of the 27th of December the North wind dropped, and after a period of calm it veered to the South. At last I was nearing the coast, admiring lovely houses dotted along the shore. Past Luhrs Rocks, I found myself in Lyall Bay, an enchanting sight, and passed between the reefs and the small lighthouse on East Point. I was running free with a fresh breeze under full sail up the channel. Off Worser, I luffed and went alongside the harbour launch to show my papers. Surprise. . . .

'Where have you come from?'

Should I say 'from America', 'from South Africa' or 'from the Cape'? I hesitated, then decided that the last might sound more familiar to them.

They looked at me strangely, obviously wondering whether I was mad or sane. I expressed myself with difficulty; my lips moved, but it seemed to me that it was not my lips that spoke.

My interrogators seemed surprised and not really convinced. They gave me a cup of tea and asked me innumerable questions while we exchanged cigarettes.

They notified the port and I received permission to proceed; and so I left these friends of a moment with whom I had broken the silence of long months. As I passed Karalck Bay people were bathing on the beach. The houses along the coast seemed to be hung on the steep slope like birdcages; they were like a great mosaic, resplendent in the sun.

From Kam Point a large circular bay opened before me; I tacked to the West and saw right at the end the docks of Wellington. The wind was now almost dead ahead. A few small sailing boats passed me, going towards the opposite shore; it was Sunday and they must have been off on a pleasure trip whilst I was finishing . . . something rather different.

I saw a Customs officer making signs at me from the pierhead and came alongside. Several people helped me to make fast and I took advantage of this to lower my sails immediately; it was not easy, for the canvas was stiff and the halyards were not running well through the blocks. From first to last it was a long hour's work before I could sit down on deck to rest. And just then someone said to me:

'I say, you can't stay there. Set your sails again and get out into that little dock over there, about 10 yards; the quarantine people will come and see you.'

I was dumbfounded.

'Oh! Oh no, I'm not budging from here,' I replied forcefully. 'Do you know what it's like to spend 104 days at sea? You saw that it took me an hour to stow my sails and now you're asking me to do another hour's work? No, and No! I'm *not* moving.'

They called a tug to take me to the appointed spot. A doctor questioned me from the quay.

'Are you in good health?'

'Very good.'

'No illness?'

'None whatever.'

He and his assistant looked at each other.

'Well, what more do you want? You've only got to look at him!'

And that was the inspection.

Once I was in my berth, crowds of people came aboard: Customs officers, police, etc. One George Law told me that he had lived many years in the Argentine; he was a Lieutenant R.N. He spoke a little Spanish, but we understood each other better with my limited English. He asked me to wait a bit and returned half an hour later with a complete meal, including fruit and cold beer.

Everyone kept asking questions: they wanted to know everything that had happened to me, how I managed to cross the immense Indian Ocean. I tried to answer but it tired me; and once confronted with George Law's marvellous feast I lapsed into silence.

I spent the night alone on board; unfortunately the berth was very bad. The ground swell could be felt and the boat was bumping about dangerously. So next day when the Commodore of the Yacht

Club and various V.I.P.s  arrived I asked to be moved. I felt that I had to leave *Lehg II* in a nice quiet spot before going to stretch my legs ashore; for the sailor must always think first of his ship.

Two hours later I moored in the Boat Harbour among American warships, a privilege which I owe to the kindness of the chief of the U.S. Naval Base.

My boat was now safe and I could think of myself.

I lived through all these little incidents with great intensity; one cannot resume normality all at once. It was not until I went ashore in a lounge suit, and at the precise moment when a young girl asked me for an autograph, that I looked back at my boat riding quietly a few yards away and realized—at last—what had happened.

Behind me lay a great part of the Impossible Route. For the first time in the history of the world a lone man had accomplished the formidable task of sailing 7,400 miles non-stop from South Africa to New Zealand. No less than 104 days of solitude had been endured on the high seas—a perilous solitude, replete with mischance, struggles, despair and faith that somehow survived to carry on in a hell where I will never, *never* sail again.

Never will it leave my memory.

And, giving one last thought to all I had left behind me, tracing the imaginary line of my route through the Tasman Sea and the grim Indian Ocean, I shuddered.

# 20

# *City of the Winds*

The central part of Wellington, called by Kipling 'The City of the Winds', is built on a narrow strip of ground bordering the bay. It is curious to see how the tramway has to wind and twist in some places to achieve net gain of a few hundred yards. But I prefer not to lose my way in detailed descriptions, firstly because they lie outside the scope of this account, and particularly because it is not possible in a few weeks to penetrate the life of a people which it has taken generations to shape. Respect for other people's work restrains me from expatiating on my own impressions. In this connexion I remember the remark of a certain newspaper correspondent. Arriving in a large city where he was supposed to spend a week, he had to remain two months because of the war. As he was leaving, an official asked him whether he intended writing of what he had seen. He replied: 'If I had stayed a week, I should certainly have done so; but as I have been here two months, I can't. I know less about you now than before I started.'

Nevertheless, a few stories of my stay in Wellington are worth telling.

Firstly, the tale of the telegram.

I had an enormous correspondence from New Zealand, generously offering me hospitality so that I could have a restful stay and exchange reminiscences of my country, also many telegrams from South America. One of these was very thrilling indeed.

One morning I was walking in the town as I usually did, when a car stopped by me and a girl from the Post Office got out.

'Good morning, Mr. Dumas,' said she, 'here's a telegram.'

I expected one of the usual messages of congratulation. But, having read it, I promptly sat down on the grass verge. A gardener stopped work and asked solicitously:

'Bad news?'

Passers-by were stopping; the girl who brought the telegram looked worried and asked:

'What's happened? Are you all right?'

I read out the telegram to my improvised audience. After congratulations, it went on: 'If you need money, ask.'

There was a general burst of merriment. And then and there I composed my reply, writing on the wing of the car. Everyone helped to make it as concise as possible; and this is what I wrote:

'Thanks. Stop. Yes. Stop. Immediately.'

Do not forget that I landed in Wellington with £2 in my pocket.

I had some very happy times in this port, sometimes in warships, sometimes in a fine flat where we did our own cooking. The oddest thing about these feasts was that we used no tables; even when ladies were present, we ate sitting on the floor like Arabs.

The days went by. Repairs to *Lehg II*, not at all serious considering the rough passage, were carried out with the kind collaboration of British and U.S. sailors who were for the moment kicking their heels in the port. I paid them with what remained of my whisky: with two bottles I could pass as a millionaire.

I spent New Year's Eve, a time of memories, in the company of some airmen friends. We sang New Year songs; but we were all far from home, voices grew sad and a laugh was not always echoed.

The house of the Meadows family became a real home for me. Their prodigal hospitality was all-embracing. Often they came with me to buy the necessary stores I was beginning to get together. Invariably after dinner we went to the pictures, then returned to the house for tea and conversation before I went back on board. And every night I went down the little staircase, Mrs. Meadows was careful to remind me:

'Don't forget: there are nine steps!'

I had to count these steps in the dark before I got to the garden path bordered with flowers and ferns. The warning was never omitted and never unheeded; I always counted the steps. I came to think of that refuge as 'the house of the nine steps'.

I used to take long walks with Mr. Meadows during which we talked largely travel. He had been very fond of roaming. He was born in England, had been in Canada and Central America, where he had learnt a fair amount of Spanish; after several voyages, he had settled in Wellington with his Scottish wife and two daughters.

And so we came to the 30th of January, the day on which I had resolved to sail.

I slept at the Meadows' house and went down the little flight of steps for the last time. It was daylight and no warning was uttered; but I counted the steps all the same. The little path with its border of flowers and ferns led me to the dark green gate with its number in white. I closed it behind me and went slowly down Tinakori Street. All the houses there are surrounded by trees and flowers; it was a sunny morning. I turned into Park Street running downhill through the older part of Wellington with its timber houses. After a few blocks I passed the largest wooden building in the world. And with my head in the clouds, hardly thinking of what I had to do, I found myself at the dockside. Mechanically I bought a number of copies of the morning paper, *Dominion*. Reality returned. Some of the pages would serve to refresh my memory, others to protect me against cold and wet, if my experiences in the Indian Ocean were to be renewed.

# 21

# The Dash for America

Some sailor friends filled my one tank with water; I had not had the broken one repaired, for with the breaker and the demi-john I should have 160 litres. Another friend gave me something precious—a pair of gum boots. I was also given a silver ashtray adorned with a kiwi (the bird of New Zealand), a hamper of fruit and vegetables, a case of beer and half a dozen bottles of lemon juice. A cinema operator recorded the scene as the Meadows family presented me with an album of views of New Zealand and a carved wood kiwi.

The wind was in the North, and as I could not get out under sail, a picket boat with the Spanish name of *Vagabundo* took me in tow. All my friends were aboard. I told the skipper to stop and wait whilst I set sail. I set the mizzen, then the staysail. At that moment, rounding the pierhead, *Lehg II* came into violent contact with a concrete pillar. The damage should have been repaired; but no. I had decided to go and go I would; the job could wait till later.

Setting the staysail was not without danger, for the wind had freshened and the sea was getting up. What would it be like outside? Having set the storm jib, I cast off the tow. Farewells were shouted, and my friends made for harbour as the heavy seas made navigation difficult.

It was 11.00 hours, Saturday the 30th of January 1943. Under her own sail, the boat soon got way in the channel and the now familiar shore-line went by.

The wind was up to 40 knots and was whipping the waves into spray. The ships anchored in the roads dipped their ensigns and I replied.

In Palliser Bay, no longer sheltered by the hills, the wind found its full force and the choppy seas, increased by the ground swell, were making their presence felt. The waves were short and high and broke on deck, drenching everything. One wave carried away a boat-hook. Taken by surprise, I had not even had time to put on my oilskin and was soaked to the skin: I was furious at getting into this state before I had even reached the open sea. At 17.00 with a tremen-

dous swell I passed Cape Palliser, the last outpost of this country
that I might never see again.

Physically I was in good shape. During my stay in Wellington
all traces of scurvy had vanished.

My eyes left the dimming coast to gaze ahead into the immense
Pacific Ocean. It was over 5,000 miles to Chile without any port
of call on my course. Only Chatham Islands lay near it, a little to
the South but very close to my point of departure. In spite of what
lay ahead of me I was very happy; once on the coast of Chile I would
be nearly round the world.

The glass remained very low at 758, the temperature at 18° and
relative humidity at 80 per cent.

I remained at the helm all night and it was not until the morning
of the 31st that, the wind having slackened off a little, I decided to
get some sleep.

The weather improved. The wind, having swung to the South,
stayed there. It was a gentle breeze; the sky was lighter and the
clouds vaporous.

On the 1st of February I crossed the 180° meridian of Greenwich
and was back in West longitude. The barometer fell to 756. Finding
myself in the tail of a cyclone travelling N.N.W. to S.S.E., I decided
to take in the mainsail. Up to the present my progress had been
excellent, but the storm was getting worse and the glass dropped
to 752. That night I narrowly escaped disaster, passing very close
to the floating trunk of an enormous tree.

*Lehg II* was making a great deal of water, no doubt through the
knock she had sustained on leaving harbour; but in this weather
repairs were out of the question.

On the morning of the 2nd the weather eased a little. A shark over
10 feet long was swimming alongside with a pilot fish in attendance.
I recognized the characteristic black stripes. The shark swam under
the keel and came so close that I could not resist the temptation to
shoot him. He was hit in the back and dived at top speed.

I took advantage of the light breeze to throw my bags of spoilt
potatoes overboard, keeping only the new potatoes that had grown
from them. My harvest! In the afternoon I saw some sharks and
whales.

During these first days in the Pacific I had to adapt myself to conditions very different from those in the Indian Ocean. The waves
are not nearly so long, the clouds are higher and I rarely noticed
any mist. The sun shone frequently. The West wind on which I
had counted refused to settle, playing between North and West.
I was suspicious of the unknown and kept my eye on the barometer
to guard against any unpleasant surprise.

On Friday the 5th I was some 600 miles East of New Zealand.
On the 8th I decided to inspect the damage to the hull, hoping that

it was only a graze; but I found a plank cracked. I repaired it with a strip of inner tube, stuck on with paint and held in place by a plank which I screwed on. No more water coming in—except for the waves that broke on deck.

The Pacific was tranquil; any mist made the sky appear grey and the sea the colour of lead. As the wind was in the North-west I could often leave the helm.

Hidden alongside a panel in the cabin I discovered one of my jack-knives which I thought was lost. Before going on deck I cut myself a piece of New Zealand bread with it: when I emerged I had the fright of my life. *Lehg II* had run on the rocks. I was paralysed for a moment.

No. The boat was only elbowing her way between two whales. With a puff of wind, she tried to climb up one of the shining backs, then slipped off again. The seconds were interminable. What was the whales' reaction going to be? Perhaps the creature being jostled by my hull thought that his companion was being playful. They seemed to be asleep. There was nothing to be done. *Lehg II* had got herself into a jam and must get herself out of it. I did not dare to move for fear of startling the monsters.

Quietly, purposefully, with exasperating slowness, the boat pushed her way through alone. At last she was clear and left these uncommon obstacles astern. I drew a deep breath and my heart resumed its beat.

My diet was more varied than on the earlier part of the voyage. Apart from the inevitable chocolate with biscuits and butter, I ate apples, peaches and various little luxuries. There were several boxes of sweets, a quantity of dried fruit, nuts, raisins and figs—even some Christmas pudding! A lordly life, in fact. *Lehg II* was making 135 miles a day. At night I saw shooting stars; the wind would blow into the quarter where they fell.

The mist became thick, like clouds of smoke whirling on the sea. This was not serious, though the humidity reached 100 per cent. The current was carrying me towards my far-off goal and there was rarely a day on which I could not see the horizon. I thought of the Indian Ocean, where it was only visible from the wave crests. Here the sea was gentle, truly Pacific, getting more tranquil as I went on. The albatrosses here were brown with black underwings (the fuliginous albatross).

Raratonga, in the Cook Islands, lay 600 miles to the North and Polynesia farther off on my port bow. Perhaps one day when the world found peace again I could go there with some kindred spirits who shared my taste for aimless wandering at sea. I was satisfied enough with my lot to daydream of other voyages; an idea that would certainly not have occurred to me in the Indian Ocean! It was marvellous not to be constantly shipping seas.

*Lehg II* sailing near Buceo Harbour at the end of the voyage.

An enthusiastic crowd waiting for Vito Dumas to go ashore at Buenos Aires harbour at the end of his voyage round the world.

Petrels appeared; sharks were abundant and I had time to watch them. I could do anything I pleased; I had banquets—menus such as: tomato soup, salmon, cheese, dessert, with beer. . . . Sometimes the wind showed signs of freshening, but it dropped at nightfall. I would predict the next day's weather by observing the sunset; for example, if the sun set fiery red I would have a day of fresh winds.

The ocean was 90 percent calm. Only the ground swell athwart my course day and night, telling of far-off gales, made the boat rock lazily. Conditions were unfamiliar and she seemed to feel it too.

At dawn on the 15th I was 240 miles from the Maria Theresa Reef and 1,300 miles South of Tahiti; the nearest island was Rapa, 900 miles to the N.N.E.

Walking carelessly on the deckhouse, I made a false step, fell down the hatch and received a violent blow in the short ribs. It was so severe as to compress the lung on that side and for a short time I felt that I was suffocating. It was extremely painful and, though I soon recovered, I was unable for a long time to stand quite upright.

The unforeseen! . . .

In this splendid weather I left the portholes open to dry out the cabin. I slept, I read and I ate. The chef would dish up *rice a la Kia-Ora*, full of delicious oddments—so named in honour of my New Zealand friends. The only snag was the pain which kept me from moving freely and obliged me to wear a bandage over my ribs.

It was at this moment that the head winds began to blow; rather than beat to windward I hove to. The barometer rose to 7800 and the temperature was 17°C.

Normally I slept all night. I had breakfast in the morning, lunch at midday, and in the evening, rice with cheese or whatever came to hand; many different things go with rice.

In this atmosphere of deep peace many ideas turned over in my mind: planning future routes, choosing friends for a cruise, building, with the knowledge born of long experience, the ideal boat. I imagined that others, too would be impelled to throw over the routine that stifles life and open their minds.

My thoughts ran, they flew: far across the sea from port to port and picture to picture. After a day of hard work in a town, human beings feel the need of 'noble leisure', as the Greeks called it; here this leisure possessed me utterly, feeding and thriving on my soul. The inner world is a gift of God and one should make the most of it. But why did my fancy stray so far? Why dream of other horizons and plan travels whilst I travelled? Strange urge, to be gone when one has not yet arrived.

One tranquil day succeeded another. I would tap the barometer and find it still at 784. My mind revolved between this happiness, the accursed pain in my ribs—for it hurt me to breathe—memories, and the thought that I still had so far to go. Then memories grow painful; and seamen mumble them over sourly as they pace the deck. The truly indispensable entertainment is work; and lacking occupation, introspection becomes a danger.

At last a freshening breeze blew me out of it. On the 18th I made 123 miles. From then on I stayed longer at the helm in order to make my runs as long as possible—sometimes as long as sixteen to eighteen hours.

I planned to make the most of the favourable winds of this latitude as far as the 90th meridian and from there work up to Valparaiso in Chile, which lies on 33° S. But the winds  seldom obeyed the Pilot Chart and were reluctant to blow from the West; furthermore, mist was 50 percent more frequent than the Chart laid down.

I had long forgotten what a cyclone was like. The relative calm of the Pacific is certainly due to the immense expanse of sea without land masses; aerial currents flow freely, whereas in the Indian Ocean the tropical heat, being unable to escape to the North, runs along the East coast of Africa. Hence the waterspouts which I experienced. West of Australia the same phenomenon occurs; the winds, interrupted in their normal course by the land mass, follow a trajectory that brings them into conflict with those of the Antarctic, producing the storms that cost me such anxiety and hardship.

This is true to the extent that the sun, setting towards the North, causes heavy mists and calm in the zone where I was now navigating.

To allow *Lehg II* to run more freely, I lightened her forward by moving the anchor chain to the foot of the mainmast.

The leak remained slight; yet I had to bale half a bucket of water every two hours to keep her dry.

The relative comfort of *Lehg II* can be judged by the fact that I had on board some silk underwear and even a dinner jacket, still quite undamaged; if I did not always cook, it was not because of the weather, for the cooker, hung in gimbals, remained horizontal whatever the angle of the boat. Justifiable inertia was the reason.

On the 20th the barometer dropped 15 mm. Elsewhere, that could mean a gale; but here, all that came was a S.W. wind that had no effect on the swell and did not make the seas break. The only point worthy of notice was ground swell from the Antarctic.

My runs varied between 100 and 130 miles: 470 miles in four days.

As the wind veered to the South, I took advantage of it to go down a bit in latitude (towards the Equator), to 42°17′; but there I found quite unreasonably calm weather. I made use of it to touch up the paint on the hull, leaning over the gunwale. I also caulked the waterways on deck: I climbed the mainmast to reinforce the steel halyard tie, which looked unsafe.

The thought of being alone in the immense Pacific was somewhat unsettling.

I did not draw away from the latitude of the 'roaring winds'; on the contrary, I sought them, I needed them. But here they roared rather gently. The barometer might fall 15 mm., they did not materialize: at the best, a light, good-tempered little breeze dispersed the clouds or herded them together, played with them and with the back of a slumbering ocean. I hoped that the conjunction of the moon and the sun would bring a change; it brought none. After wandering through the tropics I was beginning to know these vague, formless, transparent nebulosities, swimming in the atmosphere.

It worried me to see the provisions dwindling away without any corresponding progress. And it was precisely in such weather that I ate more. Lots of fuel and few miles to show for it! I rang the changes on the sails, I tried more favourable zones; I was whistling for a wind.

At the end of February I had done 2,400 miles; there were 2,700 still to go.

I was glad to see mendicant petrels again; they were not as lively or as expert in snapping up crumbs as their cousins in the Indian Ocean. Every night, phosphorescent patches such as I had seen off Australia and Tasmania lit wide stretches of sea; it was some compensation.

The log-line hung vertical from the stern.

I chewed over the idea for seventy hours before making up my mind to set the spinnaker. Once I had made the decision and got everything ready, a gentle breeze sprang up—ahead. Not wishing to get on the wrong side of luck, I packed up the whole bag of tricks. At midnight the little breeze obligingly veered; I brought up the spinnaker again and set it at last.

# 22

# *Whose Little Slipper?*

Having set the jib, I looked round and, floating on the water I saw . . . a woman's slipper, pink, with a pompon somewhat darker in shade; it seemed to be silk.

I built up a romance on it. From its appearance it must have belonged to an elegant lady, a little foot, barely size 4. However did she lose it? Headlong flight? Shipwreck? A lovers' tiff? A scene—or a moment of hesitation? Like the assorted litter of a battlefield, this small object had been swept away in the vast ocean. It was strangely touching. . . .

I was still becalmed. Cigarette ends piled up in the sardine tin, my ashtray. Whales came so near that I had to discourage them with shots or with flashes from my electric torch. Their excessive familiarity was too disturbing.

On the 4th of March I saw a westbound ship, but so far away that she could not have seen me. A little wind from the South-east broke the sheet of the spinnaker and I decided to take it in. Two days later I saw many birds, probably from Pitcairn Island, 900 miles to the North, where some descendants of the *Bounty* mutineers still live. The ship's rudder was salved in 1932.

The glass fell to 760 and this time it seemed to be in earnest. My old friends the squalls arrived with heavy gales from the North. The cross-seas took *Lehg II* by the shoulder and shook her, but, with all sail set, she travelled at top speed. I made 150 miles in twenty-four hours and stayed at the helm for forty hours at a stretch to make the most of the wind. I got very wet and tired, but anything was better than calms that prolonged the journey. When I went below after those long hours on watch I gave *Lehg II* her head, lashing the tiller on one quarter with a running knot to the other to give some elasticity; it was the only way to manage. The exact position had to be determined by trial and error for four or five hours before leaving the helm, for a couple of centimetres either way would have sent my very responsive *Lehg II* off her course. The angle of the tiller was, as a rule, 2 inches to windward of the axis of the boat.

On the 9th of March, being at 40°41′ S. by 117°15′ West, I reckoned that it would take me twenty-eight more sailing days to reach Valparaiso. But, of course, everything depended on the wind. Storms helped me along, fine weather held me back.

Up to the present I had had no occasion to use a storm trysail in the Pacific.

Once the storm had blown over, winds were variable. Squalls, mist, rain and calm succeeded each other as the days went slowly by. My log kept on repeating these words. Sometimes I saw lightning to the North.

To prevent the continued gybing of the mainsail and mizzen when becalmed, I put up false guys.

I had changed none of my tackle since leaving Buenos Aires, but squalls, gales and general strain had produced a normal degree of wear in the sails; I mended them as required. I was delighted with my equipment; maintenance had been very light and I had no complaints. My one regret was to have lost the only screwdriver on board, just as I was constructing a housing for the binnacle out of an empty box; the lamp had a bad habit of going out at crucial moments. It was an old fault; I remembered how it had let me down on that terrible 'night of breakers' during my trip from France to the Argentine in 1932.

Birds continued to fly past; an indication of the land where I was bound. A few hours' flight for them meant long days of navigation for me. I hope not to be taken for a liar when I affirm that at such times I looked back with regrets to old days of struggle against a background of awful majesty. Then, the wind drove battalions of thick clouds, charging down without respite; the boat flew and her wake melted into the enormous waves. What a contrast with present 'navigation without trace'! Then, the tense emotion of a struggle for life, second by second, upheld by a deep faith in victory, a will to survive the unbridled fury of the storm. My eyes would light on a halyard, my mind would calculate its breaking strain. And now—this languid progress, so different from the conception of the Infernal Route that the boat herself seemed bored with it. She was built to withstand harsh seas; navigation for young ladies was not her cup of tea. I was with her heart and soul, and I used to pour out my indignation on the pages of the log; and when a storm threatened I retired to the cabin. I had heard that one before.

# 23

# *The Last Slice*

On Sunday the 28th I entered the last time-belt of my circumnavigation, having passed 90° W.

I was in the cabin when I heard a noise on deck and found that the main halyards had parted. It was the work of a few moments to set the storm trysail with a flying halyard. I then took a sight and found that I had covered 330 of the 360° of the earth. All I needed now was a little jump of 15° to get home; but when I reached Valparaiso I would still have to do 3,000 miles—round Cape Horn at that—in order to cover the 700 miles, as the crow flies, that separated me from Buenos Aires.

The fall of the mainsail was an omen. A gale from the East soon turned into a raging storm. The wind was over 50 knots and I had to take in the storm trysail in order to tack to the South; by the morning of Monday the 29th, with so little sail, I made 187 miles to the South. The barometer stayed at 760. I spent most of the time lying in the cabin; it was pointless to remain on deck.

Next day the wind was very fresh, due East; my route to the South was making me drift westward; so I decided to go about and set a course to the North. The boat shuddered and creaked; we took knock upon knock, and as I badly needed something hot the stove had to go on strike. So I spent thirty hours without a chance of drinking anything really warming. Feeling thoroughly exasperated, I then had to settle down to changing the nipples of the stove; it took me four hours; but the cup of chocolate I made seemed so delicious that I could not recall ever having tasted anything better.

On April 1st the gale was so kind as to give me enough time to set the storm trysail. I resumed my course to the North-east whilst I mended the mainsail. I was 400 miles West of Mocha Island and had left latitude 40. The sea remained choppy and visibility bad; I was surrounded by mist and great masses of cloud. I had now entered the Humboldt current and felt its favourable influence.

By the 6th of April I was at 36°7' S. On this latitude, yonder in the East, lay Las Flores, a little village in the province of Buenos Aires which I know very well. I was doing 70 to 90 miles a day.

I was nearing the South American mainland after all; that was the bright side of the picture. After a bad storm some compensation usually emerges.

A mass of warm air was trying to displace the prevailing cold; I was right in the neutral zone and found myself becalmed. Luckily on the evening of the 8th the boat showed signs of answering better to the helm; I was entering a zone of wind.

An enormous cachalot cutting across my bows nearly caused a catastrophe; just as I was about to hit him, he dived with astounding speed. Nothing worse than a fright; I waved him my thanks.

I was thrilled at the thought of approaching my goal and looked forward eagerly to the moment when Point Curaumillas would show through the mists.

The next day a stiff breeze picked me up and I thought that I might very soon be there; but the 10th dawned deplorably calm. The sky, which had cleared after the bad weather, was blotted out by ever-thickening mists—so thick that a number of coastal birds seemed to have got lost. Some of them looked exhausted and alighted for a rest on *Lehg II*. I had to welcome these unexpected guests and, as a good host, to give them lunch.

What surprised me most was the total absence of shipping, only 43 miles from the coast.

On Sunday the 11th of April at 20.00 after seventy-one days out of sight of land I came on deck to see the lights of Point Curaumillas flashing ahead, a few points to starboard. There lay Valparaiso; once more my navigation had been faultless.

Next day I could see the coast, but, with the light breeze, my pace slowed down as my impatience increased. At 10.00 I saw two fishing vessels to the North, but to my regret they got no nearer. Farther off, ships coming from the North gave me a wide berth.

I was fascinated by the intense life of the sea; it was swarming with a variety of creatures. Shortly after midday, thanks to the South wind, I managed to round the lighthouse point; at that moment a sailing yacht making for the port under power appeared in the offing. I made signals but there was no response.

I was approaching Valparaiso, America, my country; how my heart bounded! Hills, mountains, houses, woods, a palette of bright colours spread out before my eyes. At nightfall I was becalmed off the Punta de los Angeles; and as a diamond lace of light crept up across the magnificent crescent of Valparaiso Bay, I could not restrain a cry of admiration. The coast was only 100 metres off, but it was not for me; I could not move. In the silence of the night I could hear the lighted motor-buses. I could also hear someone whistling—perhaps a boy. I decided to ask for his assistance.

'Muchacho,' I called.

The whistling stopped for a moment, then started again.

'Do you hear me?'

No reply. The whistling continued.

'Be a good chap and tell the Harbour Master that I'm becalmed; ask if I can get a tow.'

At these words the whistling seemed to stop. A short silence. Then it went on again.

Nothing doing; he did not understand that I needed help. I gave up. Nervously, I smoked one cigarette after another and watched the smoke, hoping that it would show the direction of any puff of air. The sails hung, nerveless. *Lehg II* rocked gently; the waves breaking on the shore were getting close. I thought I saw a rock ahead.

But . . . but it was a boat. Someone on board hailed me:

'Was it you adrift this morning?'

'Yes, it was.'

'The lighthouse keeper sent us out; here we are. . . .'

They were soon alongside. It was a naval boat manned by petty officers.

They recognized who I was and greeted me warmly. I asked them on board for a drink and gave them the book on the voyage of *Lehg I*. In the meantime, a slight breeze had sprung up and *Lehg II* started drifting away from the boat and the coast. Seeing this, they sent a line and took me in tow whilst I lowered sail. At 22.00 I came alongside the tug *Leon;* a number of sailors at once came aboard, helped me to make fast and asked me to come ashore. I replied that I was not presentable: in a pilot-coat, oilskin trousers and gum boots, I was even more of a 'filibuster' than when I arrived at Cape Town.

'That's all right,' they replied. 'We're not likely to meet many people tonight.'

The dinghy made for the pier and I went ashore with the two P.O.s who were already my friends. I then noticed an officer of the Chilean Navy and hastened to introduce myself.

'Señor, I am Vito Dumas.'

He seemed surprised; he looked me up and down and I observed my companions who were standing to attention. I felt like a prisoner under escort. Finally, I explained that my last landfall had been in New Zealand, and the officer seemed to understand. He congratulated me, not evincing any great conviction that I was telling the truth. I then asked him to excuse me.

He was certainly puzzled.

We went through several narrow streets and called at a number of those little 'ports' full of bottles that are found on all coasts of the world. I tried sopaipilla, I tried wine, and at three in the morning began to notice that it was high tide; and in view of the danger of flooding I asked my friends to take me back on board. They felt a little frustrated at missing the last two ports on that cruise. . . .

Back on the deck of *Lehg II*, I thought in my artless way that it was bedtime—at last. My friends rowed off in their boat, but a voice on board the *León* said:

'Hello! you'll have a cup of coffee before you go to bed, won't you?'

Why argue? They must be right.

I went aboard the *León*. To the light of a single candle that made shadows flicker round the little cabin, we started off again, stirring up memories: names of ports, dates, figures. They they talked about whaling. The hours revolved, the sky was turning grey. We then decided that I should only sleep for an hour, after which they would bring me a saucepan and I would make them some chocolate *a la mode de Lehg II*.

I closed my eyes, exhausted, and to the gentle rocking of the boat, slept like a log.

# 24

## *A Secret is Revealed*

At the beginning of this book I said that I was fully aware of the vicissitudes I should have to undergo in order to acquit myself with credit in an enterprise which I had christened The Impossible Route. I knew that the difficulties would be enormous; they were, in fact, worse than I expected. Yet I had studied the scheme for ten years. Having weighed these risks, I faced them; and any failure could not have been imputed to lack of foresight on my part. My enthusiasm was unconcealed. The hull had been very strongly reinforced; the sails were made of the best materials and their cut and workmanship left nothing to be desired. The rigging enabled me to face the worst weather with entire confidence. Distance travelled, seasons' average runs, all confirmed my calculations. I never trusted to luck; everything was thought out beforehand. And yet, when I arrived at Valparaiso, my joy was not complete. A shadow lay across the road back to Buenos Aires: Cape Horn. Out of the basketful of advice and opinions of this question, very little indeed coincided with my scheme, which I kept to myself. I proposed to disclose it if successful; and I can now do so.

According to the Argentine Nautical Instructions, the best season for navigation in Cape Horn waters was the time when the sun was lowest in the North, that is, between the beginning of June and the 15th of July; midwinter in the Southern Hemisphere. Winds were on an average less violent and one could hope that the passage would not be too bad. In the stillness of my home, duly impressed by horrific prognoses, I checked and re-checked the information available. And each time I felt more inclined to discount the prophets of woe and to stick to my convictions.

And so, having arrived at Valparaiso on the 11th of April, I resolved not to set sail before the end of May. Time enough for a good rest. I did not doubt the excellent intentions of those who gave me contrary advice, but I had confidence in my own plan and I intended to carry it out. A Captain in the Chilean Navy was also of my way of thinking; he believed that the season and the route I had chosen were the most favourable, especially if I could manage to be near the Cape at the full moon.

My repose was relative, for I had to attend a number of receptions. It is always a great joy to me to arrive in port; I like to be taken round by friends; I feel happy and, after so many struggles, human problems take on a new aspect. I am interested in what others are doing, in the thread of lives entirely conditioned by an unchanging environment. Their questions are normal; they are endeavouring to assimilate someone else's experience. On my side, the effort to understand their problems made me forget my own.

My health was good. Soaked practically all the time during the first two stages, I had not had a single cold. I attribute this perfect state of general health to frugal living and the sobriety imposed by circumstances. Excess is the cause of most human troubles. As the doctors say, more people die of overeating than from underfeeding.

And so, from one reception to another, time went by; a time of most pleasant memories. I shall never forget the welcome of the Chilean Naval College, where I had the honour of addressing four hundred cadets and the entire staff. The Commandant presented me with a miniature mast, flying the Chilean flag, with an inscription commemorating my voyage at the foot. Numerous societies made me an honorary member.

Thanks to Admiral Kulchewsky *Lehg II* was hauled up on a slip at the Arsenal for the first time in the voyage and had a thorough overhaul. Worn ropes were replaced; the navigation workshops repaired my chronometer and I was given the set of charts I needed for my journey. From Buenos Aires, I received an oilskin, thigh-boots—for mine were in a sorry state—and a tell-tale, the reversed compass by which the course can be checked without leaving the cabin. I spent a very happy night at Concon Beach with the Betteley family, eating local dishes of sea food. Finally, it would be impossible to enumerate all the parties given in my honour.

# 25

# *Dead Man's Road*

Early on Sunday morning, the 25th of May, I went to Mass; then I fetched my luggage from the hotel. It had been the first time in all my voyage that I had left my 'rabbit-hutch' for a bed.

The city was still asleep and the sun was not yet over the mountains when I arrived aboard *Lehg II*.

I was moored astern of the corvette *General Baquedano*, the training ship of the Chilean Navy, where I had often been a guest. With the help of my friends of the Yacht Club, I stowed my stores: wine, spirits, biscuits, quantities of tinned fish; a change from times when I had not been overburdened with such luxuries. I had stores for more than six months and 3,000 miles to sail. It was the shortest leg of the voyage, but also the most tricky. Cook, Bougainville, and all seamen who have navigated in those waters testify to the fact in their books. Hansen, the only lone sailor who had succeeded in rounding Cape Horn from East to West, lay in the depths off the coast of Ancud; only the wreckage of his boat had been found on the rocks. Bernicot and Slocum had chosen to go through the Strait of Magellan.

I knew that a strong current from the West strikes the coast between 37° and 50° S.; it then divides into two branches, one running North, the other South. The danger is the possibility of being surprised by a westerly gale for a couple of days; if the navigator has not had the prudence to steer well clear, he will inevitably be thrown on to the coast. For this reason, my plan was to follow the route of the clippers and eschew the temptation to stop at Valdivia, where the Yacht Club had invited me to call.

Many friends had come to witness my last preparations, most of them convinced that they would never see me again; and I kept stopping work to say goodbye. By 10 o'clock everything was ready; the mizzen, mainsail, staysail and jib were set. Saying goodbye for the last time on board the training ship, I noticed a plaque with the inscription:

'I have sailed the seas, carrying in my wake the prayers of Chilean mothers and in my sails the breath of the firm, indomitable spirit of our country.'

The breeze was light. My friend Weddod, accompanied by many assorted persons with whom I had spent pleasant hours, took me in tow. We passed along the line of ships at anchor, including a giant Canadian five-master. She had been lying there for a long time, a sort of black phantom and warning of what might happen to me in the far South. She carried a cargo of wood and had tried to round Cape Horn, but storms had battered her hull to such an extent that leaks had reached danger-point. Her skipper, seeing that she was near sinking, decided to give up and return to Valparaiso with all hands pumping desperately. Was something like that waiting for me? The anxious faces of my friends, whose forced smiles failed to be convincing in spite of their wish to be encouraging, their hints that it might be better to give up the attempt, were certainly not good omens for my departure.

I knew that the problem would be solved for me in the first mile; as soon as I was thrown on my own resources. To escape from outside influences, and firmly to implement my decision, was the only way to defeat 'the impossible'.

We were soon past the breakwater. I looked back at the training corvette, where the signal '*Bon voyage*' must have been flying for me; at that distance it was somewhat difficult to see.

At 16.00 hours I cast off the tow in a very light westerly breeze. I made a board to the N.N.W. to give Point Curaumillas a wide berth. The glass stood at 770, the temperature at 15°C., the humidity 88 per cent. During the evening the wind backed a little to the S.W., the coast and its beautiful colours were bathed in sunshine. One more port was behind me in a sailor's life; but this time I was headed for the imponderables of Cape Horn. What of tomorrow? The day died slowly and the sun sank in a cloudless sky. Astern, above the coastal range stood the peak of Aconcagua.

After sunset I went below; alone in my boat after more than a month—I could not help kissing a panel in a surge of affection for my 'shipmate'.

For the moment I was still a stranger to her; I was so imbued with memory of happy days in Valparaiso, the land of eternal spring, that it seemed to have been a dream. With its curious and diverse buildings, its narrow streets that wind fantastically as they climb, its romantic old houses of the colonial period, the city has something of all times and a little of every country. Valparaiso is unique.

On Monday the 31st the coast was still visible to the East, but hardly distinguishable between the clouds and the banks of morning mist. The current, stronger than the light breeze, had carried me off towards the North, although my course was set westward. About 5 miles to leeward a schooner from Juan Fernandez was heading for Valparaiso.

Although in my position 71°30′ West, I should have been well clear of anything. I thought I heard breakers; I was practically becalmed—it would be. . . . No. The noise came from an enormous school of porpoises approaching ahead.

On the 1st of June the sea was flat, without a wrinkle, with little patches of ruffled surface that hardly moved. The wind veered to North-west without freshening much; but by nightfall I was moving well and the boat left a wake of phosphorescence.

On the 2nd of June I caught a better, fresher breeze which allowed me to get some sleep; but the next day it backed to the South, then a little to the South-west. It was intensely humid. I had already travelled 240 miles! Still heading West, and rather wet, I saw ahead Juan Fernandez, 'Robinson Crusoe's' island. I came fairly close, but visibility was very bad and I could not distinguish any details whatever.

I noticed a slight leak aft but was unable to track it down. It was barely a trickle; but if it was running in easy weather, it could be a nuisance when I came to a difficult bit. So I made a painstaking search for the crack; but in vain.

On the 4th of June, my position being 34°58′ S by 77°15′ W., I began to drift to the S.W. again, which enabled me to get farther from land and reach the high latitudes.

On the 5th the wind was fairly fresh from the S.S.E.; I could not get out of sight of clouds banked up in successive layers off the coast, which they could not surmount because of the height of the continent. They form a barrier that can stretch over 400 miles from the coast.

I was in the zone of variable squalls with low visibility and other obstacles to accurate taking of sights. The number of albatrosses increased as I went down to the South-west.

Up to then I had been at the helm very little; I spent almost all my time resting in the cabin. The boat was behaving very well, both on and off the wind; the prevailing winds made it necessary to sail close-hauled.

The passage of Cape Horn was gradually taking shape. The whistling of the wind was that typical of these latitudes.

The thick mist left me in semi-darkness. None of these things made any difference to my state of mind, for I was always on the lookout for some new development. Had I begun my voyage around the world by way of Cape Horn, what I found there might have made a deep impression and caused me to worry continually; but, arriving here after such vicissitudes and so much suffering, the only effect was to make me expect the worst. Such weather as this could be compared with my best days in the Indian Ocean. The only difference was the choppiness of the seas, due to the inconsiderable depth.

On the 9th of June the wind seemed to be rising into storm. As I had rested for several days, I took the helm; the barometer had fallen

10 mm. In the daytime I headed into the waves, but at night, with visibility nil and my cow of a binnacle lamp that still persisted in going out, I would not carry on with this form of sport. The boat having lost way, a wave broke over her and me. The shock was so violent and was such a surprise that I felt I was suffocating. We were well under; it was all I could do to hold my breath; asphyxia was near. For interminable seconds I clung to the mizzen mast, or I should have been washed overboard. Slowly, desperately slowly, *Lehg II* emerged: so did I. I took a deep breath. That accursed binnacle lamp and its tricks! I was so furious that, for the first time, I lowered the mainsail and went below to sleep.

On the 10th I set the mainsail again. As I was sailing very close to the wind, the seas were constantly over the deck and it was impossible to do anything without getting completely soaked. It was only in the cockpit, behind a canvas screen that I had had installed in Chile, that I found some degree of comfort, if I may call it that.

In spite of the wind and the sea, *Lehg II* went on unshaken and that was what mattered. She was going towards her goal, but towards the cold, too. Soon it was 5°C. It was no longer much use to stay at the helm, for my hands could not endure the open air for long. Matters came to the point when, having taken in the mainsail to set the storm trysail, I had to burn matches when I went below to warm my numbed fingers. It was ten seconds before I could feel the heat of the flame.

Very close-hauled, the boat was labouring heavily, shaking, shuddering and creaking under the impact of the heavy seas. My position was 42° S. by 82°45′ W.; the wind, which in the last twenty-four hours had swung to the South, obliged me to get a little closer to the land, whereas I had been more than 400 miles off. On the 14th I was level with the Gulf of Penas; I had to bale every three hours, for I had been unable to discover the leak.

Hail came rattling down and the clouds were low. The situation was getting worse every moment. That day I reached latitude 47°. I still had another 10° to make to the South in order to round Cape Horn. Waves were crashing down on board. At night I stayed in the cabin, for it was really disagreeable to remain on deck. Not at all like trade wind sailing in the tropics, when a rainstorm is welcome. Here, wet clothes were piling up in the cabin, which was beginning to look like a slop-shop. Hanging them on a wire was useless; they would not dry. Days were short; the sun barely rose above the horizon.

I was disheartened by the recurring squall and the endless swell; but suddenly I felt that it was vital to go on deck and look round. Why? I don't know. It is one of those odd things that happen to seafaring men. A presentiment inexplicable, as far as our knowledge goes. However that may be, I went on deck . . . and saw an American

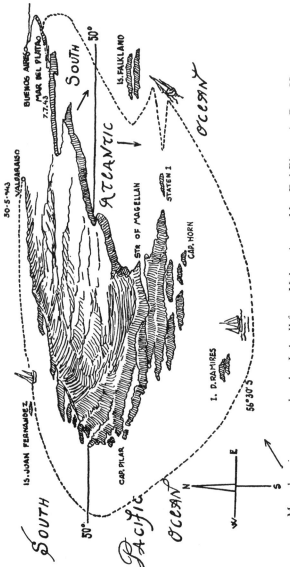

Map showing route taken by *Lehg II* from Valparaiso to Mar Del Plata, *via* Cape Horn.

warship, southward bound and pitching heavily. There were two of us shipping these dirty seas; but we could not make any signals. So we went on our course, each with a different mission.

As the margin of security I had allowed was reduced by the persistence of southerly winds, and I was beginning to get too near the coast, I made a board to the West and, in order not to go too far, took in the storm trysail. On the 16th I was at 48°2′ S. by 82°30′ W. and the wind changing to the South-west, I could resume my course to the South.

The tell-tale which I had installed in the cabin, apart from the very serious deviation caused by the proximity of masses of iron, was useless, as the gimbals had broken and I was not in a position to repair it.

After six days of gales there came a lull and I set the storm trysail once more.

I was 600 miles from Cape Horn. It was time to consider the situations that might arise when I got into the really redoubtable zone. I assessed all the aspects of the problem and drew the most logical conclusion for each of them. This study gave me a more assured plan of navigation.

The cold was so intense that I could not leave the smallest part of my face exposed; on top of the cold, wind and hail lashed down pitilessly. My daily average was 120 miles.

On the night of the 18th of June, Cape Pillar, the entrance to the Strait of Magellan, was 180 miles to the East. This passage tempted me not at all. I had decided to round Cape Horn and neither storms nor risks should shake my determination.

Although not at the helm, I was standing by to surface. Not a detail had escaped me. I had greased two gloves so that the water could not make them useless; I had done the same for my oilskin. I had prepared iron rations on a basis of chocolate, preserves and biscuit for use in the event of being surprised by a spot of weather which might keep me at the helm for several days when close to Diego Ramirez Island, some 30 miles South of the Cape. As it shows no light, constant vigilance is necessary. To keep myself awake, I had benzedrine sulphate ready. Nothing was left to chance, everything had been studied, foreseen and calculated.

I had kept a watchful eye on standing and running rigging in case of wear; they seemed capable of withstanding any unforeseen strain.

As my thigh boots were wet through, I looked about for some means of drying them; and thought of putting a light inside each.

It worked.

# 26

# *In Search of the Atlantic*

I was being carried towards the coast, in the zone of icebergs and drift ice. Numerous birds were flying about, hunting for their living. In the cabin, hermetically sealed, the temperature was 5°C.

On the 20th Cape Horn was 400 miles away to the E.S.E. Getting nearer, getting nearer!

Two days later a storm from the North obliged me to take in the storm trysail for the night. I was already sailing due East; the wind was 40 knots; *Lehg II* went on under mizzen, staysail and storm jib. I was not far from the 'mousetrap' and felt that I had to stay at the helm. At 17.00 hours I saw Tierra del Fuego to the North-east and frankly, if the seas were no heavier with the high wind that was now blowing, I could sleep in peace; I had expected worse. Perhaps my imagination had run away with me; if what I had anticipated in the Indian Ocean had been surpassed, I might have exaggerated the difficulties here. I could not deny that the wind was strong, that the waves broke; but *Lehg II* was quite equal to it and was never in danger.

What I had had to suffer to get so far! Out of respect for those gallant sailors of old Spain, for all those who have perished in those desolate regions, I had to admit that the danger existed. Still, I had the impression that I should find calm ahead; and that was what happened. I had come here expecting the worst, though convinced that no difficulty would be insurmountable; expecting the 'impossible', I came to believe that I was seeking death; maybe what was really beyond the limit did not appear so to me and I was being irreverent. The memory of the Indian Ocean must have made me feel *blasé* about all I experienced and it took the sting out of every difficulty.

Towards the end of the afternoon I ran out of the zone of wind into a calmer one, with a clearer sky. To the South I could see, shimmering whitely, the coruscating reflection of the Antarctic ice.

The current was carrying me on my road towards the East. About midday on the 24th the wind veered to the North. Numbers of cormorants came close to inspect the boat; there is nowadays so little navigation in this area that the presence of any ship is a surprise for them. I had still 90 miles to go before striking the longitude of Cape Horn.

That night the north wind had already risen to gale force. I only put my nose outside from time to time to see whether there was anything ahead.

How full of meaning and menace is the sound of those two words: Cape Horn! What a vast and terrible cemetery of seamen lies under this eternally boiling sea! Fear adds its chill to that of the atmosphere, the terror that lurks in a name and the sight of these seas.

Here, everything seems to be attracted and drawn towards the depths, as by some monstrous, supernatural magnet. Had I had a larger surface of wood under my feet, I could have calmed my nerves by pacing the deck, but no; I could not walk my thoughts under control.

Fear of the storm? No. Apprehension that sprang, I felt, from legend, for all that I had been told about these regions. Of all storms, that which lurks invisible in an atmosphere of terror is the worst.

As my boat neared the headland I tried to pierce the unknown with the sword of reason, as though this were my last opportunity to think and to live. Perhaps in a few moments all would be over.

Yet that dim light of my compass on this dark Antarctic night made me look with tenderness on these wrought planks, flesh of the beautiful trees of my country, fashioned by human knowledge into a boat. It seemed to me that they were more in their place on land, living under the murmur of warm light breezes; if they had souls, they would reject the present to which I was exposing them. My voyage had been like a stairway which I ascended step by step, until I found myself here. Here, hard by Cape Horn. Had it been announced to me as a child, I should not have believed it.

They were ringing in my ears with a note of doom, as if they came from the depths of the sea or the height of Heaven, those true words that I could not or would not understand, spoken at Valparaiso before I set out for Cape Horn.

'Wouldn't you like to leave your log here? So that your pains may not be wasted?'

The voice that spoke was trying to be persuasive without sounding ominous. What they wanted to insinuate was quite clear to me: they were not at all confident of my success; they felt that I was lost before I started. But I was full of curiosity about Cape Horn. I wanted to see it, live it, touch it, feel it. . . .

Here in my travelling library, close to me, were the records of Cook, of Bougainville, of so many other navigators, books that I had read and re-read. I remembered the enthusiasm I felt on hearing the news that Al Hansen had succeeded in rounding Cape Horn from East to West, a feat nowise diminished by his terrible end. Hansen had been powerless to escape the curse that broods between the 50° of the Atlantic and the 50° of the Pacific. I felt his Calvary in my flesh only to think of it.

Yet I had taken it upon myself to round the Cape as the only way to make port, refusing to admit any other course. All or nothing. As *Lehg II* neared the grim promontory, through hours made infinitely long by impatience and anxiety, I threw my last card on the table of life.

If luck was against me, it would be easy to say:

'It was lunacy to attempt Cape Horn alone, in a 9-tonner—barely that.'

But what if I succeeded?

Imperceptibly, perhaps, the longing of all those who would have liked to make the attempt and were unable to do so, or the hopes of those who had tried without success, crept towards me. Perhaps I had the help of those who perished in this trial; perhaps I was not quite so alone as I thought. Perhaps the seamen of all latitudes were spectators of this struggle against the squalls and the darkness. Perhaps too, this darkness would grow darker yet, that the flickering lantern would cease to glow in front of my eyes, whose lids would close to see nothing any more on earth, now, or ever. This light, of little practical use, was more of an inseparable and invisible companion, standing between me and chaos. Life shone in it, the light of illusion or hope in the possibility—perhaps—of triumph.

It was midnight. According to my speed, Cape Horn should now be abeam. The wind was high and the seas heavy. In the cabin I had to cling to hand holds to avoid being thrown against the panels.

Sitting under the light of my little paraffin lamp, I was trying to repair the tell-tale when a shock threw me forward; my face crashed near the deadlight on the other side. The pain was terrible. I was half stunned, but noticed that I was bleeding violently from the nose. Fumbling, I found some cotton-wool and held it to my face to check the bleeding. Then I let myself fall, sick and dizzy, into a corner. It took me several minutes to pull myself together. I did not know exactly what had happened. I feared that the frontal bone might be fractured, in that case, what should I do? Groggy as I was, I succeeded in grasping the situation; I remembered that the boat was still going on and thought of what could happen. I began to explore my jawbone tenderly, looking for a possible fracture. I stopped for a moment. My fingers were wet with blood. No, the chin was all right. The pain was still acute, but my mind was becoming more lucid. As I touched my nose I felt a sharp stab of pain and noticed that there was an abnormal amount of play. So I had a broken nose. Ouf! that was nothing. I decided to look for the worst, for what I most feared: the eyes. I felt them; no damage. What a relief! I continued along the supra-orbital ridge; my fingers found the lips of a wound on the forehead.

After half an hour, a long half-hour, the bleeding began to ease off.

Cape Horn had made me pay toll. Given the speed at which the boat was travelling, I should now be just past it.

For the rest of the night the wind blew furiously from the North; but in the morning it eased off and backed to S.W.

I could not observe the slightest scrap of land; only a bank of clouds to the North indicated its presence. I took advantage of the relative calm to bale; and I made a trip to the mirror to see what it had to say. My face was a horrid mess, swollen, distorted and bloodstained. But that was nothing. I was back in the Atlantic.

# 27

# *Done It!*

The 25th went by, quietly forging on under mizzen, storm trysail, staysail and jib. I remembered that I had left something behind. Oh yes! . . . Cape Horn.

How many sailors have been saddled for life with the consequences of sailing in those parts? As for me, what did I feel? How shall I express the emotion of the first man to round Cape Horn and survive?

A dead sailor was standing by me.

What a joy it was, that sunny morning in 1934, when he came to see me, signed his name on a panel of *Lehg II*, then building, and expressed his approval. He talked of the mother he had left far away in his Norwegian fjord and discussed his plans. It seemed unthinkable that he, with all his determination and optimism, should have finished as he did.

What a loss . . . that he should not have lived to tell, with more talent than I possess, what he felt on rounding Cape Horn. I realized that I was privileged. But . . . what was this privilege worth, even after those fantastic crossings—4,200, 7,400, 5,400 miles—when 1,000 miles still lay between me and my mother? Long, cruelly long were those miles. But, looking back and thinking of the sailors who got no farther, I wept with joy.

On, on I had to go, against a head wind, tacking in a zig-zag that made many miles of very few.

The cold was acute; wind and squalls made it worse, although in this zone the warm currents from the Pacific prevented the water from freezing. I could not stay at the helm for long. Sailing so near the wind, the deck was always awash. Even to catch the sun to make a point was quite a business, for at midday it was only 9° above the horizon and very hard to see. On the 26th, however, I managed to get my position as 45°56′ S. by 61°30′ W., getting clear of the zone of 21 per cent. of force 8 gales into another where the percentage was only 17. As I was only some 90 miles East of Staten Island, I decided at nightfall to make a board towards land, so as to avoid the choppy seas by the Barwood Bank.

The wounds in my mouth were a nuisance; they bled every time I tried to eat.

On the evening of the 27th I saw a seal, an indication that land was not far; so, having sailed in low visibility under an overcast sky, I preferred to go on the opposite tack in order to keep away from Staten Island; the approaches there are so dangerous and the seas so heavy that one should give them 20 miles berth. And next morning I found that I was on the bank that I had been trying to avoid; it was violently choppy and beginning to snow. It was annoying not to be able to take a sight, for I did not know how far I was from the Falkland Islands which stretch some distance to the South and include Beauchêne Island and Mintay Reef. I did not want to leave the Falklands to westward, for that would necessitate making a wide circle and take me into a current that would carry me towards the middle of the Atlantic. I could manage the wind and the sea perfectly well; the problem was to locate my position.

It was a year since I had left my country and I had just crossed the 60th meridian. What a lot of things had happened in a year! Every day meant more miles behind, fewer ahead.

It so happened the wind backed to the West late in the afternoon. I spent an uneasy night, fearing an unpleasant surprise. According to my calculations I was 30 miles from Mintay Reef. I could not see a thing: every time I went on deck the snow lashing my face drove me below again. So the only thing to do was to stay there. The wind was blowing between 30 and 40 knots with a tendency to westing, which helped me on northward. I hoped it would stay there, so that I could give the Falklands a clear berth.

Rarely have I awaited the dawn of a new day with such suspense as I did on the 29th, for in the darkness I could not see where I was sailing and feared that I was rushing on to unforeseen dangers. It was impossible to take a sight. With daylight, my anxiety decreased; but a loud crack brought me up on deck. The backstay shackle had parted under the violent wind which accompanied the rain squalls. Making the most of the rare lulls in the gale, I managed to make it fast; as I was about to go below again, I looked around and, through the squalls, saw the Beaver Islands. What a relief! I was past the Falklands. To the North of these lie the Jason Islands; but if the wind did not change, I should be past them by midnight.

On the 30th of June I was able to take a sight which showed me at 49°55′ S. by 62°30′ W.

Looking ahead now, it was only a question of days; upon my word, I already felt at home. The look of the water, the porpoises, the enormous number of birds flying round *Lehg II*, told me that I was home. No more changes. My course was set for the River Plate now. I had been a month at sea.

The shallow and uneven bottom made short seas which did not

trouble me. The mean depth is only 80 fathoms, getting shallower towards the North. The sea that can get up on these thin layers of water is so slight that neither the boat nor I would suffer much, even in the event of a storm.

I had passed Santa Cruz and the coast was some 200 miles to the East. Cape Horn was far away and with it that reasoned pessimism which compelled every other moment to work out plans for all possible contingencies. At that time, I looked forward to the black patch, Dead Man's Road, to resolve my doubts and also to taste the divine satisfaction of not having been mistaken. All that was now past. Even the hardships seemed to have shrunk, viewed at this distance as if through the wrong end of a telescope.

Thanks to sailing close-hauled, everything below was soaked with sea water. The temperature remained at 5°C., but the average runs were excellent. On the 5th of July I was 150 miles from Mar del Plata. The sun, already higher, infused the atmosphere with a friendly warmth that seemed to invite a siesta; the route was gay with birds and beautiful white-sided porpoises. With a fair wind from the West, *Lehg II* was cracking ahead, sailing without interference from me most of the time.

On the morning of the 5th of July I saw a Chilean steamer with a four-master in tow, coming from Buenos Aires. They had a cargo of coal and were bound for the Strait of Magellan. The next day at sunrise was fair; clouds and squalls were behind me.

# 28

# *Four Minutes Slow*

I was pleasantly occupied in making myself a cup of chocolate when, without any particular reason, I looked ahead . . . and there was the coast, less than 5 miles away.

What had happened?

The chronometer was four minutes slow, giving me a difference of 60 miles in longitude. It was Quenquen ahead of me. I was quite indignant, although this discrepancy was understandable; the chronometer had undergone great hardships, shaken up by many days' close sailing, and in particular the oil had congealed. My most immediate reaction was: pack up the sextant and chronometer and from now on sail by sight of land. My fury spared the compass, however . . . I forgot my chocolate and sat down at the helm for a spell of peaceful yachting, with a cigar.

Interminable beaches, yellow dunes, a little tree here and a ranch there; behind them the low hills; shallow, nile-green water. I was having fun with this type of navigation, the only kind that I had never practised in the whole of my journey. As the night fell there was the Mala Cara buoy—an 'Ugly Mug' that did not look too bad to me. The moon was in her first quarter; the wind, a gentle breeze off the land. Mar del Plata was only 18 miles away and I came in sight of it in the first minutes of the 7th of July.

The port was there—but the wind dropped. It had favoured me so far: now it was light and dead ahead. I was to the East of Punto Mogotes lighthouse; a little farther to the North the red and white lights of the breakwater marked the finishing post of my trip. Slowly I passed along Fisherman's Bank, giving *Lehg II* a gentle pat; she had been through such a lot. God must have loved her; and thanks be to Him, the end of a terrible Odyssey was very near. How beautiful were the stars! Those in the sky and those on land were twinkling, peaceful and friendly. The air was clear and the flashes from the lighthouse met no obstacle. I could hear the waves breaking on the beach; it was the only sound.

Out of thirty-eight days I had only spent seven at the helm; *Lehg II* had flown home on her own. I could imagine the surprise of people ashore when the ghost came home next day.

311

And it dawned. The fishing boats sailed by, peopling the bright morning, taking no notice. Finally one of them heard me hailing:

'Ahoy, *amigo!* When you get back from fishing, tell the harbour Master that I'm becalmed. If I could have a tow. . . .'

'We're not going in till the afternoon.'

'Never mind! Any time will do.'

Off they went. And I was the one to be surprised. They had no idea who they were talking to. So I settled down to cook a lunch which I had been hoping to eat at home. But soon I heard the popping of a motor; the boat passed near me; now she was turning. The fishermen hailed me in their dialect:

'Cap'n! We were waiting for you! We watched out all day hoping to see you come in. We didn't mean to leave you just like that without saying anything.'

I swelled with pride. They called me 'Captain'. They wanted to give me a tow.

'But you'll lose a day's fishing.'

'Bah! We fish everyday; the honour of towing you happens once in a lifetime.'

I asked them aboard. One of them helped me to furl the sails. We cracked a bottle in honour of the event. They passed a tow. I made it fast to the bitts, and *Lehg II* proceeded sedately towards the harbour. We sang sea shanties. And soon we were in port and looking for a mooring off the Yacht Club. Every face that appeared was bright with excitement. Once safely moored I set out for the Club; as I set foot on land my legs nearly let me down; they were wobbling feebly. Hands and congratulations reached out to me. As I sat on a bench of the Club House, one drew off my boots, another went to run a hot bath for me—how good it was for my chilled body!—a glass of whisky was handed to me. Now two naval officers appeared; one of them wanting to take me to the cabin prepared for me on the Coastal Patrol ship *Belgrano;* his name—believe it or not—was Amour! Everything I expected was beyond my expectations. I was staggering, stammering; all I could say was:

'I hope you're not putting yourselves out.'

'Of course not! You'll have everything you need and you'll be among sailors.'

My cup was running over. I let myself be towed along, proud as a peacock.

# 29

## *Recessional*

I could not have imagined my way of life; I had to experience it. From the Port Admiral to the last matelot, everyone fussed over me. Telegrams poured in. Receptions at the Rotary Club, at the Sailing Club, in private houses. Photographs, press interviews, autographs—I was the centre of the world.

On the 9th of July I was bidden to the ceremony of hoisting the flag at sunrise. The crews of all ships were on parade, silent and motionless in the dawn. As the rim of the sun climbed into the pale sky, a bugle call tore the silence and the flag broke from the mast. I was not alone. The great fraternity of the sea was at my side.

I offered that moment to God and murmured to myself, to that particle of the divine that each of us carries within:

'For this—I would go round the world a hundred times.'

# 30

# *A Letter*

*Lehg II* was moored near the Coastal Patrol vessel; in spite of present delights I had to sail on. I had still 200 miles to go and I could not miss Montevideo. All through the voyage my Uruguayan friends had sustained me with their encouragement. In a letter which I received at Valparaiso, one of them said to me:

'We cannot follow you to share your struggles, but our thoughts are with you, intensely and sincerely; do understand that your triumph will be not only yours but ours as well; do please heave your anchor here.'

The value of friendship is something that I have always understood. Wherever friends may be, one must go to them if possible.

That is why, when I set sail one afternoon, it was for a very short run. A huge crowd was assembled on the jetty; warships returning from an exercise saluted, fishermen going out to sea hailed me with good wishes. Only the wind was sulking; but one of the *Belgrano's* boats towed me from the jetty.

Outside, the wind was from the North and I had to luff; the sea was so calm that the boats convoying me could, and did, fill me up with mates which they passed over the side.

In order not to go too far from the coast I decided to make boards of two hours. Thus I spent a night, a day and the next night. After sailing for over thirty hours with the tiller lashed, I was level with Mar Chiquita. At 22.00 hours I made a board landward. I had only been able to sleep for an hour and a half in all.

It was perhaps 22.30 when I scrambled on deck; whether it was the current or just bad luck, but the fact remains that less than 100 yards ahead waves were breaking on the shore. The wind was practically nil. I leapt to the helm to cut it loose, but I had no knife on me. Seconds were passing. Through the mist which exaggerated its size, a high dune suddenly appeared before me; it was rushing at me. I finally succeeded in unlashing the helm and put it hard over: the boat did not respond. The breakers were very close. I tried to luff, but *Lehg II* kept straight on. She lifted on a wave and when she dropped again, I felt a heavy jolt; the keel was on the sands. The following wave broke on deck, breaking the mizzen-stay.

I was desperate; I was suffering with the boat. I kept on repeating: 'I am a bad sailor . . . a bad sailor, a bad shipmate; it's my fault. . . .' At the same time I knew that this was not the moment for lamentation; I had to save *Lehg II* by getting her as far up the beach as possible. Holding the tiller and taking advantage of each breaker, I gained inch by inch. Soon the ketch was well aground in the sand; the tiller beating to and fro with every wave.

I must lighten her. It was midnight. Drenched by the waves, I reached the beach some 15 yards away and deposited the dunnage, which I carried over my head to keep it dry. Then I began again.

By the evening of that unhappy day my task was finished and *Lehg II* considerably lighter. I had left the sails set, so that every time she eased, she would get farther inshore; she was now high and dry at low tide. From time to time I went to see how she was getting on, thinking that she would probably never sail again. Every boat that had gone ashore on these beaches had been destroyed.

# 31

# *The Rescue*

On Sunday afternoon, somewhat encouraged by the result of my efforts, I decided to go in search of help. From the top of a dune I tried to attract attention by signalling with my arms.

When I was about to give up in despair and return to my camp, a horseman rode up. I gave him a letter for his employer, Señor Arbelay, asking him to inform my friends of my lamentable plight. The man assured me that the message would reach them by Monday morning. I did not conceal the difficulties that would attend any attempt to salve *Lehg II*.

They decided on the simplest course: to pass a tow which would have to be at least a thousand metres long.

The sequel is quite a story.

On Monday afternoon the trawler *Py* and the patrol boat *Mocovi* arrived at the beach where we were stranded. They sent a ship's boat in through the breakers. Lieutenant Antonini studied the position and, as it was getting late, he assured me that he would return next morning with everything needful.

He kept his promise. The trawler, anchored about a kilometre off the coast, passed the cable which I called the 'sea serpent' because it did not sink; seeing that the boat could not possibly have brought it in; the cable had been married with another of coir fibre.

It took a whole day to pay it out and make fast to *Lehg II*. When everything was ready the order was given to the trawler: 'a kick ahead and stop'. Thus *Lehg II* was launched square on to the breakers; very gently without a scratch she was hauled off the beach and refloated. It was a real masterpiece of seamanship. Everyone was pleased; I was even more delighted.

As for myself, I was to rejoin ship by road, with my cargo, in order not to hinder the salvage. Heartfelt thanks to the Ministry of Marine!

# 32

# *The Yacht for the Job*

That night Sēnor Arbelay took me back to Mar del Plata, following the lorry which the municipality had so kindly lent me to carry my bits and pieces. I could not conceal my apprehension for the boat. Would she have sprung a leak? More wretched worry and delay to round off a voyage which was really finished, for Mar del Plata could reasonably pass as the end of my journey, after sailing across three oceans and rounding Cape Horn. Never mind, I would sleep on the beach; for over a year, I had spent only two months of relative repose on land. If the boat had to go up on the slips for repairs, would the backlash of fatigue not overcome me? What an effort, to start again. . . .

The car purred on. We had little to say to each other. Both of us would have liked to talk, to think of something else; but worry was inexorable.

We stopped for petrol; and there I heard the news. I was astounded; *Lehg II* had not made a drop of water. We started off again full of hope. Step on the gas! Now perhaps I could do something about it and be off again in a day or two. Begone, misery; roll on the happy ending!

So there we were. One afternoon, with a fresh, fair breeze from the South, I sat at the helm of my faithful companion once more.

Let's talk about her.

Her length—31 ft. 2 in., for a deep-sea yacht—is open to criticism. I admit that it may not be ideal.

When a journalist asked me my plans, I replied that, if *Lehg II* was bought for a museum, I was thinking of having a 50 ft. boat built. He replied:

'You'll be much happier with a boat like this than with a larger one.'

True enough. I was only toying with the illusion of greater convenience; but experience has proved that this length, coupled with a Norwegian stern, gives an excellent hydrostatic performance in any sea, the agility of an acrobat, and especially a flow of water along the hull without leaving eddies. There is very little drag.

The mainmast should not exceed 30 feet above the deck; the only result of making it longer would be to increase the heel in difficult weather. I had noticed that replacing the mainsail by a storm trysail with a surface of a few square metres only had no influence on my daily run. This is so true that when I set the balloon jib one day in a wind of 10 knots to see what would happen, I found that the boat got blanketed in the trough of the waves and behaved less well. The puffs only reached her on the wave crests and she showed a tendency to luff in the troughs, which gave her an abnormal heel. Instead of keeping a steady course, she yawed a great deal.

The two advantages of the Bermuda rig, which are so great that I will have nothing else on any future boat, are: the ease of taking in or setting sail even in a 25 knot wind, and the absence of spars and top-hamper required by a gaff rig; not to mention chafing against the rigging and damage due to sun and salt water. One day a block will jam, another day the lacing if not the peak thimble itself. It may be questioned that for sailing, as I did, mostly before the wind, Marconi rig is right; yet in practice it has always given me the best results.

I had no trouble with the canvas I selected—No. 8, hand-sewn— apart from some rusting of the steel luff clips; I had been unable to procure galvanized ones at the time. This is an extraordinary record for a voyage of this kind.

In 1931 I had tried the experiment of a boat with very tall masts, demonstrating to the yachting world the possibility of taking the high seas with a boat intended for racing like my 8 metre *U.I.* in which I crossed from France to the Argentine. It was the first and the last time.

In the following years naval architects showed a tendency to fine down cruising yachts, giving them relatively high masts. But for such a voyage as I had accomplished, a boat of this type would have been disastrous. Waves sometimes exceeding 60 feet and winds up to 70 knots amply confirmed my belief that a Norwegian, with continuous framing from end to end, has the cohesion necessary to withstand constant terrific shocks. For in my navigation it was no question of a storm here and there, but of an endless succession of dirty weather.

As regards a sea anchor, I have one point of view which settled the question for me: I would never give such an object ship-room. I am convinced that a boat can stand up to any sea, comfortably enough, under sail. She has freedom of movement and can lift to the seas. Should the wind force exceed 50 knots I would say, contrary to the opinion that following combers can play havoc by breaking on deck, that one of my favourite pleasures was to run through squalls on a mattress of foam. My speed on these surf-riding occasions exceeded 15 knots; I then presented the stern to another wave and began this exciting pastime anew. When a wave arrives roaring from astern and it seems impossible that the ship could lift, it stands to reason that one is frightened; but when one has ascertained that fright is not justified, one gets accustomed to the exercise. In these circumstances many people would lay-to; I at once rejected this solution, feeling, as if in my own flesh, the suffering of the boat buried under raging waves. Whatever the hurricane, it never compelled me to strike all sail; my mainsail has no reef points. The old saying which prescribed a salute to squalls by taking in sail was never adhered to in the course of my voyages; when I did take it in it was in order to get some rest.

Nor do I believe in interior ballast, which is dangerous. However carefully it is battened down, it *can* come adrift and the consequences will be disastrous. I have an example of the effect which that kind of projectile can produce in the cabin of a ship. The woodwork below carried visible scars inflicted by the handle of the capstan. I was lucky to have dodged it myself.

As for taking sights, the most frequent difficulty was the motion of the boat. Another major obstacle is the absence of a horizon, masked as it is by the infinity of planes constituted by the waves. If I tried to 'shoot the sun' standing up and leaning on the mizzen mast, the water which got into the telescope wetted and blurred the mirror and obliged me to give it up—not to speak of the danger of violent jolts which on several occasions nearly sent me overboard. The best post I have found for observation was seated on the cabin hatchway with only half my body protruding. Thus I could get the sextant under cover quickly if a wave threatened to wet it. In any case, the operation was always rather like breaking in a colt. I put the chronometer below, in full view, so that I could read it at any moment.

Several times I took circum-meridians, but I must admit that I was rarely able to note with certainty the hour when the sun reached its zenith; generally I made an approximate calculation, averaged from a series. The altitude presented another insoluble problem; the sun, practically always veiled, only allowed observation of the meridian.

I calculated longitude by a very simple method; weather permitting, by the rise and setting of the sun, sometimes in conjunction with those of the moon and a third observation at the moment of taking a sight. The correctness of my calculations was confirmed by the accuracy of landfalls in regions where visibility was very bad.

# 33

# *We're Here*

A siren shrieked.

An oil tanker came up, flying the signal: 'Congratulations and best wishes'. Passengers and crew applauded me as they passed and asked whether I needed anything. I didn't.

The ship was coming from the South coast and following the same route as myself; but she soon left me behind and by night was no more than a light ahead, soon to be duplicated by another—Querandi lighthouse.

At 21.00 hours I passed the site of my accident. Then Medanos Light appeared. If I continued at this rate I should be at Montevideo in a matter of twenty hours. All this time I could not sleep. One can do that sort of thing once. . . .

Very early in the morning I passed Cape San Antonio. But, alas! as the day wore on the wind dropped. I was steering by compass, but at night the lights of Montevideo were my guide. I did not feel tired. I was wide awake with anticipation, joy . . . and prudence. I ate pleasant food and I drank good wine. And quietly, serenely, full of hope, *Lehg II* surged on through the calm seas, to find herself off Montevideo in the morning. It was a bit slow in this calm and, caressed by the rising sun, I began to doze off in the cockpit.

I was roused by the whistle of a tug, full of friends coming to meet me. I fell on their necks, they on mine. Fatigue fled and we chatted and joked until we arrived at Flores Island, where I had been asked to wait until the next day, Saturday, to make my official entry into the port of Buceo.

What a beautiful evening I had with the charming people who live on the island at the foot of the lighthouse! And what a good rest.

On Saturday, at 17.00 hours, in splendid sunlight, very different from the squalls of a farewell which I thought might be the last, I returned.

Cheers, shouts, dinghies, boats, people crowded on the pier, tambourines—the triumphal reception of my arrival in 1943 was repeated. The only difference in the scene was the new building of the Uruguayan Yacht Club.

It would take another book to describe the triumphal progresses and the kindness that were my lot at Montevideo. When I remember these things in my retirement, I am happy to have added one little stone to a fraternity that nothing can ever destroy.

As I was expected at Buenos Aires on Sunday at 11 o'clock, *Lehg II* made the passage under tow lest the wind should fail. And on Sunday the 7th at 10 o'clock, to the deafening sounds of sirens and whistles, of cheers and shouts, I came into my home port and moored on the stroke of 11. On the deck of a Swedish ship moored close by, the Captain and an officer standing under their flag began to lower it slowly. A sudden hush fell. Extraordinary that such a simple act should silence assembled thousands.

As I came on shore the accolade of my friend Commodore Aguirre, the salutes of the officers and finally the embrace of my mother showed how this immense crowd was moved by one feeling and one wish: to celebrate my success; for I had circumnavigated the globe by the Impossible Route.

*     *     *

I am enjoying the evening in a remote place in the Sierra de Cordoba. A dog has dug himself a form to sleep in and I can hear birds twittering. It is only a very gentle whisper; colours merge into darkness, contours fade; night is creeping on the mountains. Down in the valley, lights come alive, blinking like falling stars, each one of them a boat on land that carries its own problems. Silence is falling with the dusk.

I am filled with such happiness that a silent prayer arises from the depths of my being.

'Lord, be lavish of Thy Peace and guide to all the ports of all the world those sailors who are orphaned in the immensity of the sea.'

# THE PRINCIPAL PASSAGES OF VITO DUMAS

## FIRST VOYAGE

Route No. 1. *Lehg I*

Arcachon—Buenos Aires

6,270 miles = 76 days

Arcachon: D.[1] 13.12.31
Vigo: A.[2] 22.12.31
(9 days = 550 miles)
Vigo: D. 26.12.31
Las Palmas: A. 11.1.32
(16 days = 80 miles)

Las Palmas: D. 27.1.32
Rio Grande: A. 13.3.42
(45 days = 4.200 miles)

Rio Grande: D. 5.4.32
Montevideo: A. 9.4.32
(4 days = 400 miles)

Montevideo: D. 11.4.32
Buenos Aires: A. 13.4.32
(2 days = 140 miles)

## SECOND VOYAGE

Route No. 2 *Lehg II*

Round the world (7 ports of call)

20,420 miles = 272 days

Buenos Aires: D. 27.6.42
Montevideo: A. 28.6.42
(1 day = 110 miles)

Montevideo: D. 1.7.42
Cape Town: A. 25.8.42
(55 days = 4,200 miles)

Cape Town: D. 14.9.42
Wellington: A. 27.12.42
(104 days = 7,400 miles)

Wellington: D. 30.1.43
Valparaiso: A. 12.4.43
(72 days = 5,200 miles)

Valparaiso: D. 30.5.43
Mar del Plata: A. 7.7.43
(37 days = 3,200 miles)

Mar del Plata: D. 28.8.43
Montevideo: A. 30.8.43
(2 days = 200 miles)

Montevideo: D. 6.9.43
Buenos Aires: A. 7.9.43
(1 day = 110 miles)

D. = Departure
A. = Arrival

The distances on this table correspond to the actual distance travelled, according to the wind and not to a direct line between ports. Thus, for example, the distance between Buenos Aires and Montevideo is variously drawn, as 110, 140 and 160 sea miles.

## THIRD VOYAGE

Route No. 3. *Lehg II*

Buenos Aires—New York—
  Azores Islands—Canary
  Islands—Buenos Aires

17,045 miles = 235 days

Buenos Aires: D. 1.9.45
Montevideo: A. 3.9.45
  (2 days = 110 miles)

Montevideo: D. 15.9.45
P. del Este: A. 16.9.45
  (1 day = 75 miles)

P. del Este: D. 22.9.45
Rio de Janeiro: A. 19.10.45
  (27 days = 1,300 miles)

Rio de Janeiro: D. 5.1.46
Havana: A. 9.3.46
  (61 days = 5,400 miles)

Havana: D. 2.6.46
New York
Azores Is.
Canary Is.
Cape Verde Is.
Cearâ (Brazil): A. 16.9.46
  (106 days = 7,000 miles)

Cearâ: D. 5.11.46
Montevideo: A. 10.12.36
  (35 days = 3,000 miles)

Montevideo: D. 26.1.47
Buenos Aires: A. 28.1.47
  (1 day = 110 miles)

## FOURTH VOYAGE

Route No. 4. *Sirio*

Buenos Aires—New York
  (one landfall)

7,100 miles = 117 days

Buenos Aires: D. 23.4.55
Bermuda: A. 6.8.55
  (105 days = 6,400 miles)

Bermuda: D. 2.9.55
New York: A. 23.9.55
  (12 days = 1,300 miles)

## COMMENTARY ON THE CONCEPTION AND DESIGN OF *LEHG II* BY MANUEL M. CAMPOS NAVAL ARCHITECT

This boat, which I designed in 1933 and built in 1934, was conceived for ocean voyages. Discussion with Vito Dumas led me to choose the Norwegian type as being ideal for sailing before the wind in bad weather, chiefly because of the form of the stern.

This type, which is actually as old as navigation, appears on all seas in innumerable versions. It is so common in Scandinavian countries as to be the national type of sailing vessel.

In the Argentine, before the construction of the port of Buenos Aires, the anchorage off that city was dangerous in almost all winds; hence the use of boats with double stems known as whale-boats which were probably of Spanish or Italian, certainly of Mediterranean origin.

The length of these whale-boats varied from 29 ft. 6 in. to 45 ft. or even 50 ft., but never less than 29 ft. They were peculiarly well adapted for use in this open anchorage. But the tradition had been almost forgotten when, in 1927 or 1928, people in yachting circles began to appreciate the excellent qualities of the Norwegian type. Soon after, several boats were built, copied almost exactly from Atkin's design; he in his turn had been inspired by the celebrated designer of Norwegian double-enders, Colin Archer.

Soon after, again, I received my first order to design a Norwegian; I then remembered the precise details that I had obtained from an old shipwright, shortly before his death, concerning the Rio de la Plata whale-boats of former times: their dimensions, proportions, etc.

In my efforts to collect information concerning Scandinavian boats of the 'Norwegian' type, I found that they were in the main heavily built fishing boats; naturally enough, since fishing is one of the principal industries of those countries. Others were pilot boats or lifeboats which, for use as yachts, had an excessive displacement and a considerable quantity of interior ballast with its attendant dangers.

Furthermore, their construction was too heavy and their classical gaff rigs looked old-fashioned at a time when Bermuda rig was becoming popular.

*Lehg II* is a modernized version of the old Rio de la Plata whale-boats, in which the proportion of length to beam has been reduced, after the manner of the classical 'Norwegians', and the very considerable ballast (3 tons 9 cwt.) has been converted into a cast-iron keel in order to ensure perfect stability whatever the degree of heel.

The specifications were: keel, ribs, floor timbers and deadwood in general, reinforced and benefiting from the excellent quality of Argentine woods; simplifications of the whole structure of the deck and deck-house. By this means a light and very strong structure can be achieved; all pieces were dovetailed in the traditional manner.

The rig adopted for *Lehg II* was the Marconi ketch, with moderate hoist and sail area, but quite sufficient for single-handed navigation on the high seas. The working was centralized in the cockpit.

I think I may say that the result was satisfactory. The boat turned out to be fairly fast, stable, with a high reserve of buoyancy, easy to steer in all weathers; her owner and skipper considers her fit for navigation on the high seas anywhere and in any weather.

MANUEL M. CAMPOS.

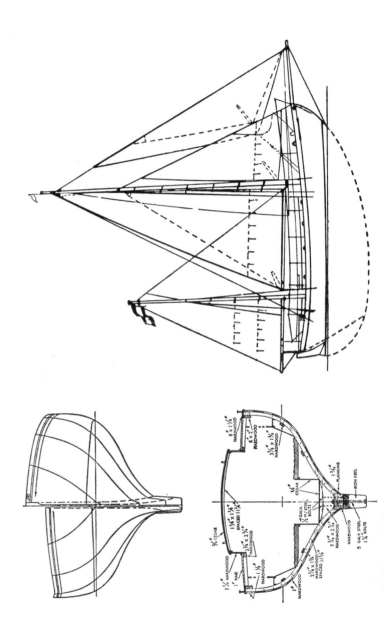

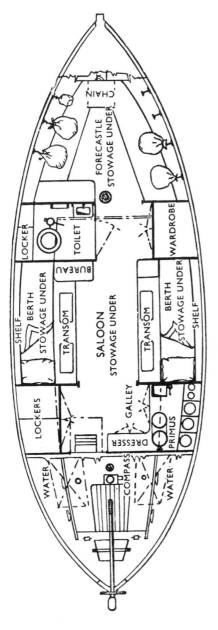

*Lehg II.* Designed by Manuel M. Campos. Length 31 ft. 2 in.; beam 10 ft. 9 in.; moulded depth 5 ft. 7 in. *Sail area*: mainsail 215 sq. ft.; mizzen 77 sq. ft.; staysail 80 sq. ft.; jib 82 sq. ft.

# OPINION OF VITO DUMAS ON *LEHG II*

To comment on the qualities of my boat before going to sea might have seemed rather daring; after having gone round the world with her I have got used to singing her praises.

The duet formed by a careful and experienced naval architect and myself, accustomed to ocean sailing in boats of various types, gave a most harmonious result.

As for myself, I am not in the habit of following other people's methods when it comes to navigation; much comment is founded on errors arising from varying interpretations of a given fact.

In the special case of a voyage round the world on the 40th parallel, the problem was complicated by the fact that no precedent existed; the only data I could gather referred to larger ships, adequately manned; and even so, all that was said of this zone was less than encouraging.

As far as my own voyage was concerned, the chief points of discussion were the characteristic features of the regions traversed and the human factors, while other elements were unfairly passed over in silence.

What could I have done on this desolate route, had I not been able to rely upon a suitable craft?

Sudden disaster is always round the corner at sea; danger lies everywhere in the waves, mast, sails, rigging, deck; the possible causes of failure could be extended indefinitely. The truth is that success is the reward of a harmonious combination of factors contributing to the desired result.

*Lehg II* shipped no water, although combers broke over her almost daily. The hollow mast out of my old boat had been made in France, in a dockyard on the Gironde, and, in spite of winds which sometimes exceeded 70 knots, in spite of the battering of the waves, it remained standing. As a human being who succeeded in surviving, my feelings during successive assaults of a raging sea were those of fair and sincere appreciation of the professional integrity of the joiners who had made that mast, of those who, in my own country, had built the hull, forged the ironwork, sewn the sails; and, last but not least, of the architect. My very real gratitude was that of a man, who, having tempted fate, felt himself sustained by the co-operation of others.

*Lehg II's* speed was good; on one occasion I made 170 miles in twenty-four hours under staysails and mizzen only; I was to beat this record a few years later with 240 miles in a day north of Brazil, assisted, it is true, by the current.

Yet the boat did not give one the sensation of speed; her progress was even and often, when in the cabin, I underestimated the storm raging outside. With her length of 31 ft. 2 in. she rode the seas perfectly; and her fittings below exceeded in their convenience every wish and every need. I could stow stores and food adequate for a year at sea.

On the other hand, it should not be forgotten that a sailor must get the feel of his boat, assimilate her characteristics, in order to get the best results.

*Lehg II* was an ideal floating house of extraordinary strength and endurance. But I must point out that the lines and construction of *Lehg II* should not be compared with other 'Norwegians' of similar appearance. I might say, to use the phraseology of prefaces to films or novels, that 'any resemblance of persons or situations is accidental'.

The proof of this is that the 'Norwegians' built at the same period as *Lehg II* carried an external ballast of 1¼ to 1½ tons at most for the same length, whereas she carried 3 tons 9 cwt.; on the other hand, I had done everything possible to minimize weight above the waterline. I carried my fad to the point of giving away bits of my rigging to various friends and clubs during earlier voyages—to one, my cross-trees; to another, the gaff of the sail I used before adopting the Marconi rig: all to increase my stability!

To give an idea of the superb construction of this boat, I will only say that when I reached Wellington after the 'impossible run' of 104 days in the Indian Ocean, an official who boarded *Lehg II* could not believe his eyes when he looked round the cabin. After 7,400 miles—and what miles—*Lehg II* looked as though she had just come out of the shipyard.

I will finish this brief description of my boat by saying that, thanks to her robust build and her first-class sailing qualities, she gave me full and complete satisfaction.

The "Spray" after she had changed her rig from a sloop to a yawl.
(From a photograph taken in Australian waters.)

# SAILING ALONE
# AROUND
# THE WORLD

BY

## Captain Joshua Slocum

ILLUSTRATED BY

Thomas Fogarty and
George Varian

# CONTENTS

## CHAPTER I

CHAPTER XIII

CHAPTER XIV

CHAPTER XV

CHAPTER XVI

CHAPTER XVII

CHAPTER XVIII

# LIST OF ILLUSTRATIONS

337

# SAILING ALONE AROUND
# THE WORLD

## CHAPTER I

A blue-nose ancestry with Yankee proclivities—Youthful fondness for the sea—Master
of the ship *Northern Light*—Loss of the *Aquidneck*—Return home from Brazil in
the canoe *Liberdade*—The gift of a "ship"—The rebuilding of the *Spray*—Conun-
drums in regard to finance and calking—The launching of the *Spray*.

In the fair land of Nova Scotia, a maritime province, there is a ridge
called North Mountain, overlooking the Bay of Fundy on one side
and the fertile Annapolis valley on the other. On the northern slope
of the range grows the hardy spruce-tree, well adapted for ship-
timbers, of which many vessels of all classes have been built. The
people of this coast, hardy, robust, and strong, are disposed to compete in the world's commerce, and it is nothing against the master
mariner if the birthplace mentioned on his certificate be Nova Scotia.
I was born in a cold spot, on coldest North Mountain, on a cold
February 20, though I am a citizen of the United States—a naturalized
Yankee, if it may be said that Nova Scotians are not Yankees in the
truest sense of the word. On both sides my family were sailors; and
if any Slocum should be found not seafaring, he will show at least
an inclination to whittle models of boats and contemplate voyages.
My father was the sort of man who, if wrecked on a desolate island,
would find his way home, if he had a jack-knife and could find a
tree. He was a good judge of a boat, but the old clay farm which
some calamity made his was an anchor to him. He was not afraid
of a capful of wind, and he never took a back seat at a camp-meeting
or a good, old-fashioned revival.

As for myself, the wonderful sea charmed me from the first. At
the age of eight I had already been afloat along with other boys on

the bay, with chances greatly in favor of being drowned. When a lad I filled the important post of cook on a fishing-schooner; but I was not long in the galley, for the crew mutinied at the appearance of my first duff, and "chucked me out" before I had a chance to shine as a culinary artist. The next step toward the goal of happiness found me before the mast in a full-rigged ship bound on a foreign voyage. Thus I came "over the bows," and not in through the cabin windows, to the command of a ship.

My best command was that of the magnificent ship *Northern Light*, of which I was part-owner. I had a right to be proud of her, for at that time—in the eighties—she was the finest American sailing-vessel afloat. Afterward I owned and sailed the *Aquidneck*, a little bark which of all man's handiwork seemed to me the nearest to per-

*Drawn by W. Taber.*

The *Northern Light*, Captain Joshua Slocum, bound for Liverpool, 1885.

fection of beauty, and which in speed, when the wind blew, asked no favors of steamers. I had been nearly twenty years a shipmaster when I quit her deck on the coast of Brazil, where she was wrecked. My home voyage to New York with my family was made in the canoe *Liberdade*, without accident.

My voyages were all foreign. I sailed as freighter and trader principally to China, Australia, and Japan, and among the Spice Islands. Mine was not the sort of life to make one long to coil up one's ropes on land, the customs and ways of which I had finally almost forgotten. And so when times for freighters got bad, as at last they did, and I tried to quit the sea, what was there for an old sailor to do? I was born in the breezes, and I had studied the sea as perhaps few men have studied it, neglecting all else. Next to attractiveness, after sea-faring, came ship-building. I longed to be master in both professions, and in a small way, in time, I accomplished my desire. From the decks of stout ships in the worst gales I had made calculations as to the size and sort of ship safest for all weather and all seas. Thus the voyage which I am now to narrate was a natural outcome not only of my love of adventure, but of my lifelong experience.

One midwinter day of 1892, in Boston, where I had been cast up from old ocean, so to speak, a year or two before, I was cogitating whether I should apply for a command, and again eat my bread and butter on the sea, or go to work at the shipyard, when I met an old acquaintance, a whaling-captain, who said: "Come to Fairhaven and I'll give you a ship. But," he added, "she wants some repairs." The captain's terms, when fully explained, were more than satis-factory to me. They included all the assistance I would require to fit the craft for sea. I was only too glad to accept, for I had already found that I could not obtain work in the shipyard without first paying fifty dollars to a society, and as for a ship to command—there were not enough ships to go round. Nearly all our tall vessels had been cut down for coal-barges, and were being ignominiously towed by the nose from port to port, while many worthy captains addressed themselves to Sailors' Snug Harbor.

The next day I landed at Fairhaven, opposite New Bedford, and found that my friend had something of a joke on me. For seven years the joke had been on him. The "ship" proved to be a very antiquated sloop called the *Spray*, which the neighbors declared had been built in the year 1. She was affectionately propped up in a field, some distance from salt water, and was covered with canvas. The people of Fairhaven, I hardly need say, are thrifty and observant. For seven years they had asked, "I wonder what Captain Eben Pierce is going to do with the old *Spray?*" The day I appeared there was a buzz at the gossip exchange: at last some one had come and was actually at work on the old *Spray*. "Breaking her up, I s'pose?" "No; going to rebuild her." Great was the amazement. "Will it pay?" was the question which for a year or more I answered by declaring that I would make it pay.

My ax felled a stout oak-tree near by for a keel, and Farmer How-ard, for a small sum of money, hauled in this and enough timbers for the frame of the new vessel. I rigged a steam-box and a pot for a boiler. The timbers for ribs, being straight saplings, were dressed and steamed till supple, and then bent over a log, where they were secured till set. Something tangible appeared every day to show for my labor, and the neighbors made the work sociable. It was a great day in the *Spray* shipyard when her new stem was set up and fastened to the new keel. Whaling-captains came from far to survey it. With one voice they pronounced it "A 1," and in their opinion "fit to smash ice." The oldest captain shook my hand warmly when the breast-hooks were put in, declaring that he could see no reason why the *Spray* should not "cut in bow-head" yet off the coast of Greenland. The much-esteemed stem-piece was from the butt of the smartest kind of a pasture oak. It afterward split a coral patch in two at the Keeling Islands, and did not receive a blemish. Better timber for a ship than pasture white oak never grew. The breast-hooks, as well as all the ribs, were of this wood, and were steamed and bent into shape as required. It was hard upon March when I began work in earnest; the weather was cold; still, there were plenty of inspectors to back me with advice. When a whaling-captain hove into sight I just rested on my adz awhile and "gammed" with him.

New Bedford, the home of whaling-captains, is connected with Fairhaven by a bridge, and the walking is good. They never "worked along up" to the shipyard too often for me. It was the charming tales about arctic whaling that inspired me to put a double set of breast-hooks in the *Spray*, that she might shunt ice.

The seasons came quickly while I worked. Hardly were the ribs of the sloop up before apple-trees were in bloom. Then the daisies and the cherries came soon after. Close by the place where the old *Spray* had now dissolved rested the ashes of John Cook, a revered Pilgrim father. So the new *Spray* rose from hallowed ground. From the deck of the new craft I could put out my hand and pick cherries that grew over the little grave. The planks for the new vessel, which I soon came to put on, were of Georgia pine an inch and a half thick. The operation of putting them on was tedious, but, when on, the calking was easy. The outward edges stood slightly open to receive the calking, but the inner edges were so close that I could not see daylight between them. All the butts were fastened by through

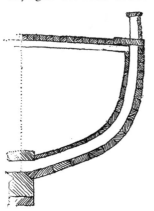

bolts, with screw-nuts tightening them to the timbers, so that there would be no complaint from them. Many bolts with screw-nuts were used in other parts of the construction, in all about a thousand. It was my purpose to make my vessel stout and strong.

Now, it is a law in Lloyd's that the *Jane* repaired all out of the old until she is entirely new is still the *Jane*. The *Spray* changed her being so gradually that it was hard to say at what point the old died or the new took birth, and it was no matter. The bulwarks I built up of white-oak stanchions fourteen inches high, and covered with seven-eighth-

Cross section of the *Spray*.

inch white pine. These stanchions, mortised through a two-inch covering-board, I calked with thin cedar wedges. They have remained perfectly tight ever since. The deck I made of one-and-a-half-inch by

"It'll crawl!"

Thomas Fogarty.

three-inch white pine spiked to beams, six by six inches of yellow or Georgia pine, placed three feet apart. The deck-inclosures were one over the aperture of the main hatch, six feet by six, for a cooking-galley, and a trunk farther aft, about ten feet by twelve, for a cabin. Both of these rose about three feet above the deck, and were sunk sufficiently into the hold to afford head-room. In the spaces along the sides of the cabin, under the deck, I arranged a berth to sleep in, and shelves for small storage, not forgetting a place for the medicine-chest. In the midship hold, that is, the space between cabin and galley, under the deck, was room for provision of water, salt beef, etc., ample for many months.

The hull of my vessel being now put together as strongly as wood and iron could make her, and the various rooms partitioned off, I set about "calking ship." Grave fears were entertained by some that at this point I should fail. I myself gave some thought to the advisability of a "professional calker." The very first blow I struck on the cotton with the calking-iron, which I thought was right, many others thought wrong. "It'll crawl!" cried a man from Marion, passing with a basket of clams on his back. "It'll crawl!" cried another from West Island, when he saw me driving cotton into the seams. Bruno simply wagged his tail. Even Mr. Ben J____, a noted authority on whaling-ships, whose mind, however, was said to totter, asked rather confidently if I did not think "it would crawl." "How fast will it crawl?" cried my old captain friend, who had been towed by many a lively sperm-whale. "Tell us how fast," cried he, "that we may get into port in time." However, I drove a thread of oakum on top of the cotton, as from the first I had intended to do. And Bruno again wagged his tail. The cotton never "crawled." When the calking was finished, two coats of copper paint were slapped on the bottom, two of white lead on the topsides and bulwarks. The rudder was then shipped and painted, and on the following day the *Spray* was launched. As she rode at her ancient, rust-eaten anchor, she sat on the water like a swan.

The *Spray's* dimensions were, when finished, thirty-six feet nine inches long, over all, fourteen feet two inches wide, and four feet two inches deep in the hold, her tonnage being nine tons net and twelve and seventy-one hundredths tons gross.

Then the mast, a smart New Hampshire spruce, was fitted, and likewise all the small appurtenances necessary for a short cruise. Sails were bent, and away she flew with my friend Captain Pierce and me, across Buzzard's Bay on a trial-trip—all right. The only thing that now worried my friends along the beach was, "Will she pay!" The cost of my new vessel was $553.62 for materials, and thirteen months of my own labor. I was several months more than that at Fairhaven, for I got work now and then on an occasional whale-ship fitting farther down the harbor, and that kept me the overtime.

# CHAPTER II

I spent a season in my new craft fishing on the coast, only to find that I had not the cunning properly to bait a hook. But at last the time arrived to weigh anchor and get to sea in earnest. I had resolved on a voyage around the world, and as the wind on the morning of April 24, 1895, was fair, at noon I weighed anchor, set sail, and filled away from Boston, where the *Spray* had been moored snugly all winter. The twelve-o'clock whistles were blowing just as the sloop shot ahead under full sail. A short board was made up the harbor on the port tack, then coming about she stood seaward, with her boom well off to port, and swung past the ferries with lively heels. A photographer on the outer pier at East Boston got a picture of her as she swept by, her flag at the peak throwing its folds clear. A thrilling pulse beat high in me. My step was light on deck in the crisp air. I felt that there could be no turning back, and that I was engaging in an adventure the meaning of which I thoroughly understood. I had taken little advice from any one, for I had a right to my own opinions in matters pertaining to the sea. That the best of sailors might do worse than even I alone was borne in upon me not a league from Boston docks, where a great steamship, fully manned, officered, and piloted, lay stranded and broken. This was the *Venetian*. She was broken completely in two over a ledge. So in the first hour of my lone voyage I had proof that the *Spray* could at least do better than this full-handed steamship, for I was already farther on my voyage than she. "Take warning, *Spray*, and have a care," I uttered aloud to my bark, passing fairylike silently down the bay.

The wind freshened, and the *Spray* rounded Deer Island light at the rate of seven knots.

Passing it, she squared away direct for Gloucester to procure there some fishermen's stores. Waves dancing joyously across Massachusetts Bay met her coming out of the harbor to dash them into myriads of sparkling gems that hung about her at every surge. The day was perfect, the sunlight clear and strong. Every particle of water thrown into the air became a gem, and the *Spray*, bounding ahead, snatched necklace after necklace from the sea, and as often threw them away. We have all seen miniature rainbows about a ship's prow, but the *Spray* flung out a bow of her own that day, such as I

347

have never seen before. Her good angel had embarked on the voyage; I so read it in the sea.

Bold Nahant was soon abeam, then Marblehead was put astern. Other vessels were outward bound, but none of them passed the *Spray* flying along on her course. I heard the clanking of the dismal bell on Norman's Woe as we went by; and the reef where the schooner *Hesperus* struck I passed close aboard. The "bones" of a wreck tossed up lay bleaching on the shore abreast. The wind still freshening, I settled the throat of the mainsail to ease the slope's helm, for I could hardly hold her before it with the whole mainsail set. A schooner ahead of me lowered all sail and ran into port under bare poles, the wind being fair. As the *Spray* brushed by the stranger, I saw that some of his sails were gone, and much broken canvas hung in his rigging, from the effects of a squall.

I made for the cove, a lovely branch of Gloucester's fine harbor, again to look the *Spray* over and again to weigh the voyage, and my feelings, and all that. The bay was feather-white as my little vessel tore in, smothered in foam. I was my first experience of coming into port alone, with a craft of any size, and in among shipping. Old fishermen ran down to the wharf for which the *Spray* was heading, apparently intent upon braining herself there. I hardly know how a calamity was averted, but with my heart in my mouth, almost, I let go the wheel, stepped quickly forward, and downed the jib. The sloop naturally rounded in the wind, and just ranging ahead, laid her cheek against a mooring-pile at the windward corner of the wharf, so quietly, after all, that she would not have broken an egg. Very leisurely I passed a rope around the post, and she was moored. Then a cheer went up from the little crowd on the wharf. "You could n't 'a' done it better," cried an old skipper, "if you weighed a ton!" Now, my weight was rather less than the fifteenth part of a ton, but I said nothing, only putting on a look of careless indifference to say for me, "Oh, that's nothing"; for some of the best sailors in the world were looking at me, and my wish was not to appear green, for I had a mind to stay in Gloucester several days. Had I uttered a word it surely would have betrayed me, for I was still quite nervous and short of breath.

I remained in Gloucester about two weeks, fitting out with the various articles for the voyage most readily obtained there. The owners of the wharf where I lay, and of many fishing-vessels, put on board dry cod galore, also a barrel of oil to calm the waves. They were old skippers themselves, and took a great interest in the voyage. They also made the *Spray* a present of a "fisherman's own" lantern, which I found would throw a light a great distance around. Indeed, a ship that would run another down having such a good light aboard would be capable of running into a light-ship. A gaff, a pugh, and a dip-net, all of which an old fisherman declared I could not sail without, were also put aboard. Then, too, from across the cove came a case of copper paint, a famous antifouling article, which stood me in good stead long after. I slapped two coats of this paint on the bottom of the *Spray* while she lay a tide or so on the hard beach.

For a boat to take along, I made shift to cut a castaway dory in two athwartships, boarding up the end where it was cut. This half-dory I could hoist in and out by the nose easily enough, by hooking the throat-halyards into a strop fitted for the purpose. A whole dory would be heavy and awkward to handle alone. Manifestly there was not room on deck for more than the half of a boat, which, after all, was better than no boat at all, and was large enough for one man. I perceived, moreover, that the newly arranged craft would answer for a washing-machine when placed athwartships, and also for a bath-tub. Indeed, for the former office my razeed dory gained such a reputation on the voyage that my washerwoman at Samoa would not take no for an answer. She could see with one eye that it was a new invention which beat any Yankee notion ever brought by missionaries to the islands, and she had to have it.

The want of a chronometer for the voyage was all that now worried me. In our newfangled notions of navigation it is supposed that a mariner cannot find his way without one; and I had myself drifted into this way of thinking. My old chronometer, a good one, had been long in disuse. It would cost fifteen dollars to clean and rate it. Fifteen dollars! For sufficient reasons I left that timepiece at home, where the Dutchman left his anchor. I had the great lantern, and a lady in Boston sent me the price of a large two-burner cabin lamp, which lighted the cabin at night, and by some small contriving served for a stove through the day.

Being thus refitted I was once more ready for sea, and on May 7 again made sail. With little room in which to turn, the *Spray*, in gathering headway, scratched the paint off an old, fine-weather craft in the fairway, being puttied and painted for a summer voyage. "Who'll pay for that?" growled the painters. "I will," said I. "With the main-sheet," echoed the captain of the *Bluebird*, close by, which was his way of saying that I was off. There was nothing to pay for above five cents' worth of paint, maybe, but such a din was raised between the old "hooker" and the *Bluebird*, which now took up my case, that the first cause of it was forgotten altogether. Anyhow, no bill was sent after me.

The weather was mild on the day of my departure from Gloucester. On the point ahead, as the *Spray* stood out of the cove, was a lively picture, for the front of a tall factory was a flutter of handkerchiefs and caps. Pretty faces peered out of the windows from the top to the bottom of the building, all smiling *bon voyage*. Some hailed me to know where away and why alone. Why? When I made as if to stand in, a hundred pairs of arms reached out, and said come, but the shore was dangerous! The sloop worked out of the bay against a light southwest wind, and about noon squared away off Eastern Point, receiving at the same time a hearty salute—the last of many kindnesses to her at Gloucester. The wind freshened off the point, and skipping along smoothly, the *Spray* was soon off Thatcher's Island lights. Thence shaping her course east, by compass, to go north to Cashes Ledge and the Amen Rocks, I sat and considered the matter all over again, and asked myself once more whether it was best to sail beyond the ledge and rocks at all. I had only said that I would sail round the world in the *Spray*, "dangers of the sea excepted," but I must have said it very much in earnest. The "charter-party" with myself seemed to bind me, and so I sailed on. Toward night I hauled the sloop to the wind, and baiting a hook, sounded for bottom-fish, in thirty fathoms of water, on the edge of Cashes Ledge. With fair success I hauled till dark, landing on deck three cod and two haddocks, one hake, and, best of all, a small halibut, all plump and spry. This, I thought, would be the place to

"'No dorg nor no cat.'"

take in a good stock of provisions above what I already had; so I put out a sea-anchor that would hold her head to windward. The current being southwest, against the wind, I felt quite sure I would find the *Spray* still on the bank or near it in the morning. Then "stradding" the cable and putting my great lantern in the rigging, I lay down, for the first time at sea alone, not to sleep, but to doze and to dream.

I had read somewhere of a fishing-schooner hooking her anchor into a whale, and being towed a long way and at great speed. This was exactly what happened to the *Spray*—in my dream! I could not shake it off entirely when I awoke and found that it was the wind blowing and the heavy sea now running that had disturbed my short rest. A scud was flying across the moon. A storm was brewing; indeed, it was already stormy. I reefed the sails, then hauled in my sea-anchor, and setting what canvas the sloop could carry, headed her away for Monhegan light, which she made before daylight on the morning of the 8th. The wind being free I ran on into Round Pond harbor, which is a little port east from Pemaquid. Here I rested a day, while the wind rattled among the pine-trees on shore. But the following day was fine enough, and I put to sea, first writing up my log from Cape Ann, not omitting a full account of my adventure with the whale.

The *Spray*, heading east, stretched along the coast among many islands and over a tranquil sea. At evening of this day, May 10, she came up with a considerable island, which I shall always think of as the Island of Frogs, for the *Spray* was charmed by a million voices. From the Island of Frogs we made for the Island of Birds, called Gannet Island, and sometimes Gannet Rock, whereon is a bright, intermittent light, which flashed fitfully across the *Spray's* deck as she coasted along under its light and shade. Thence shaping a course for Briar's Island, I came among vessels the following afternoon on the western fishing-grounds, and after speaking a fisherman at anchor, who gave me a wrong course, the *Spray* sailed directly over the southwest ledge through the worst tide-race in the Bay of Fundy, and got into Westport harbor in Nova Scotia, where I had spent eight years of my life as a lad.

The fisherman may have said "east-southeast," the course I was steering when I hailed him; but I thought he said "east-northeast," and I accordingly changed it to that. Before he made up his mind to answer me at all, he improved the occasion of his own curiosity to know where I was from, and if I was alone, and if I did n't have "no dorg nor no cat." It was the first time in all my life at sea that I had heard a hail for information answered by a question. I think the chap belonged to the Foreign Islands. There was one thing I was sure of, and that was that he did not belong to Briar's Island, because he dodged a sea that slopped over the rail, and stopping to brush the water from his face, lost a find cod which he was about to ship.

My islander would not have done that. It is known that a Briar Islander, fish or no fish on his hook, never flinches from a sea. He just tends to his lines and hauls or "saws." Nay, have I not seen my old friend Deacon W. D____, a good man of the island, while listening to a sermon in the little church on the hill, reach out his hand over the door of his pew and "jig" imaginary squid in the aisle, to the intense delight of the young people, who did not realize that to catch good fish one must have good bait, the thing most on the deacon's mind.

I was delighted to reach Westport. Any port at all would have been delightful after the terrible thrashing I got in the fierce sou'west rip, and to find myself among old schoolmates now was charming. It was the 13th of the month, and 13 is my lucky number—a fact

The deacon's dream.

registered long before Dr. Nansen sailed in search of the north pole with his crew of thirteen. Perhaps he had heard of my success in taking a most extraordinary ship successfully to Brazil with that number of crew. The very stones on Briar's Island I was glad to see again, and I knew them all. The little shop round the corner, which for thirty-five years I had not seen, was the same, except that it looked a deal smaller. It wore the same shingles—I was sure of it; for did not I know the roof where we boys, night after night, hunted for the skin of a black cat, to be taken on a dark night, to make a plaster for a poor lame man! Lowry the tailor lived there when boys were boys. In his day he was fond of the gun. He always carried his powder loose in the tail pocket of his coat. He usually had in his mouth a short dudeen; but in an evil moment he put the dudeen, lighted, in the pocket among the powder. Mr. Lowry was an eccentric man.

At Briar's Island I overhauled the *Spray* once more and tried her seams, but found that even the test of the sou'west rip had started nothing. Bad weather and much head wind prevailing outside, I was in no hurry to round Cape Sable. I made a short excursion with some friends to St. Mary's Bay, an old cruising-ground, and back to the island. Then I sailed, putting into Yarmouth the following day on account of fog and head wind. I spent some days pleasantly enough in Yarmouth, took in some butter for the voyage, also a barrel of potatoes, filled six barrels of water, and stowed all under deck. At Yarmouth, too, I got my famous tin clock, the only time-piece I carried on the whole voyage. The price of it was a dollar and a half, but on account of the face being smashed the merchant let me have it for a dollar.

Captain Slocum's chronometer.

# CHAPTER III

Good-by to the American coast—Off Sable Island in a fog—In the open sea—The man in the moon takes an interest in the voyage—The first fit of loneliness—The *Spray* encounters *La Vaguisa*—A bottle of wine from the Spaniard—A bout of words with the captain of the *Java*—The steamship *Olympia* spoken—Arrival at the Azores.

I now stowed all my goods securely, for the boisterous Atlantic was before me, and I sent the topmast down, knowing that the *Spray* would be the wholesomer with it on deck. Then I gave the lanyards a pull and hitched them afresh, and saw that the gammon was secure, also that the boat was lashed, for even in summer one may meet with bad weather in the crossing.

In fact, many weeks of bad weather had prevailed. On July 1, however, after a rude gale, the wind came out nor'west and clear, propitious for a good run. On the following day, the head sea having gone down, I sailed from Yarmouth, and let go my last hold on America. The log of my first day on the Atlantic in the *Spray* reads briefly: "9:30 A.M. sailed from Yarmouth. 4:30 P.M. passed Cape Sable; distance, three cables from the land. The sloop making eight knots. Fresh breeze N.W." Before the sun went down I was taking my supper of strawberries and tea in smooth water under the lee of the east-coast land, along which the *Spray* was now leisurely skirting.

At noon on July 3 Ironbound Island was abeam. The *Spray* was again at her best. A large schooner came out of Liverpool, Nova Scotia, this morning, steering eastward. The *Spray* put her hull down astern in five hours. At 6:45 P.M. I was in close under Chebucto Head light, near Halifax harbor. I set my flag and squared away, taking my departure from George's Island before dark to sail east of Sable Island. There are many beacon lights along the coast. Sambro, the Rock of Lamentations, carries a noble light, which, however, the liner *Atlantic*, on the night of her terrible disaster, did not see. I watched light after light sink astern as I sailed into the unbounded sea, till Sambro, the last of them all, was below the horizon. The *Spray* was then alone, and sailing on, she held her course. July 4, at 6 A.M. I put in double reefs, and at 8:30 A.M. turned out all reefs. At 9:40 P.M. I raised the sheen only of the light on the west end of Sable Island, which may also be called the Island of Tragedies. The fog, which till this moment had held off, now lowered over the sea like a pall. I was in a world of fog, shut off from the universe. I did not see any more of the light. By the lead, which I cast often, I found that a little after midnight I was passing the east point of the island, and should soon be clear of dangers of land and shoals. The wind was holding free, though it was from the foggy

354

point, south-southwest. It is said that within a few years Sable Island has been reduced from forty miles in length to twenty, and that of three lighthouses built on it since 1880, two have been washed away and the third will soon be engulfed.

" 'Good evening, sir.' "

On the evening of July 5 the *Spray*, after having steered all day over a lumpy sea, took it into her head to go without the helmsman's aid. I had been steering southeast by south, but the wind hauling forward a bit, she dropped into a smooth lane, heading southeast, and making about eight knots, her very best work. I crowded on sail to cross the track of the liners without loss of time, and to reach as soon as possible the friendly Gulf Stream. The fog lifting before night, I was afforded a look at the sun just as it was touching the sea. I watched it go down and out of sight. Then I turned my face eastward, and there, apparently at the very end of the bowsprit, was the smiling full moon rising out of the sea. Neptune himself coming over the bows could not have startled me more. "Good evening, sir," I cried; "I'm glad to see you." Many a long talk since then I have had with the man in the moon; he had my confidence on the voyage.

About midnight the fog shut down again denser than ever before. One could almost "stand on it." It continued so for a number of days, the wind increasing to a gale. The waves rose high, but I had a good ship. Still, in the dismal fog I felt myself drifting into loneliness, an insect on a straw in the midst of the elements. I lashed the helm, and my vessel held her course, and while she sailed I slept.

During those few days a feeling of awe crept over me. My memory worked with startling power. The ominous, the insignificant, the great, the small, the wonderful, the commonplace—all appeared before my mental vision in magical succession. Pages of my history were recalled which had been so long forgotten that they seemed to belong to a previous existence. I heard all the voices of the past laughing, crying, telling what I had heard them tell in many corners of the earth.

The loneliness of my state wore off when the gale was high and I found much work to do. When fine weather returned, then came the sense of solitude, which I could not shake off. I used my voice often, at first giving some order about the affairs of a ship, for I had been told that from disuse I should lose my speech. At the meridian altitude of the sun I called aloud, "Eight bells," after the custom on a ship at sea. Again from my cabin I cried to an imaginary man at the helm, "How does she head, there?" and again, "Is she on her course?" But getting no reply, I was reminded the more palpably of my condition. My voice sounded hollow on the empty air, and I dropped the practice. However, it was not long before the thought came to me that when I was a lad I used to sing; why not try that now, where it would disturb no one? My musical talent had never bred envy in others, but out on the Atlantic, to realize what it meant, you should have heard me sing. You should have seen the porpoises leap when I pitched my voice for the waves and the sea and all that was in it. Old turtles, with large eyes, poked their heads up out of the sea as I sang "Johnny Boker," and "We'll Pay Darby Doyl for his Boots," and the like. But the porpoises were, on the whole, vastly more appreciative than the turtles; they jumped a deal higher. One day when I was humming a favorite chant, I think it was "Babylon's a-Fallin'," a porpoise jumped higher than the bowsprit. Had the *Spray* been going a little faster she would have scooped him in. The sea-birds sailed around rather shy.

July 10, eight days at sea, the *Spray* was twelve hundred miles east of Cape Sable. One hundred and fifty miles a day for so small a vessel must be considered good sailing. It was the greatest run the *Spray* ever made before or since in so few days. On the evening of July 14, in better humor than ever before, all hands cried, "Sail ho!" The sail was a barkantine, three points on the weather bow, hull down. Then came the night. My ship was sailing along now without attention to the helm. The wind was south; she was heading east. Her sails were trimmed like the sails of the nautilus. They drew steadily all night. I went frequently on deck, but found all well. A merry breeze kept on from the south.

Early in the morning of the 15th the *Spray* was close aboard the stranger, which proved to be *La Vaguisa* of Vigo, twenty-three days from Philadelphia, bound for Vigo. A lookout from his masthead had spied the *Spray* the evening before. The captain, when I came near enough, threw a line to me and sent a bottle of wine across slung by the neck, and very good wine it was. He also sent his card, which bore the name of Juan Gantes. I think he was a good man, as Spaniards go. But when I asked him to report me "all well" (the *Spray* passing him in a lively manner), he hauled his shoulders much above his head; and when his mate,

"He also sent his card."

who knew of my expedition, told him that I was alone, he crossed himself and made for his cabin. I did not see him again. By sundown he was as far astern as he had been ahead the evening before.

There was now less and less monotony. On July 16 the wind was northwest and clear, the sea smooth, and a large bark, hull down, came in sight on the lee bow, and at 2:30 P.M. I spoke the stranger. She was the bark *Java* of Glasgow, from Peru for Queenstown for orders. Her old captain was bearish, but I met a bear once in Alaska that looked pleasanter. At least, the bear seemed pleased to meet me, but this grizzly old man! Well, I suppose my hail disturbed his siesta, and my little sloop passing his great ship had somewhat the effect on him that a red rag has upon a bull. I had the advantage over heavy ships, by long odds, in the light winds of this and the two previous days. The wind was light; his ship was heavy and foul, making poor headway, while the *Spray*, with a great mainsail bellying even to light winds, was just skipping along as nimbly as one could wish. "How long has it been calm about here?" roared the captain of the *Java*, as I came within hail of him. "Dunno, cap'n," I shouted back as loud as I could bawl. "I have n't been here long." At this the mate on the forecastle wore a broad grin. "I left Cape Sable fourteen days ago," I added. (I was now well across toward the Azores.) "Mate," he roared to his chief officer— "mate, come here and listen to the Yankee's yarn. Haul down the flag, mate, haul down the flag!" In the best of humor, after all, the *Java* surrendered to the *Spray*.

The acute pain of solitude experienced at first never returned. I had penetrated a mystery, and, by the way, I had sailed through a fog. I had met Neptune in his wrath, but he found that I had not treated him with contempt, and so he suffered me to go on and explore.

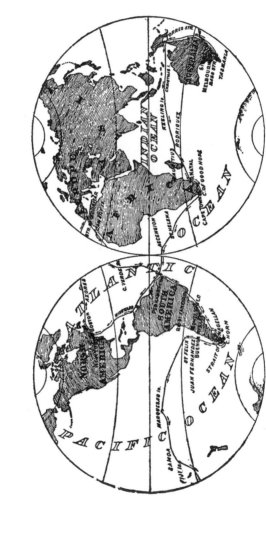

Chart of the *Spray's* course around the world—April 24, 1895, to July 3, 1898.

In the log for July 18 there is this entry: "Fine weather, wind south-southwest. Porpoises gamboling all about. The S. S. *Olympia* passed at 11:30 A.M., long. W. 34°50'."

"It lacks now three minutes of the half-hour," shouted the captain, as he gave me the longitude and the time. I admired the businesslike air of the *Olympia;* but I have the feeling still that the captain was just a little too precise in his reckoning. That may be all well enough, however, where there is plenty of sea-room. But over-confidence, I believe, was the cause of the disaster to the liner *Atlantic,* and many more like her. The captain knew too well where he was. There were no porpoises at all skipping along with the *Olympia!* Porpoises always prefer sailing ships. The captain was a young man, I observed, and had before him, I hope, a good record.

Land ho! On the morning of July 19 a mystic dome like a mountain of silver stood alone in the sea ahead. Although the land was completely hidden by the white, glistening haze that shone in the sun like polished silver, I felt quite sure that it was Flores Island. At half-past four P.M. it was abeam. The haze in the meantime had disappeared. Flores is one hundred and seventy-four miles from Fayal, and although it is a high island, it remained many years undiscovered after the principal group of the islands had been colonized.

The island of Pico.

Early on the morning of July 20 I saw Pico looming above the clouds on the starboard bow. Lower lands burst forth as the sun burned away the morning fog, and island after island came into view. As I approached nearer, cultivated fields appeared, "and oh, how green the corn!" Only those who have seen the Azores from the deck of a vessel realize the beauty of the mid-ocean picture.

At 4:30 P.M. I cast anchor at Fayal, exactly eighteen days from Cape Sable. The American consul, in a smart boat, came alongside before the *Spray* reached the breakwater, and a young naval officer, who feared for the safety of my vessel, boarded, and offered his services as pilot. The youngster, I have no good reason to doubt, could have handled a man-of-war, but the *Spray* was too small for the amount of uniform he wore. However, after fouling all the craft in port and sinking a lighter, she was moored without much damage to herself. This wonderful pilot expected a "gratification," I understood, but whether for the reason that his government, and not I, would have to pay the cost of raising the lighter, or because he did not sink the *Spray,* I could never make out. But I forgive him.

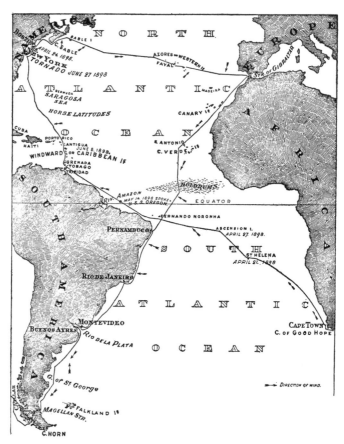

Chart of the *Spray's* Atlantic voyages from Boston to Gibraltar, thence to the Strait of Magellan, in 1895, and finally homeward bound from the Cape of Good Hope in 1898.

It was the season for fruit when I arrived at the Azores, and there was soon more of all kinds of it put on board than I knew what to do with. Islanders are always the kindest people in the world, and I met none anywhere kinder than the good hearts of this place. The people of the Azores are not a very rich community. The burden of taxes is heavy, with scant privileges in return, the air they breathe being about the only thing that is not taxed. The mother-country does not even allow them a port of entry for a foreign mail service. A packet passing ever so close with mails for Horta must deliver them first in Lisbon, ostensibly to be fumigated, but really for the tariff from the packet. My own letters posted at Horta reached the United States six days behind my letter from Gibraltar, mailed thirteen days later.

The day after my arrival at Horta was the feast of a great saint. Boats loaded with people came from other islands to celebrate at Horta, the capital, or Jerusalem, of the Azores. The deck of the *Spray* was crowded from morning till night with men, women, and children. On the day after the feast a kind-hearted native harnessed a team and drove me a day over the beautiful roads all about Fayal, "because," said he, in broken English, "when I was in America and could n't speak a word of English, I found it hard till I met some one who seemed to have time to listen to my story, and I promised my good saint then that if ever a stranger came to my country I would try to make him happy." Unfortunately, this gentleman brought along an interpreter, that I might "learn more of the country." The fellow was nearly the death of me, talking of ships and voyages, and of the boats he had steered, the last thing in the world I wished to hear. He had sailed out of New Bedford, so he said, for "that Joe Wing they call 'John.'" My friend and host found hardly a chance to edge in a word. Before we parted my host dined me with a cheer that would have gladdened the heart of a prince, but he was quite alone in his house. "My wife and children all rest there," said he, pointing to the churchyard across the way. "I moved to this house from far off," he added, "to be near the spot, where I pray every morning."

I remained four days at Fayal, and that was two days more than I had intended to stay. It was the kindness of the islanders and their touching simplicity which detained me. A damsel, as innocent as an angel, came alongside one day, and said she would embark on the *Spray* if I would land her at Lisbon. She could cook flying-fish, she thought, but her forte was dressing *bacalhao*. Her brother Antonio, who served as interpreter, hinted that, anyhow, he would like to make the trip. Antonio's heart went out to one John Wilson, and he was ready to sail for America by way of the two capes to meet his friend. "Do you know John Wilson of Boston?" he cried. "I knew a John Wilson," I said, "but not of Boston." "He had one daughter and one son," said Antonio, by way of identifying his friend. If this reaches the right John Wilson, I am told to say that "Antonio of Pico remembers him."

# CHAPTER IV

Squally weather in the Azores—High living—Delirious from cheese and plums—The pilot of the *Pinta*—At Gibraltar—Compliments exchanged with the British navy—A picnic on the Morocco shore.

I set sail from Horta early on July 24. The southwest wind at the time was light, but squalls came up with the sun, and I was glad enough to get reefs in my sails before I had gone a mile. I had hardly set the mainsail, double-reefed, when a squall of wind down the mountains struck the sloop with such violence that I thought her mast would go. However, a quick helm brought her to the wind. As it was, one of the weather lanyards was carried away and the other was stranded. My tin basin, caught up by the wind, went flying across a French school-ship to leeward. It was more or less squally all day, sailing along under high land; but rounding close under a bluff, I found an opportunity to mend the lanyards broken in the squall. No sooner had I lowered my sails when a four-oared boat shot out from some gully in the rocks, with a customs officer on board, who though he had come upon a smuggler. I had some difficulty in making him comprehend the true case. However, one of his crew, a sailorly chap, who understood how matters were, while we palavered jumped on board and rove off the new landyards I had already prepared, and with a friendly hand helped me "set up the rigging." This incident gave the turn in my favor. My story was then clear to all. I have found this the way of the world. Let one be without a friend, and see what will happen!

Passing the island of Pico, after the rigging was mended, the *Spray* stretched across to leeward of the island of St. Michael's, which she was up with early on the morning of July 26, the wind blowing hard. Later in the day she passed the Prince of Monaco's fine steam-yacht bound to Fayal, where, on a previous voyage, the prince had slipped his cables to "escape a reception" which the padres of the island wished to give him. Why he so dreaded the "ovation" I could not make out. At Horta they did not know. Since reaching the islands I had lived most luxuriously on fresh bread, butter, vegetables, and fruits of all kinds. Plums seemed the most plentiful on the *Spray*, and these I ate without stint. I had also a Pico white cheese that General Manning, the American consul-general, had given me, which I supposed was to be eaten, and of this I partook with the plums. Alas! by night-time I was doubled up with cramps. The wind, which was already a smart breeze, was increasing somewhat, with a heavy sky to the sou'-west. Reefs had been turned out, and I must turn them in again somehow.

362

Between cramps I got the mainsail down, hauled out the earings as best I could, and tied away point by point, in the double reef. There being sea-room, I should, in strict prudence, have made all snug and gone down at once to my cabin. I am a careful man at sea, but this night, in the coming storm, I swayed up my sails, which, reefed though they were, were still too much in such heavy weather; and I saw to it that the sheets were securely belayed. In a word, I should have laid to, but did not. I gave her the double-reefed mainsail and whole jib instead, and set her on her course. Then I went below, and threw myself upon the cabin floor in great pain. How long I lay there I could not tell, for I became delirious. When I came to, as I thought, from my swoon, I realized that the sloop was plunging into a heavy sea, and looking out of the companionway, to my amazement I saw a tall man at the helm. His rigid hand, grasping the spokes of the wheel, held them as in a vise. One may imagine my astonishment. His rig was that of a foreign sailor, and the large red cap he wore was cockbilled over his left ear, and all was set off with shaggy black whiskers. He would have been taken for a pirate in any part of the world. While I gazed upon his threatening aspect I forgot the storm, and wondered if he had come to cut my throat. This he seemed to divine. "Señor," said he, doffing his cap, "I have come to do you no harm." And a smile, the faintest in the world, but still a smile, played on his face, which seemed not unkind when he spoke. "I have come to do you no harm. I have sailed free," he said, "but was never worse than a *contrabandista*. I am one of Columbus's crew," he continued. "I am the pilot of the *Pinta* come to aid you. Lie quiet, señor captain," he added, "and I will guide your ship to-night. You have a *calentura*, but you will be all right to-morrow." I thought what a very devil he was to carry sail. Again, as if he read my mind, he exclaimed: "Yonder is the *Pinta* ahead; we must overtake her. Give her sail; give her sail! *Vale, vale, muy vale!*" Biting off a large quid of black twist, he said: "You did wrong, captain, to mix cheese with plums. White cheese is never safe unless you know whence it comes. *Quien sabe*, it may have been from *leche de Capra* and becoming capricious—"

"Avast, there!" I cried. "I have no mind for moralizing."

I made shift to spread a mattress and lie on that instead of the hard floor, my eyes all the while fastened on my strange guest, who, remarking again that I would have "only pains and calentura," chuckled as he chanted a wild song:

> High are the waves, fierce, gleaming,
>   High is the tempest roar!
> High the sea-bird screaming!
>   High the Azore!

I suppose I was now on the mend, for I was peevish, and complained: "I detest your jingle. Your Azore should be at roost, and would have

The apparition at the wheel.

been were it a respectable bird!" I begged he would tie a rope-yarn
on the rest of the song, if there was any more of it. I was still in agony.
Great seas were boarding the *Spray*, but in my fevered brain I thought
they were boats falling on deck, that careless draymen were throwing
from wagons on the pier to which I imagined the *Spray* was now
moored, and without fenders to breast her off. "You'll smash your
boats!" I called out again and again, as the seas crashed on the cabin
over my head. "You'll smash your boats, but you can't hurt the *Spray*.
She is strong!" I cried.

I found, when my pains and calentura had gone, that the deck, now
as white as a shark's tooth from seas washing over it, had been swept
of everything movable. To my astonishment, I saw now at broad day
that the *Spray* was still heading as I had left her, and was going like a
race horse. Columbus himself could not have held her more exactly
on her course. The sloop had made ninety miles in the night through
a rough sea. I felt grateful to the old pilot, but I marveled some that
he had not taken in the jib. The gale was moderating, and by noon the

sun was shining. A meridian altitude and the distance on the patent log, which I always kept towing, told me that she had made a true course throughout the twenty-four hours. I was getting much better now, but was very weak, and did not turn out reefs that day or the night following, although the wind felt light; but I just put my wet clothes out in the sun when it was shining, and lying down there myself, fell asleep. Then who should visit me again but my old friend of the night before, this time, of course, in a dream. "You did well last night to take my advice," said he, "and if you would, I should like to be with you often on the voyage, for the love of adventure alone." Finishing what he had to say, he again doffed his cap and disappeared as mysteriously as he came, returning, I suppose, to the phantom *Pinta*. I awoke much refreshed, and with the feeling that I had been in the presence of a friend and a seaman of vast experience. I gathered up my clothes, which by this time were dry, then, by inspiration, I threw overboard all the plums in the vessel.

July 28 was exceptionally fine. The wind from the northwest was light and the air balmy. I overhauled my wardrobe, and bent on a white shirt against nearing some coasting-packet with genteel folk on board. I also did some washing to get the salt out of my clothes. After it all I was hungry, so I made a fire and very cautiously stewed a dish of pears and set them carefully aside till I had made a pot of delicious coffee, for both of which I could afford sugar and cream. But the crowning dish of all was a fish-hash, and there was enough of it for two. I was in good health again, and my appetite was simply ravenous. While I was dining I had a large onion over the double lamp stewing for a luncheon later in the day. High living to-day!

In the afternoon the *Spray* came upon a large turtle asleep on the sea. He awoke with my harpoon in his neck, if he awoke at all. I had much difficulty in landing him on deck, which I finally accomplished by hooking the throat-halyards to one of his flippers, for he was about as heavy as my boat. I saw more turtles, and I rigged a burton ready with which to hoist them in; for I was obliged to lower the mainsail whenever the halyards were used for such purposes, and it was no small matter to hoist the large sail again. But the turtle steak was good. I found no fault with the cook, and it was the rule of the voyage that the cook found no fault with me. There was never a ship's crew so well agreed. The bill of fare that evening was turtle-steak, tea and toast, fried potatoes, stewed onions; with dessert of stewed pears and cream.

Sometime in the afternoon I passed a barrel-buoy adrift, floating light on the water. It was painted red, and rigged with a signal-staff about six feet high. A sudden change in the weather coming on, I got no more turtle or fish of any sort before reaching port. July 31 a gale sprang up suddenly from the north, with heavy seas, and I shortened sail. The *Spray* made only fifty-one miles on her course that day. August 1 the gale continued, with heavy seas. Through the night the sloop was reaching, under close-reefed mainsail and bobbed jib. At 3 P.M. the jib was washed off the bowsprit and blown to rags and ribbons. I bent the "jumbo" on a stay at the night-heads. As for the jib, let it go; I saved pieces of it, and, after all, I was in want of pot-rags.

On August 3 the gale broke, and I saw many signs of land. Bad weather having made itself felt in the galley, I was minded to try my hand at a loaf of bread, and so rigging a pot of fire on deck by which to bake it, a loaf soon became an accomplished fact. One great feature about ship's cooking is that one's appetite on the sea is always good— a fact that I realized when I cooked for the crew of fishermen in the before-mentioned boyhood days. Dinner being over, I sat for hours reading the life of Columbus, and as the day wore on I watched the birds all flying in one direction, and said, "Land lies there."

Early the next morning, August 4, I discovered Spain. I saw fires on shore, and knew that the country was inhabited. The *Spray* continued on her course till well in with the land, which was that about Trafalgar. Then keeping away a point, she passed through the Strait of Gibraltar, where she cast anchor at 3 P.M. of the same day, less than twenty-nine days from Cape Sable. At the finish of this preliminary trip I found myself in excellent health, not overworked or cramped, but as well as ever in my life, though I was as thin as a reef-point.

Two Italian barks, which had been close alongside at daylight, I saw long after I had anchored, passing up the African side of the strait. The *Spray* had sailed them both hull down before she reached Tarifa. So far as I know, the *Spray* beat everything going across the Atlantic except the steamers.

All was well, but I had forgotten to bring a bill of health from Horta,

Coming to anchor at Gibraltar.

and so when the fierce old port doctor came to inspect there was a row. That, however, was the very thing needed. If you want to get on well with a true Britisher you must first have a deuce of a row with him. I knew that well enough, and so I fired away, shot for shot, as best I could. "Well, yes," the doctor admitted at last, "your crew are healthy enough, no doubt, but who knows the diseases of your last port?"—a reasonable enough remark. "We ought to put you in the fort, sir!" he blustered; "but never mind. Free pratique, sir! Shove off, cockswain!" And that was the last I saw of the port doctor.

But on the following morning a steam-launch, much longer than the *Spray*, came alongside,—or as much of her as could get alongside,— with compliments from the senior naval officer, Admiral Bruce, saying there was a berth for the *Spray* at the arsenal. This was around at the new mole. I had anchored at the old mole, among the native craft, where it was rough and uncomfortable. Of course I was glad to shift, and did so as soon as possible, thinking of the great company the *Spray* would be in among battle-ships such as the *Collingwood*, *Balfleur*, and *Cormorant*, which were at that time stationed there, and on board all of which I was entertained, later, most royally.

"'Put it thar!' as the Americans say," was the salute I got from Admiral Bruce, when I called at the admiralty to thank him for his courtesy of the berth, and for the use of the steam-launch which towed me into dock. "About the berth, it is all right if it suits, and we'll tow you out when you are ready to go. But, say, what repairs do you want? Ahoy the *Hebe*, can you spare your sailmaker? The *Spray* wants a new jib. Construction and repair, there! will you see to the *Spray*? Say, old man, you must have knocked the devil out of her coming over alone in twenty-nine days! But we'll make it smooth for you here!" Not even her Majesty's ship the *Collingwood* was better looked after than the *Spray* at Gibraltar.

Later in the day came the hail: "*Spray* ahoy! Mrs. Bruce would like to come on board and shake hands with the *Spray*. Will it be convenient to-day?" "Very!" I joyfully shouted. On the following day Sir F. Carrington, at the time governor of Gibraltar, with other high officers of the garrison, and all the commanders of the battle-ships, came on board and signed their names in the *Spray's* log book. Again there was a hail, "*Spray* ahoy!" "Hello!" "Commander Reynolds's compliments. You are invited on board H. M. S. *Collingwood*, 'at home' at 4:30 P.M. Not later than 5:30 P.M." I had already hinted at the limited amount of my wardrobe, and that I could never succeed as a dude. "You are expected, sir, in a stovepipe hat and a claw-hammer coat!" "Then I can't come." "Dash it! come in what you have on; that is what we mean." "Aye, aye, sir!" The *Collingwood's* cheer was good, and had I worn a silk hat as high as the moon I could not have had a better time or been made more at home. An Englishman, even on his great battle-ship, unbends when the stranger passes his gangway, and when he says "at home" he means it.

The *Spray* at anchor off Gibraltar.

That one should like Gibraltar would go without saying. How could one help loving so hospitable a place? Vegetables twice a week and milk every morning came from the palatial grounds of the admiralty. "*Spray* ahoy!" would hail the admiral. "*Spray* ahoy!" "Hello!" "Tomorrow is your vegetable day, sir." "Aye, aye, sir!"

I rambled much about the old city, and a gunner piloted me through the galleries of the rock as far as a stranger is permitted to go. There is no excavation in the world, for military purposes, at all approaching these of Gibraltar in conception or execution. Viewing the stupendous works, it became hard to realize that one was within the Gibraltar of his little old Morse geography.

Before sailing I was invited on a picnic with the governor, the officers of the garrison, and the commanders of the war-ships at the station; and a royal affair it was. Torpedo-boat No. 91, going twenty-two knots, carried our party to the Morocco shore and back. The day was perfect—too fine, in fact, for comfort on shore, and so no one landed at Morocco. No. 91 trembled like an aspen-leaf as she raced through the sea at top speed. Sublieutenant Boucher, apparently a mere lad, was in command, and handled his ship with the skill of an older sailor. On the following day I lunched with General Carrington, the governor, at Line Wall House, which was once the Franciscan convent. In this interesting edifice are preserved relics of the fourteen sieges which Gibraltar has seen. On the next day I supped with the admiral at his residence, the palace, which was once the convent of the Mercenaries. At each place, and all about, I felt the friendly grasp of a manly hand, that lent me vital strength to pass the coming long days at sea. I must confess that the perfect discipline, order, and cheerfulness at Gibraltar were only a second wonder in the great stronghold. The vast amount of business going forward caused no more excitement than the quiet sailing of a well-appointed ship in a smooth sea. No one spoke above his natural voice, save a boatswain's mate now and then. The Hon. Horatio J. Sprague, the venerable United States consul at Gibraltar, honored the *Spray* with a visit on Sunday, August 24, and was much pleased to find that our British cousins had been so kind to her.

# CHAPTER V

Sailing from Gibraltar with the assistance of her Majesty's tug—The Spray's course changed from the Suez Canal to Cape Horn—Chased by a Moorish pirate—A comparison with Columbus—The Canary Islands—The Cape Verde Islands—Sea life—Arrival at Pernambuco—A bill against the Brazilian government—Preparing for the stormy weather of the cape.

Monday, August 25, the *Spray* sailed from Gibraltar, well repaid for whatever deviation she had made from a direct course to reach the place. A tug belonging to her Majesty towed the sloop into the steady breeze clear of the mount, where her sails caught a volant wind, which carried her once more to the Atlantic, where it rose rapidly to a furious gale. My plan was, in going down this coast, to haul offshore, well clear of the land, which hereabouts is the home of pirates; but I had hardly accomplished this when I perceived a felucca making out of the nearest port, and finally following in the wake of the *Spray*. Now, my course to Gibraltar had been taken with a view to proceed up the Mediterranean Sea, through the Suez Canal, down the Red Sea, and east about, instead of a western route, which I finally adopted. By officers of vast experience in navigating these seas, I was influenced to make the change. Longshore pirates on both coasts being numerous, I could not afford to make light of the advice. But here I was, after all, evidently in the midst of pirates and thieves! I changed my course; the felucca did the same, both vessels sailing very fast, but the distance growing less and less between us. The *Spray* was doing nobly; she was even more than at her best; but, in spite of all I could do, she would broach now and then. She was carrying too much sail for safety. I must reef or be dismasted and lose all, pirate or no pirate. I must reef, even if I had to grapple with him for my life.

I was not long in reefing the mainsail and sweating it up—probably not more than fifteen minutes; but the felucca had in the meantime so shortened the distance between us that I now saw the tuft of hair on the heads of the crew,—by which, it is said, Mohammed will pull the villains up into heaven,—and they were coming on like the wind. From what I could clearly make out now, I felt them to be the sons of generations of pirates, and I saw by their movements that they were now preparing to strike a blow. The exultation on their faces, however, was changed in an instant to a look of fear and rage. Their craft, with too much sail on, broached to on the crest of a great wave. This one great sea changed the aspect of affairs suddenly as the flash of a gun. Three minutes later the same wave over-

370

took the *Spray* and shook her in every timber. At the same moment the sheet-strop parted, and away went the main-boom, broken short at the rigging. Impulsively I sprang to the jib-halyards and down-haul, and instantly downed the jib. The head-sail being off, and the helm put hard down, the sloop came in the wind with a bound. While shivering there, but a moment though it was, I got the main-sail down and secured inboard, broken boom and all. How I got the boom in before the sail was torn I hardly know; but not a stitch of it was broken. The mainsail being secured, I hoisted away the jib, and, without looking round, stepped quickly to the cabin and snatched down my loaded rifle and cartridges at hand; for I made mental calculations that the pirate would by this time have recovered his course and be close aboard, and that when I saw him it would be better for me to be looking at him along the barrel of a gun. The piece was at my shoulder when I peered into the mist, but there was no pirate within a mile. The wave and squall that carried away my boom dismasted the felucca outright. I perceived his thieving crew, some dozen or more of them, struggling to recover their rigging from the sea. Allah blacken their faces!

I sailed comfortably on under the jib and forestaysail, which I now set. I fished the boom and furled the sail snug for the night; then hauled the sloop's head two points offshore to allow for the set of current and heavy rollers toward the land. This gave me the wind three points on the starboard quarter and a steady pull in the head-sails. By the time I had things in this order it was dark, and a flying-fish had already fallen on deck. I took him below for my supper, but found myself too tired to cook, or even to eat a thing already prepared. I do not remember to have been more tired before or since in all my life than I was at the finish of that day. Too fatigued to sleep, I rolled about with the motion of the vessel till near midnight, when I made shift to dress my fish and prepare a dish of tea. I fully realized now, if I had not before, that the voyage ahead would call for exertions ardent and lasting. On August 27 nothing could be seen of the Moor, or his country either, except two peaks, away in the east through the clear atmosphere of morning. Soon after the sun rose even these were obscured by haze, much to my satisfaction.

The wind, for a few days following my escape from the pirates, blew a steady but moderate gale, and the sea, though agitated into long rollers, was not uncomfortably rough or dangerous, and while sitting in my cabin I could hardly realize that any sea was running at all, so easy was the long, swinging motion of the sloop over the waves. All distracting uneasiness and excitement being now over, I was once more alone with myself in the realization that I was on the mighty sea and in the hands of the elements. But I was happy, and was becoming more and more intersted in the voyage.

Columbus, in the *Santa Maria*, sailing these seas more than four hundred yeasr before, was not so happy as I, nor so sure of success

in what he had undertaken. His first troubles at sea had already begun. His crew had managed, by foul play or otherwise, to break the
ship's rudder while running before probably just such a gale as the
*Spray* had passed through; and there was dissension on the *Santa
Maria*, something that was unknown on the *Spray*.

After three days of squalls and shifting winds I threw myself down
to rest and sleep, while, with helm lashed, the sloop sailed steadily
on her course.

September 1, in the early morning, land-clouds rising ahead told of
the Canary Islands not far away. A change in the weather came next
day: storm-clouds stretched their arms across the sky; from the east,
to all appearances, might come a fierce harmattan, or from the south
might come the fierce hurricane. Every point of the compass threat-

Chased by pirates.

ened a wild storm. My attention was turned to reefing sails, and no
time was to be lost over it, either, for the sea in a moment was confusion itself, and I was glad to head the sloop three points or more
away from her true course that she might ride safely over the waves.
I was now scudding her for the channel between Africa and the
island of Fuerteventura, the easternmost of the Canary Islands, for
which I was on the lookout. At 2 P.M., the weather becoming suddenly fine, the island stood in view, already abeam to starboard, and
not more than seven miles off. Fuerteventura is twenty-seven hundred feet high, and in fine weather is visible many leagues away.

The wind freshened in the night, and the *Spray* had a fine run
through the channel. By daylight, September 3, she was twenty-
five miles clear of all the islands, when a calm ensued, which was

the precursor of another gale of wind that soon came on, bringing with it dust from the African shore. It howled dismally while it lasted, and though it was not the season of the harmattan, the sea in the course of an hour was discolored with a reddish-brown dust. The air remained thick with flying dust all the afternoon, but the wind, veering northwest at night, swept it back to land, and afforded the *Spray* once more a clear sky. Her mast now bent under a strong, steady pressure, and her bellying sail swept the sea as she rolled scuppers under, courtesying to the waves. These rolling waves thrilled me as they tossed my ship, passing quickly under her keel. This was grand sailing.

September 4, the wind, still fresh, blew from the north-northeast, and the sea surged along with the sloop. About noon a steamship, a bullock-droger, from the river Plate hove in sight, steering northeast, and making bad weather of it. I signaled her, but got no answer. She was plunging into the head sea and rolling in a most astonishing manner, and from the way she yawed one might have said that a wild steer was at the helm.

On the morning of September 6 I found three flying-fish on deck, and a fourth one down the fore-scuttle as close as possible to the frying-pan. It was the best haul yet, and afforded me a sumptuous breakfast and dinner.

The *Spray* had now settled down to the tradewinds and to the business of her voyage. Later in the day another droger hove in sight, rolling as badly as her predecessor. I threw out no flag to this one, but got the worst of it for passing under her lee. She was, indeed, a stale one! And the poor cattle, how they bellowed! The time was when ships passing one another at sea backed their topsails and had a "gam," and on parting fired guns; but those good old days have gone. People have hardly time nowadays to speak even on the broad ocean, where news is news, and as for a salute of guns, they cannot afford the powder. There are no poetry-enshrined freighters on the sea now; it is a prosy life when we have no time to bid one another good morning.

My ship, running now in the full swing of the trades, left me days to myself for rest and recuperation. I employed the time in reading and writing, or in whatever I found to do about the rigging and the sails to keep them all in order. The cooking was always done quickly, and was a small matter, as the bill of fare consisted mainly of flying-fish, hot biscuits and butter, potatoes, coffee and cream—dishes readily prepared.

On September 10 the *Spray* passed the island of St. Antonio, the northwesternmost of the Cape Verdes, close aboard. The landfall was wonderfully true, considering that no observations for longitude had been made. The wind, northeast, as the sloop drew by the island, was very squally, but I reefed her sails snug, and steered broad from the highland of blustering St. Antonio. Then leaving the Cape Verde Islands out of sight astern, I found myself once more sailing a lonely sea and in a solitude supreme all around. When I slept I dreamed that I was alone. This feeling never left me; but, sleeping or waking, I seemed always to know the position of the sloop, and I saw my vessel moving across the chart, which became a picture before me.

One night while I sat in the cabin under this spell, the profound stillness all about was broken by human voices alongside! I sprang instantly to the deck, startled beyond my power to tell. Passing close under lee, like an apparition, was a white bark under full sail. The sailors on board of her were hauling on ropes to brace the yards, which just cleared the sloop's mast as she swept by. No one hailed from the white-winged flier, but I heard some one on board say that he saw lights on the sloop, and that he made her out to be a fisherman. I sat long on the starlit deck that night, thinking of ships, and watching the constellations on their voyage.

On the following day, September 13, a large four-masted ship passed some distance to windward, heading north.

The sloop was now rapidly drawing toward the region of doldrums, and the force of the tradewinds was lessening. I could see by the ripples that a counter-current had set in. This I estimated to be about sixteen miles a day. In the heart of the counter-current the rate was more than that setting eastward.

September 14th a lofty three-masted ship, heading north, was seen from the masthead. Neither this ship nor the one seen yesterday was within signal distance, yet it was good even to see them. On the following day heavy rain-clouds rose in the south, obscuring the sun; this was ominous of doldrums. On the 16th the *Spray* entered this gloomy region, to battle with squalls and to be harassed by fitful calms; for this is the state of the elements between the northeast and the southeast trades, where each wind, struggling in turn for mastery, expends its force whirling about in all directions. Making this still more trying to one's nerve and patience, the sea was tossed into confused cross-lumps and fretted by eddying currents. As if something more were needed to complete a sailor's discomfort in this state, the rain poured down in torrents day and night. The *Spray* struggled and tossed for ten days, making only three hundred miles on her course in all that time. I did n't say anything!

On September 23 the fine schooner *Nantasket* of Boston, from Bear River, for the river Plate, lumber-laden, and just through the doldrums, came up with the *Spray*, and her captain passing a few words, she sailed on. Being much fouled on the bottom by shellfish, she drew along with her fishes which had been following the *Spray*, which was less provided with that sort of food. Fishes will always follow a foul ship. A barnacle-grown log adrift has the same attraction for deep-sea fishes. One of this little school of deserters was a dolphin that had followed the *Spray* about a thousand miles, and had been content to eat scraps of food thrown overboard from my table; for, having been wounded, it could not dart through the sea to prey on other fishes. I had become accustomed to seeing the dolphin, which I knew by its scars, and missed it whenever it took occasional excursions away from the sloop. One day, after it had been off some hours, it returned in company with three yellowtails, a sort of cousin to the dolphin. This little school kept together, except when in danger and when foraging about the sea. Their lives were often threatened by hungry sharks that came round the vessel, and more than once they had narrow escapes. Their mode of escape interested me greatly, and I passed hours watching them. They would dart away, each in a different direcion, so that the wolf of the sea, the shark, pursuing one, would be led away from the others; then after a while they would all return and rendezvous under one side or the other of the sloop. Twice their pursuers were diverted by a tin pan, which I towed astern of the sloop, and which was mistaken for a bright fish; and while turning, in the peculiar way that sharks have when about to devour their prey, I shot them through the head.

Their precarious life seemed to concern the yellowtails very little, if at all. All living beings, without doubt, are afraid of death. Nevertheless, some of the species I saw huddle together as though they knew they were created for the larger fishes, and wished to give the least possible trouble to their captors. I have seen, on the other hand, whales swimming in a circle around a school of herrings, and with mighty exertion "bunching" them together in a whirlpool set in motion by their flukes, and when the small fry were all whirled nicely together, one or the other of the leviathans, lunging through the center with open jaws, take in a boat-load or so at a single mouthful. Off the Cape of Good Hope I saw schools of sardines or other small fish being treated in this way by great numbers of cavally-fish. There was not the slightest chance of escape for the sardines, while the cavally circled round and round, feeding from the edge of the mass. It was interesting to note how rapidly the small fry disappeared; and though it was repeated before my eyes over and over, I could hardly perceive the capture of a single sardine, so dexterously was it done.

Along the equatorial limit of the southeast tradewinds the air was heavily charged with electricity, and there was much thunder and lightning. It was hereabout I remembered that, a few years before, the American ship *Alert* was destroyed by lightning. Her people, by wonderful good fortune, were rescued on the same day and brought to Pernambuco, where I then met them.

On September 25, in the latitude of 5° N., longitude 26° 30′ W., I spoke the ship *North Star* of London. The great ship was out forty-eight days from Norfolk, Virginia, and was bound for Rio, where we met again about two months later. The *Spray* was now thirty days from Gibraltar.

The *Spray's* next companion of the voyage was a swordfish, that swam alongside, showing his tail fin out of the water, till I made a stir for my harpoon, when it hauled its black flag down and disappeared. September 30, at half-past eleven in the morning, the *Spray* crossed the equator in longitude 29° 30′ W. At noon she was two miles south of the line. The southeast trade-winds, met, rather light, in about 4° N., gave her sails now a stiff full sending her handsomely over the sea toward the coast of Brazil, where on October 5, just north of Olinda Point, without further incident, she made the land, casting anchor in Pernambuco harbor about noon: forty days from Gibraltar, and all well on board. Did I tire of the voyage in all that time? Not a bit of it! I was never in better trim in all my life, and was eager for the more perilous experience of rounding the Horn.

It was not at all strange in a life common to sailors that, having already crossed the Atlantic twice and being now half-way from Boston to the Horn, I should find myself still among friends. My determination to sail westward from Gibraltar not only enabled me to escape the pirates of the Red Sea, but, in bringing me to Pernambuco, landed me on familiar shores. I had made many voyages to this and other ports in Brazil. In 1893 I was employed as master to take the famous Ericsson ship *Destroyer* from New York to Brazil to go against the rebel Mello and his party. The *Destroyer*, by the way, carried a submarine cannon of enormous length.

In the same expedition went the *Nictheroy*, the ship purchased by the United States government during the Spanish war and renamed the *Buffalo*. The *Destroyer* was in many ways the better ship of the two, but the Brazilians in their curious war sank her themselves at Bahia. With her sank my hope of recovering wages due me; still, I could but try to recover, for to me it meant a great deal. But now within two years the whirligig of time had brought the Mello party into power, and although it was the legal government which had employed me, the so-called "rebels" felt under less obligation to me than I could have wished.

During these visits to Brazil I had made the acquaintance of Dr. Perera, owner and editor of "El Commercio Jornal," and soon after the *Spray* was safely moored in Upper Topsail Reach, the doctor, who is a very enthusiastic yachtsman, came to pay me a visit and to carry me up the waterway of the lagoon to his country residence. The approach to his mansion by the waterside was guarded by his armada, a fleet of boats including a Chinese sampan, a Norwegian pram, and a Cape Ann dory, the last of which he obtained from the *Destroyer*. The doctor dined me often on good Brazilian fare, that I might, as he said, "salle gordo" for the voyage; but he found that even on the best I fattened slowly.

Fruits and vegetables and all other provisions necessary for the voyage having been taken in, on the 23rd of October I unmoored and made ready for sea. Here I encountered one of the unforgiving Mello faction in the person of the collector of customs, who charged the

*Spray* tonnage dues when she cleared, notwithstanding that she sailed with a yacht license and should have been exempt from port charges. Our consul reminded the collector of this and of the fact—without much diplomacy, I thought—that it was I who brought the *Destroyer* to Brazil. "Oh, yes," said the bland collector; "we remember it very well," for it was now in a small way his turn.

Mr. Lungrin, a merchant, to help me out of the trifling difficulty, offered to freight the *Spray* with a cargo of gunpowder for Bahia, which would have put me in funds; and when the insurance companies refused to take the risk on cargo shipped on a vessel manned by a crew of only one, he offered to ship it without insurance, taking all the risk himself. This was perhaps paying me a greater compliment than I deserved. The reason why I did not accept the business was that in so doing I found that I should vitiate my yacht license and run into more expense for harbor dues around the world than the freight would amount to. Instead of all this, another old merchant friend came to my assistance, advancing the cash direct.

While at Pernambuco I shortened the boom, which had been broken when off the coast of Morocco, by removing the broken piece, which took about four feet off the inboard end; I also refitted the jaws. On October, 24, 1895, a fine day even as days go in Brazil, the *Spray* sailed, having had abundant good cheer. Making about one hundred miles a day along the coast, I arrived at Rio de Janeiro November 5, without any event worth mentioning, and about noon cast anchor near Villaganon, to await the official port visit. On the following day I bestirred myself to meet the highest lord of the admiralty and the ministers, to inquire concerning the matter of wages due me from the beloved *Destroyer*. The high official I met said: "Captain, so far as we are concerned, you may have the ship, and if you care to accept her we will send an officer to show you where she is." I knew well enough where she was at that moment. The top of her smoke-stack being awash in Bahia, it was more than likely that she rested on the bottom there. I thanked the kind officer, but declined his offer.

The *Spray*, with a number of old shipmasters on board, sailed about the harbor of Rio the day before she put to sea. As I had decided to give the *Spray* a yawl rig for the tempestuous waters of Patagonia, I here placed on the stern a semicircular brace to support a jigger mast. These old captains inspected the *Spray's* rigging, and each one contributed something to her outfit. Captain Jones, who had acted as my interpreter at Rio, gave her an anchor, and one of the steamers gave her a cable to match it. She never dragged Jones's anchor once on the voyage, and the cable not only stood the strain on a lee shore, but when towed off Cape Horn helped break combing seas astern that threatened to board her.

# CHAPTER VI

Departure from Rio de Janeiro—The *Spray* ashore on the sands of Uruguay—A narrow escape from shipwreck—The boy who found a sloop—The *Spray* floated but somewhat damaged—Courtesies from the British consul at Maldonado—A warm greeting at Montevideo—An excursion to Buenos Aires—Shortening the mast and bowsprit.

On November 28 the *Spray* sailed from Rio de Janeiro, and first of all ran into a gale of wind, which tore up things generally along the coast, doing considerable damage to shipping. It was well for her, perhaps, that she was clear of the land. Coasting along on this part of the voyage, I observed that while some of the small vessels I fell in with were able to outsail the *Spray* by day, they fell astern of her by night. To the *Spray* day and night were the same; to the others clearly there was a difference. On one of the very fine days experienced after leaving Rio, the steamship *South Wales* spoke the *Spray* and unsolicited gave the longitude by chronometer as 48° W., "as near as I can make it," the captain said. The *Spray*, with her tin clock, had exactly the same reckoning. I was feeling at ease in my primitive method of navigation, but it startled me not a little to find my position by account verified by the ship's chronometer.

On December 5 a barkantine hove in sight, and for several days the two vessels sailed along the coast together. Right here a current was experienced setting north, making it necessary to hug the shore, with which the *Spray* became rather familiar. Here I confess a weakness: I hugged the shore entirely too close. In a word, at daybreak on the morning of December 11 the *Spray* ran hard and fast on the beach. This was annoying; but I soon found that the sloop was in no great danger. The false appearance of the sand-hills under a bright moon had deceived me, and I lamented now that I had trusted to appearances at all. The sea, though moderately smooth, still carried a swell which broke with some force on the shore. I managed to launch my small dory from the deck, and ran out a kedge-anchor and warp; but it was too late to kedge the sloop off, for the tide was falling and she had already sewed a foot. Then I went about "laying out" the larger anchor, which was no easy matter, for my only life-boat, the frail dory, when the anchor and cable were in it, was swamped at once in the surf, the load being too great for her. Then I cut the cable and made two loads of it instead of one. The anchor, with forty fathoms bent and already buoyed, I now took and succeeded in getting through the surf; but my dory was leaking fast, and by the time I had rowed far enough to drop the anchor she was full to the gunwale and sinking. There was not a moment to spare, and I saw clearly that if I failed now all might be lost. I sprang from the oars to my feet, and lifting the anchor above my head, threw it clear just as she was turning over. I grasped her gunwale and held on as she turned bottom up, for I suddenly remembered that I could not swim. Then I tried to right her, but with too much eagerness, for she rolled clean over, and left me as before, clinging to her gunwale, while my body was still in the water. Giving a moment to cool reflection, I found that al-

though the wind was blow-
ing moderately toward the
land, the current was carrying me to sea, and that
something would have to be
done. Three times I had
been under water, in trying
to right the dory, and I was
just saying, "Now I lay
me," when I was seized by
a determination to try yet "I suddenly remembered that I could not
once more, so that no one of               swim."
the prophets of evil I had left behind me could say, "I told you so." Whatever the danger may have been, much or little, I can truly say that the moment was the most serene of my life.

After righting the dory for the fourth time, I finally succeeded by the utmost care in keeping her upright while I hauled myself into her and with one of the oars, which I had recovered, paddled to the shore, somewhat the worse for wear and pretty full of salt water. The position of my vessel, now high and dry, gave me anxiety. To get her afloat again was all I thought of or cared for. I had little difficulty in carrying the second part of my cable out and securing it to the first, which I had taken the precaution to buoy before I put it into the boat. To bring the end back to the sloop was a smaller matter still, and I believe I chuckled above my sorrows when I found that in all the haphazard my judgment or my good genius had faithfully stood by me. The cable reached from the anchor in deep water to the sloop's windlass by just enough to secure a turn and no more. The anchor had been dropped at the right distance from the vessel. To heave all taut now and wait for the coming tide was all I could do.

I had already done enough work to tire a stouter man, and was only too glad to throw myself on the sand above the tide and rest; for the sun was already up, and pouring a generous warmth over the land. While my state could have been worse, I was on the wild coast of a foreign country, and not entirely secure in my property, as I soon found out. I had not been long on the shore when I heard the patter, patter of a horse's feet approaching along the hard beach, which ceased as it came abreast of the sand-ridge where I lay shel-

A double surprise.

tered from the wind. Looking up cautiously, I saw mounted on a nag probably the most astonished boy on the whole coast. He had found a sloop! "It must be mine," he thought, "for am I not the first to see it on the beach?" Sure enough, there it was all high and dry and painted white. He trotted his horse around it, and finding no owner, hitched the nag to the sloop's bobstay and hauled as though he would take her home; but of course she was too heavy for one horse to move. With my skiff, however, it was different; this he hauled some distance, and concealed behind a dune in a bunch of tall grass. He had made up his mind, I dare say, to bring more horses and drag his bigger prize away, anyhow, and was starting off for the settlement a mile or so away for the reinforcement when I discovered myself to him, at which he seemed displeased and disappointed. "Buenos dias, muchacho," I said. He grunted a reply, and eyed me keenly from head to foot. Then bursting into a volley of questions,—more than six Yankees could ask,—he wanted to know, first, where my ship was from, and how many days she had been coming. Then he asked what I was doing here ashore so early in the morning. "Your questions are easily answered," I replied: "my ship is from the moon, it has taken her a month to come, and she is here for a cargo of boys." But the intimation of this enterprise, had I not been on the alert, might have cost me dearly; for while I spoke this child of the campo coiled his lariat ready to throw, and instead of being himself carried to the moon, he was apparently thinking of towing me home by the neck, astern of his wild cayuse, over the fields of Uruguay.

The exact spot where I was stranded was at the Castillo Chicos, about seven miles south of the dividing-line of Uruguay and Brazil, and of course the natives there speak Spanish. To reconcile my early visitor, I told him that I had on my ship biscuits, and that I wished to trade them for butter and milk. On hearing this a broad grin lighted up his face, and showed that he was greatly interested, and that even in Uruguay a ship's biscuit will cheer the heart of a boy and make him your bosom friend. The lad almost flew home, and returned quickly with butter, milk, and eggs. I was, after all, in a land of plenty. With the boy came others, old and young, from neighboring ranches, among them a German settler, who was of great assistance to me in many ways.

A coast-guard from Fort Teresa, a few miles away, also came, "to protect your property from the natives of the plains," he said. I took occasion to tell him, however, that if he would look after the people of his own village, I would take care of those from the plains, pointing, as I spoke, to the nondescript "merchant" who had already stolen my revolver and several small articles from my cabin, which by a bold front I had recovered. The chap was not a native Uruguayan. Here, as in many other places I visited, the natives themselves were not the ones discreditable to the country.

Early in the day a despatch came from the port captain of Montevideo, commanding the coastguards to render the *Spray* every assistance. This, however, was not necessary, for a guard was already on the alert, and making all the ado that would become the wreck of a steamer with a thousand emigrants aboard. The same messenger brought word from the port captain that he would despatch a steamtug to tow the *Spray* to Montevideo. The officer was as good as his word; a powerful tug arrived on the following day; but, to make a long story short, with the help of the German and one soldier and one Italian, called "Angel of Milan," I had already floated the sloop and was sailing for port with the boom off before a fair wind. The adventure cost the *Spray* no small amount of pounding on the hard sand; she lost her shoe and part of her false keel, and received other damage, which, however, was readily mended afterward in dock.

On the following day I anchored at Maldonado. The British consul, his daughter, and another young lady came on board, bringing with them a basket of fresh eggs, strawberries, bottles of milk, and a great loaf of sweet bread. This was a good landfall, and better cheer than I had found at Maldonado once upon a time when I entered the port with a stricken crew in my bark, *Aquidneck*.

In the waters of Maldonado Bay a variety of fishes abound, and fur-seals in their season haul out on the island abreast the bay to breed. Currents on this coast are greatly affected by the prevailing winds, and a tidal wave higher than that ordinarily produced by the moon is sent up the whole shore of Uruguay before a southwest gale, or lowered by a northeaster, as may happen. One of these waves having just receded before the northeast wind which brought the *Spray* in left the tide now at low ebb, with oyster-rocks laid bare for some distance along the shore. Other shellfish of good flavor were also plentiful, though small in size. I gathered a mess of oysters and mussels here, while a native with hook and line, and with mussels for bait, fished from a point of detached rocks for bream, landing several goodsized ones.

The fisherman's nephew, a lad about seven years old, deserves mention as the tallest blasphemer, for a short boy, that I met on the voyage. He called his old uncle all the vile names under the sun for not helping him across the gully. While he swore roundly in all the moods and tenses of the Spanish language, his uncle fished on, now and then congratulating his hopeful nephew on his accomplishment. At the end of his rich vocabulary the urchin sauntered off into the fields, and shortly returned with a bunch of flowers, and with all smiles handed them to me with the innocence of an angel. I remembered having seen the same flower on the banks of the river farther up, some years before. I asked the young pirate why he had brought them to me. Said he, "I don't know; I only wished to do so." Whatever the influence was that put so amiable a wish in this wild pampa boy, it must be far-reaching, thought I, and potent, seas over.

Shortly after, the *Spray* sailed for Montevideo, where she arrived on the following day and was greeted by steam-whistles till I felt embarrassed and wished that I had arrived unobserved. The voyage so far alone may have seemed to the Uruguayans a feat worthy of some recognition; but there was so much of it yet ahead, and of such an arduous nature, that any demonstration at this point seemed, somehow, like boasting prematurely.

The *Spray* had barely come to anchor at Montevideo when the agents of the Royal Mail Steamship Company, Messrs. Humphreys & Co., sent word that they would dock and repair her free of expense and give me twenty pounds sterling, which they did to the letter, and more besides. The calkers at Montevideo paid very careful attention to the work of making the sloop tight. Carpenters mended the keel and also the life-boat (the dory), painting it till I hardly knew it from a butterfly.

Christmas of 1895 found the *Spray* refitted even to a wonderful makeshift stove which was contrived from a large iron drum of some sort punched full of holes to give it a draft; the pipe reached straight up through the top of the forecastle. Now, this was not a stove by mere courtesy. It was always hungry, even for green wood; and in cold, wet days off the coast of Tierra del Fuego it stood me in good stead. Its one door swung on copper hinges, which one of the yard apprentices, with laudable pride, polished till the whole thing blushed like the brass binnacle of a P. & O. steamer.

The *Spray* was now ready for sea. Instead of proceeding at once on her voyage, however, she made an excursion up the river, sailing December 29. An old friend of mine, Captain Howard of Cape Cod and of River Plate fame, took the trip in her to Buenos Aires, where she arrived early on the following day, with a gale of wind and a current so much in her favor that she outdid herself. I was glad to have a sailor of Howard's experience on board to witness her performance of sailing with no living being at the helm. Howard sat near the binnacle and watched the compass while the sloop held her course so steadily that one would have declared that the card was nailed fast. Not a quarter of a point did she deviate from her course. My old friend had owned and sailed a pilot-sloop on the river for many years, but this feat took the wind out of his sails at last, and he cried, "I'll be stranded on Chico Bank if ever I saw the like of it!" Perhaps he had never given his sloop a chance to show what she could do. The point I make for the *Spray* here, above all other points, is that she sailed in shoal water and in a strong current, with other difficult and unusual conditions. Captain Howard took all this into account.

In all the years away from his native home Howard had not forgotten the art of making fish chowders; and to prove this he brought along some fine rockfish and prepared a mess fit for kings. When the savory chowder was done, chocking the pot securely between two boxes on the cabin floor, so that it could not roll over, we helped ourselves and swapped yarns over it while the *Spray* made her own way through the darkness on the river. Howard told me stories about the Fuegian cannibals as she reeled along, and I told him about the pilot of the *Pinta* steering my vessel through the storm off the coast of the Azores, and that I looked for him at the helm in a gale such as this. I did not charge Howard with superstition,—we are none of us superstitious,—but when I spoke about his returning to Montevideo on the *Spray* he shook his head and took a steam-packet instead.

I had not been in Buenos Aires for a number of years. The place where I had once landed from packets, in a cart, was now built up with magnificent docks. Vast fortunes had been spent in remodeling the harbor; London bankers could tell you that. The port captain,

At the sign of the comet.

after assigning the *Spray* a safe berth, with his compliments, sent me word to call on him for anything I might want while in port, and I felt quite sure that his friendship was sincere. The sloop was well cared for at Buenos Aires; her dockage and tonnage dues were all free, and the yachting fraternity of the city welcomed her with a good will. In town I found things not so greatly changed as about the docks, and I soon felt myself more at home.

From Montevideo I had forwarded a letter from Sir Edward Hairby to the owner of the "Standard," Mr. Mulhall, and in reply to it was assured of a warm welcome to the warmest heart, I think, outside of Ireland. Mr. Mulhall, with a prancing team, came down to the docks as soon as the *Spray* was berthed, and would have me go to his house at once, where a room was waiting. And it was New Year's day, 1896. The course of the *Spray* had been followed in the columns of the "Standard."

Mr. Mulhall kindly drove me to see many improvements about the city, and we went in search of some of the old landmarks. The man who sold "lemonade" on the plaza when first I visited this wonderful city I found selling lemonade still at two cents a glass; he had made a fortune by it. His stock in trade was a wash-tub and a neighboring hydrant, a moderate supply of brown sugar, and about six lemons that floated on the sweetened water. The water from time to time was renewed from the friendly pump, but the lemon "went on forever," and all at two cents a glass.

But we looked in vain for the man who once sold whiskey and coffins in Buenos Aires; the march of civilization had crushed him— memory only clung to his name. Enterprising man that he was, I fain would have looked him up. I remember the tiers of whisky-barrels, ranged on end, on one side of the store, while on the other side, and divided by a thin partition, were the coffins in the same order, of all sizes and in great numbers. The unique arrangement seemed in order, for as a cask was emptied a coffin might be filled. Besides cheap whiskey and many other liquors, he sold "cider," which he manufactured from damaged Malaga raisins. Within the scope of his enterprise was also the sale of mineral waters, not entirely blameless of the germs of disease. This man surely catered to all the tastes, wants, and conditions of his customers.

Farther along in the city, however, survived the good man who wrote on the side of his store, where thoughtful men might read and learn: "This wicked world will be destroyed by a comet! The owner of this store is therefore bound to sell out at any price and avoid the catastrophe." My friend Mr. Mulhall drove me round to view the fearful comet with streaming tail pictured large on the trembling merchant's walls.

I unshipped the sloop's mast at Buenos Aires and shortened it by seven feet. I reduced the length of the bowsprit by about five feet, and even then I found it reaching far enough from home; and more than once, when on the end of it reefing the jib, I regretted that I had not shortened it another foot.

# CHAPTER VII

Weighing anchor at Buenos Aires—An outburst of emotion at the mouth of the Plate—Submerged by a great wave—A stormy entrance to the strait—Captain Samblich's happy gift of a bag of carpet-tacks—Off Cape Froward—Chased by Indians from Fortescue Bay—A miss-shot for "Black Pedro"—Taking in supplies of wood and water at Three Island Cove—Animal life.

On January 26, 1896, the *Spray*, being refitted and well provisioned in every way, sailed from Buenos Aires. There was little wind at the start; the surface of the great river was like a silver disk, and I was glad of a tow from a harbor tug to clear the port entrance. But a gale came up soon after, and caused an ugly sea, and instead of being all silver, as before, the river was now all mud. The Plate is a treacherous place for storms. One sailing there should always be on the alert for squalls. I cast anchor before dark in the best lee I could find near the land, but was tossed miserably all night, heartsore of choppy seas. On the following morning I got the sloop under way, and with reefed sails worked her down the river against a head wind. Standing in that night to the place where pilot Howard joined me for the up-river sail, I took a departure, shaping my course to clear Point Indio on the one hand, and the English Bank on the other.

I had not for many years been south of these regions. I will not say that I expected all fine sailing on the course for Cape Horn direct, but while I worked at the sails and rigging I thought only of onward and forward. It was when I anchored in the lonely places that a feeling of awe crept over me. At the last anchorage on the monotonous and muddy river, weak as it may seem, I gave way to my feelings. I resolved then that I would anchor no more north of the Strait of Magellan.

On the 28th of January the *Spray* was clear of Point Indio, English Bank, and all the other dangers of the River Plate. With a fair wind she then bore away for the Strait of Magellan, under all sail, pressing farther and farther toward the wonderland of the South, till I forgot the blessings of our milder North.

My ship passed in safety Bahia Blanca, also the Gulf of St. Matias and the mighty Gulf of St. George. Hoping that she might go clear of the destructive tide-races, the dread of big craft or little along this coast, I gave all the capes a berth of about fifty miles, for these dangers extend many miles from the land. But where the sloop avoided one danger she encountered another. For, one day, well off the Patagonian coast, while the sloop was reaching under short sail, a tremendous wave, the culmination, it seemed, of many waves,

386

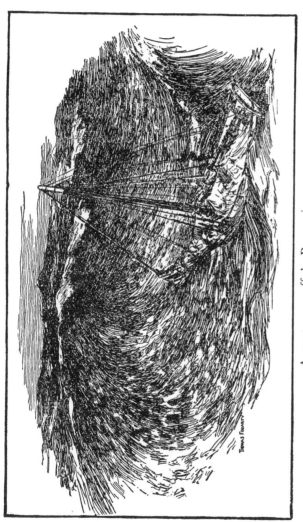

A great wave off the Patagonian coast.

rolled down upon her in a storm, roaring as it came. I had only a moment to get all sail down and myself up on the peak halliards, out of danger, when I saw the mighty crest towering masthead-high above me. The mountain of water submerged my vessel. She shook in every timber and reeled under the weight of the sea, but rose quickly out of it, and rode grandly over the rollers that followed. It may have been a minute that from my hold in the rigging I could see no part of the *Spray's* hull. Perhaps it was even less time than that, but it seemed a long while, for under great excitement one lives fast, and in a few seconds one may think a great deal of one's past life. Not only did the past, with electric speed, flash before me, but I had time while in my hazardous position for resolutions for the future that would take a long time to fulfil. The first one was, I remember, that if the *Spray* came through this danger I would dedicate my best energies to building a larger ship on her lines, which I hope yet to do. Other promises, less easily kept, I should have made under protest. However, the incident, which filled me with fear, was only one more test of the *Spray's* seaworthiness. It reassured me against rude Cape Horn.

From the time the great wave swept over the *Spray* until she reached Cape Virgins nothing occurred to move a pulse and set blood in motion. On the contrary, the weather became fine and the sea smooth and life tranquil. The phenomenon of mirage frequently occurred. An albatross sitting on the water one day loomed up like a large ship; two fur-seals asleep on the surface of the sea appeared like great whales, and a bank of haze I could have sworn was high land. The kaleidoscope then changed, and on the following day I sailed in a world peopled by dwarfs.

On February 11 the *Spray* rounded Cape Virgins and entered the Strait of Magellan. The scene was again real and gloomy; the wind, northeast, and blowing a gale, sent feather-white spume along the coast; such a sea ran as would swamp an ill-appointed ship. As the sloop neared the entrance to the strait I observed that two great tide-races made ahead, one very close to the point of the land and one farther offshore. Between the two, in a sort of channel, through combers, went the *Spray* with close-reefed sails. But a rolling sea

Entrance to the Strait of Magellan.

followed her a long way in, and a fierce current swept around the cape against her; but this she stemmed, and was soon chirruping under the lee of Cape Virgins and running every minute into smoother water. However, long trailing kelp from sunken rocks waved forebodingly under her keel, and the wreck of a great steamship smashed on the beach abreast gave a gloomy aspect to the scene.

I was not to be let off easy. The Virgins would collect tribute even from the *Spray* passing their promontory. Fitful rain-squalls from the northwest followed the northeast gale. I reefed the sloop's sails, and sitting in the cabin to rest my eyes, I was so strongly impressed with what in all nature I might expect that as I dozed the very air I breathed seemed to warn me of danger. My senses heard "*Spray* ahoy!" shouted in warning. I sprang to the deck, wondering who could be there that knew the *Spray* so well as to call out her name passing in the dark; for it was now the blackest of nights all around, except away in the southwest, where the old familiar white arch, the terror of Cape Horn, rapidly pushed up by a southwest gale. I had only a moment to douse sail and lash all solid when it struck like a shot from a cannon, and for the first half-hour it was something to be remembered by way of a gale. For thirty hours it kept on blowing hard. The sloop could carry no more than a three-reefed mainsail and forestaysail; with these she held on stoutly and was not blown out of the strait. In the height of the squalls in this gale she doused all sail, and this occurred often enough.

After this gale followed only a smart breeze, and the *Spray*, passing through the narrows without mishap, cast anchor at Sandy Point on February 14, 1896.

Sandy Point (Punta Arenas) is a Chilean coaling-station, and boasts about two thousand inhabitants, of mixed nationality, but mostly Chileans. What with sheep-farming, gold-mining, and hunting, the settlers in this dreary land seemed not the worst off in the world. But the natives, Patagonian and Fuegian, on the other hand, were as squalid as contact with unscrupulous traders could make them. A large percentage of the business there was traffic in "firewater." If there was a law against selling the poisonous stuff to the natives, it was not enforced. Fine specimens of the Patagonian race, looking smart in the morning when they came into town, had repented before night of ever having seen a white man, so beastly drunk were they, to say nothing about the peltry of which they had been robbed.

The port at that time was free, but a customhouse was in course of construction, and when it is finished, port and tariff dues are to be collected. A soldier police guarded the place, and a sort of vigilante force besides took down its guns now and then; but as a general thing, to my mind, whenever an execution was made they killed the wrong man. Just previous to my arrival the governor, himself of a jovial turn of mind, had sent a party of young bloods to foray

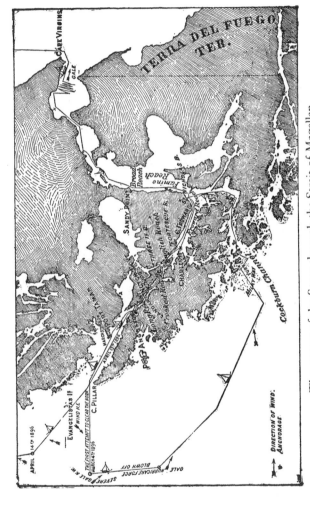

The course of the *Spray* through the Strait of Magellan.

a Fuegian settlement and wipe out what they could of it on account of the recent massacre of a schooner's crew somewhere else. Altogether the place was quite newsy and supported two papers—dailies, I think. The port captain, a Chilean naval officer, advised me to ship hands to fight Indians in the strait farther west, and spoke of my stopping until a gunboat should be going through, which would give me a tow. After canvassing the place, however, I found only one man willing to embark, and he on condition that I should ship another "mon and a doog." But as no one else was willing to come along, and as I drew the line at dogs, I said no more about the matter, but simply loaded my guns. At this point in my dilemma Captain Pedro Samblich, a good Austrian of large experience, coming along, gave me a bag of carpet-tacks, worth more than all the fighting men and dogs of Tierra del Fuego. I protested that I had no use for carpet-tacks on board. Samblich smiled at my want of experience, and maintained stoutly that I would have use for them. "You must use them with discretion," he said; "that is to say, don't step on them yourself." With this remote hint about the use of the tacks I got on all right, and saw the way to maintain clear decks at night without the care of watching.

The man who would n't ship without another "mon and a doog."

Samblich was greatly interested in my voyage, and after giving me the tacks he put on board bags of biscuits and a large quantity of smoked venison. He declared that my bread, which was ordinary sea-biscuits and easily broken, was not nutritious as his, which was so hard that I could break it only with a stout blow from a maul. Then he gave me, from his own sloop, a compass which was certainly better than mine, and offered to unbend her mainsail for me if I would accept it. Last of all, this large-hearted man brought out a bottle of Fuegian gold-dust from a place where it had been *cached* and begged me to help myself from it, for use farther along on the voyage. But I felt sure of success without this draft on a friend, and I was right. Samblich's tacks, as it turned out, were of more value than gold.

The port captain finding that I was resolved to go, even alone, since there was no help for it, set up no further objections, but ad-

A Fuegian Girl.

vised me, in case the savages tried to surround me with their canoes, to shoot straight, and begin to do it in time, but to avoid killing them if possible, which I heartily agreed to do. With these simple injunctions the offer gave me my port clearance free of charge, and I sailed on the same day, February 19, 1896. It was not without thoughts of strange and stirring adventure beyond all I had yet encountered that I now sailed into the country and very core of the savage Fuegians.

A fair wind from Sandy Point brought me on the first day to St. Nicholas Bay, where, so I was told, I might expect to meet savages; but seeing no signs of life, I came to anchor in eight fathoms of water, where I lay all night under a high mountain. Here I had my first experience with the terrific squalls, called williwaws, which extended from this point on through the strait to the Pacific. They were compressed gales of wind that Boreas handed down over the hills in chunks. A full-blown williwaw will throw a ship, even without sail on, over on her beam ends; but, like other gales, they cease now and then, if only for a short time.

February 20 was my birthday, and I found myself alone with hardly so much as a bird in sight, off Cape Froward, the southernmost point of the continent of America. By daylight in the morning I was getting my ship under way for the bout ahead.

The sloop held the wind fair while she ran thirty miles farther on her course, which brought her to Fortescue Bay, and at once among the natives' signal-fires, which blazed up now on all sides. Clouds flew over the mountain from the west all day; at night my good east wind failed, and in its stead a gale from the west soon came on. I gained anchorage at twelve o'clock that night, under the lee of a little island, and then prepared myself a cup of coffee, of which I was sorely in need; for, to tell the truth, hard beating in the heavy squalls and against the current had told on my strength. Finding that the anchor held, I drank my beverage, and named the place Coffee Island. It lies to the south of Charles Island, with only a narrow channel between.

By daylight the next morning the *Spray* was again under way, beating hard; but she came to in a cove in Charles Island, two and a half miles along on her course. Here she remained undisturbed two days, with both anchors down in a bed of kelp. Indeed, she might have remained undisturbed indefinitely had not the wind moderated; for during these two days it blew so hard that no boat could venture out on the strait, and the natives being away to other hunting-grounds, the island anchorage was safe. But at the end of the fierce wind-storm fair weather came; then I got my anchors, and again sailed out upon the strait.

Canoes manned by savages from Fortescue now came in pursuit. The wind falling light, they gained on me rapidly till coming within hail, when they ceased paddling, and a bow-legged savage stood up and called to me, "Yammerschooner! yammerschooner!" which is their begging term. I said, "No!" Now, I was not for letting on that I was alone, and so I stepped into the cabin, and, passing through the hold, came out at the fore-scuttle, changing my clothes as I went along. That made two men. Then the piece of bowsprit which I had sawed off at Buenos Aires, and which I had still on board, I arranged forward on the lookout, dressed as a seaman, attaching a line by which I could pull it into motion. That made three of us, and we did n't want to "yammerschooner"; but for all that the savages came on faster than before. I saw that besides four at the paddles in the canoe nearest to me, there were others in the bottom, and that they were shifting hands often. At eighty yards I fired a shot across the bows of the nearest canoe, at which they all stopped, but only for a moment. Seeing that they persisted in coming nearer, I fired the second shot so close to the chap who wanted to "yammer-schooner" that he changed his mind quickly enough and bellowed with fear, "Bueno jo via Isla," and sitting down in his canoe, he rubbed his starboard cat-head for some time. I was thinking of the good port captain's advise when I pulled the trigger, and must have aimed pretty straight; however, a miss was as good as a mile for Mr. "Black Pedro," as he it was, and no other, a leader in several bloody massacres. He made for the island now, and the others followed him. I knew by his Spanish lingo and by his full beard that he was the villain I had named, a renegade mongrel, and the worst murderer in Tierra del Fuego. The authorities had been in search of him for two years. The Fuegians are not bearded.

So much for the first day among the savages. I came to anchor at midnight in Three Island Cove, about twenty miles along from Fortescue Bay. I saw on the opposite side of the strait signal-fires, and heard the barking of dogs, but where I lay it was quite deserted by natives. I have always taken it as a sign that where I found birds sitting about, or seals on the rocks, I should not find savage Indians. Seals are never plentiful in these waters, but in Three Island Cove I saw one on the rocks, and other signs of the absence of savage men.

On the next day the wind was again blowing a gale, and although she was in the lee of the land, the sloop dragged her anchors, so that I had to get her under way and beat farther into the cove, where I came to in a landlocked pool. At another time or place this would

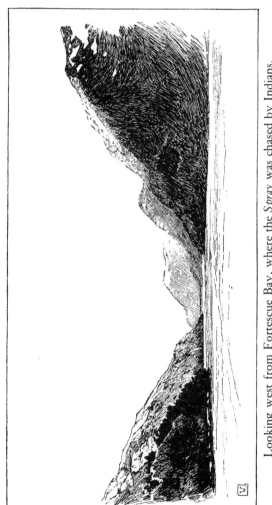

Looking west from Fortescue Bay, where the *Spray* was chased by Indians.
(From a photograph.)

have been a rash thing to do, and it was safe now only from the fact that the gale which drove me to shelter would keep the Indians from crossing the strait. Seeing this was the case, I went ashore with gun and ax on an island, where I could not in any event be surprised, and there felled trees and split about a cord of fire-wood, which loaded my small boat several times.

While I carried the wood, though I was morally sure there were no savages near, I never once went to or from the skiff without my gun. While I had that and a clear field of over eighty yards about me I felt safe.

The trees on the island, very scattering, were a sort of beech and a stunted cedar, both of which made good fuel. Even the green limbs of the beech, which seemed to possess a resinous quality, burned readily in my great drum-stove. I have described my method of wooding up in detail, that the reader who has kindly borne with me so far may see that in this, as in all other particulars of my voyage, I took great care against all kinds of surprises, whether by animals or by the elements. In the Strait of Magellan the greatest vigilance was necessary. In this instance I reasoned that I had all about me the greatest danger of the whole voyage—the treachery of cunning savages, for which I must be particularly on the alert.

The *Spray* sailed from Three Island Cove in the morning after the gale went down, but was glad to return for shelter from another sudden gale. Sailing again on the following day, she fetched Borgia Bay, a few miles on her course, where vessels had anchored from time to time and had nailed boards on the trees ashore with name and date of harboring carved or painted. Nothing else could I see to indicate that civilized man had ever been there. I had taken a survey of the gloomy place with my spy-glass, and was getting my boat out to land and take notes, when the Chilean gunboat *Huemel* came in, and officers, coming on board, advised me to leave the place at once, a thing that required little eloquence to persuade me to do. I accepted the captain's kind offer of a tow to the next anchorage, at the place called Notch Cove, eight miles farther along, where I should be clear of the worst of the Fuegians.

We made anchorage at the cove about dark that night, while the wind came down in fierce williwaws from the mountains. An instance of Magellan weather was afforded when the *Huemel*, a well-appointed gunboat of great power, after attempting on the following day to proceed on her voyage, was obliged by sheer force of the wind to return and take up anchorage again and remain till the gale abated; and lucky she was to get back!

Meeting this vessel was a little godsend. She was commanded and officered by high-class sailors and educated gentlemen. An entertainment that was gotten up on her, impromptu, at the Notch would be hard to beat anywhere. One of her midshipmen sang popular songs

A brush with Fuegians.

in French, German, and Spanish, and one (so he said) in Russian. If the audience did not know the lingo of one song from another, it was no drawback to the merriment.

I was left alone the next day, for then the *Huemel* put out on her voyage the gale having abated. I spent a day taking in wood and water; by the end of that time the weather was fine. Then I sailed from the desolate place.

A bit of friendly assistance.
(After a sketch by Midshipman Miguel Arenas.)

There is little more to be said concerning the *Spray's* first passage through the strait that would differ from what I have already recorded. She anchored and weighed many times, and beat many days against the current, with now and then a "slant" for a few miles, till finally she gained anchorage and shelter for the night at Port Tamar, with Cape Pillar in sight to the west. Here I felt the throb of the great ocean that lay before me. I knew now that I had put a world behind me, and that I was opening out another world ahead. I had passed the haunts of savages. Great piles of granite mountains of bleak and lifeless aspect were now astern; on some of them not even a speck of moss had ever grown. There was an unfinished newness all about the land. On the hill back of Port Tamar a small beacon had been thrown up, showing that some man had been there. But how could one tell but that he had died of loneliness and grief? In a bleak land is not the place to enjoy solitude.

Throughout the whole of the strait west of Cape Froward I saw no animals except dogs owned by savages. These I saw often enough, and heard them yelping night and day. Birds were not plentiful. The scream of a wild fowl, which I took for a loon, sometimes startled me with its piercing cry. The steamboat duck, so called because it propels itself over the sea with its wings, and resembles a miniature side-wheel steamer in its motion, was sometimes seen scurrying on out of danger. It never flies, but, hitting the water instead of the air with its wings, it moves faster than a rowboat or a canoe. The few fur-seals I saw were very shy; and of fishes I saw next to none at all. I did not catch one; indeed, I seldom or never put a hook over during the whole voyage. Here in the strait I found great abundance of mussels of an excellent quality. I fared sumptuously on them. There was a sort of swan, smaller than a Muscovy duck, which might have been brought down with the gun, but in the loneliness of life about the dreary country I found myself in no mood to make one life less, except in self-defense.

# CHAPTER VIII

From Cape Pillar into the Pacific—Driven by a tempest toward Cape Horn—Captain Slocum's greatest sea adventure—Reaching the strait again by way of Cockburn Channel—Some savages find the carpet-tacks—Danger from firebrands—A series of fierce williwaws—Again sailing westward.

It was the 3d of March when the *Spray* sailed from Port Tamar direct for Cape Pillar, with the wind from the northeast, which I fervently hoped might hold till she cleared the land; but there was no such good luck in store. It soon began to rain and thicken in the northwest, boding no good. The *Spray* neared Cape Pillar rapidly, and, nothing loath, plunged into the Pacific ocean at once, taking her first bath of it in the gathering storm. There was no turning back even had I wished to do so, for the land was now shut out by the darkness of night. The wind freshened, and I took in a third reef. The sea was confused and treacherous. In such a time as this the old fisherman prayed, "Remember, Lord, my ship is small and thy sea is so wide!" I saw now only the gleaming crests of the waves. They showed white teeth while the sloop balanced over them. "Everything for an offing," I cried, and to this end I carried on all the sail she would bear. She ran all night with a free sheet, but on the morning of March 4 the wind shifted to southwest, then back suddenly to northwest, and blew with terrific force. The *Spray*, stripped of her sails, then bore off under bare poles. No ship in the world could have stood up against so violent a gale. Knowing that this storm might continue for many days, and that it would be impossible to work back to the westward along the coast outside of Tierra del Fuego, there seemed nothing to do but to keep on and go east about, after all. Anyhow, for my present safety the only course lay in keeping her before the wind. And so she drove southeast, as though about to round the Horn, while the waves rose and fell and bellowed their never-ending story of the sea; but the Hand that held these held also the *Spray*. She was running now with a reefed forestaysail, the sheets flat amidship. I paid out two long ropes to steady her course and to break combing seas astern, and I lashed the helm amidship. In this trim she ran before it, shipping never a sea. Even while the storm raged at its worst, my ship was wholesome and noble. My mind as to her seaworthiness was put at ease for aye.

When all had been done that I could do for the safety of the vessel, I got to the fore-scuttle, between seas, and prepared a pot of coffee over a wood fire, and made a good Irish stew. Then, as before and afterward on the *Spray*, I insisted on warm meals. In the tide-race off Cape Pillar, however, where the sea was marvelously high, uneven, and crooked, my appetite was slim, and for a time I postponed cooking. (Confidentially, I was seasick!)

The first day of the storm gave the *Spray* her actual test in the worst sea that Cape Horn or its wild regions could afford, and in no part of the world could a rougher sea be found than at this particular point, namely, off Cape Pillar, the grim sentinel of the Horn.

Farther offshore, while the sea was majestic, there was less apprehension of danger. There the *Spray* rode, now like a bird on the crest of a wave, and now like a waif deep in the hollow between seas; and so she drove on. Whole days passed, counted as other days, but with always a thrill—yes, of delight.

On the fourth day of the gale, rapidly nearing the pitch of Cape Horn, I inspected my chart and pricked off the course and distance to Port Stanley, in the Falkland Islands, where I might find my way and refit, when I saw through a rift in the clouds a high mountain,

Cape Pillar.

about seven leagues away on the port beam. The fierce edge of the gale by this time had blown off, and I had already bent a square-sail on the boom in place of the mainsail, which was torn to rags. I hauled in the trailing ropes, hoisted this awkward sail reefed, the forestaysail being already set, and under this sail brought her at once on the wind heading for the land, which appeared as an island in the sea. So it turned out to be, though not the one I had supposed.

I was exultant over the prospect of once more entering the Strait of Magellan and beating through again into the Pacific, for it was more than rough on the outside coast of Tierra del Fuego. It was indeed a mountainous sea. When the sloop was in the fiercest squalls, with only the reefed forestaysail set, even that small sail shook her from keelson to truck when it shivered by the leech. Had I harbored the shadow of a doubt for her safety, it would have been that she might spring a leak in the garboard at the heel of the mast; but she never called me once to the pump. Under pressure of the smallest sail I could set she made for the land like a race-horse, and steering her over the crests of the waves so that she might not trip was nice work. I stood at the helm now and made the most of it.

Night closed in before the sloop reached the land, leaving her feeling the way in pitchy darkness. I saw breakers ahead before long. At this I wore ship and stood offshore, but was immediately startled by the tremendous roaring of breakers again ahead and on the lee bow. This puzzled me, for there should have been no broken water where I supposed myself to be. I kept off a good bit, then wore round, but finding broken water also there, threw her head again offshore. In this way, among dangers, I spent the rest of the night. Hail and sleet in the fierce squalls cut my flesh till the blood trickled over my face; but what of that? It was daylight, and the sloop was in the midst of the Milky Way of the sea, which is northwest of Cape Horn, and it was the white breakers of a huge sea over sunken rocks which had threatened to engulf her through the night. It was Fury Island I had sighted and steered for, and what a panorama was before me now and all around! It was not the time to complain of a broken skin. What could I do but fill away among the breakers and find a channel between them, now that it was day? Since she had escaped the rocks through the night, surely she would find her way by daylight. This was the greatest sea adventure of my life. God knows how my vessel escaped.

The sloop at last reached inside of small islands that sheltered her in smooth water. Then I climbed the mast to survey the wild scene astern. The great naturalist Darwin looked over this seascape from the deck of the *Beagle*, and wrote in his journal, "Any landsman seeing the Milky Way would have nightmare for a week." He might have added, "or seaman" as well.

The *Spray's* good luck followed fast. I discovered, as she sailed along through a labyrinth of islands, that she was in the Cockburn Channel, which leads into the Strait of Magellan at a point opposite Cape Froward, and that she was already passing Thieves' Bay, suggestively named. And at night, March 8, behold, she was at anchor in a snug cove at the Turn! Every heart-beat on the *Spray* now counted thanks.

Here I pondered on the events of the last few days, and strangely enough, instead of feeling rested from sitting or lying down, I now began to feel jaded and worn; but a hot meal of venison stew soon put me right, so that I could sleep. As drowsiness came on I sprinkled the deck with tacks, and then I turned in, bearing in mind the advice of my old friend Samblich that I was not to step on them myself. I saw to it that not a few of them stood "business end" up; for when the *Spray* passed Thieves' Bay two canoes had put out and followed in her wake, and there was no disguising the fact any longer that I was alone.

Now, it is well known that one cannot step on a tack without saying something about it. A pretty good Christian will whistle when he steps on the "commercial end" of a carpet-tack; a savage will howl and claw the air, and that was just what happened that night about twelve o'clock, while I was asleep in the cabin, where the savages thought they "had me," sloop and all, but changed their minds when they stepped on deck, for then they thought that I or somebody else had them. I had no need of a dog; they howled like a pack of hounds. I had hardly use for a gun. They jumped pell-mell, some into their canoes and some into the sea, to cool off, I suppose, and there was a deal of free language over it as they went. I fired several guns when I came on deck to let the rascals know that I was home, and then I turned in again, feeling sure I should not be disturbed any more by people who left in so great a hurry.

The Fuegians, being cruel, are naturally cowards; they regard a rifle with superstitious fear. The only real danger one could see that might come from their quarter would be from allowing them to surround one within bow-shot, or to anchor within range where they might lie in ambush. As for their coming on deck at night, even had I not put tacks about, I could have cleared them off by shots from the cabin and hold. I always kept a quantity of ammunition within reach in the hold and in the cabin and in the forepeak, so that retreating to any of these places I could "hold the fort" simply by shooting up through the deck.

"They howled like a pack of hounds."

Perhaps the greatest danger to be apprehended was from the use of fire. Every canoe carries fire; nothing is thought of that, for it is their custom to communicate by smoke-signals. The harmless brand that lies smoldering in the bottom of one of their canoes might be ablaze in one's cabin if he were not on the alert. The port captain of Sandy Point warned me particularly of this danger. Only a short time before they had fired a Chilean gunboat by throwing brands in through the stern windows of the cabin. The *Spray* had no openings in the cabin or deck, except two scuttles, and these were guarded by fastenings which could not be undone without waking me if I were asleep.

On the morning of the 9th, after a refreshing rest and a warm breakfast, and after I had swept the deck of tacks, I got out what spare canvas there was on board, and began to sew the pieces together in the shape of a peak for my square-mainsail, the tarpaulin. The day to all appearances promised fine weather and light winds, but appearances in Tierra del Fuego do not always count. While I was wondering why no trees grew on the slope abreast of the anchorage, half minded to lay by the sail-making and land with my gun for some game and to inspect a white boulder on the beach, near the brook, a williwaw came down with such terrific force as to carry the *Spray*, with two anchors down, like a feather out of the cove and away into deep water. No wonder trees did not grow on the side of that hill! Great Boreas! a tree would need to be all roots to hold on against such a furious wind.

From the cove to the nearest land to leeward was a long drift, however, and I had ample time to weigh both anchors before the sloop came near any danger, and so no harm came of it. I saw no more savages that day or the next; they probably had some sign by which they knew of the coming williwaws; at least, they were wise in not being afloat even on the second day, for I had no sooner gotten to work at sail-making again, after the anchor was down, than the wind, as on the day before, picked the sloop up and flung her seaward with a vengeance, anchor and all, as before. This fierce wind, usual to the Magellan country, continued on through the day, and swept the sloop by several miles of steep bluffs and precipices overhanging a bold shore of wild and uninviting appearance. I was not sorry to get away from it, though in doing so it was no Elysian shore to which I shaped my course. I kept on sailing in hope, since I had no choice but to go on, heading across for St. Nicholas Bay, where I had cast anchor February 19. It was now the 10th of March! Upon reaching the bay the second time I had circumnavigated the wildest part of desolate Tierra del Fuego. But the *Spray* had not yet arrived at St. Nicholas, and by the merest accident her bones were saved from resting there when she did arrive. The parting of a stay-sail-sheet in a williwaw, when the sea was turbulent and she was plunging into the storm, brought me forward to see instantly a dark cliff ahead and breakers so close under the bows that I felt surely lost, and in my thoughts cried, "Is the hand of fate against me, after all, leading me in the end to this dark spot?" I sprang aft again, unheeding the flapping sail, and threw the wheel over, expecting as the sloop came down into the hollow of a wave, to feel her timbers smash under me on the rocks. But at the touch of her helm she swung clear of the danger, and in the next moment she was in the lee of the land.

It was the small island in the middle of the bay for which the sloop had been steering, and which she made with such unerring aim as nearly to run it down. Farther along in the bay was the anchorage, which I managed to reach, but before I could get the anchor down

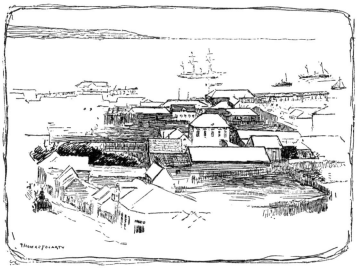

A glimpse of Sandy Point (Punta Arenas) in the Strait of Magellan.

another squall caught the sloop and whirled her round like a top and carried her away, altogether to leeward of the bay. Still farther to leeward was a great headland, and I bore off for that. This was retracing my course toward Sandy Point, for the gale was from the southwest.

I had the sloop soon under good control, however, and in a short time rounded to under the lee of a mountain, where the sea was as smooth as a mill-pond, and the sails flapped and hung limp while she carried her way close in. Here I thought I would anchor and rest till morning, the depth being eight fathoms very close to the shore. But it was interesting to see, as I let go the anchor, that it did not reach the bottom before another williwaw struck down from this mountain and carried the sloop off faster than I could pay out cable. Therefore, instead of resting, I had to "man the windlass" and heave up the anchor with fifty fathoms of cable hanging up and down in deep water. This was in that part of the strait called Famine Reach. Dismal Famine Reach! On the sloop's crab-windlass I worked the rest of the night, thinking how much easier it was for me when I could say, "Do that thing or the other," than now doing all myself. But I hove away and sang the old chants that I sang when I was a sailor. Within the last few days I had passed through much and was now thankful that my state was no worse.

It was daybreak when the anchor was at the hawse. By this time the wind had gone down, and cat's-paws took the place of willi-waws, while the sloop drifted slowly toward Sandy Point. She came within sight of ships at anchor in the roads, and I was more than half minded to put in for new sails, but the wind coming out from the northeast, which was fair for the other direction, I turned the prow of the *Spray* westward once more for the Pacific, to traverse a second time the second half of my first course through the strait.

# CHAPTER IX

Repairing the *Spray's* sails—Savages and an obstreperous anchor—A spider-fight—An encounter with Black Pedro—A visit to the steamship *Colombia*—On the defensive against a fleet of canoes—A record of voyages through the strait—A chance cargo of tallow.

I was determined to rely on my own small resources to repair the damages of the great gale which drove me southward toward the Horn, after I passed from the Strait of Magellan out into the Pacific. So when I had got back into the strait, by way of Cockburn Channel, I did not proceed eastward for help at the Sandy Point settlement, but turning again into the northwestward reach of the strait, set to work with my palm and needle at every opportunity, when at anchor and when sailing. It was slow work; but little by little the squaresail on the boom expanded to the dimensions of a serviceable mainsail with a peak to it and a leech besides. If it was not the best-setting sail afloat, it was at least very strongly made and would stand a hard blow. A ship, meeting the *Spray* long afterward, reported her as wearing a mainsail of some improved design and patent reefer, but that was not the case.

The *Spray* for a few days after the storm enjoyed fine weather, and made fair time through the strait for the distance of twenty miles, which, in these days of many adversities, I called a long run. The weather, I say, was fine for a few days; but it brought little rest. Care for the safety of my vessel, and even for my own life, was in no wise lessened by the absence of heavy weather. Indeed, the peril was even greater, inasmuch as the savages on comparatively fine days ventured forth on their marauding excursions, and in boisterous weather disappeared from sight, their wretched canoes being frail and undeserving the name of craft at all. This being so, I now enjoyed gales of wind as never before, and the *Spray* was never long without them during her struggles about Cape Horn. I became in a measure inured to the life, and began to think that one more trip through the strait, if perchance the sloop should be blown off again, would make me the aggressor, and put the Fuegians entirely on the defensive. This feeling was forcibly borne in on me at Snug Bay, where I anchored at gray morning after passing Cape Froward, to find, when broad day appeared, that two canoes which I had eluded by sailing all night were now entering the same bay stealthily under the shadow of the high headland. They were well manned, and the savages were well armed with spears and bows. At a shot from my rifle across the bows, both turned aside into a small creek out of range. In danger now of being

406

flanked by the savages in the bush close aboard, I was obliged to hoist the sails, which I had barely lowered, and make across to the opposite side of the strait, a distance of six miles. But now I was put to my wit's end as to how I should weigh anchor, for through an accident to the windlass right here I could not budge it. However, I set all sail and filled away, first hauling short by hand. The sloop carried her anchor away, as though it was meant to be always towed in this way underfoot, and with it she towed a ton or more of kelp from a reef in the bay, the wind blowing a wholesale breeze.

Meanwhile I worked till blood started from my fingers, and with one eye over my shoulder for savages, I watched at the same time, and sent a bullet whistling whenever I saw a limb or a twig move; for I kept a gun always at hand, and an Indian appearing then within range would have been taken as a declaration of war. As it was, however, my own blood was all that was spilt—and from the trifling accident of sometimes breaking the flesh against a cleat or a pin which came in the way when I was in haste. Sea-cuts in my hands from pulling on hard, wet ropes were sometimes painful and often bled freely; but these healed when I finally got away from the strait into fine weather.

After clearing Snug Bay I hauled the sloop to the wind, repaired the windlass, and hove the anchor to the hawse, catted it, and then stretched across to a port of refuge under a high mountain about six miles away, and came to in nine fathoms close under the face of a perpendicular cliff. Here my own voice answered back, and I named the place "Echo Mountain." Seeing dead trees farther along where the shore was broken, I made a landing for fuel, taking, besides my ax, a rifle, which on these days I never left far from hand; but I saw no living thing here, except a small spider, which had nested in a dry log that I boated to the sloop. The conduct of this insect interested me now more than anything else around the wild place. In my cabin it met, oddly enough, a spider of its own size and species that had come all the way from Boston—a very civil little chap, too, but mighty spry. Well, the Fuegian threw up its antennae for a fight; but my little Bostonian downed it at once, then broke its legs, and pulled them off, one by one, so dexterously that in less than three minutes from the time the battle began the Fuegian spider didn't know itself from a fly.

I made haste the following morning to be under way after a night of wakefulness on the weird shore. Before weighing anchor, however, I prepared a cup of warm coffee over a smart wood fire in my great Montevideo stove. In the same fire was cremated the Fuegian spider, slain the day before by the little warrior from Boston, which a Scots lady at Cape Town long after named "Bruce" upon hearing of its prowess at Echo Mountain. The *Spray* now reached away for Coffee Island, which I sighted on my birthday, February 20, 1896.

There she encountered another gale, that brought her in the lee of great Charles Island for shelter. On a bluff point on Charles were signal-fires, and a tribe of savages, mustered here since my first trip through

"Yammerschooner!"

the strait, manned their canoes to put off for the sloop. It was not pru-
dent to come to, the anchorage being within bow-shot of the shore,
which was thickly wooded; but I made signs that one canoe might come
alongside, while the sloop ranged about under sail in the lee of the
land. The others I motioned to keep off, and incidentally laid a smart
Martini-Henry rifle in sight, close at hand, on the top of the cabin.
In the canoe that came alongside, crying their never-ending begging
word "yammerschooner," were two squaws and one Indian, the
hardest specimens of humanity I had ever seen in any of my travels.
"Yammerschooner" was their plaint when they pushed off from shore,
and "yammerschooner" it was when they got alongside. The squaws
beckoned for food, while the Indian, a black-visaged savage, stood
sulkily as if he took no interest at all in the matter, but on my turning
my back for some biscuits and jerked beef for the squaws, the "buck"
sprang on deck and confronted me, saying in Spanish jargon that we
had met before. I thought I recognized the tone of his "yammerschooner," and his full beard identified him as the Black Pedro whom,
it was true, I had met before. "Where are the rest of the crew?" he
asked, as he looked uneasily around, expecting hands, maybe, to come
out of the fore-scuttle and deal him his just deserts for many murders.
"About three weeks ago," said he, "when you passed up here, I saw
three men on board. Where are the other two?" I answered him briefly
that the same crew was still on board. "But," said he, "I see you are
doing all the work," and with a leer he added, as he glanced at the
mainsail, "hombre valiente." I explained that I did all the work in the
day, while the rest of the crew slept, so that they would be fresh to
watch for Indians at night. I was interested in the subtle cunning of
this savage, knowing him, as I did, better perhaps than he was aware.
Even had I not been advised before I sailed from Sandy Point, I should
have measured him for an arch-villain now. Moreover, one of the
squaws, with that spark of kindliness which is somehow found in the
breast of even the lowest savage, warned me by a sign to be on my
guard, or Black Pedro would do me harm. There was no need of the
warning, however, for I was on my guard from the first, and at that moment held a smart revolver in my hand ready for instant service.

"When you sailed through here before," he said, "you fired a shot
at me," adding with some warmth that it was "muy malo." I affected
not to understand, and said, "You have lived at Sandy Point, have
you not?" He answered frankly, "Yes," and appeared delighted to
meet one who had come from the dear old place. "At the mission?" I
queried. "Why, yes," he replied, stepping forward as if to embrace an
old friend. I motioned him back, for I did not share his flattering humor.
"And you know Captain Pedro Samblich?" continued I. "Yes," said
the villain who had killed a kinsman of Samblich—"yes, indeed; he
is a great friend of mine." "I know it," said I. Samblich had told me to
shoot him on sight. Pointing to my rifle on the cabin, he wanted to
know how many times it fired. "Cuantos?" said he. When I explained

to him that the gun kept right on shooting, his jaw fell, and he spoke of getting away. I did not hinder him from going. I gave the squaws biscuits and beef, and one of them gave me several lumps of tallow in exchange, and I think it worth mentioning that she did not offer me the smallest pieces, but with some extra trouble handed me the largest of all the pieces in the canoe. No Christian could have done more. Before pushing off from the sloop the cunning savage asked for matches, and made as if to reach with the end of his spear the box I was about to give him; but I held it toward him on the muzzle of my rifle, the one that "kept on shooting." The chap picked the box off the gun gingerly enough, to be sure, but he jumped when I said "Quedao [Look out]," at which the squaws laughed and seemed not at all displeased. Perhaps the wretch had clubbed them that morning for not gathering mussels enough for his breakfast. There was a good understanding among us all.

From Charles Island the *Spray* crossed over to Fortescue Bay, where she anchored and spent a comfortable night under the lee of high land, while the wind howled outside. The bay was deserted now. They were Fortescue Indians whom I had seen at the island, and I felt quite sure they could not follow the *Spray* in the present hard blow. Not to neglect a precaution, however, I sprinkled tacks on deck before I turned in.

On the following day the loneliness of the place was broken by the appearance of a great steamship, making for the anchorage with a lofty bearing. She was no Diego craft. I knew the sheer, the model, and the poise. I threw out my flag, and directly saw the Stars and Stripes flung to the breeze from the great ship.

The wind had then abated, and toward night the savages made their appearance from the island, going direct to the steamer to "yammer-schooner." Then they came to the *Spray* to beg more, or to steal all, declaring that they got nothing from the steamer. Black Pedro here came alongside again. My own brother could not have been more delighted to see me, and he begged me to lend him my rifle to shoot a guanaco for me in the morning. I assured the fellow that if I remained there another day I would lend him the gun, but I had no mind to remain. I gave him a cooper's draw-knife and some other small implements which would be of service in canoe-making, and bade him be off.

Under the cover of darkness that night I went to the steamer, which I found to be the *Colombia*, Captain Henderson, from New York, bound for San Francisco. I carried all my guns along with me, in case it should be necessary to fight my way back. In the chief mate of the *Colombia*, Mr. Hannibal, I found an old friend, and he referred affectionately to days in Manila when we were there together, he in the *Southern Cross* and I in the *Northern Light*, both ships as beautiful as their names.

The *Colombia* had an abundance of fresh stores on board. The captain give his steward some order, and I remember that the guileless young man asked me if I could manage, besides other things, a few cans of milk and a cheese. When I offered my Montevideo gold for the supplies, the captain roared like a lion and told me to put my money up. It was a glorious outfit of provisions of all kinds that I got.

Returning to the *Spray*, where I found all secure, I prepared for an early start in the morning. It was agreed that the steamer should blow her whistle for me if first on the move. I watched the steamer, off and on, through the night for the pleasure alone of seeing her electric

A contrast in lighting—the electric lights of the *Colombia* and the canoe fires of the Fortescue Indians.

lights, a pleasing sight in contrast to the ordinary Fuegian canoe with a brand of fire in it. The sloop was the first under way, but the *Colombia*, soon following, passed, and saluted as she went by. Had the captain given me his steamer, his company would have been no worse off than they were two or three months later. I read afterward, in a late California paper, "The *Colombia* will be a total loss." On her second trip to Panama she was wrecked on the rocks of the California coast.

The *Spray* was then beating against wind and current, as usual in the strait. At this point the tides from the Atlantic and the Pacific meet, and in the strait, as on the outside coast, their meeting makes a commotion of whirlpools and combers that in a gale of wind is dangerous to canoes and other frail craft.

A few miles farther along was a large steamer ashore, bottom up.

Passing this place, the sloop ran into a streak of light wind, and then—
a most remarkable condition for strait weather—it fell entirely calm.
Signal-fires sprang up at once on all sides, and then more than twenty
canoes hove in sight, all heading for the *Spray*. As they came within
hail, their savage crews cried, "Amigo yammerschooner," "Anclas
aqui," "Bueno puerto aqui," and like scraps of Spanish mixed with
their own jargon. I had no thought of anchoring in their "good port."
I hoisted the sloop's flag and fired a gun, all of which they might con-
strue as a friendly salute or an invitation to come on. They drew up
in a semicircle, but kept outside of eighty yards, which in self-defense
would have been the death line.

In their mosquito fleet was a ship's boat stolen probably from a
murdered crew. Six savages paddled this rather awkwardly with the
blades of oars which had been broken off. Two of the savages standing
erect wore sea-boots, and this sustained the suspicion that they had
fallen upon some luckless ship's crew, and also added a hint that they
had already visited the *Spray's* deck, and would now, if they could,
try her again. Their sea-boots, I have no doubt, would have protected
their feet and rendered carpet-tacks harmless. Paddling clumsily,
they passed down the strait at a distance of a hundred yards from
the sloop, in an offhand manner as if bound to Fortescue Bay. This
I judged to be a piece of strategy, and so kept a sharp lookout over a
small island which soon came in range between them and the sloop,
completely hiding them from view, and toward which the *Spray* was
now drifting helplessly with the tide, and with every prospect of going
on the rocks, for there was no anchorage, at least, none that my cables
would reach. And, sure enough, I soon saw a movement in the grass
just on top of the island, which is called Bonet Island and is one hundred
and thirty-six feet high. I fired several shots over the place, but saw
no other sign of the savages. It was they that had moved the grass,
for as the sloop swept past the island, the rebound of the tide carrying
her clear, there on the other side was the boat, surely enough exposing
their cunning and treachery. A stiff breeze, coming up suddenly, now
scattered the canoes while it extricated the sloop from a dangerous
position, albeit the wind, though friendly, was still ahead.

The *Spray*, flogging against current and wind, made Borgia Bay on
the following afternoon, and cast anchor there for the second time. I
would now, if I could, describe the moonlit scene on the strait at midnight after I had cleared the savages and Bonet Island. A heavy cloud
bank that had swept across the sky then cleared away, and the night
became suddenly as light as day, or nearly so. A high mountain was
mirrored in the channel ahead, and the *Spray* sailing along with her
shadow was as two sloops on the sea.

The sloop being moored, I threw out my skiff, and with ax and gun
landed at the head of the cove, and filled a barrel of water from a

stream. Then, as before, there was no sign of Indians at the place. Finding it quite deserted, I rambled about near the beach for an hour or more. The fine weather seemed, somehow, to add loneliness to the place, and when I came upon a spot where a grave was marked I went no farther. Returning to the head of the cove, I came to a sort of Calvary, it appeared to me, where navigators, carrying their cross, had each set up one as a beacon to others coming after. They had anchored here and gone on, all except the one under the little mound. One of the simple marks, curiously enough, had been left there by the steamship *Colimbia*, sister ship to the *Colombia*, my neighbor of that morning.

I read the names of many other vessels; some of them I copied in my journal, others were illegible. Many of the crosses had decayed

Records of passages through the strait at the head of Borgia Bay.

NOTE.  On a small bush nearer the water there was a board bearing several other inscriptions, to which were added the words "Sloop *Spray*, March, 1896."

and fallen, and many that had put them there I had known, many a hand now still. The air of depression was about the place, and I hurried back to the sloop to forget myself again in the voyage.

Early the next morning I stood out from Borgia Bay, and off Cape Quod, where the wind fell light, I moored the sloop by kelp in twenty fathoms of water, and held her there a few hours against a three-knot current. That night I anchored in Langara Cove, a few miles farther along, where on the following day I discovered wreckage and goods washed up from the sea. I worked all day now, salving and boating off a cargo to the sloop. The bulk of the goods was tallow in casks and in lumps from which the casks had broken away; and embedded in the seaweed was a barrel of wine, which I also towed alongside. I hoisted them all in with the throat-halyards, which I took to the windlass. The weight of some of the casks was a little over eight hundred pounds.

There were no Indians about Langara; evidently there had not been any since the great gale which had washed the wreckage on shore. Probably it was from the same gale that drove the *Spray* off Cape Horn, from March 3 to 8. Hundreds of tons of kelp had been torn from beds in deep water and rolled up into ridges on the beach. A specimen stalk which I found entire, roots, leaves, and all, measured

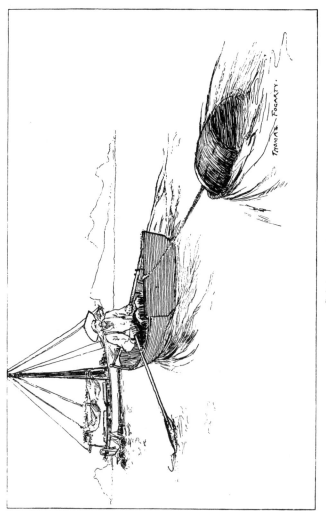

Salving wreckage.

one hundred and thirty-one feet in length. At this place I filled a barrel of water at night, and on the following day sailed with a fair wind at last.

I had not sailed far, however, when I came abreast of more tallow in a small cove, where I anchored, and boated off as before. It rained and snowed hard all that day, and it was no light work carrying tallow in my arms over the boulders on the beach. But I worked on till the *Spray* was loaded with a full cargo. I was happy then in the prospect of doing a good business farther along on the voyage, for the habits of an old trader would come to the surface. I sailed from the cove about noon, greased from top to toe, while my vessel was tallowed from keelson to truck. My cabin, as well as the hold and deck, was stowed full of tallow, and all were thoroughly smeared.

# CHAPTER X

Another gale had then sprung up, but the wind was still fair, and I had only twenty-six miles to run for Port Angosto, a dreary enough place, where, however, I would find a safe harbor in which to refit and stow cargo. I carried on sail to make the harbor before dark, and she fairly flew along, all covered with snow, which fell thick and fast, till she looked like a white winter bird. Between the storm-bursts I saw the headland of my port, and was steering for it when a flow of wind caught the mainsail by the lee, jibed it over, and dear! dear! how nearly was this the cause of disaster; for the sheet parted and the boom unshipped, and it was then close upon night. I worked till the perspiration poured from my body to get things adjusted and in working order before dark, and, above all, to get it done before the sloop drove to leeward of the port of refuge. Even then I did not get the boom shipped in its saddle. I was at the entrance of the harbor before I could get this done, and it was time to haul her to or lose the port; but in that condition, like a bird with a broken wing, she made the haven. The accident which so jeopardized my vessel and cargo came of a defective sheet-rope, one made from sisal, a treacherous fiber which has caused a deal of strong language among sailors.

I did not run the *Spray* into the inner harbor of Port Angosto, but came to inside a bed of kelp under a steep bluff on the port hand going in. It was an exceedingly snug nook, and to make doubly sure of holding here against all williwaws I moored her with two anchors and secured her, besides, by cables to trees. However, no wind ever reached there except back flaws from the mountains on the opposite side of the harbor. There, as elsewhere in that region, the country was made up of mountains. This was the place where I was to refit and whence I was to sail direct, once more, for Cape Pillar and the Pacific.

I remained at Port Angosto some days, busily employed about the sloop. I stowed the tallow from the deck to the hold, arranged my cabin in better order, and took in a good supply of wood and water. I also mended the sloop's sails and rigging, and fitted a jigger, which changed the rig to a yawl, though I called the boat a sloop just the same, the jigger being merely a temporary affair.

I never forgot, even at the busiest time of my work there, to have

416

my rifle by me ready for instant use; for I was of necessity within range of savages, and I had seen Fuegian canoes at this place when I anchored in the port, farther down the reach, on the first trip through the strait. I think it was on the second day, while I was busily employed about the decks, that I heard the swish of something through the air close by my ear, and heard a "zip"-like sound in the water, but saw nothing. Presently, however, I suspected that it was an arrow of some sort, for just then one passing not far from me struck the mainmast, where it stuck fast, vibrating from the shock—a Fuegian autograph. A savage was somewhere near, there could be no doubt about that. I did not know but he might be shooting at me, with a view to

"The first shot uncovered three Fuegians."

getting my sloop and her cargo; and so I threw up my old Martini-Henry, the rifle that kept on shooting, and the first shot uncovered three Fuegians, who scampered from a clump of bushes where they had been concealed, and made over the hills. I fired away a good many cartridges, aiming under their feet to encourage their climbing. My dear old gun woke up the hills, and at every report all three of the savages jumped as if shot; but they kept on, and put Fuego real estate between themselves and the *Spray* as fast as their legs could carry them. I took care then, more than ever before, that all my firearms should be in order and that a supply of ammunition should always be ready at hand. But the savages did not return, and although I put tacks on deck every night, I never discovered that any more visitors came, and I had only to sweep the deck of tacks carefully every morning after.

As the days went by, the season became more favorable for a chance to clear the strait with a fair wind, and so I made up my mind after six attempts, being driven back each time, to be in no further haste to sail. The bad weather on my last return to Port Angosto for shelter brought the Chilean gunboat *Condor* and the Argentine cruiser *Azopardo* into port. As soon as the latter came to anchor, Captain Mascarella, the commander, sent a boat to the *Spray* with the message that he would take me in tow for Sandy Point if I would give up the voyage and return—the thing farthest from my mind. The officers of the *Azopardo* told me that, coming up the strait after the *Spray* on her first passage through, they saw Black Pedro and learned that he had visited me. The *Azopardo*, being a foreign man-of-war, had no right to arrest the Fuegian outlaw, but her captain blamed me for not shooting the rascal when he came to my sloop.

I procured some cordage and other small supplies from these vessels, and the officers of each of them mustered a supply of warm flannels, of which I was most in need. With these additions to my outfit, and with the vessel in good trim, though somewhat deeply laden, I was well prepared for another bout with the Southern, misnamed Pacific, Ocean.

In the first week in April southeast winds, such as appear about Cape Horn in the fall and winter seasons, bringing better weather than that experienced in the summer, began to disturb the upper clouds; a little more patience, and the time would come for sailing with a fair wind.

At Port Angosto I met Professor Dusen of the Swedish scientific expedition to South America and the Pacific Islands. The professor was camped by the side of a brook at the head of the harbor, where there were many varieties of moss, in which he was interested, and where the water was, as his Argentine cook said, "muy rico." The professor had three well-armed Argentines along in his camp to fight savages. They seemed disgusted when I filled water at a small stream near the vessel, slighting their advice to go farther up to the greater brook, where it was "muy rico." But they were all fine fellows, though it was a wonder that they did not all die of rheumatic pains from living on wet ground.

Of all the little haps and mishaps to the *Spray* at Port Angosto, of the many attempts to put to sea, and of each return for shelter, it is not my purpose to speak. Of hinderances there were many to keep her back, but on the thirteenth day of April, and for the seventh and last time, she weighed anchor from that port. Difficulties, however, multiplied all about in so strange a manner that had I been given to superstitious fears I should not have persisted in sailing on a thirteenth day, notwithstanding that a fair wind blew in the offing. Many of the incidents were ludicrous. When I found myself, for instance, disentangling the sloop's mast from the branches of a tree after she had drifted three times around a small island, against my will, it seemed more than one's nerves could bear, and I had to speak about it, so I thought, or die of lockjaw, and I apostrophized the *Spray* as an impatient farmer might his horse or his ox. "Did n't you know," cried I—"did n't you know that you could n't climb a tree?" But the poor old *Spray* had essayed, and successfully too, nearly everything else in the Strait of Magellan, and my heart softened toward her when I thought of what she had gone through. Moreover, she had discovered an island. On the charts this one that she had sailed around was traced as a point of land. I named it Alan Erric Island, after a worthy literary friend whom I had met in strange by-places, and I put up a sign, "Keep off the grass," which, as discoverer, was within my rights.

Now at last the *Spray* carried me free of Tierra del Fuego. If by a close shave only, still she carried me clear, though her boom actually hit the beacon rocks to leeward as she lugged on sail to clear the point. The thing was done on the 13th of April, 1896. But a close shave and a narrow escape were nothing new to the *Spray*.

The waves doffed their white caps beautifully to her in the strait that day before the southeast wind, the first true winter breeze of the season from that quarter, and here she was out on the first of it, with every prospect of clearing Cape Pillar before it should shift. So it turned out; the wind blew hard, as it always blows about Cape Horn, but she had cleared the great tide-race off Cape Pillar and the Evangelistas, the outermost rocks of all, before the change came. I remained at the helm, humoring my vessel in the cross seas, for it was rough, and I did not dare to let her take a straight course. It was necessary to change her course in the combing seas, to meet them with what skill I could when they rolled up ahead, and to keep off when they came abeam.

On the following morning, April 14, only the tops of the highest mountains were in sight, and the *Spray*, making good headway on a northwest course, soon sank these out of sight. "Hurrah for the *Spray!*" I shouted to the seals, sea-gulls, and penguins; for there were no other living creatures about, and she had weathered all the dangers of Cape Horn. Moreover, she had on her voyage round the Horn salved a cargo of which she had not jettisoned a pound. And why should not one rejoice also in the main chance coming so of itself?

I shook out a reef, and set the whole jib, for, having sea-room, I could square away two points. This brought the sea more on her quarter, and she was the wholesomer under a press of sail. Occasionally an old southwest sea, rolling up, combed athwart her, but did no harm. The wind freshened as the sun rose half-mast or more, and the air, a bit chilly in the morning, softened later in the day; but I gave little thought to such things as these.

One wave, in the evening, larger than others that had threatened all day,—one such as sailors call "fine-weather seas,"—broke over the sloop fore and aft. It washed over me at the helm, the last that swept over the *Spray* off Cape Horn. It seemed to wash away old regrets. All my troubles were now astern; summer was ahead; all the world was again before me. The wind was even literally fair. My "trick" at the wheel was now up, and it was 5 P.M. I had stood at the helm since eleven o'clock the morning before, or thirty hours.

Then was the time to uncover my head, for I sailed alone with God. The vast ocean was again around me, and the horizon was unbroken by land. A few days later the *Spray* was under full sail, and I saw her for the first time with a jigger spread. This was indeed a small incident, but it was the incident following a triumph. The wind was still southwest, but it had moderated, and roaring seas had turned to gossiping waves that rippled and pattered against her sides as she rolled among them, delighted with their story. Rapid changes went on, those days, in things all about while she headed for the tropics. New species of birds came around; albatrosses fell back and became scarcer and scarcer; lighter gulls came in their stead, and pecked for crumbs in the sloop's wake.

On the tenth day from Cape Pillar a shark came along, the first of its kind on this part of the voyage to get into trouble. I harpooned him and took out his ugly jaws. I had not till then felt inclined to take the life of any animal, but when John Shark hove in sight my sympathy flew to the winds. It is a fact that in Magellan I let pass many ducks that would have made a good stew, for I had no mind in the lonesome strait to take the life of any living thing.

From Cape Pillar I steered for Juan Fernandez, and on the 26th of April, fifteen days out, made that historic island right ahead.

The blue hills of Juan Fernandez, high among the clouds, could be seen about thirty miles off. A thousand emotions thrilled me when I saw the island, and I bowed my head to the deck. We may mock the Oriental salaam, but for my part I could find no other way of expressing myself.

The wind being light through the day, the *Spray* did not reach the island till night. With what wind there was to fill her sails she stood close in to shore on the northeast side, where it fell calm and remained so all night. I saw the twinkling of a small light farther along in a cove,

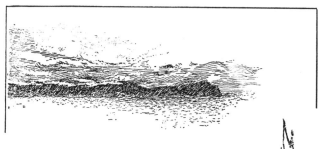

The *Spray* approaching Juan Fernandez, Robinson Crusoe's Island.

and fired a gun, but got no answer, and soon the light disappeared altogether. I heard the sea booming against the cliffs all night, and realized that the ocean swell was still great, although from the deck of my little ship it was apparently small. From the cry of animals in the hills, which sounded fainter and fainter through the night, I judged that a light current was drifting the sloop from the land, though she seemed all night dangerously near the shore, for, the land being very high, appearances were deceptive.

Soon after daylight I saw a boat putting out toward me. As it pulled near, it so happened that I picked up my gun, which was on the deck, meaning only to put it below; but the people in the boat, seeing the piece in my hands, quickly turned and pulled back for shore, which was about four miles distant. There were six rowers in her, and I observed that they pulled with oars in oar-locks, after the manner of trained seamen, and so I knew they belonged to a civilized race; but their opinion of me must have been anything but flattering when they mistook my purpose with the gun and pulled away with all their might. I made them understand by signs, but not without difficulty, that I did not intend to shoot, that I was simply putting the piece in the cabin, and that I wished them to return. When they understood my meaning they came back and were soon on board.

One of the party, whom the rest called "king," spoke English; the others spoke Spanish. They had all heard of the voyage of the *Spray* through the papers of Valparaiso, and were hungry for news concerning it. They told me of a war between Chile and the Argentine, which I had not heard of when I was there. I had just visited both countries, and I told them that according to the latest reports, while I was in Chile, their own island was sunk. (This same report that Juan Fernandez had sunk was current in Australia when I arrived there three months later.)

I had already prepared a pot of coffee and a plate of doughnuts, which, after some words of civility, the islanders stood up to and discussed with a will, after which they took the *Spray* in tow of their boat and made toward the island with her at a rate of a good three knots. The man they called king took the helm, and with whirling it up and down he so rattled the *Spray* that I thought she would never carry herself straight again. The others pulled away lustily with their oars. The king, I soon learned, was king only by courtesy. Having lived longer on the island than any other man in the world,—thirty years,— he was so dubbed. Juan Fernandez was then under the administration of a governor of Swedish nobility, so I was told. I was also told that his daughter could ride the wildest goat on the island. The governor, at the time of my visit, was away at Valparaiso with his family, to place his children at school. The king had been away once for a year or two, and in Rio de Janiero had married a Brazilian woman who followed his fortunes to the far-off island. He was himself a Portuguese and a native of the Azores. He had sailed in New Bedford whale-ships and had steered a boat. All this I learned, and more too, before we reached the anchorage. The sea-breeze, coming in before long, filled the *Spray's* sails, and the experienced Portuguese mariner piloted her to a safe berth in the bay, where she was moored to a buoy abreast the settlement.

# CHAPTER XI

The islanders at Juan Fernandez entertained with Yankee doughnuts—The beauties of
Robinson Crusoe's realm—The mountain monument to Alexander Selkirk—Robinson Crusoe's cave—A stroll with the children of the island—Westward ho! with a
friendly gale—A month's free sailing with the Southern Cross and the sun for guides—
Sighting the Marquesas—Experience in reckoning.

The *Spray* being secured, the islanders returned to the coffee and doughnuts, and I was more than flattered when they did not slight my buns,
as the professor had done in the Strait of Magellan. Between buns and
doughnuts there was little difference except in name. Both had been
fried in tallow, which was the strong point in both, for there was
nothing on the island fatter than a goat, and a goat is but a lean beast,
to make the best of it. So with a view to business I hooked my steelyards
to the boom at once, ready to weigh out tallow, there being no custom's officer to say, "Why do you do so?" and before the sun went
down the islanders had learned the art of making buns and doughnuts.
I did not charge a high price for what I sold, but the ancient and curious
coins I got in payment, some of them from the wreck of a galleon
sunk in the bay no one knows when, I sold afterward to antiquarians
for more than face-value. In this way I made a reasonable profit. I
brought away money of all denominations from the island, and nearly
all there was, so far as I could find out.

Juan Fernandez, as a place of call, is a lovely spot. The hills are well
wooded, the valleys fertile, and pouring down through many ravines
are streams of pure water. There are no serpents on the island, and no
wild beasts other than pigs and goats, of which I saw a number, with
possibly a dog or two. The people lived without the use of rum or beer
of any sort. There was not a police officer or a lawyer among them.
The domestic economy of the island was simplicity itself. The fashions
of Paris did not affect the inhabitants; each dressed according to his
own taste. Although there was no doctor, the people were all healthy,
and the children were all beautiful. There were about forty-five souls
on the island all told. The adults were mostly from the mainland of
South America. One lady there, from Chile, who made a flying-jib
for the *Spray*, taking her pay in tallow, would be called a belle at Newport. Blessed island of Juan Fernandez! Why Alexander Selkirk ever
left you was more than I could make out.

A large ship which had arrived some time before, on fire, had been
stranded at the head of the bay, and as the sea smashed her to pieces
on the rocks, after the fire was drowned, the islanders picked up the
timbers and utilized them in the construction of houses, which naturally

The house of the king.

presented a ship-like appearance. The house of the king of Juan Fernandez, Manuel Carroza by name, besides resembling the ark, wore a polished brass knocker on its only door, which was painted green. In front of this gorgeous entrance was a flag-mast all ataunto, and near it a small whale-boat painted red and blue, the delight of the king's old age.

I of course made a pilgrimage to the old lookout place at the top of the mountain, where Selkirk spent many days peering into the distance for the ship which came at last. From a tablet fixed into the face of the rock I copied these words, inscribed in Arabic capitals:

IN MEMORY

OF

## ALEXANDER SELKIRK,

MARINER,

A native of Largo, in the county of Fife, Scotland, who lived on this island in complete solitude for four years and four months. He was landed from the *Cinque Ports* galley, 96 tons, 18 guns, A.D. 1704, and was taken off in the *Duke*, privateer, 12th February, 1709. He died Lieutenant of H. M. S. *Weymouth*, A.D. 1723,[1] aged 47. This tablet is erected near Selkirk's lookout, by Commodore Powell and the officers of H. M. S. *Topaze*, A.D. 1868.

The cave in which Selkirk dwelt while on the island is at the head of the bay now called Robinson Crusoe Bay. It is around a bold headland west of the present anchorage and landing. Ships have anchored there, but it affords a very indifferent berth. Both of these anchorages

---

[1]Mr. J. Cuthbert Hadden, in the "Century Magazine" for July, 1899, shows that the tablet is in error as to the year of Selkirk's death. It should be 1721.

are exposed to north winds, which, however, do not reach home with much violence. The holding-ground being good in the first-named bay to the eastward, the anchorage there may be considered safe, although the undertow at times makes it wild riding.

I visited Robinson Crusoe Bay in a boat, and with some difficulty landed through the surf near the cave, which I entered. I found it dry and inhabitable. It is located in a beautiful nook sheltered by high mountains from all the severe storms that sweep over the island, which

Robinson Crusoe's cave.

are not many; for it lies near the limits of the trade-wind regions, being in latitude $35\frac{1}{2}°$S. The island is about fourteen miles in length, east and west, and eight miles in width; its height is over three thousand feet. Its distance from Chile, to which country it belongs, is about three hundred and forty miles.

Juan Fernandez was once a convict station. A number of caves in which the prisoners were kept, damp, unwholesome dens, are no longer in use, and no more prisoners are sent to the island.

The pleasantest day I spent on the island, if not the pleasantest on my whole voyage, was my last day on shore,—but by no means because it was the last,—when the children of the little community, one and all, went out with me to gather wild fruits for the voyage. We found quinces, peaches, and figs, and the children gathered a basket of each. It takes very little to please children, and these little ones, never hearing a word in their lives except Spanish, made the hills ring with mirth at the sound of words in English. They asked me the names of all manner of things on the island. We came to a wild fig-tree loaded with fruit, of which I gave them the English name. "Figgies, figgies!" they cried, while they picked till their baskets were full. But when I told them that the *cabra* they pointed out was only a goat, they screamed with laughter, and rolled on the grass in wild delight to think that a man had come to their island who would call a cabra a goat.

The first child born on Juan Fernandez, I was told, had become a beautiful woman and was now a mother. Manuel Carroza and the good soul who had followed him here from Brazil had laid away their only child, a girl, at the age of seven, in the little churchyard on the point. In the same half-acre were other mounds among the rough lava rocks, some marking the burial-place of native-born children, some the resting-places of seamen from passing ships, landed here to end days of sickness and get into a sailor's heaven.

The greatest drawback I saw in the island was the want of a school.

The man who called a cabra a goat.

A class there would necessarily be small, but to some kind soul who loved teaching and quietude life on Juan Fernandez would, for a limited time, be one of delight.

On the morning of May 5, 1896, I sailed from Juan Fernandez, having feasted on many things, but on nothing sweeter than the adventure itself of a visit to the home and to the very cave of Robinson Crusoe. From the island the *Spray* bore away to the north, passing the island of St. Felix before she gained the trade-winds, which seemed slow in reaching their limits.

If the trades were tardy, however, when they did come they came with a bang, and made up for lost time; and the *Spray*, under reefs, sometimes one, sometimes two, flew before a gale for a great many days, with a bone in her mouth, toward the Marquesas, in the west, which she made on the forty-third day out, and still kept on sailing. My time was all taken up those days—not by standing at the helm; no man, I think, could stand or sit and steer a vessel round the world: I did better than that; for I sat and read my books, mended my clothes, or cooked my meals and ate them in peace. I had already found that it was not good to be alone, and so I made companionship with what there was around me, sometimes with the universe and sometimes with my own insignificant self; but my books were always my friends, let fail all else. Nothing could be easier or more restful than my voyage in the trade-winds.

I sailed with a free wind day after day, marking the position of my ship on the chart with considerable precision; but this was done by intuition, I think, more than by slavish calculations. For one whole month my vessel held her course true; I had not, the while, so much as a light in the binnacle. The Southern Cross I saw every night abeam. The sun every morning came up astern; every evening it went down ahead. I wished for no other compass to guide me, for these were true. If I doubted my reckoning after a long time at sea I verified it by reading the clock aloft made by the Great Architect, and it was right.

There was no denying that the comical side of the strange life appeared. I awoke, sometimes, to find the sun already shining into my cabin. I heard water rushing by, with only a thin plank between me and the depths, and I said, "How is this?" But it was all right; it was my ship on her course, sailing as no other ship had ever sailed before in the world. The rushing water along her side told me that she was sailing at full speed. I knew that no human hand was at the helm; I knew that all was well with "the hands" forward, and that there was no mutiny on board.

The phenomena of ocean meteorology were interesting studies even here in the trade-winds. I observed that about every seven days the wind freshened and drew several points farther than usual from the direction of the pole; that is, it went round from east-southeast to south-southeast, while at the same time a heavy swell rolled up from the southwest. All this indicated that gales were going on in the anti-trades. The wind then hauled day after day as it moderated, till it stood again at the normal point, east-southeast. This is more or less the constant state of the winter trades in latitude 12°S., where I "ran down the longitude" for weeks. The sun, we all know, is the creator of the trade-winds and of the wind system all over the earth. But ocean meteorology is, I think, the most fascinating of all. From Juan Fernandez to the Marquesas I experienced six changes of these great palpitations of sea-winds and of the sea itself, the effect of far-off gales. To know the laws that govern the winds, and to know that you know them, will give you an easy mind on your voyage round the world; otherwise you may tremble at the appearance of every cloud. What is true of this in the trade-winds is much more so in the variables, where changes run more to extremes.

To cross the Pacific Ocean, even under the most favorable circumstances, brings you for many days close to nature, and you realize the vastness of the sea. Slowly but surely the mark of my little ship's course on the track-chart reached out on the ocean and across it, while at her utmost speed she marked with her keel still slowly the sea that carried her. On the forty-third day from land,—a long time to be at sea alone,—the sky being beautifully clear and the moon being "in distance" with the sun, I threw up my sextant for sights. I found from the result of three observations, after long wrestling with lunar tables, that her longitude by observation agreed within five miles of that by dead reckoning.

This was wonderful; both, however, might be in error, but somehow I felt confident that both were nearly true, and that in a few hours more I should see land; and so it happened, for then I made the island of Nukahiva, the southernmost of the Marquesas group, clear-cut and lofty. The verified longitude when abreast was somewhere between the two reckonings; this was extraordinary. All navigators will tell you that from one day to another a ship may lose or gain more than five miles in her sailing-account, and again, in the matter of lunars, even expert lunarians are considered as doing clever work when they average within eight miles of the truth.

I hope I am making it clear that I do not lay claim to cleverness or to slavish calculations in my reckonings. I think I have already stated that I kept my longitude, at least, mostly by intuition. A rotator log always towed astern, but so much has to be allowed for currents and for drift, which the log never shows, that it is only an approximation, after all, to be corrected by one's own judgment from data of a thousand voyages; and even then the master of the ship, if he be wise, cries out for the lead and the lookout.

Unique was my experience in nautical astronomy from the deck of the *Spray*—so much so that I feel justified in briefly telling it here. The first set of sights, just spoken of, put her many hundred miles west of my reckoning by account. I knew that this could not be correct. In about an hour's time I took another set of observations with the utmost care; the mean result of these was about the same as that of the first set. I asked myself why, with my boasted self-dependence, I had not done at least better than this. Then I went in search of a discrepancy in the tables, and I found it. In the tables I found that the column of figures from which I had got an important logarithm was in error. It was a matter I could prove beyond a doubt, and it made the difference as already stated. The tables being corrected, I sailed on with self-reliance unshaken, and with my tin clock fast asleep. The result of these observations naturally tickled my vanity, for I knew that it was something to stand on a great ship's deck and with two assistants take lunar observations approximately near the truth. As one of the poorest of American sailors, I was proud of the little achievement alone on the sloop, even by chance though it may have been.

I was *en rapport* now with my surroundings, and was carried on a vast stream where I felt the buoyancy of His hand who made all the worlds. I realized the mathematical truth of their motions, so well known that astronomers compile tables of their positions through the years and the days, and the minutes of a day, with such precision that one coming along over the sea even five years later may, by their aid, find the standard time of any given meridian on the earth.

To find local time is a simpler matter. The difference between local and standard time is longitude expressed in time—four minutes, we all know, representing one degree. This, briefly, is the principle on which longitude is found independent of chronometers. The work of the lunarian, though seldom practised in these days of chronometers, is beautifully edifying, and there is nothing in the realm of navigation that lifts one's heart up more in adoration.

# CHAPTER XII

To be alone forty-three days would seem a long time, but in reality,
even here, winged moments flew lightly by, and instead of my
hauling in for Nukahiva, which I could have made as well as not, I
kept on for Samoa, where I wished to make my next landing. This
occupied twenty-nine days more, making seventy-two days in all.
I was not distressed in any way during that time. There was no end
of companionship; the very coral reefs kept me company, or gave
me no time to feel lonely, which is the same thing, and there were
many of them now in my course to Samoa.

First among the incidents of the voyage from Juan Fernandez to
Samoa (which were not many) was a narrow escape from collison
with a great whale that was absent-mindedly plowing the ocean at
night while I was below. The noise from his startled snort and the
commotion he made in the sea, as he turned to clear my vessel, brought
me on deck in time to catch a wetting from the water he threw up
with his flukes. The monster was apparently frightened. He headed
quickly for the east; I kept on going west. Soon another whale passed,
evidently a companion, following in its wake. I saw no more on this
part of the voyage, nor did I wish to.

Hungry sharks came about the vessel often when she neared islands
or coral reefs. I own to a satisfaction in shooting them as one would
a tiger. Sharks, after all, are the tigers of the sea. Nothing is more
dreadful to the mind of a sailor, I think, than a possible encounter
with a hungry shark.

A number of birds were always about; occasionally one poised
on the mast to look the *Spray* over, wondering, perhaps, at her odd
wings, for she now wore her Fuego mainsail, which, like Joseph's
coat, was made of many pieces. Ships are less common on the Southern seas than formerly. I saw not one in the many days crossing the
Pacific.

My diet on these long passages usually consisted of potatoes and
salt cod and biscuits, which I made two or three times a week. I had
always plenty of coffee, tea, sugar, and flour. I carried usually a
good supply of potatoes, but before reaching Samoa I had a mishap
which left me destitute of this highly prized sailors' luxury. Through

meeting at Juan Fernandez the Yankee Portuguese named Manuel Carroza, who nearly traded me out of my boots, I ran out of potatoes in mid-ocean, and was wretched thereafter. I prided myself on being something of a trader; but this Portuguese from the Azores by way of New Bedford, who gave me new potatoes for the older ones I had got from the *Colombia*, a bushel or more of the best, left me no ground for boasting. He wanted mine, he said, "for changee the seed." When I got to sea I found that his tubers were rank and unedible, and full of fine yellow streaks of repulsive appearance. I tied the sack up and returned to the few left of my old stock, thinking that maybe when I got right hungry the island potatoes would improve in flavor.

Meeting with the whale.

Three weeks later I opened the bag again, and out flew millions of winged insects! Manuel's potatoes had all turned to moths. I tied them up quickly and threw all into the sea.

Manuel had a large crop of potatoes on hand, and as a hint to whalemen, who are always eager to buy vegetables, he wished me to report whales off the island of Juan Fernandez, which I have already done, and big ones at that, but they were a long way off.

Taking things by and large, as sailors say, I got on fairly well in the matter of provisions even on the long voyage across the Pacific. I found always some small stores to help the fare of luxuries; what I lacked in fresh meat was made up in fresh fish, at least while in the trade-winds, where flying-fish crossing on the wing at night would hit the sails and fall on deck, sometimes two or three of them, sometimes a dozen. Every morning except when the moon was large I got a bountiful supply by merely picking them up from the lee scuppers. All tinned meats went begging.

First exchange of courtesies in Samoa.

On the 16th of July, after considerable care and some skill and hard work, the *Spray* cast anchor at Apia, in the kingdom of Samoa, about noon. My vessel being moored, I spread an awning, and instead of going at once on shore I sat under it till late in the evening, listening with delight to the musical voices of the Samoan men and women.

A canoe coming down the harbor, with three young women in it, rested her paddles abreast the sloop. One of the fair crew, hailing with the naïve salutation, "Talofa lee" ("Love to you, chief"), asked:

"Schoon come Melike?"

"Love to you," I answered, and said, "Yes."

"You man come 'lone?"

Again I answered, "Yes."

"I don't believe that. You had other mans, and you eat 'em."

At this sally the others laughed. "What for you come long way?" they asked.

"To hear you ladies sing," I replied.

"Oh, talofa lee!" they all cried, and sang on. Their voices filled the air with music that rolled across to the grove of tall palms on the other side of the harbor and back. Soon after this six young men came down in the United States consul-general's boat, singing in parts and beating time with their oars. In my interview with them I came off better than with the damsels in the canoe. They bore an invitation from General Churchill for me to come and dine at the consulate. There was a lady's hand in things about the consulate at Samoa. Mrs. Churchill picked the crew for the general's boat, and saw to it that they wore a smart uniform and that they could sing the Samoan boatsong, which in the first week Mrs. Churchill herself could sing like a native girl.

Next morning bright and early Mrs. Robert Louis Stevenson came to the *Spray* and invited me to Vailima the following day. I

Vailima, the home of Robert Louis Stevenson.

was of course thrilled when I found myself, after so many days of adventure, face to face with this bright woman, so lately the companion of the author who had delighted me on the voyage. The kindly eyes, that looked me through and through, sparkled when we compared notes of adventure. I marveled at some of her experiences and escapes. She told me that, along with her husband, she had voyaged in all manner of rickety craft among the islands of the Pacific, reflectively adding, "Our tastes were similar."

Following the subject of voyages, she gave me the four beautiful volumes of sailing directories for the Mediterranean, writing on the fly-leaf of the first:

To CAPTAIN SLOCUM. These volumes have been read and re-read many times by my husband, and I am very sure that he would be pleased that they should be passed on to the sort of seafaring man that he liked above all others.

FANNY V. DE G. STEVENSON.

Mrs. Stevenson also gave me a great directory of the Indian Ocean. It was not without a feeling of reverential awe that I received the books so nearly direct from the hand of Tusitala, "who sleeps in the forest." Aolele, the *Spray* will cherish your gift.

The novelist's stepson, Mr. Lloyd Osbourne, walked through the Vailima mansion with me and bade me write my letters at the old desk. I thought it would be presumptuous to do that; it was sufficient for me to enter the hall on the floor of which the "Writer of Tales," according to the Samoan custom, was wont to sit.

Coming through the main street of Apia one day, with my hosts, all bound for the *Spray*, Mrs. Stevenson on horseback, I walking by her side, and Mr. and Mrs. Osbourne close in our wake on bicycles, at a sudden turn in the road we found ourselves mixed with a remarkable native procession, with a somewhat primitive band of music, in front of us, while behind was a festival or a funeral, we could not tell which. Several of the stoutest men carried bales and bundles on poles. Some were evidently bales of tapa-cloth. The burden of one set of poles, heavier than the rest, however, was not so easily made out. My curiosity was whetted to know whether it was a roast pig or something of a gruesome nature, and I inquired about it. "I don't know," said Mrs. Stevenson, "whether this is a wedding or a funeral. Whatever it is, though, captain, our place seems to be at the head of it."

The *Spray* being in the stream, we boarded her from the beach abreast, in the little razeed Gloucester dory, which had been painted a smart green. Our combined weight loaded it gunwale to the water, and I was obliged to steer with great care to avoid swamping. The adventure pleased Mrs. Stevenson greatly, and as we paddled along she sang, "They went to sea in a pea-green boat." I could understand her saying of her husband and herself, "Our tastes were similar."

As I sailed farther from the center of civilization I heard less and less of what would and what would not pay. Mrs. Stevenson, in speaking of my voyage, did not once ask me what I would make out of it. When I came to a Samoan village, the chief did not ask the price of gin, or say, "How much will you pay for roast pig?" but, "Dollar, dollar," said he; "white man know only dollar."

"Never mind dollar. The *tapo* has prepared ava; let us drink and rejoice." The tapo is the virgin hostess of the village; in this instance it was Taloa, daughter of the chief. "Our taro is good; let us eat. On the tree there is fruit. Let the day go by; why should we mourn over that? There are millions of days coming. The breadfruit is yellow in the sun, and from the cloth-tree is Taloa's gown. Our house, which is good, cost but the labor of building it, and there is no lock on the door."

While the days go thus in these Southern islands we at the North are struggling for the bare necessities of life.

For food the islanders have only to put out their hand and take what nature has provided for them; if they plant a banana-tree, their only care afterward is to see that too many trees do not grow. They have great reason to love their country and to fear the white man's yoke, for once harnessed to the plow, their life would no longer be a poem.

The chief of the village of Caini, who was a tall and dignified Tonga man, could be approached only through an interpreter and talking man. It was perfectly natural for him to inquire the object of my visit, and I was sincere when I told him that my reason for casting anchor in Samoa was to see their fine men, and fine women, too. After a considerable pause the chief said: "The captain has come a long way to see so little; but," he added, "the tapo must sit nearer the captain." "Yack," said Taloa, who had so nearly learned to say yes in English, and suiting the action to the word, she hitched a peg nearer, all hands sitting in a circle upon mats. I was no less taken with the chief's eloquence than delighted with the simplicity of all he said. About him there was nothing pompous; he might have been taken for a great scholar or statesman, the least assuming of the men I met on the voyage. As for Taloa, a sort of Queen of the May, and the other tapo girls, well, it is wise to learn as soon as possible the manners and customs of these hospitable people, and meanwhile not to mistake for overfamiliarity that which is intended as honor to a guest. I was fortunate in my travels in the islands, and saw nothing to shake one's faith in native virtue.

To the unconventional mind the punctilious etiquette of Samoa is perhaps a little painful. For instance, I found that in partaking of ava, the social bowl, I was supposed to toss a little of the beverage over my shoulder, or pretend to do so, and say, "Let the gods drink," and then drink it all myself; and the dish, invariably a cocoanut-shell, being empty, I might not pass it politely as we would do, but politely throw it twirling across the mats at the tapo.

My most grievous mistake while at the islands was made on a nag, which, inspired by a bit of good road, must needs break into a smart trot through a village. I was instantly hailed by the chief's deputy, who in an angry voice brought me to a halt. Perceiving that I was in trouble, I made signs for pardon, the safest thing to do, though I did not know what offense I had committed. My interpreter coming up, however, put me right, but not until a long palaver had ensued. The deputy's hail, liberally translated, was: "Ahoy, there, on the frantic steed! Know you not that it is against the law to ride thus through the village of our fathers?" I made what apologies I could, and offered to dismount and, like my servant, lead my nag by the bridle. This, the interpreter told me, would also be a grievous wrong, and so I again begged for pardon. I was summoned to appear before a chief; but my interpreter, being a wit as well as a bit of a rogue, explained that I was myself something of a chief, and should not be detained, being on a most important mission. In my own behalf I could only say that I was a stranger, but, pleading all this, I knew I still deserved to be roasted, at which the chief showed a fine row of teeth and seemed pleased, but allowed me to pass on.

The chief of the Tongas and his family at Caini, returning my visit, brought presents of tapa-cloth and fruits. Taloa, the princess, brought a bottle of cocoanut-oil for my hair, which another man might have regarded as coming late.

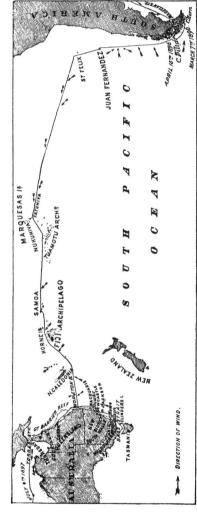

The *Spray's* course from the Strait of Magellan to Torres Strait.

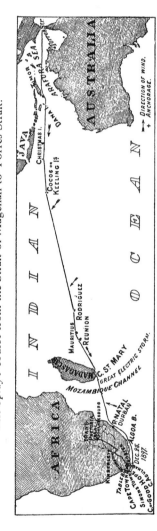

The *Spray's* course from Australia to South Africa.

It was impossible to entertain on the *Spray* after the royal manner in which I had been received by the chief. His fare had included all that the land could afford, fruits, fowl, fishes, and flesh, a hog having been roasted whole. I set before them boiled salt pork and salt beef, with which I was well supplied, and in the evening took them all to a new amusement in the town, a rocking-horse merry-go-round, which they called a "kee-kee," meaning theater; and in a spirit of justice they pulled off the horses' tails, for the proprietors of the show, two hard-fisted countrymen of mine, I grieve to say, unceremoniously hustled them off for a new set, almost at the first spin. I was not a little proud of my Tonga friends; the chief, finest of them all, carried a portentous club. As for the theater, through the greed of the proprietors it was becoming unpopular, and the representatives of the three great powers, in want of laws which they could enforce, adopted a vigorous foreign policy, taxing it twenty-five per cent. on the gate-money. This was considered a great stroke of legislative reform!

It was the fashion of the native visitors to the *Spray* to come over the bows, where they could reach the head-gear and climb aboard with ease, and on going ashore to jump off the stern and swim away; nothing could have been more delightfully simple. The modest natives wore *lava-lava* bathing-dresses, a native cloth from the bark of the mulberry-tree, and they did no harm to the *Spray*. In summerland Samoa their coming and going was only a merry every-day scene.

One day the head teachers of Papauta College, Miss Schultze and Miss Moore, came on board with their ninety-seven young women students. They were all dressed in white, and each wore a red rose, and of course came in boats or canoes in the cold-climate style. A merrier bevy of girls it would be difficult to find. As soon as they got on deck, by request of one of the teachers, they sang "The Watch on the Rhine," which I had never heard before. "And now," said they all, "let's up anchor and away." But I had no inclination to sail from Samoa so soon. On leaving the *Spray* these accomplished young women each seized a palm-branch or paddle, or whatever else would serve the purpose, and literally paddled her own canoe. Each could have swum as readily, and would have done so, I dare say, had it not been for the holiday muslin.

It was not uncommon at Apia to see a young woman swimming alongside a small canoe with a passenger for the *Spray*. Mr. Trood, an old Eton boy, came in this manner to see me, and he exclaimed, "Was ever king ferried in such state?" Then, suiting his acton to the sentiment, he gave the damsel pieces of silver till the natives watching on shore yelled with envy. My own canoe, a small dugout, one day when it had rolled over with me, was seized by a party of fair bathers, and before I could get my breath, almost, was towed around and around the *Spray*, while I sat in the bottom of it, wondering what they would do next. But in this case there were six of them, three on a side, and I could not help myself. One of the sprites, I remember, was a young English lady, who made more sport of it than any of the others.

# CHAPTER XIII

Samoan royalty—King Malietoa—Good-by to friends at Vailima—Leaving Fiji to the south—Arrival at Newcastle, Australia—The yachts of Sydney—A ducking on the *Spray*—Commodore Foy presents the sloop with a new suit of sails—On to Melbourne—A shark that proved to be valuable—A change of course—The "Rain of Blood"—In Tasmania.

At Apia I had the pleasure of meeting Mr. A. Young, the father of the late Queen Margaret, who was Queen of Manua from 1891 to 1895. Her grandfather was an English sailor who married a princess. Mr. Young is now the only survivor of the family, two of his children, the last of them all, having been lost in an island trader which a few months before had sailed, never to return. Mr. Young was a Christian gentleman, and his daughter Margaret was accomplished in graces that would become any lady. It was with pain that I saw in the newspapers a sensational account of her life and death, taken evidently from a paper in the supposed interest of a benevolent society, but without foundation in fact. And the startling head-lines saying, "Queen Margaret of Manua is dead," could hardly be called news in 1898, the queen having then been dead three years.

While hobnobbing, as it were, with royalty, I called on the king himself, the late Malietoa. King Malietoa was a great ruler; he never got less than forty-five dollars a month for the job, as he told me himself, and this amount had lately been raised, so that he could live on the fat of the land and not any longer be called "Tin-of-salmon Malietoa" by graceless beach-combers.

As my interpreter and I entered the front door of the palace, the king's brother, who was viceroy, sneaked in through a taro-patch by the back way, and sat cowering by the door while I told my story to the king. Mr. W—— of New York, a gentleman interested in missionary work, had charged me, when I sailed, to give his remembrance to the king of the Cannibal Islands, other islands of course being meant; but the good King Malietoa, notwithstanding that his people had not eaten a missionary in a hundred years, received the message himself, and seemed greatly pleased to hear so directly from the publishers of the "Missionary Review," and wished me to make his compliments in return. His Majesty then excused himself, while I talked with his daughter, the beautiful Faamu-Sami (a name signifying "To make the sea burn"), and soon reappeared in the full-dress uniform of the German commander-in-chief, Emperor William himself; for, stupidly enough, I had not sent my credentials ahead that the king might be in full regalia to receive me.

Calling a few days later to say good-by to Faamu-Sami, I saw King Malietoa for the last time.

Of the landmarks in the pleasant town of Apia, my memory rests first on the little school just back of the London Missionary Society coffee-house and reading-rooms, where Mrs. Bell taught English to about a hundred native children, boys and girls. Brighter children you will not find anywhere.

"Now, children," said Mrs. Bell, when I called one day, "let us show the captain that we know something about the Cape Horn he passed in the *Spray*," at which a lad of nine or ten years stepped nimbly forward and read Basil Hall's fine description of the great cape, and read it well. He afterward copied the essay for me in a clear hand.

Calling to say good-by to my friends at Vailima, I met Mrs. Stevenson in her Panama hat, and went over the estate with her. Men were at work clearing the land, and to one of them she gave an order to cut a couple of bamboo-trees for the *Spray* from a clump she had planted four years before, and which had grown to the height of sixty feet. I used them for spare spars, and the butt of one made a serviceable jib-boom on the homeward voyage. I had then only to take ava with the family and be ready for sea. This ceremony, important among Samoans, was conducted after the native fashion. A Triton horn was sounded to let us know when the beverage was ready, and in response we all clapped hands. The bout being in honor of the *Spray*, it was my turn first, after the custom of the country, to spill a little over my shoulder; but having forgotten the Samoan for "Let the gods drink," I repeated the equivalent in Russian and Chinook, as I remembered a word in each, whereupon Mr. Osbourne pronounced me a confirmed Samoan. Then I said "Tofah!" to my good friends of Samoa, and all wishing the *Spray bon voyage*, she stood out of the harbor August 20, 1896, and continued on her course. A sense of loneliness seized upon me as the islands faded astern, and as a remedy for it I crowded on sail for lovely Australia, which was not a strange land to me; but for long days in my dreams Vailima stood before the prow.

The *Spray* had barely cleared the islands when a sudden burst of the trades brought her down to close reefs, and she reeled off one hundred and eighty-four miles the first day, of which I counted forty miles of current in her favor. Finding a rough sea, I swung her off free and sailed north of the Horn Islands, also north of Fiji instead of south, as I had intended, and coasted down the west side of the archipelago. Thence I sailed direct for New South Wales, passing south of New Caledonia, and arrived at Newcastle after a passage of forty-two days, mostly of storms and gales.

One particularly severe gale encountered near New Caledonia foundered the American clippership *Patrician* farther south. Again, nearer the coast of Australia, when, however, I was not aware that the gale was extraordinary, a French mail-steamer from New Cale-

The accident at Sydney.

donia for Sydney, blown considerably out of her course, on her arrival reported it an awful storm, and to inquiring friends said: "Oh, my! we don't know what has become of the little sloop *Spray*. We saw her in the thick of the storm." The *Spray* was all right, lying to like a duck. She was under a goose's wing mainsail, and had had a dry deck while the passengers on the steamer, I heard later, were up to their knees in water in the saloon. When their ship arrived at Sydney they gave the captain a purse of gold for his skill and seamanship in bringing them safe into port. The captain of the *Spray* got nothing of this sort. In this gale I made the land about Seal Rocks, where the steamship *Catherton*, with many lives, was lost a short time before. I was many hours off the rocks, beating back and forth, but weathered them at last.

I arrived at Newcastle in the teeth of a gale of wind. It was a stormy season. The government pilot, Captain Cumming, met me at the harbor bar, and with the assistance of a steamer carried my vessel to a safe berth. Many visitors came on board, the first being the United States consul, Mr. Brown. Nothing was too good for the *Spray* here. All government dues were remitted, and after I had rested a few days a port pilot with a tug carried her to sea again, and she made along the coast toward the harbor of Sydney, where she arrived on the following day, October 10, 1896.

I came to in a snug cove near Manly for the night, the Sydney harbor police-boat giving me a pluck into anchorage while they gathered data from an old scrap-book of mine, which seemed to interest them. Nothing escapes the vigilance of the New South Wales police; their reputation is known the world over. They made a shrewd guess that I could give them some useful information, and they were the first to meet me. Some one said they came to arrest me, and—well, let it go at that.

Summer was approaching, and the harbor of Sydney was blooming with yachts. Some of them came down to the weather-beaten *Spray* and sailed round her at Shelcote, where she took a berth for a few days. At Sydney I was at once among friends. The *Spray* remained at the various watering-places in the great port for several weeks, and was visited by many agreeable people, frequently by officers of H.M.S. *Orlando* and their friends. Captain Fisher, the commander, with a party of young ladies from the city and gentlemen belonging to his ship, came one day to pay me a visit in the midst of a deluge of rain. I never saw it rain harder even in Australia. But they were out for fun, and rain could not dampen their feelings, however hard it poured. But, as ill luck would have it, a young gentleman of another party on board, in the full uniform of a very great yacht club, with brass buttons enough to sink him, stepping quickly to get out of the wet, tumbled holus-bolus, head and heels, into a barrel of water I had been coopering, and being a short man, was soon out of sight, and nearly drowned before he was rescued. It was the nearest to a casualty on the *Spray* in her whole course, so far as I know. The young man having come on board with compliments made the mishap most embarrassing. It had been decided by his club that the *Spray* could not be officially recognized, for the reason that she brought no letters from yacht-clubs in America, and so I say it seemed all the more embarrassing and strange that I should have caught at least one of the members, in a barrel, and too, when I was not fishing for yachtsmen.

The typical Sydney boat is a handy sloop of great beam and enormous sail-carrying power; but a capsize is not uncommon, for they carry sail like vikings. In Sydney I saw all manner of craft, from the smart steam-launch and sailing-cutter to the smaller sloop and canoe pleasuring on the bay. Everybody owned a boat. If a boy in Australia has not the means to buy him a boat he builds one, and it is usually one not to be ashamed of. The *Spray* shed her Joseph's coat, the Fuego mainsail, in Sydney, and wearing a new suit, the handsome present of Commodore Foy, she was flagship of the Johnstone's Bay Flying Squadron when the circumnavigators of Sydney harbor sailed in their annual regatta. They "recognized" the *Spray*

Captain Slocum working the *Spray* out of the Yarrow River, a part of Melbourne harbor.

as belonging to "a club of her own," and with more Australian sentiment than fastidiousness gave her credit for her record.

Time flew fast those days in Australia, and it was December 6, 1896, when the *Spray* sailed from Sydney. My intention was now to sail around Cape Leeuwin direct for Mauritius on my way home, and so I coasted along toward Bass Strait in that direction.

There was little to report on this part of the voyage, except changeable winds, "busters," and rough seas. The 12th of December, however, was an exceptional day, with a fine coast wind, northeast. The

*Spray* early in the morning passed Twofold Bay and later Cape Bundooro in a smooth sea with land close aboard. The lighthouse on the cape dipped a flag to the *Spray's* flag, and children on the balconies of a cottage near the shore waved handkerchiefs as she passed by. There were only a few people all told on the shore, but the scene was a happy one. I saw festoons of evergreen in token of Christmas, near at hand. I saluted the merrymakers, wishing them a "Merry Christmas," and could hear them say, "I wish you the same."

From Cape Bundooro I passed Cliff Island in Bass Strait, and exchanged signals with the lightkeepers while the *Spray* worked up under the island. The wind howled that day while the sea broke over their rocky home.

A few days later, December 17, the *Spray* came in close under Wilson's Promontory, again seeking shelter. The keeper of the light at that station, Mr. J. Clark, came on board and gave me directions for Waterloo Bay, about three miles to leeward, for which I bore up at once, finding good anchorage there in a sandy cove protected from all westerly and northerly winds.

Anchored here was the ketch *Secret*, a fisherman, and the *Mary* of Sydney, a steam ferry-boat fitted for whaling. The captain of the *Mary* was a genius, and an Australian genius at that, and smart. His crew, from a sawmill up the coast, had not one of them seen a live whale when they shipped; but they were boatmen after an Australian's own heart, and the captain had told them that to kill a whale was no more than to kill a rabbit. They believed him, and that settled it. As luck would have it, the very first one they saw on their cruise, although an ugly humpback, was a dead whale in no time, Captain Young, the master of the *Mary*, killing the monster at a single thrust of a harpoon. It was taken in tow for Sydney, where they put it on exhibition. Nothing but whales interested the crew of the gallant *Mary*, and they spent most of their time here gathering fuel along shore for a cruise on the grounds off Tasmania. Whenever the word "whale" was mentioned in the hearing of these men their eyes glistened with excitement.

We spent three days in the quiet cove, listening to the wind outside. Meanwhile Captain Young and I explored the shores, visited abandoned miners' pits, and prospected for gold ourselves.

Our vessels, parting company the morning they sailed, stood away like sea-birds each on its own course. The wind for a few days was moderate, and, with unusual luck of fine weather, the *Spray* made Melbourne Heads on the 22d of December, and, taken in tow by the steam-tug *Racer*, was brought into port.

Christmas day was spent at a berth in the river Yarrow, but I lost little time in shifting to St. Kilda, where I spent nearly a month.

The *Spray* paid no port charges in Australia or anywhere else on the voyage, except at Pernambuco, till she poked her nose into

The shark on the deck of the *Spray*.

the custom-house at Melbourne, where she was charged tonnage dues; in this instance, sixpence a ton on the gross. The collector exacted six shillings and sixpence, taking off nothing for the fraction under thirteen tons, her exact gross being 12.70 tons. I squared the matter by charging people sixpence each for coming on board, and when this business got dull I caught a shark and charged them sixpence each to look at that. The shark was twelve feet six inches in length, and carried a progeny of twenty-six, not one of them less than two feet in length. A slit of a knife let them out in a canoe full of water, which, changed constantly, kept them alive one whole day. In less than an hour from the time I heard of the ugly brute it was on deck and on exhibition, with rather more than the amount of the *Spray's* tonnage dues already collected. Then I hired a good Irishman, Tom Howard by name,—who knew all about sharks, both on the land and in the sea, and could talk about them,—to answer questions and lecture. When I found that I could not keep abreast of the questions I turned the responsibility over to him.

Returning from the bank, where I had been to deposit money early in the day, I found Howard in the midst of a very excited crowd, telling imaginary habits of the fish. It was a good show; the people wished to see it, and it was my wish that they should; but owing to his over-stimulated enthusiasm, I was obliged to let Howard resign. The income from the show and the proceeds of the tallow I had gatherd in the Strait of Magellan, the last of which I had disposed of to a German soap-boiler at Samoa, put me in ample funds.

January 24, 1897, found the *Spray* again in tow of the tug *Racer*, leaving Hobson's Bay after a pleasant time in Melbourne and St. Kilda, which had been protracted by a succession of southwest winds that seemed never-ending.

In the summer months, that is, December, January, February, and sometimes March, east winds are prevalent through Bass Strait and round Cape Leeuwin; but owing to a vast amount of ice drifting up from the Antarctic, this was all changed now and emphasized with much bad weather, so much so that I considered it impracticable to pursue the course farther. Therefore, instead of thrashing round cold and stormy Cape Leeuwin, I decided to spend a pleasanter and more profitable time in Tasmania, waiting for the season for favorable winds through Torres Strait, by way of the Great Barrier Reef, the route I finally decided on. To sail this course would be taking advantage of anticyclones, which never fail, and besides it would give me the chance to put foot on the shores of Tasmania, round which I had sailed years before.

I should mention that while I was at Melbourne there occurred one of those extraordinary storms sometimes called "rain of blood," the first of the kind in many years about Australia. The "blood" came from a fine brick-dust matter afloat in the air from the deserts.

Varian Photo

On board at St. Kilda. Retracing on the chart the course of the *Spray* from Boston.

A rain-storm setting in brought down this dust simply as mud; it fell in such quantities that a bucketful was collected from the sloop's awnings, which were spread at the time. When the wind blew hard and I was obliged to furl awnings, her sails, unprotected on the booms, got mud-stained from clue to earing.

The phenomena of dust-storms, well understood by scientists, are not uncommon on the coast of Africa. Reaching some distance out over the sea, they frequently cover the track of ships, as in the case of the one through which the *Spray* passed in the earlier part of her voyage. Sailors no longer regard them with superstitious fear, but our credulous brothers on the land cry out "Rain of blood!" at the first splash of the awful mud.

The rip off Port Phillip Heads, a wild place, was rough when the *Spray* entered Hobson's Bay from the sea, and was rougher when she stood out. But, with sea-room and under sail, she made good weather immediately after passing it. It was only a few hours' sail to Tasmania across the strait, the wind being fair and blowing hard. I carried the St. Kilda shark along, stuffed with hay, and disposed of it to Professor Porter, the curator of the Victoria Museum of Launceston, which is at the head of the Tamar. For many a long day to come may be seen there the shark of St. Kilda. Alas! the good but mistaken people of St. Kilda, when the illustrated journals with pictures of my shark reached their news-stands, flew into a passion, and swept all papers containing mention of fish into the fire; for St. Kilda was a watering-place—and the idea of a shark *there!* But my show went on.

The *Spray* was berthed on the beach at a small jetty at Launceston while the tide driven in by the gale that brought her up the river was unusually high; and she lay there hard and fast, with not enough water around her at any time after to wet one's feet till she was ready to sail; then, to float her, the ground was dug from under her keel.

In this snug place I left her in charge of three children, while I made journeys among the hills and rested my bones, for the coming voyage, on the moss-covered rocks at the gorge hard by, and among the ferns I found wherever I went. My vessel was well taken care of. I never returned without finding that the decks had been washed and that one of the children, my nearest neighbor's little girl from across the road, was at the gangway attending to visitors, while the others, a brother and sister, sold marine curios such as were in the cargo, on "ship's account." They were a bright, cheerful crew, and people came a long way to hear them tell the story of the voyage, and of the monsters of the deep "the captain had slain." I had only to keep myself away to be a hero of the first water; and it suited me very well to do so and to rusticate in the forests and among the streams.

# CHAPTER XIV

A testimonial from a lady—Cruising round Tasmania—The skipper delivers his first lecture on the voyage—Abundant provisions—An inspection of the *Spray* for safety at Devonport—Again at Sydney—Northward bound for Torres Strait—An amateur shipwreck—Friends on the Australian coast—Perils of a coral sea.

February 1, 1897, on returning to my vessel I found waiting for me the letter of sympathy which I subjoin:

A lady sends Mr. Slocum the inclosed five-pound note as a token of her appreciation of his bravery in crossing the wide seas on so small a boat, and all alone, without human sympathy to help when danger threatened. All success to you.

To this day I do not know who wrote it or to whom I am indebted for the generous gift it contained. I could not refuse a thing so kindly meant, but promised myself to pass it on with interest at the first opportunity, and this I did before leaving Australia.

The season of fair weather around the north of Australia being yet a long way off, I sailed to other ports in Tasmania, where it is fine the year round, the first of these being Beauty Point, near which are Beaconsfield and the great Tasmania gold-mine, which I visited in turn. I saw much gray, uninteresting rock being hoisted out of the mine there, and hundreds of stamps crushing it into powder. People told me there was gold in it, and I believed what they said.

I remember Beauty Point for its shady forest and for the road among the tall gum-trees. While there the governor of New South Wales, Lord Hampden, and his family came in on a steam-yacht, sight-seeing. The *Spray*, anchored near the landing-pier, threw her bunting out, of course, and probably a more insignificant craft bearing the Stars and Stripes was never seen in those waters. However, the governor's party seemed to know why it floated there, and all about the *Spray*, and when I heard his Excellency say, "Introduce me to the captain," or "Introduce the captain to me," whichever it was, I found myself at once in the presence of a gentleman and a friend, and one greatly interested in my voyage. If any one of the party was more interested than the governor himself, it was the Honorable Margaret, his daughter. On leaving, Lord and Lady Hampden promised to rendezvous with me on board the *Spray* at the Paris Exposition in 1900. "If we live," they said, and I added, for my part, "Dangers of the seas excepted."

From Beauty Point the *Spray* visited Georgetown, near the mouth

449

of the river Tamar. This little settlement, I believe, marks the place where the first footprints were made by whites in Tasmania, though it never grew to be more than a hamlet.

Considering that I had seen something of the world, and finding people here interested in adventure, I talked the matter over before my first audience in a little hall by the country road. A piano having been brought in from a neighbor's, I was helped out by the severe thumping it got, and by a "Tommy Atkins" song from a strolling comedian. People came from a great distance, and the attendance all told netted the house about three pounds sterling. The owner of the hall, a kind lady from Scotland, would take no rent, and so my lecture from the start was a success.

From this snug little place I made sail for Devonport, a thriving place on the river Mersey, a few hours' sail westward along the coast, and fast becoming the most important port in Tasmania. Large steamers enter there now and carry away great cargoes of farm produce, but the *Spray* was the first vessel to bring the Stars and Stripes to the port, the harbor-master, Captain Murray, told me, and so it is written in the port records. For the great distinction the *Spray* enjoyed many civilities while she rode comfortably at anchor in her port duster awning that covered her from stem to stern.

From the magistrate's house, "Malunnah," on the point, she was saluted by the Jack both on coming in and on going out, and dear Mrs. Aikenhead, the mistress of Malunnah, supplied the *Spray* with jams and jellies of all sorts, by the case, prepared from the fruits of her own rich garden—enough to last all the way home and to spare. Mrs. Wood, farther up the harbor, put up bottles of raspberry wine for me. At this point, more than ever before, I was in the land of good cheer. Mrs. Powell sent on board chutney prepared "as we prepare it in India." Fish and game were plentiful here, and the voice of the gobbler was heard, and from Pardo, farther up the country, came an enormous cheese; and yet people inquire: "What did you live on? What did you eat?"

I was haunted by the beauty of the landscape all about, of the natural ferneries then disappearing, and of the domed forest-trees on the slopes, and was fortunate in meeting a gentleman intent on preserving in art the beauties of his country. He presented me with many reproductions from his collection of pictures, also many originals, to show to my friends.

By another gentleman I was charged to tell the glories of Tasmania in every land and on every occasion. This was Dr. McCall, M.L.C. The doctor gave me useful hints on lecturing. It was not without misgivings, however, that I filled away on this new course, and I am free to say that it is only by the kindness of sympathetic audiences that my oratorical bark was held on even keel. Soon after my first talk the kind doctor came to me with words of approval.

As in many other of my enterprises, I had gone about it at once and without second thought. "Man, man," said he, "great nervousness is only a sign of brain, and the more brain a man has the longer it takes him to get over the affliction; but," he added reflectively, "you will get over it." However, in my own behalf I think it only fair to say that I am not yet entirely cured.

The *Spray* was hauled out on the marine railway at Devonport and examined carefully top and bottom, but was found absolutely free from the destructive teredo, and sound in all respects. To pro-

The *Spray* in her port duster at Devonport, Tasmania, February 22, 1897.

tect her further against the ravage of these insects the bottom was coated once more with copper paint, for she would have to sail through the Coral and Arafura seas before refitting again. Everything was done to fit her for all the known dangers. But it was not without regret that I looked forward to the day of sailing from a country of so many pleasant associations. If there was a moment in my voyage when I could have given it up, it was there and then; but no vacancies for a better post being open, I weighed anchor April 16, 1897, and again put to sea.

The season of summer was then over; winter was rolling up

from the south, with fair winds for the north. A foretaste of winter wind sent the *Spray* flying round Cape Howe and as far as Cape Bundooro farther along, which she passed on the following day, retracing her course northward. This was a fine run, and boded good for the long voyage home from the antipodes. My old Christmas friends on Bundooro seemed to be up and moving when I came the second time by their cape, and we exchanged signals again, while the sloop sailed along as before in a smooth sea and close to the shore.

The weather was fine, with clear sky the rest of the passage to Port Jackson (Sydney), where the *Spray* arrived April 22, 1897, and anchored in Watson's Bay, near the heads, in eight fathoms of water. The harbor from the heads to Parramatta, up the river, was more than ever alive with boats and yachts of every class. It was, indeed, a scene of animation, hardly equaled in any other part of the world.

A few days later the bay was flecked with tempestuous waves, and none but stout ships carried sail. I was in a neighboring hotel then, nursing a neuralgia which I had picked up alongshore, and had only that moment got a glance of just the stern of a large, unmanageable steamship passing the range of my window as she forged in by the point, when the bell-boy burst into my room shouting that the *Spray* had "gone bung." I tumbled out quickly, to learn that "bung" meant that a large steamship had run into her, and that it was the one of which I saw the stern, the other end of her having hit the *Spray*. It turned out, however, that no damage was done beyond the loss of an anchor and chain, which from the shock of the collision had parted at the hawse. I had nothing at all to complain of, though, in the end, for the captain, after he clubbed his ship, took the *Spray* in tow up the harbor, clear of all dangers, and sent her back again, in charge of an officer and three men, to her anchorage in the bay, with a polite note saying he would repair any damages done. But what yawing about she made of it when she came with a stranger at the helm! Her old friend the pilot of the *Pinta* would not have been guilty of such lubberly work. But to my great delight they got her into a berth, and the neuralgia left me then, or was forgotten. The captain of the steamer, like a true seaman, kept his word, and his agent, Mr. Collishaw handed me on the very next day the price of the lost anchor and chain, with something over for anxiety of mind. I remember that he offered me twelve pounds at once; but my lucky number being thirteen, we made the amount thirteen pounds, which squared all accounts.

I sailed again, May 9, before a strong southwest wind, which sent the *Spray* gallantly on as far as Port Stevens, where it fell calm and then came up ahead; but the weather was fine, and so remained for many days, which was a great change from the state of the weather experienced here some months before.

Having a full set of admiralty sheet-charts of the coast and Barrier Reef, I felt easy in mind. Captain Fisher, R. N., who had steamed through the Barrier passages in H. M. S. *Orlando*, advised me from the first to take this route, and I did not regret coming back to it now.

The wind, for a few days after passing Port Stevens, Seal Rocks, and Cape Hawk, was light and dead ahead; but these points are photographed on my memory from the trial of beating round them. some months before when bound the other way. But now, with a good stock of books on board, I fell to reading day and night, leaving this pleasant occupation merely to trim sails or tack, or to lie down and rest, while the *Spray* nibbled at the miles. I tried to compare my state with that of old circumnavigators, who sailed exactly over the route which I took from Cape Verde Islands or farther back to this point and beyond, but there was no comparison so far as I had got. Their hardships and romantic escapes—those of them who escaped death and worse sufferings—did not enter into my experience, sailing all alone around the world. For me is left to tell only of pleasant experiences, till finally my adventures are prosy and tame.

I had just finished reading some of the most interesting of the old voyages in woe-begone ships, and was already near Port Macquarie, on my own cruise, when I made out, May 13, a modern dandy craft in distress, anchored on the coast. Standing in for her, I found that she was the cutter-yacht *Akbar*,[1] which had sailed from Watson's Bay about three days ahead of the *Spray*, and that she had run at once into trouble. No wonder she did so. It was a case of babes in the wood or butterflies at sea. Her owner, on his maiden voyage, was all duck trousers; the captain, distinguished for the enormous yachtman's cap he wore, was a Murrumbidgee[2] whaler before he took command of the *Akbar;* and the navigating officer, poor fellow, was almost as deaf as a post, and nearly as stiff and immovable as a post in the ground. These three jolly tars comprised the crew. None of them knew more about the sea or about a vessel than a newly born babe knows about another world. They were bound for New Guinea, so they said; perhaps it was as well that three tenderfeet so tender as those never reached that destination.

The owner, whom I had met before he sailed, wanted to race the poor old *Spray* to Thursday Island en route. I declined the challenge, naturally, on the ground of the unfairness of three young yachtsmen in a clipper against an old sailor all alone in a craft of coarse build; besides that, I would not on any account race in the Coral Sea.

"*Spray* ahoy!" they all hailed now. "What's the weather goin' t'be? Is it a-goin' to blow? And don't you think we'd better go back t' r-r-refit?"

---

[1]*Akbar* was not her registered name, which need not be told.

[2]The Murrumbidgee is a small river winding among the mountains of Australia, and would be the last place in which to look for a whale.

"'Is it a-goin' to blow?'"

I thought, "If ever you get back, don't refit," but I said: "Give me the end of a rope, and I'll tow you into yon port farther along; and on your lives," I urged, "do not go back round Cape Hawk, for it's winter to the south of it."

They purposed making for Newcastle under jurysails; for their mainsail had been blown to ribbons, even the jigger had been blown away, and her rigging flew at loose ends. The *Akbar*, in a word, was a wreck.

"Up anchor," I shouted, "up anchor, and let me tow you into Port Macquarie, twelve miles north of this."

"No," cried the owner; "we'll go back to Newcastle. We missed Newcastle on the way coming; we did n't see the light, and it was not thick, either." This he shouted very loud, ostensibly for my hearing, but closer even than necessary, I thought, to the ear of the navigating officer. Again I tried to persuade them to be towed into the port of refuge so near at hand. It would have cost them only the trouble of weighing their anchor and passing me a rope; of this I assured them, but they declined even this, in sheer ignorance of a rational course.

"What is your depth of water?" I asked.

"Don't know; we lost our lead. All the chain is out. We sounded with the anchor."

"Send your dinghy over, and I'll give you a lead."

"We've lost our dinghy, too," they cried.

"God is good, else you would have lost yourselves," and "Farewell" was all I could say.

The trifling service proffered by the *Spray* would have saved their vessel.

"Report us," they cried, as I stood on—"report us with sails blown away, and that we don't care a dash and are not afraid."

"Then there is no hope for you," and again "Farewell."

I promised I would report them, and did so at the first opportunity, and out of humane reasons I do so again. On the following day I spoke the steamship *Sherman*, bound down the coast, and reported the yacht in distress and that it would be an act of humanity to tow her somewhere away from her exposed position on an open coast. That she did not get a tow from the steamer was from no lack of funds to pay the bill; for the owner, lately heir to a few hundred pounds, had the money with him. The proposed voyage to New Guinea was to look that island over with a view to its purchase. It was about eighteen days before I heard of the *Akbar* again, which was on the 31st of May, when I reached Cooktown, on the Endeavor River, where I found this news:

May 31, the yacht *Akbar*, from Sydney for New Guinea, three hands on board, lost at Crescent Head; the crew saved.

So it took them several days to lose the yacht, after all.

After speaking the distressed *Akbar* and the *Sherman*, the voyage for many days was uneventful save in the pleasant incident on May 16 of a chat by signal with the people on South Solitary Island, a dreary stone heap in the ocean just off the coast of New South Wales, in latitude 30° 12′ south.

"What vessel is that?" they asked, as the sloop came abreast of their island. For answer I tried them with the Stars and Stripes at the peak. Down came their signals at once, and up went the British ensign instead, which they dipped heartily. I understood from this that they made out my vessel and knew all about her, for they asked no more questions. They did n't even ask if the "voyage would pay," but they threw out this friendly message, "Wishing you a pleasant voyage," which at that very moment I was having.

May 19 the *Spray*, passing the Tweed River, was signaled from

Danger Point, where those on shore seemed most anxious about the state of my health, for they asked if "all hands" were well, to which I could say, "Yes."

On the following day the *Spray* rounded Great Sandy Cape, and, what is a notable event in every voyage, picked up the trade-winds, and these winds followed her now for many thousands of miles, never ceasing to blow from a moderate gale to a mild summer breeze, except at rare intervals.

From the pitch of the cape was a noble light seen twenty-seven miles; passing from this to Lady Elliott Light, which stands on an island as a sentinel at the gateway of the Barrier Reef, the *Spray* was at once in the fairway leading north. Poets have sung of beacon-light and of pharos, but did ever poet behold a great light flash up before his path on a dark night in the midst of a coral sea? If so, he knew the meaning of his song.

The *Spray* had sailed for hours in suspense, evidently stemming a current. Almost mad with doubt, I grasped the helm to throw her head off shore, when blazing out of the sea was the light ahead. "Excalibur!" cried "all hands," and rejoiced, and sailed on. The *Spray* was now in a protected sea and smooth water, the first she had dipped her keel into since leaving Gibraltar, and a change it was from the heaving of the misnamed "Pacific" Ocean.

The Pacific is perhaps, upon the whole, no more boisterous than other oceans, though I feel quite safe in saying that it is not more pacific except in name. It is often wild enough in one part or another. I once knew a writer who, after saying beautiful things about the sea, passed through a Pacific hurricane, and he became a changed man. But where, after all, would be the poetry of the sea were there no wild waves? At last here was the *Spray* in the midst of a sea of coral. The sea itself might be called smooth indeed, but coral rocks are always rough, sharp, and dangerous. I trusted now to the mercies of the Maker of all reefs, keeping a good lookout at the same time for perils on every hand.

Lo! the Barrier Reef and the waters of many colors studded all about with enchanted islands! I behold among them after all many safe harbors, else my vision is astray. On the 24th of May, the sloop, having made one hundred and ten miles a day from Danger Point, now entered Whitsunday Pass, and that night sailed through among the islands. When the sun rose next morning I looked back and regretted having gone by while it was dark, for the scenery far astern was varied and charming.

# CHAPTER XV

On the morning of the 26th Gloucester Island was close aboard, and the *Spray* anchored in the evening at Port Denison, where rests, on a hill, the sweet little town of Bowen, the future watering place and health-resort of Queensland. The country all about here had a healthful appearance.

The harbor was easy of approach, spacious and safe, and afforded excellent holding-ground. It was quiet in Bowen when the *Spray* arrived, and the good people with an hour to throw away on the second evening of her arrival came down to the School of Arts to talk about the voyage, it being the latest event. It was duly advertised in the two little papers, "Boomerang" and "Nully Nully," in the one the day before the affair came off, and in the other the day after, which was all the same to the editor, and, for that matter, it was the same to me.

Besides this, circulars were distributed with a flourish, and the "best bellman" in Australia was employed. But I could have keel-hauled the wretch, bell and all, when he came to the door of the little hotel where my prospective audience and I were dining, and with his clattering bell and fiendish yell made noises that would awake the dead, all over the voyage of the *Spray* from "Boston to Bowen, the two Hubs in the cart-wheels of creation," as the "Boomerang" afterward said.

Mr. Myles, magistrate, harbor-master, land commissioner, gold warden, etc., was chairman, and introduced me, for what reason I never knew, except to embarrass me with a sense of vain ostentation and embitter my life, for Heaven knows I had met every person in town the first hour ashore. I knew them all by name now, and they all knew me. However, Mr. Myles was a good talker. Indeed, I tried to induce him to go on and tell the story while I showed the pictures, but this he refused to do. I may explain that it was a talk illustrated by stereopticon. The views were good, but the lantern, a thirty-shilling affair, was wretched, and had only an oil-lamp in it.

I sailed early the next morning before the papers came out, thinking it best to do so. They each appeared with a favorable column, however, of what they called a lecture, so I learned afterward, and they had a kind word for the bellman besides.

From Port Denison the sloop ran before the constant trade-wind, and made no stop at all, night or day, till she reached Cooktown, on the Endeavor River, where she arrived Monday, May 31, 1897, before a furious blast of wind encountered that day fifty miles down the coast. On this parallel of latitude is the high ridge and backbone of the trade-winds, which about Cooktown amount often to a hard gale.

I had been charged to navigate the route with extra care, and to feel my way over the ground. The skilled officer of the Royal navy who advised me to take the Barrier Reef passage wrote me that H. M. S. *Orlando* steamed nights as well as days through it, but that I, under sail, would jeopardize my vessel on coral reefs if I undertook to do so.

Confidentially, it would have been no easy matter finding anchorage every night. The hard work, too, of getting the sloop under way every morning was finished, I had hoped, when she cleared the Strait of Magellan. Besides that, the best of admiralty charts made it possible to keep on sailing night and day. Indeed, with a fair wind, and in the clear weather of that season, the way through the Barrier Reef Channel, in all sincerity, was clearer than a highway in a busy city, and by all odds less dangerous. But to any one contemplating the voyage I would say, beware of reefs day or night, or, remaining on the land, be wary still.

"The *Spray* came flying into port like a bird," said the longshore daily papers of Cooktown the morning after she arrived; "and it seemed strange," they added, "that only one man could be seen on board working the craft." The *Spray* was doing her best, to be sure, for it was near night, and she was in haste to find a perch before dark.

Tacking inside of all the craft in port, I moored her at sunset nearly abreast the Captain Cook monument, and next morning went ashore to feast my eyes on the very stones the great navigator had seen, for I was now on a seaman's consecrated ground. But there seemed a question in Cooktown's mind as to the exact spot where his ship, the *Endeavor*, hove down for repairs on her memorable voyage around the world. Some said it was not at all at the place where the monument now stood. A discussion of the subject was going on one morning where I happened to be, and a young lady present, turning to me as one of some authority in nautical matters, very flatteringly asked my opinion. Well, I could see no reason why Captain Cook, if he made up his mind to repair his ship inland, could n't have dredged out a channel to the place where the monument now stood, if he had a dredging-machine with him, and afterward fill it up again; for Captain Cook could do 'most anything, and nobody ever said that he had n't a dredger along. The young lady seemed to lean to my way of thinking, and following up the story of the historical voyage, asked if I had visited the point farther down the harbor where the great circumnavigator was murdered. This took my breath, but a bright school-boy coming along relieved my embarrassment, for, like all boys, seeing that information was wanted, he voluteered to supply it. Said he: "Captain Cook was n't murdered 'ere at all, ma'am; 'e was killed in Hafrica: a lion et 'im."

The *Spray* leaving Sydney, Australia, in the new suit of sails
given by Commodore Foy of Australia
(From a photograph.)

Here I was reminded of distressful days gone by. I think it was in 1866 that the old steamship *Soushay*, from Batavia for Sydney, put in at Cooktown for scurvy-grass, as I always thought, and "incidentally" to land mails. On her sick-list was my fevered self; and so I did n't see the place till I came back on the *Spray* thirty-one years later. And now I saw coming into port the physical wrecks of miners from New Guinea, destitute and dying. Many had died on the way and had been buried at sea. He would have been a hardened wretch who could look on and not try to do something for them.

The sympathy of all went out to these sufferers, but the little town was already straitened from a long run on its benevolence. I thought of the matter, of the lady's gift to me at Tasmania, which I had promised myself I would keep only as a loan, but found now, to my embarrassment, that I had invested the money. However, the good Cooktown people wished to hear a story of the sea, and how the crew of the *Spray* fared when illness got aboard of her. Accordingly the little Presbyterian church on the hill was opened for a conversation; everybody talked, and they made a roaring success of it. Judge Chester, the magistrate, was at the head of the gam, and so it was bound to succeed. He it was who annexed the island of New Guinea to Great Britain. "While I was about it," said he, "I annexed the blooming lot of it." There was a ring in the statement pleasant to the ear of an old voyager. However, the Germans made such a row over the judge's mainsail haul that they got a share in the venture.

Well, I was now indebted to the miners of Cooktown for the great privilege of adding a mite to a worthy cause, and to Judge Chester all the town was indebted for a general good time. The matter standing so, I sailed on June 6, 1897, heading away for the north as before.

Arrived at a very inviting anchorage about sundown, the 7th, I came to, for the night, abreast the Claremont light-ship. This was the only time throughout the passage of the Barrier Reef Channel that the *Spray* anchored, except at Port Denison and at Endeavor River. On the very night following this, however (the 8th), I regretted keenly, for an instant, that I had not anchored before dark, as I might have done easily under the lee of a coral reef. It happened in this way. The *Spray* had just passed M Reef light-ship, and left the light dipping astern, when, going at full speed, with sheets off, she hit the M Reef itself on the north end, where I expected to see a beacon.

She swung off quickly on her heel, however, and with one more bound on a swell cut across the shoal point so quickly that I hardly knew how it was done. The beacon was n't there; at least, I did n't see it. I had n't time to look for it after she struck, and certainly it did n't much matter then whether I saw it or not.

But this gave her a fine departure for Cape Greenville, the next point ahead. I saw the ugly boulders under the sloop's keel as she flashed over them, and I made a mental note of it that the letter M, for which the reef was named, was the thirteenth one in our alphabet, and that thirteen, as noted years before, was still my lucky number. The natives of Cape Greenville are notoriously bad, and I was advised to give them the go-by. Accordingly, from M Reef I steered outside of the adjacent islands, to be on the safe side. Skipping along now, the *Spray* passed Home Island, off the pitch of the cape, soon after midnight, and squared away on a westerly course. A short time later she fell in with a steamer bound south, groping her way in the dark and making the night dismal with her own black smoke.

From Home Island I made for Sunday Island, and bringing that abeam, shortened sail, not wishing to make Bird Island, farther along, before daylight, the wind being still fresh and the islands being low, with dangers about them. Wednesday, June 9, 1897, at daylight, Bird Island was dead ahead, distant two and a half miles, which I considered near enough. A strong current was pressing the sloop forward. I did not shorten sail too soon in the night! The first and only Australian canoe seen on the voyage was encountered here standing from the mainland, with a rag of sail set, bound for this island.

A long, slim fish that leaped on board in the night was found on deck this morning. I had it for breakfast. The spry chap was no longer around than a herring, which it resembled in every respect, except that it was three times as long; but that was so much the better, for I am rather fond of fresh herring, anyway. A great number of fisher-birds were about this day, which was one of the pleasantest on God's earth. The *Spray*, dancing over the waves, entered Albany Pass as the sun drew low in the west over the hills of Australia.

At 7:30 P.M. the *Spray*, now through the pass, came to anchor in a cove in the mainland, near a pearl-fisherman, called the *Tarawa*, which was at anchor, her captain from the deck of his vessel directing me to a berth. This done, he at once came on board to clasp hands. The *Tarawa* was a Californian, and Captain Jones, her master, was an American.

On the following morning Captain Jones brought on board two pairs of exquisite pearl shells, the most perfect ones I ever saw. They were probably the best he had, for Jones was the heart-yarn of a sailor. He assured me that if I would remain a few hours longer some friends from Somerset, near by, would pay us all a visit, and one of the crew, sorting shells on deck, "guessed" they would. The mate "guessed" so, too. The friends came, as even the second mate and cook had "guessed" they would. They were Mr. Jardine, stockman, famous throughout the land, and his family. Mrs. Jardine was the niece of King Malietoa, and cousin to the beautiful Faamu-Sami ("To make the sea burn"), who visited the *Spray* at Apia. Mr. Jardine was himself a fine specimen of a Scotsman. With his little family about him, he was content to live in this remote place, accumulating the comforts of life.

The fact of the *Tarawa* having been built in America accounted for the crew, boy Jim and all, being such good guessers. Strangely enough, though, Captain Jones himself, the only American aboard, was never heard to guess at all.

After a pleasant chat and good-by to the people of the *Tarawa*, and to Mr. and Mrs. Jardine, I again weighed anchor and stood across for Thursday Island, now in plain view, mid-channel in Torres Strait, where I arrived shortly after noon. Here the *Spray* remained over until June 24. Being the only American representative in port, this tarry was imperative, for on the 22d was the Queen's diamond jubilee. The two days over were, as sailors say, for "coming up."

Meanwhile I spent pleasant days about the island. Mr. Douglas, resident magistrate, invited me on a cruise in his steamer one day among the islands in Torres Strait. This being a scientific expedition in charge of Professor Mason Bailey, botanist, we rambled over Friday and Saturday islands, where I got a glimpse of botany. Miss Bailey, the professor's daughter, accompanied the expedition, and told me of many indigenous plants with long names.

The 22d was the great day on Thursday Island, for then we had not only the jubilee, but a jubilee with a grand corroboree in it, Mr. Douglas having brought some four hundred native warriors and their wives and children accross from the mainland to give the celebration the true native touch, for when they do a thing on Thursday Island they do it with a roar. The corroboree was, at any rate, a howling success. It took place at night, and the performers, painted in fantastic colors, danced or leaped about before a blazing fire. Some were rigged and painted like birds and beasts, in which the emu and kangaroo were well represented. One fellow leaped like a frog. Some had the human skeleton painted on their bodies, while they jumped about threateningly, spear in hand, ready to strike down some imaginary enemy. The kangaroo hopped and danced with natural ease and grace, making a fine figure. All kept time to music, vocal and instrumental, the instruments (save the mark!) being bits of wood, which they beat one against the other, and saucer-like bones, held in the palm of the hands, which they knocked together, making a dull sound. It was a show at once amusing, spectacular, and hideous.

The warrior aborigines that I saw in Queensland were for the most part lithe and fairly well built, but they were stamped always with repulsive features, and their women were, if possible, still more ill favored.

I observed that on the day of the jubilee no foreign flag was waving in the public grounds except the Stars and Stripes, which along with the Union Jack guarded the gateway, and floated in many places, from the tiniest to the standard size. Speaking to Mr. Douglas, I ventured a remark on this compliment to my country. "Oh," said he, "this is a family affair, and we do not consider the Stars and Stripes a foreign flag." The *Spray* of course flew her best bunting, and hoisted the Jack as well as her own noble flag as high as she could.

On June 24 the *Spray*, well fitted in every way, sailed for the long voyage ahead, down the Indian Ocean. Mr Douglas gave her a flag as she was leaving his island. The *Spray* had now passed nearly all the dangers of the Coral Sea and Torres Strait, which, indeed, were not a few; and all ahead from this point was plain sailing and a straight course. The trade-wind was still blowing fresh, and could be safely counted on now down to the coast of Madagascar, if not beyond that, for it was still early in the season.

I had no wish to arrive off the Cape of Good Hope before midsummer, and it was now early winter. I had been off that cape once in July, which was, of course, midwinter there. The stout ship I then commanded encountered only fierce hurricanes, and she bore them ill. I wished for no winter gales now. It was not that I feared them more, being in the *Spray* instead of a large ship, but that I preferred fine weather in any case. It is true that one may encounter heavy gales off the Cape of Good Hope at any season of the year, but in the summer they are less frequent and do not continue so long. And so with time enough before me to admit of a run ashore on the islands en route, I shaped the course now for Keeling Cocos, atoll islands, distant twenty-seven hundred miles. Taking a departure from Booby Island, which the sloop passed early in the day, I decided to sight Timor on the way, an island of high mountains.

Booby Island I had seen before, but only once, however, and that was when in the steamship *Soushay*, on which I was "hove-down" in a fever. When she steamed along this way I was well enough to crawl on deck to look at Booby Island. Had I died for it, I would have seen that island. In those days passing ships landed stores in a cave on the island for shipwrecked and distressed wayfarers. Captain Airy of the *Soushay*, a good man, sent a boat to the cave with his contribution to the general store. The stores were landed in safety, and the boat, returning, brought back from the improvised post-office there a dozen or more letters, most of them left by whalemen, with the request that the first homeward-bound ship would carry them along and see to their mailing, which had been the custom of this strange postal service for many years. Some of the letters brought back by our boat were directed to New Bedford, and some to Fairhaven, Massachusetts.

There is a light to-day on Booby Island, and regular packet communication with the rest of the world, and the beautiful uncertainty of the fate of letters left there is a thing of the past. I made no call at the little island, but standing close in, exchanged signals with the keeper of the light. Sailing on, the sloop was at once in the Arafura Sea, where for days she sailed in water milky white and green and purple. It was my good fortune to enter the sea on the last quarter of the moon, the advantage being that in the dark nights I witnessed the phosphorescent light effect at night in its greatest splendor. The sea, where the sloop disturbed it, seemed all ablaze, so that by its light I could see the smallest articles on deck, and her wake was a path of fire.

On the 25th of June the sloop was already clear of all the shoals and dangers, and was sailing on smooth sea as steadily as before, but with speed somewhat slackened. I got out the flying-jib made at Juan Fernandez, and set it as a spinnaker from the stoutest bamboo that Mrs. Stevenson had given me at Samoa. The spinnaker pulled like a sodger, and the bamboo holding its own, the *Spray* mended her pace.

Several pigeons flying across to-day from Australia toward the islands bent their course over the *Spray*. Smaller birds were seen flying in the opposite direction. In the part of the Arafura that I came to first, where it was shallow, sea-snakes writhed about on the surface and tumbled over and over in the waves. As the sloop sailed farther on, where the sea became deep, they disappeared. In the ocean, where the water is blue, not one was ever seen.

In the days of serene weather there was not much to do but to read and take rest on the *Spray*, to make up as much as possible for the rough time off Cape Horn, which was not yet forgotten, and to forestall the Cape of Good Hope by a store of ease. My sea journal was now much the same from day to day—something like this of June 26 and 27, for example:

```
On the log at noon is ................................. 130 miles
Subtract correction for slip ........................... 10  ″
                                                        120  ″
Add for current ....................................... 10  ″
                                                        130  ″
```

Latitude by observation at noon, 10° 23′ S.
Longitude as per mark on the chart.

There was n't much brain-work in that log, I'm sure. June 27 makes a better showing, when all is told:

First of all, to-day, was a flying-fish on deck; fried it in butter.
133 miles on the log.
For slip, off, and for current, on, as per guess, about equal—let it go at that.
Latitude by observation at noon, 10° 25′ S.

For several days now the *Spray* sailed west on the parallel of 10° 25′ S., as true as a hair. If she deviated at all from that, through the day or night,—and this may have happened,—she was back, strangely enough, at noon, at the same latitude. But the greatest science was in reckoning the longitude. My tin clock and only time-piece had by this time lost its minute-hand, but after I boiled her she told the hours, and that was near enough on a long stretch.

On the 2d of July the great island of Timor was in view away to the nor'ard. On the following day I saw Dana Island, not far off, and a breeze came up from the land at night, fragrant of the spices or what not of the coast.

On the 11th, with all sail set and with the spinnaker still abroad, Christmas Island, about noon, came into view one point on the star-

board bow. Before night it was abeam and distant two and a half
miles. The surface of the island appeared evenly rounded from the
sea to a considerable height in the center. In outline it was as smooth
as a fish, and a long ocean swell, rolling up, broke against the sides,
where it lay like a monster asleep, motionless on the sea. It seemed
to have the proportions of a whale, and as the sloop sailed along
its side to the part where the head would be, there was a nostril, even,
which was a blow-hole through a ledge of rock where every wave
that lashed threw up a shaft of water, lifelike and real.

It had been a long time since I last saw this island; but I remember
my temporary admiration for the captain of the ship I was then in,
the *Tanjore*, when he sang out one morning from the quarter-deck,
well aft, "Go aloft there, one of ye, with a pair of eyes, and see Christmas Island." Sure enough, there the island was in sight from the
royal-yard. Captain M__ had thus made a great hit, and he never
got over it. The chief mate, terror of us ordinaries in the ship, walking never to windward of the captain, now took himself very humbly
to leeward altogether. When we arrived at Hong-Kong there was a
letter in the ship's mail for me. I was in the boat with the captain
some hours while he had it. But do you suppose he could hand a
letter to a seaman? No, indeed; not even to an ordinary seaman. When
we got to the ship he gave it to the first mate; the first mate gave it
to the second mate, and he laid it, michingly, on the capstan-head,
where I could get it!

# CHAPTER XVI

To the Keeling Cocos Islands was now only five hundred and fifty miles; but even in this short run it was necessary to be extremely careful in keeping a true course else I would miss the atoll.

On the 12th, some hundred miles southwest of Christmas Island, I saw anti-trade clouds flying up from the southwest very high over the regular winds, which weakened now for a few days, while a swell heavier than usual set in also from the southwest. A winter gale was going on in the direction of the Cape of Good Hope. Accordingly, I steered higher to windward, allowing twenty miles a day while this went on, for change of current; and it was not too much, for on that course I made the Keeling Islands right ahead. The first unmistakable sign of the land was a visit one morning from a white tern that fluttered very knowingly about the vessel, and then took itself off westward with a businesslike air in its wing. The tern is called by the islanders the "pilot of Keeling Cocos." Farther on I came among a great number of birds fishing, and fighting over whatever they caught. My reckoning was up, and springing aloft, I saw from half-way up the mast cocoanut-trees standing out of the water ahead. I expected to see this; still, it thrilled me as an electric shock might have done. I slid down the mast, trembling under the strangest sensations; and not able to resist the impulse, I sat on deck and gave way to my emotions. To folks in a parlor on shore this may seem weak indeed, but I am telling the story of a voyage alone.

I did n't touch the helm, for with the current and heave of the sea the sloop found herself at the end of the run absolutely in the fairway of the channel. You could n't have beaten it in the navy! Then I trimmed her sails by the wind, took the helm, and flogged her up the couple of miles or so abreast the harbor landing, where I cast anchor at 3:30 P.M., July 17, 1897, twenty-three days from Thursday Island. The distance run was twenty-seven hundred miles as the crow flies. This would have been a fair Atlantic voyage. It was a delightful sail! During those twenty-three days I had not spent altogether more than three hours at the helm, including the time occupied in beating into Keeling harbor. I just lashed the helm and let her go; whether the wind was abeam or dead aft, it was all the same: she always sailed on her course. No part of the voyage up to this point, taking it by and large, had been so finished as this.[1]

The Keeling Cocos Islands, according to Admiral Fitzroy, R. N., lie between the latitudes of 11° 50′ and 12° 12′ S., and the longitudes of 96° 51′ and 96° 58′ E. They were discovered in 1608-9 by Captain William Keeling, then in the service of the East India Company. The southern group consists of seven or eight islands and islets on the atoll, which is the skeleton of what some day, according to the history of coral reefs, will be a continuous island. North Keeling has no harbor, is seldom visited, and is of no importance. The South Keelings are a strange little world, with a romantic history all their own. They have been visited occasionally by the floating spar of some hurricane-swept ship, or by a tree that has drifted all the way from Australia, or by an ill-starred ship cast away, and finally by man. Even a rock once drifted to Keeling, held fast among the roots of a tree.

After the discovery of the islands by Captain Keeling, their first notable visitor was Captain John Clunis-Ross, who in 1814 touched in the ship *Borneo* on a voyage to India. Captain Ross returned two years later with his wife and family and his mother-in-law, Mrs. Dymoke, and eight sailor-artisans, to take possession of the islands, but found there already one Alexander Hare, who meanwhile had marked the little atoll as a sort of Eden for a seraglio of Malay women which he moved over from the coast of Africa. It was Ross's own brother, oddly enough, who freighted Hare and his crowd of women to the islands, not knowing of Captain John's plans to occupy the little world. And so Hare was there with his outfit, as if he had come to stay.

On his previous visit, however, Ross had nailed the English Jack to a mast on Horsburg Island, one of the group. After two years shreds

---

[1]Mr. Andrew J. Leach, reporting, July 21, 1897, through Governor Kynnersley of Singapore, to Joseph Chamberlain, Colonial Secretary, said concerning the *Iphegenia's* visit to the atoll: "As we left the ocean depths of deepest blue and entered the coral circle, the contrast was most remarkable. The brilliant colors of the waters, transparent to a depth of over thirty feet, now purple, now of the bluest sky-blue, and now green, with the white crests of the waves flashing under a brilliant sun, the encircling . . . palm-clad islands, the gaps between which were to the south undiscernible, the white sand shores and the whiter gaps where breakers appeared, and, lastly, the lagoon itself, seven or eight miles across from north to south, and five to six from east to west, presented a sight never to be forgotten. After some little delay, Mr. Sidney Ross, the eldest son of Mr. George Ross, came off to meet us, and soon after, accompanied by the doctor and another officer, we went ashore.

"On reaching the landing-stage, we found, hauled up for cleaning, etc., the *Spray* of Boston, a yawl of 12.70 tons gross, the property of Captain Joshua Slocum. He arrived at the island on the 17th of July, twenty-three days out from Thursday Island. This extraordinary solitary traveler left Boston some two years ago single-handed, crossed to Gibraltar, sailed down to Cape Horn, passed through the Strait of Magellan to the Society Islands, thence to Australia, and through the Torres Strait to Thursday Island."

of it still fluttered in the wind, and his sailors, nothing loath, began at once the invasion of the new kingdom to take possession of it, women and all. The force of forty women, with only one man to command them, was not equal to driving eight sturdy sailors back into the sea.[1]

From this time on Hare had a hard time of it. He and Ross did not get on well as neighbors. The islands were too small and too near for characters so widely different. Hare had "oceans of money," and might have lived well in London; but he had been governor of a wild colony in Borneo, and could not confine himself to the tame life that prosy civilization affords. And so he hung on to the atoll with his forty women, retreating little by little before Ross and his sturdy crew, till at last he found himself and his harem on the little island known to this day as Prison Island, where, like Bluebeard, he confined his wives in a castle. The channel between the islands was narrow, the water was not deep, and the eight Scotch sailors wore long boots. Hare was now dismayed. He tried to compromise with rum and other luxuries, but these things only made matters worse. On the day following the first St. Andrew's celebration on the island, Hare, consumed with rage, and no longer on speaking terms with the captain, dashed off a note to him, saying: "DEAR ROSS: I thought when I sent rum and roast pig to your sailors that they would stay away from my flower-garden." In reply to which the captain, burning with indignation, shouted from the center of the island, where he stood, "Ahoy, there, on Prison Island! You Hare, don't you know that rum and roast pig are not a sailor's heaven?" Hare said afterward that one might have heard the captain's roar across to Java.

The lawless establishment was soon broken up by the women deserting Prison Island and putting themselves under Ross's protection. Hare then went to Batavia, where he met his death.

My first impression upon landing was that the crime of infanticide had not reached the islands of Keeling Cocos. "The children have all come to welcome you," explained Mr. Ross, as they mustered at the jetty by hundreds, of all ages and sizes. The people of this country were all rather shy, but, young or old, they never passed one or saw one passing their door without a salutation. In their musical voices they would say, "Are you walking?" ("Jalan, jalan?") "Will you come along?" one would answer.

For a long time after I arrived the children regarded the "one-man ship" with suspicion and fear. A native man had been blown away to sea many years before, and they hinted to one another that he might have been changed from black to white, and returned in the sloop. For some time every movement I made was closely

---

[1] In the accounts given in Findlay's "Sailing Directory" of some of the events there is a chronological discrepancy. I follow the accounts gathered from the old captain's grandsons and from record on the spot.

watched. They were particularly interested in what I ate. One day, after I had been "boot-topping" the sloop with a composition of coal-tar and other stuff, and while I was taking my dinner, with the luxury of blackberry jam, I heard a commotion, and then a yell and a stampede, as the children ran away yelling: "The captain is eating coal-tar! The captain is eating coal-tar!" But they soon found out that this same "coal-tar" was very good to eat, and that I had brought a quantity of it. One day when I was spreading a sea-biscuit thick with it for a wide-awake youngster, I heard them whisper, "Chut-chut!" meaning that a shark had bitten my hand, which they observed was lame. Thenceforth they regarded me as a hero, and I had not fingers enough for the little bright-eyed tots that wanted to cling to them and follow me about. Before this, when I held out my hand and said, "Come!" they would shy off for the nearest house, and say, "Dingin" ("It 's cold"), or "Ujan" ("It 's going to rain"). But it was now accepted that I was not the returned spirit of the lost black, and I had plenty of friends about the island, rain or shine.

The *Spray* ashore for "boot-topping" at the Keeling Islands.
(From a photograph.)

One day after this, when I tried to haul the sloop and found her fast in the sand, the children all clapped their hands and cried that a *kpeting* (crab) was holding her by the keel; and little Ophelia, ten or twelve years of age, wrote in the *Spray's* log-book:

> A hundred men with might and main
> 　On the windlass hove, yeo ho!
> The cable only came in twain;
> 　The ship she would not go;
> For, child, to tell the strangest thing,
> The keel was held by a great kpeting.

This being so or not, it was decided that the Mohammedan priest, Sama the Emim, for a pot of jam, should ask Mohammed to bless the voyage and make the crab let go the sloop's keel, which it did, if it had hold, and she floated on the very next tide.

On the 22d of July arrived H. M. S. *Iphegenia*, with Mr. Justice Andrew J. Leech and court officers on board, on a circuit of inspection among the Straits Settlements, of which Keeling Cocos was a dependency, to hear complaints and try cases by law, if any there were to try. They found the *Spray* hauled ashore and tied to a cocoanut-tree. But at the Keeling Islands there had not been a grievance to complain of since the day that Hare migrated, for the Rosses have always treated the islanders as their own family.

If there is a paradise on this earth it is Keeling. There was not a case for a lawyer, but something had to be done, for here were two ships in port, a great man-of-war and the *Spray*. Instead of a lawsuit a dance was got up, and all the officers who could leave their ship came ashore. Everybody on the island came, old and young, and the governor's great hall was filled with people. All that could get on their feet danced, while the babies lay in heaps in the corners of the room, content to look on. My little friend Ophelia danced with the judge. For music two fiddles screeched over and over again the good old tune, "We won't go home till morning." And we did not.

The women at the Keelings do not do all the drudgery, as in many places visited on the voyage. It would cheer the heart of a Fuegian woman to see the Keeling lord of creation up a cocoanut-tree. Besides cleverly climbing the trees, the men of Keeling build exquisitely modeled canoes. By far the best workmanship in boat-building I saw on the voyage was here. Many finished mechanics dwelt under the palms at Keeling, and the hum of the band-saw and the ring of the anvil were heard from morning till night. The first Scotch settlers left there the strength of Northern blood and the inheritance of steady habits. No benevolent society has ever done so much for any islanders as the noble Captain Ross, and his sons, who have followed his example of industry and thrift.

Admiral Fitzroy of the *Beagle*, who visited here, where many things are reversed, spoke of "these singular though small islands, where crabs eat cocoanuts, fish eat coral, dogs catch fish, men ride on turtles, and shells are dangerous man-traps," adding that the greater part of the sea-fowl roost on branches, and many rats make their nests in the tops of palm-trees.

My vessel being refitted, I decided to load her with the famous mammoth tridacna shell of Keeling, found in the bayou near by. And right here, within sight of the village, I came near losing "the crew of the *Spray*"—not from putting my foot in a man-trap shell, however, but from carelessly neglecting to look after the details of a trip across the harbor in a boat. I had sailed over oceans; I have since completed a course over them all, and sailed round the whole world without so nearly meeting a fatality as on that trip across a lagoon, where I trusted all to some one else, and he, weak mortal that he was, perhaps trusted all to me. However that may be, I found myself with a thoughtless African negro in a rickety bateau that was fitted with a rotten sail, and this blew away in mid-channel in a squall, that sent us drifting helplessly to sea, where we should have been incontinently lost. With the whole ocean before us to leeward, I was dismayed to see, while we drifted, that there was not a paddle or an oar in the boat! There was an anchor, to be sure, but not enough rope to tie a cat, and we were already in deep water. By great good fortune, however, there was a pole. Plying this as a paddle with the utmost energy, and by the merest accidental flaw in the wind to favor us, the trap of a boat was worked into shoal water, where we could touch bottom and push her ashore. With Africa, the nearest coast to leeward, three thousand miles away, with not so much as a drop of water in the boat, and a lean and hungry negro—well, cast the lot as one might, the crew of the *Spray* in a little while would have been hard to find. It is needless to say that I took no more such chances. The tridacna were afterward procured in a safe boat, thirty of them taking the place of three tons of cement ballast, which I threw overboard to make room and give buoyancy.

On August 22, the kpeting, or whatever else it was that held the sloop in the islands, let go its hold, and she swung out to sea under all sail, heading again for home. Mounting one or two heavy rollers on the fringe of the atoll, she cleared the flashing reefs. Long before dark Keeling Cocos, with its thousand souls, as sinless in their lives as perhaps it is possible for frail mortals to be, was left out of sight, astern. Out of sight, I say, except in my strongest affection.

The sea was rugged, and the *Spray* washed heavily when hauled on the wind, which course I took for the island of Rodriguez, and which brought the sea abeam. The true course for the island was west by south, one quarter south, and the distance was nineteen hundred miles; but I steered considerably to the windward of that to allow for the heave of the sea and other leeward effects. My sloop on this course ran under reefed sails for days together. I naturally tired of the never-ending motion of the sea, and, above all, of the

Captain Slocum drifting out to sea.

wetting I got whenever I showed myself on deck. Under these heavy weather conditions the *Spray* seemed to lag behind on her course; at least, I attributed to these conditions a discrepancy in the log, which by the fifteenth day out from Keeling amounted to one hundred and fifty miles between the rotator and the mental calculations I had kept of what she should have gone, and so I kept an eye lifting for land. I could see about sundown this day a bunch of clouds that stood in one spot, right ahead, while the other clouds floated on; this was a sign of something. By midnight, as the sloop sailed on, a black object appeared where I had seen the resting clouds. It was still a long way off, but there could be no mistaking this: it was the high island of Rodriguez. I hauled in the patent log, which I was now towing more from habit than from necessity, for I had learned the *Spray* and her ways long before this. If one thing was clearer than another in her voyage, it was that she could be trusted to come out right and in safety, though at the same time I always stood ready to give her the benefit of even the least doubt. The officers who are over-sure, and "know it all like a book," are the ones, I have observed, who wreck the most ships and lose the most lives. The cause of the discrepancy in the log was one often met with, namely, coming in contact with some large fish; two out of the four blades of the rotator were crushed or bent, the work probably of a shark. Being sure of the sloop's position, I lay down to rest and to think, and I felt better for it. By daylight the island was abeam, about three miles away. It wore a hard, weather-beaten appearance there, all alone, far out in the Indian Ocean, like land adrift. The windward side was uninviting, but there was a good port to leeward, and I hauled in now close on the wind for that. A pilot came out to take me into the inner harbor, which was reached through a narrow channel among coral reefs.

It was a curious thing that at all of the islands some reality was insisted on as unreal, while improbabilities were clothed as hard facts; and so it happened here that the good abbé, a few days before, had been telling his people about the coming of Antichrist, and when they saw the *Spray* sail into the harbor, all feather-white before a gale of wind, and run all standing upon the beach, and with only one man aboard, they cried, "May the Lord help us, it is he, and he has come in a boat!" which I say would have been the most improbable way of his coming. Nevertheless, the news went flying through the place. The governor of the island, Mr. Roberts, came down immediately to see what it was all about, for the little town was in a great commotion. One elderly woman, when she heard of my advent, made for her house and locked herself in. When she heard that I was actually coming up the street she barricaded her doors, and did not come out while I was on the island, a period of eight days. Governor Roberts and his family did not share the fears of their people, but came on board at the jetty, where the sloop was berthed, and their example induced others to come also. The governor's young boys took charge of the *Spray's* dinghy at once, and my visit cost his Excellency, besides great hospitality to me, the building of a boat for them like the one belonging to the *Spray*.

My first day at this Land of Promise was to me like a fairy-tale. For many days I had studied the charts and counted the time of my arrival at this spot, as one might his entrance to the Islands of the Blessed, looking upon it as the terminus of the last long run, made irksome by the want of many things with which, from this time on, I could keep well supplied. And behold, here was the sloop, arrived, and made securely fast to a pier in Rodriguez. On the first evening ashore, in the land of napkins and cut glass, I saw before me still the ghosts of hempen towels and of mugs with handles knocked off. Instead of tossing on the sea, however, as I might have been, here was I in a bright hall, surrounded by sparkling wit, and dining with the governor of the island! "Aladdin," I cried, "where is your lamp? My fisherman's lantern, which I got at Gloucester, has shown me better things than your smoky old burner ever revealed."

The second day in port was spent in receiving visitors. Mrs. Roberts and her children came first to "shake hands," they said, "with the *Spray*." No one was now afraid to come on board except the poor old woman, who still maintained that the *Spray* had Antichrist in the hold, if, indeed, he had not already gone ashore. The governor entertained that evening, and kindly invited the "destroyer of the world" to speak for himself. This he did, elaborating most effusively on the dangers of the sea (which, after the manner of many of our frailest mortals, he would have had smooth had he made it); also by contrivances of light and darkness he exhibited on the wall pictures of the places and countries visited on the voyage (nothing like the countries, however, that he would have made), and of the people seen, savage and other, frequently groaning, "Wicked world! Wicked world!" When this was finished his Excellency the governor, speaking words of thankfulness, distributed pieces of gold.

On the following day I accompanied his Excellency and family on a visit to San Gabriel, which was up the country among the hills. The good abbé of San Gabriel entertained us all royally at the convent, and we remained his guests until the following day. As I was leaving his place, the abbé said, "Captain, I embrace you, and of whatever religion you may be, my wish is that you succeed in making your voyage, and that our Saviour the Christ be always with you!" To this good man's words I could only say, "My dear abbé, had all religionists been so liberal there would have been less bloodshed in the world."

At Rodriguez one may now find every convenience for filling pure and wholesome water in any quantity, Governor Roberts having built a reservoir in the hills, above the village, and laid pipes to the jetty, where, at the time of my visit, there were five and a half feet at high tide. In former years well-water was used, and more or less sickness occurred from it. Beef may be had in any quantity on the island, and at a moderate price. Sweet potatoes were plentiful and cheap; the large sack of them that I bought there for about four shillings kept unusually well. I simply stored them in the sloop's dry hold. Of fruits, pomegranates were most plentiful; for two shillings I obtained a large sack of them, as many as a donkey could pack from the orchard, which, by the way, was planted by nature herself.

# CHAPTER XVII

On the 16th of September, after eight restful days at Rodriguez, the mid-ocean land of plenty, I set sail, and on the 19th arrived at Mauritius, anchoring at quarantine about noon. The sloop was towed in later on the same day by the doctor's launch, after he was satisfied that I had mustered all the crew for inspection. Of this he seemed in doubt until he examined the papers, which called for a crew of one all told from port to port, throughout the voyage. Then finding that I had been well enough to come thus far alone, he gave me pratique without further ado. There was still another official visit for the *Spray* to pass farther in the harbor. The governor of Rodriguez, who had most kindly given me, besides a regular mail, private letters of introduction to friends, told me I should meet, first of all, Mr. Jenkins of the postal service, a good man. "How do you do, Mr. Jenkins?" cried I, as his boat swung alongside. "You don't know me," he said. "Why not?" I replied. "From where is the sloop?" "From around the world," I again replied, very solemnly. "And alone?" "Yes; why not?" "And you know me?" "Three thousand years ago," cried I, "when you and I had a warmer job than we have now" (even this was hot). "You were then Jenkinson, but if you have changed your name I don't blame you for that." Mr. Jenkins, forbearing soul, entered into the spirit of the jest, which served the *Spray* a good turn, for on the strength of this tale it got out that if any one should go on board after dark the devil would get him at once. And so I could leave the *Spray* without the fear of her being robbed at night. The cabin, to be sure, was broken into, but it was done in daylight, and the thieves got no more than a box of smoked herrings before "Tom" Ledson, one of the port officials, caught them red-handed, as it were, and sent them to jail. This was discouraging to pilferers, for they feared Ledson more than they feared Satan himself. Even Mamode Hajee Ayoob, who was the day-watchman on board,—till an empty box fell over in the cabin and frightened him out of his wits,—could not be hired to watch nights, or even till the sun went down. "Sahib," he cried, "there is no need of it," and what he said was perfectly true.

At Mauritius, where I drew a long breath, the *Spray* rested her

The *Spray* at Mauritius.

wings, it being the season of fine weather. The hardships of the voyage, if there had been any, were now computed by officers of experience as nine tenths finished, and yet somehow I could not forget that the United States was still a long way off.

The kind people of Mauritius, to make me richer and happier, rigged up the opera-house, which they had named the "Ship *Pantai*."[1] All decks and no bottom was this ship, but she was as stiff as a church. They gave me free use of it while I talked over the *Spray*'s adventures. His Honor the mayor introduced me to his Excellency the governor from the poop-deck of the *Pantai*. In this way I was also introduced again to our good consul, General John P. Campbell, who had already introduced me to his Excellency. I was becoming well acquainted, and was in for it now to sail the voyage over again. How I got through the story I hardly know. It was a hot night, and I could have choked the tailor who made the coat I wore for this occasion. The kind governor saw that I had done my party trying to rig like a man ashore, and he invited me to Government House at Reduit, where I found myself among friends.

[1] Guinea-hen.

It was winter still off stormy Cape of Good Hope, but the storms might whistle there. I determined to see it out in milder Mauritius, visiting Rose Hill, Curipepe, and other places on the island. I spent a day with the elder Mr. Roberts, father of Governor Roberts of Rodriguez, and with his friends the Very Reverend Fathers O'Loughlin and McCarthy. Returning to the *Spray* by way of the great flower conservatory near Moka, the proprietor, having only that morning discovered a new and hardy plant, to my great honor named it "Slocum," which he said Latinized it at once, saving him some trouble on the twist of a word; and the good botanist seemed pleased that I had come. How different things are in different countries! In Boston, Massachusetts, at that time, a gentleman, so I was told, paid thirty thousand dollars to have a flower named after his wife, and it was not a big flower either, while "Slocum," which came without the asking, was bigger than a mangel-wurzel!

I was royally entertained at Moka, as well as at Reduit and other places—once by seven young ladies, to whom I spoke of my inability to return their hospitality except in my own poor way of taking them on a sail in the sloop. "The very thing! The very thing!" they all cried. "Then please name the time," I said, as meek as Moses. "To-morrow!" they all cried. "And, aunty, we may go, may n't we, and we 'll be real good for a whole week afterward, aunty! Say yes, aunty dear!" All this after saying "To-morrow"; for girls in Mauritius are, after all, the same as our girls in America; and their dear aunt said "Me, too" about the same as any really good aunt might say in my own country.

I was then in a quandary, it having recurred to me that on the very "to-morrow" I was to dine with the harbor-master, Captain Wilson. However, I said to myself, "The *Spray* will run out quickly into rough seas; these young ladies will have *mal de mer* and a good time, and I 'll get in early enough to be at the dinner, after all." But not a bit of it. We sailed almost out of sight of Mauritius, and they just stood up and laughed at seas tumbling aboard, while I was at the helm making the worst weather of it I could, and spinning yarns to the aunt about sea-serpents and whales. But she, dear lady, when I had finished with stories of monsters, only hinted at a basket of provisions they had brought along, enough to last a week, for I had told them about my wretched steward.

The more the *Spray* tried to make these young ladies seasick, the more they all clapped their hands and said, "How lovely it is!" and "How beautifully she skims over the sea!" and "How beautiful our island appears from the distance!" and they still cried, "Go on!" We were fifteen miles or more at sea before they ceased the eager cry, "Go on!" Then the sloop swung round, I still hoping to be back to Port Louis in time to keep my appointment. The *Spray* reached the island quickly, and flew along the coast fast enough; but I made a mistake in steering along the coast on the way home, for as we came abreast of Tombo Bay it enchanted my crew. "Oh, let 's anchor here!" they cried. To this no sailor in the world would say nay. The sloop came to anchor, ten minutes later, as they wished, and a young man on the cliff abreast, waving his hat, cried, "*Vive la Spray!*" My passengers said, "Aunty, may n't we have a swim in the surf along the shore?" Just then the harbor-master's launch hove in sight, coming out to meet us; but it was too late to get the sloop into Port Louis that night. The launch was in time, however, to land my fair crew for a swim; but they were determined not to desert the ship. Meanwhile I prepared a roof for the night on deck with the sails, and a Bengali man-servant arranged the evening meal. That night the *Spray* rode in Tombo Bay with her precious freight. Next morning bright and early, even before the stars were gone, I awoke to hear praying on deck.

The port officers' launch reappeared later in the morning, this time with Captain Wilson himself on board, to try his luck in getting the *Spray* into port for he had heard of our predicament. It was worth something to hear a friend tell afterward how earnestly the good harbor-master of Mauritius said, "I 'll find the *Spray* and I 'll get her into port." A merry crew he discovered on her. They could hoist sails like old tars, and could trim them, too. They could tell all about the ship's "hoods," and one should have seen them clap a bonnet on the jib. Like the deepest of deep-water sailors, they could heave the lead, and—as I hope to see Mauritius again!—any of them could have put the sloop in stays. No ship ever had a fairer crew.

The voyage was the event of Port Louis; such a thing as young ladies sailing about the harbor, even, was almost unheard of before.

While at Mauritius the *Spray* was tendered the use of the military dock free of charge, and was thoroughly refitted by the port authorities. My sincere gratitude is also due other friends for many things needful for the voyage put on board, including bags of sugar from some of the famous old plantations.

The favorable season now set in, and thus well equipped, on the 26th of October, the *Spray* put to sea. As I sailed before a light wind the island receded slowly, and on the following day I could still see the Puce Mountain near Moka. The *Spray* arrived next day off Galets, Réunion, and a pilot came out and spoke her. I handed him a Mauritius paper and continued on my voyage; for rollers were running heavily at the time, and it was not practicable to make a landing. From Réunion I shaped a course direct for Cape St. Mary, Madagascar.

The sloop was now drawing near the limits of the trade-wind, and the strong breeze that had carried her with free sheets the many thousands of miles from Sandy Cape, Australia, fell lighter each day until October 30, when it was altogether calm, and a motionless sea held her in a hushed world. I furled the sails at evening, sat down on deck, and enjoyed the vast stillness of the night.

October 31 a light east-northeast breeze sprang up, and the sloop passed Cape St. Mary about noon. On the 6th, 7th, 8th, and 9th of November, in the Mozambique Channel, she experienced a hard gale of wind from the southwest. Here the *Spray* suffered as much as she did anywhere, except off Cape Horn. The thunder and lightning preceding this gale were very heavy. From this point until the sloop arrived off the coast of Africa, she encountered a succession of gales of wind, which drove her about in many directions, but on the 17th of November she arrived at Port Natal.

This delightful place is the commercial center of the "Garden Colony," Durban itself, the city, being the continuation of a garden. The signalman from the bluff station reported the *Spray* fifteen miles off. The wind was freshening, and when she was within eight miles he said: "The *Spray* is shortening sail; the mainsail was reefed and set in ten minutes. One man is doing all the work."

This item of news was printed three minutes later in a Durban morning journal, which was handed to me when I arrived in port. I could not verify the time it had taken to reef the sail, for as I have already said, the minute-hand of my timepiece was gone. I only knew that I reefed as quickly as I could.

The same paper, commenting on the voyage, said: "Judging from the stormy weather which has prevailed off this coast during the past few weeks, the *Spray* must have had a very stormy voyage from Mauritius to Natal." Doubtless the weather would have been called stormy by sailors in any ship, but it caused the *Spray* no more inconvenience than the delay natural to head winds generally.

The question of how I sailed the sloop alone, often asked, is best answered, perhaps, by a Durban newspaper. I would shrink from repeating the editor's words but for the reason that undue estimates have been made of the amount of skill and energy required to sail a sloop of even the *Spray's* small tonnage. I heard a man who called himself a sailor say that "it would require three men to do what it was claimed" that I did alone, and what I found perfectly easy to do over and over again; and I have heard that others made similar nonsensical remarks, adding that I would work myself to death. But here is what the Durban paper said:

As briefly noted yesterday, the *Spray*, with a crew of one man, arrived at this port yesterday afternoon on her cruise round the world. The *Spray* made quite an auspicious entrance to Natal. Her commander sailed his craft right up the channel past the main wharf, and dropped his anchor near the old *Forerunner* in the creek, before any one had a chance to get on board. The *Spray* was naturally an object of great curiosity to the Point people and her arrival was witnessed by a large crowd. The skilful manner in which Captain Slocum steered his craft about the vessels which were occupying the waterway was a treat to witness.

The *Spray* was not sailing in among greenhorns when she came to Natal. When she arrived off the port the pilot-ship, a fine, able steam-tug, came out to meet her, and led the way in across the bar, for it was blowing a smart gale and was too rough for the sloop to be towed with safety. The trick of going in I learned by watching the steamer; it was simply to keep on the windward side of the channel and take the combers end on.

Captain Joshua Slocum.

I found that Durban supported two yacht-clubs, both of them full of enterprise. I met all the members of both clubs, and sailed in the crack yacht *Florence* of the Royal Natal, with Captain Spradbrow and the Right Honorable Harry Escombe, premier of the colony. The yacht's center-board plowed furrows through the mud-banks, which according to Mr. Escombe, Spradbrow afterward planted with potatoes. The *Florence*, however, won races while she tilled the skipper's land. After our sail on the *Florence* Mr. Escombe offered to sail the *Spray* round the Cape of Good Hope for me, and hinted at his famous cribbage-board to while away the hours. Spradbrow in retort, warned me of it. Said he, "You would be played out of the sloop before you could round the cape." By others it was not thought probable that the premier of Natal would play cribbage off the Cape of Good Hope to win even the *Spray*.

It was a matter of no small pride to me in South Africa to find that American humor was never at a discount, and one of the best American stories I ever heard was told by the premier. At Hotel Royal one day, dining with Colonel Saunderson, M.P., his son, and Lieutenant Tipping, I met Mr. Stanley. The great explorer was just from Pretoria, and had already as good as flayed President Krüger with his trenchant pen. But that did not signify, for everybody has a whack at Oom Paul, and no one in the world seems to stand the joke better than he, not even the Sultan of Turkey himself. The colonel introduced me to the explorer, and I hauled close to the wind, to go slow, for Mr. Stanley was a nautical man once himself,—on the Nyanza, I think,—and of course my desire was to appear in the best light before a man of his experience. He looked me over carefully, and said, "What an example of patience!" "Patience is all that is required," I ventured to reply. He then asked if my vessel had water-tight compartments. I explained that she was all water-tight and all compartment. "What if she should strike a rock?" he asked. "Compartments would not save her if she should hit the rocks lying along her course," said I; adding, "she must be kept away from the rocks." After a considerable pause Mr. Stanley asked, "What if a swordfish should pierce her hull with its sword?" Of course I had thought of that as one of the dangers of the sea, and also of the chance of being struck by lightning. In the case of the swordfish, I ventured to say that "the first thing would be to secure the sword." The colonel invited me to dine with the party on the following day, that we might go further into this matter, and so I had the pleasure of meeting Mr. Stanley a second time, but got no more hints in navigation from the famous explorer.

It sounds odd to hear scholars and statesmen say the world is flat; but it is a fact that three Boers favored by the opinion of President Krüger prepared a work to support that contention. While I was at Durban they came from Pretoria to obtain data from me, and they seemed annoyed when I told them that they could not prove it by my experience. With the advice to call up some ghost of the dark ages for research, I went ashore, and left these three wise men poring over the *Spray's* track on a chart of the world, which, however, proved nothing to them, for it was on Mercator's projection, and behold, it was "flat." The next morning I met one of the party in a clergyman's garb, carrying a large Bible, not different from the one I had read. He tackled me, saying, "If you respect the Word of God, you must admit that the world is flat." "If the Word of God stands on a flat world—" I began. "What!" cried he, losing himself in a passion, and making as if he would run me through with an assagai. "What!" he shouted in astonishment and rage, while I jumped aside to dodge the imaginary weapon. Had this good but misguided fanatic been armed with a real weapon, the crew of the *Spray* would have died a martyr there and then. The next day, seeing him across the street, I bowed and made curves with my hands. He responded with a level, swimming movement of his hands, meaning "the world is flat." A pamphlet by these Transvaal geographers, made up of arguments from sources high and low to prove their theory, was mailed to me before I sailed from Africa on my last stretch around the globe.

While I feebly portray the ignorance of these learned men, I have great admiration for their physical manhood. Much that I saw first and last of the Transvaal and the Boers was admirable. It is well known that they are the hardest of fighters, and as generous to the fallen as they are brave before the foe. Real stubborn bigotry with them is only found among old fogies, and will die a natural death, and that, too, perhaps long before we ourselves are entirely free from bigotry. Education in the Transvaal is by no means neglected, English as well as Dutch being taught to all that can afford both; but the tariff duty on English school-books is heavy, and from necessity the poorer people stick to the Transvaal Dutch and their flat world, just as in Samoa and other islands a mistaken policy has kept the natives down to Kanaka.

I visited many public schools at Durban, and had the pleasure of meeting many bright children.

But all fine things must end, and December 14, 1897, the "crew" of the *Spray*, after having a fine time in Natal, swung the sloop's dinghy in on deck, and sailed with a morning land-wind, which carried her clear of the bar, and again she was "off on her alone," as they say in Australia.

# CHAPTER XVIII

Rounding the "Cape of Storms" in olden time—A rough Christmas—The *Spray* ties up for a three months' rest at Cape Town—A railway trip to the Transvaal—President Krüger's odd definition of the *Spray's* voyage—His terse sayings—Distinguished guests on the *Spray*—Cocoanut fiber as a padlock—Courtesies from the admiral of the Queen's navy—Off for St. Helena—Land in sight.

The Cape of Good Hope was now the most prominent point to pass. From Table Bay I could count on the aid of brisk trades, and then the *Spray* would soon be at home. On the first day out from Durban it fell calm, and I sat thinking about these things and the end of the voyage. The distance to Table Bay, where I intended to call, was about eight hundred miles over what might prove a rough sea. The early Portuguese navigators, endowed with patience, were more than sixty-nine years struggling to round this cape before they got as far as Algoa Bay, and there the crew mutinied. They landed on a small island, now called Santa Cruz, where they devoutly set up the cross, and swore they would cut the captain's throat if he attempted to sail farther. Beyond this they thought was the edge of the world, which they too believed was flat; and fearing that their ship would sail over the brink of it, they compelled Captain Diaz, their commander, to retrace his course, all being only too glad to get home. A year later, we are told, Vasco da Gama sailed successfully round the "Cape of Storms," as the Cape of Good Hope was then called, and discovered Natal on Christmas or Natal day; hence the name. From this point the way to India was easy.

Gales of wind sweeping round the cape even now were frequent enough, one occurring, on an average, every thirty-six hours; but one gale was much the same as another, with no more serious result than to blow the *Spray* along on her course when it was fair, or to blow her back somewhat when it was ahead. On Christmas, 1897, I came to the pitch of the cape. On this day the *Spray* was trying to stand on her head, and she gave me every reason to believe that she would accomplish the feat before night. She began very early in the morning to pitch and toss about in a most unusual manner, and I have to record that, while I was at the end of the bowsprit reefing the jib, she ducked me under water three times for a Christmas box. I got wet and did not like it a bit: never in any other sea was I put under more than once in the same short space of time, say three minutes. A large English steamer passing ran up the signal, "Wishing you a Merry Christmas." I think the captain was a humorist; his own ship was throwing her propeller out of water.

483

Two days later, the *Spray*, having recovered the distance lost in the gale, passed Cape Agulhas in company with the steamship *Scotsman*, now with a fair wind. The keeper of the light on Agulhas exchanged signals with the *Spray* as she passed, and afterward wrote me at New York congratulations on the completion of the voyage. He seemed to think the incident of two ships of so widely different types passing his cape together worthy of a place on canvas, and he went about having the picture made. So I gathered from his letter. At lonely stations like this hearts grow responsive and sympathetic, and even poetic. This feeling was shown toward the *Spray* along many a rugged coast, and reading many a kind signal thrown out to her gave one a grateful feeling for all the world.

One more gale of wind came down upon the *Spray* from the west after she passed Cape Agulhas, but that one she dodged by getting into Simons Bay. When it moderated she beat around the Cape of Good Hope, where they say the *Flying Dutchman* is still sailing. The voyage then seemed as good as finished; from this time on I knew that all, or nearly all, would be plain sailing.

Here I crossed the dividing-line of weather. To the north it was clear and settled, while south it was humid and squally, with, often enough, as I have said, a treacherous gale. From the recent hard weather the *Spray* ran into a calm under Table Mountain, where she lay quietly till the generous sun rose over the land and drew a breeze in from the sea.

The steam-tug *Alert*, then out looking for ships, came to the *Spray* off the Lion's Rump, and in lieu of a larger ship towed her into port. The sea being smooth, she came to anchor in the bay off the city of Cape Town, where she remained a day, simply to rest clear of the bustle of commerce. The good harbor-master sent his steam-launch to bring the sloop to a berth in dock at once, but I preferred to remain for one day alone, in the quiet of a smooth sea, enjoying the retrospect of the passage of the two great capes. On the following morning the *Spray* sailed into the Alfred Dry-docks, where she remained for about three months in the care of the port authorities, while I traveled the country over from Simons Town to Pretoria, being accorded by the colonial government a free railroad pass over all the land.

The trip to Kimberley, Johannesburg, and Pretoria was a pleasant one. At the last-named place I met Mr. Krüger, the Transvaal president. His Excellency received me cordially enough; but my friend Judge Beyers, the gentleman who presented me, by mentioning that I was on a voyage around the world, unwittingly gave great offense to the venerable statesman, which we both regretted deeply. Mr. Krüger corrected the judge rather sharply, reminding him that the world is flat. "You don't mean *round* the world," said the president; "it is impossible! You mean *in* the world. Impossible!" he said, "impossible!" and not another word did he utter either to the judge, or to me. The judge looked at me and I looked at the judge, who should have

Cartoon printed in the Cape Town "Owl" of March 5, 1898, in connection with an item about Captain Slocum's trip to Pretoria.

known his ground, so to speak, and Mr. Krüger glowered at us both. My friend the judge seemed embarrassed, but I was delighted; the incident pleased me more than anything else that could have happened. It was a nugget of information quarried out of Oom Paul, some of whose sayings are famous. Of the English he said, "They took first my coat and then my trousers." He also said, "Dynamite is the corner-stone of the South African Republic." Only unthinking people call President Krüger dull.

Soon after my arrival at the cape, Mr. Krüger's friend Colonel Saunderson, [1] who had arrived from Durban some time before, invited me to Newlands Vineyard, where I met many agreeable people. His Excellency Sir Alfred Milner, the governor, found time to come aboard with a party. The governor, after making a survey of the deck, found a seat on a box in my cabin; Lady Muriel sat on a keg, and Lady Saunderson sat by the skipper at the wheel, while the colonel, with his kodak, away in the dinghy, took snap shots of the sloop and her distinguished visitors. Dr. David Gill, astronomer royal, who was of the party, invited me the next day to the famous Cape Observatory. An hour with Dr. Gill was an hour among the stars. His discoveries in stellar photography are well known. He showed me the great astronomical clock of the observatory, and I showed him the tin clock on the *Spray*, and we went over the subject of standard time at sea, and how it was found from the deck of the little sloop without the aid of a clock of any kind. Later it was advertised that Dr. Gill would preside at a talk about the voyage of the *Spray:* that alone secured for me a full house. The hall was packed, and many were not able to get in. This success brought me sufficient money for all my needs in port and for the homeward voyage.

After visiting Kimberley and Pretoria, and finding the *Spray* all right in the docks, I returned to Worcester and Wellington, towns famous for colleges and seminaries, passed coming in, still traveling as the guest of the colony. The ladies of all these institutions of learning wished to know how one might sail round the world alone, which I thought augured of sailing-mistresses in the future instead of sailing-masters. It will come to that yet if we men-folk keep on saying we "can't."

On the plains of Africa I passed through hundreds of miles of rich but still barren land, save for scrub-bushes, on which herds of sheep were browsing. The bushes grew about the length of a sheep apart, and they, I thought, were rather long of body; but there was still room for all. My longing for a foothold on land seized upon me here, where so much of it lay waste; but instead of remaining to plant forests and reclaim vegetation, I returned again to the *Spray* at the Alfred Docks, where I found her waiting for me, with everything in order, exactly as I had left her.

[1]Colonel Saunderson was Mr. Krüger's very best friend, inasmuch as he advised the president to avast mounting guns.

Captain Slocum, Sir Alfred Milner (with the tall hat), and Colonel
Saunderson, M. P., on the bow of the *Spray* at Cape Town.

I have often been asked how it was that my vessel and all appurtenances were not stolen in the various ports where I left her for days
together without a watchman in charge. This is just how it was: The
*Spray* seldom fell among thieves. At the Keeling Islands, at Rodriguez,
and at many such places, a wisp of cocoanut fiber in the door-latch,
to indicate that the owner was away, secured the goods against even
a longing glance. But when I came to a great island nearer home, stout
locks were needed; the first night in port things which I had always
left uncovered disappeared, as if the deck on which they were stowed
had been swept by a sea.

A pleasant visit from Admiral Sir Harry Rawson of the Royal
Navy and his family brought to an end the *Spray's* social relations
with the Cape of Good Hope. The admiral, then commanding the
South African Squadron, and now in command of the great Channel
fleet, evinced the greatest interest in the diminutive *Spray* and her
behavior off Cape Horn, where he was not an entire stranger. I have
to admit that I was delighted with the trend of Admiral Rawson's
questions, and that I profited by some of his suggestions, notwithstanding the wide difference in our respective commands.

On March 26, 1898, the *Spray* sailed from South Africa, the land of distances and pure air, where she had spent a pleasant and profitable time. The steam-tug *Tigre* towed her to sea from her wonted berth at the Alfred Docks, giving her a good offing. The light morning breeze, which scantily filled her sails when the tug let go the towline, soon died away altogether, and left her riding over a heavy swell, in full view of Table Mountain and the high peaks of the Cape of Good Hope. For a while the grand scenery served to relieve the

T. FOGARTY.

"Reading day and night."

monotony. One of the old circumnavigators (Sir Francis Drake, I think), when he first saw this magnificent pile, sang, " 'T is the fairest thing and the grandest cape I 've seen in the whole circumference of the earth."

The view was certainly fine, but one has no wish to linger long to look in a calm at anything, and I was glad to note, finally, the short heaving sea, precursor of the wind which followed on the second day. Seals playing about the *Spray* all day, before the breeze came, looked with large eyes when, at evening, she sat no longer like a lazy bird with folded wings. They parted company now, and the *Spray* soon sailed the highest peaks of the mountains out of sight, and the world changed from a mere panoramic view to the light of a homeward-bound voyage. Porpoises and dolphins, and such other fishes as did not mind making a hundred and fifty miles a day, were her companions now for several days. The wind was from the southeast; this suited the *Spray* well, and she ran along steadily at her best speed, while I dipped into the new books given me at the cape, reading day and night. March 30 was for me a fast-day in honor of them. I read on, oblivious of hunger or wind or sea, thinking that all was going well, when suddenly a comber rolled over the stern and slopped saucily into the cabin, wetting the very book I was reading. Evidently it was time to put in a reef, that she might not wallow on her course.

March 31 the fresh southeast wind had come to stay. The *Spray* was running under a single-reefed mainsail, a whole jib, and flying-jib besides, set on the Vailima bamboo, while I was reading Stevenson's delightful "Inland Voyage." The sloop was again doing her work smoothly, hardly rolling at all, but just leaping along among the white horses, a thousand gamboling porpoises keeping her company on all sides. She was again among her old friends the flying-fish, interesting denizens of the sea. Shooting out of the waves like arrows, and with outstretched wings, they sailed on the wind in graceful curves; then falling till again they touched the crest of the waves to wet their delicate wings and renew the flight. They made merry the livelong day. One of the joyful sights on the ocean of a bright day is the continual flight of these interesting fish.

One could not be lonely in a sea like this. Moreover, the reading of delightful adventures enhanced the scene. I was now in the *Spray* and on the Oise in the *Arethusa* at one and the same time. And so the *Spray* reeled off the miles, showing a good run every day till April 11, which came almost before I knew it. Very early that morning I was awakened by that rare bird, the booby, with its harsh quack, which I recognized at once as a call to go on deck; it was as much as to say, "Skipper, there 's land in sight." I tumbled out quickly, and sure enough, away ahead in the dim twilight, about twenty miles off, was St. Helena.

My first impulse was to call out, "Oh, what a speck in the sea!" It is in reality nine miles in length and two thousand eight hundred and twenty-three feet in height. I reached for a bottle of port-wine out of the locker, and took a long pull from it to the health of my invisible helmsman—the pilot of the *Pinta*.

# CHAPTER XIX

In the isle of Napoleon's exile—Two lectures—A guest in the ghostroom at Plantation House—An excursion to historic Longwood—Coffee in the husk, and a goat to shell it—The *Spray's* ill luck with animals—A prejudice against small dogs—A rat, the Boston spider, and the cannibal cricket—Ascension Island.

It was about noon when the *Spray* came to anchor off Jamestown, and "all hands" at once went ashore to pay respects to his Excellency the governor of the island, Sir. R. A. Sterndale. His Excellency, when I landed, remarked that it was not often, nowadays, that a circumnavigator came his way, and he cordially welcomed me, and arranged that I should tell about the voyage, first at Garden Hall to the people of Jamestown, and then at Plantation House—the governor's residence, which is in the hills a mile or two back—to his Excellency and the officers of the garrison and their friends. Mr. Poole, our worthy consul, introduced me at the castle, and in the course of his remarks asserted that the sea-serpent was a Yankee.

Most royally was the crew of the *Spray* entertained by the governor. I remained at Plantation House a couple of days, and one of the rooms in the mansion, called the "west room," being haunted, the butler, by command of his Excellency, put me up in that— like a prince. Indeed, to make sure that no mistake had been made, his Excellency came later to see that I was in the right room, and to tell me all about the ghosts he had seen or heard of. He had discovered all but one, and wishing me pleasant dreams, he hoped I might have the honor of a visit from the unknown one of the west room. For the rest of the chilly night I kept the candle burning, and often looked from under the blankets, thinking that maybe I should meet the great Napoleon face to face; but I saw only furniture, and the horseshoe that was nailed over the door opposite my bed.

St. Helena has been an island of tragedies—tragedies that have been lost sight of in wailing over the Corsican. On the second day of my visit the governor took me by carriage-road through the turns over the island. At one point of our journey the road, in winding around spurs and ravines, formed a perfect W within the distance of a few rods. The roads, though tortuous and steep, were fairly good, and I was struck with the amount of labor it must have cost to build them. The air on the heights was cool and bracing. It is said that, since hanging for trivial offenses went out of fashion, no one has died there, except from falling over the cliffs in old age, or from being crushed by stones rolling on them from the steep mountains! Witches at one time were persistent at St. Helena, as with us in America in

490

the days of Cotton Mather. At the present day crime is rare in the island. While I was there, Governor Sterndale, in token of the fact that not one criminal case had come to court within the year, was presented with a pair of white gloves by the officers of justice.

Returning from the governor's house to Jamestown, I drove with Mr. Clark, a countryman of mine, to "Longwood," the home of Napoleon. M. Morilleau, French consular agent in charge, keeps the place respectable and the buildings in good repair. His family at Longwood, consisting of wife and grown daughters, are natives of courtly and refined manners, and spend here days, months, and years of contentment, though they have never seen the world beyond the horizon of St. Helena.

On the 20th of April the *Spray* was again ready for sea. Before going on board I took luncheon with the governor and his family at the castle. Lady Sterndale had sent a large fruit-cake, early in the morning, from Plantation House, to be taken along on the voyage. It was a great high-decker, and I ate sparingly of it, as I thought, but it did not keep as I had hoped it would. I ate the last of it along with my first cup of coffee at Antigua, West Indies, which, after all, was quite a record. The one my own sister made me at the little island in the Bay of Fundy, at the first of the voyage, kept about the same length of time, namely, forty-two days.

After luncheon a royal mail was made up for Ascension, the island next on my way. Then Mr. Poole and his daughter paid the *Spray* a farewell visit, bringing me a basket of fruit. It was late in the evening before the anchor was up, and I bore off for the west, loath to leave my new friends. But fresh winds filled the sloop's sails once more, and I watched the beacon-light at Plantation House, the governor's parting signal for the *Spray*, till the island faded in the darkness astern and became one with the night, and by midnight the light itself had disappeared below the horizon.

When morning came there was no land in sight, but the day went on the same as days before, save for one small incident. Governor Sterndale had given me a bag of coffee in the husk, and Clark, the American, in an evil moment, had put a goat on board, "to butt the sack and hustle the coffee-beans out of the pods." He urged that the animal, besides being useful, would be as companionable as a dog. I soon found that my sailing-companion, this sort of dog with horns, had to be tied up entirely. The mistake I made was that I did not chain him to the mast instead of tying him with grass ropes less securely, and this I learned to my cost. Except for the first day, before the beast got his sea-legs on, I had no peace of mind. After that, actuated by a spirit born, maybe, of his pasturage, this incarnation of evil threatened to devour everything from flying-jib to stern-davits. He was the worst pirate I met on the whole voyage. He began depredations by eating my chart of the West Indies, in the cabin, one day, while I was about my work for'ard, thinking that the critter was securely tied on deck by the pumps. Alas! there was not a rope in the sloop proof against that goat's awful teeth!

It was clear from the very first that I was having no luck with animals on board. There was the tree-crab from the Keeling Islands. No sooner had it got a claw through its prison-box than my sea-jacket, hanging within reach, was torn to ribbons. Encouraged by this success, it smashed the box open and escaped into my cabin, tearing up things generally, and finally threatening my life in the dark. I had hoped to bring the creature home alive, but this did not prove feasible. Next the goat devoured my straw hat, and so when I arrived in port I had nothing to wear ashore on my head. This last unkind stroke decided his fate. On the 27th of April the *Spray* arrived at Ascension, which is garrisoned by a man-of-war crew, and the boatswain of the island came on board. As he stepped out of his boat the mutinous goat climbed into it, and defied boatswain and crew. I hired them to land the wretch at once, which they were only too willing to do, and there he fell into the hands of a most excellent Scotchman, with the chances that he would never get away. I was destined to sail once more into the depths of solitude, but these experiences had no bad effect upon me; on the contrary, a spirit of charity and even benevolence grew stronger in my nature through the meditations of these supreme hours on the sea.

In the loneliness of the dreary country about Cape Horn I found myself in no mood to make one life less in the world, except in self-defense, and as I sailed this trait of the hermit character grew till the mention of killing food-animals was revolting to me. However well I may have enjoyed a chicken stew afterward at Samoa, a new self rebelled at the thought suggested there of carrying chickens to be slain for my table on the voyage, and Mrs. Stevenson, hearing my protest, agreed with me that to kill the companions of my voyage and eat them would be indeed next to murder and cannibalism.

As to pet animals, there was no room for a noble large dog on the *Spray* on so long a voyage, and a small cur was for many years associated in my mind with hydrophobia. I witnessed once the death of a sterling young German from that dreadful disease, and about the same time heard of the death, also by hydrophobia, of the young gentleman who had just written a line of insurance in his company's books for me. I have seen the whole crew of a ship scamper up the rigging to avoid a dog racing about the decks in a fit. It would never do, I thought, for the crew of the *Spray* to take a canine risk, and with these just prejudices indelibly stamped on my mind, I have, I am afraid, answered impatiently too often the query, "Did n't you have a dog?" with, "I and the dog would n't have been very long in the same boat, in any sense." A cat would have been a harmless animal, I dare say, but there was nothing for puss to do on board, and she is an unsociable animal at best. True, a rat got into my vessel at the Keeling Cocos Islands, and another at Rodriguez, along with a centipede stowed away in the hold; but one of them I drove out of the ship, and the other I caught. This is how it was: for the first one with infinite pains I made a trap, looking to its capture and destruction; but the wily rodent, not to be deluded, took the hint and got ashore the day the thing was completed.

It is, according to tradition, a most reassuring sign to find rats coming to a ship, and I had a mind to abide the knowing one of Rodriguez; but a breach of discipline decided the matter against him. While I slept one night, my ship sailing on, he undertook to walk over me, beginning at the crown of my head, concerning which I am always sensitive. I sleep lightly. Before his impertinence had got him even to my nose I cried "Rat!" had him by the tail, and threw him out of the companionway into the sea.

As for the centipede, I was not aware of its presence till the wretched insect, all feet and venom, beginning, like the rat, at my head, wakened me by a sharp bite on the scalp. This also was more than I could tolerate. After a few applications of kerosene the poisonous bite, painful at first, gave me no further inconvenience.

From this on for a time no living thing disturbed my solitude; no insect even was present in my vessel, except the spider and his wife, from Boston, now with a family of young spiders. Nothing, I say, till sailing down the last stretch of the Indian Ocean, where mosquitos came by hundreds from rain-water poured out of the heavens. Simply a barrel of rain-water stood on deck five days, I think, in the sun, then music began. I knew the sound at once; it was the same as heard from Alaska to New Orleans.

Again at Cape Town, while dining out one day, I was taken with the song of a cricket, and Mr. Branscombe, my host, volunteered to capture a pair of them for me. They were sent on board next day in a box labeled, "Pluto and Scamp." Stowing them away in the binnacle in their own snug box, I left them there without food till I got to sea—a few days. I had never heard of a cricket eating anything. It seems that Pluto was a cannibal, for only the wings of poor Scamp were visible when I opened the lid, and they lay broken on the floor of the prison-box. Even with Pluto it had gone hard, for he lay on his back stark and stiff, never to chirrup again.

Ascension Island, where the goat was marooned, is called the Stone Frigate, R. N., and is rated "tender" to the South African Squadron. It lies in 7°55′ south latitude and 14°25′ west longitude, being in the very heart of the southeast trade-winds and about eight hundred and forty miles from the coast of Liberia. It is a mass of volcanic matter, thrown up from the bed of the ocean to the height of two thousand eight hundred and eighteen feet at the highest point above sea-level. It is a strategic point, and belonged to Great Britain before it got cold. In the limited but rich soil at the top of the island, among the clouds, vegetation has taken root, and a little scientific farming is carried on under the supervision of a gentleman from

Canada. Also a few cattle and sheep are pastured there for the garrison mess. Water storage is made on a large scale. In a word, this heap of cinders and lava rock is stored and fortified, and would stand a seige.

Very soon after the *Spray* arrived I received a note from Captain Blaxland, the commander of the island, conveying his thanks for the royal mail brought from St. Helena, and inviting me to luncheon with him and his wife and sister at headquarters, not far away. It is hardly necessary to say that I availed myself of the captain's hospitality at once. A carriage was waiting at the jetty when I landed, and a sailor, with a broad grin, led the horse carefully up the hill to the captain's house, as if I were a lord of the admiralty, and a governor besides; and he led it as carefully down again when I returned. On the following day I visited the summit among the clouds, the same team being provided, and the same old sailor leading the horse. There was probably not a man on the island at that moment better able to walk than I. The sailor knew that. I finally suggested that we change places. "Let me take the bridle," I said, "and keep the horse from bolting." "Great Stone Frigate!" he exclaimed, as he burst into a laugh, "this 'ere 'oss would n't bolt no faster nor a turtle. If I did n't tow 'im 'ard we 'd never get into port." I walked most of the way over the steep grades, whereupon my guide, every inch a sailor, became my friend. Arriving at the summit of the island, I met Mr. Schank, the farmer from Canada, and his sister, living very cozily in a house among the rocks, as snug as conies, and as safe. He showed me over the farm, taking me through a tunnel which led from one field to the other, divided by an inaccessible spur of mountain. Mr. Schank said that he had lost many cows and bullocks, as well as sheep, from breakneck over the steep cliffs and precipices. One cow, he said, would sometimes hook another right over a precipice to destruction, and go on feeding unconcernedly. It seemed that the animals on the island farm, like mankind in the wide world, found it all too small.

On the 26th of April, while I was ashore, rollers came in which rendered launching a boat impossible. However, the sloop being securely moored to a buoy in deep water outside of all breakers, she was safe, while I, in the best of quarters, listened to well-told stories among the officers of the Stone Frigate. On the evening of the 29th, the sea having gone down, I went on board and made preparations to start again on my voyage early next day, the boatswain of the island and his crew giving me a hearty handshake as I embarked at the jetty.

For reasons of scientific interest, I invited in mid-ocean the most thorough investigation concerning the crew-list of the *Spray*. Very few had challenged it, and perhaps few ever will do so henceforth; but for the benefit of the few that may, I wished to clench beyond doubt the fact that it was not at all necessary in the expedition of a sloop around the world to have more than one man for the crew, all told, and that the *Spray* sailed with only one person on board. And so, by appointment, Lieutenant Eagles, the executive officer, in the morning, just as I was ready to sail, fumigated the sloop, rendering it impossible for a person to live concealed below, and proving that only one person was on board when she arrived. A certificate to this effect, besides the official documents from the many consulates, health offices, and custom-houses, will seem to many superfluous; but this story of the voyage may find its way into hands unfamiliar with the business of these offices and of their ways of seeing that a vessel's papers, and above all, her bills of health, are in order.

The lieutenant's certificate being made out, the *Spray*, nothing loath, now filled away clear of the sea-beaten rocks, and the tradewinds, comfortably cool and bracing, sent her flying along on her course. On May 8, 1898, she crossed the track, homeward bound, that she had made October 2, 1895, on the voyage out. She passed Fernando de Noronha at night, going some miles south of it, and so I did not see the island. I felt a contentment in knowing that the *Spray* had encircled the globe, and even as an adventure alone I was in no way discouraged as to its utility, and said to myself, "Let what will happen, the voyage is now on record." A period was made.

# CHAPTER XX

On May 10 there was a great change in the condition of the sea; there could be no doubt of my longitude now, if any had before existed in my mind. Strange and long-forgotten current ripples pattered against the sloop's sides in grateful music; the tune arrested the ear, and I sat quietly listening to it while the *Spray* kept on her course. By these current ripples I was assured that she was now off St. Roque and had struck the current which sweeps around that cape. The trade-winds, we old sailors say, produce this current, which, in its course from this point forward, is governed by the coast-line of Brazil, Guiana, Venezuela, and, as some would say, by the Monroe Doctrine.

The trades had been blowing fresh for some time, and the current, now at its height, amounted to forty miles a day. This, added to the sloop's run by the log, made the handsome day's work of one hundred and eighty miles on several consecutive days. I saw nothing of the coast of Brazil, though I was not many leagues off and was always in the Brazil current.

I did not know that war with Spain had been declared, and that I might be liable, right there, to meet the enemy and be captured. Many had told me at Cape Town that, in their opinion, war was inevitable, and they said: "The Spaniard will get you! The Spaniard will get you!" To all this I could only say that, even so, he would not get much. Even in the fever-heat over the disaster to the *Maine* I did not think there would be war; but I am no politician. Indeed, I had hardly given the matter a serious thought when, on the 14th of May, just north of the equator, and near the longitude of the river Amazon, I saw first a mast, with the Stars and Stripes floating from it, rising astern as if poked up out of the sea, and then rapidly appearing on the horizon, like a citadel, the *Oregon!* As she came near I saw that the great ship was flying the signals "C B T," which read, "Are there any men-of-war about?" Right under these flags, and larger than the *Spray's* mainsail, so it appeared, was the yellowest Spanish flag I ever saw. It gave me nightmare some time after when I reflected on it in my dreams.

I did not make out the *Oregon's* signals till she passed ahead, where I could read them better, for she was two miles away, and I had no binoculars. When I had read her flags I hoisted the signal "No," for

The *Spray* passed by the *Oregon*.

I had not seen any Spanish men-of-war; I had not been looking for any. My final signal, "Let us keep together for mutual protection," Captain Clark did not seem to regard as necessary. Perh'aps my small flags were not made out; anyhow, the *Oregon* steamed on with a rush, looking for Spanish men-of-war, as I learned afterward. The *Oregon's* great flag was dipped beautifully three times to the *Spray's* lowered flag as she passed on. Both had crossed the line only a few hours before. I pondered long that night over the probability of a war risk now coming upon the *Spray* after she had cleared all, or nearly all, the dangers of the sea, but finally a strong hope mastered my fears.

On the 17th of May, the *Spray*, coming out of a storm at daylight, made Devil's Island, two points on the lee bow, not far off. The wind was still blowing a stiff breeze on shore. I could clearly see the dark-gray buildings on the island as the sloop brought it abeam. No flag or sign of life was seen on the dreary place.

Later in the day a French bark on the port tack, making for Cayenne, hove in sight, close-hauled on the wind. She was falling to leeward fast. The *Spray* was also closed-hauled, and was lugging on sail to secure an offing on the starboard tack, a heavy swell in the night having thrown her too near the shore, and now I considered the matter of supplicating a change of wind. I had already enjoyed my share of favoring breezes over the great oceans, and I asked myself if it would be right to have the wind turned now all into my sails while the Frenchman was bound the other way. A head current, which he stemmed, together with a scant wind, was bad enough for him. And so I could only say, in my heart, "Lord, let matters stand as they are, but do not help the Frenchman any more just now, for what would suit him well would ruin me!"

I remembered that when a lad I heard a captain often say in meeting that in answer to a prayer of his own the wind changed from southeast to northwest, entirely to his satisfaction. He was a good man, but did this glorify the Architect—the Ruler of the winds and the waves? Moreover, it was not a trade-wind, as I remember it, that changed for him, but one of the variables which will change when you ask it, if you ask long enough. Again, this man's brother maybe was not bound the opposite way, well content with a fair wind himself, which made all the difference in the world.[1]

On May 18, 1898, is written large in the *Spray's* log-book: "To-night, in latitude 7°13′ N., for the first time in nearly three years I see the north star." The *Spray* on the day following logged one hundred and forty-seven miles. To this I add thirty-five miles for current sweeping her onward. On the 20th of May, about sunset, the island of Tobago, off the Orinoco, came into view, bearing west

---

[1] The Bishop of Melbourne (commend me to his teachings) refused to set aside a day of prayer for rain, recommending his people to husband water when the rainy season was on. In like manner, a navigator husbands the wind, keeping a weather-gage where practicable.

by north, distant twenty-two miles. The *Spray* was drawing rapidly toward her home destination. Later at night, while running free along the coast of Tobago, the wind still blowing fresh, I was startled by the sudden flash of breakers on the port bow and not far off. I luffed instantly offshore, and then tacked, heading in for the island. Finding myself, shortly after, close in with the land, I tacked again offshore, but without much altering the bearings of the danger. Sail whichever way I would, it seemed clear that if the sloop weathered the rocks at all it would be a close shave, and I watched with anxiety, while beating against the current, always losing ground. So the matter stood hour after hour, while I watched the flashes of light thrown up as regularly as the beats of the long ocean swells, and always they seemed just a little nearer. It was evidently a coral reef,—of this I had not the slightest doubt,—and a bad reef at that. Worse still, there might be other reefs ahead forming a bight into which the current would sweep me, and where I should be hemmed in and finally wrecked. I had not sailed these waters since a lad, and lamented the day I had allowed on board the goat that ate my chart. I taxed my memory of sea lore, of wrecks on sunken reefs, and of pirates harbored among coral reefs where other ships might not come, but nothing that I could think of applied to the island of Tobago, save the one wreck of Robinson Crusoe's ship in the fiction, and that gave me little information about reefs. I remembered only that in Crusoe's case he kept his powder dry. "But there she booms again," I cried, "and how close the flash is now! Almost aboard was that last breaker! But you 'll go by, *Spray*, old girl! 'T is abeam now! One surge more! and oh, one more like that will clear your ribs and keel!" And I slapped her on the transom, proud of her last noble effort to leap clear of the danger, when a wave greater than the rest threw her higher than before, and, behold, from the crest of it was revealed at once all there was of the reef. I fell back in a coil of rope, speechless and amazed, not distressed, but rejoiced. Aladdin's lamp! My fisherman's own lantern! It was the great revolving light on the island of Trinidad, thirty miles away, throwing flashes over the waves, which had deceived me! The orb of the light was now dipping on the horizon, and how glorious was the sight of it! But, dear Father Neptune, as I live, after a long life at sea, and much among corals, I would have made a solemn declaration to that reef! Through all the rest of the night I saw imaginary reefs, and not knowing what moment the sloop might fetch up on a real one, I tacked off and on till daylight, as nearly as possible in the same track, all for the want of a chart. I could have nailed the St. Helena goat's pelt to the deck.

My course was now for Grenada, to which I carried letters from Mauritius. About midnight of the 22d of May I arrived at the island, and cast anchor in the roads off the town of St. George, entering the inner harbor at daylight on the morning of the 23d, which made forty-two days' sailing from the Cape of Good Hope. It was a good run, and I doffed my cap again to the pilot of the *Pinta*.

Lady Bruce, in a note to the *Spray* at Port Louis, said Grenada was a lovely island, and she wished the sloop might call there on the voyage home. When the *Spray* arrived, I found that she had been fully expected. "How so?" I asked. "Oh, we heard that you were at Mauritius," they said, "and from Mauritius, after meeting Sir Charles Bruce, our old governor, we knew you would come to Grenada." This was a charming introduction, and it brought me in contact with people worth knowing.

The *Spray* sailed from Grenada on the 28th of May, and coasted along under the lee of the Antilles, arriving at the island of Dominica on the 30th, where, for the want of knowing better, I cast anchor at the quarantine ground; for I was still without a chart of the islands, not having been able to get one even at Grenada. Here I not only met with further disappointment in the matter, but was threatened with a fine for the mistake I made in the anchorage. There were no ships either at the quarantine or at the commerical roads, and I could not see that it made much difference where I anchored. But a negro chap, a sort of deputy harbor-master, coming along, thought it did, and he ordered me to shift to the other anchorage, which, in truth, I had already investigated and did not like, because of the heavier roll there from the sea. And so instead of springing to the sails at once to shift, I said I would leave outright as soon as I could procure a chart, which I begged he would send and get for me. "But I say you mus' move befo' you gets anyt'ing 't all," he insisted, and raising his voice so that all the people alongshore could hear him, he added, "An' jes now!" Then he flew into a towering passion when they on shore snickered to see the crew of the *Spray* sitting calmly by the bulwark instead of hoisting sail. "I tell you dis am quarantine," he shouted, very much louder than before. "That's all right, general," I replied: "I want to be quarantined anyhow." "That's right, boss," some one on the beach cried, "that's right; you get quarantined," while others shouted to the deputy to "make de white trash move 'long out o' dat." They were about equally divided on the island for and against me. The man who had made so much fuss over the matter gave it up when he found that I wished to be quarantined, and sent for an all-important half-white, who soon came alongside, starched from clue to earing. He stood in the boat as straight up and down as a fathom of pump-water—a marvel of importance. "Charts!" cried I, as soon as his shirt-collar appeared over the sloop's rail; "have you any charts?" "No, sah," he replied with much-stiffened dignity; "no, sah; cha'ts do's n't grow on dis island." Not doubting the information, I tripped anchor immediately, as I had intended to do from the first, and made all sail for St. John, Antigua, where I arrived on the 1st of June, having sailed with great caution in midchannel all the way.

The *Spray*, always in good company, now fell in with the port officer's steam-launch at the harbor entrance, having on board Sir

Francis Fleming, governor of the Leeward Islands, who, to the delight of "all hands," gave the officer in charge instructions to tow my ship into port. On the following day his Excellency and Lady Fleming, along with Captain Burr, R. N., paid me a visit. The court-house was tendered free to me at Antigua, as was done also at Grenada, and at each place a highly intelligent audience filled the hall to listen to a talk about the seas the *Spray* had crossed, and the countries she had visited.

# CHAPTER XXI

Clearing for home—In the calm belt—A sea covered with sargasso—The jibstay parts in a gale—Welcomed by a tornado off Fire Island—A change of plan—Arrival at Newport—End of a cruise of over forty-six thousand miles—The *Spray* again at Fairhaven.

On the 4th of June, 1898, the *Spray* cleared from the United States consulate, and her license to sail single-handed, even round the world, was returned to her for the last time. The United States consul, Mr. Hunt, before handing the paper to me, wrote on it, as General Roberts had done at Cape Town, a short commentary on the voyage. The document, by regular course, is now lodged in the Treasury Department at Wahsington, D.C.

On June 5, 1898, the *Spray* sailed for a home port, heading first direct for Cape Hatteras. On the 8th of June she passed under the sun from south to north; the sun's declination on that day was 22°54′, and the latitude of the *Spray* was the same just before noon. Many think it is excessively hot right under the sun. It is not necessarily so. As a matter of fact the thermometer stands at a bearable point whenever there is a breeze and a ripple on the sea, even exactly under the sun. It is often hotter in cities and on sandy shores in higher latitudes.

The *Spray* was booming joyously along for home now, making her usual good time, when of a sudden she struck the horse latitudes, and her sail flapped limp in a calm. I had almost forgotten this calm belt, or had come to regard it as a myth. I now found it real, however, and difficult to cross. This was as it should have been, for, after all of the dangers of the sea, the dust-storm on the coast of Africa, the "rain of blood" in Australia, and the war risk when nearing home, a natural experience would have been missing had the calm of the horse latitudes been left out. Anyhow, a philosophical turn of thought now was not amiss, else one's patience would have given out almost at the harbor entrance. The term of her probation was eight days. Evening after evening during this time I read by the light of a candle on deck. There was no wind at all, and the sea became smooth and monotonous. For three days I saw a full-rigged ship on the horizon, also becalmed.

Sargasso, scattered over the sea in bunches, or trailed curiously along down the wind in narrow lanes, now gathered together in great fields, strange sea-animals, little and big, swimming in and out, the most curious among them being a tiny sea-horse which I captured and brought home preserved in a bottle. But on the 18th of June a gale began to blow from the southwest, and the sargasso was dispersed again in windrows and lanes.

On this day there was soon wind enough and to spare. The same might have been said of the sea. The *Spray* was in the midst of the turbulent Gulf Stream itself. She was jumping like a porpoise over the uneasy waves. As if to make up for lost time, she seemed to touch only the high places. Under a sudden shock and strain her rigging began to give out. First the main-sheet strap was carried away, and then the peak halyard-block broke from the gaff. It was time to reef and refit, and so when "all hands" came on deck I went about doing that.

The 19th of June was fine, but on the morning of the 20th another gale was blowing, accompanied by cross-seas that tumbled about and shook things up with great confusion. Just as I was thinking about taking in sail the jibstay broke at the mast-head, and fell, jib and all, into the sea. It gave me the strangest sensation to see the bellying sail fall, and where it had been suddenly to see only space. However, I was at the bows, with presence of mind to gather it in on the first wave that rolled up, before it was torn or trailed under the sloop's bottom. I found by the amount of work done in three minutes' or less time that I had by no means grown stiff-jointed on the voyage; anyhow, scurvy had not set in, and being now within a few degrees of home, I might complete the voyage, I thought, without the aid of a doctor. Yes, my health was still good, and I could skip about the decks in a lively manner, but could I climb? The great King Neptune tested me severely at this time, for the stay being gone, the mast itself switched about like a reed, and was not easy to climb; but a gun-tackle purchase was got up, and the stay set taut from the masthead, for I had spare blocks and rope on board with which to rig it, and the jib, with a reef in it, was soon pulling again like a "sodger" for home. Had the *Spray's* mast not been well stepped, however, it would have been "John Walker" when the stay broke. Good work in the building of my vessel stood me always in good stead.

On the 23d of June I was at least tired, tired, tired of baffling squalls and fretful cobble-seas. I had not seen a vessel for days and days, where I had expected the company of at least a schooner now and then. As to the whistling of the wind through the rigging, and the slopping of the sea against the sloop's sides, that was well enough in its way, and we could not have got on without it, the *Spray* and I; but there was so much of it now, and it lasted so long! At noon of that day a winterish storm was upon us from the nor'west. In the Gulf Stream, thus late in June, hailstones were pelting the *Spray*, and lightning was pouring down from the clouds, not in flashes alone, but in almost continuous streams. By slants, however, day and night I worked the sloop in toward the coast, where, on the 25th of June, off Fire Island, she fell into the tornado which, an hour earlier, had swept over New York city with lightning that wrecked buildings and sent trees flying about in splinters; even ships at docks had parted their moorings and smashed into other ships, doing great damage. It was the climax storm of the voyage, but I saw the unmistakable character of it in time to have all snug aboard and receive it under bare poles. Even so, the sloop shivered when it struck her, and she heeled over unwillingly on her beam ends: but rounding to, with a sea-anchor ahead, she righted and faced out the storm. In the midst of the gale I could do no more than look on, for what is a man in a storm like this? I had seen one electric storm on the voyage, off the coast of Madagascar, but it was unlike this one. Here the lightning kept on longer, and thunderbolts fell in the sea all about. Up to this time I was bound for New York; but when all was over I rose, made sail, and hove the sloop round from starboard to port tack, to make for a quiet harbor to think the matter over; and so, under short sail, she reached in for the coast of Long Island, while I sat thinking and watching the lights of coasting-vessels which now began to appear in sight. Reflections of the voyage so nearly finished stole in upon me now; many tunes I had hummed again and again came back once more. I found myself repeating fragments of a hymn often sung by a dear Christian woman of Fairhaven when I was rebuilding the *Spray*. I was to hear once more and only once, in profound solemnity, the metaphorical hymn:

> By waves and wind I'm tossed and driven.

And again:

> But still my little ship outbraves
> The blust'ring winds and stormy waves.

After this storm I saw the pilot of the *Pinta* no more.

The experiences of the voyage of the *Spray*, reaching over three years, had been to me like reading a book, and one that was more and more interesting as I turned the pages, till I had come now to the last page of all, and the one more interesting than any of the rest.

When daylight came I saw that the sea had changed color from dark green to light. I threw the lead and got soundings in thirteen fathoms. I made the land soon after, some miles east of Fire Island, and sailing thence before a pleasant breeze along the coast, made for Newport. The weather after the furious gale was remarkably fine. The *Spray* rounded Montauk Point early in the afternoon; Point Judith was abeam at dark; she fetched in at Beavertail next. Sailing on, she had one more danger to pass—Newport harbor was mined. The *Spray* hugged the rocks along where neither friend nor foe could come if drawing much water, and where she would not disturb the guard-ship in the channel. It was close work, but it was safe enough so long as she hugged the rocks close, and not the mines. Flitting by a low point abreast of the guard-ship, the dear old *Dexter*, which I knew well, some one on board of her sang out, "There goes a craft!" I threw up a light at once and heard the hail, "*Spray*, ahoy!" It was the voice of a friend, and I knew that a friend would not fire on the *Spray*. I eased off the main-sheet now, and the *Spray* swung off for the beacon-lights of the inner harbor. At last she reached port in safety, and there at 1 A.M. on June 27, 1898, cast anchor, after the cruise of more than forty-six thousand miles round the world, during an absence of three years and two months, with two days over for coming up.

Was the crew well? Was I not? I had profited in many ways by the voyage. I had even gained flesh, and actually weighed a pound more than when I sailed from Boston. As for aging, why, the dial of my life was turned back till my friends all said, "Slocum is young again." And so I was, at least ten years younger than the day I felled the first tree for the construction of the *Spray*.

My ship was also in better condition than when she sailed from Boston on her long voyage. She was still as sound as a nut, and as tight as the best ship afloat. She did not leak a drop—not one drop! The pump, which had been little used before reaching Australia, had not been rigged since that at all.

The first name on the *Spray's* visitors' book in the home port was written by the one who always said, "The *Spray* will come back." The *Spray* was not quite satisfied till I sailed her around to her birth-place, Fairhaven, Massachusetts, farther along. I had myself a desire to return to the place of the very beginning whence I had, as I have said, renewed my age. So on July 3, with a fair wind, she waltzed beautifully round the coast and up the Acushnet River to Fairhaven, where I secured her to the cedar spile driven in the bank to hold her when she was launched. I could bring her no nearer home.

If the *Spray* discovered no continents on her voyage, it may be that there were no more continents to be discovered; she did not seek new worlds, or sail to powwow about the dangers of the seas. The sea has been much maligned. To find one's way to lands already discovered is a good thing, and the *Spray* made the discovery that even the worst sea is not so terrible to a well-appointed ship. No king, no country, no treasury at all, was taxed for the voyage of the *Spray*, and she accomplished all that she undertook to do.

To succeed, however, in anything at all, one should go understandingly about his work and be prepared for every emergency. I see, as I look back over my own small achievement, a kit of not too elaborate carpenters' tools, a tin clock, and some carpet-tacks, not a great many, to facilitate the enterprise as already mentioned in the story. But above all to be taken into account were some years of schooling, where I studied with diligence Neptune's laws, and these laws I tried to obey when I sailed overseas; it was worth the while.

And now, without having wearied my friends, I hope, with detailed scientific accounts, theories, or deductions, I will only say that I have endeavored to tell just the story of the adventure itself. This, in my own poor way, having been done, I now moor ship, weather-bitt cables, and leave the sloop *Spray*, for the present, safe in port.

APPENDIX

Again tied to the old stake at Fairhaven.

# APPENDIX

From a feeling of diffidence toward sailors of great experience, I refrained, in the preceding chapters as prepared for serial publication in the "Century Magazine," from entering fully into the details of the *Spray's* build, and of the primitive methods employed to sail her. Having had no yachting experience at all, I had no means of knowing that the trim vessels seen in our harbors and near the land could not all do as much, or even more, than the *Spray*, sailing, for example, on a course with the helm lashed.

I was aware that no other vessel had sailed in this manner around the globe, but would have been loath to say that another could not do it, or that many men had not sailed vessels of a certain rig in that manner as far as they wished to go. I was greatly amused, therefore, by the flat assertions of an expert that it could not be done.

The *Spray*, as I sailed her, was entirely a new boat, built over from a sloop which bore the same name, and which, tradition said, had first served as an oysterman, about a hundred years ago, on the coast of Delaware. There was no record in the custom-house of where she was built. She was once owned at Noank, Connecticut, afterward in New Bedford and when Captain Eben Pierce presented her to me, at the end of her natural life, she stood, as I have already described, propped up in a field at Fairhaven. Her lines were supposed to be those of a North Sea fisherman. In rebuilding timber by timber and plank by plank, I added to her freeboard twelve inches amidships, eighteen inches forward, and fourteen inches aft, thereby increasing her sheer, and making her, as I thought, a better deep-water ship. I will not repeat the history of the rebuilding of the *Spray*, which I have detailed in my first chapter, except to say that, when finished, her dimensions were thirty-six feet nine inches over all, fourteen feet two inches wide, and four feet two inches deep in the hold, her tonnage being nine tons net, and twelve and seventy one-hundredths tons gross.

I gladly produce the lines of the *Spray*, with such hints as my really limited fore-and-aft sailing will allow, my seafaring life having been spent mostly in barks and ships. No pains have been spared to give them accurately. The *Spray* was taken from New York to Bridge-port, Connecticut, and, under the supervision of the Park City Yacht Club, was hauled out of water and very carefully measured in every way to secure a satisfactory result. Captain Robins produced the model. Our young yachtsmen, pleasuring in the "lilies of the sea," very naturally will not think favorably of my craft. They have a right to their opinion, while I stick to mine. They will take exceptions to her short ends, the advantage of these being most apparent in a heavy sea.

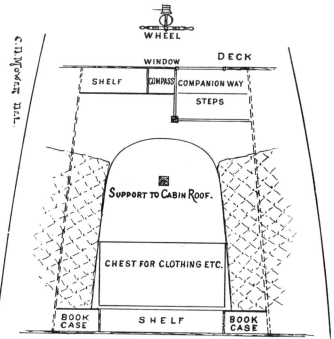

Plan of the after cabin of the *Spray*.

Some things about the *Spray's* deck might be fashioned differently without materially affecting the vessel. I know of no good reason why for a party-boat a cabin trunk might not be built amidships instead of far aft, like the one on her, which leaves a very narrow space between the wheel and the line of the companion way. Some even say that I might have improved the shape of her stern. I do not know about that. The water leaves her run sharp after bearing her to the last inch, and no suction is formed by undue cutaway.

Smooth-water sailors say, "Where is her overhang?" They never crossed the Gulf Stream in a nor'easter, and they do not know what is best in all weathers. For your life, build no fantail overhang on a craft going offshore. As a sailor judges his prospective ship by a "blow of the eye" when he takes interest enough to look her over at all, so I judged the *Spray*, and I was not deceived.

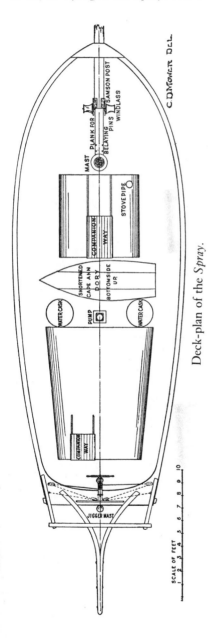

Deck-plan of the *Spray*.

C D MOWER DEL.

In a sloop-rig the *Spray* made that part of her voyage reaching from Boston through the Strait of Magellan, during which she experienced the greatest variety of weather conditions. The yawl-rig then adopted was an improvement only in that it reduced the size of a rather heavy mainsail and slightly improved her steering qualities on the wind. When the wind was aft the jigger was not in use; invariably it was then furled. With her boom broad off and with the wind two points on the quarter the *Spray* sailed her truest course. It never took long to find the amount of helm, or angle of rudder, required to hold her on her course, and when that was found I lashed the wheel with it at that angle. The mainsail then drove her, and the main-jib, with its sheet boused flat amidships or a little to one side or the other, added greatly to the steadying power. Then if the wind was even strong or squally I would sometimes set a flying-jib also, on a pole rigged out on the bow-sprit, with the sheets hauled flat amidships, which was a safe thing to do, even in a gale of wind. A stout downhaul on the gaff was a necessity, because without it the mainsail might not have come down when I wished to lower it in a breeze. The amount of helm required varied according to the amount of wind and its direction. These points are quickly gathered from practice.

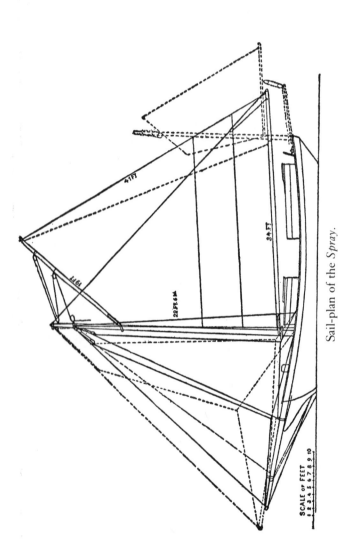

**SCALE OF FEET**
1 2 3 4 5 6 7 8 9 10

41 FT

19 FT

22 FT. 6 IN

34 FT

## Sail-plan of the *Spray*.

The solid lines represent the sail-plan of the *Spray* on starting for the long voyage. With it she crossed the Atlantic to Gibraltar, and then crossed again southwest to Brazil. In South American waters the bowsprit and boom were shortened and the jigger-sail added to form the yawl-rig with which the rest of the trip was made, the sail-plan of which is indicated by the dotted lines. The extreme sail forward is a flying jib occasionally used, set to a bamboo stick fastened to the bowsprit. The manner of setting and bracing the jigger-mast is not indicated in this drawing, but may be partly observed in the plans on page 511 and 513.

Briefly I have to say that when close-hauled in a light wind under all sail she required little or no weather helm. As the wind increased I would go on deck, if below, and turn the wheel up a spoke more or less, relash it, or, as sailors say, put it in a becket, and then leave it as before.

To answer the questions that might be asked to meet every contingency would be a pleasure, but it would overburden my book. I can only say here that much comes to one in practice, and that, with such as love sailing, mother-wit is the best teacher, after experience. Labor-saving appliances? There were none. The sails were hoisted by hand; the halyards were rove through ordinary ships' blocks with common patent rollers. Of course the sheets were all belayed aft.

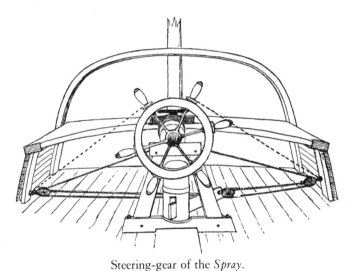

Steering-gear of the *Spray*.

The dotted lines are the ropes used to lash the wheel. In practice the loose ends were belayed, one over the other, around the top spokes of the wheel.

The windlass used was in the shape of a winch, or crab, I think it is called. I had three anchors, weighing forty pounds, one hundred pounds, and one hundred and eighty pounds respectively. The windlass and the forty-pound anchor, and the "fiddle-head," or carving, on the end of the cutwater, belonged to the original *Spray*. The ballast, concrete cement, was stanchioned down securely. There was no iron or lead or other weight on the keel.

If I took measurements by rule I did not set them down, and after sailing even the longest voyage in her I could not tell offhand the length of her mast, boom, or gaff. I did not know the center of effort in her sails, except as it hit me in practice at sea, nor did I care a rope yarn about it. Mathematical calculations, however, are all right in a good boat, and the *Spray* could have stood them. She was easily balanced and easily kept in trim.

Some of the oldest and ablest shipmasters have asked how it was possible for her to hold a true course before the wind, which was just what the *Spray* did for weeks together. One of these gentlemen, a highly esteemed shipmaster and friend, testified as government expert in a famous murder trial in Boston, not long since, that a ship would not hold her course long enough for the steersman to leave the helm to cut the captain's throat. Ordinarily it would be so. One might say that with a square-rigged ship it would always be so. But the *Spray*, at the moment of the tragedy in question, was sailing around the globe with no one at the helm, except at intervals more or less rare. However, I may say here that this would have had no bearing on the murder case in Boston. In all probability Justice laid her hand on the true rogue. In other words, in the case of a model and rig similar to that of the tragedy ship, I should myself testify as did the nautical experts at the trial.

But see the run the *Spray* made from Thursday Island to the Keeling Cocos Islands, twenty-seven hundred miles distant, in twenty-three days, with no one at the helm in that time, save for about one hour, from land to land. No other ship in the history of the world ever performed, under similar circumstances, the feat on so long and continuous a voyage. It was, however, a delightful midsummer sail. No one can know the pleasure of sailing free over the great oceans save those who have had the experience. It is not necessary, in order to realize the utmost enjoyment of going around the globe, to sail alone, yet for once and the first time there was a great deal of fun in it. My friend the government expert, and saltest of salt sea-captains, standing only yesterday on the deck of the *Spray*, was convinced of her famous

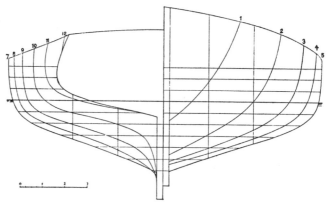

Body-plan of the *Spray*.

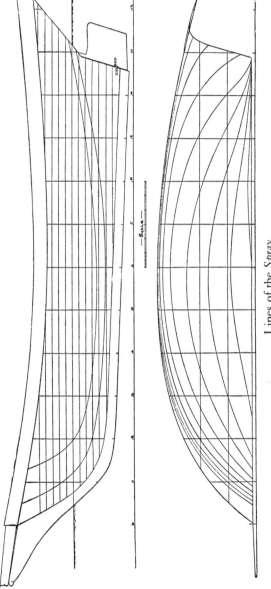

Lines of the *Spray*.

qualities, and he spoke enthusiastically of selling his farm on Cape Cod and putting to sea again.

To young men contemplating a voyage I would say go. The tales of rough usage are for the most part exaggerations, as also are the stories of sea danger. I had a fair schooling in the so-called "hard ships" on the hard Western Ocean, and in the years there I do not remember having once been "called out of my name." Such recollections have endeared the sea to me. I owe it further to the officers of all the ships I ever sailed in as boy and man to say that not one ever lifted so much as a finger to me. I did not live among angels, but among men who could be roused. My wish was, though, to please the officers of my ship wherever I was, and so I got on. Dangers there are, to be sure, on the sea as well as on the land, but the intelligence and skill God gives to man reduce these to a minimum. And here comes in again the skilfully modeled ship worthy to sail the seas.

To face the elements is, to be sure, no light matter when the sea is in its grandest mood. You must then know the sea, and know that you know it, and not forget that it was made to be sailed over.

I have given in the plans of the *Spray* the dimensions of such a ship as I should call seaworthy in all conditions of weather and on all seas. It is only right to say, though, that to insure a reasonable measure of success, experience should sail with the ship. But in order to be a successful navigator or sailor it is not necessary to hang a tar-bucket about one's neck. On the other hand, much thought concerning the brass buttons one should wear adds nothing to the safety of the ship.

I may some day see reason to modify the model of the dear old *Spray*, but out of my limited experience I strongly recommend her wholesome lines over those of pleasure-fliers for safety. Practice in a craft such as the *Spray* will teach young sailors and fit them for the more important vessels. I myself learned more seamanship, I think, on the *Spray* than on any other ship I ever sailed, and as for patience, the greatest of all the virtues, even while sailing through the reaches of the Strait of Magellan, between the bluff mainland and dismal Fuego, where through intricate sailing I was obliged to steer, I learned to sit by the wheel, content to make ten miles a day beating against the tide, and when a month at that was all lost, I could find some old tune to hum while I worked the route all over again, beating as before. Nor did thirty hours at the wheel, in storm, overtax my human endurance, and to clap a hand to an oar and pull into or out of port in a calm was no strange experience for the crew of the *Spray*. The days passed happily with me wherever my ship sailed.